S0-DUT-993

hed by SMITHSONIAN INSTITUTION SCHOLARLY PRESS

Box 37012
C 957
shington, D.C. 20013-7012
w.scholarlypress.si.edu

over design: Piper Wallis

Library of Congress Cataloging-in-Publication Data

Science diplomacy : science, Antarctica, and the governance of international spaces / Paul Arthur Berkman, Michael A. Lang, David W. H. Walton, and Oran R. Young, editors.

p. cm.

"A Smithsonian Contribution to Knowledge."

"This book is a product of the keynote addresses, plenary presentations, panel discussions, workshops and posters from the Antarctic Treaty Summit: Science-Policy Interactions in International Governance at the Smithsonian Institution during 30 November through 3 December 2009"—Preface.

Includes bibliographical references and index.

ISBN 978-1-935623-06-9 (alk. paper)

1. Antarctica—International status—Congresses. 2. Polar regions—Research—International cooperation—Congresses. I. Berkman, Paul Arthur.

KWX60.S26 2011

341.4'2—dc22 2010045415

∞ The paper used in this publication meets the minimum requirements of the American National Standard for Permanence of Paper for Printed Library Materials Z39.48–1992.

Science Di

Antarctica, Scien Governance of Interna

Edited by
Paul Arthur Berkman, Micha
David W. H. Walton, and Ora

A Smithsonian Contribution to Kn

Smithsonian Institution
Scholarly Press

WASHINGTON D.C.
2011

Publi
P.O.
MR
Wa
ww
C

Contents

SCIENCE FOR MANAGEMENT

SCIENCE FOR INTERNATIONAL COLLABORATION

Foreword

As is the case wherever the problem of environmental protection arises, the major issue for international negotiation is that of the interface between scientific research and policy making, and that was the case in Copenhagen. It is also that of the transformation of scientific truth into collective choice. Such transformation is never easy, nor natural.

Regardless of their accuracy, scientific facts cannot conceal the complexity of decisions that must include other issues and take into account other interests. This is why it is so important to be able to examine the case of the Antarctic Treaty, which is both exemplary and, alas, unique.

Fifty years ago when 12 countries decided to pool their efforts to preserve the Antarctic from all territorial claims, they probably had no idea of the meaning their action would take in light of the current situation. They could not imagine that saving our now endangered planet would become our main concern. They could not have known that the poles, until now the embodiment of the power of wilderness and wild expanses, would become the symbols of their new vulnerability. It is true that the Madrid Protocol provided a useful addition to the treaty in 1991, giving it an essential environmental dimension. In fact, all it did was reassert its original spirit, that of an area dependent on the shared responsibility of mankind, a continent whose collective importance requires defining the boundaries of special interests.

The spirit of the Antarctic Treaty Summit was to emphasize the primordial importance of these deserted expanses for mankind, expanses with almost no human beings but also without which all of us could no longer exist as we have so far. This is why I spoke of a case that is both exemplary and unique. The Antarctic Treaty political decision preceded scientific certainty; in a way, it even preceded the threat.

But beyond realities of its time, it also set out a universal philosophy for the preservation of higher interests of mankind. The treaty made it possible for nearly 10% of the Earth's surface to escape national interests and be dedicated to peaceful purposes. Given today's very different realities, this is the success that should inspire us. It will be difficult but not impossible since we have other assets, including the certainties acquired by scientists in the past 50 years. We now know the challenge confronting us, what is at stake, our prime interests, our very survival. Threat and fear often trigger new momentum.

I was able and honored to go to Antarctica in January 2009, where I was able to visit 26 different research stations with dozens of researchers of different nationalities. I would like to pay tribute to their dedication, their passion, their selflessness. These men and women devote years of their lives trying to understand the complexities of our world. We must recognize today that their work is often insufficiently heeded by those who should be its natural extension, political decision makers. In recent decades scientists have been warning us of our planet's degradation, yet for decades our economies and short-term interests have been privileged. The international agenda is brimming with more urgent tragedies and crises with more immediate effects. Fortunately, things are beginning to change since scientists have succeeded in mobilizing increasingly vigilant public opinions. The world over, we can now see the emergence of renewed global awareness, our most valuable asset.

Regardless of the time it will take, we can now believe that progress will end up being the rule. We cannot afford, however, to lose too much time. We have already too long postponed making the right decisions to preserve the Earth and its resources and likely to guarantee a viable environment for future generations.

In Antarctica more than anywhere else we can observe the devastating effects of climate change year after year. The problem is all the more acutely felt in the Arctic as well, which does not benefit from any true protection by any treaty. Today, we can observe that the threats weighing on the Arctic no longer concern only degradation of the biotype. The strategic stakes are now very clear, and the ambitions are more and more openly voiced. Economic appetites are aroused, of course, by scientific estimations that one-fifth of the planet is still undiscovered, where technically exploitable energy resources are located in the Arctic zone. In addition to economic appetites there are often, unfortunately, strategic appetites. In the face of these threats we must take action. The importance of the resources at stake can only aggravate the situation in future years. This is why it is imperative for us to set up as soon as possible a lasting international solution taking into account everyone's interests. Everyone meaning not only the five states surrounding the Arctic Ocean and its shores, part of whose indigenous populations are seeing their traditional lifestyles profoundly disrupted, but also the international community as a whole since, I repeat, the future of the Arctic is crucial for all of us.

Without any specific international treaty, the 1982 United Nations Convention on the Law of the Sea serves as the basis for the protection of the Arctic. It is on this basis that all five of the coastal countries recently "agreed to take measures to ensure protection and conservation of the fragile marine environment of the Arctic Ocean." Can this statement weigh against the inexorable almost daily advance of the new conquerors of these icy expanses given the interests involved, their power and complexity? It is highly unlikely that any binding agreement can help move ahead in the coming years.

Thus, international negotiations cannot solve all problems. Although an effective global Arctic Treaty must remain our long-term objective, we must also explore parallel courses, short-term measures for good governance, less ambitious but just as necessary. In particular, we must envisage the creation of sanctuaries and protected areas for preserving biodiversity, including at sea, as has already been done, for example, by my country Monaco, France, and Italy in the Mediterranean with the Pelagos Sanctuary. This approach also applies to all phenomena linked to global warming, including the very important issue of acidification of the ocean and the threats against biodiversity. In the face of these challenges we must be flexible and inventive in combining different levels of actions that are both daring and complement each other. This is why it is so important for scientists to intensify their pressure. They represent a respected, independent moral force. Today, their voice is capable of going beyond specific interests and contingencies of topicality. While policy makers struggle to convert the conclusions of their work into appropriate choices, we must continue to rely on them so that we can reasonably triumph tomorrow.

As Secretary of State Hillary Clinton declared for the 50th anniversary of the Antarctic Treaty, the challenges of the poles will offer nations the opportunity of meeting in the twenty-first century as we did 50 years ago in the twentieth century, to reinforce peace and security, encourage sustainable development, and protect the environment. These are very strong words that trace a course that is now our own. This is, at any rate, the way that I see my fight for the poles as a determinant focal point for the future of our world.

Prince Albert II
Sovereign Prince of Monaco
May 2010

Preface

Meeting in Washington, D.C., on 1 December 1959, 12 nations came together to adopt the Antarctic Treaty in the interest of all mankind. The elegance of the treaty was in its simplicity of only 14 articles that would provide the basis for the governance of nearly 10% of the Earth "for peaceful purposes only." Territorial issues were set aside. "Substantial research" activities became the criterion for nations to consult on "matters of common interest" and to make decisions by consent of all parties.

The 1959 Antarctic Treaty has succeeded remarkably well during its first 50 years. Scientific and technical advice has become a central element of the Antarctic Treaty System, especially from the Scientific Committee on Antarctic Research. Institutional offspring have emerged, most notably the 1980 Convention on the Conservation of Antarctic Marine Living Resources. Divisive issues, particularly potential mineral resources, have been successfully addressed. In 1991, the Antarctic Treaty Consultative Parties adopted a comprehensive Protocol on Environmental Protection to the Antarctic Treaty to safeguard the continent for future generations as the largest conservation area on Earth.

Following the International Geophysical Year of 1957–1958, with science as a tool of diplomacy, the Antarctic Treaty System has provided lessons that are relevant to the governance of transboundary systems as well as the other international spaces beyond sovereign jurisdictions (i.e., outer space, the deep sea, and the high seas) that together cover nearly 70% of the Earth's surface. With vision and hope for the future, the challenge of the Antarctic Treaty Summit was to identify and assess these science-policy lessons of international cooperation that have enabled both the flexibility and the resilience of the Antarctic Treaty since it was adopted at the height of the Cold War.

The Antarctic Treaty Summit was convened in the spirit of being international, interdisciplinary, and inclusive. Discussions were open, engaging, and collaborative. Participants came from 27 nations and included diplomats, scientists, legislators, administrators, lawyers, historians, artists, writers, educators, entrepreneurs, students, and other members of civil society. The Antarctic Treaty Summit involved plenary presentations with panel discussions during the first three days followed by a final day of topical workshops. The plenary sessions were

1. Origin of the Antarctic Treaty,
2. Development of the Antarctic Treaty System,
3. Antarctica's Role in Global Science,
4. Scientific Advice in the Antarctic Treaty System,
5. International Cooperation in Antarctica,
6. Interactions Between the Antarctic Treaty System and other International Regimes, and
7. Governing International Spaces: Lessons from Antarctica.

The topical workshops on the fourth day considered (1) Arctic Governance—Lessons from Antarctica and (2) History of International Spaces, with a luncheon dialogue on Building Bridges: Communicating Science with Policy Makers. Authors of this book include key contributors to the Antarctic Treaty System along its timeline over the past half century.

The Antarctic Treaty Summit adopted the Forever Declaration, which was finalized with participant contributions in open discussion and made available for signature via the internet for anyone anywhere in the world (http://www.atsummit50.aq). A concurrent resolution (Recognizing the 50th Anniversary of the Signing of the Antarctic Treaty) was adopted with unanimous consent by the U.S. House of Representatives (H. Con. Res. 51) and the U.S. Senate (S. Res. 365) during the first session of the 111th Congress in 2009, encouraging "international and interdisciplinary collaboration in the Antarctic Treaty Summit to identify lessons from 50 years of international cooperation under the Antarctic Treaty that have legacy value for humankind." In addition, His Excellency Ban Ki-moon (Secretary-General of the United Nations) delivered a video address to the Antarctic Treaty Summit on 1 December 2009, celebrating 50 years of international cooperation and peace promoted by the Antarctic Treaty.

There have been many summits, generally seen as important government meetings and usually involving heads of state. We were, indeed, fortunate to have the participation of His Serene Highness Prince Albert II of Monaco in this summit. The notion of summit also involves climbing and overcoming challenges. During the past half century, humankind has been climbing together along the route blazed by the original 12 Antarctic Treaty signatories, who have welcomed increasing participation in Antarctic governance from many other nations, which now include nearly 50 signatories. Importantly, summits offer special vistas, not only of the mountain climbed, but of all that surrounds. Such perspective was the central goal of the Antarctic Treaty Summit.

This volume brings together key elements of the Antarctic Treaty Summit (the plenary lectures, discussion panels, and workshops) to examine lessons we can learn for the future governance of the Antarctic and other international spaces beyond sovereign jurisdictions, as well as for resources that cross the boundaries of nations. The book is organized to highlight lessons about science-policy interactions in the origin, design, development, and applications of the Antarctic Treaty System as a governance case study that has global relevance. Chapters from the keynote speakers, complemented by the shorter vignettes from other experts involved with the summit, illustrate these lessons with international and interdisciplinary balance. The final conclusions provide a further synthesis of Antarctic lessons for science diplomacy and good governance, offering hope and inspiration for us all.

"With the interests of science and the progress of all mankind," on behalf of the International Board and our benefactors, patrons, sponsors, endorsing organizations, and participants in the Antarctic Treaty Summit, we invite you to share our challenge and opportunity in assessing the lessons of international cooperation promoted by the Antarctic Treaty during its first 50 years.

Paul Arthur Berkman, University of Cambridge
Michael A. Lang, Smithsonian Institution
David W. H. Walton, British Antarctic Survey
Oran R. Young, University of California

Acknowledgments

This book is a product of the keynote addresses, plenary presentations, panel discussions, workshops, and posters from the Antarctic Treaty Summit: Science-Policy Interactions in International Governance at the Smithsonian Institution during 30 November through 3 December 2009 (http://www.atsummit50.aq).

The international, interdisciplinary, and inclusive spirit of this golden anniversary celebration for the Antarctic Treaty stemmed from the collaboration among its board members: Professor Paul Arthur Berkman (Chair, United States); Dr. Maj De Poorter (New Zealand); Professor Edith Fanta (Brazil); Dr. Marie Jacobsson (Sweden); Dr. Yeadong Kim (Republic of Korea); Mr. Michael Lang (United States); Dr. José Retamales (Chile); Professor David W. H. Walton (Vice-Chair, United Kingdom); Judge Rüdiger Wolfrum (Germany); Professor Oran R. Young (United States); and Professor Abdul Hamid Zakri (Malaysia). We gratefully acknowledge the authors of this book and the participants from the 27 nations who contributed to the Antarctic Treaty Summit as well as the 40 national or international government agencies, nongovernmental organizations, foundations, corporations, and universities from around the world that made this celebration a success.

We especially thank the following three summit benefactors who provided essential support for the Antarctic Treaty Summit. With continuous enthusiasm from the start, the Tinker Foundation enabled the overall summit planning and implementation, and we are grateful for the support from Ms. Renate Rennie (Chief Executive Officer and President). The Prince Albert II of Monaco Foundation (Monaco Office) provided key support for the speakers and panelists to attend this event in Washington, D.C., and we gratefully acknowledge the personal involvement from His Serene Highness Prince Albert II. Without enthusiastic support from the Smithsonian Institution, through the Office of the Under-Secretary for Science and the Office of Special Events and Protocol, we would not have had use of the prestigious National Museum of Natural History and National Air and Space Museum or the timely publication of this book, and we especially thank Dr. G. Wayne Clough (12th Secretary of the Smithsonian Institution) for his commitment to the summit activities.

We thank the summit patrons who supported key elements of the Antarctic Treaty Summit. The U.S. Marine Mammal Commission supported the Web site and subsequent archive (http://www.atsummit50.aq) as well as a mini-documentary about the Antarctic Treaty System and other outreach strategies. The Office of Polar Programs at the U.S. National Science Foundation supported the poster session and video interviews that were integrated into the mini-documentary about the lasting values of the Antarctic Treaty for humankind. TransPolar (a Raytheon/AECOM company) supported the gala at the National Air and Space Museum on the 50th anniversary of the Antarctic Treaty. The Prince Albert II of Monaco Foundation (U.S. Office) contributed to the audiovisual logistics for the plenary presentations and panel discussions as well as the performance by the Keystone State Boychoir. The Eisenhower Institute at Gettysburg College contributed to the lunches and coffee breaks that promoted interactions among participants. The United States–United Kingdom Fulbright Commission supported critical coordination and networking through the University of Cambridge.

We thank the summit sponsors who contributed to the diverse participation and logistics for the Antarctic Treaty Summit. Contract management was through the University of California, Santa Barbara (Bren School of Environmental Science and Management), with additional fiscal administration by the University of Cambridge (Scott Polar Research Institute). The following organizations contributed to the travel, lodging, and registration costs of participants: American Geophysical Union, Foundation for the Good Governance of International Spaces, Greenpeace, Japan Polar Research Association, KBR, Korean Polar Research Institute, Korea Supporters Association for Polar Research, Lindblad Expeditions, Pew Charitable Trusts, Stanford University (Department of Earth Sciences), United Nations Environmental Programme, Universiti Sains Malaysia (Centre for Global Sustainability Studies), and World Wildlife Fund–Australia (Antarctica and Southern Ocean Initiative). The Association for Polar Early Career Scientists conducted the Antarctic Treaty essay contest (which involved submissions from 12 nations), and The Explorers Club covered the costs for the winning essayist. The U.S. Geological Survey covered the costs of the musical performance by Rive Gauche at the gala. The Arctic Governance Project and Aspen Institute (Dialogue and Commission on Arctic Climate Change) contributed to the workshop on Antarctic lessons for the Arctic. The Scientific Committee on Antarctic Research contributed to the workshop on the history of international spaces.

We thank the organizations that provided key outreach through their summit endorsements: American Association for the Advancement of Science, Fulbright Academy of Science and Technology, International Council of Science/World Meteorological Organization Joint Committee for the International Polar Year, National Geographic Society, The Royal Society, United Nations University (Institute of Advanced Studies), the U.S. House of Representatives, and the U.S. Senate.

Finally, such a complex meeting could not have been executed so smoothly without professional assistance of the highest order, and we thank Linder & Associates for their excellent event management, which was contributed with creative enthusiasm. Importantly, as editors, we are grateful to the many reviewers who provided thoughtful assessments of the papers in this volume.

Building the International Legal Framework for Antarctica

Marie Jacobsson

INTRODUCTION

Imagine a pristine continent, cold as ice, extremely windy and dry, almost as giant as Latin America and clearly larger than Europe, but with little or negligible human activities, yet a continent in which states, some explorers, and scientists are taking an increasing interest. Imagine that, outlandish as it may seem, this continent was about to become a scene of international discord and that you had to solve the problem. What would you do? It is clear that you would need a political and a legal solution, a solution that would last and that everybody could live with. There is no room for one winner; there is no room for any loser. There is only room for numerous winners.

This was the situation that a number of particularly concerned states faced in the 1940s when they needed to address how Antarctica should be managed. Their challenges were

- to find a solution that would be accepted domestically,
- to settle the issue among the most concerned states (internal accommodation),
- to meet the challenges of states not involved in the discussions, the nonstate parties (external accommodation), and
- to meet the challenges of nonstate actors (public opinion).

This article will address the development of a legal framework for Antarctica, not only the 50 years of the Antarctic Treaty but also the decades preceding the treaty. These are phases of developments that mirrored, mirror, and will continue to mirror international and domestic political developments, including the expectations of civil society.[1]

Marie Jacobsson, Swedish Ministry for Foreign Affairs, Department of International Law, Human Rights and Treaty Law, SE-103 39 Stockholm, Sweden. Correspondence: marie.jacobsson@foreign.ministry.se; marie.jacobsson@swipnet.se.

THE DEVELOPMENT OF THE LEGAL FRAMEWORK FOR ANTARCTICA

The necessity for a new power structure was already apparent during the Second World War and so was the need for new principles of law and politics to be inaugurated and upheld.[2] The post–Second World War political discussions on Antarctica were no doubt influenced by the adoption of the United Nations (UN) Charter in San Francisco in 1945. "Regional" solutions became a sanctioned and encouraged means of conflict moderation, explicitly addressed in Article 52 of the UN Charter. At least the two Latin American claimants have endeavoured to regard Antarctica as a regional matter. The United States regarded Antarctica as a sphere of interest among a group of powers friendly to the United States. It was not until the Soviet Union claimed the right to participate in the political discussions on the future of Antarctica that the question of Antarctica developed into one of global interest, or rather, Antarctica became a pawn in global politics.

The Most Important Steps

Before I recount what took place at the intergovernmental level, let me state that the interest in Antarctic issues has never been limited to governmental interests alone. On the contrary, popular interest in the polar regions has always been considerable. The post–Second World War situation stimulated individuals as well as international organizations to bring forward ideas pertaining to the administration of the polar areas. The role of the newborn United Nations seemed self-evident to many. So, for instance, the Women's International League for Peace and Freedom favoured control and administration of the uninhabited polar areas by one or two mandate commissions under the Trusteeship Council of the United Nations. Such administration was expected to result in, inter alia, equal and free access to raw materials (including to mineral resources), organized and adequate scientific research, and surveys whose results should be available to all those interested. The organization also argued for equitable arrangements regarding fishing and whaling rights, as well as prevention of "destructive methods in connection with whaling and sealing".[3] This proposal was brought to the attention of the UN Trusteeship Council, which, however, decided to take no action. A similar proposal was made in 1947 by the Commission to Study the Organization of the Peace. Dr. Julian Huxley, the first Director-General of the UN Educational, Scientific and Cultural Organization (UNESCO), wished to see UNESCO set up an "International Antarctic Research Institute." A member of the British parliament, Lord Edward Shackleton, son of the explorer Ernest Shackleton, argued in favour of involvement by the United Nations in the settlement of the Antarctic question. Others, such as Dr. Dana Coman, president of the American Polar Society, proposed, in an internal discussion at the State Department, that Antarctica should be made the first "international park."

There was, in short, a newly awoken interest in Antarctic political affairs that presumably stemmed from reading press reports on the growing friction in Antarctica and, furthermore, mirrored a confidence in the newly established United Nations.

Although the Second World War had brought with it a decrease in scientific activities in Antarctica, the political predicament with respect to Antarctica and, in particular, to the question of sovereignty over Antarctic territory had become more and more tense as British, U.S., Argentine, and Chilean activities during and after the ending of WWII clearly showed. It is often forgotten that all these states had sent military expeditions to Antarctica and undertook military operations there between 1943 and 1948.

The obviously increasing tension in Antarctica, together with the growing embarrassment to the United States of having three of its allies, namely, Chile, Argentina, and the United Kingdom, as antagonists with respect to sovereignty disputes in Antarctica, no doubt contributed to a conviction in the State Department that there was a compelling need for a more vigorous solution to the question of Antarctica.[4] There was also a fear that the Soviet Union would exploit the situation.[5]

The United States had to come up with a proposal that not only struck a balance between the United States' interest in Antarctica and the claimant states' interests but, at the same time, circumvented the perceived risk of Soviet involvement. The United States therefore became a key player in initiating the consultations on Antarctica in the late 1940s. But the United States was not alone.

The Proposals for a Solution, 1939–1959

In fact, the suggestions and initiatives related to the future management of Antarctica were numerous, and it is not possible to address all of them in this paper. I will focus on only a few initiatives while asking readers to bear in mind that discussions were ongoing throughout the period from 1939 onward, with the exception of the WWII period.[6]

In sum, one can say that the first post-WWII initiative came from Chile and the action that led to the Antarctic Treaty came from the United Kingdom.

In October 1947, Chile, in reference to an initiative by the United States in 1939, asked the United States about its view on a possible convocation of an Antarctic Conference and of the likelihood of a territorial claim by the United States.[7] The background to the Chilean query is that in late 1939, the United States had put forward the idea of a common inter-American policy with regard to the Antarctic. This policy consisted, inter alia, of an arrangement should the investigations and surveys show that natural resources might be developed and utilized. According to the U.S. proposal, all these governments should enjoy equal opportunities to participate in such development and utilization.[8] The 1939 initiative was clearly related to the claims and the issue of enjoying equal rights in possible development and utilisation.

Argentina had also put forward the idea of a conference on Antarctica in 1940 in proposing that an international conference among states claiming rights and interests in Antarctica should be assembled, with the objective of determining the "juridico-political status of that region".[9]

The United States' initiative in 1939–1941 on a common inter-American policy on Antarctica was unsuccessful. For obvious reasons, the Second World War overshadowed the Antarctic question, and it was temporarily set aside. In the meantime, the global geopolitical map changed. When Chile chose to resurrect the U.S. idea in 1947, the United States was already in the process of reconsidering its Antarctic policy. The U.S. response therefore conveyed the message that the time was not then opportune for such a conference, while also assuring that the "United States attitude remains essentially the same as it was at that time".[10] While the internal discussion in the United States went on, the tension between the United Kingdom, Argentina, and Chile sharpened, and the United Kingdom contemplated taking the Antarctic controversy to the International Court of Justice.

Draft Agreement on Antarctica, 1948

During the early months of 1948 the Draft Agreement on Antarctica was prepared in the State Department. It should be noted that the draft recommended the establishment of an international status for Antarctica and also that the United States should make official claim to areas in the Antarctic, so as to place the United States "on an equal footing with the other seven powers." The claim was not to be announced until after an international settlement had been obtained.[11] The draft contained a proposal for the establishment of a trusteeship under the United Nations and joint sovereignty over the continent among eight countries, namely, Argentina, Australia, Chile, France, Norway, New Zealand, the United Kingdom, and the United States.

In reality, the United States' draft was a combination of a trusteeship proposal and a condominium. Not surprisingly, the idea of "pooling claims" did not to appeal to the claimant states,[12] irrespective of the U.S. ambitions to blur this by the attempts to launch the proposal as a "trusteeship proposal."[13]

Although the draft agreement contains no explicit reference to the freedom of scientific research in the area, it was "intended to provide for complete liberty of bona fide scientific research."[14] This ambition was underlined by the obligation on the parties to foster free access to and freedom of transit through or over the area, although under rules prescribed by the commission that was proposed to be set up. It should be noted that, at that time, it was not a U.S. objective to declare Antarctica a demilitarised area,[15] notwithstanding the major objective to lower the tensions in the area.[16]

The basic postulates that resulted in the proposal were an identified need to solve territorial disputes and a belief that a collective solution to the question of Antarctica would best prevent disturbances between the current claimant states, particularly since it was judged that such disturbances could be exploited by the Soviet Union. There was, furthermore, an assumption that no significant exploitable resources existed in Antarctica and that the value of Antarctica was primarily scientific.

The U.S. proposal was designed to legitimise the collective administration of Antarctica and to prevent certain "external interference" (read: the Soviet Union and its so-called "satellite states").[17] The proposal foresaw the possibility of admitting states other than the eight original states that had a "legitimate interest" in Antarctica. It was in this context that the idea of a retrospective "activity criteria" as a key to admittance surfaced.[18] The draft was also designed to meet possible criticism of "by-passing and weakening the United Nations" since it was considered important for the United States to fully support the United Nations.[19]

During the course of developing the proposal, the United States consulted few other governments. The consultations with the United Kingdom, and later with Chile, were, however, crucial to the development.[20] The British reaction caused the State Department to elaborate a revised draft agreement "to provide for a condominium."[21]

The Escudero Proposal, 1948

A few months later, in July 1948, a representative of the State Department arrived in Santiago and thereafter in Buenos Aires to discuss the Antarctic question. It was during the discussion in Santiago that the Chilean representative, Professor Escudero, expressed doubts as to whether the trusteeship would be applicable under the UN Charter and voiced the idea of a joint declaration by a limited group of states, which would freeze the current legal rights and interests in Antarctica for a period of 5 or 10 years. During that period, actions in Antarctica by the states party to the declaration would have no legal effects on their rights. This was the so-called modus vivendi proposal and the embryonic form of "the Escudero proposal"[22] presented later and designed to be a means of conflict moderation as well as to prevent any interpretation that Chile (or other claimants) would relinquish claims to sovereignty.

New U.S. Proposal

At this early stage the United States neglected the Chilean idea of a modus vivendi agreement and decided instead to present the new version of its previous proposal to a wider circle of interested states, which included Chile and also Argentina, Australia, France, New Zealand, Norway, and the United Kingdom. This version was built on the comments made by the United Kingdom.[23] The trusteeship idea was abandoned and turned into a pure proposal for a condominium.[24]

The obligation to cooperate with the specialised agencies of the United Nations now constituted the only connection with the United Nations. Furthermore, the commission was to constitute "the actual government" with "full executive and administrative powers," and decisions on matters of substance were to be taken by a two-thirds majority.

Not surprisingly, the proposal was not embraced wholeheartedly by the recipients, most of whom neither seemed to have had much idea about what was going on, nor had seen the proposal in advance. Hence, the responses varied on a scale from disapproval to sceptical consent. Argentina declared a clearly negative view to any international regime. Chile disapproved of the condominium solution but underlined a favourable attitude to a modus vivendi solution. Norway considered the establishment of an international administration "unnecessary." Having taken an initially unfavourable view, Australia and New Zealand declared their willingness to "go along," but New Zealand underlined that a closer relationship with the United Nations was preferable. France was reluctant and asked for clarification. The United Kingdom cautiously advised its acceptance "in principle and as a basis for discussion".[25] None of the claimants were prepared to waive their claim and turn it into a "pooled" sovereignty.

However, the United States made its initiative public on 28 August 1948.[26] According to the press release, the suggested solution ("some form of internationalization") should best be such as to promote scientific investigation and research. The question of cooperation in scientific research as such was not addressed.[27] Reactions from states that had not been consulted did not fail to appear. South Africa and Belgium declared that they considered themselves entitled to participate in an Antarctic settlement.[28]

Chile was, as mentioned, still in favour of an international "understanding" in the form of a declaration. Chile had formally rejected the U.S. proposal. Instead, Chile proposed an agreement to exchange scientific data and including nonstrengthened claims by activity. Chile came back to the idea voiced by Escudero in the earlier bilateral discussions.

The negative responses to the specific proposal by the United States, together with the positive views expressed on an international solution to parts of the Antarctic question, such as scientific cooperation, led the United States to reconsider its proposal. It was concluded that the Chilean proposal offered the best prospect if it were modified on certain points[29] since it was considered to be too temporary and declaratory in nature.

The U.S. Draft Declaration on Antarctica, 1950

A new blueprint entitled Draft Declaration on Antarctica was therefore elaborated by the Department of State in early 1950. Prior to the new outline, the United Kingdom had been consulted, and its suggestions were incorporated in the United States' draft.[30] The new proposal now contained the Chilean idea of "freezing of claims."

Irrespective of the fact that the new draft was labelled "declaration" and not "agreement," its content resembled more an agreement than a declaration, although it had entirely left out the ideas on pooling of sovereign claims and collective governance. Instead, the Draft Declaration was an agreement on cooperation, to the benefit of all individual participants. Conscientiously drafted, it contained a provision that the parties to the declaration were disposed to discuss territorial problems in Antarctica and to freeze the claims. The area of application was identified as the territory south of 60°S latitude. Freedom of scientific research among the parties and its nationals and the exchange of scientific information were cornerstones of the declaration. A committee should be created, to which governments should report, but it would have no decision-making power. The question of third states' activities in Antarctica was cautiously addressed by stating that the committee could make recommendations in relation to third states wishing to conduct scientific research. If such expeditions were carried out, they would not be recognised as a basis for territorial claims. The declaration was of limited duration (5 or 10 years was proposed) but foresaw a possible future Antarctic Conference and, hence, an in-built opportunity to prolong the agreement.[31]

Soviet Reactions

The State Department had calculated in 1948 that its first motion would prevent Soviet intervention in the process.[32] The exclusion of the Soviet Union from any future Antarctic solution remained a paramount objective.

The first indication that this was not a procedure that the Soviet government would observe in silence came via articles in *Pravda* and *Izvestiya* on 11 February 1949. The articles reported of a meeting of the All-Union Geographic Society, during which the president of the society, Lev Semyonovich Berg, declared that the Soviet Union had a valid claim to Antarctic territory based on the discoveries of the "Russian" navigators Bellingshausen and Lazarev.[33] Furthermore, the states that had an interest in Antarctica should be those that formed an Antarctic regime. A resolution with such content was adopted by the meeting of the society.[34] The wording of the resolution is almost identical to that of the Soviet diplomatic note to be delivered later. These news articles were observed, inter alia, in the United States and the United Kingdom but elicited no formal reactions on the part of the countries involved in the Antarctica discussions.

On 8 June 1950, the Soviet Union sent a memorandum to the United States, the United Kingdom, France, Norway, New Zealand, Australia, and Argentina stating that "the Soviet Government cannot recognize as legal any decision regarding the regime of the Antarctic taken without its participation."[35]

U.S. Proposal on a Modus Vivendi, 1951

It has been maintained that "the negotiations ceased" after "the Soviet Note of June 1950 and the outbreak of the Korean War" on 25 June 1950. This belief does not seem to be correct. Despite the Korean conflict, Chile and the United States continued to exchange revised versions of the modus vivendi proposal during 1950 and 1951. However, the Korean situation no doubt put a damper on the discussions.[36]

The State Department sent a new draft, now labelled Modus Vivendi, to the Chilean Embassy on 14 November 1951.[37] It differed little from the previous proposal. The United States stated that the only substantive change was that it addressed the collection of fees, so as to meet Chile's concern. Under the new proposal, the collection of fees would not prejudice the right of any other party. There was, however, another substantial change. The article on the right to perform scientific research in Antarctica had been redrafted. Chile returned to the proposal in the autumn of 1953.[38]

In the meantime, the U.S. policy on Antarctica was under continuous assessment, and it was therefore anything but clear and consistent.[39] The interest focused primarily on the pro et contra arguments in relation to a pronouncement of a U.S. claim, the forthcoming U.S. expedition, and the emerging plans for an International Geophysical Year (IGY).[40] The idea of a modus vivendi was not entirely abandoned, but in view of the fact that the United States had had no official activity in Antarctica since 1948, the character of the argumentation was modified.[41] President Eisenhower accentuated the option of focusing the politics on a reaffirmation of U.S. rights and claims, rather than announcing a claim.[42] Documents from 1954 indicate that the United States had now deserted the idea of an internationalisation of Antarctica while "still being in favour of a standstill agreement between friendly powers."[43] The primary objectives, laid down by the National Security Council, were a solution to the territorial problems of Antarctica so as to "ensure maintenance of control by United States [sic] and friendly powers and exclude our most probable enemies" and freedom of scientific research and exchange of scientific data "for nationals of the United States and friendly powers."[44]

Antarctica surfaced as a global political factor—an element in the politics of containment.

Political Development in the Mid-1950s

In 1955, the United Kingdom filed the Antarctica Case at the International Court of Justice, but the case was removed from the court's list since the court found that it did not have any acceptance by Argentina to deal with the dispute.[45]

In January 1956, the New Zealand prime minister, the former Labour leader of the opposition Walter Nash, proposed that Antarctica should be a UN trusteeship.[46] Nash also proposed the abandonment of claims in Antarctica.[47] Allegedly inspired by Nash,[48] India proposed in early 1956 that the question of Antarctica be included in the agenda of the UN General Assembly. According to an explanatory memorandum, the reason for the initiative was that India wanted "to affirm that the area will be utilised entirely for peaceful purposes and for the general welfare." Another objective was to secure "the development of Antarctica's resources for peaceful purposes".[49]

The Indian request was evidently caused by a concern that Antarctica would be utilised for nuclear testing. There was no attempt to transfer the issue of territorial claims to the UN agenda, but rather, the attempt was to secure the peaceful use of Antarctica, a concern that the United States tried to meet by assuring that the United States had no intention in using Antarctica as a nuclear site.[50] Documents disclose U.S. concern that the Indian move was inspired by the Soviet Union and that it would attract "neutral states." The claimant states were also clearly negative to the Indian proposal, and Argentina and Chile argued that it would be contrary to Article 2, paragraph 7, of the UN Charter.[51] The Indian proposal was withdrawn by 4 December 1956.[52]

A Revival of the U.S. Condominium Proposal, 1957

The United States became more and more aware of the urgent need to revise (or rather to formulate) an Antarctic policy before the IGY, not least in light of the controversy among the United Kingdom, Chile, and Argentina and the Indian proposal to include the question of Antarctica at the UN. The U.S. fear of a UN involvement seems to have been related to anxiety about getting the Soviet Union involved.

A condominium was considered preferable to a trusteeship. By the spring of 1957 the U.S. plans for proposing a condominium had come to fruition.[53] It was considered that a condominium would be consistent with the assertion of claims, which was the only way to persuade most of the claimants to accept the idea. A condominium, it was argued, could be designed "to facilitate the further development of the area in the interest of all mankind." The idea of a condominium could "be presented as a dramatic Free World initiative." Although the idea was not a watertight way of keeping the Soviet Union outside the condominium, it was assessed that such ambitions on the part of the Soviet Union could be curbed.[54] This assessment was wrong.

The United Kingdom's Proposal

Before the United States had formulated a policy on the future of Antarctica and decided on how to proceed however, the United Kingdom proposed quadripartite talks among the United States, Australia, New Zealand, and the United Kingdom. These quadripartite talks were apparently preceded by talks in London between Australia, New Zealand, South Africa, and the United Kingdom.[55] A major difference between the British and U.S. perspectives at the time was the view on Soviet participation. The United Kingdom's more realistic view of the situation apparently presupposed that the Soviet Union could not be left outside an agreement and hence calculated that it would be included, whereas the United States remained negative to such inclusion.[56] The British initiative is yet another example of the role the United Kingdom played in setting in motion the negotiations of the Antarctic Treaty. The four-power talks prepared the ground for entering into the more formal Preparatory Meeting.

On 15 July 1958, a new attempt to include the question of Antarctica on the UN agenda was made by India. The attempt was unsuccessful.[57] At that time, the IGY was in full progress, the United States had convened a Conference on Antarctica, and the Preparatory Meeting had commenced.

Elements That Bore Fruit from the Early Proposals

Several elements in the Antarctic Treaty can be traced back to the earlier proposals. A brief recounting gives the following list.

1. *The removal of Antarctica from the arena of international disputes.* The objective survived, although the motives did not, namely, the fear that the Soviet Union might exploit the potential conflict and that the United States did not benefit from such friction.

2. *Safeguarding individual interests; limited participation by states with special interests.* During the course of discussions on the proposals, no one seems to have proposed an open-ended group of participants. From the outset, and from the U.S. perspective, there was a clearly identified group of states with so-called special interests. No other state claimed the right to participate, nor was there a discussion on the "legitimacy" of the states to regulate. Those states that claimed the right to participate in an Antarctic solution later became original signatories to the Antarctic Treaty.

3. *Obligation to cooperate with the United Nations and other organisations.* The obligation to cooperate with the United Nations underwent a negative transition during the discussions from a clear trusteeship proposal, under which an Antarctic trusteeship would have been a UN-sanctioned administration, or a condominium, possibly sanctioned by the UN, to an obligation to cooperate with specialised agencies of the UN.

4. *Freedom of scientific research, freedom of movement, and cooperation.* The question of "freedom of scientific research" was directly related to the identified group of participants, or "friendly powers." Freedom of scientific research on the high seas would still prevail under international law. However, the idea of cooperation in other areas as well and the obligation to cooperate developed in the Antarctic Treaty.

5. *Public interest and the benefit of scientific progress to "people."* Public interest in Antarctica is well documented, and it had the benefit of bringing in funds and economic support for the poorly funded scientific community. The general assertion that mankind would benefit from scientific progress was considered a fact rather than a matter to be debated.

6. *Demilitarisation; peaceful use.* Even if the proposals were aimed at preventing Antarctica from becoming an arena for international conflicts, there was no direct proposal with respect to a demilitarisation of the area.

7. *Exploitation and conservation of resources.* At the time, it was judged that there were no economically exploitable resources in Antarctica, with the possible exception of marine living resources, which were considered not to be included in an agreement because fishing activities were subject to the freedom of the high seas. Regulation and conservation of resources (except whaling) were therefore not an issue.

8. *Territorial scope: south of 60°S Latitude.* A clear distinction is made between the continent and the water areas south of 60°S latitude. This distinction is less clear in the Antarctic Treaty. It was clear throughout the discussions that the high-seas freedoms south of 60°S latitude could not be limited.

9. *Consensus.* Attempts to have a decision-making procedure by majority rule failed. The claimant states were not prepared to accept any decision-making procedure that would not have given them a veto. The consensus principle was a prerequisite.

10. *Duration.* The discussions on the duration of the agreement mirrored, at an early stage, the tension between the wish to have a stable agreement and the concern on the part of the claimant states not to give the impression that they were relinquishing their claims. It was important to find a formula that satisfied the two aspects.

It is therefore maintained that most elements in the Antarctic Treaty can be traced back to the previous proposals, especially to those based on the so-called Escudero proposal in 1948, which despite its ambiguity, would have been constructive enough to serve as a foundation for a stable agreement. The political ambitions alone did not lead to a result until 1957, when help came from a seemingly nonpolitical arrangement, namely, the IGY.

The International Geophysical Year

The IGY exercise helped transfer the question of Antarctica from the table of diplomacy to the table of science, which was, indeed, a fortunate catalytic process for future legal and political development.

The agreement and achievements of the IGY are also of relevance to lawyers.[58] One of the most important steps was the move by French Colonel (later General) Georges Laclavère to not allow political controversies to prevail over scientific efforts. From the very outset, namely, at the first Antarctic Conference in Paris in 1955, Georges Laclavère, the conference chairman, stated that there was no room for political considerations and underlined, in his opening address, the technical character of the conference. Political questions were not the concern of the conference since it was a conference about science.[59] This declaration led to the conference unanimously adopting a resolution that ensured that "the objectives of the conference are exclusively of a scientific nature."[60] The political innovations of the IGY, such as the gentlemen's agreement, "some international administration," and the exchange of scientists between bases, were "political" elements that were later sanctioned and given a legal meaning in the Antarctic Treaty.

The primary reason why the IGY remains relevant in the Antarctic context is that Article II of the Antarctic Treaty contains a cross-reference to the IGY. This cross-reference is one component of the two prerequisites for the material application of the very fundamental provision in the Antarctic Treaty that deals with the right to perform scientific research in Antarctica. According to this article, "freedom of scientific investigation and co-operation toward that end, *as applied during the International Geophysical Year,* shall continue, subject to the provisions of the Antarctic Treaty" (my emphasis). This formulation is the result of a compromise. In order to understand the meaning of the wording of Article II of the Antarctic Treaty, it is necessary to examine what the relevant features of the IGY were.

First, the IGY was a decision made by scientists, which was supported by an understanding by governments, to put aside political and legal struggles—the gentlemen's agreement—and to concentrate on the overall scientific aim. The gentlemen's agreement survived in essence and is now reflected in Article IV of the Antarctic Treaty. Second, it featured participation and openness. Third, it outlined the importance of presence and activities in Antarctica. The "activity requirement" is reflected in Article IX, paragraph 2, but had precedents in earlier U.S. proposals. Fourth, it specified access to scientific data and cooperation. Also, the exchange of data and scientists between stations commenced with the IGY.[61] This practice is reflected in Articles II and III of the Antarctic Treaty. Fifth, it required unanimity in decision making. The IGY conferences could make decisions for their own organisation of work. On such occasions the conferences worked under "the rule of unanimity." This procedural rule is codified in the Antarctic Treaty, Articles IX, XII, and XIII.

In conclusion, most of the provisions in the Antarctic Treaty that relate to the performance of scientific research in Antarctica have their origin in the IGY. They were, as will be shown, taken up during the preparatory meetings before the Washington Conference, and from there, they found their way into the Antarctic Treaty. The treaty itself elaborated science as part of the requirement for acceptance of the treaty.

THE DEVELOPMENT FROM ONE SINGLE TREATY, THE ANTARCTIC TREATY, TO THE ANTARCTIC TREATY SYSTEM

The Antarctic Treaty

It is not my intention to go through the provisions of the Antarctic Treaty but, rather, to shed light on what is not there, namely, resource management and administrative structures, despite attempts to regulate them in the treaty. Many, if not all, articles of the Antarctic Treaty are, of course, of utmost importance, but the heart of the treaty is Article IV (the article that deals with the claims). However, for the issue of building a legal regime for Antarctica, Article IX is of paramount importance since it is the legal basis for the administration of Antarctica. Article IX is structured around two basic components. The first relates to the meetings under the Antarctic Treaty (when, where, and how they can be held) and who can participate in those meetings. The second component relates to the mandate for these meetings and what measures can be taken during such meetings and by whom.

It is on the basis of this article that the entire legal management of the Antarctic region has been built. In short, Article IX is the foundation of the Antarctic Treaty System.

The Agreed Measures for the Conservation of Antarctic Fauna and Flora

The Agreed Measures for the Conservation of Antarctic Fauna and Flora (AMCAFF), adopted by the Consultative Parties at Antarctic Treaty Consultative Meeting (ATCM) III (1964), was the first more-ambitious attempt to adopt elaborate conservation measures for Antarctica. The potential need for measures with respect to the preservation and conservation of living resources in Antarctica was foreseen in the Antarctic Treaty. The First Consultative Meeting had already addressed the issue in Recommendation I-VIII, and it could be said that AMCAFF grew out of that recommendation. The Agreed Measures for the Conservation of Antarctic Fauna and Flora was not labelled a convention, but its form indirectly indicates its status as a treaty under the Antarctic Treaty. The Agreed Measures for the Conservation of Antarctic Fauna and Flora is considered by the Treaty Parties and by some authors as a comprehensive successful international instrument for wildlife conservation. It foreshadows a development within the treaty system with respect to environmental protection, transparency, information sharing, and the role of international organisations, namely, the Scientific Committee on Antarctic Research (SCAR).

The Convention on the Conservation of Antarctic Seals

The next step was to regulate Antarctic seals, probably not so much because seals were threatened but because this step was part of a much-larger objective, namely, to accustom reluctant parties to the Antarctic Treaty to the idea that it was appropriate to deal with matters or conservation. The parties to the Antarctic Treaty took it upon themselves to regulate their potential activities in the high-seas area. In this respect, the convention resembles a traditional fishery-conservation agreement.

New and important features of the Antarctic Treaty System[62] were introduced by the negotiations on, and conclusion (in 1972) of, the Convention on the Conservation of Antarctic Seals (CCAS). First of all, the negotiations were held parallel to the ATCM and outside the Antarctic Treaty. The negotiating Antarctic Treaty Parties recognised that negotiation of the matters dealt with under the CCAS did not fall within the framework of the Antarctic Treaty. They further recognised that states, not parties to the Antarctic Treaty, could have a legitimate interest in the conservation and commercial exploitation of seals. The view that management of resources in the maritime areas south of 60°S latitude was outside the frame of the Antarctic Treaty was later to be modified. The Treaty Parties had obvious problems in tackling the question of whether the Antarctic Treaty was applicable to sea areas or not, hence the issue of high-seas rights.

Second, the CCAS was the first treaty to address how to manage the economic exploitation of an Antarctic resource and also the management of a resource not yet economically exploited.

Third, the CCAS introduced an "open accession formula." There is no formal requirement that parties *in spe* be parties to the Antarctic Treaty. The CCAS strengthened the role of SCAR, and the participation in 1972 of representatives from a specialised agency of the UN as observers and their de facto liberty to circulate documents were new instruments in opening up the system. Today, nongovernmental organizations and UN specialised agencies definitely have a role of their own within the Antarctic Treaty System.

Wolfrum claims that the CCAS is interesting from a "Rechtssystematisch" (systematic) perspective, in that Consultative Parties as "selbstbestellte Sachwalter" (self-appointed guardians) for the Antarctic environment are established.[63] Although I agree with such a conclusion, it is important to stress that such a situation was, indeed, facilitated by neglect of the issue on the part of the remaining international community. The Antarctic Treaty Parties were later to learn that being a self-appointed trustee is not easily recognised. Yet it should be stressed that if AMCAFF is regarded as a treaty, this development had been started by the conclusion of AMCAFF.

The Convention on the Conservation of Antarctic Marine Living Resources

Despite the lack of enthusiasm for addressing the issue of the preservation and conservation of marine living resources at the Washington Conference, this convention only lasted until the first Antarctic Treaty Consultative Meeting (1961), when four proposals were presented with respect to the conservation of living resources in the treaty area. The Scientific Committee on Antarctic Research also recommended that conservation measures be taken.[64]

The Antarctic Treaty Parties decided in 1977 to commence negotiations. The participants included the 12 signatories to the Antarctic Treaty and states that had acceded to the treaty, namely, the German Democratic Republic, the Federal Republic of Germany, and Poland. A number of international organisations participated as observers: the European Community, the UN Food and Agriculture Organization (FAO), the International Whaling Commission, the Intergovernmental Oceanographic Commission, the International Union for Conservation of Nature, the Scientific Committee on Oceanic Research, and SCAR.

Signals from the FAO and UN Development Programme for the need to exploit resources were met with strong reactions from the Treaty Parties.[65] Other UN representatives spoke with a slightly different, more conservationist, voice. The UN Environment Programme suggested that it should be "involved in the protection of the Antarctic environment and the establishment of ecologically sound guidelines for exploration and exploitation of resources."[66] Nontreaty parties were also interested in exploitation. It was time for the Treaty Parties to secure control, and the CCAS had opened the door for the regulation of resources in international waters.

The aim of the Treaty Parties was to conclude a treaty before the end of 1978. As was the case with AMCAFF and the CCAS, the discussions had revealed that the area of application of such regulation was not self-evident, nor were the contents, nor the form of agreement. Questions were also raised as to who should participate in the development of a regime, what kind of institutional arrangements were needed, if any, how conservation measures could be enforced, and whether a dispute settlement procedure was needed. Yet the negotiations were fruitful. By agreeing to the Convention on the Conservation of Antarctic Marine Living Resources (CCAMLR), the parties to the Antarctic Treaty recognized among themselves a functional, efficient, regional treaty that applies both to areas that have the legal status of high seas and to areas that are, or are claimed to be, the territorial seas and exclusive economic zones of claimant states. It is a treaty that applies to areas that third parties clearly have rights to and interests in, as well as certain obligations, for example, under the UN Convention on the Law of the Sea. In addition, the CCAMLR brought about the first "institutionalisation" of Antarctica through the establishment of the commission and the Scientific Committee under the commission. Since the conclusion of the treaty, the CCAMLR has shown that it is capable of developing and adjusting to the requirements of the time.

When the Antarctic Treaty Consultative Parties (ATCPs) took control of the situation and decided to tackle the question of marine living resources, they acted preemptively. Any attempts by third states to exploit marine living resources in a claimed area would most likely have disturbed peaceful Antarctic cooperation; to use the wording of the Antarctic Treaty, they would have threatened to make Antarctica a scene or object of international discord.

Convention on the Regulation of Antarctic Mineral Resources

The decision to start negotiations on a minerals regime had had a long prelude. Many states realised at the time of the Washington Conference that there was a need to reach agreement on living and nonliving resources, but the issue was, at the time, far too complicated to even attempt accomplishing.

New Zealand raised the question of Antarctic mineral resources at a Preparatory Meeting before ATCM VI (1970), and there were many countries that saw the need for raising this issue, not least the United Kingdom. The decision to commence negotiations on a minerals convention was underlined by the aspiration to negotiate a minerals regime before any commercial exploitation had commenced. Only the Consultative Parties were initially allowed to attend the session of that meeting. That restriction changed after ATCM XII (1983), when Non-Consultative Parties (NCPs) were invited for the first time to attend a Consultative Meeting. As a result, NCPs were also invited to attend the mineral negotiations. There is little doubt that the parallel development at the UN General Assembly (that is, an increasing criticism of the alleged "closed and secret nature" of the Antarctic Treaty) inspired the Consultative Parties to make that decision.

The Convention on the Regulation of Antarctic Mineral Resource Activities (CRAMRA) was adopted in Wellington on 2 June 1988, but it never entered into force, although not because of the external criticism stemming from the UN General Assembly. Instead, a revolution from within the Treaty Parties posed a great challenge. The treaty process was interrupted by Australian and French political turnabout. Belgium and Italy soon sided with France and Australia.[67]

The Convention on the Regulation of Antarctic Mineral Resource Activities is an interesting legal conception since it was negotiated as a regime for the management of resources that were known or believed to exist, but without any evidence that they would become economically exploitable. The negotiation of CRAMRA was not so much about the exploitation of resources as it was a tool to prevent disharmony and conflict in Antarctica. Hence, the Treaty Parties were obliged to address this delicate issue, although that was not how the nontreaty parties saw it. On the contrary, one of the main criticisms against the Antarctic Treaty Parties was the alleged lack of a mandate to negotiate a minerals regime since the Antarctic Treaty lacks any reference to mineral resources.

From a political perspective, CRAMRA is, at present, of marginal interest. However, the legal constructions in CRAMRA, the balance of interests between claimant and nonclaimant states, might serve as an example when the time is right to address other resource issues.

Protocol on Environmental Protection to the Antarctic Treaty

As has been shown, the initiatives to protect the Antarctic environment did not start with the Environmental Protocol. At the Preparatory Meeting (1989) to ATCM XV, Chile suggested that the question of "comprehensive measures" for the protection of the Antarctic environment ought to be addressed.[68] Behind the choice of obscure words was the diplomatic insight that the time was not right for discussions on yet another convention, particularly in light of a situation in which the future of CRAMRA was at stake. A series of formal meetings were held, and the negotiations resulted in a proposal on a protocol to the Antarctic Treaty that was adopted in Madrid in 1991 and entered into force in 1998.

With the Environmental Protocol, the Treaty Parties took a step toward more-modern management of the Antarctic environment. In short, the protocol institutionalised the protection of the Antarctic environment, not only by requiring environmental impact assessments before activities take place but also by establishing the Committee on Environmental Protection.

The Liability Annex

The Environmental Protocol, Article 16, foresees the adoption of a liability regime to elaborate rules and procedures relating to liability for damage arising from activities taking place in the Antarctic Treaty area and covered by the protocol. The first step in that direction was taken by the adoption of the so-called Liability Annex, at ATCM XXVII in Stockholm in 2005.[69] Despite the fact that this annex is not yet in force, its conclusion meant that the Treaty Parties showed their preparedness to tackle difficult and serious issues relating to the prevention and restoration of the Antarctic environment.

CONCLUDING REMARKS AND A LOOK INTO THE CRYSTAL BALL

Article IV is clearly the heart of the Antarctic Treaty and the Antarctic Treaty System.[70] However, Article IX, the article that allows for management of the continent, is an absolute legal and political necessity for stable cooperation and the peaceful use of Antarctica. No progress would have been possible without the so-called "measures" taken, according to the article.[71] The establishment of a secretariat serves to facilitate the interactions of the claimants; the decision-making power remains with the ATCPs operating through the ATCM. In the meantime, the ATCPs have considerably developed, strengthened, and adapted the Antarctic Treaty System.

After more than 20 years of debate, the Question of Antarctica was effectively taken off the agenda of the UN General Assembly in 2005[72]; at that time, the assembly did not request the secretary-general to submit a report to a forthcoming session and did not include it on the agenda of forthcoming sessions but only wished to "remain sized of the matter." This decision can be seen as an important recognition of the successful management of Antarctica under and within the Antarctic Treaty System. The present secretary-general of the United Nations, Ban Ki-moon, was the first sitting UN secretary-general to visit Antarctica.[73]

It is sometimes claimed that it is the issue of illegal, unregulated, and unreported (IUU) fishing or tourism that constitutes the challenges to the Antarctic Treaty System. I do not share that view. The IUU fishing is certainly a threat to the Antarctic marine ecosystem, but not to the Antarctic Treaty System as such. The issue of IUU fishing is well taken care of within the context of CCAMLR,[74] and management by CCAMLR has not been politically challenged by nonstate parties, nor has there been a proposal that the management of marine living resources would be better handled elsewhere.

The same goes for the issue of tourism. Tourism is a legitimate use of Antarctica, and tourists and individual explorers bring about a greater interest in the Antarctic region. The tourism industry has, in fact, helped to buttress the legitimacy of the Antarctic Treaty System, and the tourism industry is now a natural "party" to the system, though not legally, of course.

However, other issues are likely to pose more of a challenge, such as the continental shelf issue and the issues of bioprospecting and genetic resources. The reason is that these issues are so closely related to Article IV and the issue of claims. These issues are further complicated by the fact that we are discussing not only shelf areas stemming from the Antarctic continent but also shelf areas extending from north of 60°S latitude into the Antarctic Treaty Area.

I believe that these issues need to be more effectively and preemptively addressed by all the Antarctic Treaty Parties. The continental shelf issue is not an issue solely for those countries that have expressed claims or potential claims to the continent. This issue is, indeed, related to ensuring that the Antarctic will not become the scene of international discord. The Antarctic Treaty is a model for international cooperation at its best. It shows that cooperation is possible even in situations when sovereignty, the fight for resources, and different political aims are at stake. It is a heritage that needs to be nurtured.

NOTES

1. This article is based on the research I did for my doctoral thesis "The Antarctic Treaty System: *Erga Omnes or Inter Partes*?" which was presented at the University of Lund, Sweden, on 31 January 1998. The dissertation is available through a few Swedish libraries and from the author. It is accepted for publication. The original text is, for obvious reasons, overloaded with footnotes. For the benefit of the reader I have only retained a selected number of footnotes.

2. The contents of what was to come were already foreshadowed by the famous joint declaration by President Roosevelt and Prime Minister Churchill in 1941. The declaration put forth eight basic principles for the conduct of states in their international relations. Declaration of Principles issued by the President of the United States and the Prime Minister of the United Kingdom, released to the press by the White House on 14 August 1941, reprinted in *American Journal of International Law* 35 (official supplement) (1941): 191–192.

3. Emily Greene Balch, 1948, "The Polar Regions as Part of One World," *Survey Graphic* 37(9): 392–393. Professor Balch had become a Nobel Peace Prize Laureate in 1946. The International Executive Committee of the Women's International League for Peace and Freedom voted in favour of the appointment of an ad hoc committee to consider and report on the proposal to internationalise all uninhabited polar areas at a meeting in May 1947 in Geneva.

4. The development was closely followed by the U.S. press, which took an active interest in the matter and thereby put a certain pressure on the government, for instance, by asking about the U.S. view on an international conference for the settlement of the claims to Antarctica. The Secretary of State to the Embassy in London, Telegram, Washington, January 30, 1947, in *Foreign Relations of the United States, 1947*, vol. I (Washington, D.C.: U.S. Government Printing Office, 1971), p. 1050.

5. Paper Prepared by the Policy Planning Staff, [Washington,] June 9, 1948, in *Foreign Relations, 1948*, vol. I, pt. 2, p. 979; and The Department of State to the British Embassy, Aide-Mémoire, Washington, June 25, 1948, in *Foreign Relations, 1948*, vol. I, pt. 2, p. 988.

6. A brief account of the background history is found in John Hanessian, "The Antarctic Treaty 1959," *International and Comparative Law Quarterly* 9 (1960): 436–480. (Hereinafter Hanessian, ICLQ 1960.)

7. The Chilean Embassy to the Department of State, 13 October 1947, in *Foreign Relations, 1947*, vol. I, p. 1052.

8. See "United States Instructions to Diplomatic Officers of the United States in the American Republics Proposing a Common Inter-American Policy with Reference to the Antarctic," extracts reprinted as US11121939 in W. M. Bush, *Antarctica and International Law. A Collection of Inter-state and National Documents* (London: Oceana Publications Inc., 1988), vol. 3, pp. 446–447. This document was preceded by, inter alia, an instruction of 8 August 1939 to diplomatic officers of the United States in the 21 American republics to give notice of the United States Antarctic Service expedition (The Acting Secretary of State to Diplomatic Officers in the American Republics, Washington, August 8, 1939, in *Foreign Relations, 1939*, vol. II, pp. 9–10). The instruction is an indicator of (or at least leaves open) the possibility of a future U.S. claim. Simultaneously, President Roosevelt instructed Admiral Byrd, who was the commanding officer of the United States Antarctic Service, to take appropriate steps "which might assist in supporting a sovereignty claim by the United States Government" (President Roosevelt to the Commanding Officer of the United States Antarctic Service (Byrd) Washington, November 25, 1939, in *Foreign Relations, 1939*, vol. II, p. 13). As to the development at the Second Meeting of Ministers of Foreign Affairs of the American Republics in Havana in 1940, see Bush, *Antarctica and International Law*, vol. 1, p. 604. See also United Nations Treaty Series, vol. 161, p. 253, Article XVIII, which excluded Antarctica from any part of trusteeship.

9. Argentinean Memorandum to the United Kingdom proposing a Conference to determine the juridico-political status of the Antarctic, reprinted in translation as AR11091940 in Bush, *Antarctica and International Law,* vol. 1, p. 605. The proposal was reiterated on several occasions (Bush, *Antarctica and International Law,* vol. 1, p. 606).

10. Department of State to the Chilean Embassy, Memorandum, Washington, November 3, 1947, in *Foreign Relations, 1947*, vol. I, p. 1052. The same message was also conveyed by the president at a press conference on 7 January 1947 (The Secretary of State to the Embassy in the United Kingdom, Telegram, Washington, January 30, 1947, in *Foreign Relations, 1947*, vol. I, p. 1050). At the same time, the internal discussions in the United States were intense. Although the United States at first favoured a trusteeship solution, other alternatives were contemplated, primarily an international administration in the form of a condominium. The initial attention given to a trusteeship solution under the UN Charter foresaw an identified group of especially interested countries as primarily responsible and who would "safe-guard special interests of certain countries by giving them permanent control of trusteeship administration"; see The Acting Secretary of State to the Embassy in the United Kingdom, Telegram, Washington, September 22, 1947, in *Foreign Relations, 1947*, vol. I, p. 1051.

11. Draft Agreement Prepared by the Department of State, [Washington, n.d.], in *Foreign Relations, 1948*, vol. I, pt. 2, p. 984. This document was circulated together with a Paper Prepared by the Policy Planning Staff [Washington], June 9, 1948 [PPS-31] (hereinafter PPS-31), which, in turn, was the result of a series of internal consultations during the spring of 1948; see Editorial Note, in *Foreign Relations, 1948*, vol. I, pt. 2, pp. 976–977. The paper was also submitted to the National Security Council (Editorial Note, p. 977, note 1). See also Editorial Note (p. 982) for reference to an international status. In addition, Hanessian (ICLQ 1960, p. 437, note 4) refers to a "Draft Communication Regarding the Antarctic," Department of State, February 19, 1948.

12. R. E. Guyer, "The Antarctic System," Recueil des cours 139, no. II (1973): 171.

13. The draft text proposed that the eight states were to be "designated jointly as the administering authority of the trust territory" and that a commission, also consisting of the eight states, should be created and decisions be taken by a two-thirds majority. There was a prescribed duty for the commission to cooperate with appropriate specialised agencies of the United Nations and international scientific bodies. The tasks for the commission were to draw up plans for, inter alia, scientific research as well as to prescribe appropriate procedures under which states and private expeditions might be granted permission to conduct scientific investigations, develop resources, or carry out other activities consistent with the purposes of the agreement.

14. Department of States to the French Embassy, Aide-Mémoire, Washington, September 28, 1948, in *Foreign Relations, 1948*, vol. I, pt. 2, p. 1005.

15. The Secretary of Defense (Forrestal) to the Secretary of State, Washington, 12 April 1948, in *Foreign Relations, 1948*, vol. I, pt. 2, p. 973. Cf. Hanessian, ICLQ 1960, p. 439 and note 12, who refers to a Department of State Memorandum (EUR) of 25 February 1948, Washington, D.C. Hanessian asserts that an "important new element, providing for the demilitarisation of the area," was also included. Such an element cannot be found in the documents from this period reprinted in *Foreign Relations*.

16. The draft agreement provided for accession by other states. The proposed territorial scope of the agreement was "the Antarctic continent and all islands south of 60° South latitude except the South Shetland and South Orkney groups." The area of application did not include the sea areas, the reason being that the United States did not wish to involve these areas for reasons of defence, security, and whaling.

17. This was by no means only a U.S. interest. Lord Shackleton claims that the proposals for a solution on the Antarctic question that had a UN involvement were not popular because such a solution could have attracted the Soviet Union to Antarctica. Shackleton in House of Lords Debate (1960), p. 167.

18. The Secretary of the Interior (Krug) to the Acting Secretary of State, Washington, January 8, 1948, in *Foreign Relations, 1948*, vol. I, pt. 2, p. 962. See note 22.

19. It is difficult to see how the Soviet Union could have been kept outside the regime proposed in the draft agreement since Article 86, paragraphs 1a and 1b, of the UN Charter (together with Article 23) would have provided for the Soviet Union to be a member of the Trusteeship Council.

20. The United Kingdom, which was the first country to be informed, indicated that an eight-power condominium was preferable to a trusteeship under the United Nations since a trusteeship solution would allow for the Soviet Union to interfere. The role of the United Kingdom, and in particular of the legendary Brian B. Roberts, in these early stages of the development is still hidden in the closed archives of the Foreign and Commonwealth Office.

21. Editorial Note, in *Foreign Relations, 1948*, vol. I, pt. 2, p. 992. Cf. F. M. Auburn, *British Yearbook of International Law* 43 (1971), who asserts that "the very word condominium brought shivers to the Foreign Office" (p. 86), "presumably due to the intractable problems detailed in D. P. Connell, 'The Condominium of the New Hebrides'" (note 12). Auburn's conclusion is difficult to reconcile with the information in *Foreign Relations* that the United Kingdom preferred a condominium to a trusteeship; see, e.g., Position Paper Prepared in the Office of the United Nations Political and Security Affairs, in *Foreign Relations, 1955–1957*, p. 647; and the observation of Hanessian, ICLQ 1960, p. 440.

22. The Ambassador in Chile (Bowers) to the Secretary of State, Telegram, Santiago, July 19, 1948, *Foreign Relations, 1948*, vol. I, pt. 2, p. 995. Professor Escudero was an acknowledged Chilean expert on Antarctic matters. He had, inter alia, in 1939 been appointed to study Antarctic questions and their bearing on Chilean interests; see Bush, "CH07091939," in *Antarctica and International Law,* vol. 2, pp. 307–308. It should be noted that the discussions in Argentina did not lead to a continuing discussion between the United States and Argentina like the meeting in Chile did between the United States and Chile. The prime concern voiced by the Argentine representative was that it was inadmissible that countries outside the Western Hemisphere should be given a voice within the American quadrant; see The Chargé in Argentina (Ray) to the Secretary of State, Telegram, Buenos Aires, July 21, 1948, *Foreign Relations, 1948*, vol. 1, pp. 995–996. This was a shift in attitude; cf. note 18.

23. *Foreign Relations, 1948*, vol. I, pt. 2, p. 997, note 2.

24. The Department of State to the French Embassy, Aide-Mémoire, Washington, September 28, 1948, in *Foreign Relations, 1948*, vol. I, pt. 2, p. 1005. See also, Bush, *Antarctica and International Law,* vol. 2, pp. 2, 165.

25. For the views of the consulted states, see *Foreign Relations, 1948*, vol. I, pt. 2: Chile, p. 997, note 2, and Memorandum of Conversation, by the Under Secretary of State (Lovett), [Washington,] August 16, 1948, p. 1002; Argentina, p. 997, note 2, and The Ambassador in Argentina (Bruce) to the Secretary of State, Telegram, Buenos Aires, November 1, 1948, p. 1011; Australia, Memorandum of Conversation, by

the Secretary of State, [Washington,] August 17, 1948, p. 1003, and The Ambassador in the United Kingdom (Douglas) to the Secretary of State, p. 1014; New Zealand, The Minister in New Zealand (Scotten) to the Secretary of State, Telegram, Wellington, September 7, 1948, p. 1005; United Kingdom, The Ambassador in the United Kingdom (Douglas) to the Secretary of State, Telegram, London, November 24, 1948, p. 1014; France, p. 1005, note 1; Norway, The Norwegian Ambassador (Morgenstierne) to the Acting Secretary of State, Washington, November 15, 1948, pp. 1011–1013; United Kingdom, p. 997, note 2, and Editorial Note, p. 1015; and a summary of views in Paper Prepared in the Department of State, [Washington, n.d.], in *Foreign Relations, 1949*, vol. I, pp. 800–801. See also Hanessian, ICLQ 1960, p. 445 (Argentina).

26. Editorial Note, in *Foreign Relations, 1948*, vol. I, pt. 2, p. 1004. The press release can be found in the File on Antarctica, Swedish Ministry for Foreign Affairs, Doss. HP 53 P (1), containing the Department of State Press Release, August 28, 1948, No. 689. Apparently, the British Foreign Office and the Chilean Ministry for Foreign Affairs had already issued statements regarding the discussions on Antarctica. See also *Department of State Bulletin* 19, No. 479 (5 Sept. 1948).

27. Chile explicitly stated an interest in scientific cooperation, Hanessian, ICLQ 1960, p. 441.

28. Memorandum of Conversation by the Chief, Division of Northern European Affairs (Hulley), [Washington,] October 1, 1948, in *Foreign Relations, 1948*, vol. I, pt. 2, pp. 1007–1010. The notes from which the South African chargé d'affaires spoke are reprinted as an annex. It is worth noticing that parallel to this, consultations between the United Kingdom, Argentina, and Chile had commenced, so as to avoid "naval displays" in the southern latitudes. These consultations resulted in a tripartite declaration on 18 January 1949 not to send warships south of 60°S latitude, apart from customary routine movements.

29. Paper prepared in the Department of State, [Washington, n.d.], in *Foreign Relations, 1949*, vol. I, pp. 800–803; and Memorandum by the Secretary of State for the Executive Secretary of the National Security Council (Souers), Washington, August 29, 1949, in *Foreign Relations, 1949*, vol. I, p. 805. See also Memorandum of Conversation, by the Chief of the Division of Northern European Affairs (Hulley), [Washington,] March 23, 1949, in *Foreign Relations, 1949*, vol. I, p. 795.

30. Draft Declaration on Antarctica Prepared by the Department of State, [Washington, n.d.], in *Foreign Relations, 1950*, vol. I, pp. 905–906. The Chileans were apparently not informed about the British involvement. Memorandum of Conversation, by the Chief of the Division of Northern European Affairs, Washington, September 13, 1949, in *Foreign Relations, 1949*, vol. I, p. 806. For a similar vein of handling the matter, see *Foreign Relations, 1950*, vol. I, p. 907, note 2; and Memorandum by the Officer in Charge of British Commonwealth and Northern European Affairs (Hulley) to the Director of the Officer of North and West Coast Affairs (Mills) [Washington,] January 4, 1950, in *Foreign Relations, 1950*, vol. I, p. 905.

31. Draft Declaration on Antarctica Prepared by the Department of State, [Washington, n.d.], in *Foreign Relations, 1950*, vol. I, p. 905–906.

32. PPS-31, Washington, June 9, 1948, in *Foreign Relations, 1948*, vol. I, pt. 2, p. 982.

33. *Foreign Relations, 1949*, vol. I, p. 794, note 1. Bellingshausen was, however, Estonian, rather than Russian, although he sailed a Russian ship. He was received with lukewarm interest when he returned to Russia, but his achievement has, in recent times, been described as "second only to that of Cook." G. E. Foggs and David Smith, *The Explorations of Antarctica* (London: Cassell Publishers Limited, 1990), p. 28. See Headland (Chronology), p. 115, index no. 433.

34. The Embassy in Moscow to the Minister for Foreign Affairs, 22 February 1947, Swedish Ministry for Foreign Affairs, File on Antarctica, Doss. HP 53 P. See also Department of State Policy Statement, [Washington,] July 1, 1951, *Foreign Relations, 1951*, vol. I, p. 1727.

35. The Embassy of the Soviet Union to the Department of State, Memorandum Washington, June 8, 1950, in *Foreign Relations, 1950*, vol. I, pp. 911–913. Chile and the Soviet Union had no diplomatic relations, Klotz (America), p. 24.

36. F. M. Auburn, *Antarctic Law and Politics* (Bloomington: Indiana University Press, 1982), p. 86; Philip W. Quigg, *A Pole Apart: The Emerging Issue of Antarctica* (New York: McGraw-Hill Book Company, 1983), p. 136; and Bush, *Antarctica and International Law*, vol. 1, p. 57. But cf. Memorandum of Conversation, by the Officer in Charge of British Commonwealth and Northern European Affairs (Hulley), [Washington,] September 7, 1950, in *Foreign Relations, 1950*, vol. I, pp. 917–919, and Memorandum of Conversation, by Mr .Grant G. Hilliker of the Office of British Commonwealth and Northern European Affairs, [Washington,] March 5, 1951, in *Foreign Relations, 1951*, vol. I, pp. 1717–1718. See also Hanessian, ICLQ 1960, p. 447.

37. Draft Declaration on Antarctica, Prepared in the Department of State, [Washington, November 14, 1951], *Foreign Relations, 1951*, vol. I, pp. 1734–1736.

38. Hanessian, ICLQ 1960, p. 447.

39. *Foreign Relations, 1952–1954*, vol. X, p. 1738, note 5.

40. See the documents in *Foreign Relations, 1952–1954*, in particular, Draft Statement of Policy Proposal by the National Security Council, [Washington,] June 28, 1954, pp. 1744–1756, but also see Quigg, *A Pole Apart*, pp. 137–138.

41. Draft Statement of Policy Proposed by the National Security Council, [Washington,] June 28, 1954, in *Foreign Relations, 1952–1954*, vol. I, pp. 1754–1761. The debate was, to a large extent, a budgetary discussion; it is costly to fulfil and maintain a claim.

42. Memorandum of Discussion at the 206th Meeting of the National Security Council on Thursday, July 15, 1954, in *Foreign Relations 1952–1954*, vol. I, p. 1758. President Eisenhower is quoted as having said that he "would rather offend the British than our Latin American friends regarding issues in Antarctica." See also, Klotz, *America*, p. 25.

43. Statement of Policy by the National Security Council, [Washington,] July 16, 1954, in *Foreign Relations, 1951–1954*, vol. I, p. 1761 (approved by the president; see p. 1760).

44. Statement of Policy by the National Security Council, [Washington,] July 16, 1954, in *Foreign Relations, 1951–1954*, vol. I, p. 1761 (approved by the president; see p. 1760).

45. *Antarctica Case, United Kingdom v. Argentina*, ICJ Report of Judgment, Advisory Opinions and Orders 1956, Order 16, March 1956, p. 14.

46. John Hanessian Jr., New Zealand and the Antarctic. Part II: International Political Aspects, in Polar Area Series, vol. II, No.3, (Antarctica) American Universities Field Staff. Report Service, (New York?) 1962, especially pp. 3–8. As Labour leader of the opposition, Nash had proposed international control over Antarctica. His ideas did not receive support from the New Zealand government, but when back in power, he pursued the idea of international control of the area and also that the United Nations should approve of, but not necessarily administer, such a regime. Nash had previously in 1948, as acting foreign minister, expressed a positive attitude to the U.S. proposal on a condominium (Hanessian, New Zealand and the Antarctic, p. 3).

47. New Zealand orally maintained this idea up to the stage of the commencement of the Washington Conference. See Opening Statement

by the New Zealand representative A. D. McIntosh, C.M.G. in Doc. 6 at the Washington Conference. It is stated that New Zealand had been "prepared to consider the relinquishment of national rights and claims in Antarctica if such a step towards the establishment of a wider regime were generally agreed" (p. 1). "This is why my Prime Minister has put forward the view that the establishment of a completely international regime for Antarctica would require countries to forego their national claims . . . only on this basis that a fully effective administration of the whole of Antarctica could be achieved—an administration that could coordinate all activities and ensure the permanent neutralization of the area. Such an international regime could prepare for the eventual use of resources of Antarctica in a regulated and orderly manner" (p. 2).

48. Hanessian, New Zealand and the Antarctic, p. 3.

49. S. Chaturvedi, *The Dawning of Antarctica* (New Delhi: Segment Books, 1990), p. 72. See also Memorandum From the Assistant Secretary of State for European Affairs (Merchant) to the Under-Secretary of State (Hoover), Washington, February 24, 1956 and Telegram From the Department of State to the Mission at the United Nations, Washington, September 3, 1956, in *Foreign Relations, 1955–1957*, vol. XI, pt. II, pp. 643–645. The date of the request was 19 February 1956, and the explanatory memorandum was presented to the U.S. mission on 3 September.

50. Memorandum From the Assistant Secretary of State for European Affairs (Merchant) to the Under-Secretary of State (Hoover), Washington, February 24, 1956 and Telegram From the Department of State to the Mission at the United Nations, Washington September 3, 1956, in *Foreign Relations, 1955–1957*, vol. XI, pt. II, pp. 643–645.

51. See the document "Question of Antarctica" attached to a Position Paper Prepared in the Office of the United Nations Political and Security Affairs, in turn attached to a Memorandum From the Director of the Office of the United Nations Political and Security Affairs (Adams) to the Assistant Secretary of 1956, in *Foreign Relations, 1955–1957*, p. 648.

52. Memorandum From the Acting Assistant Secretary of State for Inter-American Affairs (Rubottom) to the Secretary of State, Washington, December 4, 1956, in *Foreign Relations, 1955–1957*, p. 652.

53. Memorandum From the Director of the National Security Council Secretariat (Boggs) to the National Security Council Planning Board, including enclosures, among others a Draft Statement of Policy by the National Security Council on Antarctica, in *Foreign Relations, 1955–1957*, vol. XI, pp. 675–689.

54. Paper Prepared in the Department of State [n.d.], Subject: Establishment of a Condominium of Antarctica, in *Foreign Relations, 1955–1957*, pp. 681–682. It was perceived that this "would not preclude the Soviets from claiming the right to participate in the administration of the area based on such claims as it might make, and while it would not force or necessarily bring about the withdrawal of Soviet personnel from the area, it would provide a basis for the U.S. and the present claimant powers to question its [sic] validity of Soviet presence in the area."

55. Telegram from the Department of State to the Embassy in the United Kingdom, Washington, August 23, 1957, in *Foreign Relations, 1955–1957*, vol. XI, pp. 710–711. The United States informs London, Canberra, and Wellington that it is prepared to participate in such quadripartite talks. The telegram also reveals the U.S. plan to gradually establish and expand a condominium over Antarctica and that these plans were to remain secret until after the IGY.

56. Telegram from the Department of State to the Embassy in the United Kingdom, Washington, August 23, 1957, in *Foreign Relations, 1955–1957*, vol. XI, pp. 710–711. When the United States advised that it was prepared to participate in such quadripartite talks, it declared that [the State Department's] "first reaction to British suggestion is that creation of condominium including USSR would not best serve interests and security free world and would be inconsistent with present U.S. policy." See also Hanessian, ICLQ 1960, p. 452. As to the British role, see Ivo Meisner, "Evolution of the Antarctic Treaty System: Responding to Special Interests" (doctoral thesis, Scott Polar Research Institute, Cambridge, 1986). The contents of and comprehensiveness of the British role remains to be examined.

57. Chaturvedi, *The Dawning*, p. 72.

58. For a historic perspective of the IGY, see Cornelia Lüdecke, "Parallel Precedents for the Antarctic Treaty," in *Science Diplomacy: Antarctica, Science, and the Governance of International Spaces*, ed. Paul A. Berkman, Michael A. Lang, David W. H. Walton, and Oran R. Young (Washington, D.C.: Smithsonian Institution Scholarly Press, 2011, this volume), pp. 253–263.

59. This took place at the First International Geophysical Year Antarctic Conference in Paris on 6–10 July 1955; see Marjorie M. Whiteman, *Digest of International Law*, vol. 2, Department of State Publication 7553 (Washington, D.C.: U.S. Department of State, 1963), p. 1242. Also at a meeting of the Comité Special de l'Année Geophysique Internationale (CSAGI) in Brussels, 8–14 September 1955, the president of CSAGI, Dr. Chapman, emphasised that CSAGI was a strictly nonpolitical organisation; Sullivan (Assault) p. 277. In this light, it is particularly interesting that the (unofficial) "U.S. programs in Antarctica in connection with the IGY" should be designed in support of a policy designed to protect the U.S. national interest; see Memorandum of Discussion at the 272nd Meeting of the National Security Council, Washington, January 12, 1956, in *Foreign Relations, 1955–1957*, vol. XI, p. 642.

60. Resolution 1 approved by the conference on 10 July 1955, reprinted in Bush, "GE10071955," in *Antarctica and International Law*, vol. I, p. 501. For the text of the Argentine and Chilean statements, see Whiteman, *Digest*, pp. 1242–1243.

61. As to coordination of scientific observations, see T. Nagata, pp. 73–74, Shapley, p. 88. A scientist from the U.S. Weather Bureau wintered at Mirny Base, and a group of scientists, including a Soviet meteorologist, wintered at a U.S. base.

62. The notion of the Antarctic Treaty System had not yet been conceived by the time of the negotiations of CCAS.

63. Rüdiger Wolfrum, *Die Internationalisierung* (Location: Publisher, 1984), pp. 80–81.

64. Sec. paper/8, 10 July 1961, Suggested Form of Measures to Promote Conservation of Nature in the Antarctic, SCAR document. David W. H. Walton, "The Scientific Committee on Antarctic Research and the Antarctic Treaty," in *Science Diplomacy: Antarctica, Science, and the Governance of International Spaces*, ed. Paul A. Berkman, Michael A. Lang, David W. H. Walton, and Oran R. Young (Washington, D.C.: Smithsonian Institution Scholarly Press, 2011, this volume), pp. 75–88.

65. James N. Barnes, "The Emerging Convention on the Conservation of Antarctic Marine Living Resources: An Attempt to Meet New Realities of Resource Exploitation in the Southern Ocean," in *The New Nationalism and the Use of Common Spaces*, ed. Jonathan I. Charney (Totowa, N.J.: Allanheld, Osmun & Co. Publishers Inc., 1982), p. 278, note 35.

66. Matthew Howard, "The Convention on the Conservation of Antarctic Marine Living Resources: A Five-Year Review," *International and Comparative Law Quarterly* 38 (1989), p. 111.

67. For a more detailed analysis, see T. Scully, "The Development of the Antarctic Treaty System," in *Science Diplomacy: Antarctica, Science, and the Governance of International Spaces*, ed. Paul A. Berkman,

Michael A. Lang, David W. H. Walton, and Oran R. Young (Washington, D.C.: Smithsonian Institution Scholarly Press, 2011, this volume), pp. 29–38.

68. Information paper, presented by the Delegation of Chile, PREP/WP/1 and attachment, both are undated. On file with the author.

69. Annex VI to the Protocol on Environmental Protection to the Antarctic Treaty Liability Arising From Environmental Emergencies.

70. Its importance has been stressed by Gillian Triggs; see Gillian Triggs, "The Antarctic Treaty System: A Model of Legal Creativity and Cooperation," in *Science Diplomacy: Antarctica, Science, and the Governance of International Spaces*, ed. Paul A. Berkman, Michael A. Lang, David W. H. Walton, and Oran R. Young (Washington, D.C.: Smithsonian Institution Scholarly Press, 2011, this volume), pp. 39–49. For an analysis of Article IV, see G. Triggs, *International Law and Australian Sovereignty in Antarctic* (Sydney: Legal Books PTY, 1986), pp. 137–150.

71. They were initially called recommendations but were subsequently renamed to decisions, measures, or resolutions, depending on their legal character. The importance of governance through the decisions, measures, and resolutions is dealt with in other contributions to this volume (e.g., Scully, this volume).

72. See UN General Assembly, Sixtieth Session, A/60/PV.61 GA Resolution 60/47, adopted without a vote on 8 December 2005 on the basis of a Report of the First Committee (A/60/454).

73. He returned to the UN and declared (at a briefing to an informal meeting of the General Assembly, New York, 21 November 2007) that "in the ice shelves of Antarctica, the glaciers of Torres del Paine and the rainforests of the Amazon, I saw up-close how some of the most delicate and precious treasures of our planet are being threatened by the actions of our own species. Antarctica's message was chillingly simple: the continent's glaciers are melting, far faster than we used to think. If large quantities of Antarctica's ice were to vanish, sea levels could rise catastrophically."

74. Denzil Miller, "Sustainable Management in the Southern Ocean: CCAMLR Science," in *Science Diplomacy: Antarctica, Science, and the Governance of International Spaces*, ed. Paul A. Berkman, Michael A. Lang, David W. H. Walton, and Oran R. Young (Washington, D.C.: Smithsonian Institution Scholarly Press, 2011, this volume), pp. 103–121.

President Eisenhower, the Antarctic Treaty, and the Origin of International Spaces

Paul Arthur Berkman

ABSTRACT. The late 1940s and early 1950s was a dangerous period of cold war posturing, with few bridges between the United States and Soviet Union. Nuclear weapons were a reality, and ballistic missiles were inevitable. It was during this period in the wake of World War II (as revealed in minutes of U.S. National Security Council meetings from 1954 to 1959) when President Eisenhower became the catalyst for an unprecedented mixture of global strategies to achieve "a day of freedom and of peace for all mankind." One of the possibilities was to create an international status for the Antarctic area, as suggested in the draft agreement that was circulated by the United States to the seven claimant nations in 1948. Planning also was underway for the International Geophysical Year (IGY) in 1957–1958 with scientific satellites anticipated to advance upper atmospheric research and promote the freedom of space, which was seen to be analogous to the long-standing concept of the freedom of the seas. In support of this space policy, the White House restrained the Army Ballistic Missile Agency from launching its Jupiter-C rocket into orbit in September 1956, which enabled the freedom of space to emerge with the IGY launch of Sputnik in October 1957. Building on this momentum of scientific cooperation, in May 1958, President Eisenhower invited the Soviet Union and the 10 other nations involved with Antarctic research to begin secret negotiations that would result in adoption of the Antarctic Treaty in Washington, D.C., on 1 December 1959, creating an international space "forever to be used exclusively for peaceful purposes . . . with the interests of science and the progress of all mankind." Following the 1958 Convention on the High Seas that had created the initial international space beyond sovereign jurisdictions, the Antarctic Treaty also became the first nuclear arms agreement with nonarmament and peaceful-use provisions that would become precedents for the outer-space and the deep-sea regimes that further established these areas as international spaces. The statesmanship of President Eisenhower that led to the Antarctic Treaty and the other international spaces demonstrates the role of science as a tool of diplomacy to build on the common interests of allies and adversaries alike for the lasting benefit of all humanity.

Paul Arthur Berkman, Scott Polar Research Institute, University of Cambridge, Lensfield Road, Cambridge CB2 1ER, UK, and Donald Bren School of Environmental Science and Management, University of California, Santa Barbara, California 93106-5131, USA. Correspondence: pb426@cam.ac.uk.

INTRODUCTION

The Antarctic Treaty was signed by 12 nations in Washington, D.C., on 1 December 1959 (Figure 1). The following year, during ratification hearings in the U.S. Senate, it was suggested (Gould, 1960) that "the Antarctic Treaty is indispensable to the world of science which knows no national or other political

FIGURE 1. Signature of the Antarctic Treaty on 1 December 1959 in Washington, D.C., by Ambassador Herman Phleger from the United States, who chaired the Conference on Antarctica from 15 October to 1 December 1959 (Department of State, 1960). The inscription reads, "To Laurence Gould without whom there would be no Antarctic Treaty. Warm Regards Herman Phleger". Permission to reproduce the photograph courtesy of the Carleton College Archives.

boundaries; but it is much more than that . . . it is a document unique in history which may take its place alongside the Magna Carta and other great symbols of man's quest for enlightenment and order."

This comparison may seem presumptuous. Our civilization has nearly eight centuries of learning from England's Great Charter of 1215, which has ensured that "no freeman shall be captured or imprisoned . . . except by lawful judgment of his peers or by the law of the land." Even today, after 50 years, the Antarctic Treaty is still in its infancy relative to the Magna Carta, which has served as a worldwide precedent for constitutional law and national democracy.

The great symbol of the Antarctic Treaty and the quest for enlightenment and order were the genius of a man from Denison, Texas, who later served as the supreme commander of the Allied forces in Europe during the Second World War and then as 34th president of the United States. When President Dwight David Eisenhower entered office on 20 January 1953, he understood firsthand the devastation of global conflict as well as the dangers of a world with nuclear weapons (Eisenhower, 1953a): "The world and we have passed the midway point of a century of continuing challenge. We sense with all our faculties that forces of good and evil are massed and armed and opposed as rarely before in history."

Yet, rather than pandering to the prevailing paranoia in the United States, with McCarthyism rampant (Fried, 1997), President Eisenhower envisioned options for cooperation between the United States and Soviet Union, asking in his first inaugural address (Eisenhower, 1953a): "Are we nearing the light—a day of freedom and of peace of all mankind?"

For President Eisenhower, this question was more than rhetoric. He was shaping postwar policy (Eisenhower, 1965; Bowie and Immerman, 1998), as elaborated early in his administration with his "chance for peace" speech to the American Society of Newspaper Editors on 16 April 1953. This speech, which was delivered the month after the death of Joseph Stalin, identified five precepts of international relations that resonate still (Eisenhower, 1953b):

> First: No people on earth can be held, as a people, to be an enemy, for all humanity shares the common hunger for peace and fellowship and justice.
>
> Second: No nation's security and well-being can be lastingly achieved in isolation but only in effective cooperation with fellow-nations.
>
> Third: Every nation's right to a form of government and an economic system of its own choosing is inalienable.
>
> Fourth: Any nation's attempt to dictate to other nations their form of government is indefensible.
>
> And fifth: A nation's hope of lasting peace cannot be firmly based upon any race in armaments but rather upon just relations and honest understanding with all other nations.

It takes a visionary head of state to articulate such international balance and build on "common" interests. However, it takes a statesman to actually achieve peace, which is what President Eisenhower accomplished with the Antarctic Treaty in establishing a firm foundation for nearly 10% of the Earth "forever to be used exclusively for peaceful purposes" (as stated in the Antarctic Treaty, Preamble).

Projecting forward, the Antarctic Treaty may be analogous to the Magna Carta at the international scale, revealing a grand experiment that will take centuries to assess for its value in our civilization. This story is as much about the origin of the Antarctic Treaty and international spaces as it is about the statesman who rose to the occasion by using science as a tool of diplomacy for the benefit of all humanity. This story is about hope for future generations.

CONVERGING SECURITY MATTERS

The late 1940s and early 1950s was a dangerous period of cold war posturing, as the United States and Soviet Union raced to create ballistic missiles that could deliver nuclear weapons across continents (Joint Chiefs of Staff, 1957). Few bridges were being considered, much less built, between these superpowers. It was during this period of turbulence in the wake of World War II, as revealed in minutes of U.S. National Security Council meetings from 1954 to 1959 (Table 1), when President Eisenhower became the catalyst for an unprecedented mixture of global security elements (ballistic missiles, geophysical research, and international spaces) that will remain forever as part of our civilization.

The world was inexorably introduced to nuclear weapons after their 1945 deployment by the United States to end World War II in Japan. By 1949, the Union of Soviet Socialist Republics also had proven capacity to detonate atomic weapons (Rhodes, 1996). The risk of deployment was not limited to air delivery by planes, as was the case during World War II, it was the inevitability of nuclear weapons that could be delivered by rockets with ranges across continents.

Both the United States and Soviet Union clearly understood that such intercontinental ballistic missiles would become an enduring security threat to the welfare of all nations, people, and living systems on our home planet. However, with the iron curtain of the cold war descending (Churchill, 1946), cooperation between the two superpowers (especially regarding military topics, such as rockets) was at a standstill, with both nations independently pursuing the development of missiles that could annihilate the other. According to John Foster Dulles, US Secretary of State, it was a time of "brinkmanship" (Shepley, 1956:78): "The ability to get to the verge without getting into war is the necessary art. If you cannot master it, you inevitably get into war. If you try to run away from it, if you are scared to go to the brink, you are lost."

After World War II, discussions began appearing about the establishment of institutions to govern regions beyond the boundaries of nations, international spaces that today extend across nearly 70% of the Earth's surface (Kish, 1973). Among the first international spaces was Antarctica, where the United States had proposed "establishment of an international area" in its 9 August 1948 Aide-Memoire and Draft Agreement (Department of State, 1948). These documents were circulated in secret by the United States to the embassies of the seven claimant nations (United Kingdom, New Zealand, France, Australia, Norway, Chile, and Argentina) with specific exclusion of the Soviet Union. The associated Draft Agreement included eight articles that defined a "special regime" for the "Antarctic continent and all islands south of 60 degrees south latitude, except the South Shetland and South Orkney Groups." Although issues of resource exploitation and sovereignty were explicit, the Aide-Memoire clarified,

TABLE 1. Mapping of topics discussed in National Security Council (NSC) meetings that specifically referenced Antarctica or the International Geophysical Year (IGY) during the Eisenhower Administrations from 1954 to 1959, determined from copies of documents from the Eisenhower Presidential Library

	Antarctic		Nuclear			Science			
Reference	Governance	Resources	Weapons	Stockpiles	Missiles	Safety	IGY	Space	Satellites
NSC (1954a)	X[a,b,c,d]						X		
NSC (1954b)	X[a,b,c]								
NSF (1955a)					X		X	X	X[c]
NSC (1955b)	X[b,c]		X		X[c]				
NSC (1955c)	X[a,b,c,e]	X							
NSC (1956)	X[a]	X		X	X	X	X		
NSC (1957a)	X[a,b]	X	X[c]						
NSC (1957b)	X				X				
NSC (1957c)	X[a,b,c,f,g,h]	X			X		X		
NSC (1958a)	X[a,b,c,f,g,i]	X					X		
NSC (1958b)	X[a,b,c,f,g]		X		X		X	X	
NSC (1958c)	X		X		X		X	X	X
NSC (1958d)	X[a,b,c,f,g]				X		X		
NSC (1959)	X[a,b,c,f,g,j]						X		

[a] References the Antarctic claimant nations (Argentina, Australia, Chile, France, New Zealand, Norway, and United Kingdom).
[b] References possible claim by the United States.
[c] References the Union of Soviet Socialist Republics.
[d] Includes map of Antarctica with the Antarctic Convergence and map of claimant sectors.
[e] Includes map of Antarctic claimant sectors.
[f] Includes nonclaimant nations participating in IGY research in Antarctica (Belgium, Japan, South Africa, Union of Soviet Socialist Republics, and United States).
[g] References the United Nations.
[h] Includes map of Antarctic claims.
[i] Includes 9 August 1948 U.S. Aide Memoire and Draft Agreement on Antarctica and 10 June 1950 Soviet Memorandum on the Antarctic.
[j] Includes 10 June 1950 Soviet Memorandum on the Antarctic; 2 May 1958 note delivered by the United States to the other 11 nations participating in Antarctic research during the IGY; and 3 May 1958 Statement by the president.

"The foreseeable values of Antarctica are predominantly scientific rather than strategic or economic. An international regime would be well calculated to promote the exploitation of these scientific values."

Moreover, the United States and other governments increasingly recognized that "without scientific progress no amount of achievement in other directions can insure our health, prosperity, and security as a nation in the modern world" (Bush, 1945). Although the value of science was largely seen in terms of "new products, new industries, and more jobs," there was nascent recognition that the "most recent example of large-scale international cooperation is to be found in the Second International Polar Year of 1932–33" (Roberts, 1949). Soon after, on 5 April 1950, in a historic meeting at the home of James Van Allen, the 3rd International Polar Year (IPY) was conceived, initially with a focus on upper atmospheric research (Korsmo, 2007). Studying the upper atmosphere would involve rockets, and it was this geophysical research tool that facilitated convergence between ballistic missiles and the international governance of Antarctica.

With a global focus under the auspices of the International Council of Scientific Unions (ICSU), the 3rd IPY was renamed in 1952 as the International Geophysical Year, the IGY (Jones, 1959; Berkman, 2003). At that time, the Soviet Union had yet to become effectively engaged in either ICSU or planning the IGY from 1 June 1957 through 31 December 1958, even though Russia had contributed to the 2nd IPY (Laursen, 1959) as well as the 1st IPY in 1882–1883 (Heathcote and Armitage, 1959). Soviet engagement largely began only after the October 1954 ICSU meeting in Rome, where the United States proposed that satellite launches should become a significant component of the IGY (Siddiqi, 2000; Bulkeley, 2008).

Still, in 1954, the United States had no intention to interact with the Soviet Union in managing Antarctica, as reflected by the statements in the National Security Council (1954a): "Orderly progress toward a solution of the territorial problem of Antarctica which would ensure maintenance of control by the United States and friendly powers and exclude our most probable enemies." It was further believed that "any increase in activity in Antarctica, particularly by the U.S., may result in the announcement of claims by the USSR." More specifically, it was decided on 15 July 1954 "to make sure that Russia was not invited to take part in any discussions or negotiations respecting Antarctica" (National Security Council, 1954b).

These U.S. Antarctic policies began to reverse with active involvement of the Soviet Union in the IGY, as noted in a White House memorandum from the special assistant to President Eisenhower on 17 May 1955 (Rockefeller, 1955):

> B. I am informed that the IGY in its Rome meeting last year endorsed the launching of a satellite as a desirable scientific step.
>
> C. Since Russia is represented in this organization it would be in a position to know immediately of any U.S. offer made by the Government through the U.S. National Committee to launch a satellite.

The outcome of such discussions emerged on 20 May 1955 with the United States' first space policy to "endeavor to launch a small scientific satellite under international auspices, such as the International Geophysical Year, in order to emphasize its peaceful purposes" (National Security Council, 1955a): "a program for a small scientific satellite could be developed from existing missile programs already underway within the Department of Defense . . . the IGY affords an excellent opportunity to mesh a scientific satellite program with the cooperative world-wide geophysical observational program." Unknown at the time, the IGY was opening a new channel for U.S.-Soviet dialogue, and by 13 July 1955, with information about "plans of the Soviet Government for an expedition to Antarctica in connections with the International Geophysical Year," there was "desirability of a review of U.S. policy toward Antarctica" (National Security Council, 1955b).

ROCKET PRIORITIES

Quite separate from the IGY, satellites clearly were linked to ballistic missiles and government considerations about the eventuality of humankind in space (National Security Council, 1955a):

> The inference of such a demonstration of advanced technology and its unmistakable relationship of intercontinental ballistic missile technology might have important repercussions on the political determination of free world countries to resist Communist threats, especially if the USSR were to be the first to establish a satellite. Furthermore, a small scientific satellite will provide a test of the principle of "Freedom of Space."

The concept of the "Freedom of Space" was seen to be analogous to the freedom of the seas (Hall, 1995). As a legal construct, freedom of the seas had been evolving for centuries. Notably, the Dutch jurist Hugo de Groot had written *Mare Liberum* in 1609 to describe certain freedoms beyond sovereign jurisdictions enjoyed by all humankind in the sea (Bull et al., 1990). The freedom of space would become a next step for humanity.

Recognizing the challenge of "weapons many, many times more destructive . . . than ever known or imagined before," President Eisenhower then introduced his Open Skies proposal in Geneva on 21 July 1955 (Eisenhower, 1955). Noting that "disarmament agreements without adequate reciprocal inspection increase the dangers of war and do not brighten the prospects of peace," President Eisenhower went on to propose that the United States and the Soviet Union would give each other a "complete blueprint of our military establishments" as part of a system of mutual aerial reconnaissance.

Before the day ended, Chairman of the Soviet Council of Ministers Nikolai Bulganin and First Secretary of the Communist Party Nikita Khrushchev rejected Open Skies as an obvious American attempt to "accumulate target information" (Hall, 1995). This result was not surprising to President Eisenhower, who later indicated in an interview that "we knew the Soviets wouldn't accept it" (Parmet, 1972; Rostow, 1983). Immediately afterward, on 29 July 1955, the White House publicly disclosed its intention to create a scientific satellite program as part of the IGY under the principle of the Freedom of Space (Hagerty, 1955): "On behalf of the President, I am now announcing that the President has approved plans for this country for going ahead with the launching of small earth-circling satellites as part of the United States participation in the International Geophysical Year."

Throughout this period, the United States also was continuing its rocket development programs through the Navy, Air Force, and Army (Erickson, 2005). An Advisory Group Committee on Special Capabilities was appointed to determine which of these military branches would be in charge of launching the IGY satellites (Green and Lomask, 1970; Baker, 1978; Day, 2007).

Ultimately, the Navy was given responsibility for launching the IGY satellite with their Vanguard rockets, "first, to accent the scientific purposes of the satellite and, second, to avoid interference with topic priority missile programs" (National Security Council, 1957d). The most notable rocket progress, however, was under the technical direction of Wernher von Braun at the Redstone arsenal, which became the site of the Army Ballistic Missile Agency on 1 February 1956 to weaponize rockets and develop the Jupiter Intermediate Range Ballistic Missile (von Braun and Ordway, 1975).

As expressed with firsthand knowledge by von Braun's co-worker, Frederick I. Ordway III (F. I. Ordway, personal communication, 17 March 2007), it was during 1956 when an order was given to the Army Ballistic Missile Agency that it should not plan for, or attempt, a satellite launch because (Murphree, 1956) "satellite effort using the JUPITER reentry test vehicle may have the effect of disrupting our relations with the non-military scientific community and international elements of the IGY group." This order was given despite the "considerable prestige and psychological benefits [that] will accrue to the nation which first is successful in launching a satellite" (National Security Council, 1955a). What happened next is nothing short of amazing.

On 20 September 1956, the four-stage Jupiter-C (Composite Re-entry Test Vehicle) RS-27 was launched from Redstone with the fourth stage intentionally inactivated and filled with sand (Lethbridge, 2000), which continued in subsequent nose cone retrieval tests (Logsdon et al., 1999). The Jupiter-C RS-27 attained a range of 3335 miles (5367 km) and an altitude of 682 miles (1098 km) and "could have obtained sufficient velocity to place it in orbit, if the last stage had been activated" (Wade, 2008), more than a year before the IGY launch of Sputnik 1 by the Soviet Union on 4 October 1957 (Killian, 1977).

The fact that the United States deliberately did not utilize all means available to become the first nation in space is inescapable. The Sputnik 1 launch was no surprise considering the United States had intelligence in July 1957 that the President of the Soviet Academy of Sciences had stated (Dulles, 1957), "soon, literally in the next few months, the earth will get its second satellite." Moreover, in his press conference on 9 October 1957 regarding the Sputnik 1 launch, President Eisenhower indicated (Eisenhower, 1957): "There never has been one nickel asked for accelerating the program. Never has it been considered as a race; merely an engagement on our part to put up a vehicle of this kind during the period [i.e., International Geophysical Year] that I have already mentioned."

Launching the first satellite would neither have accelerated nor impeded the ballistic missile capacity of the United States. What did the United States have to gain or lose by withholding the Jupiter C?

Finally, on 31 January 1958 (three months after the world's first artificial satellite), following the failure of the Vanguard rockets, the United States successfully launched the Explorer 1 satellite using a fourth-stage-activated Jupiter-C rocket. Although this rocket chronology is well known (e.g., Green and Lomask, 1970), it still begs the question of why the United States chose not to be the first in space, in stark contrast to the race for "priority" that has motivated nations and explorers alike throughout human history. The answer is revealed in a White House meeting with President Eisenhower four days after Sputnik 1, when the originator of the Freedom of Space doctrine and the person who appointed the ad hoc Group on Special Capabilities, Deputy Secretary of Defense Donald Quarles, observed (McDougall, 1985): "There was no doubt . . . that the Redstone, had it been used could have orbited a satellite a year or more ago. The Russians have in fact done us a good turn, unintentionally, in establishing the concept of freedom of international space."

The implication of Quarles' statement is that a U.S. weapons system as the first in space would have exacerbated the cold war, which was a serious concern since the Soviet Union already had nuclear weapons that could be delivered by manned aircraft and there were "possibilities of a future war" (National Security Council, 1956): "The President asked the National Security Council to imagine a situation in which the United States had actually won a thermonuclear war. With so much destruction heaped on the country and with our ports in ruins . . ."

This question reflects the underlying philosophy that President Eisenhower had been developing since his 1953 "atoms of peace" speech to the United Nations General Assembly, seeking "an acceptable solution to the atomic armaments race which over shadows not only the peace, but the very life, of the world" (Eisenhower, 1953c). President Eisenhower was building toward a commitment from the Soviet Union not to weaponize space (Eisenhower, 2004).

Launching the first human-made satellite with the Jupiter-C, especially in 1956 before the IGY had even begun, would have contravened the first U.S. space policy (National Security Council, 1955a) and undermined the peaceful objectives of the IGY, very likely leading to the weaponization of space. Establishing "priority" with the Jupiter-C also would have destabilized international scientific cooperation, which was growing in national security importance because the "major emphasis of U.S. programs in Antarctica was placed upon scientific activities in support of the International Geophysical Year" (National Security Council, 1957b).

PEACEFUL PURPOSES ONLY

With the Soviet Union and United States both in outer space by early 1958, Antarctica "assumed some strategic importance in the light of recent technological advances and increased Soviet activity" (National Security Council, 1958a). This "strategic importance" of Antarctica provided the catalyst for the United States to finalize the governance of this international space, which had been considered on an ongoing basis since the Aide-Memoire in 1948 (Table 1).

Since 1948, the United States had been suggesting that the "promotion of scientific investigation in Antarctica and the solution of conflicting claims might be accomplished by some form of internationalization" (National Security Council, 1958a; Table 1). Alternatives for this internationalization included a "condominium," whereby Antarctic claims would be merged, as well as a United Nations' "trusteeship" that could be established over part or all of Antarctica.

By February 1958, with "urgency to the need to reconsider U.S. policy in Antarctica", the United States also was considering (National Security Council, 1958a): "the conclusion of a multilateral treaty—which would include provision for an Antarctic organization—among the countries having direct and substantial interests in Antarctica, including the USSR."It is noteworthy that this new policy position was opposed by the Joint Chiefs of Staff, who "wished to exclude the USSR from any voice in the administration of Antarctica" (National Security Council, 1958b).

However, as noted by Secretary of State Dulles, the interests of the United States were to "demilitarize the entire area," and there was "no way to push the Soviet Union out of Antarctica without resort to force" (National Security Council, 1958b). Moreover, the United States was specifically concerned about "Antarctica's becoming a scene of East-West conflict or being used for military or nuclear development purposes" (National Security Council, 1958a). It also was recognized that the Soviet Union would agitate against any multilateral treaty for Antarctica if they were not a party.

In the end, as reasoned by the Department of State (National Security Council, 1958a), the pros outweighed the cons for Soviet involvement, and on 3 May 1958, President Eisenhower extended an invitation to all nations conducting Antarctic research during the IGY (Eisenhower, 1958):

> The United States is dedicated to the principle that the vast uninhabited wastes of Antarctica shall be used only for peaceful purposes. We do not want Antarctica to become an object of political conflict. Accordingly, the United States has invited eleven other countries, including the Soviet Union, to confer with us to seek an effective joint means of achieving this objective.

Within three months of President Eisenhower's invitation, "all countries invited accepted; and preliminary information discussions with representatives of the 11 countries concerned have been held regularly in Washington since June 13, 1958" (National Security Council, 1959).

Over the next 14 months, at the height of the cold war, the two superpowers and the other 10 IGY Antarctic nations contributed to 60 secret preparatory meetings in Washington, D.C., to hammer out a firm foundation for the Antarctic Treaty (*Washington Post*, 1959). This "secret advance consultation" was conceived for these nations "to reach agreement on the broad basis for an Antarctic organization" with the overarching objective "toward a peaceful solution of the problem of Antarctica" (National Security Council, 1958a). As a contingency, the "secret advance consultation" also enabled the United States to "prepare the way for cooperative arrangements . . . in the event of failure to achieve such an Antarctic organization which includes the USSR."

With science as the "keystone common interest" (Berkman, 2002), the final negotiations were convened with the Conference on Antarctica at the Department of State annex on 1776 Pennsylvania Avenue in Washington, D.C., from 15 October to 1 December 1959, when the Antarctic Treaty was signed by the seven claimant and five non-claimant nations, which included the United States and Soviet Union (Department of State, 1960). Beyond prohibiting "any measure of a military nature," the Antarctic Treaty became the first nuclear arms agreement in our world (Office of the Deputy Assistant to the Secretary of Defense for Nuclear Matters, 2007) by establishing that "any nuclear explosions in Antarctica and the disposal there of radioactive waste material shall be prohibited." Moreover, the Antarctic Treaty instituted international inspection innovations that built on the Open Skies concepts proposed by President Eisenhower in 1955, so that unilateral "aerial observation may be carried out at any time over any or all areas of Antarctica by any of the Contracting Parties." Although other nations were involved in negotiating the Antarctic Treaty, particularly with regard to territorial claims, the nuclear arms and inspection provisions were directed by the two cold war superpowers for their cooperation in that part of the world initially. As heralded by the press that week in December 1959 (*Cleveland Plain Dealer*, 1959), "Cold War Thaws in Antarctic."

The Antarctic Treaty, which has been unchanged since it was signed an half century ago, is groundbreaking in its 14-article simplicity and breadth to ensure that that the region south of 60°S latitude "shall not become the scene or object of international discord" (Antarctic Treaty, Preamble). As the catalyst for the Antarctic Treaty, the IGY demonstrates how science can serve as a tool of diplomacy that facilitates successful negotiations among nations beyond political, economic, or cultural barriers.

Moreover, with critical contributions, especially from the Scientific Committee on Antarctic Research (Summerhayes, 2008), the Antarctic Treaty has evolved into a resilient system (Polar Research Board, 1986) that has come to include diverse components such as the 1980 Convention on the Conservation of Antarctic Marine Living Resources and the 1991 Protocol on Environmental Protection to the Antarctic Treaty. Continuity of the Antarctic Treaty reflects the role of science as a "substantial" activity that inspires ongoing consultation among nations to resolve issues "in the interest of all mankind."

BALANCING INTERESTS GLOBALLY

As a fundamental transition period in our civilization, the twentieth century was when we became a global community (Figure 2). The first half of the twentieth century was marred by devastating conflicts among nations on a global scale: the concept of world wars. In contrast, the second half of the twentieth century opened the door to a steep learning curve of international cooperation to resolve environmental and ecosystem issues that extend across as well as beyond the boundaries of nations.

Amid the stockpiling of nuclear weapons (Rosenberg, 1983) and cold war posturing for a nuclear war (e.g., Kissinger, 1957), President Eisenhower pursued peaceful alternatives to engage the Soviet Union in cooperative dialogues. He proposed Open Skies in 1955 (Eisenhower, 1955), and when that strategy was unsuccessful, he promoted the Freedom of Space and the launch of scientific satellites during the IGY (National Security Council, 1955a). Because priority in space had not been pursued at any cost, he preserved leverage to establish the peaceful use of regions beyond sovereign jurisdictions, "international space" as Secretary Quarles had presented to him in 1957 (McDougall, 1985).

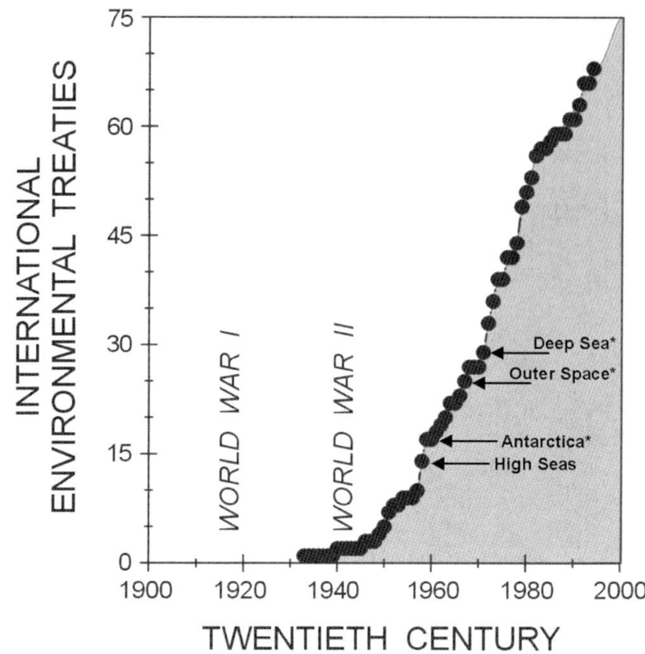

FIGURE 2. Emergence of global interdependence in our civilization during the twentieth century. Nearly 95% of the international ecosystem and environmental treaties and conventions that entered into force were signed after 1950. These frameworks for international cooperation are in stark contrast to the global conflicts represented by the two world wars during the first half of the twentieth century. Originating during the administration of President Eisenhower, international legal frameworks to establish international spaces beyond sovereign jurisdictions (arrows) were signed for the high seas and Antarctica in 1958 and 1959, respectively (Table 2). The 1959 Antarctic Treaty was the first nuclear arms agreement and the precedent for the nonarmament regimes (denoted with an asterisk, *) that were subsequently signed for outer space and the deep sea in 1967 and 1971, respectively (Table 2). Elaborated from Berkman (2002).

During his watch, the 1958 Convention on the High Seas established the legal framework for the first international space "open to all nations, no State may validly purport to subject any part of them to its sovereignty." President Eisenhower then invited allies and adversaries alike (including the Soviet Union) to negotiate the 1959 Antarctic Treaty, which also was envisioned in relation to space law (National Security Council, 1958c): "If, by analogy to the Antarctic proposal of the United States, international agreement can be reached in space and the rules and regulations to be followed with respect thereto, problems of sovereignty may be avoided or at least deferred."

With its adoption, the Antarctic Treaty also reinforced the international status of the high seas (Antarctic Treaty, Article VI): "nothing in the present Treaty shall prejudice or in any way affect the rights, or the exercise of the rights, of any State under international law with regard to the high seas within that area." Importantly, the peaceful-use and nonarmament provisions of the Antarctic Treaty as well as its firm foundation on common interests became the precedent for the outer-space and the deep-sea regimes, establishing those areas as international spaces as well (Berkman, 2009).

More than accelerating the development of international legal frameworks to resolve environmental and ecosystem issues across national boundaries, President Eisenhower paved the way for humankind to establish international spaces across most of the Earth and in the cosmos (Table 2). With Antarctica as the centerpiece among the international spaces, he established strategies for balancing national interests and common interests for the lasting benefit of all. The vision President Eisenhower presented in his first inaugural address (Eisenhower, 1953a) remains a guiding light. With hope and inspiration, the signature day of the Antarctic Treaty, December 1st, deserves to be celebrated forever as "a day of freedom and of peace for all mankind." In this spirit, 'Antarctica Day' was inaugurated on 1 December 2010 (Antarctic Treaty Summit Website Archive, 2010).

Acknowledgments

This article emerged from international planning for the Antarctic Treaty Summit: Science-Policy Interactions in International Governance (http://www.atsummit50.aq) that was convened at the Smithsonian Institution in Washington, D.C., from 30 November to 3 December 2009. I especially thank my colleagues and friends on the International Board for the Antarctic Treaty Summit: Maj De Poorter, Edith Fanta, Marie Jacobsson, Yeadong Kim, Michael A. Lang, José Retamales, David W. H. Walton, Rüdiger Wolfrum, Oran R. Young, and Abdul Hamid Zakri. I also thank Susan Eisenhower and Ernest Fredrick Roots for their helpful comments on this manuscript. Support for this manuscript was generously provided by the Prince Albert II of Monaco Foundation, Tinker Foundation, and U.S.-UK Fulbright Commission. The paper is a contribution from the Arctic Ocean Geopolitics Programme of the Scott Polar Research Institute and Judge Business School at the University of Cambridge.

TABLE 2. Initial agreements to establish international spaces beyond sovereign jurisdictions in the high seas, Antarctica, outer space and the deep sea.

Agreement name	Signature location and date	Entry into force	Peaceful purposes	Nonarmament region
Convention on the High Seas	Geneva, 29 April 1958	30 September 1962	Not Specified	Not established
Antarctic Treaty	Washington, D.C., 1 December 1959	23 June 1961	Matters of common interest	Yes
Treaty on Principles Governing the Activities of States in the Exploration and Use of Outer Space, Including the Moon and Other Celestial Bodies	London, Moscow, Washington, D.C., 27 January 1967	10 October 1967	Common interest of all mankind	Yes
Treaty on the Prohibition of the Emplacement of Nuclear Weapons and Other Weapons of Mass Destruction on the Seabed and the Ocean Floor and in the Subsoil	London, Moscow, Washington, D.C., 11 February 1971	18 May 1972	Common interest of mankind	Yes

LITERATURE CITED

Antarctic Treaty Summit Website Archive. http://www.atsummit50.aq (accessed 3 December 2010).

Baker, D. 1978. *The Rocket: The History and Development of Rocket and Missile Technology*. London: New Cavendish Books.

Berkman, P. A. 2002. *Science into Policy: Global Lessons from Antarctica*. London: Academic Press.

———. 2003. International Polar Year 2007–2008. *Science*, 301:1669.

———. 2009. International Spaces Promote Peace. *Nature*, 462:412–413.

Bowie, R. R., and R. H. Immerman. 1998. *Waging Peace: How Eisenhower Shaped an Enduring Cold War Strategy*. New York: Oxford University Press.

Bull, H., B. Kingsbury, and A. Roberts, eds. 1990. *Hugo Grotius and International Relations*. New York: Oxford University Press.

Bulkeley, R. 2008. Aspects of the Soviet IGY. *Russian Journal of Earth Sciences*, 10:1–17.

Bush, V. 1945. *Science the Endless Frontier: A Report to the President*. Washington, D.C.: Office of Scientific Research and Development.

Cleveland Plain Dealer. 1959. "Cold War Thaws in Antarctic." 6 December.

Churchill, W. 1946. "The Sinews of Peace." Speech delivered at Westminster College, Fulton, Mo., 5 March.

Day, D. A. 2007. Tinker, Tailor, Satellite, Spy. The Space Review. http://www.thespacereview.com/article/989/1 (accessed 3 December 2010).

Department of State. 1948. U.S. Aide-Memoire and Draft Agreement on Antarctica. August 9, 1948. In National Security Council 1958a, pp. 30–31.

———. 1960. *The Conference on Antarctica. Washington October 15–December 1, 1959*. Department of State Publication 7060. International Organization and Conference Series 13. Washington, D.C.: Government Printing Office.

Dulles, A. W. 1957. Letter to Deputy Secretary of Defense, Donald Quarles. 9 July 1957. Central Intelligence Agency, Washington, D.C.

Eisenhower, D. D. 1953a. Presidential Inaugural Address. Washington, D.C., 20 January.

———. 1953b. "The Chance for Peace." Speech delivered before the American Society of Newspaper Editors, Washington, D.C., 15 April.

———. 1953c. "Atoms for Peace." Speech delivered before United Nations General Assembly, New York, 8 December.

———. 1955. "'Open Skies' Proposal. 21 July 1955." In *Public Papers of the Presidents, Dwight D. Eisenhower, Documents of American History II*. pp. 713–716. Washington, D.C.: Government Printing Office.

———. 1957. Official White House Transcript of President Eisenhower's Press and Radio Conference 123 (Filmed, Taped and Shorthand Reported). Held in Room 474, Executive Office Building, Thursday, October 9, 1957. At 10:29 O'clock a.m. White House, Washington, D.C. (see: http://www.eisenhower.archives.gov/research/digital_documents/NASA/Binder1.pdf; accessed 3 December 2010)

———. 1958. Statement by the President Concerning Antarctica. 3 May 1958. *Department of State Bulletin*, 38:911.

———. 1965. *Waging Peace, 1956–1961: The White House Years*. Garden City, N.Y.: Doubleday.

Eisenhower, S. 2004. *Partners in Space: U.S.-Russian Cooperation after the Cold War*. Washington, D.C.: Eisenhower Institute.

Erickson , M. 2005. *Into the Unknown Together: The DOD, NASA and Early Spaceflight*. Maxwell Air Force Base, Ala.: Air University Press.

Fried, A. 1997. *McCarthyism: The Great American Red Scare: A Documentary History*. New York: Oxford University Press.

Green, C. M., and M. Lomask. 1970. *Vanguard: A History*. The NASA Historical Series. NASA SP-4202. Washington, D.C.: National Aeronautics and Space Administration.

Gould, L. M. 1960. Testimony to the U.S. Congress, Senate, Committee on Foreign Relations, Regarding the Ratification of the Antarctic Treaty. 14 June.

Hall, R. C. 1995. "Origins of U.S. Space Policy: Eisenhower, Open Skies, and Freedom of Space." In *Volume 1: Organizing for Exploration*, ed. J. M. Logsdon, L. G. Lear, J. Warren-Findley, R. A. Williamson, and D. A. Day, pp. 213–229, *Exploring the Unknown: Selected Documents in the History of the U.S. Civil Space Program*. NASA SP-4407. Washington, D.C.: NASA.

Hagerty, J. C. 1955. Public Statement by White House Press Secretary. Washington, D.C., 28 July.

Heathcote, N. H. de V., and A. Armitage. 1959. The First International Polar Year. *Annals of the International Geophysical Year*, 1:6–101.

Joint Chiefs of Staff. 1957. Chronology of Significant Events and Decisions Relating to the U.S. Missile and Earth Satellite Development Programs May 1942 through October 1957. Washington, D.C.: Historical Section, Joint Chiefs of Staff. 22 November.

Jones, H. S. 1959. The Inception and Development of the International Geophysical Year. *Annals of the International Geophysical Year*, 1:383–414.

Killian, J. R. 1977. *Sputnik, Scientists, and Eisenhower: A Memoir of the First Special Assistant to the President for Science and Technology*. Boston: MIT Press.

Kish, J. 1973. *The Law of International Spaces*. Leiden, Netherlands: A. W. Sijthoff.

Kissinger, H. A. 1957. *Nuclear Weapons and Foreign Policy*. New York: Harper & Brothers.

Korsmo, F. 2007. The Birth of the International Geophysical Year. *The Leading Edge*, 26(10):1312–1316.

Laursen, V. 1959. The Second International Polar Year. *Annals of the International Geophysical Year*, 1:211–234.

Lethbridge, C. 2000. Chronology of Major Events Leading to the Launch of Explorer I. http://www.spacearium.com/special/spaceline/spaceline.org/explorerchron.html (accessed 3 December 2010).

Logsdon, J. M., R. A. Williamson, R. D. Launius, R. J. Acker, S. J. Garber, and J. L. Friedman, eds. 1999. *Exploring the Unknown. Selected Documents in the History of the U.S. Civil Space Program*, vol. 4, *Accessing Space*. NASA SP-4407. Washington, D.C.: National Aeronautics and Space Administration.

McDougall, W. A. 1985. Sputnik, the Space Race, and the Cold War. *Bulletin of the Atomic Scientists*, 41(5):20–25.

Murphree, E. V. 1956. *Use of the JUPITER Re-entry Test Vehicle as a Satellite*. Memorandum prepared for Deputy Secretary of Defense. Washington, D.C., 5 July. In Logsdon et al. 1999, p. 49.

National Security Council. 1954a. Notes by the Executive Secretary to the National Security Council on Antarctica. NSC 5424. 28 June 1954. Washington, D.C.

———. 1954b. Discussion at the 206th Meeting of the National Security Council, Thursday, July 15, 1954. Washington, D.C.

———. 1955a. U.S. Scientific Satellite Program. NSC 5520. May 20, 1955. Washington, D.C.

———. 1955b. Discussion at the 258th Meeting of the National Security Council, Thursday, September 8, 1955. Washington, D.C.

———. 1955c. Antarctica. NSC 5528. December 12, 1955. Washington, D.C.

———. 1956. Discussion at the 272nd Meeting of the National Security Council, Thursday, January 12, 1956. Washington, D.C.

———. 1957a. Discussion at the 321st Meeting of the National Security Council, Thursday, May 2, 1957. Washington, D.C.

———. 1957b. Memorandum. Discussion at the 327th Meeting of the National Security Council, Thursday, June 20, 1957. Washington, D.C.

———. 1957c. Antarctica. NSC 5715/1. June 29, 1957. Washington, D.C.

———. 1957d. Memorandum. Implications of the Soviet Earth Satellite for U.S. Security. October 11, 1957. Washington, D.C.

———. 1958a. Antarctica. NSC 5804. February 25, 1958. Washington, D.C.

———. 1958b. Memorandum. Discussion at the 357th Meeting of the National Security Council, Thursday, March 6, 1958. Washington, D.C.

———. 1958c. U.S. Policy on Outer Space. NSC 5814. June 20, 1958. Washington, D.C.

———. 1958d. Memorandum. Discussion at the 375th Meeting of the National Security Council, Thursday, August 7, 1958. Washington, D.C.

———. 1959. *U.S. Policy on Antarctica. NSC 5905. 25 March 1959.* Washington, D.C.

Office of the Deputy Assistant to the Secretary of Defense for Nuclear Matters. 2007. International Treaties and Agreements. http://www.acq.osd.mil/ncbdp/nm/print/printinternational.html (accessed 3 December 2010).

Parmet, H. W. 1972. *Eisenhower and the American Crusades*. New York: MacMillan Company.

Polar Research Board. 1986. *Antarctic Treaty System: An Assessment: Proceedings of a Workshop Held at Beardmore South Field Camp, Antarctica, January 7–13, 1985*. Washington, D.C.: National Academies Press.

Rhodes, R. 1996. *Dark Sun: The Making of The Hydrogen Bomb*. New York: Simon and Schuster.

Rockefeller, N. A. 1955. White House Memorandum on U.S. Scientific Satellite Program. May 17, 1955. Washington, D.C.

Roberts, B. 1949. International Organizations for Polar Exploration. *Polar Record*, 5:352–354.

Rosenberg, D. A. 1983. The Origins of Overkill. Nuclear Weapons and American Strategy, 1945–1960. *International Security*, 7(4):3–71.

Rostow, W. W. 1983. *Open Skies: Eisenhower's Proposal of July 21, 1955*. Austin: University of Texas Press.

Shepley, J. 1956. "How Dulles Averted War." *Life*, 16 January: 70–80.

Siddiqi, A. A. 2000. "Korolev, Sputnik, and the International Geophysical Year." In *Reconsidering Sputnik: Forty Years since the Soviet Satellite*, ed. R. D. Launius, J. M. Logsdon, and R. W. Smith, pp. 43–72. Amsterdam: Harwood Academic.

Summerhayes, C. 2008. International Collaboration in Antarctica: The International Polar Years, the International Geophysical Year, and the Scientific Committee on Antarctic Research. *Polar Record*, 44:321–334.

von Braun, W., and F. I. Ordway III. 1975. *History of Rocketry and Space Travel*. New York: Crowell.

Wade, M. 2008. Encyclopedia Astronautica. http://www.astronautix.com/sites/capallc5.htm (accessed 3 December 2010).

Washington Post. 1959. "Twelve Nations Agree to Peaceful Antarctic." 21 October.

The Development of the Antarctic Treaty System

Tucker Scully

ABSTRACT. This paper will examine the evolution of the Antarctic Treaty from the perspective of governance, looking at the Antarctic Treaty as a mechanism for anticipating, identifying, and responding to new circumstances or activities requiring common action. It will inevitably touch upon both substance (what has been achieved under the Antarctic Treaty) and process (how it has been achieved). As such, it will address the story of the development of the Antarctic Treaty into what is now known as the Antarctic Treaty System.

THE TREATY

Negotiation of the Antarctic Treaty of 1959 may be viewed as an effort to provide for a system of governance for scientific research in the most remote and inhospitable region of the planet. In fact, its direct antecedent was the International Geophysical Year (IGY) of 1957–1958. The IGY confirmed the unique opportunities for scientific research of worldwide importance offered by Antarctica and the importance of international cooperation to take advantage of those opportunities.

The IGY grew out of proposals for a third international polar year, with a priority accorded to research in the Antarctic. Antarctica was the least studied region of the planet, and earlier polar years had concentrated on the Arctic. Rapid advances in technology and logistics, spurred in part by World War II, opened previously unavailable opportunities to pursue geophysical and other sciences in the extreme conditions of Antarctica.

Twelve nations joined in the IGY's cooperative program of research and associated logistics support activities in Antarctica: Argentina, Australia, Belgium, Chile, France, Japan, New Zealand, Norway, South Africa, the Soviet Union, the United Kingdom, and the United States. The IGY represented an unprecedented and extremely successful program of scientific collaboration. Groundbreaking research was carried out in a variety of disciplines, including geology, glaciology, geomagnetism, meteorology, and upper-atmosphere physics.

For IGY activities to go forward in Antarctica, its planners had to deal with the political realities of Antarctica in the mid-twentieth century, including, specifically, the potential for international conflict there. Such potential arose first from

R. Tucker Scully, 1517 P Street, N.W., Apt. #3, Washington, D.C. 20005, USA. Correspondence: leetucker@verizon.net.

disputes over territorial sovereignty in Antarctica and second from the ideological and military competition between the United States and its allies and the Soviet Union and its allies that emerged from World War II (the cold war).

The issue of territorial sovereignty, the legal status of Antarctica, did not become a major issue during the first century of human activities in and around the continent. In the twentieth century, however, seven countries asserted claims to territorial sovereignty to parts of Antarctica. These were Argentina, Australia, Chile, France, New Zealand, Norway, and the United Kingdom. Three of these claims overlap. Basically, Argentina, Chile, and the United Kingdom all claim the Antarctic Peninsula as their territory. Moreover, a significant part of Antarctica, Marie Byrd Land, was unclaimed. These seven countries participated in the IGY. Other nations, including the other five IGY participants (Belgium, Japan, South Africa, the Soviet Union (Russia), and the United States), neither asserted nor recognized claims to territorial sovereignty.

The stationing of military forces in the Antarctic Peninsula during World War II to counter possible German use of the area as a base for naval operations created tensions between Argentina and the United Kingdom that continued to grow in the postwar decade, raising fears of actual conflict.

On the global level, the question of governance of Antarctica was raised in the United Nations, and a proposal was made for some type of UN trusteeship over the continent. That idea was rejected by claimant countries. Another idea that emerged was for an eight-nation condominium to oversee Antarctica, with the seven existing claimants plus the United States (which presumably was to claim Marie Byrd Land) as the overseers.

This latter idea drew a strong reaction from the Soviet Union. Citing both early Russian explorations and more-recent Soviet scientific activities, the Soviet Union warned that it would disregard any decisions on Antarctica in which it did not take part. The Soviet position raised the prospect of cold war competition and conflict being added to the disputes over territorial sovereignty.

In the face of this political climate, the IGY planners, essentially, their national academies of science, opted for including the Soviet Union fully in the scientific programs and persuaded their governments to temporarily set aside their differences over territorial sovereignty. In return, IGY participants undertook to share in advance plans for all scientific investigations and to make fully available the results of such activities after their completion.

The informal arrangements worked out for the IGY were so successful, and the resulting research so productive, that the scientists pressed their governments to establish them on a continuing and binding basis. As a consequence, the United States took the initiative to convene a conference of the 12 IGY countries. Negotiations initiated in mid-1958 bore fruit with the signing of the Antarctic Treaty on 1 December 1959. It entered into force on 30 June 1961.

The Antarctic Treaty's basic objectives center upon the freedom of scientific research and scientific cooperation in Antarctica and reserving Antarctica exclusively for peaceful purposes. These objectives are converted into binding obligations in the operative articles of the Antarctic Treaty.

The Antarctic Treaty applies to the area south of 60°S latitude, including all ice shelves, but nothing in the Antarctic Treaty is to prejudice or in any way affect the rights, or the exercise of the rights by any state, under international law with regard to the high seas within that area (Article VI). Freedom of scientific investigation in Antarctica and cooperation therein as applied in the IGY shall continue (Article II). To promote such cooperation, the parties to the Antarctic Treaty agree to share information regarding plans for scientific programs in Antarctica in advance of the research activities, to exchange scientific personnel between expeditions and stations in Antarctica, and to ensure that the observations and results of scientific research in Antarctica are shared and made freely available (Article III.1). There is also provision for the establishment of cooperative working relations with those specialized agencies of the United Nations and other international organizations having a scientific or technical interest in Antarctica (Article III.2).

Antarctica shall be used for peaceful purposes only; military activities are prohibited, including the establishment of military bases and fortifications, military maneuvers, and the testing of weapons (Article I). Nuclear explosions and the disposal of radioactive waste in Antarctica are also prohibited (Article V).

In support of these basic obligations, the Antarctic Treaty provides for a system of on-site inspection (Article VII). Each party has the right to designate observers with free access to all areas of and to all stations and installations in Antarctica to ensure observance of the provisions of the Antarctic Treaty.

Articles I and V establish Antarctica as a nuclear-free zone of peace. An important objective of these provisions was to remove the threat of cold-war-generated conflict from Antarctica. The Soviet Union, as an important player in polar science, had participated in the IGY, but there was concern that its inclusion in the governance of Antarctica would bring cold war competition and conflict to the area. The zone of peace provisions respond to this concern.

Perhaps even more importantly, achievement of the Antarctic Treaty's substantive objectives required that it deal with the basic disagreement over the legal and political status of Antarctica: the issue of claims to territorial sovereignty. As mentioned, 7 of the 12 original parties to the Antarctic Treaty (Argentina, Australia, Chile, France, New Zealand, Norway, and the United Kingdom) assert claims to territorial sovereignty in Antarctica. Three of these claims overlap. The other five original parties to the Antarctic Treaty (Belgium, Japan, South Africa, the Soviet Union (Russia), and the United States) neither assert nor recognize claims to territorial sovereignty. Two of the five, the United States and the Soviet Union, although neither asserting claims nor recognizing the claims of others, maintained that their past activities in Antarctica gave them the basis for making claims in the future if circumstances dictated. The Antarctic Treaty addresses this disagreement in the juridical accommodation reflected in Article IV.

Nothing in the Antarctic Treaty is to be interpreted as a renunciation of previously asserted rights of or claims to territorial sovereignty in Antarctica and any basis of such claim or as prejudicing the position of any party regarding recognition or nonrecognition of claims. No activities taking place while the Antarctic Treaty is in force shall constitute a basis for asserting, supporting, or denying a claim to sovereignty in Antarctica or create any rights of sovereignty there. Further, no new claim or enlargement of an existing claim may be asserted while the Antarctic Treaty is in force.

Article IV is sometimes described, not surprisingly, as freezing the respective positions on territorial sovereignty. In the sense of preserving a balance in these positions I would agree.

Equally important, Article IV's juridical accommodation, combined with the other substantive provisions of the Antarctic Treaty, allows its Parties to agree on how activities actually take place in Antarctica. The Antarctic Treaty applies what has been called a bifocal approach, which permits application of common sets of obligations to those activities with which the Antarctic Treaty deals and in a way that each side, claimant and nonclaimant alike, can view as consistent with its basic legal position.

This bifocal approach can be illustrated by the example of a scientist from the United States undertaking research in the area claimed by New Zealand. New Zealand would assert that in exercise of its sovereignty over this area, it has the exclusive right to authorize scientific research there and to determine conditions for its conduct. As a party to the Antarctic Treaty, however, New Zealand can take the position that it has given its consent for scientists of other Antarctic Treaty parties to carry out research in its claimed area provided that they observe the obligations applicable to such research set forth in the Antarctic Treaty.

The United States, on the other hand, would disagree with New Zealand's interpretation since, in the U.S.'s view, there is no territorial sovereignty in Antarctica. It would assert, therefore, that pursuant to its jurisdiction over its nationals wherever they are, it has the exclusive right to authorize research by U.S. scientists anywhere in Antarctica and determine conditions for their conduct. As a party to the Antarctic Treaty, however, the United States can take the position that it has exercised this exclusive jurisdiction in authorizing the research and requiring observation of the obligations on such research set forth in the Antarctic Treaty.

Each side, therefore, can assert that the research is taking place in a manner consistent with its legal position. In spite of the differences in their legal positions, however, each side agrees that the research go forward under commonly agreed conditions.

The bifocal approach is a basic element in Antarctic governance. It reflects a fundamental principle of restraint by all parties, in effect, recognition that the effort to determine which position is to prevail on the question of territorial sovereignty or jurisdiction in Antarctica is not only unnecessary but also undesirable. Removal of this imperative also removes a potentially potent source of conflict.

The Antarctic Treaty includes a mechanism to develop specific measures to implement or further elaborate its substantive obligations. Article IX provides for regular meetings of the parties for the purpose of consulting together on matters of common interest concerning Antarctica and developing recommended measures in furtherance of the principles and objectives of the Antarctic Treaty (called Consultative Meetings).

In this regard, there are two other important elements in establishing the basis for achieving and building upon the Antarctic Treaty's substantive obligations: the activities criterion and consensus decision making. Participation in the Consultative Meetings is open to the 12 original parties (all of whom had initiated scientific programs in Antarctica during the IGY) and to any other country that becomes party to the Antarctic Treaty during such time as that party demonstrates its interest in Antarctica by the conduct of substantial scientific research there. Decision-making competence, therefore, is linked to research activities in Antarctica. Those parties participating in Consultative Meetings with decision-making authority are known as Consultative Parties.

Measures recommended at Consultative Meetings become effective when approved by all Consultative Parties. Under the rules of procedures for Consultative Meetings, recommendations for such measures require approval of all representatives present. These rules have been applied, in practice, on a no-objection or consensus basis.

The Antarctic Treaty's consensus-based decision-making system adds important political reinforcement to the juridical accommodation set forth in Article IV. Each party is provided the assurance that it cannot be outvoted on decisions that could affect the issues of sovereignty dealt with in Article IV.

The activities criterion, tying decision-making authority to actual activities in Antarctica, is an important stimulus for cooperation there. Decisions on activities in Antarctica are taken by those actually carrying them out: an incentive to base decisions on the common and shared experience of Antarctica and a deterrent to politicizing issues. This activities criterion tends to restrain possible abuse of the power to object in consensus decision making.

These legal and political provisions have been essential ingredients in the practical achievement of the objectives that lie at the heart of the Antarctic Treaty. Antarctica has been and remains an effective zone of peace and the scene of cutting-edge scientific research.

THE EVOLUTION OF THE ANTARCTIC TREATY

The success of the Antarctic Treaty in securing Antarctica as an area free of conflict and the scientific understanding of the continent and surrounding waters promoted by the Antarctic Treaty have been preconditions for extending the experiment, i.e., for the evolution of the Antarctic Treaty as a system of governance. It is important to remember that the Antarctic Treaty was, at the outset, a limited-purpose agreement. It dealt with freedom of scientific investigation in Antarctica and establishing it as a zone of peace. The legal and political accommodations in the Antarctic Treaty applied to these obligations and activities related thereto but did not apply to activities not mentioned in the Antarctic Treaty, such as the exploitation of resources.

At the same time, the drafters of the Antarctic Treaty anticipated the need for its future evolution in providing for the regular Consultative Meetings to adopt recommendations in furtherance of the principles and purposes of the Antarctic Treaty (Article IX). This is also reflected in the provision for establishing cooperative working relationships with international organizations having a scientific or technical interest in Antarctica (Article III, paragraph 2). Interest in Antarctica as a basis for interaction with other organizations, a variation on the activities criterion, has been an important theme in the evolution of the Antarctic Treaty.

In addressing the evolution of the Antarctic Treaty, the role played by the Scientific Committee on Antarctic Research (SCAR) should also be highlighted. A nongovernmental body and member of the International Council of Scientific Unions (now the International Council for Science), SCAR originated as a scientific mechanism for coordinating activities in Antarctica for the IGY. Following the IGY, it became a permanent body to provide a continuing means for coordinating and facilitating scientific research activities and for identifying scientific priorities in Antarctica.

Science has played a key role in the evolution of the Antarctic Treaty. The results of scientific research and observations in Antarctica have contributed importantly to the definition of issues that require intergovernmental agreement and are an important basis for evaluating the intergovernmental response to such issues once identified. SCAR has been central to this aspect of the Antarctic Treaty's evolution by providing a valuable source of scientific advice and peer review for the Antarctic Treaty and from a nongovernmental perspective.

As a result of the work of Antarctic Treaty Consultative Meetings, a wide range of measures have been adopted to extend the principles and purposes of the Antarctic Treaty to human activities in Antarctica and to avoid adverse impacts of those activities. These include measures on the facilitation of scientific research and logistic support thereof; conservation of Antarctic fauna and flora and protection of the Antarctic environment; designation of protected areas, historical sites, and monuments; cooperation in meteorology, telecommunication, and emergency response; air safety; tourism; and the operation of the Antarctic Treaty itself.

A perhaps even more important impetus of the evolution of the Antarctic Treaty to what is known as the Antarctic Treaty System was the effort to deal with possible resource activities in Antarctica: first, Antarctic marine living resources and, second, Antarctic mineral resources.

ANTARCTIC MARINE LIVING RESOURCES

The preservation and conservation of living resources in Antarctica was cited in the Antarctic Treaty itself as a subject for measures to be adopted at Antarctic Treaty Consultative Meetings (Article IX, paragraph 9(f)). Recommendation I-VIII, adopted at the First Antarctic Treaty Consultative Meeting in 1961, recognized the urgent need to conserve and protect living resources in the area of the Antarctic Treaty.

A first result was the Agreed Measures for the Conservation of Antarctic Fauna and Flora adopted in 1964. The agreed measures were aimed at ensuring that human activities in Antarctica, then primarily scientific research and associated logistics support activities, did not adversely affect Antarctic fauna and flora. They prohibited the taking of native species except for compelling scientific purposes and set forth far-reaching measures to avoid harmful interference with populations of such species and to protect their habitats. The reach of the measures was to the continent and its ice shelves, not to adjacent offshore waters.

The second major initiative to deal with marine living resources was a new agreement designed to deal with the possible reemergence of commercial exploitation of seals, in particular, crabeater seals. It was recognized that any effort to reinitiate commercial exploitation of seals would need to cover pack ice areas of the high seas. In light of the potentially differing interpretations of the application of a measure adopted under the Antarctic Treaty to the high-seas areas (Article VI), the Consultative Parties, therefore, with significant scientific input from SCAR, set out to negotiate a freestanding agreement on pelagic sealing.

The resulting Convention on the Conservation for Antarctic Seals (CCAS), concluded in 1972, established sealing zones and precautionary catch limits in those zones; SCAR was designated as the scientific advisory body for the convention. Commercial-scale sealing, in fact, did not emerge. Nonetheless, CCAS represents one of the first, if not the first, international effort to put into place a mechanism to regulate commercial exploitation of living resources before the initiation of those activities.

SCAR identified and synthesized data and information on the pack ice seal populations and provided the scientific framework for the precautionary approach to conservation included in CCAS. It also promoted and coordinated study and understanding of the Antarctic marine ecosystem as a whole. This work, brought together in SCAR's Biological Investigations of Marine Antarctic Systems and Stocks (BIOMASS) Program in 1976, spotlighted the central role played by Antarctic krill (shrimplike crustaceans) in the Antarctic marine ecosystem. It also identified the potential of krill for human consumption as well as the potentially severe impacts of large-scale harvesting not only on krill populations themselves but also on the numerous other species dependent upon krill.

As a result of the pioneering research on the Antarctic marine ecosystem coordinated by SCAR, in 1977 the Consultative Parties agreed to initiate negotiation on an agreement to "provide for the effective conservation of the marine living resources of the Antarctic ecosystem as a whole" (Recommendation IX-2 [London, 1977]).

A special negotiating process was established, in part, because it was widely recognized that the form of the regime would need to be, like CCAS, a freestanding convention. This recognition also reflected commitment to cover the entire marine ecosystem, which extends north of the area of the Antarctic Treaty (north of 60°S latitude). The negotiations were initiated in 1978 and were concluded in 1980.

The Convention on the Conservation of Antarctic Marine Living Resources (CCAMLR), which entered into force in 1982, is a principal component of the system built upon the Antarctic Treaty and reflects the innovative and precedent-setting character of its parent. CCAMLR is the first international agreement that defines its area of application by reference to an ecosystem and seeks to describe the components and spatial extent of that ecosystem.

The northern limit of the CCAMLR area is defined by reference to the Antarctic Convergence, or Polar Front, an oceanic transition zone that separates colder Antarctic waters from subantarctic waters to the north. It forms an environmental barrier that many species do not cross and is considered the northern limit of many Antarctic species. CCAMLR sets forth geographic coordinates that approximate the location of this zone for regulatory purposes.

Antarctic marine living resources are defined as the populations of all species of living organisms found south of the convergence, and the Antarctic marine ecosystem is defined as the complex of relationships of Antarctic marine living resources with each other and with their physical environment.

CCAMLR is also the first international agreement to incorporate an ecosystem approach to the management of living resources. CCAMLR defines its objective as the conservation of Antarctic marine living resources, with conservation understood to include rational use of such resources.

The ecosystem approach is set forth in three obligations applicable to harvesting activities (Article II, paragraph 3, of CCAMLR). All such activities are to be conducted so as to (1) maintain populations that are the target of harvesting at healthy levels (preventing their decrease to levels below those necessary to ensure stable recruitment), (2) maintain ecological relationships between harvested, dependent, and related populations of Antarctic marine living resources and restoration of depleted populations to meet the first standard, and (3) prevent irreversible change (not potentially reversible over two or three decades) in the Antarctic marine ecosystem as a whole.

CCAMLR recognizes that the implementation of an ecosystem approach to conservation and management is data dependent. Therefore, CCAMLR includes extensive and detailed provisions on data collection and reporting, both as obligations of the parties and as priority functions of the institutions.

With respect to institutions, CCAMLR represented a significant evolution in the Antarctic Treaty system. It establishes a commission to determine management measures, a scientific committee to provide advice to the commission, and a secretariat to serve both. Substantive decisions in the commission are taken by consensus of its members, and membership is also based on an activities criterion, in this case, harvesting of or substantial research on Antarctic marine living resources.

CCAMLR draws directly upon the juridical accommodation reflected in Article IV of the Antarctic Treaty and applies it to assertions of maritime jurisdiction south of 60°S latitude derived from claims to territorial sovereignty there. The parties also set forth understandings to reflect the fact that there is recognized sovereignty and recognized maritime jurisdiction in the CCAMLR area north of 60°S latitude.

CCAMLR also incorporates imaginative provisions to deal with the divided competence between the European Union (EU) and its member states with respect to matters covered by CCAMLR. The EU and relevant member states are members of the commission, but with safeguards against double voting.

CCAMLR's provisions for a scientific committee merit attention. The members of the Scientific Committee, as with most regional fisheries bodies, represent governments rather than serving in an individual expert capacity. However, in addition to carrying out such activities as may be directed by the commission, the committee is accorded specific and independent functions to develop the basis for implementing CCAMLR's ecosystem management approach. The committee's relationship with SCAR, also provided for in CCAMLR, has operated to reinforce the independence of the committee. As noted earlier, SCAR, in effect, acts as a peer-review body of the committee's work. The fact that many of the scientists representing governments are also active participants in SCAR has contributed to the objectivity of the committee's deliberations.

An important challenge to the successful implementation of CCAMLR arose at the outset, in the start-up of the Scientific Committee. The committee was charged with recommending agreed rules of procedure for its operation to the commission for final approval. The issue turned on whether the consensus decision-making system provided in CCAMLR for the commission should also apply to the Scientific Committee. Several parties took the position that a consensus of all committee members was required for the provision of scientific advice or recommendations to the commission. This position could have prevented the commission from receiving any advice; it could have deprived the commission of the understanding of where and why scientific views diverged, and it would have involved the Scientific Committee in political decisions, properly the purview of the commission. The majority of members expressed fundamental objection to this position. The resulting impasse prevented the adoption of rules for over a year. Those opposed to subjecting the Scientific Committee's advice to consensus decision making held firm, however, and prevailed at the committee's second meeting. The relevant rule (Rule 3, Rules of Procedure of the Scientific Committee) provides the following:

- Scientific recommendations and advice to be provided by the Scientific Committee pursuant to the Convention shall normally be determined by consensus.
- Where consensus cannot be achieved the Committee shall set out in its report all views advanced on the matter under consideration.
- Reports of the Scientific Committee to the Commission shall reflect all the views expressed at the Committee on the matters discussed.
- If a Member or group of Members in the Committee so wishes, additional views of that Member or group of Members on any particular questions may be submitted directly to the Commission.
- Where the Committee takes decisions, it will do so in accordance with Article XII of the Convention.

Resolution of the dispute in this fashion was critical to establishing a healthy interaction between the scientific and technical requirements for management and the political process for taking management decisions. Getting the science-policy interaction right is necessary to ensure that risk and uncertainty are given proper weight in management decisions; CCAMLR's ability to do so has been a key element in the success it has had in the ongoing attempt to put ecosystem management into practice.

Although it is beyond the scope of this paper to analyze the operation of CCAMLR, since its entry into force in 1982, it should be noted that CCAMLR's Commission has been at the international forefront of the complex task of converting ecosystem management into practical measures, in precautionary, risk-based management of fisheries; in establishing healthy science-policy interaction; in dealing with harmful fisheries practices, in particular, seabird by-catch; and in coming to grips with illegal, unreported, and unregulated (IUU) fishing, through such measures as its innovative catch documentation scheme.

ANTARCTIC MINERAL RESOURCES

Following the completion of the negotiation of CCAMLR in 1980, the Consultative Parties turned their attention to the issue of Antarctic mineral resources, an issue that had emerged in the mid-1970s to threaten the Antarctic Treaty's experiment in international governance.

This challenge derived from inferences that there were valuable mineral resources in Antarctica and was driven by worldwide concern over possible resource scarcity, in particular, fears of oil shortages following the formation of the Organization of Petroleum Exporting Countries (OPEC). Governments and resource companies, therefore, sought to determine the resource potential of previously uninvestigated regions, including the most remote areas of the planet, such as Antarctica.

The search for valuable resources in Antarctica was certainly not a new phenomenon. The appetite for new sealing and whaling grounds was an important element in the exploration of Antarctica from the outset. The pattern of harvesting followed by overharvesting of marine mammal populations became an all-too-familiar feature in the history of Antarctica.

Dealing with possible exploitation of mineral resources, however, was viewed as more difficult than managing living resources. They are not renewable and were perceived as more valuable. Moreover, the authority to manage and profit from mineral resource development is one of the most jealously guarded aspects of sovereignty. Here again, it should be recalled that the Antarctic Treaty is a limited-purpose agreement and its imaginative governance provisions did not extend to possible mineral resource activities.

Under these circumstances, the Treaty Parties decided that it was necessary to have a mechanism in place for determining the acceptability of mineral resource development in Antarctica before, rather than after, any valuable deposits were identified. Research on basic geological and geophysical processes in Antarctica was inexorably expanding information about the possible occurrence of mineral resources. Reaching agreement on what to do after any such deposits had been identified could have proved impossible.

Therefore, in 1981, the Consultative Parties agreed to negotiate a regime to deal with possible oil development and mining in Antarctica. As with the case of CCAMLR, their objective was to conclude a freestanding agreement, separate from, but closely tied to, the Antarctic Treaty, and they established a special negotiating process to that end.

The resulting negotiations were extraordinarily complex and difficult, as well as fascinating for those like myself who took part in them. They were initiated at a time of deep division, east/west and north/south, over international economic and resource distribution issues that focused international attention on Antarctica. They also became the catalyst for concerted environmental campaigns within many of the Consultative Parties opposing any possible Antarctic mineral resource activities. Environmental groups called for designating Antarctica as a world park in which mineral resource development and perhaps other commercial activities would be prohibited.

The growing power of this environmental movement was obscured by the progress being made in the negotiations, and in 1988, after seven years of intense bargaining, the Consultative Parties adopted the Convention on the Regulation of Antarctic Mineral Resource Activities (CRAMRA). Its adoption by consensus was a remarkable negotiating achievement.

This consensus, however, was short-lived. Shortly after adoption of CRAMRA, Australia and France announced that they would no longer support it and would work instead for a permanent prohibition of mineral resource activities in Antarctica. It became clear that the ratifications necessary to bring CRAMRA into force would not be forthcoming.

CRAMRA, though it has been shelved, included environmental standards, including unique sufficiency of information criteria as a precondition for making decisions, arguably the most stringent standards ever developed for possible resource activities. Many of its provisions have served as precedents for subsequent environmental agreements.

The problem with CRAMRA, however, was that it could be seen to allow the possibility of mineral development. Even the term "regulation" in its title was taken to imply that mineral resource exploitation would inevitably flow from CRAMRA, a reality by no means foreordained in its substantive provisions. Nonetheless, this possibility, however remote, became the catalyst for an effective public campaign against CRAMRA. Environmental organizations concerned with Antarctica recognized the extraordinary emotive value and popular appeal of declaring Antarctica forever off-limits to mineral resource development. The force of this movement proved to be irresistible.

The demise of CRAMRA converted what had been a challenge to the Antarctic Treaty's system of governance into a potential crisis. Some observers characterized it as a significant failure of the Antarctic Treaty system and questioned the viability of the treaty as a mechanism for dealing with environmental protection. There certainly was deep division among the Consultative Parties. The division was not just over a ban on mineral activities.

The Consultative Parties that first advocated a permanent ban on mineral resource activities called for a new comprehensive agreement on the protection of the Antarctic environment. This comprehensive convention not only would prohibit mineral resource activities that were not covered by the Antarctic Treaty but would also apply to activities directly regulated by the Antarctic Treaty, e.g., facilitation of science and associated logistics in support of science, tourism, and other visitation. There were also proposals to substitute a qualified majority system for consensus decision-making procedures. The effect of these proposals was to call into question the Antarctic Treaty as the framework for governance.

Under these circumstances, the Consultative Parties returned to the negotiating table. The crisis was overcome through agreement on the Protocol on Environmental Protection to the Antarctic Treaty, sometimes called the Madrid Protocol, which was concluded in 1991 and entered into force in 1998.

The Madrid Protocol, which forms an integral part of the Antarctic Treaty itself, incorporates a prohibition on mineral resource activities in Antarctica along with provisions strengthening and rationalizing the Antarctic Treaty's framework for environmental protection.

Specifically, the Madrid Protocol, in addition to including the minerals ban (Article 7), elaborates environmental principles applicable to human activities in Antarctica and sets out mandatory rules in a series of annexes. These include the following:

- Annex I on Environmental Impact Assessment, which requires that the environmental impact of proposed activities in Antarctica be assessed before they take place;
- Annex II on the Conservation of Antarctic Fauna and Flora, which prohibits taking of taking of native animals and plants without a permit (available only for compelling scientific purposes); prohibits harmful interference with native populations; prohibits introduction of nonnative species; and basically strengthens and extends the Agreed Measures of 1964;
- Annex III on Waste Disposal and Waste Management, which provides for strict regulation of waste disposal and waste management at stations and field camps, including the requirement that most types of waste must be removed from Antarctica, a ban on open burning of waste, and prohibition of the introduction of polychlorinated biphenyls (PCBs), polystyrene packaging, pesticides, or nonsterile soil into Antarctica;
- Annex IV on Prevention of Marine Pollution, which prohibits disposal into the sea of oil, chemicals, including plastics, and garbage (other than food waste) from ships and stations; sets forth restrictions on disposal of sewage and food waste; and calls for prompt and effective response to accidents and environmental emergencies; and
- Annex V on Protected Areas, which provides for establishment of Antarctic Specially Protected Areas (ASPA), areas of outstanding wilderness, scientific, and environmental value that require a management plan and permit for entry (available only for compelling scientific purposes), and of Antarctic Specially Managed Areas (ASMA), areas where human activities need to be coordinated, requiring management plans but not permits for entry.

The Madrid Protocol provides for additional annexes to be negotiated and incorporated into this framework in the future. Annex VI on Liability from Environmental Emergencies has been concluded but has not yet entered into force. The Madrid Protocol also includes provisions for compulsory settlement of disputes regarding interpretation or application of its provisions, matters relating to Article IV of the Antarctic Treaty excepted.

The conclusion of the Protocol on Environmental Protection to the Antarctic Treaty, which, as previously noted, forms an integral part of the Antarctic Treaty, represented the restoration of consensus among the Consultative Parties on the issue of mineral resources and environmental protection in Antarctica. As with CCAMLR, the Madrid Protocol represents a major expansion in the Antarctic Treaty System by extending the Antarctic Treaty's system of governance.

Moreover, the negotiations over the 10-year period leading up to the Madrid Protocol were a catalyst to the elaboration of the techniques of Antarctic governance. That decade witnessed major changes in the participation and operation of the Antarctic Treaty System, what has been called the "greening" of the system. The intense interest generated by the issue of Antarctic mineral resources played an important part in the emergence of new actors seeking to play a role in Antarctic matters.

In 1959, the 12 countries that had negotiated the Antarctic Treaty were, in effect, responsible for the governance of Antarctica. Those 12—the Consultative Parties and only those parties—participated in the Consultative Meetings held under the Antarctic Treaty. During the first two decades of the operation of the Antarctic Treaty, only one acceding party to the Antarctic Treaty, Poland, had sought and achieved recognition as a Consultative Party (in 1977).

This situation changed dramatically with the emergence of the issue of potential development of mineral resources in Antarctica. By the conclusion of the Madrid Protocol in 1991, the number of Consultative Parties had doubled to 26. Among the new Consultative Parties were a number of developing countries, including Brazil, India, and China. There are now 28 Consultative Parties.

The negotiations also gave impetus to efforts by acceding parties to the Antarctic Treaty (those parties that had not achieved consultative status, or Non-Consultative Parties) to secure involvement in the work of Consultative Meetings, calls for opening Consultative Meetings to observers, and efforts in the United Nations by countries not party to the Antarctic Treaty, led by Malaysia, to challenge the legitimacy of the Antarctic Treaty. The Consultative Parties successfully responded to each of these challenges in a manner that extended and strengthened the Antarctic Treaty's system of governance.

First, in 1983, agreement was reached that Non-Consultative Parties had the right to participate in Consultative Meetings as observers with the ability to take part in discussions without decision-making powers. This agreement put an end to the anomalous situation in which parties to the Antarctic Treaty who had accepted their obligations but had not, or had not yet, met the activities criterion for consultative status had been unable even to attend Consultative Meetings. There are now 19 Non-Consultative Parties to the Antarctic Treaty.

Second, in 1987, agreement was reached on providing for attendance at Consultative Meetings by international organizations, both intergovernmental and nongovernmental. Representatives of components of the Antarctic Treaty System (SCAR, the Commission for the Conservation of Antarctic Marine Living Resources, and the Council of Managers of National Antarctic Programs) are entitled to attend as observers. In addition, experts may be invited from international organizations that may contribute to the work of Consultative Meetings, based on the provisions for establishing cooperative working relations with international organizations set forth in Article III, paragraph 2. At the most recent Consultative Meeting (ATCM XXXII, held in the United States in 2009) observers and experts from 14 international organizations (intergovernmental and nongovernmental) attended.

Finally, the Consultative Parties coordinated a unified response to the campaign in the United Nations that questioned the legitimacy of the Antarctic Treaty system as a forum for dealing with mineral resources or other issues of concern to the international community. In reply to contentions that the Antarctic Treaty was a closed club based on an undemocratic decision-making system, the Consultative Parties took the position that issues relating to Antarctica were appropriately dealt with only by consensus, whether within the Antarctic Treaty's mechanisms or in the United Nations General Assembly.

Consensus could not be achieved at the assembly, and those questioning the legitimacy of the Antarctic Treaty sought the adoption of General Assembly resolutions by majority vote. The Consultative Parties responded by not participating in such votes. Faced with a united front of Consultative Parties and with ongoing growth and diversification in the make up of the Consultative Parties themselves, the United Nations debates took on an increasingly hollow character. Finally, in 1994, consensus was achieved (following the conclusion of the Environmental Protocol and set forth in preliminary fashion in the agenda of the 1992 Earth Summit in Rio de Janeiro). This consensus involved international recognition of the legitimacy and value of the Antarctic Treaty System as a system of governance coupled with emphasis on the fulfillment of the obligations of Antarctic Treaty Parties to provide information about the operation of the Antarctic Treaty and the scientific research it promotes.

ANTARCTIC GOVERNANCE AFTER 50 YEARS

The entry into force of the Protocol on Environmental Protection to the Antarctic Treaty in 1998 and its implementation in the decade that followed, including the related establishment of the Antarctic Treaty Secretariat, mark the evolution of the Antarctic Treaty from a limited-purpose, albeit unique and precedent setting, agreement into an overall system of governance. Among international instruments, the Antarctic Treaty has been uniquely successful in achieving its objectives. It has done so during five decades of rapid and significant change, not only in the international landscape but also in the numbers and interests of those participating in the Antarctic Treaty itself. Its innovative and precedent-setting conflict resolution and disarmament provisions and its guarantees of freedom of scientific research remain relevant and vital today. These achievements constitute the most important results of 50 years of operation of the Antarctic Treaty and make it one of the most successful efforts at conflict prevention and political cooperation in modern history.

This same dynamism has been reflected in the evolution of the Antarctic Treaty System, in particular, CCAMLR. The provisions, practices, and conservation measures of CCAMLR continue to be widely emulated worldwide as a model and inspiration for efforts to conserve fishery and other living resources.

The governance elements that derive from the Antarctic Treaty itself, in particular, the bifocal approach reflected in Article IV, consensus-based decision making, and the activities criterion, provide essential bases for Antarctic problem solving, whether under the Antarctic Treaty or in subsequent instruments built upon the Antarctic Treaty. I would also add to the suite of techniques that characterize Antarctic governance the ecosystem management approach of CCAMLR as well as the precautionary, risk-based management techniques and the process of science-policy interactions that have evolved under it. A final element is reliance on the results of scientific research and observations in Antarctica as a basis for Consultative Party action and for evaluating the effectiveness of such action once implemented.

The Antarctic Treaty System: A Model of Legal Creativity and Cooperation

Gillian Triggs

ABSTRACT. The Antarctic Treaty System (ATS), founded upon the Antarctic Treaty of 1959, has proved to be one of the successes of twentieth century international law and diplomacy. Over the last 50 years, the Antarctic Treaty has preserved the Antarctic continent as a zone of peace and cooperative scientific research and provided an effective model for the management of regions beyond the limits of national jurisdiction according to common values. The reasons for this success are, however, by no means obvious to the casual observer. The language of the treaty itself and of the related conventions on seals, marine living resources, and minerals and the Protocol on Environmental Protection is deliberately ambiguous and vague. The regime has weak inspection, enforcement, and governance mechanisms and has been slow to respond to conflict in the Southern Ocean over whaling and unregulated fishing. A key to understanding both the successes and limitations of the ATS lies in the differing juridical positions of the member states on sovereign claims to Antarctic territory. Every ATS agreement, measure, and decision and state practices in respect to Antarctica should be viewed through the prism of these national perspectives on sovereignty. This paper sets out the evolution of the ATS and explores the fundamental role of Article IV and "sovereign neutrality" as the glue that binds the Antarctic Treaty and its interlinked measures, decisions, and agreements. Article IV has enabled the Consultative Parties to sidestep potential conflicts over territorial claims and to manage activities in Antarctica in the wider interests of the international community. For the second decade of the twenty-first century, the vital question is whether the ATS is capable of responding effectively to the challenges posed by illegal fishing and whaling, climate change, commercial tourism, energy, and human security. The litigation in the *Japanese Whaling* case, brought by the Humane Society International in the Australian Federal Court, provides a salutary warning of the risks to the ATS of unilateral assertions of national jurisdiction over activities in the Antarctic region. The Consultative Parties are now on notice to justify the legitimacy of their mandate and to demonstrate the capacity of the ATS to respond to contemporary Antarctic issues. The 50-year historical evolution of the ATS and its demonstrated capacity for dynamic growth suggest that the regime and its members have the flexibility and political will to maintain its success in the future.

INTRODUCTION

The Antarctic Treaty System (ATS) of interlinked conventions, measures, and recommendations, founded upon the Antarctic Treaty of 1959, has proved

Gillian Triggs, Sydney Law School, University of Sydney, Sydney, NSW, 2006, Australia. Correspondence: g.triggs@usyd.edu.au.

to be one of the successes of contemporary international law and diplomacy. For the last 50 years a tenth of the Earth has been regulated peacefully and in the interest of scientific research. Negotiated during the cold war, the treaty has ensured that potential conflict over the seven largely unrecognised and disputed claims to territorial sovereignty in Antarctica has been avoided. Indeed, as Phillip C. Jessup argued before the U.S. Senate Committee on Foreign Relations, the importance of the Antarctic Treaty "lies . . . in the fact that it will permit the last great empty continent from becoming an international bone of contention, a scene of controversy and actual fighting."[1]

The ATS has achieved this and much more. It has become a model for regional environmental management founded upon agreed common values of cooperative scientific research and peaceful purposes. It was negotiated by 12 states, 7 of which claimed rights as territorial sovereigns, at a time when there were as few as 55 states in the international community as a whole. Today, it might be questioned whether the 192 states that are now members of the United Nations (UN) are in any way bound by such a grandiose gesture that purported, over 50 years ago, to regulate activities on the largest continent on earth. The life of the law lies, of course, in experience. In fact, the Antarctic Treaty has withstood the tests of time and political, technological, and economic change. It now has 46 members, representing a significant majority of the world's population. The resilience of the treaty was, for example, demonstrated recently when, despite global concerns for energy security, the 28 Antarctic Treaty Consultative Parties (ATCPs) confirmed their commitment to a prohibition on mineral resource exploitation.[2]

The 14 articles of the Antarctic Treaty, by today's standards a model of elegant, concise simplicity, have ensured that the world's largest, coldest, driest, and most inhospitable continent has been preserved for scientific research and peaceful purposes as a nonnuclear region. An understanding of the contribution of Antarctica to the global climate system is now recognised as vital, and the culture of free exchange of scientific data has, for example, facilitated unprecedented cooperation in understanding the causes of the ozone hole and the melting of glaciers.

Laurence Gould has claimed that the Antarctic Treaty is "unique in history which may take its place alongside the Magna Carta and other great symbols of man's quest for enlightenment and order."[3] Such hyperbole on the fiftieth anniversary of the signing of the treaty prompts reflection upon the reasons for its success as a regime for governance under international law. This chapter considers the evolution of the ATS and explores the fundamental role of Article IV and sovereign neutrality as the glue that binds the regime together by sidestepping potential conflicts over territorial claims, enabling Consultative Parties to manage activities in Antarctica in the wider interests of the international community. Also considered is a vital question for the twenty-first century: is the ATS capable of responding effectively to the challenges posed by unregulated fishing and whaling, climate change, commercial tourism, energy, and human security? The litigation in the *Japanese Whaling* case, brought by the Humane Society International in the Australian Federal Court, is examined as a salutary warning of the risks to the ATS of unilateral assertions of national jurisdiction over activities in the Antarctic region. The Consultative Parties are now on notice to justify the legitimacy of their mandate and to demonstrate the capacity of the ATS to respond to contemporary Antarctic issues.

HISTORY

To those who are new to it, the Antarctic Treaty System may seem to be an unnecessarily ambiguous, contrived, and suboptimal regime. A moment's reflection on the history of the evolution of the regime explains its current structure, procedures, and limitations. The historical background also illumines the dynamic, evolutionary nature of a legal regime that has responded to diverse political, economic, and resource priorities over the last 50 years. The treaty was negotiated during the cold war, completed shortly after Castro took over Havana, and has survived efforts to open it up for mineral exploitation. Antarctica was on the agenda of the UN General Assembly for over 30 years, but as an indication of the stability of the ATS, the "Question of Antarctica" was removed from the agenda in 2006.[4] There have also been calls for Antarctica to be declared a "world park" and to be adopted as the "common heritage of mankind."[5] Along the way, the evolving ATS has told us much about effective international governance in the face of apparently insurmountable legal obstacles. We have also come to understand how international law and diplomatic language can play a creative role in global problem solving.

The early twentieth century negotiating history for an Antarctic regime reflects the predominant concern of claimant states, and states conducting scientific research activities there, to protect their interests. Claims to territorial sovereignty over sectors in Antarctica have been made by the United Kingdom (1908), Chile (1940), France (1924), Norway (1939), and Argentina (1927–1957) on the traditional legal grounds of discovery, effective occupation, and geographical proximity.[6] The claims by New Zealand and Australia are founded in the transfer of claimant status by the United Kingdom in 1923 and 1933, respectively, and have since been maintained on the grounds of occupation and exploration. Of these claimants, only five, Australia, New Zealand, Norway, France, and the United Kingdom, mutually recognise the claims of the others. Overwhelmingly, the international community has either objected to the claims on the grounds, among others, that Antarctica is not amendable to territorial sovereignty or ignored them. Although the United States and the Soviet Union had made the most extensive commitment of resources to Antarctic research and exploration by the 1940s, neither had made a claim to sovereignty. Rather, each reserved the right to do so in the future.[7] Other states, such as Belgium, Japan, and South Africa, had historical and research interests in Antarctica and sought to ensure a role in determining the future governance of the region. Although India, Brazil, Uruguay, and Peru had also expressed their interests in Antarctic affairs, they were ultimately not included in negotiations for an agreement.[8]

The potential for conflict in the wider area of the Southern Ocean was already apparent by the 1940s, when the United Kingdom and the United States established bases on Stonington Island. Quite apart from the profound legal perspectives that separated the negotiating states, the late 1950s were politically unstable times. This period was one of intense anxiety during the cold war, and 1959 was the year Castro invaded Cuba. A legal solution was not likely to be achieved. In 1955, the United Kingdom unsuccessfully attempted to have the question of the validity of Antarctic claims made by Argentina and Chile adjudicated by the International Court of Justice.[9]

In the summers of 1946/1947 and 1947/1948, Argentine and Chile sent naval expeditions to the Falkland Islands Dependencies to assert their historic claims to the area.[10] Indeed, the press wrote of the "scramble for Antarctica" as early as 1947, and the United Kingdom, Chile, and Argentina adopted the policy of barring naval demonstrations and manoeuvres below the 60th parallel to reduce rising temperatures in the "South American Quadrant."[11] It had become clear both that some form of joint administration of the subantarctic area was needed and that any agreement should preserve the diversity of legal perspectives of the states with interests in the Antarctic and Southern Ocean.

The first national proposal to consider some form of international regulation of Antarctica was made by Norway in 1934.[12] The planned conference was then cancelled because of the impending threat of war. Subsequently, further proposals for internationalisation, including a UN trusteeship under Chapter XII of the UN Charter or a condominium, were made by the United States, the Soviet Union, Australia, New Zealand, the United Kingdom, and India, respectively. The first glimmerings of the precepts upon which the ATS came to be founded were proposed in 1939 by Julio Escudero, an international lawyer from Chile, who argued that any international agreement should not prejudice sovereign rights in Antarctica, that territorial claims should be "frozen" through a moratorium, and that scientific cooperation should be ensured.[13] He addressed the sovereignty issue by arguing that any agreement should provide that activities south of 60°S latitude should not prejudice sovereign rights in Antarctica.

With the end of the Second World War came renewed attempts to seek a solution to the problem of Antarctic governance. Although the driving force for negotiation of an agreement lay in protection of national interests, science was well recognised by leaders such as President Eisenhower as a "tool of diplomacy" during this period. In addition to support among the scientific community for free access to Antarctica, the wider "internationalist" objectives of nongovernmental organizations, diplomats, and private citizens should not be forgotten. In December 1947, for example, three petitions were made by the Woman's International League for Peace and Freedom urging the creation of a UN committee to take control of both the Arctic and Antarctic, an idea that was rejected, as the UN had no competence in polar regions.

In 1948, the United States proposed that some form of internationalisation should be considered and emphasised the importance of scientific research in Antarctica. Chile responded that any attempt to unite all claims through internationalisation would be antithetical to its 'full and absolute sovereignty'.[14] Australia, Argentina, and Chile remained implacable in defending their sovereignty claims. In contrast, New Zealand was, at this time, willing to consider the establishment of Antarctica as a world territory under the auspices of the UN. In February 1956 and again in 1957, India proposed that the question of Antarctica should be considered by the General Assembly.[15] The U.S. proposal had the cathartic effect of prompting the Soviet Union to consider its interests. In February 1949, the Geographical Society of the USSR resolved that the Soviet Union had "irrefutable rights . . . to participate in a solution of problems of the Antarctic" and that the Soviet Union had priority in discovering the continent. In 1957, the United Kingdom, Australia, and New Zealand proposed renewed consideration of an agreement to create an international consortium to ensure free access to scientific research and nonmilitarisation of Antarctica, a proposal that was rejected by Chile and Argentina on sovereignty grounds. France also remained steadfast in its objection to the creation of an international regime and joined Chile, Argentina, and Australia in rejecting any form of permanent secretariat or organisational structure. The juridical battle lines were thus drawn.

These tentative initiatives for Antarctic governance were shortly to be overtaken by preparations for the International Geophysical Year (IGY) from 1 July 1957 to 31 December 1958. Antarctic scientific research was a major focus of the IGY, and the Special Committee for Antarctic Research (SCAR) was set up under the International Council for Scientific Unions. Although the IGY provided an opportunity for the Soviet Union and the United States to cooperate on scientific research in Antarctica, the politics of the cold war intruded as the bases established in the name of science on the continent might, it was feared, be used subsequently to undermine sovereignty claims. The Australians most particularly understood the point that Soviet bases established during the IGY within the Australian Antarctic Territory (AAT) were not likely to be dismantled. It is possible that recognition of the permanence of these bases encouraged Australia to view some form of wider governance as the better means of protecting its interests.[16] With some prescience, Argentina and Chile had earlier insisted at the 1955 IGY Conference in Paris that scientific research should "not modify the existing status in the Antarctic regarding the relations of the participating countries." Their insistence on maintaining the status quo appears to have subsequently formed the basis of a "gentlemen's agreement" by which participating governments agreed not to "engage in legal or political argumentation" over Antarctic sovereignty during the IGY.[17]

Although it is doubtful that such an understanding had any legal validity, the idea of putting aside differing juridical views on sovereignty fell on fertile ground. The United States took the initiative in 1958 to adopt a strategy of "quiet, confidential and informal" discussions with interested states.[18] The United States suggested adopting the earlier Chilean modus vivendi, which would maintain the status quo with respect to sovereignty and ensure nonmilitarisation and scientific cooperation. In May 1958, with the close of the IGY, the United States invited 11 states with a "direct interest" in Antarctica to attend a conference in Washington, D.C., in October 1959. These states were the seven territorial claimants, states which reserved the right to make a claim in the future (United States and Soviet Union), and those with research activities in Antarctica during the IGY (South Africa, Belgium, and Japan). The mooted inclusion of Brazil, Poland, and India proved too problematic, and they were not invited. Somewhat surprisingly, and with caveats, each invited state agreed to take part in the negotiations. An informal preparatory working group was established to produce a draft agreement adopting the core principles that the status quo with respect to sovereignty claims would be maintained and that nonmilitarisation of Antarctica and scientific cooperation would be guaranteed.

By today's standards, the negotiations were breathtakingly fast. The conference met over six weeks (15 October to 1 December 1959), and the Antarctic Treaty was adopted on 1 December 1959, coming into force 18 months later on 23 June 1961. As Hanessian points out, apart from the 1958 Law of the Sea Conventions and the creation of the International Atomic Energy Agency, the Antarctic Treaty was to be the only important treaty to include all the major powers of the time since the Second World War.[19]

This then was all the more reason to marvel that the leaders of delegations at the negotiating table were so generous in their commitment to the core principles of the proposed treaty. Sir Esler Dening, the UK representative, in particular, appreciated the responsibility that lay with the 12 negotiating states. When explaining to third states that "might question the right of any single group of countries even to give the appearance of legislating on a matter of world-wide concern," he argued that the "Treaty is, in fact, to be almost entirely a self-denying ordinance on the part of the signatories, who will derive from it virtually no privileges but only obligations."[20]

Such a high-minded sentiment, although optimistic at the time, has resonance today. Viewed 50 years later, survival of the ATS may well depend upon the success of the "self-denying" vision of Treaty Parties in meeting contemporary needs for Antarctic environmental governance.

The Antarctic Treaty is disarmingly simple. It applies to the area south of 60°S latitude, including ice shelves, but does not affect the rights of states under international law in respect of the high seas. Only the most minimal institutional structure is permitted in order to achieve the primary objectives that "Antarctica shall be used for peaceful purposes only," that any measures of a military nature and nuclear explosions or disposal of radioactive waste are prohibited, and that there should be freedom of scientific investigation. The treaty requires the Contracting Parties to exchange information and scientific personnel and establishes a process for inspections by observers. A slender process for Antarctic governance is created by the agreement that Contracting Parties can meet as determined by them. Those states that were listed in the preamble to the treaty are entitled to attend meetings, along with acceding states who meet the criterion that they can demonstrate their interest in Antarctica by conducting "substantial scientific research" there. These states have become known as the Consultative Parties, as distinct from those acceding states that are not able to demonstrate the appropriate level of research activity. The vital point of difference is that only the Consultative Parties are entitled to vote at, or attend, meetings. In contrast, the Non-Consultative Parties are invited to such meetings. Consultative Party Meetings are now held every year for two weeks to discuss matters of common interest and for representatives to make recommendations to their governments. Formal "measures" can also be adopted by the Consultative Parties on issues such as the preservation and conservation of natural resources and jurisdiction. It is a weakness of the treaty that measures will only become binding when all Consultative Parties have subsequently approved them by consensus. The requirement of unanimity reflects the differing juridical positions on sovereignty but has a limiting effect on effective governance.

This brief survey of the Antarctic Treaty has thus far failed to mention two of the most important and controversial provisions. The first concerns the means by which the treaty was to protect all possible juridical perspectives on Antarctica. The second is the constraint imposed by the treaty on the excise of jurisdiction by contracting states over nonnationals.

SOVEREIGN NEUTRALITY

The idea of sovereign neutrality has been the vital building block for the development of the Antarctic Treaty System. Indeed, all aspects of Antarctic governance need to be viewed through the prism of differing juridical perspectives on sovereignty. Article IV provides that

> Nothing in the present Treaty shall be interpreted as:
>
> A renunciation by any contracting party of previously asserted rights or claims to territorial sovereignty in Antarctica;
>
> A renunciation or diminution by any Contracting Party of any basis of claim to territorial sovereignty in Antarctica which it may have whether as a result of its activities or those of its nationals in Antarctica, or otherwise;
>
> Prejudicing the position of any Contracting Party as regards its recognition or non-recognition of any other State's right of or claim or basis of claim to territorial sovereignty in Antarctica.

To paraphrase, the treaty should not be interpreted as a renunciation of previously asserted rights or basis of a claim, nor is the treaty to prejudice the position of any party as regards its recognition or nonrecognition of any other state's right of claim or basis of a claim. The words "any basis of claim" in paragraph 1(b) may protect the prior interests of nonclaimant states such as the United States and the Soviet Union, which had not previously sought to assert a claim but which might do so in the future. The words "or those of its nationals" will cover claims made on behalf of, but not ratified by, the state concerned. In this way, the potential claimants may protect their "rights" to make a claim in the future. Nonclaimants may also be protected by Article IV, paragraph 1(c), which provides that a Contracting Party does not prejudice its position as "regards its recognition or non-recognition of the rights or claims of other states." This provision also protects claimants who have already recognised the Antarctic sovereignty of other states. Claimants are further protected by Article IV, paragraph 1(a), which provides that the treaty is not a renunciation of "previously asserted rights or claims to territorial sovereignty." Similarly, Article IV, paragraph 1(b), provides that "any basis of claim" that a state may have is not to be reduced or diminished by the treaty.

The words of Article IV are circuitous and ambiguous, leaving each state free to interpret the provision as it deems necessary to protect its juridical position. Despite this, few legal clauses have proved to be as successful in international dispute resolution as Article IV. Few such clauses have formed the foundation for so extensive a superstructure of interlinked treaties for the governance of so large a part of the world. Deliberately obscure, creating what Marcoux described as a "purgatory of ambiguity,"[21] Article IV has enabled states with diametrically inconsistent juridical positions on Antarctic sovereignty to engage cooperatively and fruitfully in one of the most effective regimes for global governance to be established within the international community.

Not only does Article IV enable states with differing legal perspectives on Antarctica to participate in the Antarctic Treaty, but it has also formed the glue for the subsequently negotiated interlinked agreements that now compose the regime. Parties to the Antarctic Fisheries Convention are, for example, bound by Article IV of the Antarctic Treaty in their relations with each other, even though they may not all be parties to the Antarctic Treaty.[22]

Important though it is to understand the function of Article IV within the ATS, it is also clear, as the United Kingdom's Sir Arthur Watts pointed out in 1986, that the provision has not "solved" the sovereignty problem.

National claims to territorial sovereignty or interests in Antarctica are "still very much alive."[23] Fifty years after the treaty was negotiated, the claimant states remain adamant that they have valid and genuine claims to sovereignty. Moreover, there are no strategic reasons why claimant states should relinquish their juridical positions. If at any time the major interests of the claimant states are not met through the ATS, for example, in the event of weak environmental protection or overfishing, the trump card of sovereignty remains to be played. The Antarctic Treaty cannot, however, arrest time. New ideas of "common spaces" and a growing intolerance for traditional notions of territorial sovereignty in a pristine and beautiful continent suggest that it will be difficult to gain international support for national claims in Antarctica.

EVOLUTION OF THE ANTARCTIC TREATY SYSTEM

Before setting out the evolution of the regime created under the Antarctic Treaty umbrella, it might be useful to review the technical means of Antarctic law making. Under Article IX the Consultative Parties are required to meet at "suitable intervals and places" for, among other things, "recommending to their Governments, measures in furtherance of the principles and objectives of the Treaty." Any such measures could be either mandatory or hortatory, the majority being the latter. In 1995, by Decision 1, the term "recommendation" was deleted, and new terms were adopted. The term "measures" is to address mandatory obligations under Article IX. "Decisions" are also mandatory, but as they are administrative in nature, they do not require subsequent Article IX approval by all Consultative Parties. For the future, "resolutions" were to be hortatory only. This new terminology and legal status for Consultative Party determinations are vital to understanding the governance mechanisms adopted over the life of the treaty.

The states negotiating the Antarctic Treaty were not initially concerned with resource issues and referred to environmental matters only in Article IX, paragraph 1(f), calling for "preservation and conservation of living resources in Antarctica." Despite the primary geopolitical objectives of the treaty, the Consultative Parties rapidly came to appreciate that a primary function of Antarctic governance for the future was to preserve and conserve the environment. Indeed, it has been a feature of Antarctic governance that the Consultative Parties attempted to be "proactive" in negotiating measures and agreements that addressed issues before they became politically too difficult to address.

Employing the mechanism for regulation under the Antarctic Treaty, the Agreed Measures for the Conservation of Antarctic Fauna and Flora were adopted in 1964. These measures provide for the adoption of "specially protected areas" of outstanding scientific interest and for a permit system for the taking of designated species. Two voluntary standards were subsequently adopted: the 1975 Code of Conduct to protect against human interference in the Antarctic environment and a Statement of Accepted Principles and Good Conduct Guide for Tourist Groups.

The first separate treaty to be negotiated by the Antarctic Treaty Consultative Parties was the Convention for the Conservation of Antarctic Seals (CCAS) in 1972. It was believed that pelagic seals on the floating ice pack of the Southern Ocean and high seas could not be regulated by the Antarctic Treaty itself as the treaty has no application to the high seas. In Article 1 of CCAS, the Consultative Parties agreed to affirm the provisions of Article IV of the Antarctic Treaty so that nothing in CCAS could prejudice the maritime claims of the parties in Antarctica. The Convention for the Conservation of Antarctic Seals is intended to promote and achieve the objectives of "protection, scientific study and rational use of Antarctic seals, and to maintain a satisfactory balance within the ecological system." Certain species are not to be killed or captured by nationals of the parties within the seas south of 60°S latitude.

The technique of drafting a separate treaty to deal with a specific issue while maintaining dominance by the Antarctic Treaty Parties and protected by a sovereign neutrality clause provided a valuable precedent for the subsequent negotiation in 1980 of the Convention on the Conservation of Antarctic Marine Living Resources (CCAMLR). The ATCPs had recognised at the Eighth Consultative Meeting in 1975 that international interest in exploiting krill and other marine living resources of the Southern Ocean demanded effective regulation. By the late 1960s commercial and unregulated fishing was making considerable inroads in certain fish stocks, such as the marbled rockcod in the waters around South Georgia. Yet another motivation for speedy negotiation of CCAMLR was recognition that a failure to regulate the living resources in the area south of 60° parallel could jeopardise the interests of the claimant states and undermine the authority of the ATCPs to manage the area. CCAMLR has been one of the most successful agreements within the ATS in that, in contrast to the Antarctic Treaty itself, the ATCPs succeeded in creating an international organisation with legal personality, headquarters, an executive secretary, and staff. A commission has been established that meets annually and has a decision-making capacity based on consensus rather than unanimity.

Rather more controversial than the protection of marine resources or the environment was the question of how to regulate mineral exploration and exploitation in Antarctica. Again, the Consultative Parties adopted the, by now familiar, technique of negotiating a new treaty with interlinking, sovereignty-neutral clauses. The Convention on the Regulation of Antarctic Mineral Resource Activities was completed in 1988 but never came into force.[24] It was almost immediately made redundant by the Madrid Protocol on Environmental Protection to the Antarctic Treaty (Madrid Protocol) of 1991 that prohibited any activity relating to mineral resources, other than scientific research.[25] In effect, an indefinite prohibition on mining exploration and exploitation has been agreed. After 50 years any Consultative Party may request a conference to review the operation of the protocol. A three-quarters majority of Consultative Parties will then be required to overturn the prohibition. The protocol establishes a Committee for Environmental Protection (CEP) to advise and make recommendations to the parties and to report to the annual Antarctic Treaty Consultative Meetings (ATCM). Of critical importance to the effectiveness of the protocol has been the recent agreement upon the terms of Annex VI, with respect to the strict liability of operators in Antarctica. Under Article 6, an operator who fails to take a "prompt and effective response action to environmental emergencies arising from its activities shall be liable to pay the costs of response action taken by the Parties." The terms "prompt," "effective," and "respond" are not defined and remain to be interpreted in the practices of the ATS.

Finally, and importantly for the future of the ATS, the Consultative Parties agreed at the 24th ATCM in St. Petersburg in 2001 to create a permanent secretariat with headquarters in Buenos Aires, Argentina. This new body does not have international personality and plays an essentially support role for the ATCMs and the CEP, with further responsibilities under the Liability Annex. The Consultative Parties have responded to concerns that the activities of the ATS are not transparent by establishing a Web site, and the secretariat has been effective in supporting the activities of the ATS. Nonetheless, the Consultative Parties remain reluctant to agree to the secretariat exercising any real autonomy or discretionary power.

JURISDICTION: *HUMANE SOCIETY INTERNATIONAL V. KYOTO SENPAKU KAISHA LTD (JAPANESE WHALING CASE)*

A potent risk to the stability of the ATS is the temptation for claimant states to exercise jurisdiction within their claimed sectors. Although it is a sine qua non of national sovereignty that the state may assert jurisdiction over all persons found within its territory or territorial seas, Article VIII of the Antarctic Treaty confines jurisdiction over observers and scientific personnel and their staff to the Contracting Party of which they are nationals. It is "one of the major unresolved questions" raised by the Antarctic Treaty that it leaves open whether foreign nationals may, in other circumstances, be subject to the jurisdiction of other states in respect of their Antarctic activities.[26] In practice, claimant states have routinely confined the exercise of jurisdiction over acts and persons within their Antarctic territories to their nationals and have refrained from applying domestic laws to the nationals of other states. The long-standing state practice of restricting the traditional jurisdictional reach of a territorial state has avoided clashes over sovereignty and enabled cooperation on the primary objectives of Antarctic science.[27]

A challenge to this amicable compromise of juridical positions has recently arisen in the litigation before the Federal Court of Australia in the *Humane Society International v. Kyoto Senpaku Kaisha Ltd (Japanese Whaling Case)*.[28] The international legal problem arose in the following way. A Japanese company, Kyodo Senpaku Kaish Ltd, had taken over 400 minke whales in the Australian Whale Sanctuary that had been declared off the coast of the AAT, throughout Australia's exclusive economic zone (EEZ). The taking of whales in the sanctuary was contrary to the Environment Protection and Biodiversity Conservation Act 1999 (EPBC), which makes it an offence to kill or interfere with marine mammals.[29] The act extended to foreign fishing vessels and their crews. The Federal Court of Australia declared that whaling by the Japanese company was illegal and issued an injunction restraining it from further whaling in the area. The declaration of a whale sanctuary in the waters off the AAT is a legally consistent element of Australia's sovereignty claim.[30] However, to enforce Australian legislation against a nonnational, in this case the Japanese company, is contrary to Article VIII of the Antarctic Treaty.

In the usual course of events, Australia would take action to enforce an injunction properly issued by the Federal Court of Australia. The Australian government chose not to do that, on the grounds that the act should not be enforced against foreign citizens unless they had submitted to the jurisdiction of the Australian courts.[31] The Australian government thus avoided the deeply divisive consequences within the Antarctic Treaty System that were likely to have been sparked had the injunction been enforced. There is also the risk that the International Court of Justice or the International Tribunal for the Law of the Sea might gain jurisdiction over the dispute, in which case

Article IV would provide little protection for Australia's position at international law.

Although confrontation with Japan was avoided, the *Japanese Whaling* case exposes the vulnerability of the ATS where state parties threaten to take unilateral action to enforce their laws in and around Antarctica. The litigation also illustrates the embarrassing consequences for governments of giving procedural capacity to a private entity, e.g., the Humane Society International, to apply directly to a court to apply national legislation. Had Australia decided to enforce the injunction against the Japanese company, the weaknesses of Australia's international legal position in Antarctica would potentially have been open to international scrutiny. Enforcement against a nonnational would have exposed not only the difficulties in substantiating Australia's 42% claim under international law but also the questionable validity of its proclamation of a 200 nautical mile EEZ adjacent to its claimed territory.[32] Apart from the complications arising from an assertion by Australia of maritime jurisdiction in Antarctica, the unilateral exercise of jurisdiction over a nonnational might prompt other Antarctic claimants to apply their legislation to foreign nationals. Although, for the most part, an Antarctic claimant state has every reason to avoid disputes over sovereignty and to act within the constraints of the Antarctic Treaty, there will be occasions when popular demand for the application of more stringent and enforceable national legislation, especially to protect the environment, seems attractive. For the Australian government to enforce a court injunction to prevent Japanese whaling in the Southern Ocean would have been popular, both within the national and international spheres. Where national environmental legislation is more stringent and effective than the measures and decisions of the ATS, the temptation to act outside the boundaries of the Antarctic Treaty may become increasingly attractive, although it also carries considerable risks.

TWENTY-FIRST CENTURY CHALLENGES TO THE ANTARCTIC TREATY SYSTEM

Successful though the ATS has been over its 50 year evolution, the twenty-first century poses some new, sensitive, and complex challenges to the authority of the regime.

Collaboration with Other International Organisations

The *Japanese Whaling* case exposes the imperative that the ATS should interact collaboratively with other international organisations that have interests in the Southern Ocean and Antarctica. The Antarctic Treaty itself does not deal with whales, the rationale being that the International Convention for the Regulation of Whaling (ICRW), established 10 years earlier in 1949, was the international institution specifically empowered to regulate whales. The International Whaling Commission has not, however, been able to take effective action against Japan for its "scientific whaling" in the Southern Ocean. This failure has arguably stimulated litigation by the Humane Society International to enforce national legislation, with all the attendant risks discussed above.

It may now be time to reconsider the traditional position taken within the ATS that it should not attempt to regulate whaling in the Southern Ocean. The Madrid Protocol is, for example, sufficiently widely drafted to include marine mammals. Article 2 provides that parties are committed to protect the "dependent and associated ecosystems" of the Antarctic.[33] Such language appears to include migratory whales. It is also relevant that the environmental principles of the protocol extend to activities in the Antarctic Treaty area, including whaling by ships. Article 3 of the protocol requires that all activities in the area are "planned and conducted so as to avoid . . . further jeopardy to endangered or threatened species."[34] It is not easy, however, to harmonise obligations under the protocol with other, apparently contrary, provisions within the ATS. Article VI of CCAMLR, for example, provides that the convention is not to "derogate from the rights and obligations . . . under the ICRW." Reports commissioned by the Paris, Sydney, and Canberra Working Groups on Whaling have attempted to resolve such treaty conflicts through traditional legal techniques of interpretation. These technical legal arguments are not entirely convincing in their efforts to harmonise international agreements that grew like Topsy to provide solutions to contemporary issues. The agreements within the ATS and other treaties with interests in the Southern Ocean are jostling for space with each other as activities there increase. Rationalisation and good faith collaboration are now required.

Beyond the specific issue of whaling in the Southern Ocean is the wider question of overlapping mandates under other international agreements and institutions with growing interests in Antarctica. The parties to the Madrid Protocol are obliged to "consult and cooperate" with parties to other international institutions.[35] Such bodies could include the UN International Seabed Authority, the International Maritime Organisation, the International Whaling Commission, the UN Continental

Shelf Commission, the UN Food and Agriculture Organisation, the World Health Organisation, the UN Environment Programme, the International Hydrographic Organisation, the Antarctic and Southern Ocean Coalition, the International Union for Conservation of Nature, the International Association of Antarctica Tour Operators, and regional fisheries organisations. All these bodies may be invited to ATCM and meetings of CCAMLR. There is evidence of some commendable collaboration emerging, including that among the East Antarctic coastal states (South Africa, France, New Zealand, and Australia) in response to unreported fishing of Patagonian tooth fish and the South Indian Ocean fishing arrangement. It is hoped that greater efforts to act through strategic alliances and to develop thematic regional cooperation will develop in the future.

Antarctic Continental Shelf Delimitation

For the claimant states, their Antarctic territory automatically brings with it sovereign rights to the resources of the continental shelf under the 1982 UN Law of the Sea Convention. The importance of the continental shelf lies in its significant oil resources. The U.S. Energy Information Administration reported in 2000 that the Weddell and Ross seas hold 50 billion barrels of oil, similar to Alaska's known reserves.[36] Before long, it might be expected that the UN Continental Shelf Commission will be asked to consider the limits of an Antarctic continental shelf claim. Any such request will, in turn, beg the question of the validity of the relevant claim to territorial sovereignty. A request for recognition of an Antarctic continental shelf will, moreover, pose yet another unanswered question of interpretation of Article IV, paragraph 2, prohibiting any "new claim, or enlargement of an existing claim, to territorial sovereignty in Antarctica." It is strongly arguable that delineation of the limits of the continental shelf is not a new "claim" for the purposes of Article IV, paragraph 2, because delineation is merely an assertion of sovereign rights that derive from the existing territorial claim. The commission is more likely to challenge the validity of the territorial claim itself, rather than the rights that arise from that claim. Although Australia has submitted the delimitation of its Antarctic continental shelf to the commission, it has asked that the commission refrain from making any ruling on the issue at present. In this way, the legal question of interpretation has been avoided for the time being. It might be observed, however, that not all states have adopted the Australian approach. New Zealand and the United Kingdom have, for example, relied on a more "minimalist" approach by making a partial submission only, reserving their right to submit their delineations for an extended continental shelf at some time in the future, if they decide to do so.

Threats to Security within the Antarctic Region

As Antarctica and the Southern Ocean are vulnerable to increasing threats from terrorism and conflict, we may need to view the effectiveness of the ATS through the prism of wider concerns for security. There have been, for example, several maritime incidents that may be a harbinger of future threats to the Antarctic area. Whereas in the past it might validly be claimed that the Antarctic Treaty system was effective in confining the Falklands conflict to the subantarctic region, the terrorist attack on the *Rainbow Warrior* in New Zealand, the fire on the *Nissin Maru* of the Japanese fleet in February 2007, and recent activities by the Sea Shepherd Conservation Society in January 2008 in respect to Japanese whaling suggest that the region might well be a theatre of conflict in the future. Threats are also posed to human security within the Southern Ocean (though not yet within the region of Antarctica) by piracy and by rising numbers of asylum seekers, posing questions about the efficacy of search and rescue capacities.

It is, moreover, likely that global concerns for security from conflict will expand to wider concerns for energy, food, and the security of economic opportunities in the Antarctic. Tourism poses a risk to the environment and is also a human risk in the event of a serious shipping incident in which the many thousands of tourists on a single vessel are likely to strain rescue operations. Commercial risks to sustainable fishing are also likely in the future, with unreported fishing in the Southern Ocean of Patagonian tooth fish and southern bluefin tuna. Further, largely untapped, opportunities for commercial gain lie in clean water and bioprospecting. Resource security is thus a potential challenge to the current mining moratorium.

CONCLUSIONS

New thinking and initiatives are required to strengthen the system. The ATS is, fairly or otherwise, seen by many as insular and nontransparent, incapable of enforcing its measures, and slow to respond to contemporary threats. What are the solutions?

- It would be wise to make modest suggestions for reform that do not include significant legal change.

For example, the ATCM might adopt the model of CCAMLR by creating an Antarctic Treaty Commission with legal personality. Under such a structure, the chair of the ATCM might be granted power to act on behalf of the ATCM. It will be necessary to develop any such proposal by reference to its objects and purposes and powers to achieve them.

- Some form of independent performance review, similar to those adopted by CCAMLR and the Indian Ocean Tuna Commission, would add credibility to the governance of the ATS.
- Greater resources need to be devoted to the region to plan for and manage risks on a "be prepared" basis.
- The well-recognized lack of capacity to enforce measures agreed by the Consultative Parties against nonparty states may become a more significant impediment to governance. Increased efforts to encourage further accessions to the ATS by the international community should be made.
- The two-week annual meeting of the ATCPs seems, on its face, to be inadequate. Although it is recognized that the committees, such as the Scientific Committee, meet much more regularly and report to the ATCM, the need for more-active governance suggests additional resources will be necessary in the future.
- The reporting obligations of the Antarctic Treaty System are not met by most state parties, and basic functions such as monitoring and administration are only minimally carried out. These obligations need to be implemented and monitored.

One of the factors contributing to the success of the Antarctic Treaty has been that it created a "process, not just a piece of paper".[37] This means that the treaty provides the means by which, in an organic way, the states parties could develop principles and procedures for Antarctic governance that would ensure its primary objectives while leaving intact their respective views on sovereignty.

The ATS provides a valuable model for the evolution of international regimes that avoids irresolvable sovereignty and boundary issues. As access to living and nonliving resources becomes a vital matter of national and global security over the coming years, the ATS provides an exemplar for the promotion of peaceful problem solving. The ATS also demonstrates how regions beyond national jurisdiction might be managed in the future according to identified common interests and values that are more comprehensive those of traditional national sovereignty.

NOTES

1. Senate Committee on Foreign Relations, ExB, 86th Cong., 2nd sess., 14 June 1960, 48.

2. Antarctic Treaty Consultative Meeting XXXII in Washington, D.C., 6 April 2009.

3. British Antarctic Survey, "Antarctic Treaty 50th Anniversary—2009," http://www.antarctica.ac.uk/about_antarctica/geopolitical/treaty/anniversary.php (accessed 5 June 2009).

4. P. J. Beck, "The United Nations and Antarctica: The End of the Question of Antarctica?" *Polar Record* 217 (2006): 222–252.

5. The first call for Antarctica to be the "common heritage of mankind" was made in the UN General Assembly by Malaysia's Prime Minister Mahatir in September 1982; UN General Assembly, 37th Sess., UN Doc. A/37/PV 10, 1982. In 1987 Greenpeace established the World Park Base in the Ross Dependency, claimed by New Zealand, to press its demand that Antarctica be declared a world park within which commercial exploitation and pollution should be prohibited and research limited.

6. Argentina's claim to sovereignty was incremental in the sense that from 1904 it occupied islands such as the South Orkneys and South Shetlands.

7. The remaining unclaimed sector, about one fifth of the continent, is Marie Byrd Land, between the Chilean and New Zealand sectors; Russia, although making no formal claim, cites the explorations by Admiral Bellingshausen in the 1830s as giving it a priority interest in Antarctic affairs.

8. R. D. Hayton, "The Antarctic Settlement of 1959," *American Journal of International Law* 54 (1960): 352; The Argentine and Chilean claims spring from their inheritance of Spanish title, which in turn, rests on the fifteenth century Treaty Of Tordesillas, which gave all lands to the west of the 46th meridian to Spain and all lands to the east to Portugal; Chile also relies on a grant in 1539 of all territories to the south of the Strait of Magellan; E. W. Hunter Christie, *The Antarctic Problem* (London: Allen & Unwin, 1949), 277; British sovereignty was founded in "effective occupation" from at least 1908.

9. ICJ Reports 1956, pp. 12, 15.

10. C .H. M. Waldock, "Disputed Sovereignty in the Falkland Islands Dependencies," *British Yearbook of International Law* 25 (1948): 311–353; J. Hanessian "The Antarctic Treaty 1959," *International and Comparative Law Quarterly* 9 (1960): 436.

11. *Washington Post*, "Antarctic Claims," 2 January 1947; Hanessian, "Antarctic Treaty," p. 436; Hayton, "Antarctic Settlement," p. 350.

12. R. Bulkeley writes that individuals also played a role by advocating internationalisation, including T. W. Balch, an international lawyer, in 1910, with the support of the *New York Times,* and Herbert Brown a weather forecaster, "The Political Origins of the Antarctic Treaty," in "Invited Reflections on the Antarctic Treaty," *Polar Record* 46(1):9–11.

13. Hanessian, "Antarctic Treaty," p. 444.

14. Hanessian, "Antarctic Treaty," p. 441.

15. G. Triggs, *International Law and Australian Sovereignty in Antarctica* (Sydney: Legal Books, 1986), p. 277.

16. Hayton, "Antarctic Settlement."

17. Triggs, *Australian Sovereignty*, p. 423; M. M. Whiteman, *Digest of International Law,* vol. 11 (Washington: U.S. Department of State, 1963–1973), p. 1238.

18. Hanessian, "Antarctic Treaty," p. 455.

19. Hanessian, "Antarctic Treaty," p. 467.

20. Hayton, "Antarctic Settlement," p. 356.

21. J. M. Marcoux, "Natural Resource Jurisdiction on the Antarctic Continental Margin," *Virginia Journal of International Law* 11 (1971): 379.

22. Article III, CCAMLR.

23. Cited by D. K. Anton, "Australian Jurisdiction and Whales in Antarctica", *Asia Pacific Journal of Environmental Law* 11, nos. 3 & 4 (2008): 188.

24. The Convention on the Regulation of Antarctic Mineral Resource Activities has not been ratified by any state.

25. In force, 1998.

26. D. Rothwell, "Japanese Whaling in Antarctica," *Asia Pacific Journal of Environmental Law* 11, nos. 3 & 4 (2008): 142.

27. It is arguable that state practice now supports a customary rule that prohibits the exercise of jurisdiction against nonnationals for their acts or omissions in the treaty area, Anton, "Whales in Antarctica," p. 179.

28. *Humane Society International v. Kyoto Senpaku Kaisha Ltd (Japanese Whaling Case)*, [2004] FCA 1510; [2005] FCA 678; [2006] FCAFC 116; [2007] FCA 124; [2008] FCA 3 (granting injunction on declaration that there was a breach of Australian law); [2008] FCA 36 (leave for substituted service of orders).

29. Sec. 475 gives interested persons standing to seek orders restraining breaches of the act.

30. Australia claims a 12 nautical mile territorial sea off the AAT, a 200 nautical mile EEZ (the Antarctic EEZ is "excepted waters" in respect of the Australian Fisheries Zone and not subject to the Fisheries Management Act of 1991 [EPBC], sec. 3), and a juridical continental shelf of 200 nautical miles; Australia made its submission in 2004 to the UN Commission on the Limits of the Continental Shelf under Article 76 of The United Nations Convention on the Law of the Sea, but asked that the commission should "not take any action for the time being with respect to the Antarctic area," 1 July 2008.

31. The attorney-general's submissions to the Federal Court of Australia suggested that restraint was required by international law, a view that is legally questionable, www.envlaw.com.au/whale7.pdf; the EPBC Act does not include any provision making the act subject to Australia's obligations under international law and gives an enforcement capacity to any interested persons under sec. 475.

32. Only four states, France, New Zealand, Norway, and the United Kingdom, accept Australia's territorial claim since 1933; more specifically, Japan has been consistent in refusing to recognize Australia's claim, including in 2006 when the Humane Society International attempted to serve Kyodo with the Federal Court of Australia injunction, [2008] FCA 3[20]; Australia is vulnerable to the argument that all the maritime claims (except with respect to the continental shelf claim made in 1953) are in breach of Article IV, paragraph 2, because they are new sovereign claims or extensions of claims; if so, Australia would have no jurisdiction over the activities of a nonnational in the waters of the Southern Ocean off the AAT.

33. The meaning of the phrase "dependent and associated ecosystems" is unclear and was adopted in the protocol to ensure that any major pollution incidents stemming from mineral exploration or exploitation would be covered in respect of the waters adjacent to Chile.

34. Article 3, paragraph 2(b)(v).

35. The protocol is, in any event, subservient to the Antarctic Treaty, and it is arguable that it does not regulate whaling activities in Antarctic Treaty area. The CCAMLR Commission, through its Scientific Committee, has the stronger claim to take action in respect to whaling, although it has thus far chose to tread carefully.

36. Cited by Anton, "Whales in Antarctica," p. 192.

37. British Antarctic Survey, "50th Anniversary."

Balancing Sovereign Interests beyond National Jurisdictions

Vladimir Golitsyn

Fifty years ago on 2 May 1958 the government of the United States of America circulated a note to the 12 states most actively involved in scientific research in Antarctica during the International Geophysical Year, initiating discussions regarding the convening of a conference on Antarctica and the conclusion of an international treaty for this area. Shortly after the circulation of the note, on 10 June 1958, these 12 states, namely, Argentina, Australia, Belgium, Chile, France, Japan, New Zealand, Norway, South Africa, the United Kingdom, the United States, and the Union of Soviet Socialist Republics (USSR), started informal preliminary discussions in Washington that resulted in the convening of an international conference in Washington on 15 October 1959. On 1 December 1959 the conference resulted in the signing of the Antarctic Treaty, which entered into force on 23 June 1961 and currently defines an international regime for this vast area of our planet. The Antarctic Treaty turned out to be one of the most successful international agreements concluded by states belonging to two opposite ideological and military blocks, despite the extreme tension existing between them during the cold war period. It is also remarkable that the 12 states concerned managed to overcome a disagreement that existed and continues to exist among them regarding the legal status of the Antarctic continent in general and certain parts thereof that are considered by seven of them, namely, Argentina, Australia, Chile, France, New Zealand, Norway, and the United Kingdom, to be part of their territory.

A lot was said at the Antarctic Treaty Summit: Science-Policy Interactions in International Governance about the important role played by the Antarctic Treaty in ensuring close international cooperation in Antarctica, in providing solid ground for development of scientific research in Antarctica in the interest of all mankind, and in preserving Antarctica as an area of peace and stability, free of military rivalry and confrontation. Therefore, I will concentrate only on one aspect of the Antarctic Treaty that, in my view, is crucial for understanding what constitutes a foundation of the treaty and for retaining Antarctica as an area of peace and stability in the interests of future generations. I refer to the provisions of Article IV of the Antarctic Treaty.

In a balanced way, Article IV reflects the positions of the three groups of states that negotiated the Antarctic Treaty: states that consider the respective

Vladimir Golitsyn, International Tribunal for the Law of the Sea, Am Internationalen Seegerichtshof 1, D-22609 Hamburg, Germany. Correspondence: vgolitsyn@gmail.com.

parts of the Antarctic continent as their territory; states that did not claim any sovereignty in Antarctica at the time of the conclusion of the treaty but consider that they may have legitimate right to do so; and states that take the position that no state can claim sovereignty in Antarctica. The position of the first group of states is reflected in paragraph 1(a) of Article IV, which states that nothing contained in the present treaty shall be interpreted as "a renunciation by any Contracting Party of previously asserted rights of or claims to territorial sovereignty in Antarctica." Paragraph 1(b) conveys the position of the second group by providing that nothing contained in the present treaty shall be interpreted as "a renunciation or diminution by any Contracting Party of any basis of claim to territorial sovereignty in Antarctica which it may have whether as a result of its activities or those of its nationals in Antarctica, or otherwise." Finally, paragraph 1(c) reflects the position of the third group, which currently constitutes the overwhelming majority of the Treaty Parties; it states that nothing contained in the present treaty shall be interpreted as "prejudicing the position of any Contracting Party as regards its recognition or nonrecognition of any other State's right of or claim or basis of claim to territorial sovereignty in Antarctica."

The above provisions are supplemented by an important commitment contained in paragraph 2 of Article IV, which states that "no acts or activities taking place while the present Treaty is in force shall constitute a basis for asserting, supporting or denying a claim to territorial sovereignty in Antarctica or create any rights of sovereignty in Antarctica. No new claim, or enlargement of an existing claim, to territorial sovereignty in Antarctica shall be asserted while the present Treaty is in force."

What is important to understand in relation to Article IV of the treaty is that contrary to widespread perception, the Antarctic Treaty does not freeze claims to territorial sovereignty in Antarctica. The Antarctic Treaty proclaims noble goals and contains concrete provisions aimed at ensuring their implementation. It states that Antarctica shall be used for peaceful purposes only and in this regard prohibits any measure of a military nature, such as the establishment of military bases and fortifications, the carrying out of military manoeuvres, and the testing of any type of weapon. In addition, it prohibits nuclear explosions in Antarctica and the disposal there of radioactive waste material. The treaty guarantees freedom of scientific investigation in Antarctica and cooperation toward that end and provides for the exchange of information regarding plans for scientific programs, scientific observations, and results from Antarctica and the exchange of scientific personnel in Antarctica. None of the objectives of the Antarctic Treaty could have been achieved on the basis of the position of only one of the groups of states referred to above. In order to achieve these objectives, which represented the common interests of the drafters of the treaty, the 12 original parties to the treaty agreed to retain status quo in Antarctica; in other words, they agreed to freeze the settlement of the issue of territorial claims in Antarctica. The Antarctic Treaty Parties agreed to assume obligations that correspond to the objectives of the treaty, but they retained at the same time their respective positions with regard to the issue of sovereignty.

Why is it so important to understand the role of Article IV of the Antarctic Treaty? The answer is because any new activity in Antarctica that goes beyond the scope of the Antarctic Treaty requires revisiting the provisions of Article IV to determine whether that activity could be accommodated by extending the application of Article IV. The development of the so-called Antarctic Treaty System has demonstrated that so far, the Antarctic Treaty Parties have been willing and capable of applying the understandings embodied in Article IV of the treaty to some new activities by adjusting such understandings as required. The Antarctic Treaty System is a set of complex arrangements made for the purpose of coordinating relations among states with respect to Antarctica and includes the Antarctic Treaty itself, recommendations adopted at meetings of the Antarctic Treaty Consultative Parties, the Protocol on Environmental Protection to the Antarctic Treaty, and two separate conventions, the Conservation of Antarctic Seals (London, 1972) and the Conservation of Antarctic Marine Living Resources (Canberra, 1980). The Antarctic Treaty System also includes the results of Meetings of Experts and the decisions of Special Consultative Meetings and, at a nongovernmental level, reflects the work of the Scientific Committee on Antarctic Research (SCAR) on all aspects of the system.

However, efforts of the Antarctic Treaty Parties have not always been successful. The Convention for the Regulation of Antarctic Mineral Resource Activities (Wellington, 1988) has not been ratified by any state and, consequently, has never entered into force. This lack of ratification occurred not only because of deficiency of or dissatisfaction with its provisions concerning protection of environment but also, as I will try to demonstrate, because of reasons related to the issue of sovereignty. Consequently, the future of the Antarctic Treaty and the system that has evolved on the basis of its provisions will depend, to a great extent, on the ability of these three groups of states to continue to work together within the framework of the treaty to accommodate new activities, in particular, those relating to the potential use of Antarctic mineral resources, both on land and off the shore.

As we are celebrating the 50th anniversary of the conclusion of the Antarctic Treaty and look with pride on the past achievements, we should be mindful of what lies ahead, be realistic, and have the courage to acknowledge that there are serious perils on the horizon that may endanger the delicate balance of interests preserved by the Antarctic Treaty System, the cornerstone of which is the treaty itself. Recent submissions to the Commission on the Limits of the Continental Shelf by states claiming sovereignty in Antarctica have clearly demonstrated that rivalry over the territorial status of Antarctica is still present. It has not vanished over the last 50 years despite all the achievements of the Antarctic Treaty System; it is still alive and raises questions about the ability of the Antarctic Treaty System to withstand challenges posed by the potential opening of Antarctic mineral resources for exploitation.

According to Article VI of the Antarctic Treaty, its provisions apply to the area south of 60°S latitude, including all ice shelves. This is an artificial boundary as it does not represent the geographical boundary of Antarctica. Presumably, this latitude was selected because all land that is disputed and viewed by many states as territorial claims is located south of 60°S latitude.

The first time that the Antarctic Treaty Parties had to deal with the regulation of a commercial activity in Antarctica related to its resources was in 1972 in the case of the Convention for the Conservation of Antarctic Seals. Although there had been no attempt to exploit Antarctic seals commercially since 1964, the SCAR Group of Specialists on Antarctic Seals continued to monitor the taking of seals for scientific purposes, and the Treaty Parties came to the conclusion that there was a need to develop an international mechanism to protect the conservation of Antarctic seals. The Antarctic Treaty Parties had the choice of incorporating the agreement in the form of an Antarctic Treaty Recommendation or of adopting a freestanding instrument, and they chose the latter option. As there was no commercial activity related to the exploitation of Antarctic seals, the Antarctic Treaty Parties easily agreed that this convention should apply to the seas south of 60°S latitude (Article 1, "Scope of the Convention"), in respect of which the Contracting Parties affirmed the provisions of Article IV of the Antarctic Treaty.

However, eight years later in the case of Antarctic marine living resources the Antarctic Treaty Parties were confronted with a serious challenge to reach an agreement on how it would be possible, if at all, to apply the provisions of Article IV of the treaty to the activities related to the use of these resources. In the 1970s, the Antarctic waters were gradually becoming an area of quite extensive fishery activities. The Antarctic Consultative Parties recognized that there was an urgent need to establish some form of regulatory mechanism that would ensure conservation and sustainable use of the Antarctic marine living resources. At that time, negotiations on the Law of the Sea Convention had not been completed yet. However, it was more or less accepted by all states that the new convention would entitle coastal states to establish zones extending up to 200 nautical miles, within which they would have the sovereign rights for the purpose of exploiting, conserving, and managing its living resources. On 26 September 1977 New Zealand adopted a new law regarding the territorial sea and the exclusive economic zone, and in 1979 Australia adopted new legislation on the 200 nautical mile fishery zone. The states claiming sovereignty in Antarctica took and continue to maintain a position that the establishment of such zones is an act of exercise of their sovereign rights under international law and therefore does not constitute an extension of the existing claim to territorial sovereignty, which is prohibited by paragraph 2 of Article IV of the Antarctic Treaty. States that do not recognize claims to territorial sovereignty in Antarctica took and continue to maintain the opposite position.

Marine living resources do not recognize boundaries. To be effective, their conservation and management should be organized on a regional basis covering all areas of their migration. It should be acknowledged as a significant achievement of the Antarctic Treaty Parties in the 1970s that, first, they agreed to approach the conservation and management of Antarctic marine living resources by negotiating a convention applying to the entire area of the Antarctic marine ecosystem and, second, in the process of such negotiations conducted within the framework of a Special Consultative Meeting convened for this purpose, they managed to reach a common understanding on how the provisions of Article IV of the treaty could be extended to this new activity while preserving, with respect to the issue of sovereignty, the status quo enshrined in the Antarctic Treaty.

The Convention on the Conservation of Antarctic Marine Living Resources, which was concluded in Canberra, Australia, in May 1980 and entered into force on 7 April 1982, applies to the entire area of the Antarctic marine ecosystem and is limited in the north by the Antarctic Convergence, a major circum-Antarctic biogeographic boundary where the cold, northerly moving waters dip beneath warmer, southerly moving subtropical waters. Article I, paragraph 1, of this convention provides that the convention applies to the Antarctic marine living resources of the area south of 60°S latitude and to the Antarctic marine living resources of the area between that latitude and the Antarctic Convergence, which form part of the Antarctic marine ecosystem.

The issue of territorial sovereignty, as in the case of the Antarctic Treaty, is addressed in Article IV of the convention. Since the convention is open to states and entities (e.g., the European Union) who are not parties to the Antarctic Treaty, the convention contains an important condition that binds all parties to the convention by the provisions of Article IV of the treaty. Paragraph 1 of Article IV of the convention states that with respect to the Antarctic Treaty area, all Contracting Parties, whether or not they are parties to the Antarctic Treaty, are bound by Articles IV and VI of the Antarctic Treaty in their relations with each other. Article VI of the Antarctic Treaty relates to freedoms of high seas.

The compromise between the three groups of states as reflected in Article IV of the convention contains three main elements. Paragraph 2(a) of that article reiterates their basic positions and states that nothing in the convention and no acts or activities taking place while it is in force shall constitute a basis for asserting, supporting, or denying a claim to territorial sovereignty in the Antarctic Treaty area or create any rights of sovereignty in the Antarctic Treaty area. Paragraph 2(d) addresses the issue of the extension of sovereign claims and provides that nothing in the convention and no acts or activities taking place while it is in force affect the provision of Article IV, paragraph 2, of the Antarctic Treaty that no new claim, or enlargement of an existing claim, to territorial sovereignty in Antarctica shall be asserted while the Antarctic Treaty is in force.

Paragraphs 2(b) and (c) deal with coastal state jurisdiction and reflect the positions of claimant and nonclaimant states on this issue. They respectively provide that nothing in the convention and no acts or activities taking place while it is in force shall be interpreted as a renunciation or diminution by any Contracting Party of, or as prejudicing, any right or claim or basis of claim to exercise coastal state jurisdiction under international law within the area to which this convention applies or be interpreted as prejudicing the position of any Contracting Party as regards its recognition or nonrecognition of any such right, claim, or basis of claim.

Despite their disagreement regarding coastal state jurisdiction in Antarctica, reflected in Article IV of the convention, both claimant and nonclaimant states as parties to the convention agreed to entrust the responsibility for the conservation and management of Antarctic marine living resources to the Commission for the Conservation of Antarctic Marine Living Resources established pursuant to Article VII of the convention. The commission is empowered under the convention, inter alia, to identify conservation needs and analyze the effectiveness of conservation measures; to formulate, adopt, and revise conservation measures on the basis of the best scientific evidence available; to implement the system of observation and inspection established under Article XXIV of this convention; and to carry out such other activities as are necessary to fulfil the objective of the convention. The conservation measures that may be adopted by the commission include the designation of the quantity of any species which may be harvested in the area to which this convention applies; the designation of regions and subregions based on the distribution of populations of Antarctic marine living resources; the designation of the quantity which may be harvested from the populations of regions and subregions; the designation of protected species; the designation of the size, age, and, as appropriate, sex of species which may beharvested; the designation of open and closed seasons for harvesting; the designation of the opening and closing of areas, regions, or subregions for purposes of scientific study or conservation, including special areas for protection and scientific study; and regulation of the effort employed and methods of harvesting, including fishing gear, with a view, inter alia, to avoiding undue concentration of harvesting in any region or subregion.

The compromise achieved in Article IV of the convention was possible because of the good will of all the parties concerned who shared the view that effective conservation and management of Antarctic marine living resources requires a regional approach and that such a regime should apply to the whole area of the Antarctic marine ecosystem. However, in addition to Article IV, the convention also includes other provisions that guarantee that no activities will take place in Antarctica on the basis of the convention if they are not acceptable to the states, whose interests are protected by Article IV of the convention. These guarantees are embodied in Articles IX and XII of the convention. Article XII provides that decisions of the Commission for the Conservation of Antarctic Marine Living Resources on matters of substance are taken by consensus, which allows any claimant or nonclaimant state to block the adoption of a decision by the commission if that state disagrees with it. According to Article IX, paragraph 6(b), conservation measures adopted by the commission become binding upon all members of the commission 180 days after the receipt of a notification from the commission about their adoption. However, pursuant to paragraph 6(c) of this article, if a member of the commission, within 90 days following such notification, informs the commission that it is unable to accept the conservation measure, in whole or in part, the respective measure shall not, to the extent stated, be binding upon that member of the commission.

The Antarctic Treaty Parties found themselves in a much more complex situation in the case of mineral resources, namely, in determining whether it would be likewise possible to find common ground regarding a minerals regime that should govern their exploration and exploitation. In the mid-1970s some geophysical prospecting companies started making inquiries about the possibility of prospecting for mineral resources in the Southern Ocean surrounding Antarctica. At the time of the negotiation of the Antarctic Treaty the question was raised as to whether the treaty should also cover mineral exploration and exploitation, and it was concluded that to do so would be premature. However, in the mid-1970s it was understood by the Antarctic Treaty Parties that the question of how Antarctic mineral activity was to be regulated, were it ever to occur, would not go away.

As a first step the Antarctic Treaty Consultative Parties agreed, by adopting Recommendation IX-1 at the Ninth Consultative Meeting, to "urge their nationals and other States to refrain from all exploration and exploitation of Antarctic mineral resources while [they are] making progress towards the timely adoption of an agreed regime." Negotiations on a minerals regime, which lasted for almost 10 years and were conducted within the framework of the Fourth Special Consultative Meeting convened for that purpose, culminated in the adoption of the Convention on the Regulation of Antarctic Mineral Resources Activities (CRAMRA) on 2 June 1988 in Wellington, New Zealand.

The first problem that the Antarctic Treaty Parties needed to resolve in elaborating a minerals regime was the question of the potential area of its application. Pursuant to Article 1, paragraph 1(a) of the Convention on the Law of the Sea (UNCLOS), to which, with one exception, all Antarctic Treaty Parties are members, the seabed and ocean floor and subsoil thereof beyond the limits of national jurisdiction constitute the "Area." In accordance with Articles 136 and 137 of UNCLOS, the Area and its resources are the common heritage of mankind and no state shall claim or exercise sovereignty or sovereign rights over any part of the Area or its resources, nor shall any state or natural or juridical person appropriate any part thereof, and no such claim or exercise of sovereignty or sovereign rights nor such appropriation shall be recognized.

If there is no sovereignty over land mass in Antarctica, theoretically, there should be no continental shelf in Antarctica, which according to Article 76 of UNCLOS, constitutes the natural prolongation of the land territory of a state up to the outer edge of the continental margin. The Antarctic Treaty Parties sidestepped the problem of the origin of rights to the continental shelf by adopting an approach implying that if a minerals regime is elaborated that is applicable to the land mass in Antarctica, irrespective of its status (in other words, applicable to the Antarctic continent and surrounding islands), then it should logically be extended to what constitutes the natural prolongation of this land mass in submarine areas appertaining to that land mass. Article 5, paragraphs 2 and 3, of CRAMRA provide that the convention "shall regulate Antarctic mineral resource activities which take place on the continent of Antarctica and all Antarctic islands, including all ice shelves, south of 60° south latitude and in the seabed and subsoil of adjacent offshore areas up to the deep seabed" and that "for the purposes of this Convention 'deep seabed' means the seabed and subsoil beyond the geographic extent of the continental shelf as the term continental shelf is defined in accordance with international law."

In the Final Act of the Fourth Special Antarctic Treaty Consultative Meeting that adopted the convention it is clarified that the area of regulation of Antarctic mineral resource activities defined in Article 5, paragraph 2, of the convention does not extend to any continental shelf appurtenant in accordance with international law to islands situated north of 60°S latitude. It is further clarified in the Final Act that the geographic extent of the continental shelf as referred to in Article 5, paragraph 3, of the convention would be determined by reference to all the criteria and the rules embodied in paragraphs 1–7 of Article 76 of UNCLOS.

Article 9 of CRAMRA, "Protection of Legal Positions under the Antarctic Treaty," is aimed at extending the balance reflected in Article IV of the Antarctic Treaty to new activities related to mineral resources and follows the format of Article IV of the Convention on the Conservation of Antarctic Marine Living Resources. It contains three main elements. Paragraph (a) of this article reiterates the basic positions of the three groups of states and provides that nothing in the convention and no acts or activities taking place while it is in force shall constitute a basis for asserting, supporting, or denying a claim to territorial sovereignty in the Antarctic Treaty area or create any rights of sovereignty in the Antarctic Treaty area. Paragraph 2(d) addresses the issue of extension of sovereign claims and states that nothing in the convention and no acts or activities taking place while it is in force shall affect the provision of Article IV, paragraph 2, of the Antarctic Treaty that no new claim, or enlargement of an existing claim, to territorial sovereignty in Antarctica shall be asserted while the Antarctic Treaty is in force.

Paragraphs (b) and (c) of Article 9 deal with potential rights to the continental shelf and therefore the text of paragraph (b) is slightly different from the text of the similar paragraph in Article IV of the Convention on the Conservation of Antarctic Marine Living Resources (paragraph 2(b)). Paragraphs (b) and (c) of Article 9 of CRAMRA respectively provide that nothing in the convention and no acts or activities taking place while it is in force shall be interpreted as a renunciation or diminution by any party of, or as prejudicing, any right or claim or basis of claim to territorial sovereignty in Antarctica or to exercise coastal state jurisdiction under international law or be interpreted as prejudicing the position of any party as regards its recognition or nonrecognition of any such right, claim, or basis of claim.

In addition, the issue of territorial claims is also addressed in a special preamble paragraph stating that a regime for Antarctic mineral resources must be consistent with Article IV of the Antarctic Treaty and in accordance therewith be without prejudice and be acceptable to those states which assert rights of or claims to territorial sovereignty in Antarctica and those states which neither recognise nor assert such rights or claims, including those states which assert a basis of claim to territorial sovereignty in Antarctica.

Although the above provisions reiterate that the status quo is preserved in Antarctica in the case of the minerals regime, from my point of view, they are mostly symbolic in nature because as in the case of living resources the real issue is whether other substantive provisions of the minerals convention confirm that respective interests of the three groups of states are adequately protected. Analysis of substantive provisions of CRAMRA raise doubts in this regard.

Two main institutions that are envisaged to be established under CRAMRA are the Antarctic Mineral Resources Commission (hereinafter "the Commission") and the Antarctic Mineral Resources Regulatory Committees (hereinafter "the Regulatory Committees").

Membership in the Commission, inter alia, includes all states that were Antarctic Treaty Consultative Parties on the date of the opening of the convention for signature, which includes all states that assert rights of or claims to territorial sovereignty in Antarctica, the two states that assert a basis of claim to territorial sovereignty in Antarctica (the United States and the Russian Federation/former USSR), and all other states that do not recognize any such rights or claims (Article 18, paragraph 2(a)). So, on the surface, the balance of Article IV is preserved.

However, decision-making provisions of CRAMRA provide that the Commission shall take its decisions on matters of substance by a three-quarters majority of the members present and voting (Article 22, paragraph 1). It is true that according to paragraph 2 of Article 22, some decisions can be taken by the Commission only by consensus. However, most of them relate to budgetary/financial matters (Articles 21, paragraph 1(p), (q), and 35, paragraphs 1–5), which are important but secondary in nature; the elaboration of the principle of nondiscrimination (Article 21, paragraph 1(i)); and the identification of an area for possible exploitation. Consensus, however, is not required for decisions of the Commission concerning the determination of disposition of revenues received from the exploitation of the mineral resources (Articles 21, paragraph 1(r), and 35, paragraph 7). The only clause that addresses, in a rather oblique form, this sensitive and most important issue for states whose positions are reflected in Article IV of the Antarctic Treaty is the statement in paragraph 7(b) of Article 35 providing that the Commission, in determining the disposition of revenues accruing to it, shall ensure that the interests of the members of Regulatory Committees who have the most direct interest in the matter in relation to the areas in question are respected in any disposition of that surplus.

The fact that decisions of the Commission on such an important issue as revenue sharing are to be taken by three-quarters majority of those present and voting raises the question as to whether this is a fair procedure that adequately and in a balanced way preserves the interests of at least two groups of states referred to in Article IV of the Antarctic Treaty, namely, those who assert rights of or claims to territorial sovereignty in Antarctica and those who assert a basis of claim to territorial sovereignty in Antarctica. In my view, at least the rights of the Russian Federation, which asserted a basis of claim, are not adequately protected by voting procedures in the Commission.

Another institution that plays a crucial role in the implementation of the convention is a Regulatory Committee. Under the convention a 10-member Regulatory Committee is to be established for each area identified by the Commission as a coherent unit for the purposes of resource management.

Provisions on membership in Regulatory Committees are contained in Article 29 of the convention. Membership of each such Regulatory Committee should always include the member, if any, or if there is more than one, those members of the Commission identified by reference to Article 9, paragraph (b), which assert rights or claims in the identified area (Article 29, paragraph 2(a)), in other words, claimant states. Such membership should also include the two members of the Commission, also identified by reference to Article 9, paragraph (b), who assert a basis of claim in Antarctica (Article 29, paragraph 2(b)). These two countries are the United States and the Russian Federation. In general, under the convention the 10-member composition of each Regulatory Committee, which is determined by the Commission, should include four members identified by reference to Article 9, paragraph (b), who assert rights or claims, including the member or members, if any, referred to in paragraph (a) of Article 29, and six members who do not assert rights or claims as described in Article 9, paragraph (b), including the two members referred to in paragraph (b) of Article 29, the two states that asserted basis of claim.

The Final Act of the Fourth Special Antarctic Treaty Consultative Meeting includes some additional clarifications with regard to membership in Regulatory Committees. In relation to Article 29 it states that the meeting agreed that the member or members of the Commission mentioned in Article 29, paragraph 2(a), are those identified by reference to Article IV, paragraph 1(a), of the Antarctic Treaty. The members of the Commission mentioned in Article 29, paragraph 2(b), are those identified by reference to Article IV, paragraph 1(b), of the Antarctic Treaty.

It is obvious from the description of the functions of Regulatory Committees defined in Article 31 of the convention that they will play a crucial role in the development of Antarctic mineral resources. The functions of each Regulatory Committee, inter alia, shall include the consideration of applications for exploration and development permits; approval of management schemes; issuance of exploration and development permits; and monitoring of exploration and development activities.

Decision-making procedures in Regulatory Committees are defined in Article 32 of the convention. It provides that decisions by a Regulatory Committee regarding approval of the management scheme (Article 48) and its modification (Article 54, paragraph 5) require a two-thirds majority of the members present and voting, which majority should include a simple majority of those present and voting referred to in Article 29, paragraph 2(c)(i), in other words, states that asserted rights or claims. It also requires a simple majority of members present and voting referred to in Article 29, paragraph 2(c)(ii), which means two states that asserted a basis of claim and states that do not recognize territorial claims in Antarctica (Article 32, paragraph 1). Decisions by a Regulatory Committee on guidelines identifying the general requirements for exploration and development in its area of competence and their revision (Article 43, paragraphs 3 and 5) require a two-thirds majority of the members present and voting, which majority shall include at least half of members of two groups referred to in Article 29, paragraphs 2(c)(i) and (ii) (Article 32, paragraph 2). Decisions by a Regulatory Committee on other matters of substance require a two-thirds majority of the members present and voting (Article 32, paragraph 3). Finally, Article 32, paragraph 5, provides that nothing in it shall be interpreted as preventing a Regulatory Committee, in taking decisions on matters of substance, from endeavouring to reach a consensus.

The above rather complex decision-making formulas, despite repeated references to states asserting rights or claims and states asserting basis of claim, do not sufficiently protect their interests because they do not exclude the adoption of decisions that may not be acceptable to them. It is obvious from the provisions on decision-making procedures that although efforts to reach consensus should be endeavoured and a simple majority of the interested group of states is required, in the end, decisions on substance will be taken in a Regulatory Committee by a two-thirds majority and a country with the most vested interest in the concerned area will be unable to block a decision that is unacceptable to it.

It appears that the efforts by the drafters of CRAMRA to transfer the balance of interest embodied in the provisions of the Antarctic Treaty, which was successfully reinstated in the case of marine living resources, to potential activities related to the use of Antarctic mineral resources failed to produce the required result. Leaving aside the question of whether CRAMRA is deficient because it does not provide sufficient guarantees for an adequate protection of the very fragile Antarctic environment, a conclusion may be reached that the respective provisions of the convention that are supposed to accommodate the interests of the three groups of states referred to in Article IV of the Antarctic Treaty do not preserve the required balance of interest and leave no doubt that some key states will find it difficult to accept the convention. The lesson to be learned from this experience is that only a convention that provides guarantees for real involvement in mineral resource activities and revenue sharing of all states whose interests are reflected in Article IV of the Antarctic

Treaty, if and when such activities take place there, and a decision-making mechanism that is based on general agreement and not one that is based on majority vote can have good chance of achieving true and lasting balance of interest in Antarctica and therefore ensure continuation of stability in the area.

The Protocol on Environmental Protection to the Antarctic Treaty was hastily drafted by the Eleventh Antarctic Treaty Consultative Meeting after it became clear that CRAMRA had little chance to enter into force. Most of the provisions of the protocol, which supplements the Antarctic Treaty but neither modifies nor amends it, draw in large part from recommendations adopted earlier by the Consultative Parties (Article 4). The protocol prohibits in Article 7 any activity relating to mineral resources, other than scientific research. With respect to Article 7, the protocol provides in paragraph 5 of Article 25 that the prohibition on Antarctic mineral resource activities contained therein shall continue unless there is in force a binding legal regime on Antarctic mineral resource activities that includes an agreed means for determining whether, and if so, under which conditions, any such activities would be acceptable. It is further emphasized in Article 25 that the legal regime on Antarctic mineral resources shall fully safeguard the interests of all states referred to in Article IV of the Antarctic Treaty and apply the principles thereof. No reservations to the protocol are permitted (Article 24).

It follows that any use of Antarctic mineral resources in the future will require negotiation of a legally binding regime and such a regime should fully safeguard the interests of all states referred to in Article IV of the Antarctic Treaty. In this regard, it is worth recalling that in their submission to the Commission on the Limits of the Continental Shelf, most of the states that have asserted rights or claims to sovereignty in Antarctica have either submitted or reserved the right to submit information regarding areas of their continental shelf in Antarctica, the extent of which has yet to be defined. They also stated in communications to the commission that they have regard to the legal and political status of Antarctica under the provisions of the Antarctic Treaty, including its Article IV, and consider that it is open to the states concerned to submit information to the commission that would not be examined by the commission for the time being. These actions, as expected, have not been answered by states that do not recognize territorial claims or that assert a basis of claim in Antarctica.

Thus, rivalry over the legal status of Antarctica is still present and very much alive. The success of any negotiations on a minerals regime, if any, for Antarctica will depend on whether appropriate lessons are drawn from the positive and negative experiences in negotiating CRAMRA.

Origin and Limitations of the Antarctic Treaty

Aant Elzinga

INTRODUCTION

As a philosopher and historian of science it strikes me how two mutually opposite kinds of retrospective accounts of the emergence of the Antarctic Treaty have evolved. There is the naive view, according to which the International Geophysical Year (IGY) and the Antarctic Treat (AT) simply succeeded because politics was entirely set to one side. And there is the cynical view, according to which both the IGY and the advent of the AT were a matter of politics all the way. Both of these views are untenable. Instead, I want to argue for a critical realist perspective that focuses on both the science and its geopolitical context.

THE DUAL FUNCTION OF SCIENCE IN THE ANTARCTIC TREATY

As cold war archives have opened, recent scholarship has shown that there was a great deal more politics behind the scenes than we were previously told. However, on some basic issues differences were successfully set aside or frozen, and fundamental principles were agreed upon: the question of claims (sovereign neutrality), the question of carrying out atomic tests (prohibited), demilitarization, and the use of science as a criterion for full participation in the management regime that was set up. It was not because of the application of altruism that this was possible. On the contrary, national interests and agendas were still there, but the extreme cost of the alternative, perpetuating conflict, was too great. Thus, realism, pragmatism, and willingness to compromise on the basis of mutual benefit were the effective principles at work.

The AT involves a mechanism of inclusion/exclusion based on scientific performance. Performing substantial scientific research as an entry ticket for new countries to manifest their presence and participate in the management of the Antarctic continent's future is key. I call this the sublimation of politics in science. Science has a dual function, both advancing new knowledge and manifesting a country's serious interest and presence. Politics in this context is not a bad thing, but rather a good thing, an incentive to do good research that will,

Aant Elzinga, Department of Philosophy, Linguistics and Theory of Science, University of Gothenburg, Box 200, SE-405 30 Gothenburg, Sweden. Correspondence: Aant.Elzinga@theorysc.gu.se.

in turn, give a country clout at the decision-making table. The success of the AT lies in the fact that it gave science a dual function, including its status as a kind of symbolic capital in a political arena, an arm's-length function that reinforced rather than undermined the multinational intergovernmental political management regime.

THREE PRINCIPLES OF SCIENTIFIC INTERNATIONALISM

Even though the science criterion has become more flexible with time, a challenge for the future is still the question of internationalism—how far and what kind. In this respect, three dimensions of internationalism can be distinguished.

1. The *epistemological,* or knowledge, principle states that truth knows no boundaries and scientific results belong to all. This is also called the principle of universality. One way to operationalize it is to measure the frequency of multiauthor, multinational publications to see if this has increased over time and to what extent nontreaty countries are represented.
2. The o*rganizational* principle pertains to the need to cooperate and exchange results. Division of labor helps prevent costly and unnecessary duplication. It is also a matter of what the sociologist of science Robert Merton called the need for "organized skcpticism," what we today call peer review, to enhance the quality of research and its results. One can furthermore distinguish a scale of cooperation ranging from simply multilateral coordination of efforts to actual cooperation and, further, to close multinational collaboration in projects and at research stations.
3. The w*elfare* principle involves solidarity and the application of the fruits of science for the benefit of all humankind, including the distribution of its goods. Joseph Needham, the first science director of the United Nations Educational, Scientific and Cultural Organization (UNESCO) called it the periphery principle. He had in mind the dissemination of science from its world centers to the peripheries in the third world. Julian Huxley, the first director general of UNESCO, used it to argue for organizing Antarctic research within an international institute (see Elzinga and Landström, 1996).

When it comes to the epistemological principle, the AT does quite well. Regarding the second principle, it has been unable to live up to the ideals already expressed in the statutes of the International Polar Commission (IPC) of 1908, which Lüdecke (this volume) considers an important episode in the history of Antarctic research and exploration. Representatives of 12 countries (but not the United Kingdom, Germany, and Norway)[1] agreed to establish closer relations between polar explorers; to standardize methods of observation in key fields; to cooperate in the discussion and interpretation of results; to provide advice and assistance to new polar enterprises, with emphasis on scientific criteria; and to provide for the need for continuity in activities by, for example, introducing research bases for a five-year period, with rotation of participating researchers who might come from different countries. This far-reaching ideal of internationalism and planning was eclipsed by World War I and the cold war in science that followed when, under the auspices of the then newly established International Research Council (IRC), the victor countries boycotted research communities in Germany, Austria, the Soviet Union, and some other countries, a situation that only changed (in part) when the IRC was replaced by the International Council of Scientific Unions (ICSU) in 1931.

When the idea of setting up the Special Committee on Antarctic Research (SCAR) emerged in 1957 and was implemented the following year, several countries were, at first, opposed to or dubious concerning a strong internationalist thrust in this context; not least, the Australian government objected because it felt this might lead to acts of occupancy on its claimed territory.[2] This concern is evident, for example, in the actions of Keith Bullen, a seismologist at the University of Sydney who attended SCAR's constitutional meeting in The Hague and was elected its vice-president. On his return to Australia he reported back to government officials that in line with Australian policy, he had succeeded in getting a clause that had proposed that SCAR should directly organize the whole scientific program in Antarctica removed from the draft SCAR constitution. Thus, SCAR shied away from the kind of dirigiste approach to cooperation in science that Henryk Arctowski had advocated for in the old IPC in 1906. In 1958–1959 it was, however, more than just a research management principle that was at issue, it was a matter of politics.

With respect to the welfare principle in internationalism, the AT still has some way to go. Two alternatives to the AT have been suggested; one is the notion of Antarctica as part of the heritage of humankind, from which stems the idea that it should be placed under the auspices of the United Nations. The other is the notion of Antarctica as a world natural park, an idea proposed by international environmentalist nongovernmental organizations. Both of these concepts have been unsuccessful, but they have contributed to some accommodation of the AT to broader internationalist and environmental conservation principles. In light of these changes it appears that the most viable road for continued and farther-reaching internationalism should involve the introduction of international research stations. This point is briefly discussed at the end of this paper.

THE DECISION NOT TO LET THE COLD WAR SPILL OVER INTO ANTARCTICA

Regarding the negotiations prior to the signing of the AT, first, 60 secret meetings were held, and then the formal conference opened in October 1959, culminating in the signing of the treaty on 1 December. The process was not an easy one. As Ambassador Oscar Pinochet de la Barra recalled at the symposium "On the Future of the Antarctic Treaty" held in Ushuaia, Argentina, on 20–24 March 1995, "some delegates were in favour of freedom of science, others were against it; some supported the freezing of sovereignty, some did not; some wanted a treaty for 30 years, others a more permanent treaty; some said yes and some said no to observers; and so on" (Jackson, 1995:9).

It is a pity that so little is known about the role of the Soviet Union and that so few Russian participants attended the conference on which this volume is based. Russian accounts of the process (e.g., that of Yuri M. Rybakov at the 25th anniversary of the treaty during the Beardmore conference in Antarctica, 1985) maintain that the Soviets pushed to keep atomic tests out of Antarctica and that there were some parties that wanted to allow for experimentation with "non-military atomic blasts" provided prior forewarning was given; of course, it was difficult to draw a line between military and civilian "blasts." (see Rybakov's comments in Polar Research Board report, 1986). It would be useful to know more about this topic.

It is clear that it was ultimately the attitudes, insights, and mutual understanding between the two superpowers that was very important to the decision not to let the cold war spill over into the Antarctic. This understanding was not an expression of altruism but rather an expression of hardheaded realpolitik with mutual benefit and pragmatic considerations as a guiding principle.

THE IMMEDIATE POST-IGY PERIOD

In many recent periodizations of the history of Antarctic exploration and research the IGY 1957/1958 marks a definitive benchmark. Pre-IGY periods are depicted as ones of conflict and tension between countries with political and economic interests in Antarctica, whereas the post-IGY era is mostly portrayed as one of harmony, one where science is able to flourish. This portrayal is also a misconception.

Once the Antarctic Treaty was in place, national interests and rivalries still existed when it came to advancing research projects because by and of itself, the science, or the basic research motive, is not enough to establish new forms of large-scale multinational collaboration within the ATS framework. More often than not, a definitive political will on the part of the participating countries, along with the possibility of significant mutual benefit at economic and political levels, is needed. The role of leading (hybrid) scientific personalities who might act as champions for specific projects with transnational and transdisciplinary collaboration is also important. It may be instructive to consider a visionary proposal for European research collaboration in Antarctica that arose in the early 1970s; ultimately, this proposal failed because even if the will was there in relevant scientific communities, other factors controlled by decision makers at several political levels constituted hindrances.

Generally speaking, in the decade after IGY at least four related factors converged to raise interest in European scientific collaboration in the Antarctic. First, new technological developments made it possible to pursue new research agendas. Second, there was a shift from description and observation to an interest in explaining processes, such as changes in the mass balance of glacial ice sheets. Third, an epistemic differentiation took place on the disciplinary landscape within the sciences, with glaciology becoming more prominent. Fourth, mission orientation of science in the wake of reformulations of economic and environmental motives for research was also important, allowing glaciology to play a special role in advancing the understanding of environmental change.[3]

THE EUROPEAN ANTARCTIC PROJECT OF THE 1970s: A VISIONARY COLLABORATIVE PROJECT

In the early 1970s, several new international research programs were underway (for details and references pertinent to the European Antarctic Project [EAP], see Elzinga, 2009a, and also Stauffer, 2009; for details on the policies of the Netherlands, Belgium, and Germany during 1957–1990, see Abbink, 2009). In May 1969 the United States,

Soviet Union, Australia, and France joined together in the International Antarctic Glaciological Programme (IAGP; with the United Kingdom joining 1972), focusing on East Antarctica, e.g., the Vostok ice dome. In 1970 an ad hoc group within SCAR led by glaciologist J. H. Zumberge set up the Ross Ice Shelf Project (RISP), and later, the Filchner-Ronne Ice Shelf Project (FRISP) was set up, which involved Germany, the United Kingdom, the Soviet Union, and the United States.

The Glaciology of the Antarctic Peninsula project, involving the United Kingdom, Argentina, Chile, and the United States, emerged in 1973 out of a symposium at the Scott Polar Research Institute in Cambridge where airborne radio echo sounding and isotope analysis of ice cores were discussed. Throughout the 1970s, there were significant efforts to standardize methods in glaciology, with the IAGP producing comprehensive standardization guidelines endorsed by SCAR in 1972 for measuring along traverse lines and taking geophysical measurements, including radar, seismic refraction profiles, magnetic profiling, physical and chemical properties of ice, traces of radioactivity. It is in this context that the significance of the idea of a joint European glaciological project may be appreciated.

Initially, the idea for the EAP came up during the SCAR meeting and symposium on Earth sciences held in Oslo in 1970. At that meeting there was discussion not only on geology and mineral deposits but also on the question of environmental change, which might have left traces in the archive of the Antarctic ice sheet. Tony van Autenboer and Hugo Decleir, two veterans of the Belgian IGY expedition to Antarctica, sounded the idea for the EAP out with a French researcher, Jacques Nougier, who suggested the Council of Europe (CoE; created in 1949) might be interested. This discussion led to a preliminary meeting hosted in Brussels (3 November 1970), chaired by Baron Gaston de Gerlache Gomery, who later became the chairman of the "bureau" of a European working group for polar research under the auspices of the Committee on Science and Technology (CST) of the CoE. At the time, it was noted how only two European countries maintained permanent research stations in Antarctica (France and the United Kingdom) and that three other countries (Norway, Belgium, and the Netherlands) had a constant interest but only intermittent activity. West Germany, Italy, Sweden, and Switzerland also expressed interests (for more detail, see Stauffer, 2009).

Increasing sophistication of research and prohibitive costs of logistic and technical support had made it virtually impossible for smaller countries to maintain a permanent effort except as part of a joint European effort. When articulated, the concept was soon linked to environmental interests. A central task was ice core drilling to facilitate studies of past climate change and to predict future change, including the influence of human activities, much along the lines of the European Project for Ice Coring in Antarctica (EPICA) 20 years later.

Such a project, it was decided, might play an important role in providing several additional countries with the possibility of participating in and developing what "would represent a spectacular and significant manifestation of *l'esprit européen*."(Nougier et al., 1971: 115). With travel and hospitality costs funded by the European Council's CST, the Working Party for European Polar Research (WPEPR), consisting of scientists plus a CST representative, held at least 16 meeting in various European cities from 1970 to 1974, with the most intensity in Paris from the autumn of 1972 to the spring of 1973. A draft report was widely circulated. The scientific concept that evolved concentrated on deep drilling, first and foremost in what appears to be the area of present-day Dome Fuji on Dronning Maud Land. Drilling was to be supplemented by several traverses along three types of lines, namely, glacial ice flow lines, dividing lines between major ice field regions, and lines following 2500 m elevation contours. In addition, the plan called for drilling on the ice shelf, a geodetic program, and a radio echo program. Operations were to be during the austral summer seasons over a period of five years.

SCIENTIFIC CHALLENGES AND PRACTICAL HINDRANCES ASSOCIATED WITH THE EAP OF THE 1970s

At the first Paris meeting (1971) of the European polar working group, glaciologists Claude Lorius and Hans Oeschger emphasized the importance of the climatic environment in the world as a factor affecting human life, pointing to the great significance of the Antarctic venture in this context, an argument that made an impact at the CoE. However, intergovernmental consensus was not forthcoming. The main obstacles were the great expense and a failure to come to an agreement with regard to the project's managerial structure and the financial formula for sharing the cost between participating countries. The problem was the larger countries.

Having decided to join the IAGP, the United Kingdom withdrew from the EAP effort by June of 1972, saying that it was prepared to help but did not want to be an official partner since partnership entailed costs that would cut severely into the normal operating budget of the British

Antarctic Survey. The United Kingdom also committed itself to a program for the Glaciology of the Antarctic Peninsula, a venture that was politically more important since it covered the region of British Antarctic territorial claims. Furthermore, the Scott Polar Research Institute had become heavily involved in a very fruitful collaborative effort with U.S. scientists and Danish radio engineers in pioneering activities to successively map bedrock profiles under the Antarctic ice sheet over vast areas of the continent using airborne radio echo techniques (radioglaciology, as it was also called in some scientific and engineering circles at the time; see Dean et al., 2008). For this effort, the U.S. Navy provided the planes and logistical support, and the National Science Foundation in Washington, D.C., was responsible for a major portion of the funding. Collaboration with the United States proved to be simpler and cheaper while yielding substantial scientific payoff.

The West German delegate to the EAP working group meetings, Walther Hofmann, had his sights set upon an expedition to Greenland and succeeded in getting his government to vote against a joint European Antarctic endeavor. Thus, the $3 million it was hoped Germany would contribute also disappeared. France, on the other hand, became all the more adamant as the rightful defender of the European standard. Representatives of smaller countries like Belgium worked hard to revamp the project and, in response to a request in 1974 by the CoE (before a final decision in 1975), scaled it down to a more acceptable level of costs by extending the time frame from five to seven years.

DIFFERENCES OVER PRIORITIES AND RIVAL MODELS OF SCIENTIFIC COOPERATION

It was not only the high cost that constituted a stumbling block. There were also technological difficulties. First, at the time, technology for ice core drilling had not yet been sufficiently developed to meet the requirements of deep drilling at temperatures below −40°C. Second, for logistics purposes in the earlier plan there was a need for a large ski-equipped transport aircraft of the CL-130 type, something only the U.S. Navy possessed.

Some delegates argued that the EAP should be converted to participation in the IAGP instead since there the two superpowers supplied long-distance logistics. French scientists put a lot of energy into trying to shape up the original plan of 1972 to make it acceptable. The West German representative, Walther Hofmann, was particularly strongly opposed to the French rationalist top-down approach. A professor in geodesy who had experience from Greenland, he was, moreover, not interested in Antarctica and pushed for a project on Greenland instead, arguing that it was much closer and less costly, in which case the United States might even be relied on for long-distance transport of equipment.

In opposition to the French "integrated" model, Hofmann introduced an à la carte model of financing and management according to which each country would be responsible on both counts for only a part or parts of the scientific program. His motivation was that it could not be expected that national institutions and funding bodies "promote the means of research work which is carried out and exploited by other countries." (CoE, 1972:2). Large-country chauvinism thus ended up undermining the whole enterprise. Van Autenboer's conclusion, in retrospect, is that the greatest fault all along lay in the failure to do the extensive political groundwork needed for a project like the EAP. Also, the role of individual personalities and their interests proved to be important. Hofmann, for example, turned out to be the wrong man for the role of "delegate" on behalf of West Germany (Van Autenboer in an interview with Peter Abbink; see Abbink, 2009).

POLITICAL GROUNDWORK IN THE 1970s AS A BOON TO EPICA

Despite a good scientific program and a constructive approach to logistics the plan for the EAP came to naught and was abandoned in 1975. The CoE was relieved when Norway offered to finance a European pilot study on Spitsbergen before anything else was done. Substantial parts of the scientific program that was developed did, however, find their way into other international programs. When EPICA came into being, it was largely thanks to much better political groundwork and the fact that two of its major champions, Gotthilf Hempel of West Germany and Claude Lorius of France, acted in unison at the Grand Challenges conference in Bremen in September 1994.

Since little has been written about how the political groundwork for EPICA was prepared, I will provide further detail on this point. The experience in ice core drilling accumulated by European scientists both in Greenland and Antarctica by the early 1990s warranted a return to the old idea of an all-European joint venture in Antarctica. The situation by then was completely different compared to that in the early 1970s when the plan for the EAP had to be abandoned. As Heinz Miller related, a new Antarctic project "was already there in our heads before we started drilling in Greenland."[4] The scientific arguments for a major Antarctic ice coring program were strong. To avoid the mistake made with the EAP in the early 1970s, leading scientists worked hard to anchor the idea politically. A number of contemporary events converged to make it easier. Within the ICSU the International Geosphere-Biosphere Programme (IGBP) was initiated in 1986, and it soon identified one of its themes as "documenting and predicting climate change." Within the UN framework the idea of an Intergovernmental Panel on Climate Change was implemented in 1988. European scientists were centrally involved in both of these developments. Paleoclimatology based on data from ice cores was important. The Greenland Ice Core Project (GRIP; and the Vostok effort in Antarctica) demonstrated that European expertise in ice core studies was excellent, logistics efficient, and collaboration good. According to reliable assessments, GRIP with its smaller drill and core (4-inch diameter) gave a much better scientific payback per unit cost investment than the core (6-inch diameter) brought up by the U.S. group with its larger and much heavier drill within Greenland Ice Sheet Project 2 (GISP2).[5] The "Antarctic Science–Global Concerns" conference hosted by SCAR in Bremen in 1991 helped bring polar researchers more closely into harmony with the international research programs on global climate change.[6] The linkages with pertinent international programs helped the paleoclimatic community establish credentials when they made their case in their respective countries for a new collaborative ice coring effort on a grander scale.

Generally, some form of institutionalization is invaluable for large-scale projects in order to gain network stability, ensuring better continuity over time. At the European level this occurred with the creation of the European Committee for Ocean and Polar Science (ECOPS) in 1990 as a liaison (existing for five years) between the European Science Foundation and the European Commission's (EC) Directorate General XII (for Science) (DG XII), constituted as an ad hoc joint scientific advisory body at arm's-length from politics.[7] Two important functions were served. First, as a hybrid forum of scientists and policy makers ECOPS became a vehicle for science diplomacy at national and intergovernmental levels. Second, the hybrid forum provided a neutral space where visions and project ideas could be articulated, tested, and gain purchase in the worlds of science and politics simultaneously, allowing for a coproduction of new scientific and political orders.

The ECOPS's influence lay in suggesting and promoting big science projects, immensely helped by the fact that it was an ad hoc committee and had a very dynamic chairman, Gotthilf Hempel, who knew how to cut red tape and lobby politicians. As the committee was ad hoc, Hempel had the mandate to select the committee members via national representative bodies in different countries. Thus, ECOPS could operate quite freely and flexibly as a group of "wise men." It acted from the top down in identifying themes and sketching possible approaches to large-scale European projects and then elicited bottom-up input from scientific communities by broad consultations through workshops to develop special programs and networks around them. The very first workshop (1990) related to the ECOPS Grand Challenges thrust was on Antarctic ice cores.[8]

Still, EC politicians and bureaucrats were not immediately won over. In the very first round when a first phase for EPICA was proposed to the EC DG XII in January 1992, it was rejected. The proposal was met with the argument that Europe is far away from and has nothing to do with Antarctica. Resistance hinged particularly on the extreme cost of the project, 8 million Ecu (European Currency Unit, now called Euro), which was a large amount and would eat into the potential budgets of other areas of European science, for example, oceanography, where there were also plans for new projects. The oceanographic research community was older, better established, and strong in Europe. Thus, EPICA had quite a number of opponents and doubtful friends in the beginning, at least when it came to proceeding from vision to action.

Hempel himself, being an ocean scientist, was at first not in favor of EPICA, but once he came around, he became a strong supporter. Although more or less neutral concerning the four suggested grand challenge projects, his response to the bureaucratic inertia within the EC was important. Further lobbying occurred during the course of the European Ocean and Polar Science symposium he organized in Obernai, France, in October 1992. At that symposium ECOPS met with about 50 chief administrators and scientists of national funding bodies, and a new draft proposal for EPICA was also presented to the EC. The timing was good. It followed the UN conference in Rio that marked an important turning point at the political level. The idea of global change began to take hold with politicians, and countries needed to show that they took it seriously. The GRIP results were coming in, research in Antarctica gained media coverage, and it became clear that uncertainties pertaining to climate change might be reduced by further work on ice cores. Moreover, EPICA promised a much longer time series than what was available from Greenland. A new deep core from Antarctica was needed because the old Vostok one had a different resolution; it was different and lower, making it unreliable to compare with the Greenland ice cores. In fact, two new

Antarctic cores were projected, one from Dome C, where the bottom ice would be very old, and one with a higher resolution and reflecting the influence of the Atlantic sector, obtainable in the Dronning Maud Land sector, where snow accumulation is much higher than at Dome C. For the implementation of EPICA the European conference Ice-Sheet-Climate Interaction in 1993 was also very important, laying the groundwork for a breakthrough a year later in Bremen.

The ECOPS continued to flesh out four major projects. When summarized at the Grand Challenges conference in 1994 (Bremen) organized by the Alfred Wegener Institute (AWI), EPICA stood out as an absolute winner, a model project, well anchored in relevant scientific communities and politically opportune for Europe in the period after Rio. The enthusiasm, scientific prowess, personal persistence, and diplomatic skills of a few leading scientists had paid off: Claude Lorius, the eminent glaciologist of Antarctic Vostok core fame; David Drewry, a leading personality at the British Antarctic Survey; and Gotthilf Hempel, then head of AWI, the man with the political acumen. Resistance still came from the oceanographic community, which had their own grand challenge project competing for extraordinary funding. Years of networking activities orchestrated by EPICA's leading scientists, however, were now revealed to have been instrumental in fostering the bottom-up process of enrollment through the earlier series of European workshops and conferences. The relevant research communities stood sufficiently united, and policy support was forthcoming around a long-term commitment to deep coring in Antarctica. The process was aided by coincidence with specific conjunctures in the upsurge of the global change issue together with integration with existing international research programs, along with other ones stemming from activities under the auspices of SCAR. This concurrence, in turn, made it easier for scientists in the various countries involved to obtain funding from their respective national science councils.

Ultimately, then, changing conjunctures in geopolitics can make or break possible implementation of such collaboration in any individual case. This is a lesson that has to be remembered and viewed in the long-term perspective of the institutionalization of Antarctic polar research. In the long term, one should also not forget that there is always the possibility in future that the Antarctic Treaty will meet strong challenges in the event that forces of economic globalization press for exploitation of Antarctic mineral resources.

At present, the Madrid Protocol on Environmental Protection to the Antarctic Treaty (and therewith as moratorium on minerals prospecting) is in place. The protocol replaced (and incorporated important elements of) CRAMRA, which momentarily existed—on paper—in 1988–1989 after eight years of negotiations but was never ratified. Currently, interest in gas and oil in the seabed is concentrated on the Arctic region, where the melting of ice in tandem with climate change has triggered a lot of scientific activity linked to Arctic rim countries' efforts to get a better picture of the lay of the continental shelf and the Lomonosov Ridge (among others) to make a case for extending their seabed territories, claims that will be reviewed by the Continental Shelf Commission (CSC) of UNCLOS. Looking 30 years into the future, with continued economic globalization and an entirely new generation of technologies being developed, one should not be entirely surprised if strong stakeholder interests try to push the situation in the Antarctic and its surrounding oceans in a similar direction.

IMPORTANCE OF COINCIDENCE BETWEEN POLITICAL AND SCIENTIFIC AGENDAS

In view of the examples above, of the failed European Antarctic Project of the 1970s and the later success of EPICA in the 1990s and also the present quest for minerals exploitation in the Arctic, there are definite historical lessons to be drawn. The historical record suggests that as long as Antarctic research does not represent a political threat, either in content, organization, or logistical support systems, researchers will have complete freedom of choice in the selection of topics, choice of collaborators, and modes of evaluating results. If, on the other hand, the primary interests of governments, politicians, or high-level (leading scientists or hybrid) civil servants become threatened, conditions of cooperation will degenerate. Whether or not research facilitates international cooperation in real terms or only symbolically will depend on the context, vested interests, and political conjunctures. When it works, we see science as the continuation of politics by other means; in the case at hand, it is in and through the IGY and the ATS regime that followed it. To a large extent, knowledge interests of scientists and the symbolic-instrumental interests of politicians have been more or less convergent in Antarctica, which is what made the IGY and the ATS regime that followed it possible in the first place. This convergence was possible because of some very special geopolitical conditions combined with new technological capabilities in the 1950s.

In the Antarctic, because of the treaty, which suspends territorial claims and makes science the ticket into the club of decision makers, research continued to represent a form of symbolic capital. There was/is a special kind of tradeoff with politicians whereby scientists are provided with funds to do research, but in doing this research they also perform a political task, advancing the national interest of their own country in a geographical arena. In doing so, they can influence the growth of science. Crudely put, one might say that politicians in the major nations after the advent of the AT did not need to worry so much about the kind of work their scientists do, as long as they were there in Antarctica and could show a "significant performance of research." The symbolic value lies primarily in the very presence of a country's scientists in this cold continent, but of course, international recognition of high-quality scientific effort enhances the symbolic value of a country's research on the political arena. Probably, with time the latter aspect became more important, but then again, this varied from one country to another depending on the prevailing political climate, the national science policy doctrine, and overriding institutional motives. In some cases a country might desire to join or use its presence in the club to influence the course of international science.

Sometimes the rhetorical import of research activities may be more important to politicians than their actual scientific value. This means not only that projects that are poor from a scientific point of view get endorsed or that the siting of new research stations is based on expediency and the political need to demonstrate a presence (hence the location of so many stations on King George Island, which was easily accessible for new players) but also that scientifically interesting projects and plans for multinational collaboration on a scientific basis get frustrated and are unable to proceed. Thus, the image of letting the scientists more or less follow their own agenda (and hence natural prominence of good-quality basic research) does not always run true.

INTERNATIONAL RESEARCH STATIONS: A SCENARIO OF THE FUTURE?

In principle, once the Antarctic Treaty was in place, there is no reason why, theoretically, nations might not get together to create an international research station, flying the flag of SCAR or perhaps UNESCO in place of a national flag. In practice, of course, such an international station would probably once again open up the issue of sovereignty, both between and within the nations involved. In other cases of multinational European collaboration in science one finds that under certain conditions such collaboration under a common "European" flag is possible. Two examples are nuclear research (European Organization for Nuclear Research, CERN) and astronomy (the European Southern Observatory, ESO, in Chile).

For future research into the history of science it is interesting to clearly identify the factors that made possible far-reaching collaboration in nuclear physics and astronomy but were not present in the 1970s in Antarctic science. Comparisons with the peaceful uses of atomic energy and collaboration in astronomy are particularly instructive if one is interested in teasing out the limits of internationalism and the institutional motives at play behind scientific efforts.

To summarize, first, it is clear that science during the IGY played an important role as a mutual confidence-building measure. Second, the incrementalist character of the treaty, with the possibility of layering one agreement, convention, or protocol over the next, leading to a whole network of imperatives by which participating parties are bound, has been important. Third, the flexibility built into the treaty, allowing for interpretative flexibility of basic concepts in its institutional architecture, for example, the science criterion, is significant. At the same time, for the future this criterion will require further reinterpretation in what some scholars call the postcolonial era. The challenge is to find ways and means of further broadening participation of additional countries in Antarctic research and policy making in line with a more robust form of internationalism.

NOTES

1. Norway and Britain particularly benefitted from the whaling industry that took off in 1905 and brought great wealth to private entrepreneurs and their national treasuries. In science today, we speak of investing 3% of a country's Gross National Product into research and development; if 3% of the profits (a kind of proscience tax) from the lucrative and ecologically questionable whaling industry had been put into Antarctic polar science, continuity in research might have evolved in an entirely different manner than what actually happened. When contemplating the gap between internationalism in words and in deeds, it is sometimes instructive to think counterfactually in this way.

2. The idea was discussed at an ad hoc conference under the auspices of the International Council of Scientific Unions (ICSU) held in Stockholm on 9–11 September 1959. The Swedish glaciologist Valter Schytt, who had been a member of the Norwegian-British-Swedish Expedition to Dronning Maud Land in 1949–1952, served as secretary of the conference and became the first secretary of the Special Committee on Antarctic Research (SCAR; later called the Scientific Committee), doing a lot of the preparatory work. His diary (Schytt, 1957–1958), covering incoming and outgoing letters to the conference organizers in Stockholm, and the first draft of SCAR's statutes for the organization's constitutional meeting in The Hague on 3–5 February 1958 bear witness to a distinctive

internationalist spirit that was subsequently somewhat tempered by political realities of the time. See also Elzinga (2007).

3. For a historical review of changes in the conditions of research, its goals, and epistemological "style" during the course of four international polar years from 1882–1883 to 2007–2009, see Elzinga (2009b).

4. Heinz Miller, AWI, Germany, interview by Carsten Krueck (of the Science and Technology Studies Department at the University of Bielefeld, Germany), 2 November 1998.

5. Bernhard Stauffer, Climate and Environment Physics, Physics Institute, University of Bern, Bern, Switzerland, interview by the author, 26 August 1998.

6. Hempel (1995). An important outcome of the conference was the creation of the Group of Specialists on Global Change and the Antarctic (GLOCHANT), which, in turn, spawned a long-term project with six core projects, one of them on paleoenvironmental records from ice sheets and marine and land sediments.

7. Ibb Troen and Klaus Bruening, European Commission Directorate General XII, Brussels, Belgium, interview by Carsten Krueck and Jutta Borchers (affiliation as above in note 4), 9 June 1998.

8. It was organized by Claude Lorius and held in Grenoble, France, 29–31 October 1990; "Modelling of Dynamics of Large Polar Ice Sheets" was the name of another workshop, one organized by David Drewry and C. Doake in Cambridge, 29 April to 1 May 1991.

LITERATURE CITED

Abbink, P. 2009. *Antarctic Policymaking and Science in the Netherlands, Belgium and Germany (1957–1990)*. Circumpolar Studies 6. Groningen, Netherlands: Arctic Centre.

CoE (Council of Europe). 1972. Science and Technology Committee. Minutes of the Study Group on Glaciology, June 1972 (for specific archival details see Abbink, 2009 and Stauffer, 2009).

Dean, K., S. Naylor, and M. Siegert. 2008. Data in Antarctic Science and Politics. *Social Studies of Science,* 38(4):571–604.

Elzinga, A. 2007. "Swedish Non-participation in the Antarctic Leg of IGY 1957/58." In *Steps of Foundation of Institutionalized Antarctic Research: Proceedings of the 1st SCAR Workshop on the History of Antarctic Research*, ed. C. Lüdecke, pp. 142–162. Berichte zur Polar- und Meeresforschung 250. Bremerhaven, Germany: Alfred-Wegener-Institut für Polar- und Meeresforschung. http://epic.awi.de/Publications/Lde2007b.pdf (accessed 22 June 2010).

———. 2009a. "Geopolitics, Science and Internationalism—The Cases of CERN, ESO and EAP (a Failed European Antarctic Project)." In *2nd SCAR Workshop on the History of Antarctic Research. Boletín Antárctico Chileno*. Punte Arenas: Chilean Antarctic Institute (Instituto Antártico Chileno–INACH) http://www.inach.cl/InachWebNeo/Controls/Neochannels/Neo_CH6139/deploy/boletinhistorico.pdf accessed 22 June 2010).

———. 2009b. Through the Lens of the Polar Years: Changing Characteristics of Polar Research in Historical Perspective. *Polar Record,* 45(235):313–326.

Elzinga, A., and C. Landström. 1996. *Internationalism and Science*. London: Taylor Graham.

Hempel, G. ed. 1995. *The Ocean and the Poles: Grand Challenges for European Cooperation*. Jena and New York: G. Fischer Verlag.

Jackson, A., ed. 1995. *On the Antarctic Horizon. Proceedings of the International Symposium on the Future of the Antarctic Treaty System. Ushuaia, Argentina 20–24 March 1995*. Hobart: Australian Antarctic Foundation.

Lüdecke, C. 2011 (this volume). "Parallel Precedents for the Antarctic Treaty." In *Science Diplomacy: Antarctica, Science, and the Governance of International Spaces*, ed. P. A. Berkman, M. A. Lang, D. W. H. Walton, and O. R. Young, pp. 253–263. Washington, D.C.: Smithsonian Institution Scholarly Press.

Nougier, J., T. van Autenboer and C. Swithenbank. 1971. "European Antarctic Collaboration", *IUGS Geological Newsletter*, 1971(2);112–116.

Polar Research Board. 1986. Antarctic Treaty System: an Assessment: Proceedings of a Workshop held at Beardsmore, South Field Camp, Antarctic, January 7–13, 1985. Washington D.C.: National Academy Press.

Schytt, V. 1957–1958. Logbook for SCAR Secretariat. Schytt Archive, Swedish Royal Academy of Sciences, Stockholm.

Stauffer, B. 2009. Early Attempts for an European Antarctic Programme 1970–1974. *Polarforschung,* 78(3):113–118.

Background and Evolution of Some Ideas and Values That Have Led to the Antarctic Treaty

Ernest Frederick Roots

The story of exploration of the polar regions is a fascinating story of the role of new knowledge—science—in the evolution of public and political consciousness and opportunity regarding the world and its resources. The story involves the interplay of the attributes of curiosity, personal ambition, greed, drive for national prestige, and impulse to control that are characteristic of human impulses and activities anywhere, but in the polar regions they have been manifest in individual actions against a harsh and unforgiving natural environment that brings to light successes and failures in a dramatic fashion. In the Antarctic, this interplay of forces has led, through a number of faltering steps over the last century, to significant recent progress, in global human terms, in cooperation and shared responsibility for the management of a portion of the planet and its environment. The evolution of science, and its attendant evolution of technology, has been a key factor in achieving this progress and in recognising the key role that Antarctica plays in global processes.

The story of the activities and the policies that have led eventually to the Antarctic Treaty is also a story of individual persons of strength, determination, and perseverance, whose knowledge, ability to make contacts, and influence governments has shaped polar history. Each has used the science of the day as a tool for diplomacy, used it to develop new paradigms of what is progress, and used new knowledge as a force for change in national and public attitudes in ways that were not apparent at the time.

The story of the evolving concepts concerning the polar regions is also a tale of the interplay between the impulse to explore and to exploit a new region or its resources, on the one hand, and to govern and control it, on the other. Both these contrasting impulses have used progressive scientific knowledge, or the desire for new knowledge, as a tool for their particular ends. The result has been that scientific investigation has been an integral part of the exploration and development of the polar regions throughout its history. Today, the Antarctic Treaty enshrines the twin values of "peace" and "science."

The history of the growth of these concepts, and the tension between the impulses of exploitation and of governance, can in many ways be traced back to the Treaty of Tordesillas of 1494, which formalized the papal bull of Pope Alexander VI and addressed the competing claims of Spain and Portugal to

Ernest Frederick Roots, Environment Canada, 6790 East Sooke Road, Sooke, British Columbia V9Z 1A6, Canada. Correspondence: fred.roots@ec.gc.ca.

exploit and control the wealth they might obtain anywhere in the world through their newly developed technology and navigational science, based on rot-resistant ropes, the magnetic compass, and the astrolabe, that enabled them to travel the world oceans. Chinese ships had, indeed, roamed throughout the Pacific and beyond nearly a century earlier, perhaps into high latitudes, but simply as explorers and traders, and there seems to be no evidence that they were interested in governance or control. The Treaty of Tordesillas extended from pole to pole and granted to Portugal all wealth and territories that were "not already under the mandate of a Christian king" east of a line west of the Azores Islands and to Spain a similar right west of that line. The boundary on the other side of the world was not defined. This treaty had a strong influence in spurring northern European nations to explore their northern regions in order to bypass the decree laid down by the Catholic Church, which impeded their access to the wealth of the Indies and Cathay. This exploration led to long-continuing interest and efforts to discover a practical Northeast Passage and a Northwest Passage. The northern expertise thus developed served as a basis for later actions in southern polar regions.

An important step, in political terms, in the development of national attitudes toward new territories and the ownership of polar regions was taken during the reign of Queen Elizabeth I of England when Martin Frobisher, on his first voyage to what is now Arctic Canada, after his ship had capsized in the mid-Atlantic and lost a mast, came to a headland of Baffin Island and named it "Queen Elizabeth's Foreland." This is the first time that a newly discovered land had been named and claimed for a reigning monarch. Queen Elizabeth asked her adviser, the polymath John Dee (who also had instructed Frobisher, a private citizen, in navigation), to produce an argument for her rights to undiscovered and uncontested lands claimed in her name. In 1585 Dee presented a document, which is still preserved in the British Library, stating the basis by which the monarch had legal rights to accept newly discovered lands claimed by her citizens "compassing . . . even unto the North Pole." This statement, although it had no immediate geographical effect, linked discovery of new lands to the claims of expanding empire and undoubtedly was an influence in building a continuing interest in Britain in polar exploration. That interest and "right" in due course extended to southern polar regions. It led to similar or competing intentions and actions by other nations.

At the same time that several nations were developing an appetite for competition in discovery of polar territories for political or commercial reasons, the progress of science was raising questions about natural phenomena that could only be answered by observations in the high latitudes. Questions about the ocean currents and ice, magnetism, astronomical navigation, and the pull of gravity and the shape and dimensions of planet Earth were becoming preoccupations in academies of science in several countries, and although many of these topics had practical application for navigation, trade, and economy, they were not the prerogative of any one country, and new scientific information was exchanged freely across national boundaries. Thus, by the eighteenth century, in many countries a difference in orientation developed between the geographical institutions, whose polar interests were to a large extent focused on discoveries of new lands in the name of the exploring country, and the scientific institutions, whose aim was to uncover new natural facts, new species, and new relationships and make them known regardless of the country or countries involved. This difference in attention had an influence on the course of subsequent exploration in Antarctica and the involvement of different countries in subsequent international investigative activities such as the International Polar Years, the International Geophysical Year, and the Antarctic Treaty.

The Royal Society of Britain became a dominant influence in the pursuit of scientific knowledge in polar regions in the eighteenth century. After his successful expedition to the South Pacific in 1768–1771 to measure the transit of the planet Venus in front of the illuminated disc of the Sun and thus enable the dimensions of the solar system to be more accurately calculated, James Cook was commissioned to determine the existence and position of the continent of Antarctica, whose presence had been a persistent feature in myths, stories, and intellectual philosophy for many centuries. The name Antarctica had been used by Greek cosmologists two thousand years previously for the supposed lands opposite on the planet to those in the north under the celestial bear Arctos (anti-Arctos = Antarctic). In pursuit of this objective, in 1772–1775 Cook went as far south as he could sail his ship and circumnavigated the edge of the ice pack surrounding Antarctica but never sighted the continent.

Just as Cook was returning from his frustrating circumnavigation of Antarctica, in 1775 the Royal Society launched the first truly multidisciplinary scientific expedition to the polar regions, "a voyage towards the North-Pole to be of service to the promotion of natural knowledge."[1] This expedition, commanded by Constantine Phipps, had a genuine international background: the plan had been proposed by a French explorer (de Bougainville), and German, Dutch, and Swiss scientists had contributed. A very large number of observations and experiments were successfully completed. The first substantive information was obtained on the depth, chemistry, and currents of the subarctic ocean and on pack ice, marine fauna, magnetism, and the aurora; gravity measurements were made that led to calculations of the curvature of the Earth, and some imaginative but ultimately useless experiments on the expansion of materials at low temperatures were carried out to determine whether there was a "latitude" effect. This was the first truly careful scientific examination of the polar regions. It added substantially to world scientific knowledge. Yet, except for the fact that the polar bear carries the scientific name *Thalacrtos maritimus Phipps*, this very productive expedition remained unknown or ignored in geographical circles and by the public because it did not discover, or try to discover, new physical territories for national glory. Likewise, the more limited but still important scientific accomplishments of Cook's Antarctic voyages were submerged or publicly forgotten in the attention given to geographic discovery.

However, national ambitions for empire, or the nonnational incentives for new knowledge, can become overridden by commercial and financial opportunities. Cook was pessimistic about whether the world would benefit from further discoveries in Antarctica, "lands doomed by nature to everlasting frigidness," but he also noted, and recorded, the abundance of seals on the subantarctic islands among which he passed.[2] Within a decade of his expedition, commercial sealing was in full swing. By 1804, an estimated 100 sealing ships were operating in the subantarctic waters. Some ships reported taking up to 100,000 seals per season. Most of the ships and their sponsoring companies were British or American, but ships from several other countries were involved. Although several of the islands had been claimed in the name of a "home" country, there was no government control, and the whole Antarctic region was considered *terra nullis*. The sites of exploitation shifted periodically, as ruthless slaughter of seals reduced the local resource in one island area after another to unprofitability and the sealers searched for new resources. Despite occasional pleas for restraint of indiscriminate slaughter in order to maintain the productivity of the resources,[3] uncontrolled exploitation continued. By 1824, the sealing frenzy subsided, as the fur seal populations in most of the subantarctic islands were nearly exterminated. Some taking of elephant seals, for oil, and of small right whales with hand-launched harpoons continued. After 1870, when the explosive harpoon came into use and the whales in the Arctic waters, formerly "as numerous as carps in a pond."[4] became rare and with the establishment of a whaling station on South Georgia in 1904, harvesting of large whales became a principal commercial activity in the south polar waters. Then followed another "exploitation explosion." By 1912–1913 there were 6 land stations, 21 floating factory ships, and 62 catcher boats collecting nearly 11,000 whales in subantarctic waters; by 1930–1931 the harvest was 400,000. This high level of exploitation continued until and after the Second World War. In realization that most of the once-abundant marine mammal resource was inevitably being destroyed, the International Whaling Commission was formed in 1946. It has had mixed results. One consequence has been the polarization of public attitudes and some policies about use and conservation of natural resources in polar regions.

During the period of uncontrolled private exploitation of resources, scientific interest and the urge to explore the undiscovered Antarctica arose at intervals, and governments of several countries took an interest in exploration and research. Between 1819 and 1840 eight expeditions, sponsored by the governments of Russia, the United Kingdom, United States, and France added much to the knowledge of the geography of the Antarctic coastline and surrounding seas and of the features of its oceanography, meteorology, and geophysics. National interests, both scientific and commercial and based on country prestige, dominated. By the end of the nineteenth century, territorial claims were beginning to be recognized by governments, and following a precedent in the Arctic, a "national sector" concept began to emerge. Progressively, between 1923 and 1943 governments of seven countries laid formal claims to sectors of almost the whole Antarctic continent and parts of the surrounding waters, although three of those claims overlapped and one "sector" remained unclaimed.

The challenge to investigate the interior of the Antarctic continent, and specifically to reach the South Pole, arose at the end of the nineteenth and beginning of the twentieth century, mainly from the ambitions of a few determined individuals, who cultivated a broad public interest that then took on aspects of national rivalry. On top of "the race to the pole" was added, in some cases, some excellent scientific investigation. But once the pole had been reached, interest subsided. A world war followed by a worldwide economic depression meant that little attention was paid to polar regions. The declining activity in marine mammal exploitation became ostensibly the responsibility of the respective governments who now claimed territorial sectors, although there was little effective management. The few expeditions to the continent between the First and Second World Wars were privately organized, although some had government contributions

(United Kingdom, United States, Norway, Germany), and focussed on geographical exploration, including, for the first time, aerial mapping.

During the Second World War, the possibility that Antarctic and subantarctic territories might be used as havens by enemy interests prompted the United Kingdom, France, Australia, Argentina, and Chile to take protective measures in areas of their responsibility. Although the reasons for the establishments of stations and patrols on the continent and subantarctic islands were political, some of the activities made contributions to scientific knowledge. They helped to create a new corps of scientists and technicians with polar experience and interest and to develop a notion, which had originally been forcefully expounded by Karl Weyprecht in the 1880s in connection with the International Polar Year, that scientific knowledge itself was a valuable justification for investigation in polar regions.

In 1945, at the close of the Second World War, a proposal was made by a Swedish scientist, Hans Ahlmann, that a purely scientific multidiscipline international research expedition, sponsored jointly by Norway, Sweden, and the United Kingdom, be undertaken in the hitherto unvisited part of Antarctica, within the sector claimed by Norway, part of which had been photographed from the air by a German expedition in 1938–1939. The proposal was supported by senior scientists and endorsed by institutions with polar interests in the three countries concerned. The result, after considerable negotiation, was the Norwegian-British-Swedish Antarctic Expedition, 1949–1952.

The Norwegian-British-Swedish Antarctic Expedition was the first modern, genuinely international scientific expedition in the polar regions without territorial pretentions. Scientists from five countries participated The expedition consciously and openly endorsed and demonstrated the principles for polar research that had been expressed by Weyprecht 70 years previously for the first International Polar Year: that science was not a territory for national possession or international discord, that all nations have a role to play in polar research, and that the results of polar scientific investigation should be freely shared without discrimination.[5] It prepared the way, in the sense of the advantages it demonstrated of political cooperation as well as nonnational cooperation between scientific institutions from different countries, for the Third International Polar Year, which became the International Geophysical Year, 1957–1958, and, in turn, helped set the stage for the Antarctic Treaty.

NOTES

1. Minutes, Council of the Royal Society (London), meeting 19 January 1773. London: The Royal Society Library and Archive.

2. "Lands doomed by nature to everlasting frigidness and never once to feel the warmth of the sun's rays; such are the lands we have discovered, what may we expect those to be which lie more to the south, for we may reasonably suppose that we have seen the best as lying most to the north, whoever has the resolution and perseverance to clear up this point by proceeding farther than I have done, I shall not envy him the honour of the discovery but I will be bold to say that the world will not be benefitted by it." *The Journal of Captain James Cook*, Vol. II, 1776. Reprinted 1969 with agenda and corrigenda, ed. R. A. Skelton. Extra Series No. 36. 1647 pp. London: The Hakluyt Society.

3. Capt. James W. Budington (a Connecticut sealer), testimony to the US Congress 1892.

4. C. M. Scammon, 1874. *The Marine Mammals of the Northwestern Coast of North America*. San Francisco: John H. Carmany and Company Publishers.

5. N. H. deV. Heathcoate, and A. Armitage. 1959. "The First International Polar Year (1882–1883)." In *Annals of the International Geophysical Year*, Vol. I, pp. 3–302. London: Permagon Press.

Japan and the Antarctic Treaty after World War II

Yoshio Yoshida

On behalf of my friends, colleagues, and predecessors, please allow me to share my sincere gratitude on the occasion of the 50th anniversary of the Antarctic Treaty that was signed in Washington, D.C., on 1 December 1959.

The government of Japan decided in 1955 to participate in the cooperative Antarctic investigations organized during the International Geophysical Year (IGY). Among the 12 nations who were conducting Antarctic research at that time, Japan was the only one who had been defeated during World War II. We also were the only Asian nation with a history of active interest in Antarctica, going back to the 1910–1912 expeditions of Nobu Shirase (Shirase, 2011).

The international scientific community and victorious governments warmly accepted Japanese collaboration in Antarctic research during the IGY. The station for the first Japanese Antarctic Research Expedition (JARE) was established in January 1957 at 69°00′S, 39°35′E on East Ongul Island, Lützow-Holm Bay, East Antarctica, and has been occupied ever since.

I was on the replacement team (JARE-2) on February 1958, and our team was forced to abandon 15 Sakhalin sled dogs at the unmanned Syowa Station because of the poor sea ice conditions. Upon their 14 January 1959 arrival, the JARE-3 team was surprisingly greeted by two of the huskies— Taro and Jiro— who had survived on their own for 11 months, possibly living on seal dung and penguins. I then served as the geomorphologist and dog handler during the 1960/1961 seasons, working with Taro and Jiro along with the 11 other dogs that we brought to Syowa for the winter. Over the years, it has been amazing to watch these two sled dogs became heroes in the hearts of the Japanese people as symbols of courage and survival, with museum statues and feature movies to their credit, awakening a national sense of pride in Antarctic research.

Japan formally abandoned all territorial rights in Antarctica (based on the early twentieth century exploration of Shirase) on the occasion of signing the Treaty of Peace with Japan on 8 September 1951 in San Francisco. Thus, as a nonclaimant nation, Japan contributed to the Antarctic Treaty negotiations in Washington, D.C., with Minister T. Shimoda as the first secretary of the Japanese Embassy (Sugihara, 1988).

In 2008–2009, an international team of scientists led by the National Institute of Polar Research participated in JARE-50. Throughout, Japan has been a

Yoshio Yoshida, Japan Polar Research Association, Street/mailing address, Tokyo, Japan, Rissho University, Tokyo, Japan, and National Institute of Polar Research, Tokyo, Japan. Correspondence: yoyosida@vmail.plala.or.jp.

strong supporter of the Scientific Committee on Antarctic Research (SCAR) and the Antarctic Treaty System. For example, Japan hosted the 6th Antarctic Treaty Consultative Meeting (ATCM) in Tokyo in 1970 and the 18th ATCM in Kyoto in 1994 as well as the Special Meetings on Antarctic Mineral Resources in 1984 and 1986 in Tokyo. Similarly, Japan hosted the SCAR General Assembly in 1968 and 2000 in Tokyo as well as various SCAR symposia over the years (e.g., Yoshida et al., 1991).

Over the past half century, Japanese scientists and the general public as well as decision makers have learned much about the importance of science as well as international cooperation. I recall the determination of our leading scientists and the statesmen who promoted these Antarctic research opportunities during a very hard time for Japan, only 10 years after the Second World War.

Antarctic research in Japan during the first 50 years of the Antarctic Treaty has built bridges of cooperation with the world. I hope the experience of Japan will help those developing countries that will participate in Antarctic research in the future.

LITERATURE CITED

Shirase, N. and Antarctic Expedition Supporters Association. 2011. *Antarctica: The Japanese South Polar Expedition of 1910–12*. Translated from the Japanese by Lara Dagnell and Hilary Shibata. Bluntisham: Bluntisham Books and Erskine Press.

Sugihara, S. 1988. *Kyokuchi* [Polar News], 24(1).

Yoshida, Y., K. Kaminuma, and K. Shiraishi, eds. 1991. *Recent Progress in Antarctic Earth Science*. Tokyo: National Institute of Polar Research.

The Scientific Committee on Antarctic Research and the Antarctic Treaty

David W. H. Walton

ABSTRACT. The Scientific Committee on Antarctic Research (SCAR) had its antecedents in the Special Committee on Antarctic Research of the International Geophysical Year, and thus its establishment in 1958 predates the Antarctic Treaty. As a body of the International Council for Science (ICSU, formerly the International Council of Scientific Unions) it is a nongovernmental organization, yet it has been intimately linked to the governmental discussions at the Antarctic Treaty since the first Antarctic Treaty meeting in 1961. Its primary role has always been to develop and coordinate international scientific research, but it has also provided independent advice to Treaty Parties on many scientific and environmental questions, initially through national government delegations. Only in 1987 was SCAR itself granted the status of observer and the right to attend Antarctic Treaty Consultative Meetings (ATCMs) and to submit information and working papers. This paper looks at the changing relationship between SCAR and the Treaty Parties, at some of its most important science inputs to the ATCM, and at the way SCAR itself has changed. Its earliest input to governance was advice on conservation that became the Agreed Measures for the Conservation of Antarctic Fauna and Flora of 1964, and for the first 40 years of the Antarctic Treaty, SCAR provided major input on protected areas and protected species, as well as environmental impact and monitoring. Its proposals for seal conservation and management gave it a specific role in the Convention for the Conservation of Antarctic Seals, and its Biological Investigations of Marine Antarctic Systems and Stocks (BIOMASS) programme laid the foundations for the Convention for the Conservation of Antarctic Marine Living Resources (CCAMLR). Its nonpolitical stance has allowed it to provide the only unified gazetteer for the Antarctic. The organization of SCAR remained virtually unchanged for around 30 years until the logisticians split to form the Council of Managers of National Antarctic Programs (COMNAP) in 1989. The organization was languishing, but a major review of structure and function changed that in 2000, resulting in the establishment of Open Science Conferences, major new international programmes, increased educational outreach, and a greater input to the annual Antarctic Treaty meetings, often on controversial subjects like marine acoustics or specially protected species. There are currently 31 full members with 4 associate members and 9 ICSU union members.

David W. H. Walton, British Antarctic Survey, Natural Environment Research Council, High Cross, Madingley Road, Cambridge CB3 0ET, UK. Correspondence: dwhw@bas.ac.uk.

INTRODUCTION

The International Geophysical Year (1956–1957) was one of the most important international events in the history of twentieth century science. The original idea for this was apparently conceived by a small group of physicists led by Lloyd Berkner in the United States and Sidney Chapman in the United Kingdom over dinner at the house of James van Allen in the spring of 1950 (Belanger, 2006). The proposal was for a coordinated series of measurements of many key geophysical variables using agreed protocols, especially in the polar regions. The proposers enlisted the support of the National Academy of Sciences and the Royal Society as well as many of their colleagues, and the International Council of Scientific Unions (ICSU) Executive Board rapidly and with enthusiasm endorsed the theme when it was proposed in 1951. In response to a suggestion by the World Meteorological Organization that the polar focus was too narrow, Chapman widened it and suggested the International Geophysical Year (IGY) rather than just an International Polar Year (Belanger, 2006). From its small beginnings it grew initially to involve scientists from 46 countries, but by the time it ended scientists from 67 countries were taking part. It was, to a large part, modelled on the previous International Polar Years, and it was therefore significant that the organizers had declared that there were two scientific frontiers that should be attacked: outer space and the Antarctic. Both constituted major unknowns at that time, and developments in technology, especially in rocketry, made the scientific prospects much more attractive than they had ever been before.

Twelve countries finally decided that they would work in the Antarctic. Several (Argentina, Australia, Chile, France, and the United Kingdom) already had stations there but intended to augment their work, whereas the new countries (Belgium, Japan, New Zealand, Norway, South Africa, the Union of Soviet Socialist Republics (USSR), and the United States) all needed to establish themselves there. After some arguments the sites for all the stations were agreed and the IGY got under way.

It is difficult to imagine 50 years on just how revolutionary this international programme was. The aftermath of the Second World War, the expansion of Soviet military activities and the spread of communism, and the militarization and aggressive stance of the United States threw a pall across the world. The research turned out to be even more productive than the scientists expected, and the international collaboration engendered was, during the time of the Cold War, a very positive and surprising result. The scientific community soon began to lobby for a continuation of the Antarctic work, citing the need to get a long-term return on the infrastructure investment and the value of the data that were being produced and pooled for all to use. Unknown to them, President Eisenhower had already decided that a permanent agreement was necessary, both to stop the arguments between Chile, Argentina, and the United Kingdom over sovereignty and to ensure that the Soviets were not able to militarize the Antarctic and escalate the arms race to a new level. He used the pleas from the science community as window dressing to support his initiation of secret talks in 1957 between the 12 countries toward a new Antarctic Treaty for the continent (Berkman, this volume).

Meanwhile, the ICSU Comité Speciale de l'Année Géophysique Internationale (CSAGI) had already decided at its fourth meeting that a more permanent international focus for Antarctic science would be necessary and recommended to ICSU that a Special Committee on Antarctic Research should be formed. This was the beginning of SCAR.

This paper will examine the development of the relationship between the Antarctic Treaty Parties and SCAR, using examples to indicate how scientific advice has laid the foundations for both law and policy.

EARLY DAYS

The first meeting of SCAR was organized at The Hague in February 1958. The ICSU had decided that it would be attended by delegates from the 12 countries active in the Antarctic as well as representatives of the five most relevant scientific unions (International Union of Geodesy and Geophysics [IUGG], the International Geographical Union [IGU], the International Union of Biological Sciences [IUBS], the International Union of Pure and Applied Physics [IUPAP], and the Union Radio Scientifique Internationale [URSI]) and one from the World Meteorological Organization. They gathered for a three-day meeting that laid the firm foundations for what would follow over five decades.

All the participating nations except New Zealand and South Africa were there as well as two of the unions, all represented by scientists except Chile (whose ambassador attended as an observer). Only Belgium, the USSR, and the United States brought advisors along, so it was a small meeting of 18 people (Figure 1). R. Fraser and E. Herbays represented ICSU, W. Schytt IGU, A. Bruun IUBS, and G. Laclavère IUGG whilst N. Herlofson chaired the meeting. The main objectives were to agree to a constitution for the committee, elect officers, frame a budget, and prepare a scientific plan for the years after IGY. A draft constitution had been prepared, apparently by Valter Schytt, based on other ICSU constitutions, and circulated in advance. It was commendably short at this stage!

The sterling international work done during IGY ensured the unopposed election of Georges Laclavère from France as president, with Keith Bullen from Australia as

FIGURE 1. Participants in the first SCAR meeting, The Hague, February 1958. 1, Dr. L. M. Gould, United States; 2, Dr. Ronald Fraser, ICSU; 3, Dr. N. Herlofson, convenor; 4, Colonel E. Herbays, ICSU; 5, Professor T. Rikitake, Japan; 6, Professor Leiv Harang, Norway; 7, Dr. Valter Schytt, IGU; 8, Dr. Anton F. Bruun, IUBS; 9, Mr. J. J. Taljaard, South Africa; 10, Captain F. Bastin, Belgium; 11, Captain Luis de la Canal, Argentina; 12, Sir James Wordie, United Kingdom; 13, Professor K. E. Bullen, Australia; 14, Dr. H. Wexler, United States; 15, Ingénieur Général Georges Laclavère, IUGG; 16, Ingénieur Général André Gougenheim, France; 17, Mr. Luis Renard, Chile; 18, Dr. M. M. Somov, USSR; 19, Prof. J. van Mieghen, Belgium. From Wolff (2010).

vice-president and Valter Schytt as secretary. Costs were estimated at $6000 per year, so the initial contribution was set at $500 per nation with the intention to move to a sliding scale in future years based on the number of overwintering staff. The establishment of the World Data Centres by ICSU had already removed one potential task from their list of key scientific activities, but the range of science within IGY needed to be broadened now that the emphasis was not principally on geophysics. The meeting set up three working groups to discuss future research programmes: WGI Meteorology, Oceanography, Cosmic Physics, Biology & Physiology; WGII Geology, Glaciology, Morphology & Cartography, and WGIII Seismology, Gravity & Vulcanology. Given the limited information on biology, this initial disciplinary listing seems still heavily biased to Earth science and physics and is probably a reflection of the expertise around the table. This structure of working groups changed at later meetings as more scientists became directly involved. In addition, it was agreed that SCAR's area of interest would be determined principally by scientific features. The SCAR scientists agreed on the Antarctic Convergence (Polar Front) as the general northern boundary but then decided that some islands lying north of this would need to be included for biological reasons: Ile Amsterdam, Iles Crozet, Gough Island, Iles de Kerguelen, Macquarie Island, Prince Edward Islands, Ile Saint-Paul, South Georgia, and Tristan da Cunha. They also agreed to establish the *SCAR Bulletin* to provide a reporting link to the global community.

Most importantly, they stated that "the continuation of scientific activity in Antarctic research should be regarded as being inspired by the interest aroused by the activities of IGY but was in no way an extension of the IGY."(SCAR, 1959). This statement was clearly a get-out clause for politicians who wanted to draw a line under their national involvement and had, at that stage, the potential to severely limit future involvement.

As a component body of ICSU SCAR had to adopt their normal method of national representation, which was through a committee constituted within the national academy of sciences. Since all 12 countries were already ICSU members, this did not cause any problem, but it did take a little time for all of them to establish committees, not all of which have functioned effectively over the past 50 years. Although at the time this must have seemed a logical and effective route for communicating with the active scientists, within a few years it became clear that this would be a troublesome and ineffective linkage for many countries.

Political wrangling was continuing over who would continue to work in Antarctica and just how extensive that work would be. The politicians worried over the escalating bill for, as some saw it, scientists to have a good time at the taxpayers' expense. The impetus seemed to be failing when, at the Fifth CSAGI Meeting in Moscow in August 1958, a formal proposal from Soviet scientists to continue Antarctic research galvanized both the scientists and their politicians. It seemed that the Soviet scientists were desperate to maintain the international links that the IGY had fostered as well as capitalising on the international recognition gained by the launch of Sputnik 1. To assuage the politicians, they needed to find a new name for the one-year extension and the "Year of International Geophysical Co-operation" became the new title, but however it was dressed up it was clear that if the USSR was staying, so were the Americans and many others.

SCAR AND THE ANTARCTIC TREATY

The State Department pushed ahead with its plan for a new governance system, capitalizing on the wave of scientific enthusiasm. The 60 secret meetings in Washington eventually resulted in sufficient agreement for the countries to decide that a more formal and public negotiation could take place to finalize the details of the Antarctic Treaty (Hanessian, 1960). Meeting in Washington, D.C., starting on 15 October 1959, the Contracting Parties, as they styled themselves, finally signed the Antarctic Treaty on 1 December 1959. In the process of agreeing to the Antarctic Treaty the Contracting Parties had found a way of setting to one side the sovereignty claims and disputes, had demilitarized a continent and ensured that it could not be used for dumping nuclear waste, had established an international inspection procedure (which was effectively the first nuclear arms treaty), and had formally recognized that the continent should be used only for peace and science for the good of all mankind. Given the range of national objectives, the superpower struggle for supremacy, and the history of animosity between many of the participating countries, this was a remarkable achievement.

The parties had recognized at an early stage that to govern the continent they would need good scientific advice. Although SCAR is not mentioned in the Antarctic Treaty itself, right from the first Consultative Meeting in Canberra in 1961 the importance of input from SCAR was formally recognized. Indeed, many of the delegations contained scientists associated with SCAR: e.g., for Australia, R. Carrick, F. J. Jacka, and P. G. Law; for France, G. Laclavère; for New Zealand, E. I. Robertson; for Norway, A. K. Corvin; for South Africa, M. P. van Rooy; for the United Kingdom, B. B. Roberts; for the USSR, M. M. Somov; and for the United States, T. Jones.

In the final report of the First Antarctic Treaty Consultative Meeting (ATCM, 1961) the first four recommendations all dealt with science, and Recommendation I-IV was specifically devoted to SCAR:

> The Representatives agree without prejudice to the rights of Governments, to make such arrangements as they deem necessary to further the objectives of scientific co-operation set forth in the Treaty:
>
> 1) That the free exchange of information and views among scientists participating in SCAR, and the recommendations concerning scientific programmes and co-operation formulated by this body constitute a most valuable contribution to international scientific co-operation in Antarctica,
> 2) That since these activities of SCAR constitute the kind of activity templated in Article II of the Treaty, SCAR should be encouraged to continue its advisory work which has so effectively facilitated international co-operation in scientific investigations.

At that same meeting the Contracting Parties took the first steps to rectify the lack of any specific conservation measure in the Antarctic Treaty itself. Using a report published by SCAR in 1960 (Carrick, 1960), they agreed to Recommendation I-VIII, "Conservation of the Antarctic Flora and Fauna," establishing an interim measure that in 1964 they would turn into Recommendation III-VIII, "Agreed Measures for the Conservation for the Antarctic Fauna and Flora." Linked to this was Recommendation III-X asking that SCAR should continue to report on conservation matters especially with respect to proposals for specially protected species and specially protected areas.

At the Fourth Meeting of SCAR in October 1961 in Wellington the Biology Working Group seized on the progress toward the Agreed Measures and promptly drew up a list of suggested protected areas, as well as recommending that the Ross seal and the fur seals should be designated as specially protected species. At IV ATCM in Santiago in 1966, 15 new protected areas were designated, and the Ross and fur seals were formally given special protection. Interestingly, the Biology Working Group had completed its 1961 report with the statement that "research in Antarctic biology would suffer if SCAR becomes too involved in the political and economic aspects of conservation, as distinct from the formulation of principles and recommendations based upon scientific work." Clearly, SCAR had already recognized the difficult balancing act it would need to achieve if its inputs to policy were to be valued yet its nonpolitical status was to be protected.

THE DEVELOPMENT OF THE CONVENTION FOR THE CONSERVATION OF ANTARCTIC SEALS

There were other politics on the horizon that drew SCAR in even more closely to the Antarctic Treaty. The notification by Norway that a pilot sealing expedition would go to Antarctica in 1964 drew immediate attention to the history of sealing and its disastrous consequences for fur seals. The Consultative Parties quickly passed Recommendation III-11 urging that any pelagic sealing be undertaken in such a way as not to disrupt the ecosystem nor threaten the integrity of species. They followed this at the next meeting with Interim Guidelines on the Voluntary Regulation of Antarctic Pelagic Sealing (Recommendation IV-21) and urged SCAR to continue its interest (Recommendation IV-22) in the subject. The SCAR had, indeed, been active, with the Biology Working Group first producing a statement on pelagic sealing in August 1964 and establishing a Subcommittee on Seals to consider the problems in more detail. Returning to the subject in 1968 the Biology Working Group had the report of the subcommittee to consider. This report proposed a revision of the Antarctic Treaty's Interim Guidelines, changing many of the details and laying out details of permissible catches in Annex A and the location of sealing zones in Annex B. An important element in the SCAR response was the acceptance of the principle that seals were a resource that could be sustainably harvested and that, despite the wishes of some scientists, it was not possible to argue for a complete ban on commercial sealing.

This concern over seals finally resulted in the first of the additional conventions to the Antarctic Treaty. The Convention for the Conservation of Antarctic Seals (CCAS), agreed by the Consultative Parties in 1972 in London, specifically mandates SCAR to provide scientific advice on stock sizes and management. To involve an independent nongovernmental ICSU body directly in this way was certainly unusual, and indeed, the signing of the instrument was delayed until 2 June 1972 , the day after SCAR formally accepted the task. One longer-term commitment by SCAR as a result of CCAS was the formation and support of a new Group of Specialists on Seals, part of whose role was to be prepared to provide advice to CCAS if needed. Since commercial sealing has never restarted, the convention has never been used, but SCAR continues to collect data annually on seal numbers killed in scientific research.

BIOMASS AND CCAMLR

Others beside the seal biologists had also become alarmed at the prospect of major changes in the Southern Ocean. American biologists at the Second SCAR Biology Symposium in 1968 (Holdgate, 1970) had noticed the way in which the Soviet Union was researching krill; they recognized not only how little was really known about krill but also that it did appear to be a keystone species in the Southern Ocean food web. The Soviet Union had both research vessels and trawler fleets in the Southern Ocean and was actively catching krill, having mastered the technical problems of processing the animals prior to freezing them, as well as catching large quantities of fish. There were no controls on any of these actions as the Antarctic Treaty specifically did not cover the high seas.

These U.S. scientists persuaded the National Science Foundation to fund the first multidisciplinary oceanographic cruise on board the USNS *Eltanin* in 1972 to study the structure and function of the Ross Sea ecosystem (El-Sayed, 1973). Meanwhile, at the SCAR Biology Working Group meeting in August 1972 in Canberra a strong case was made for a new focus on marine resources, and a new Subcommittee on Marine Resources was established, with S. Z. El-Sayed as its chairman. Meeting in Montreal in 1974, the subcommittee made rapid progress, and in 1975 the SCAR Executive Committee established it as a new Group of Specialists on Southern Ocean Ecosystems and their Living Resources. In November of the same year the Scientific Committee on Oceanic Research (SCOR) agreed to cosponsor the group, as did the International Association for Biological Oceanography (IABO) and the Advisory Committee on Marine Resources Research of the United Nations Food and Agriculture Organization. Activities increased as VIII ATCM asked SCAR to provide a report on progress on Antarctic marine living resources. The group met in 1975 in Cambridge and then again in Woods Hole in August 1976, where, in a much larger conference format, the proposal for cooperative studies in the Southern Ocean was developed, and Dick Laws devised its new acronym, BIOMASS: Biological Investigations of Marine Antarctic Systems and Stocks.

The BIOMASS programme was on a much larger scale than anything SCAR had attempted before. It lasted over 10 years, with three international field seasons, involving many ships from 11 countries. Its scientific outputs were considerable (El-Sayed, 1994), but just as important was the way in which this research activity stimulated the Treaty Parties to develop a new system of governance and management for the Southern Ocean. In 1977 at IX ATCM the parties agreed to establish a new convention for the sustainable management of marine living resources and thus was born the Convention for the Conservation of Antarctic Marine Living Resources (CCAMLR), which was signed on 20 May 1980 and came into force on 7 April 1982. The SCAR scientists were closely involved in advising on the scientific basis for the convention, which was established on a new principle: maximum sustainable yield without disturbing the existing ecological relationships between species. Equally important was the acceptance by the politicians of the scientific argument that the CCAMLR boundary should not be that of the Antarctic Treaty but a relevant biological one: the Antarctic Polar Front (Antarctic Convergence). As Nigel Bonner has said (Bonner, 1987:145), "CCAMLR is a philosophical scientist's convention. It is certainly not a convention for fisheries managers," yet it has been made to work and its principles have since been adopted for other regional fisheries.

The SCAR was granted the status of observer at the CCAMLR Scientific Committee once it was established, but since so many SCAR scientists were already involved in national delegations, it initially rarely took up the role. Later, it appointed a marine scientist as the official SCAR representative to ensure that requests to SCAR could be formally targeted and to allow for an independent report to the Biology Working Group at the following SCAR meeting.

These early exchanges set the model for the relationship between SCAR and the Antarctic Treaty for the first 25 years where SCAR's ideas, suggestions, and recommendations were filtered into the ATCMs through national delegations. Some authors (e.g., Herr, 1996) have included SCAR as a part of the Antarctic Treaty System, but that suggests an equality of legal persona that has never existed between governmental and nongovernmental representation. Of course, SCAR scientists were included within many of the national delegations, but the organization itself did not initially have any formal representation.

Vidas (1996) has suggested that the changes (the admission of observers and experts as well as the Acceding Parties) were largely a response to the charge at the United Nations that the Antarctic Treaty System (ATS) was an "exclusive club" of rich and powerful states and that their discussions were veiled in secrecy, with the hope of defusing further criticism. Certainly, the latter charge was true, and it is difficult to understand at this distance why secrecy was apparently so important in the governance of an uninhabited continent. Perhaps the first and natural refuge of diplomats in any intergovernmental meeting at that time was to deprive the public they represented of any useful information so that they could work untrammelled by public opinion.

Criticism eventually had some effect. The Consultative Parties responded to increasing public concern in 1983 by first allowing Non-Consultative Parties to attend the meetings, then admitting as Consultative Parties India, Brazil, China, and Uruguay (undermining the argument at the United Nations that only developed states could achieve the highest status), and finally inviting both observers and experts to attend the meetings, thus meeting the criticisms from the international environmental lobby.

So, finally, at XIV ATCM in 1987 in Rio de Janeiro, SCAR and CCAMLR were both formally invited to take their place as observers and were requested to provide reports of their activities to the plenary. Since then, SCAR's input to the Antarctic Treaty meetings has steadily increased, not only in terms of providing information and working papers but also in the institution of a SCAR science lecture to the plenary, the first of which was given by Claude Lorius (then president of SCAR) at XV ATCM in Paris.

CONSERVATION INITIATIVES

Having had a major hand in establishing CCAMLR, SCAR was already moving on. The Biology Working Group Subcommittee on Conservation was chaired by Nigel Bonner, a seal biologist, then head of Life Sciences Division at the British Antarctic Survey. Bonner had watched with interest the development of a World Conservation Strategy by the International Union for the Conservation of Nature

(IUCN, 1980) with assistance from the United Nations Environment Program (UNEP) and the World Wildlife Fund (WWF). The IUCN had observed continuing and accelerating degradation of habitats globally, widespread pollution, and damage from the development of infrastructure, a lack of adequate conservation legislation, and governments whose priorities were short-term and economic rather than long-term and strategic. Published in 1980 (IUCN, 1980), the objective of the strategy was to integrate conservation and development in a global framework within which national and regional strategies could be developed. Section 18 was devoted to the Global Commons and drew particular attention to the need to manage the Southern Ocean living resources sustainably. In 1982 IUCN proposed that a joint meeting be held with SCAR to bring conservationists together with Antarctic scientists. Following this, at the 16th IUCN General Assembly in 1984 Antarctica was designated as a region in which IUCN should actively promote the protection, management, and conservation of the environment and natural resources.

The IUCN formally approached SCAR, and Bonner was designated to work with their convenor (Martin Angel) on developing such a regional conservation strategy for the Antarctic, covering both the land and the surrounding ocean. With support from both sides the joint IUCN/SCAR Symposium on Requirements for Antarctic Conservation was held in Bonn in April 1985. Out of this was developed the Strategy for Antarctic Conservation (IUCN, 1991). For whatever reason, IUCN and SCAR failed to send the strategy to the ATCM, which at that point, was rather absorbed in agreeing the Protocol on Environmental Protection to the Antarctic Treaty, and the valuable lessons that could have been utilized were lost. Indeed, the strategy was not written in a user-friendly fashion, and its published format was not well designed. Despite all the effort put into drafting and agreeing it, the strategy failed to make any substantive mark on Antarctic environmental governance.

FINDING A CONCENSUS ON MINERALS

The Antarctic Treaty is silent on all forms of resource, not only because the extent and value of Antarctic resources were unknown in the 1950s but also because achieving agreement on these, even as abstract aspirations, would have been too difficult for the Washington talks. Although marine living resources (first as seals and then as fish and krill) were the initial resources legislated for, the question of mineral resources was already floating steadily upward. Interest in Antarctic minerals was first expressed at VI ATCM in Tokyo in 1970, in an attempt to interest Contracting Parties in developing a minerals regime ahead of the need for one (Joyner, 1996). This proved to be excellent timing as the actions of the Organization of Petroleum Exporting Countries (OPEC) in 1973 in restricting the world supply of hydrocarbons and causing a quadrupling of the price jerked governments into considering all sorts of new possibilities for future hydrocarbon development. In addition, in 1971–1972 drilling by the *Glomar Challenger* in the Ross Sea had discovered traces of methane but no oil, fuelling media speculation that there could be extensive oil reserves in Antarctica. The VII ATCM in Wellington began the discussions ostensibly as part of a concern that mineral extraction would have serious impacts on the environment. At their next meeting in Oslo in 1975 their Recommendation VIII-14 invited SCAR to make an assessment of the possible environmental impacts of mineral exploration and exploitation.

The SCAR was immediately apprehensive about this, and at XIV SCAR in Mendoza there was very spirited discussion about what should be done to provide a reply. Some biologists were concerned that any response by SCAR would be seen as supporting mineral exploitation whilst others from the geological sciences saw this as an opportunity to lay out what little was really known about economic mineral resources and correct many widely publicized misunderstandings. In the end, SCAR established the Group of Specialists on Environmental Impact Assessment of Mineral Resource Exploration and Exploitation in the Antarctic (EAMREA), chaired by Jim Zumberge, a geologist, but containing a wide range of both geologists and biologists. Parts of their report submitted to IX ATCM proved politically unacceptable (especially to the USSR), and the Antarctic Treaty then established its own Intergovernmental Group of Experts which produced a parallel report (Bonner, 1993b).

The Antarctic Treaty soon saw that such a contentious subject would need lengthy negotiations away from public view and these could not be contained within the normal ATCM agenda. A series of Special Consultative Meetings was begun under the chairmanship of Chris Beeby from New Zealand, leading in 1988 to a consensus in the form of the Convention on the Regulation of Antarctic Mineral Resource Activities (CRAMRA). During the course of these negotiations SCAR was again asked for advice, producing a new report "Antarctic Environmental Implications of Possible Mineral Exploration and Exploitation" in 1986.

All this effort appeared to be in vain because although all parties signed CRAMRA, the refusal first by Australia and then by France and New Zealand to ratify it effectively consigned it to limbo. Yet the new environmental thinking that went into the safeguards in CRAMRA was to find an unexpected outlet in a more general instrument for environmental protection.

THE FORMATION OF THE COUNCIL OF MANAGERS OF NATIONAL ANTARCTIC PROGRAMS

The SCAR Working Group on Logistics had been one of the first formed after SCAR was established. It never sat easily alongside the other purely scientific working groups, but it did have the advantage of ensuring that science and logistics periodically met together and talked. In its early days it was tasked with responding to several Antarctic Treaty requests on communications, transport, and even data management. As SCAR membership increased, the diversity of appointments of national programme managers increased, with some from science backgrounds, others from technical and engineering backgrounds, and some, from South American countries in particular, managers from diplomatic or military backgrounds. The degree of autonomy that each had varied widely and, with it, the degree of political control, as well as the extent of resources that each controlled. Organizing the working group proved a continuing problem, yet SCAR felt strongly that having the managers within the SCAR um brella was the most effective way to keep communications going and integrate the science and logistics for efficiency.

When Edward Todd was Director of the Office of Polar Programs (OPP), he apparently developed some strong views on SCAR, believing that SCAR was interfering in the way that the United States made its decisions about science programs and logistics. In 1983 he wrote, with respect to the Logistics Working Group, "some SCAR participants forget that commitments to SCAR are not governmental commitments by most SCAR participants who have no such charter; this confusion has led SCAR to assume management direction of research activities to which governments are not committed, and to unwarranted criticism of governments that have declined the presumed commitment of resources necessary to implement them" (Fowler, 2000:32). This streak of irritability persisted in the United States, and the appointment of Peter Wilkness as Director of the National Science Foundation Office of Polar Programs exacerbated it further. Wilkness saw the working group as an ineffective anachronism and questioned how government employees (the managers) could realistically make themselves subservient to a nongovernmental body (SCAR Executive Committee). He began to talk up the need for change in San Diego in 1986 and reinforced this at a special meeting in Boulder in 1987. In all this he found a willing supporter in Jim Bleasel, the director of the Australian Antarctic Division and the chairman of the Working Group on Logistics. Together they persuaded the managers that their rightful place was in their own autonomous organisation. Discussions continued through into the next SCAR meeting in Hobart, where on 15 September 1988 the Council of Managers of National Antarctic Programs (COMNAP) was formed. To try to find a face-saving formula, the new organization was described as being "federated" to SCAR, but in reality, the managers had broken free completely, appointing David Drewry as the first chairman and Al Fowler as executive secretary in a new independent secretariat (Fowler, 2000).

Appearing at the next ATCM in Bonn in their own right, COMNAP made a major impression on the Contracting Parties as a well organized and professional body and immediately began to undertake studies at the request of the Consultative Parties. This impression was, of course, helped by the extensive resources under the control of the managers, who could easily divert both staff and thousands of dollars into exercises they thought politically important. This was in sharp contrast to SCAR whose report, presented by Dick Laws as President, had suggested that SCAR had problems funding the work necessary to meet the constant stream of requests from the Antarctic Treaty. In particular, he said, "If the ATCPs do not give reasonable weight to the views of SCAR and if SCAR is unable to attract the relatively substantial (but absolutely small) extra funds required it may be obliged to concentrate on primary science and withdraw from giving advice on applied or management problems. The ATCPs have not responded to SCAR requests for extra funding to enable it to carry out the applied science function. To help SCAR make a decision it asks the ATCPs to make clear their intentions" (ATCM, 1992:232). He went on to lay out what should be the relevant responsibilities of Treaty Parties, SCAR, and COMNAP and cautioned against the Consultative Parties taking advice from environmental pressure groups. This sort of straight talking was not to the liking of some Consultative Parties, who questioned the role of SCAR and, by inference, its temerity in telling governments what should be done. Although many Consultative Parties came to the rescue of SCAR, no funding was forthcoming, and by breaking the implicit rules that govern discussions at Antarctic Treaty meetings, this report made the role of SCAR at ATCMs harder to achieve immediately afterward.

THE PROTOCOL REVOLUTION

The sudden demise of CRAMRA and the rapid negotiation of the Protocol on Environmental Protection to the Antarctic Treaty have been well documented (Chaturvedi, 1996). By pulling many of the environmental protection elements from CRAMRA and rationalizing the many conservation and management recommendations already agreed, the Consultative Parties were able to draft the protocol much more quickly than might have been expected for such a key international document. Such was the speed that SCAR, although present, was largely left out of the loop as the meetings concentrated on agreeing the form of the text and its limitations rather than dealing in detail with its implementation. As far as science is concerned the Protocol on Environmental Protection established a much more coherent approach to conservation and environmental management and finally brought some much needed tools (like environmental impact assessment) into normal use. As is often the case with Antarctic Treaty legislation, it provides careful ambiguity in some key areas (for example, what exactly are "associated and dependent ecosystems" or "minor or transitory impacts") and sets out goals with little indication of how they can be achieved. Nevertheless, by establishing the Committee for Environmental Protection (CEP) it provided a potentially powerful forum for developing environmental advice independent of SCAR.

The SCAR saw both opportunities and drawbacks in the new system. In order to cope with the increased number of environmental requests from the Antarctic Treaty, the SCAR Executive Committee had decided in 1988 to convert the Subcommittee on Conservation to the Group of Specialists on Environmental Affairs and Conservation (GOSEAC). Initially chaired by Nigel Bonner and then later by David Walton, it was required (SCAR, 1988)

> to advise SCAR on matters directly related to environmental affairs and conservation in the SCAR area of interest, in particular:
>
> - identification of environmental criteria relating to research activities and associated logistic support, as well as to relevant commercial activities and the selection of sites for all types of stations,
> - environmental aspects of waste disposal
> - protected areas in the Antarctic
> - additional protective measures.

Thus, SCAR was well prepared for engaging with the CEP when it finally came into being and provided a wide range of assistance, including workshops organized on protected areas, subantarctic island management, and environmental education; a handbook for the preparation of protected area management plans; detailed protocols for environmental monitoring of human impacts; checklists for inspections of protected areas and incinerator emissions; input to the Liability Annex discussions, bioprospecting, and marine acoustic impacts; and a detailed revision of every management plan for a Specially Protected Area or Site of Special Scientific Interest proposed or revised.

GEOGRAPHICAL NAMES

In undertaking science in Antarctica it has always been necessary to be able to name topographic features so that specimen collection localities can be identified and maps produced of biological and geological observations. The early expeditions provided some names, but as exploration and then the IGY progressed, names began to be a problem.

The disputes over sovereignty were a major part of the problem the Consultative Parties had in acting at the Antarctic Treaty level, and as more and more maps began to appear with duplicate names the possibility of chaos loomed. The SCAR Working Group on Geodesy and Geographic Information had been tracking the problem for many years, noting how individual countries promulgated new names for existing named features, the lack of any agreed nomenclature for describing features, and the poor positional data that often accompanied new names. By scientific standards many countries were doing a very poor job. At XXII SCAR in 1992 in Bariloche the working group resolved to compile a composite gazetteer, with Italy volunteering to compile the database and Germany developing a set of toponymic rules for naming. The SCAR Composite Gazetteer of Antarctica was first published in 1998 (SCAR, 1998) and has been continually updated ever since. Although originally issued as a printed publication, it soon became available online.

None of this work was either requested or supported by Treaty Parties, yet the arrival of the final product gave a new tool to everyone. Since SCAR had been careful to include all names that could be validated without suggesting which one should be used, the gazetteer was as politically anodyne as it could be and is now the basic reference source for all.

MARINE ACOUSTICS

Sometimes actions for environmental protection can have major consequences for science, and SCAR has had to employ considerable resources over a long period in order to ensure that policies are based on the best science available rather than on political agendas. An excellent example is the difficulties raised by a licensing authority over certain types of marine research.

There have been a variety of cases around the world where whale stranding appears to have been associated with marine noise or where some measure of disturbance has been credited to nearby military, commercial, or scientific activities (Weilgart and Whitehead, 2004), but the evidence is very confusing, partial, and possibly species specific. In 1998 Germany decided that the deployment of seismic instruments in the Southern Ocean was likely to cause unacceptable impact on marine mammals. Since German ships needed a permit from the Federal Environment Agency (Umwelt Bundes Amt) to operate, this effectively stopped all marine geophysics programmes. The German SCAR Committee asked if there really was evidence to support this contention. The SCAR decided to establish an ad hoc group to look at marine acoustics and produced an initial information paper for the ATCM promising to follow up with more detailed evidence (SATCM, 2000). The output from a SCAR workshop in Cambridge in 2001 (O'Brien, 2004) provided the basis for two papers to the Antarctic Treaty (ATCM, 2002a, 2002b) whose general conclusions were that the evidence available did not justify a ban on seismic surveys or scientific echo sounders in Antarctic waters but that mitigation strategies should be used as a precautionary measure. There was a further paper in Madrid (ATCM, 2003), and then SCAR held another international workshop in Cadiz. The final discussion on marine acoustics took place at the Edinburgh ATCM in 2006, where SCAR provided a report on the Cadiz workshop (which included a new risk assessment system for seismic studies) (ATCM, 2006a)and a case study of ship noise based on the *Polarstern* (ATCM, 2006b) and COMNAP provided a detailed breakdown of all seismic equipment on Antarctic research vessels (ATCM, 2006c). Meanwhile, in 2002 the Conference on the Impact of Acoustics on Marine Organisms had been organized in Berlin, under the auspices of Deutsche Forschungsgemeinschaft, which added some more details to the SCAR publications and again highlighted the lack of any solid data from the Antarctic on which to base regulations (Anonymous, 2004). For some within Germany this information was not sufficient, and they turned to promoting the application of the precautionary principle instead. It was made clear to the Consultative Parties by SCAR on several occasions that a sensible regime needed new research to establish not only which species might be affected, the degree of impact, and its severity but also the effectiveness of the mitigation measures proposed. It would appear that the appeal fell on deaf ears, and no such research was funded. Although the *Polarstern* initially used foreign licences to operate multinational geophysics cruises, there were eventually changes in the restrictions on low-power seismic systems, and some science was able to be undertaken. No other Consultative Party followed Germany in restricting its geophysics research, and there are still no new data from the Southern Ocean to substantiate the need for restrictions.

ACCESS TO DATA

One of the fundamental elements of the Antarctic Treaty (Article III, paragraph 1(c)) is that all data collected within the Antarctic Treaty area should be freely available to all. The development of databases in World Data Centres during and after IGY was an important step in this direction for some scientific fields. However, these centres did not encompass all aspects of Antarctic science, and it became clear that a new initiative was necessary to allow access to the very considerable amounts of data that were being produced. In 1985 at the XIII ATCM, during discussions on human impacts on the environment, Consultative Parties decided that there was scope for improvement in data management and, in Recommendation XIII-5, asked SCAR what steps could be taken to improve the comparability and accessibility of scientific data. The SCAR-COMNAP ad hoc Planning Group on Antarctic Data Management was formed in June 1992, and its first report proposed developing an Antarctic Data Directory System comprising National Antarctic Data Centres linked through an Antarctic Master Directory. This proposal was reported to the Antarctic Treaty (ATCM, 1992), and these ideas, elaborated at the second meeting (SCAR, 1994), became the basis for all future developments.

In 1997 COMNAP and SCAR finally reached agreement on joint funding and joint oversight for the committee, and the ad hoc committee became the Joint Committee for Antarctic Data Management (JCADM). It is fair to say that SCAR took the leading role in developing the framework of National Data Centres and the establishment of the metadata directory, and although the joint nature of the funding continued for some years, COMNAP never provided any serious input into what it considered to be a wholly scientific exercise. It was, of course, also meant to incorporate COMNAP data, but managers were unwilling to entrust any of their data to it.

Despite the efforts of many people JCADM grew more slowly than expected, not least because some national operators were apparently unable to establish a national Antarctic data centre. Recommendation XXII-4 addressed this point directly but failed to get all the managers to act. After a major review in 2005 a reorganization of both the role and objectives has ensured that JCADM is now firmly linked into the new SCAR programme structure, and the objectives of the original Antarctic Treaty recommendation are closer to being met. One of the key objectives of SCAR in recent years has been the development of a comprehensive data and information management strategy for the Antarctic, into which the activities of JCADM would fit. Such a strategy was developed in time for the XXX SCAR meeting in St. Petersburg in 2008. At that meeting, delegates endorsed the strategy and, following COMNAP's decision to discontinue partially funding JCADM, agreed that JCADM should become the Standing Committee on Data and Information Management (SCADM). The SCAR intends to draw the attention of the Consultative Parties to the new data strategy, as a means of getting it widely applied for the benefit of all.

REORGANISING SCAR

Elzinga (2009) has suggested that the pressure from new applicants to SCAR, enthusiastic to gain Consultative Status at the ATCM before CRAMRA came into operation, as well as the admission of SCAR to the ATCM as an official observer, triggered the development of a strategy discussion within the organisation. Although these were certainly relevant factors, there were many others, including the increasing importance of scientific conservation issues, a change in the Executive Secretary, the formation of COMNAP and the Standing Committee on Antarctic Logistics and Operations (SCALOP), and a determination by several presidents, including Claude Lorius and Dick Laws, to reexamine the objectives of the organization in the light of science trends. It also seems likely to have been influenced by the identification of Antarctic ozone depletion in 1985, the recognition that ice cores could provide key palaeoclimatic data, and the identification that the Southern Ocean was a major carbon sink, all combining to suddenly thrust what was considered regional science onto a global stage. This point was commented on by David Drewry in the first editorial in the new journal *Antarctic Science* (Drewry, 1989). The establishment of the Intergovernmental Panel on Climate Change (IPCC) in 1988 as well as the continuing development of the International Geosphere-Biosphere Program (IGBP) all pointed toward the need for a more-integrated cross-disciplinary approach to science, including that from the Antarctic, which was reflected in the development of a new SCAR programme on global change (SCAR, 1992).

In addition to internal discussions of change the General Council of ICSU decided to undertake a review of SCAR using an international panel chaired by Rita Colwell from the United States. The SCAR did not initially handle this review well but, rather late in the day, was able to provide the indications that ICSU needed to guarantee their support for the continuation of SCAR. The review committee's report was both supportive of what had been achieved and critical of the internal organisation, not least because the available funds were insufficient to meet an increasingly demanding role both in science coordination and in advice to the Antarctic Treaty. In addition, the report suggested that a merger with International Arctic Science Committee (IASC) might be considered to form a single polar committee and that an Antarctic Science Foundation could be formed to raise more funding (Colwell, 1993).

Delegates to XXII SCAR in Bariloche spent some time discussing the report and suggesting changes to the SCAR strategy as well as responses to the ICSU report. The SCAR responded to the report by disagreeing with the proposals for a foundation and especially with a merger with IASC but welcoming the recognition that funding was too low. The SCAR Executive Committee clearly felt that the report failed to understand the political dimension of interactions with the Antarctic Treaty, where a lack of sound science advice could seriously disadvantage Antarctic research in the future (SCAR, 1993). However, the comments on internal efficiency did strike home, and some minor changes were made to improve information flow.

The SCAR then lapsed back into complacency, apparently not recognizing that its structure and organization were woefully inadequate in a fast-moving and rapidly changing world. The Executive Committee did decide to make some changes, but little progress was made at either XXIII SCAR or at XXIV SCAR, and it was not until XXV SCAR in Concepción in 1998 that a force for change appeared. Six strategy papers were tabled, addressing a wide range of possibilities, but it was only when Chris Rapley from the United Kingdom and Jörn Thiede from Germany challenged the slow pace of change, and proposed an ad hoc review group with an independent chair, that change really became the focus of attention. This ad hoc group was chaired by Phil Smith from the United States, whose Antarctic credentials went back to IGY, and its remit was drawn widely enough for all possibilities to be examined. Its report was discussed by the SCAR Executive Committee in 2001, and implementation was agreed at XXVII SCAR in 2002. The most fundamental changes were the appointment of an executive director, the establishment of major peer-reviewed science programmes, an increase in funding, etc. The effect of all of these changes began to be felt immediately as new five-year programmes were devised; delegate committees were given new responsibilities for oversight; existing committees were merged, changed, or closed; and an experienced international scientist became the first executive director. The SCAR had suddenly woken up!

THE FUTURE

According to Herr (1996), the role played by SCAR in the development of the ATS was well beyond a passive legitimating influence. He says (p. 106), "SCAR helped to make the ATS work in terms of effectiveness by acting as a facilitator for regime objectives, providing a clearing house for scientific information. Moreover, its constituent organs at the national level in many countries served as a lobby group for both resources and support for the ATS regime." Indeed, others from the more militant elements of the nongovernmental organisation sector have seen this role as far too quiescent, gaining influence by being co-opted into the system rather than questioning it. This fine line between policy and science, between advocacy and reporting, is one that SCAR has been walking for the last 50 years. As Zumberge (1987:8), a previous president of SCAR, wrote, "The line between science and politics has become more finely drawn, and SCAR must exercise constant vigilance to avoid becoming tangled in policy matters that, while they may relate to scientific activities, are the business of the Consultative Parties that administer the Antarctic Treaty and related agreements." Keeping to the right side of the line can be very difficult at Antarctic Treaty meetings when it is clear that inexperienced delegates are proposing unsound policies that will have serious impacts on science! The scientific contributions made to discussions at the Antarctic Treaty owe a great deal to the activities of Nigel Bonner, David Walton, and Steven Chown, whose presentations and explanations at the Antarctic Treaty meetings have provided a much higher profile for SCAR science than before.

Nigel Bonner (1993a) had suggested, rather pessimistically, that the formation of COMNAP, the establishment of the Scientific Committee of CCAMLR, and the development of the Committee for Environmental Protection (CEP) would all lead to a weakening of SCAR's role and influence. Although at that point the future did, indeed, seem rather grey, now almost 20 years later the situation appears to have changed significantly. Although there are more experts providing science input to the CEP, the Consultative Parties now seem much more able to recognize the good science from the dressed-up polemic. The new working relationships with both CEP and CCAMLR have provided SCAR with many opportunities to respond to requests and to take the initiative, and the relationship with COMNAP is functional, although still far from perfect. The role of science in the ATS continues to be a strong one, with SCAR providing the lead.

The development of a new form of interaction between the CEP and SCAR has taken some time. The special status of SCAR in providing advice to the Antarctic Treaty is clearly indicated in the Protocol on Environmental Protection, but the final wording adopted is less supportive than that originally proposed by Sweden (Bonner, 1993b, p. 107): "In carrying out its functions, the Committee shall have regard to the work of the Scientific Committee on Antarctic Research . . . To that end, SCAR shall be invited to present their views and to comment on proposals within their competence put forward by the Committee. Such comments shall be presented together with the report from the Committee." After almost 40 years of SCAR providing a wide range of environmental and conservation advice the Consultative Parties clearly thought that the CEP was immediately going to provide a scientific committee for the Antarctic Treaty. This it failed to do, not only because for many years it lacked adequate expertise but also because the CEP also decided that a number of areas where SCAR had previously provided advice and assistance would now be dealt with by the Consultative Parties. The SCAR was told its help was no longer required, especially in areas like management plans for protected areas. Tension developed between the CEP and SCAR, not least when it became clear that the outputs being agreed were much less satisfactory than when SCAR had provided them.

As the CEP has matured and grown in expertise, although more slowly than most people had hoped, it has also redeveloped its links with SCAR, so that for the immediate future the two sides are agreeing a work plan. This plan will deliver well-considered science advice at a pace that SCAR can manage and the CEP can properly consider by ensuring that the energy and time of the CEP is properly focused at each meeting on a smaller number of key topics. The SCAR has, of course, continued to pursue its own science agenda and, where appropriate, passed its findings to the Antarctic Treaty. The latest input, one of the most important for many years, has been the synthesis on Antarctic climate and the environment (Turner et al., 2009).

Meanwhile, SCAR has also approached IUCN about revising the Antarctic conservation strategy to meet the needs of the twenty-first century. The IUCN is now actively engaged in seeking possible sponsorship for this (IUCN, 2009). Linked to this, there is a need for more-detailed information on the natural biodiversity in Antarctica so that non-native species can be more easily identified, and considerable work is needed to rationalize the protected areas on land and develop, with CCAMLR, a sensible range of marine protected areas.

Environmental monitoring of activities is a continuing requirement for which SCAR and COMNAP have provided a wide range of reports. However, the monitoring of tourism activities and the potential use of the data to manage areas by closure or visitor limits is a contentious area that so far has defied agreement and funding. Equally important is the provision of pattern and trend data to the CEP and to the IPCC on the effects of climate change.

The SCAR is at present flourishing as never before. It has 31 members, with another four countries as associate members. Its programmes are addressing global science questions where the data are relevant not only to the Antarctic Treaty Parties but to many other countries and organizations. Its relationship with IASC and SCOR continues to develop, and its Open Science conferences every two years now attract over 1,000 scientists.

Although this paper has necessarily focused on the history of interactions between SCAR and the ATS, a much fuller account of the first 50 years of SCAR activities is contained in Walton and Clarkson (In press). The SCAR has undertaken a remarkable range of activities over the past 50 years in support of good governance of the Antarctic. Throughout this entire period it has not received any financial support from the ATCM whatever the size of the task that was proposed. Now, with a permanent secretariat, the Consultative Parties are still unwilling to use its potential and allow the secretariat to service the CEP more directly by holding databases and working directly with science organisations like SCAR to ensure that the right information is available at the right time. It could even commission small pieces of work if it was provided with minimal funds, but this seems unlikely to happen given the level of control that some Parties insist on exerting over the secretariat. The symbiosis between the Antarctic Treaty and SCAR will, however, continue because it is in the long-term interests of both sides to ensure that the governance of a continent for peace and science is, indeed, underpinned by good science.

Acknowledgements

I am grateful to Dr. Peter Clarkson and Professor Jörn Thiede for their comments on a draft version. I am indebted to Dr Torben Wolff who supplied the image for Figure 1.

LITERATURE CITED

Anonymous. 2004. Proceedings of the Conference on Impact of Acoustics on Marine Organisms, 17–19 June 2002, Berlin. *Polarforschung*, 72(2/3):59–144.

Antarctic Treaty Consultative Meeting (ATCM). 1961. Report of First Consultative Meeting, Canberra, 10–24 July 1961.

———. 1991. "SCAR Report." In *Report of Sixteenth Antarctic Treaty Consultative Meeting, Bonn, Germany, 7–18 October 1991*, pp. 230–246.

———. 1992. SCAR Report. In *Report of the Seventeenth Antarctic Treaty Consultative Meeting, Venice , Italy, 11–20 November 1992*, pp. 199–214.

———. 2002a. Marine Acoustic Technology and the Environment. Working Paper 23. XXV ATCM Warsaw, Poland, 10–20 September 2202.

———. 2002b. Marine Acoustic Technology and the Environment. Information Paper 24. XXV ATCM Warsaw, Poland, 10–20 September 2202.

———. 2003. Acoustic Technology and the Marine Ecosystem. XXVI ATCM Madrid, Spain, 9–20 June 2003.

———. 2006a. SCAR Report on Marine Acoustics and the Southern Ocean. Working Paper 41. XXIX ATCM Edinburgh, UK, 12–23 June 2006.

———. 2006b. Broadband Calibration of Marine Seismic Sources—a case study. Information Paper 98. XXIX ATCM Edinburgh, UK, 12–23 June 2006

———. 2006c. Marine Acoustic Systems Used by National Antarctic Program Vessels. Information Paper 84. XXIX ATCM Edinburgh, UK,12–23 June 2006.

Belanger, D. O. 2006. *Deep Freeze—The United States, the International Geophysical Year and the Origins of Antarctica's Age of Science*. Boulder: University Press of Colorado.

Berkman, P. 2011 (this volume). "President Eisenhower, the Antarctic Treaty, and the Origin of International Spaces." In *Science Diplomacy: Antarctica, Science, and the Governance of International Spaces*, ed. P. A. Berkman, M. A. Lang, D. W. H. Walton, and O. R.

Young, pp. 17–27. Washington, D.C.: Smithsonian Institution Scholarly Press.

Bonner, W. N. 1987. "Recent Developments in Antarctic Conservation." In *The Antarctic Treaty Regime: Law, Environment and Resources*, ed. G. Triggs, pp. 143–149. Cambridge: Cambridge University Press.

———. 1993a. "The Development of the Science/Politics Interface in the Antarctic Treaty and the Role of Scientific Advice." In *Changing Trends in Antarctic Research*, ed. A. Elzinga, pp. 36–40. Dordrecht: Kluwer Academic Publishers.

———. 1993b. "The Science/Politics Interface in Development." In *Changing Trends in Antarctic Research*, ed. A. Elzinga, pp. 103–110. Dordrecht: Kluwer Academic Publishers.

Carrick, R. 1960. Conservation of Nature in Antarctica. SCAR Bulletin No. 6. *Polar Record*, 10: 299–305.

Chaturvedi, S. 1996. *The Polar Regions—A Political Geography*. Chichester, U.K.: John Wiley.

Colwell, R. R. 1993. "Some Views on Antarctic Research." In *Changing Trends in Antarctic Research*, ed. A. Elzinga, pp. 140–149. Dordrecht: Kluwer Academic Publishers.

Drewry, D. J. 1989. Science in Antarctica—A Matter of Quality. *Antarctic Science*, 1:2.

El-Sayed, S. Z. 1973. Biological Oceanography. *Antarctic Journal of the United States*, 8:93–100.

———, ed. 1994. *Southern Ocean Ecology: The BIOMASS Perspective*. Cambridge: Cambridge University Press.

Elzinga, A. 2009. Through the Lens of the Polar Years: Changing Characteristics of Polar Research in Historical Perspective. *Polar Record*, 45:313–336.

Fowler, A. N. 2000. *COMNAP—The National Managers in Antarctica*. Baltimore: American Literary Press.

Hanessian, J. 1960. The Antarctic Treaty 1959. *International and Comparative Law Quarterly*, 9:436–480.

Herr, R. 1996. "The Changing Role of NGOs in the ATS." In *Governing the Antarctic—The Effectiveness and Legitimacy of the Antarctic Treaty System*, ed. O. S. Stokke and D. Vidas, pp. 91–110. Cambridge: Cambridge University Press.

Holdgate, M. W., ed. 1970. *Antarctic Ecology*. London: Academic Press.

International Union for the Conservation of Nature (IUCN). 1980. *World Conservation Strategy*. Gland, Switzerland: IUCN

———. 1991. *Strategy for Antarctic Conservation*. Gland, Switzerland: IUCN

———. 2009. *Strategy for IUCN's Programme and Policy on Antarctic Issues*. Gland, Switzerland: IUCN

Joyner, C. C. 1996. "The Effectiveness of CRAMRA." In *Governing the Antarctic—The Effectiveness and Legitimacy of the Antarctic Treaty System*, ed. O. S. Stokke and D. Vidas, pp. 152–73. Cambridge: Cambridge University Press.

O'Brien, P. E. 2004. Report on the SCAR *ad hoc* Group on Marine Acoustic Technology and the Environment Workshop, September 2001. *Polarforschung*, 72:69.

Scientific Committee on Antarctic Research (SCAR). 1959. Aims and Establishment of S.C.A.R. *SCAR Bulletin* 1, 1–13.

———. 1988. Meeting of SCAR Executive Committee, Paris, France, 28–31 March 1988. *SCAR Bulletin* 90, 1–5.

———. 1992. *The Role of the Antarctic in Global Change: An International Plan for a Regional Research Programme*. Cambridge: SCAR.

———. 1993. Meeting of SCAR Executive Committee, Stockholm, Sweden, 13–14 and 16 April 1993. *SCAR Bulletin*, 111:1–20.

———. 1994. SCAR-COMNAP *ad hoc* Planning Group on Antarctic Data Management. Report of the Second Meeting. Boulder, Colorado, USA, September 1993. *SCAR Bulletin*, 114:5–17.

———. 1998. *Composite Gazetteer of Antarctica (South of Latitude 60°S)*. Cambridge: SCAR.

Special Antarctic Treaty Consultative Meeting (SATCM). 2000. Impacts of Acoustic Techniques in the Marine Environment. Information Paper 42. Special Antarctic Treaty Consultative Meeting XII, 11–15 September 2000, The Hague, Netherlands.

Turner, J., R. Bindschadler, C. P. Summerhayes, P. Convey, G. Di Prisco, E. Fahrbach, J. Gutt, D. A. Hodgson, and P. Mayewski. 2009. *Antarctic Climate and the Environment*. Cambridge: SCAR. 554pp.

Vidas, D. 1996. "The Antarctic Treaty in the International Community: An Overview." In *Governing the Antarctic—The Effectiveness and Legitimacy of the Antarctic Treaty System*, ed. O. S. Stokke and D. Vidas, pp 35–60. Cambridge: Cambridge University Press.

Walton, D. W. H., and P. D. Clarkson. In press. *Science in the Snow: 50 Years of the Scientific Committee on Antarctic Research*. Cambridge: SCAR.

Weilgart, L., and H. Whitehead. 2004. The Threat of Underwater Noise on Whales: Management in Light of Scientific Limitations. *Polarforschung*, 72:99–101.

Wolff, T. 2010. The birth and first years of the Scientific Committee on Oceanic Research (SCOR). SCOR History Report #1, 1–95. Newark:SCOR.

Zumberge, J. H. 1987. "Introduction." In *International Research in the Antarctic*, ed. R. Fifield, pp. 1–8. Oxford: Oxford University Press.

The Antarctic Treaty: Toward a New Partnership

Johannes Huber

INTRODUCTION

The Antarctic Treaty was adopted in 1959 to deal with a geopolitical vacuum around the southern continent that was a source of tension and conflict. It was also inspired by the success of the scientific cooperation under the International Geophysical Year, 1957–1958. The treaty created the conditions for Antarctica to become a continent for peaceful international scientific cooperation. In terms of its original purposes, the treaty has been a tremendous success. Even at times of considerable tension in regions close to Antarctica, the treaty regime of disarmament and peaceful cooperation in Antarctica has been maintained without interruption.

In addition, on the basis of the treaty a legal regime for the protection of the Antarctic environment was built up, which is now enshrined in the Protocol on Environmental Protection to the Antarctic Treaty (Environment Protocol) of 1991 and its six annexes. This regime is still being developed further through the measures of the Antarctic Treaty Consultative Meeting (ATCM).[1]

As an active participant in the ATCM from 1997 to 2004 and then as its senior official at the head of the Antarctic Treaty Secretariat from 2004 to 2009, I am proud to have made a contribution to its work. At the same time, my experience with the ATCM has also given me concerns about its ability to meet the challenges that are facing it in the twenty-first century.

In this chapter I will argue that although the Antarctic Treaty Parties and the ATCM established a comprehensive regulatory system to manage Antarctica, they have never shown much interest in the practical questions of ensuring its implementation or even its maintenance as a clear and consistent set of regulations. To put it in another way, the regulatory regime has outstripped the capacity of the parties to implement it. Without aiming at a systematic treatment, I will discuss some reasons for this gap between theory and practice, one of which is the resistance of the parties and the ATCM to institutional development. In a time of increasing pressure on the Antarctic environment resulting from technological and economic development, the regime needs to be strengthened; I believe this could be done, however, without changing the basic features of the Antarctic Treaty System.

Johannes Huber, Antarctic Treaty Secretariat, Av. Leandro N. Alem 884 Piso 4, C1001AAQ, Buenos Aires, Argentina. Correspondence: jansr@huber.nl.

BACKGROUND

When the Antarctic Treaty was adopted 50 years ago, Antarctica was a remote, dangerous place, where survival was only ensured by heroic efforts and mutual cooperation against the continuous threat of a hostile environment. No wonder that a lot of the early measures of the ATCM concerned mutual cooperation between stations!

Fifty years later, Antarctica can be reached by regular air connections from three continents. Scientists on the stations are connected to the Internet and can pick up the phone and call their loved ones. Antarctica is a regular stop for the worldwide cruise industry, and tens of thousands of tourists visit it every year. Furthermore, the main business before the ATCM is no longer concerned with demilitarization, but rather protection of the Antarctic environment against the consequences of mankind's increasing access to the continent.

The evolution of the Antarctic Treaty from a geopolitical agreement to prevent conflict over Antarctica into the core of a regulatory system managing Antarctica started from the beginning of the Antarctic Treaty. The first ATCM, held in Canberra in 1962, adopted Recommendation I-VIII, "General Rules of Conduct for Preservation and Conservation of Living Resources in Antarctica," and a more comprehensive set of rules was outlined in the Agreed Measures for the Conservation of Antarctic Fauna and Flora (adopted with Recommendation III-VIII, Brussels, 1964). Conservation activities on a global scale were only just beginning at that time, of course, so the ATCM was acting in the spirit of the times. More measures were added regularly, and the Protocol on Environmental Protection to the Antarctic Treaty (Madrid, 1991) organized all of this into a single scheme, bringing much of Antarctic conservation into line with developments outside.

The administration and implementation of a comprehensive regulatory regime for Antarctica was, however, not foreseen in the procedures of Article IX, and with the conclusion of the Environment Protocol in 1991 it became clear that some adaptations would have to be made to the functioning of the Antarctic Treaty system.

Some steps were, in fact, taken. In the first place, in the Environment Protocol the Committee on Environmental Protection (CEP) was established. If one could say that the institution of the CEP represents the first step toward institutionalization taken by the ATCM (the CEP has a Chair and Vice-Chairs who are elected for specified terms, unlike their counterparts in the ATCM who are appointed at each meeting only for that meeting), one would have to add that it was a very cautious one. The CEP does not have any powers of its own; its only function is to "provide advice and formulate recommendations to the Parties in connection with the implementation of this Protocol, including the operation of its Annexes, for consideration at Antarctic Treaty Consultative Meetings."[2]

The second change was to amend the procedures for dealing with measures adopted by the ATCM. According to the provisions of Article IX, measures adopted by the ATCM "become effective when approved by all [Consultative Parties] entitled to participate in the meetings held to consider those measures," a process that even in the early days took years and became ever more time-consuming with the increase in the number of parties. This process was too cumbersome to deal with the measures necessary to put into effect the Environment Protocol, and so in the annexes of the protocol provision was made for the automatic entry into effect of certain types of measures. A few years later, at the 19th ATCM in Seoul in 1995 the Consultative Parties made a more general change and decided to reserve the application of this provision only to texts containing provisions intended to be legally binding, to be called from then on Measures with a capital *M*. The other types of measures adopted by the ATCM, divided into Decisions (dealing with internal organizational matters) and Resolutions (containing hortatory texts), are not subject to this procedure and consequently enter into force immediately.[3]

The third step was the decision in principle taken at the 17th ATCM in Venice in 1992 to set up a permanent secretariat of the treaty. The ATCM had been meeting for 30 years without feeling the need for any permanent institution, and initiatives for a secretariat had been routinely dismissed until that time, but the establishment of a comprehensive system of environmental regulations made such a situation untenable. The fact that the ATCM occupied itself for 12 years, from 1992 to 2004, deciding where to locate its secretariat may indicate a certain lack of urgency.[4]

These changes were necessary and could be regarded as the first steps toward an effective regime. A brief look at some features of the present situation, however, will make clear that much progress still has to be made.

THE CURRENT SITUATION

The Approval Process

If the process for reaching unanimous agreement on a recommendation appears tortuous, then at least it benefits from undivided attention of all those attending the ATCM. Once agreement has been reached and the delegates return home, the Antarctic appears to go to the bottom of the attention pile, and often, very little national action is taken to implement the items agreed. As mentioned before, with the increase in the number of Antarctic Treaty Parties to the Antarctic Treaty the time spent on completion of the approval process according to Article IX, paragraph 4, has increased greatly; indeed, one might say to a ludicrous extent. Some recommendations of the 1990s, such as Recommendation XVIII-1 (Venice, 1992), which established the basic guidelines for tourism in Antarctica, have not yet become effective almost 20 years after they were adopted.[5]

To take a more recent example, the 27th ATCM (Capetown, 2004) adopted Measure 4 (2004), "Insurance and Contingency Planning for Tourism and Non Governmental Activities in the Antarctic Treaty Area." This measure provides that Antarctic Treaty Parties must require operators "organising or conducting tourist or other non-governmental activities in the Antarctic Treaty Area" to have "appropriate contingency plans and sufficient arrangements for health and safety, search and rescue (SAR), and medical care and evacuation" in place before the start of any activity, together with insurance covering the costs.

These safety issues have received much attention from the ATCM in recent years. At a special seminar by the International Hydrographic Organization during the 31st ATCM in Kyiv in 2008, the National Hydrographer of the United Kingdom, Rear Admiral Ian Moncrief, stated that the question was not *if* a serious accident would occur with a tourist ship in Antarctic waters, but when. And yet, up to now, the ATCM has no specific legal basis in its own measures for the regulation of tourist vessels in the Antarctic Treaty area. Nevertheless, despite frequent expressions of concern in the ATCM, in the five years after adoption of the Measure 4 only 9 of the necessary 28 Consultative Parties have gotten around to approving it.[6]

A similar case is that of Annex VI of the Environment Protocol, which introduces the principle that operators should under some circumstances be liable for the consequences of environmental emergencies caused by them. It took 12 years to negotiate and even then contains far less substance than many originally envisaged, and at the current pace it will take at least that long to be approved and enter into force. At the time of writing, five years after its adoption, it had been approved by only four Antarctic Treaty Parties.

Which Measures Are in Effect?

Lack of a permanent secretariat meant that until 2004 each party hosting an ATCM had the entire responsibility for assembling the documentation for the meeting, collecting the documents submitted to it, and drawing up and distributing its report. Under such circumstances, in which every year a new team had to start from scratch organizing the meeting, it is not surprising that the legislative record of the ATCM, consisting of several hundreds of measures, is full of discontinuities, gaps, and duplications. This situation has not been helped by the fact that the rapid turnover of delegates in most national delegations has ensured a weak collective memory of what has gone before. When adopting a new measure, the ATCM did not, until recently, necessarily indicate which earlier measures were invalidated or replaced. After 50 years, this means that the question of which measures are currently in effect and applicable to any particular issue does not have a clear and unambiguous answer.

This issue was first raised some 20 years ago, when some Antarctic Treaty Parties that had recently acceded to the Antarctic Treaty were trying to find out which previous measures they would have to approve in order to meet their obligations. The matter has been discussed on and off since then, but progress has been very slow. After many years of discussion, the 25th ATCM in Warsaw adopted a decision declaring 24 previous recommendations "spent." Despite the establishment in the meantime of the Antarctic Treaty Secretariat, no further progress was made until 2007, when a further 13 former measures were declared "no longer current." Even with the Secretariat now doing the analytical work preparing these decisions, nothing has happened at the next two meetings. Considering that possibly up to half of the 400 odd measures on the books are actually out of date, this is slow progress indeed![7]

Implementation Problems

Because of the nature of the Antarctic Treaty itself, especially Article IV on the sovereignty claims over parts of Antarctica, implementation of the Antarctic Treaty regime has always been a complicated question. Possible solutions, such as a condominium or full internationalization, had been discussed before, but by 1959 the Antarctic Treaty Parties had come to the conclusion that these were not viable options. Instead, they chose a supremely pragmatic approach, basically setting the claims aside without providing any definitive solution to the sovereignty issue and concentrating on practical cooperation to let the scientists get on with their research.

The compromise represented by the Antarctic Treaty has worked marvelously well. Its legal basis, however, is weak, as the status of the area it is dealing with is not settled in the treaty, and attempts at a more precise definition of that status usually run into opposition from the Treaty Parties, especially those with sovereignty claims. The result is that implementation of the environmental regime, which is comprehensive in its aims, has to be left entirely to the national governments of the Antarctic Treaty Parties, with all their different legal and institutional systems.

A tourist ship cruising through the Antarctic Treaty area and calling at various stations will encounter a different situation in each one. In one place it will be greeted by officials of one Antarctic Treaty Party who act almost as if they are the territorial authority exercising port state control and in another by officials of another Party who are mostly concerned with minimizing interruption of their station's research activities.

A system like this, which does not have an international organization for its implementation but, instead, relies on the purely national efforts of the participating countries, needs strong provisions on transparency and information sharing. Thanks to the wisdom of its framers, the Treaty actually provides a solid foundation in these areas. Article VII of the Antarctic Treaty establishes that "all areas of Antarctica, including all stations, installations and equipment within those areas, and all ships and aircraft at points of discharging or embarking cargoes or personnel in Antarctica, shall be open at all times to inspection" by the observers designated by the Antarctic Treaty Parties. At the same time, the Parties are required to inform each other beforehand of, among others things, "all expeditions to and within Antarctica, on the part of its ships or nationals, and all expeditions to Antarctica organized in or proceeding from its territory; all stations in Antarctica occupied by its nationals." Article VII was the foundation for a system of information exchange covering many aspects of all activities, whether official or nonofficial, on Antarctica, and with the adoption of the Environment Protocol the basic operational information about expeditions, stations, ships, aircraft, and personnel was expanded to include many kinds of environmental information, such as environmental impact assessments, permits to visit protected areas, permits to take fauna and flora, waste management plans, etc.

Access to this kind of information is a precondition for any kind of management system, so one of the first priorities of the Antarctic Treaty Secretariat, after its establishment in 2004, was the development of a central database to collect all the many kinds of information exchanged under this system, as had been decided at the 24th ATCM in St. Petersburg.[8] After three years of development work, at the 31st ATCM in Kyiv the ATCM instructed the Secretariat to put the Electronic Information Exchange System into operation.[9]

Unfortunately, the observance of Article VII by the Antarctic Treaty Parties is inadequate, both with regard to inspection and with regard to information exchange. Of course, Article VII does not require Parties to carry out inspections. Considering the importance of inspection activities, however, it is disappointing that more than half of all Consultative Parties have never engaged in any inspections at all and some long-occupied stations have never been visited by an inspection team.

Much more serious is the failure of the Antarctic Treaty Parties to fulfill their obligation to report on their activities. The mandatory information exchange requirements are clearly laid down in the treaty, the Environmental Protocol, and the subsequent measures adopted by the ATCM, but many parties are in breach of these rules year after year. With an electronic system now in operation, compliance has become much easier, and so the number of Antarctic Treaty Parties providing information is growing, but it still is far from satisfactory. To give an example, at the time of writing, when the 2009/2010 Antarctic season is already over, only 16 of the 28 Consultative Parties had provided their preseason information![10]

An important reason for the various failings to maintain and implement the regime is a lack of human and financial resources. Except for a small number of the major Antarctic Treaty Parties, most Treaty countries do not have adequate personnel or expertise, either at headquarters or in the field, for a credible implementation of the regulatory regime they have legally instituted. The personnel in the field are fully occupied keeping their stations going, and the human resources devoted to Antarctica at home are very limited. Most Consultative Parties have only one or two officials in their capitals occupied with Antarctic Treaty matters and often on a part-time basis at that. It's all they can do to prepare adequately for the annual ATCM.

The ATCM

The inheritor and guardian of a glorious tradition of cooperation and comradeship with regard to Antarctica, the ATCM is a unique forum and is, by far, the most harmonious and constructive international diplomatic circle that I have ever encountered in my career. To some extent, however, it is the victim of its own success. Speakers in the ATCM often refer in a self-congratulatory manner to the Antarctic tradition and the contribution it has made to maintaining Antarctica as a continent of "peace, scientific cooperation and environmental protection." It is a tradition to be proud of. At the same time, the ATCM is also an intensely conservative and complacent group where agreements are negotiated in a confidential, clubby atmosphere, far away from the public and the media, and where change is usually resisted.

The ATCM functions on the basis of Article IX of the Treaty, which determines who may take part in the meetings: representatives of the original 12 signatories and of those parties that conduct "substantial scientific research activity" on Antarctica, together called the Consultative Parties. According to Article IX, the meetings are held for the purpose of "exchanging information, consulting together on matters of common interest pertaining to Antarctica, and formulating and considering, and recommending to their Governments, measures in furtherance of the principles and objectives of the Treaty."

Even after 50 years, this is still a faithful description of the work of the ATCM. The trouble is that the entire context in which the meeting takes place has changed out of all recognition. The first ATCM, held in Canberra in 1962, united representatives of the 12 original signatories and scientists, including veterans of the IGY. Now, the ATCM is held yearly and includes representatives of more than 40 Antarctic Treaty Parties, both Consultative and Nonconsultative, international organizations, and scientific and other nongovernmental organizations.

Not only has the ATCM grown, but the issues facing it and the environment in which it operates have changed. Besides being a diplomatic conference to negotiate new measures, the ATCM is also a forum bringing together the governments responsible for the de facto administration of an entire continent.

Questions relating to the effectiveness of this administration, however, are rarely discussed. It is characteristic for the ATCM that it is happy to hold long discussions on the precise interpretation of certain provisions relating to environmental impact assessments—the terms "a minor or transitory impact" come to mind—but one would look in vain for any attempt to compare the application of environmental impact assessments (EIAs) in practice between different countries as this would have potentially embarrassing political consequences, exposing some Antarctic Treaty Parties as grossly negligent in the way they approach this activity. The ATCM functions like a continuous diplomatic conference, ever negotiating new refinements of the original agreements. Avoiding the sensitivities of the Parties, and of various groups of the Parties—countries with claims, countries with a "basis of claim,"[11] countries that don't recognize any claims—is the all-important objective. Questions relating to the current status and the consistency of the body of legislation created by the ATCM do not have a great priority, let alone questions relating to its implementation and effectiveness.

One of the most sensitive points in this continuing diplomatic negotiation is the question of institutional development. Especially to some of the Antarctic Treaty Parties that maintain a claim or a "basis of claim" of sovereignty to parts of Antarctica, the development of any institutions is very easily seen as a threat to the power of national administrations. Of course, the chance that any national claim will ever be recognized by the rest of the world is practically zero, so the claims being protected are largely theoretical in nature and mostly relevant only to the domestic politics of the nations concerned. At the same time, they do make the development of the Antarctic Treaty System in the direction of an effective and efficient cooperative system of governance much more complicated.

In the view of some Parties, the ATCM is nothing more than a diplomatic conference, and so it has no continuing existence between its meetings. Nevertheless, the CEP (admittedly only an advisory body to the ATCM) has a Chair and Vice-Chairs who are elected according to formal procedures for definite periods. When a proposal was made at the 31st ATCM in Kyiv in 2008 to amend the Rules of Procedure and provide for the election of the chairs of the working groups of the ATCM for periods of two years, it was rejected, as some delegates considered this would "limit flexibility."[12] The traditional system, in which the chairs of the working groups magically emerge from the meeting of the heads of delegation the day before the start of the ATCM, was retained.

An even more serious "problem" for some parties is the existence of the Antarctic Treaty Secretariat, which is a definite institution, incorporated according to the laws of Argentina, with physical premises, employees, and a budget. When the instruments establishing the secretariat were negotiated, Antarctic Treaty Parties worried about the Secretariat as a potential rival to their own authority peppered the texts with clauses to the effect that the Secretariat does not have an independent existence but only functions as an instrument of the ATCM. Thus, Article 1 of Measure 1 (2003), the measure establishing the Secretariat, does not actually specify its purpose or function, but merely states, "The Secretariat shall constitute an organ of the ATCM. As such it shall be subordinated to the ATCM"; similar phrases are repeated frequently in the measure. The only trouble is, What is the ATCM? If it is purely a diplomatic conference existing only two weeks every year, how can it possibly exercise the oversight described in the Secretariat instruments?

TOWARD A NEW PARTNERSHIP

In the preceding passages I have sketched some ways in which the Antarctic Treaty, the Environmental Protocol, and the measures of the ATCM, considered as the de facto regulatory regime to manage Antarctica, fall short in practice. At the same time, technological and economic development brings an ever-increasing involvement of the rest of the world with Antarctica, especially in the form of visitors by sea and by air. The demand for access to Antarctica for all kinds of purposes will continue to grow for a long time to come. Also, changes in the global climate system pose a growing threat to the survival of the Antarctic ecosystems.

A new partnership between the Antarctic Treaty Parties is needed to deal with these challenges and to preserve Antarctica as the world's largest natural reserve, unspoiled by the humankind. Such a partnership would focus on joint, rather than purely national, implementation of the regulatory regime established through the ATCM.

Although a basic support structure now exists in the form of the Antarctic Treaty Secretariat, setting up an effective, up-to-date management system for Antarctica will need an increase in manpower and resources, both in national capitals and in the field. There is no need for any elaborate new legal or institutional development. What is needed, however, is a change of thinking, moving away from a narrow focus on the execution of purely national programs to a joint administration of Antarctica.

Also, as the basic approach will continue to be that of national implementation of all Antarctic regulation, the Antarctic Treaty Parties should urgently consider working out cooperative agreements, including open-ended coordination arrangements in the field, to minimize the gaps that inevitably will occur.

Possible elements of such a new approach might be the following:

- The assignment of informative, monitoring, and administrative functions related to the Antarctic regulatory regime to government personnel active in Antarctica. In some cases, dedicated personnel might be needed; in other cases these functions could be carried out by existing program personnel.
- Conclusion of flexible, open-ended liaison and coordination arrangements between the parties on a regional basis, on the model of the arrangements made for the administration of Antarctic Specially Managed Areas, to make sure all areas are covered for monitoring and implementation purposes.
- Strengthening the Electronic Information Exchange System so that it can provide, through the existing information exchange requirements, real-time information concerning permits, EIAs, contingency plans, etc., directly to government personnel in Antarctica tasked with implementing the management regime.
- Establishment of periodic monitoring and reporting systems on the state of the Antarctic environment as a whole and the successes and failures of the regulatory system.
- Adoption by the ATCM of provisions for the automatic entry into effect of Measures as a rule, maintaining, of course, exceptions in case any party would object within a certain period.
- Greater efforts by the Consultative Parties to deal with the national approval procedures of Measures adopted by the ATCM in a timely manner. Revision and updating by the ATCM of its body of legislation adopted by the ATCM and an active policy of publication and outreach with regard to the Antarctic Treaty System.
- Establishment by the ATCM of standing committees to oversee the work of the secretariat, monitor the implementation of the regulatory regime, and deal with emergencies.
- Allowing the establishment of standing committees of the CEP (as the Convention on the Conservation of Antarctic Marine Living Resources [CCAMLR] has) that can meet and report without simultaneous translation.

These are just examples of actions the Antarctic Treaty Parties might take. The Antarctic Treaty system has been a great success for 50 years, but it would be a mistake to take it for granted and to let it drift along and possibly lose relevance to the fast-developing situation of the Antarctic. Instead, by adopting a more active approach and taking a few modest institutional steps the Treaty Parties have a marvelous opportunity to show the world that its last remaining true wilderness can be managed on behalf of mankind by the countries active in Antarctica in a pragmatic and efficient way.

NOTES

1. The measures of the ATCM were previously called recommendations, as they are recommended to the governments of the Antarctic Treaty Parties and, according to Article IX, paragraph 4, only enter into effect after their approval by all parties concerned. In 1995 this procedure was amended; since then, the measures subject to the Article

IX, paragraph 4, procedure are called Measures with a capital *M*. In this article, measures without capitalization will refer to all categories. Aside from the Treaty, the Protocol, and the measures of the ATCM, the Antarctic Treaty System also includes other agreements (Convention on the Conservation of Antarctic [CCAS] and CCAMLR) and measures adopted by the CCAMLR Commission; to simplify the argument, I will not treat these agreements here.

2. Environment Protocol, Article 12.

3. Decision 1 (1995).

4. See my article, "Notes on the Past, Present and Future of the Antarctic Treaty Secretariat," *Diplomacia* 120 (2009): 35–43

5. Consultative Parties are not obliged, of course, to approve Measures, even if they have participated in their adoption at the ATCM. There are precedents for a party to come to the conclusion, after the adoption of a Measure, that circumstances had occurred that prevented them from approving it. In such cases they will usually inform the other parties at subsequent ATCMs of these circumstances. This is not the case with Recommendation XVIII-1, however, which has never encountered any opposition from any party.

6. Details on the approval process can be found in the Antarctic Treaty Database on the Antarctic Treaty Secretariat Web site (http://www.ats.aq).

7. See J. Huber, "Notes on the ATCM Recommendations and Their Approval Process," in *The Antarctic Legal System and Environmental Issues,* ed. G. Tamburelli, (Milan: Giuffrè Editore, 2006), pp. 17–31.

8. Resolution 6 (2001).

9. Decision 5 (2008).

10. Information Exchange section of the Antarctic Treaty Secretariat Web site.

11. Article IV of the treaty safeguards the position of both the seven countries that have asserted claims of sovereignty (Argentina, Australia, Chile, France, New Zealand, Norway, and the United Kingdom) and the countries that have asserted a "basis of claim" (Russia and the United States).

12. ATCM XXXI (Kyiv, 2008) WP1 "Proposal by Australia, the United Kingdom and Norway to Amend Rule 11 of the Rules of Procedure of the ATCM"; Final Report, paragraph 35.

Potential Challenges to the Antarctic Treaty

Christopher C. Joyner

The 1959 Antarctic Treaty has as its principal purposes to ensure "in the interests of all mankind that Antarctica shall continue forever to be used exclusively for peaceful purposes and shall not become the scene or object of international discord" and to use the science performed there to benefit the entire planet.[1] More than 50 years on, this accord has proved to be a remarkable multilateral instrument and, in many ways, is unique among international legal agreements. It is simple, straightforward, and succinct. It consists of 2,364 words contained in only seven pages set out elegantly in a preamble and 14 articles. Notwithstanding its conspicuous brevity, and the fact that seven of the original treaty parties assert claims to territory on the continent,[2] what the treaty provides for in those legal provisions is huge, indeed. Moreover, the Antarctic Treaty has also demonstrated considerable adaptability and resiliency as it evolved from a single instrument into a robust regional regime containing four new instruments since its inception: the 1964 Agreed Measures for the Protection of Flora and Fauna,[3] the 1972 Convention on the Conservation of Antarctic Seals,[4] the 1980 Convention on the Conservation of Antarctic Marine Living Resources (CCAMLR),[5] and the 1991 Protocol on Environmental Protection to the Antarctic Treaty (Environmental Protocol).[6] Notwithstanding the successful evolution of this legal regime,[7] in recent years three issues have surfaced that could challenge the legal integrity and political viability of this regional treaty regime.

The first challenge involves the possible conflict between claimant and non-claimant governments over access to possible hydrocarbon resources offshore the continent. At the regulatory heart of this potential rush to secure access to as yet undiscovered south polar hydrocarbons lies Article 76 of the 1982 United Nations Convention on the Law of the Sea (UNCLOS).[8] Indeed, Article 76 provides the legal means by which coastal states can gain sovereignty over vast areas of submarine continental shelf areas offshore their coasts, areas that might hold enormous reserves of hydrocarbon resources. To that end, Antarctic claimant states have made either full or partial submissions to the UN Commission on the Limits of the Continental Shelf (CLCS), as provided for in Article 76, concerning the possibility of asserting continental shelf claims offshore their claimed Antarctic territories. Australia was the first claimant to make a submission to the CLCS and did so in November 2004.[9] The submission by New Zealand was

Christopher C. Joyner, Department of Government, Georgetown University, Washington, D.C. 20057, USA. Correspondence: joynerc@georgetown.edu

filed with the CLCS in April 2006, although it excluded a prospective outer continental shelf claim offshore its claimed sector in Antarctica.[10] Argentina made its submission with the CLCS in April 2009, which included a map and geographical coordinating for outer continental shelf limits overlapping the Antarctic Peninsula.[11] Norway filed a partial submission to the CLCS in May 2009, in which Dronning Maud Land was included.[12] Chile made its submission in the form of a "Preliminary Information" statement to the CLCS in May 2009.[13] The United Kingdom made two public communications concerning its outer continental shelf claims in the Antarctic, one in a note on 9 May 2008 to the UN Secretary General, which indicated that United Kingdom would be making in 2009 "a partial submission" that "will not include areas of the continental shelf areas appurtenant to Antarctica, for which a submission may be made later."[14] Although France has not formulated any specific outer continental shelf claim offshore its clamed territory in Antarctica (Adelie Land), it did note in a "partial submission" to the UN Secretary General in February 2009 that such an offshore zone might well exist, for which a submission may later be made.[15]

The implications of potential continental shelf claims and the possibility of mineral and hydrocarbon resource development clearly weigh on the minds of many Antarctic Treaty Consultative Party (ATCP) governments. That these concerns are real was demonstrated in April 2009 in the Ministerial Declaration on the Fiftieth Anniversary of the Antarctic Treaty, issued at the beginning of the 32nd Antarctic Treaty Consultative Meeting.[16] In that document, the Consultative Parties pledged to "Reaffirm the importance they attach to the contribution made by the Treaty, and by Article IV in particular, to ensuring the continuance of international harmony in Antarctica." Likewise, the ATCPs also pledged to "Reaffirm their commitment to Article 7 of the Environmental Protocol, which prohibits any activity relating to mineral resources, other than scientific research." The declaration was designed to reiterate support for the basic tenets of the Antarctic Treaty System, especially key elements such as Article IV of the treaty and Article 7 of the Environmental Protocol. These two elements were emphasized in particular because they remain fundamental to the continuing health of the Antarctic Treaty regime.

In sum, two potential political problems are posed by these partial claimant state continental shelf submissions, either of which could have unsettling impacts on the stability of the Antarctic Treaty. First, if pushed on to full submission, these claimant state assertions would resurrect the dispute over the status of national sovereignty claims on the continent. Second, the allegation is bound to arise from nonclaimant governments that these submissions are actually extensions of claims made prior to 1959 or even new claims made by each state. Since 1961 when the Antarctic Treaty entered into force, both these critical complications have been held in check by the ingenious construction of its Article IV, and the political willingness of the claimant government not to push the sovereignty issue. Prudence suggests that all the ATCPs ought to view their national interest as being best served by preserving the integrity of the present system, rather than risk politically unraveling it for the sake of asserting claims over unknown (and very likely unrecoverable) continental shelf hydrocarbon resources.

A second potential challenge to the integrity of the Antarctic Treaty is biological prospecting, or bioprospecting, in the region and the potential conflicts these activities might generate among Treaty Parties. Increasing scientific research on flora and fauna in and around Antarctica is being conducted with the aim of discovering commercially beneficial genetic and biochemical resources. Growing commercial interest in Antarctic genetic resources is evident, as indicated by the fact that products from Antarctic genetic resources are already being marketed by several companies, including nutraceuticals from krill oil, antifreeze proteins, anticancer drugs, enzymes, and compounds for cosmetic products. Much of this commercial activity focuses on the marine environment, in particular, the crustacean krill. Nearly 200 research organizations and companies from 27 states are undertaking research for commercial purposes in the Antarctic. Amongst the major sponsoring states are Japan, United States, Spain, United Kingdom, Korea, Canada, Sweden, Russia, China, Chile, New Zealand, France, Belgium, India, Denmark, the Netherlands, Germany, and Poland, all ATCPs. The most entries in the recently constructed Antarctic Bioprospecting Database originate from Japan and mainly focus on organisms in the marine environment, principally Antarctic krill. The second largest number of entries originate from United States, most of which also focus on marine biota, especially krill, bacteria, and fish.

The raison d'être of the Antarctic Treaty is to ensure peaceful uses only and opportunities for scientists to exchange freely information, personnel, and investigation results from research conducted in the Antarctic Treaty area. For the foreseeable future, it seems that bioprospecting in Antarctica mainly will be confined to the collection and discovery of new biological resources. Such activities should fall under the ambit of Article III since they address cooperation among scientific programs and scientific personnel and the exchange of scientific observations and research results. Important also is that reporting requirements will likely furnish information about many of these activities, but such reports are not likely to include information about the commercial application of these resources. This consequence brings up two obvious concerns: First, can the desire to ensure commercial confidentiality and patent protection be reconciled with the legal requirements of scientific exchange and cooperation in the treaty's Article III? Second, can intellectual property rights be preserved as a useful means for promoting and encouraging the exchange of scientific information? During these early years of bioprospecting in Antarctica, such queries remain unanswered by scientists, commercial investors, and statesmen involved in the region.

Certain unresolved bioprospecting issues could pose serious challenges within the ATCPs, particularly between claimant and nonclaimant states. For example, there is the lack of a consensus definition of biological prospecting as a research activity. Another legal concern relates to who has the authority to determine access to genetic resources in Antarctica. Consequently, although Article IV provides that "no acts or activities taking place while the present Treaty is in force shall constitute a basis for asserting, supporting or denying a claim to territorial sovereignty in Antarctica or create any rights of sovereignty in Antarctica," what degree of legal authority, if any, do claimant states possess to regulate access to Antarctic genetic resources in their claimed sectors? No less important, would this "authority" give claimant states the right of refusal to a prospective bioprospector? Moreover, how and with whom should monetary and other benefits acquired from genetic resource research be shared? Who retains how much of the profits, if any, derived from bioprospecting research? Are all benefits to be retained solely by the company who invests most heavily in the research? Should claimant states figure into any exclusive scheme for apportioning benefits derived from genetic resources in their sector claim? Should the ATCPs receive benefits as a special group? Or should there be a common fund so that peoples worldwide might gain from Antarctica's resources? Finally, with respect to the freedom of scientific research in the Antarctic Treaty area, should a distinction be made between basic scientific research, applied scientific research, and commercial use within the context of benefit sharing? These are important questions affecting bioprospecting activities that could trigger disruptive political reactions among the ATCPs. For the foreseeable future, however, most Antarctic Treaty parties seem content to allow bioprospecting activities to go forward, so long as conflict of interests can be avoided among research organizations, claimant governments, and nonclaimant governments.

In the search for answers to these critical questions, it would seem prudent and practical that lessons for bioprospecting might be learned from the experience during the 1980s of negotiating the prospecting phase for the Antarctic minerals regime, as well as by consulting the text of its nonoperational instrument, the Convention on the Regulation of Antarctic Mineral Resource Activities (CRAMRA), especially its Chapter III, which constitutes the prospecting section in that instrument.

A third potentially serious challenge to the integrity of the Antarctic Treaty lies in the political tensions arising between Japan and Australia, both Antarctic Treaty Consultative Parties, over the former's practice of lethal whaling in the Southern Ocean. The international body created to watch over national whaling operations is the International Whaling Commission (IWC), which in 1986 adopted a moratorium on commercial whaling that still remains in effect. In 1994 the IWC created the Southern Ocean Whale Sanctuary, which prohibits all commercial whaling within its borders, consisting of nearly all of the Antarctic Southern Ocean.[17] Even so, Japan in 2005 announced its intention to undertake Whale Research Program under Special Permit in the Antarctic (JARPA II), a large-scale Antarctic program, which began the next season. It is widely reported that much of the whale meat generated by JARPA II ends up for sale in fish markets for human consumption.

The conflict between Japan's "scientific whaling" program and the Australian government became joined in 1980. That year Australia's Parliament repealed the Whaling Act 1960 and replaced it with the Whale Protection Act of 1980. Legal protection for whales under Australian law was again reinforced in 1999 as Parliament enacted new legislation, the Environment Protection and Biodiversity Conservation Act 1999 (EPBC Act). The act establishes an Australian Whale Sanctuary (AWS) to help assure the conservation of whales and other cetaceans and acknowledges the "formal recognition of the high level of protection and management afforded to cetaceans" by Australia's government.

Australia's steadfast antiwhaling position over the past 20 years concentrated on Japan and boiled over into Australia's Federal Court in 2004. The case was brought by Humane Society International (HSI), a public interest organization, against Kyodo Senpaku Kaisha Ltd. (Kyodo), a Japanese company engaged in killing whales in the Southern Ocean, specifically in the AWS, within the claimed exclusive economic zone (EEZ) off the Australian Antarctic Territory (AAT).

The key questions raised by HSI's suit are, first, whether Japan had violated the EPBC Act and, second, whether Australia had the capacity to impose legal authority over the Japanese whaling fleet. The court reasoned that within the context of the 1982 UNCLOS and the provisions of the EPBC Act, Australia's EEZ and attendant whale sanctuary did extend into Antarctic circumpolar waters. Therefore, the court concluded that because the Japanese killed whales within the AAT, they violated the Australian EPBC Act. Subsequently, the court issued an injunction to Kyodo, effective 15 January 2008, to refrain from the further killing, injuring, taking, or interfering with any Antarctic minke, fin, or humpback whales in the AWS bordering the AAT. Australia thus became the first state to judicially find that Japan's whaling in the Southern Ocean Sanctuary was unlawful under national or international law. Significant to note, however, is that Japan publicly indicated in 2008 that it would ignore the Australian Federal Court's ruling. The justification for this was not unreasonable. Japan, along with 187 other states, does not recognize Australia's sovereignty on the continent nor its legal authority to declare jurisdictional zones (i.e., an Australian EEZ or a whale sanctuary) offshore Antarctica. Nearly all states, including Japan, interpret this to mean that all circumpolar Antarctic seas should be considered high seas, simply because no recognized sovereign coastal states exist within the Antarctic Treaty area.

The facts described above underscore the situation that Australia and Japan, two original parties to the Antarctic Treaty, remain at serious loggerheads over the Japanese government's continued support for whaling in the Southern Ocean, most particularly in waters offshore the AAT. Their treaty relationship is no doubt further strained by the cosmetic character of Japan's legal rationale for whaling, i.e., through special permits issued for "scientific research."

This whaling dispute escalated to a new legal level on 1 June 2010, when Australia instituted proceedings before the International Court of Justice against the Japanese government, alleging that "Japan's continued pursuit of a large scale programme of whaling under the Second Phase of its Japanese Whale Research Programme under Special Permit in the Antarctic ('JARPA II') [is] in breach of obligations assumed by Japan under the International Convention for the Regulation of Whaling ('ICRW'), as well as its other international obligations for the preservation of marine mammals and marine environment."[18] Japan has agreed to go before the court to respond to these allegations and could eventually win on grounds that whaling for "scientific research" is permitted by Article VIII of the ICRW. Nonetheless, it appears certain that Australia is aiming to have Japan's whaling activity judged to be unlawful or at least shamed internationally in the court of world public opinion.

The issue still remains as to whether Japan's whaling policy threatens the very purpose and intent of other ATS instruments. For example, what environmental risks to the marine ecosystem in the Southern Ocean are posed by the activities of Japanese whalers? Can whaling as an activity be viewed as undermining the environmental principles set out in the Antarctic Treaty's Environmental Protocol? That is, does JARPA II as a national Japanese activity undercut the "protection of the Antarctic environment and dependent and [its] associated ecosystems and the intrinsic value of Antarctica, including its wilderness and aesthetic and dependent and associated ecosystems"? Specifically in this regard, do Japanese whaling activities produce "detrimental changes in the distribution, abundance or productivity of species of populations of species of fauna and flora" or cause "further jeopardy to endangered or threatened species or populations of such species" or lead to "degradation of, or substantial risk to, areas of biological, scientific, historic, aesthetic or wilderness significance" in the Antarctic marine ecosystem, as provided for in Article 3 of the Environmental Protocol? Should the aggressive confrontations between Japanese whaling vessels and environmental activists in Antarctic waters be viewed as a breach of the fiat that the Antarctic area must be used exclusively for peaceful purposes and not become the scene or object of international discord? Notwithstanding the mandate in Article VI of CCAMLR, might the Commission on the Conservation of Antarctic Marine Living Resources be empowered to take a bolder approach toward assessing the environmental impacts of Japan's whaling activities on species within the Antarctic Treaty area? Although these queries remain more hypothetical than realistic suggestions, they should not be dismissed outright.

A final challenge unrelated to political differences amongst the ATCPs merits mention. This is the impact of global forces, especially climate change, upon the Antarctic Treaty System. Scientists generally agree that global temperatures and levels of carbon dioxide in the atmosphere are rising. Of all the world's regions, the Antarctic Peninsula is particularly sensitive to small rises in the annual average temperature, which has increased by nearly 3°C since the Antarctic Treaty was negotiated. This is about 10 times faster than the average for the rest of the world, which makes the peninsula area worthy of serious scientific scrutiny. The rapid disintegration of the Larson

Ice Shelf in 2002, the collapse of the Wilkins Ice Shelf in 2008, and the calving since 1995 of giant icebergs the size of Delaware, Rhode Island, and Connecticut all graphically demonstrated the impacts that warmer waters are having around Antarctica's perimeter ice shelves. In addition, most glaciers on the Antarctic Peninsula are in pronounced retreat because of climate change, and 40% of the sea ice off the West Antarctic Peninsula has disappeared in the last 25 years. In the peninsula area, these climate changes have disrupted local penguin colonies and even compelled some of them to migrate south. The remaining 96% of the continent, however, shows no notable signs of either temperatures rise or loss of ice, a circumstance largely attributable to the cooling effects of the ozone hole over East Antarctica.

How best might the ATCPs deal with global climate disruption in the Antarctic? The answer lies in mobilizing more extensive scientific research efforts through the Scientific Committee on Antarctic Research to better understand the nature of the climate change problem and its impacts on the continent, circumpolar waters, and the indigenous wildlife, especially in the peninsula region. Ways and means must be devised to achieve closer coordination and collaboration in the ATCPs' efforts to tackle the serious effects of climate change on marine resources in the Southern Ocean, including Antarctic krill, the critical prey species in the Antarctic marine ecosystem. Global climate disruption has intensified the urgency of these concerns as rising temperatures continue to melt sea ice, thus destroying key habitat and nursery areas for Antarctic krill. Less sea ice means fewer Antarctic krill, and fewer krill means less food for penguins, seals, whales, finfish, and squid in the region.

The immediate impact of human activity on natural climate cycles, from ice sheet dynamics to wind and ocean currents, remains unclear. A practical strategy would be for leading ATCP science governments, the United States, Russia, Australia, the United Kingdom, Japan, and Germany, to place highest scientific priority on research aimed at studying climate disruption in the Antarctic. By so doing, greater efforts might be brought to bear on understanding these impacts, which might then lead to new insights and strategies that the ATCPs can apply in dealing with the causes and managing the effects of climate change in the circumpolar south. Although there is no silver bullet for solving global climate disruption in the Antarctic, the best scientific minds in the ATCPs could mobilize considerable energy and revenues toward seeking viable, long-term solutions.

Over the past five decades, the Antarctic Treaty has proved itself to be among the most successful multilateral agreements negotiated in the twentieth century. It demilitarizes, denuclearizes, and guarantees freedom of scientific research, exchange of information, and programmatic cooperation between its member states over one-tenth of the Earth's surface. But we now live in an era of accelerating technological development, rapidly unfolding globalization, and escalating natural resource demands. New pressures of economic need and political circumspection could generate negative impacts upon the cooperative character of the Antarctic Treaty regime. These include the possibility that claimant states might opt to implement national continental shelf claims offshore Antarctica or that companies or governments might undertake widespread unregulated bioprospecting activities in the treaty area or that tensions might become more exacerbated between Japan and Australia and antagonistic environmental activists over Japanese whaling in Antarctic waters. If any of these scenarios should occur, real risks and potentially high costs might be imposed upon the security of the Antarctic Treaty. Given the potentially grave consequences that these challenges could portend, they should be taken very seriously by all the Treaty Parties, but especially so by the ATCPs who have the most to lose by the treaty's unraveling.

NOTES

1. "The Antarctic Treaty," done 1 December 1959, entered into force 23 June 1961, 12 *United States Treaties and Other International Agreements* (UST) 794, *Treaties and Other International Acts Series* (TIAS) No. 4780, 402 *United Nations Treaty Series* (UNTS) 71.

2. The seven claimants are Argentina, Australia, Chile, France, New Zealand, Norway, and the United Kingdom. These seven plus Belgium, Japan, South Africa, the Soviet Union, and the United States were the original treaty members. By 2010, 47 states had become Treaty Parties. Of those, the original 12 and 16 others attained the status of Antarctic Treaty Consultative Parties (ATCPs), which are the participant decision-making governments that negotiate and adopt policies under the treaty. The acceding ATCPs are Brazil, Bulgaria, China, Ecuador, Finland, Germany, India, Italy, Republic of Korea, the Netherlands, Peru, Poland, Spain, Sweden, Ukraine, and Uruguay. The 19 Non-Consultative Parties are Austria, Belarus, Canada, Colombia, Cuba, Czech Republic, Democratic People's Republic of Korea, Denmark, Estonia, Greece, Guatemala, Hungary, Monaco, Papua New Guinea, Romania, Slovak Republic, Switzerland, Turkey, and Venezuela.

3. "Recommendation III-VIII," approved June 2, 1964, entered into force November 1, 1982, 17 UST 996, TIAS No. 6058 (1965), as modified in 24 UST 992, TIAS No. 7692 (1973),. The Agreed Measures were superseded by Annex II to the 1991 Protocol on Environmental Protection to the Antarctic Treaty when the protocol entered into force in 1998.

4. Done in London 1 June 1972, entered into force 11 March 1978, 29 UST 441, TIAS No. 8826.

5. Done in Canberra on 20 May 1980, entered into force 7 April 1982, 1329 UNTS 47.

6. "Protocol on Environmental Protection to the Antarctic Treaty," Doc. XI ATSCM/2, 21 June 1991, adopted 4 October 1991, entered into force 14 January 1998.

7. A highly detailed and lengthy instrument, the Convention on the Regulation of Antarctic Mineral Resource Activities, was negotiated by the ATCPs between 1982 and 1988. See Done 2 June 1988 in Wellington, New Zealand, opened for signature 25 November 1988, Doc. AMR/SCM/88/78 of 2 June 1988, reprinted in 28 *International Legal Materials* (ILM) 859 (1988). However, owing to critical public protests from environmental activists in France and Australia over the possibility of minerals development in Antarctica, the agreement was indefinitely shelved and never entered into force.

8. United Nations Convention on the Law of the Sea, Art. 76, para. 1, Dec. 10, 1982, 1833 U.N.T.S. 397, http://www.un.org/Depts/los/convention_agreements/texts/unclos/unclos_e.pdf [Hereinafter 1982 UNCLOS] (accessed 18 November 2010).

9. Commission on the Limits of the Continental Shelf (CLCS) Outer limits of the continental shelf beyond 200 nautical miles from the baselines: Submissions to the Commission: Submission by Australia, http://www.un.org/Depts/los/clcs_new/submissions_files/submission_aus.htm (accessed 18 November 2010).

10. Commission on the Limits of the Continental Shelf (CLCS).

11. Outer Limit of the Continental Shelf, Argentine Submission, Executive Summary, pp.11–16, 22, http://www.un.org/Depts/los/clcs_new/submissions_files/arg25_09/arg2009e_summary_eng.pdf (accessed 18 November 2010).

12. Continental Shelf Submission of Norway with respect to Bouvetoya and Dronning Maud Land (Executive Summary), http://www.un.org/Depts/los/clcs_new/submissions_files/nor30_09/nor2009_executive summary.pdf (accessed 18 November 2010).

13. Continental Shelf Preliminary Information of Chile, http://www.un.org/Depts/los/clcs_new/submissions_files/preliminary/chl2009 preliminaryinformation.pdf (accessed 18 November 2010).

14. United Kingdom, Note No. 168/08 (9 May 2008), http://www.un.org/Depts/los/clcs_new/submissions_files/gbr08/gbr_nv_9may2008.pdf (accessed 18 November 2010); Submission by United Kingdom of Great Britain and Northern Ireland, 11 May 2009, http://www.un.org/Depts/los/clcs_new/submissions_files/submission_gbr_45_2009.htm (accessed 18 November 2010).

15. Permanent Mission of France to the United Nations, Note No.HR/cl No. 69, February 2009, http://www.un.org/Depts/los/clcs_new/submissions_files/fra09/fra_note_feb2009e.pdf (accessed 18 November 2010).

16. Bureau of Oceans and International Environmental and Scientific Affairs, "Antarctic Treaty Consultative Meeting XXXII, Washington, Ministerial Declaration on the Fiftieth Anniversary of the Antarctic Treaty," 6 April 2009, http://www.state.gov/g/oes/rls/other/2009/121339.htm (accessed 23 April 2010).

17. The IWC is considering a proposal that would reauthorize commercial whale hunting in exchange for reducing the number of whales killed each year. Not surprisingly, this has touched off a serious controversy between IWC members and environmentalists. See Juliet Eilperin, "Panel Proposes Whaling Ban Compromise," *Washington Post*, A2, 24 April 2010.

18. International Court of Justice, "Australia Institutes Proceedings against Japan for Alleged Breach of International Obligations Concerning Whaling," Press Release No. 2010/16, 1 June 2010.

Sustainable Management in the Southern Ocean: CCAMLR Science

Denzil Miller

ABSTRACT. The Antarctic Treaty System promotes science as the basis for conserving and managing Antarctic resources. The 1980 Convention on the Conservation of Antarctic Marine Living Resources (CAMLR Convention) further advocates science, as well as a precautionary approach and ecosystem perspective to manage harvesting of Antarctic marine living resources. This review presents case studies to illustrate the CAMLR Commission's (CCAMLR) use of science, precaution, and an ecosystem approach to managing Antarctic fisheries. The case studies illustrate CCAMLR's use of small-scale management units, bycatch measures, spatial management measures, and ecosystem-directed initiatives. These various studies highlight the value of science to CCAMLR's management efforts and the utility of CCAMLR as a model of large-scale marine ecosystem management.

INTRODUCTION

The 1959 Antarctic Treaty stands alone as an instrument of conflict prevention, strategic accommodation, and political cooperation, largely because of the sovereignty accommodations in Article IV (Zumberge and Kimball, 1986). Most notably, Articles II and III of the Antarctic Treaty provide for "freedom of scientific investigation in Antarctica" and promote "international cooperation in scientific investigation." Consequently, the freedom of scientific investigation in Antarctica may be viewed as a key element in the Antarctic Treaty's promotion of peace, cooperation, and the progress of all humankind.

However, things were not always this way. During the nineteenth and twentieth centuries, sealers and whalers hunted fur seals (*Arctocephalus gazellae*), elephant seals (*Mirounga leonina*), and the great whales (predominantly baleen whales, *Baleonoptera* spp.) in the Southern Ocean nearly to extinction.[1] Indeed, the Antarctic Treaty responds to this history by seeking to preserve and conserve the Antarctic's living resources (Article IX, paragraph 1(f)).

Two subsequent agreements underscored the Antarctic Treaty's conservation "ethic": the 1964 Agreed Measures for the Conservation of Antarctic Fauna and Flora (Agreed Measures) and the 1972 Convention for the Conservation of Antarctic Seals (CCAS). The latter aims to "promote and achieve the objectives of protection, scientific study and rational use of Antarctic seals, and to maintain a satisfactory balance within the ecological system." Together, the

Denzil Miller, Institute for Marine and Antarctic Studies, University of Tasmania, Private Bag 129, Hobart, TAS, 7001 Australia. Correspondence: denzilgmiller@gmail.com.

Antarctic Treaty, Agreed Measures, and CCAS became the founding elements of the Antarctic Treaty System (ATS).[2]

Extensive harvesting of finfish in the Subantarctic during the late 1960s and mid-1970s and an emerging interest in large-scale krill (*Euphausia superba*) exploitation raised concerns about fisheries sustainability in the Antarctic Treaty area (south of 60°S) and beyond. In response, Recommendation VIII-10 from the 1975 Eighth Antarctic Treaty Consultative Meeting (ATCM VIII) noted the need to "promote and achieve within the framework of the Antarctic Treaty, the objectives of protection, scientific study and rational use of [Antarctic] marine living resources." Again, the importance of science was recognised as a basis for the protection and rational (i.e., sustainable) use of such resources.

In 1977, the Scientific Committee on Antarctic Research (SCAR) and the Scientific Committee on Oceanic Research (SCOR) sponsored the Biological Investigations of Marine Antarctic Systems and Stocks (BIOMASS) program to "gain a deeper understanding of the structure and dynamic functioning of the Antarctic marine ecosystem as a basis for the future management of potential living resources" (El-Sayed, 1994:3). Together with three United Nations Food and Agriculture Organisation reports (Eddie, 1977; Everson, 1977; Grantham, 1977), BIOMASS highlighted the importance of krill as a keystone species in the Antarctic marine ecosystem.

Growing recognition of the ecosystem role of krill heightened concerns that its large-scale exploitation could have severe repercussions for Antarctic birds, seals, and whales that depend on it (Mitchell and Sandbrook, 1980). Over the next eight years, BIOMASS sponsored substantial research (including the first large-scale acoustic assessment of krill abundance in 1981, the First International BIOMASS Experiment) to investigate the ecosystem vulnerability of unsustainable krill harvesting (El-Sayed, 1994).

At the same time, Recommendation IX-2 from the Ninth Antarctic Treaty Consultative Meeting (1977) called on Treaty Parties to contribute to scientific research on Antarctic marine living resources, observe interim guidelines on their conservation, and schedule a special meeting to establish a conservation regime for these resources. This Second Special Antarctic Consultative Meeting comprised a series of meetings from 1978 to 1980 and concluded with the signing of the Convention on the Conservation of Antarctic Marine Living Resources (CAMLR Convention, hereinafter referred to as the "Convention" unless otherwise indicated) in Canberra on 20 May 1980.[3] The Convention entered into force on 7 April 1982.

Although developed under the Antarctic Treaty's patronage, the CAMLR Convention stands alone as a legally binding agreement, and its attached Commission has its own legal personality.[4] The Convention applies to a broader area than the Antarctic Treaty and sets the northern boundary of the Antarctic marine ecosystem as the Antarctic Convergence, now known as the Antarctic Polar Front (Convention Article I) (Figure 1). The convergence is a circum-Antarctic, biogeographic boundary where cold, northward-flowing Antarctic waters sink beneath warmer southward-moving subtropical waters. South of the convergence, krill is the dominant species (Miller and Hampton, 1988) and therefore key to understanding and managing the Antarctic ecosystem.

Article I of the CAMLR Convention identifies Antarctic marine living resources as "populations of fin fish, molluscs, crustaceans and all other species of living organisms, including birds, found south of the Antarctic Convergence." The Antarctic marine ecosystem is defined as the "complex of relationships of Antarctic marine living resources with each other and the physical environment."

In the remainder of this paper, I use case studies to illustrate the crucial role of science in addressing the Convention's key objectives. It will be shown that science has come to underpin CCAMLR's standing as "the leader to follow" (Willock and Lack, 2006) in sustainable management of marine living resources.

CONVENTION OBJECTIVES AND THE ROLE OF SCIENCE

Convention Objectives

The Convention's primary objective is "the conservation of Antarctic marine living resources" (Article II, paragraph 2), with the term "conservation" being considered to include "rational use." Article II, paragraph 3, indicates that any harvesting and associated activities in the Convention area should be conducted in accordance with the Convention and with the principles of conservation outlined in paragraphs 3(a) to 3(c). These principles include

- "prevention of decrease in the size of any harvested population to levels below those which ensure its stable recruitment";
- "maintenance of the ecological relationships between harvested, dependent and related populations of Antarctic marine living resources"; and

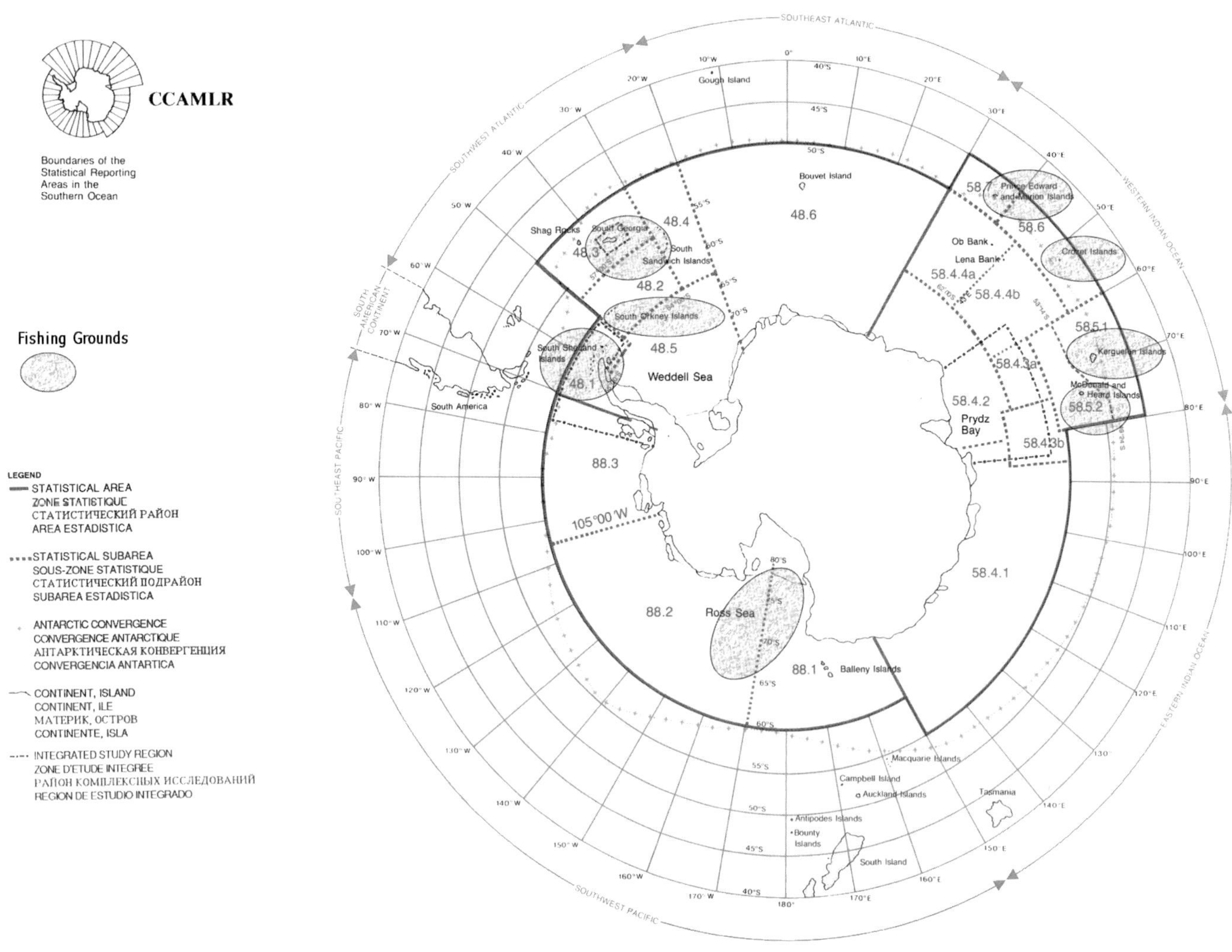

FIGURE 1. The CCAMLR area, showing boundaries, statistical areas, and fishing grounds.

- "prevention of changes or minimisation of the risk of changes in the marine ecosystem which are not potentially reversible over two or three decades."

The potential changes specifically identified include direct and indirect impacts of harvesting, the effects of alien (i.e., introduced) species, and the effects of environmental change(s). Under Article II, the management approach adopted by CCAMLR is characterised as being

- "precautionary," which means that CCAMLR collects data as it can, then weighs the extent and effect of uncertainties and gaps (i.e., "deficiencies") in such data before taking a management decision; and
- based on an "ecosystem" approach, which ideally takes into account the delicate and complex relationships between organisms (of all sizes) and physical processes (such as currents, sea temperature, etc.) that constitute or impact the Antarctic marine ecosystem.

The Convention thus not only regulates fishing for target species but also aims to ensure that "harvesting activity" does not compromise other species or harm the environment.

Since the Convention's entry into force, the ecosystem and precautionary approaches in Article II have both directed and challenged CCAMLR's conservation efforts (Constable et al., 2000; Miller, 2002). The ecological uncertainties associated with full and effective implementation of the Convention's provisions have forced innovative thinking to provide a holistic, scientific, and ecologically based approach to regulate fishing on target resources and minimise the indirect effects of harvesting on the Antarctic marine ecosystem as a whole.

The Role of Science

Article IX, paragraph 1(f), requires that CCAMLR Conservation Measures (CMs) be formulated, adopted, or revised on "the basis of the best scientific evidence available" subject to the provisions of paragraph 5 in the same article.[5] For that purpose, CCAMLR must take full account of any relevant measures or regulations adopted by the ATCM or by existing fisheries commissions that manage target species that enter the Convention area. This requirement raises questions as to what scientific evidence is required and how that evidence is to be integrated into the CCAMLR management process.

The Scientific Basis for CCAMLR Management

General Basis

The term "scientific evidence" in Convention Article IX, paragraph 1(f), implies that scientific information, or advice, should be formally presented to CCAMLR for management purposes. In 1990 (CCAMLR, 1990: paragraph 7.6), the Commission clearly endorsed this assumption and agreed that "it should regard the Scientific Committee as the source of the best scientific evidence available," an agreement that effectively endorses the provenance of the Scientific Committee's scientific advice.[6]

One of the first scientific challenges faced by CCAMLR was to use a spatially explicit, iterative, interactive, and scientific process to describe the scale-dependent organization of species such as krill (Figure 2). To that end, CCAMLR's approach to fishery management can be viewed as a series of interdependent ecological associations of which fishing (Miller, 2000), individual species, and their ecological interactions are bound in space and time. By specifically accounting for key ecological factors, this approach facilitates assessment of "ecosystem status" and "health," as well as the scientific and systematic development of sustainable management measures for krill in particular (Everson, 2002).[7]

Much has been written about CCAMLR's management approach (e.g. Agnew, 1997; Constable et al., 2000; Constable, 2002; Everson, 2002; Miller, 2002), and Figure 3 summarises its early evolution for the krill fishery. Nevertheless, the question of how to manage fisheries in an ecosystem (i.e., multispecies) context is an ongoing and difficult issue, as well as one that particularly vexes CCAMLR (Constable, 2005).

CCAMLR Ecosystem Monitoring Program

The CCAMLR Ecosystem Monitoring Program (CEMP) was initiated in 1985 (Agnew, 1997) to improve CCAMLR's understanding of potential interactions between fisheries, harvested species, and the environment. To follow an ecosystem-based management approach, Constable (2002) has indicated (Figure 4) that CCAMLR should take explicit account of harvesting on target, dependent, and related species. To that end, CEMP focuses on monitoring key life history parameters of selected dependent, or "indicator," species likely to be affected by the availability of harvested species (Agnew, 1997; Miller, 2007).

Therefore, CCAMLR must not only take into account the best available scientific information in their quest to meet the Convention's objectives, but also specifically allow for incomplete knowledge of ecosystem function(s) and uncertainty in the available information (Miller, 2007). To the extent possible, actual resource use is preceded and/or accompanied by surveys to assess resource potential, to monitor resource status, and to provide for associated analyses of ancillary data. The approach is not to manage the Antarctic marine ecosystem per se but, rather, to regulate human activities (i.e., harvesting) in that system. Science is the means to achieve this operationally (Butterworth, 1986), a point well illustrated by the temporal and spatial confines of "biophysical" interactions and the "fishery" illustrated in Figure 2.

CCAMLR's scientifically based management approach relies on four key actions to achieve the conservation principles outlined in Convention Article II, paragraph 3: (1) development of operational objectives ("measures") to determine the desired/agreed status for relevant species or ecosystem features, (2) development of methods to assess ecosystem status, (3) elaboration of decision rules to control harvesting in a manner that meets the Convention's objectives, and (4) development of methods to address uncertainty (including ecosystem functional ["physical world"] uncertainty). The outcomes of such an approach aim to establish scientific consensus in such a way that the consequence of various management actions can be identified and clearly understood.

To be effective, the CCAMLR management approach relies on clearly identified scientific requirements. In effect,

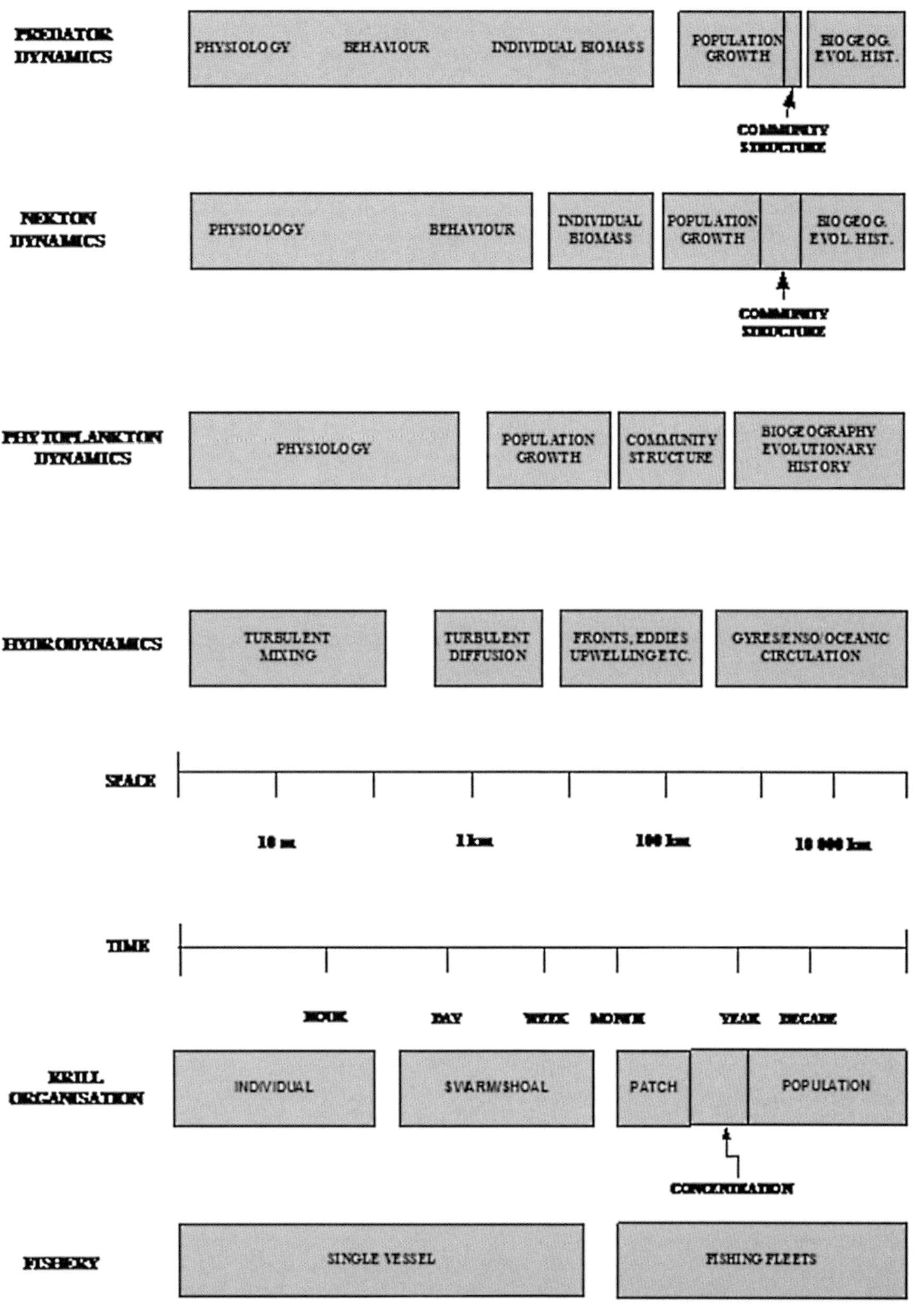

FIGURE 2. The spatial and temporal structure of krill distribution in relation to other Antarctic marine ecosystem components, the physical environment, and the fishery (after Miller, 2002).

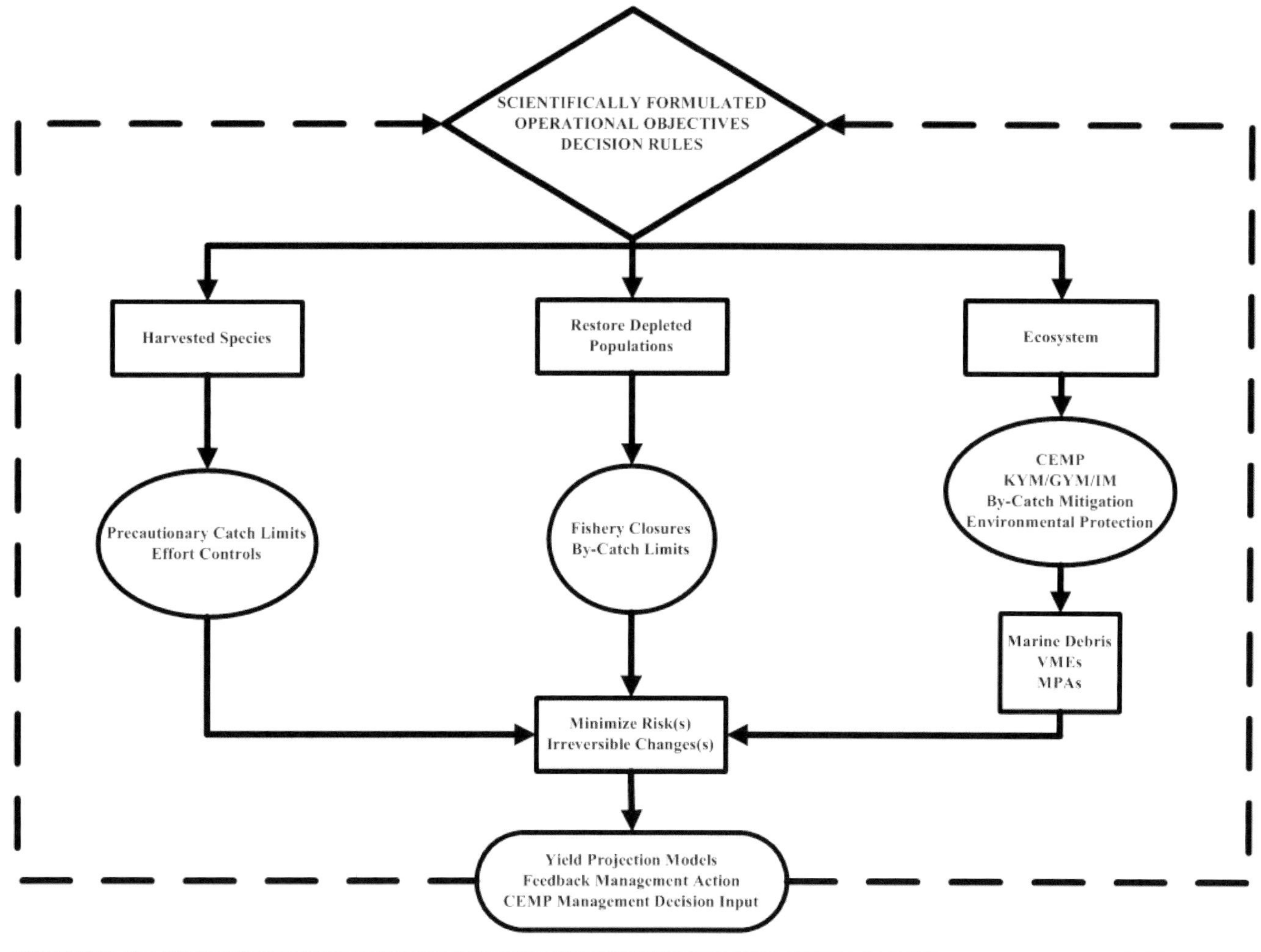

FIGURE 3. The CCAMLR's management approach to address Convention Article II objectives (after Miller, 2002). See text for explanation of various acronyms and activities.

it highlights the need, mandated by Article II, to (1) apply correct and timely decisions consistent with CCAMLR conservation principles, (2) undertake monitoring of sufficient power to prevent harvests from negatively affecting dependent predators, (3) allow sufficient time to detect and rectify harvest-induced changes in the ecosystem within two or three decades, and (4) refine precautionary assessments of harvested stock yield to account for new estimates of key demographic parameters. The approach also requires that (5) the precautionary yield of a target species such as krill is equally divided into small-scale management units (SSMUs) of appropriate scale to improve predictive power and spread any risk of irreversible ecosystem changes and (6) the development of operational objectives for nonharvested species to account for uncertainties is associated with ecosystem function and dynamic relationships among predators, particularly between predators and prey. All these considerations require scientific definition, elaboration, and monitoring.

The overall CCAMLR management procedure thus comprises a set of rules to adjust harvest levels on the basis of scientifically objective assessments (Kock, 2000). These rules are sufficiently rigorous and flexible to ensure that the conservation objectives illustrated have a high probability of being met. In practice, the status ("health") of the Antarctic marine ecosystem is effectively observed through monitoring (i.e., via CEMP). Ideally, regular assessments account for uncertainty associated with ecosystem function as well as potential relationships between monitoring and key ecosystem components and properties, including

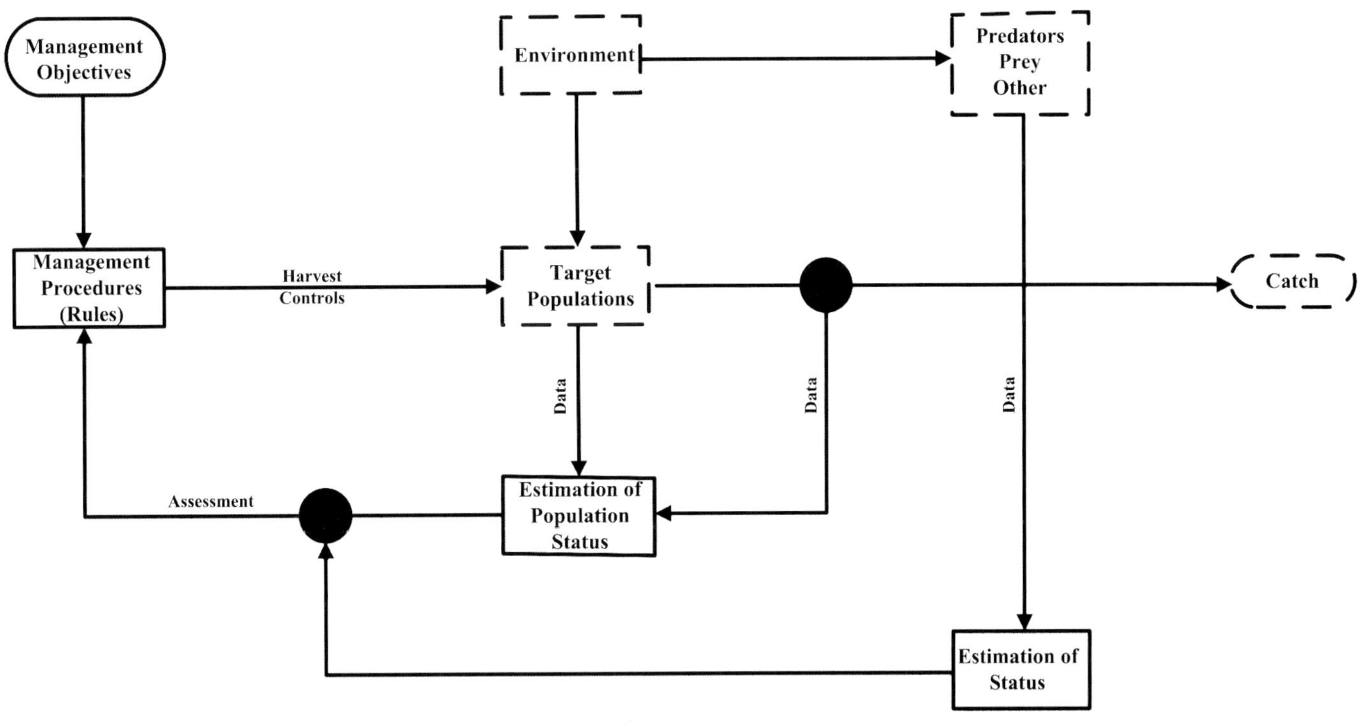

FIGURE 4. An ecosystem-based approach to manage effects of fishing on dependent and related species (adapted from Constable, 2002, with permission). Assessments (solid boxes) lead to decision rules for adjusting harvest controls to meet operational objectives. The physical world (dashed boxes) reflects ecosystem's actual state as observed by monitoring (e.g., via CEMP). Assessments take into account the uncertainty about how the physical world functions as well as how the monitoring program and physical world are related.

the physical environment. Full elaboration of the latter remains an important priority for CCAMLR in terms of fulfilling Convention Article II requirements.

CASE STUDIES

The case studies below outline CCAMLR's approach to managing krill and finfish fisheries; they include aspects of ecosystem management and protection. In each case the scientific aspects of the various approaches are emphasised. Although Convention Article II objectives address an essentially "new management ethos" and "conservation ethic" (Hewitt and Linen Low, 2000), the various case studies clearly show that CCAMLR has not relied on a single management approach alone. Rather, associated decisions are scientifically driven, iterative, and ongoing in an effort to address the key conservation challenges being faced. These challenges include

- assessing and monitoring harvested populations;
- defining and quantifying ecological interactions between harvested and other species (either dependent on or related to them); and
- estimating levels of depletion in order to effectively monitor restoration of depleted populations.

Fisheries Management

Finfish

Large-scale finfish harvesting preceded the Convention's entry into force and many stocks in the Convention area were seriously depleted by 1982 (Kock, 1992). Therefore, the first task CCAMLR faced was to seek scientific advice on sustainable catch levels for species other than krill (Agnew, 1997; Miller, 2002). Such advice initially came from available fishery data, and to determine catch limits, CCAMLR used Beverton and Holt's (1957) approach to estimate the maximum sustainable yield. By 1987, CCAMLR had begun to develop other measures to set fishing levels (Scientific Committee for the Conservation of Antarctic Marine Living Resources [SC-CAMLR], 1987). The introduction of $F_{0.1}$ (see Hilborn and Walters, 1992, for description) followed as a management standard for selected finfish species in the Convention area and fishery independent scientific survey data were used to "tune" estimates of stock yield (Kock, 2000).

In cases where stock assessments are data-scarce or where estimates of yield are largely uncertain, CCAMLR has come to mandate fishery-independent surveys as a prerequisite for opening any fishery. It also applies measures that ensure that fishery development proceeds at a pace commensurate with the ability to collect essential data for management (Sabourenkov and Miller, 2004).

During the early 1990s, CCAMLR became concerned that a management approach based on fishing mortality (F) alone might undermine Article II conservation principles if available yield(s) are not maximised and recruitment of young animals is compromised. As a consequence, CCAMLR began developing model-based approaches for dealing with uncertainty "unambiguously and unanimously" (Constable et al., 2000). These approaches are based on the conviction that spawning stock "escapement" is vital in determining sustainable levels of F (Kock, 2000). They use scientifically based, stochastic projection methods to incorporate and account for uncertainty in key biological parameters and to allow for random recruitment fluctuations (Constable et al., 2000).

Krill

For various reasons, the CCAMLR scientific community quickly realised that a single-species management approach for the krill fishery would be unlikely to safeguard ecosystem health, given the species' low trophic status, disparate distribution, and interactions with other species (Beddington and May, 1980; Miller, 2002). Recognising its management challenges, SC-CAMLR and the Committee developed an empirically based management procedure for krill comprising three inter-related elements (Miller, 1991): (1) collection and compilation of essential data, (2) analysis of such data to determine target stock status, and (3) ongoing action to align management objectives (including evaluation of analysed data and implementation of appropriate action).

The above procedures facilitated development of general concepts for implementing Article II provisions. These were accepted by SC-CAMLR and the Commission as being to

- keep the krill biomass at a level higher than might be the case if only single-species considerations are of concern so as to ensure sufficient krill escapement to meet reasonable predator requirements;
- accept that krill dynamics have a stochastic component and therefore focus on the lowest biomass that might occur over a future period, rather than on a mean biomass at the end of the period as might be the case in a single-species context; and
- ensure that any reduction of food to predators which may arise from krill harvesting does not affect land-based predators with restricted foraging ranges disproportionately compared to predators present in pelagic habitats.

The above concepts also provided the basis for the 1994 adoption of pre-agreed decision rules for setting annual krill yield (Table 1) over time. These rules were based on Beddington and Cooke's (1983) approach as modified by Butterworth et al. (1991). The modified approach is known as the krill yield model (KYM) and calculates annual krill yield (Y) as a proportion (λ) of estimated preexploitation biomass (B_0). Initially, the KYM allowed for more refined determinations of λ, using recruitment variability information from survey data, with particular attention being paid to the relationship between such

TABLE 1. CCAMLR three-part decision rule for selecting the proportionality coefficient γ value to set krill precautionary catch limits where yield (Y) is calculated as a proportion (γ) of preexploitation biomass (B_0) such that $Y = \gamma B_0$ (SC-CAMLR, 1994).

Rule	Proportionality Coefficient	Action
1	γ_1	γ is chosen so that the probability of the spawning stock biomass dropping below 20% of the preexploitation median level over a 20-year harvesting period is 10%
2	γ_2	γ is chosen so that the median krill escapement over a 20-year harvesting period is 75%
3	lower of γ_1 or γ_2	The lower of γ_1 and γ_2 is selected as the level for γ for the calculation of krill yield

variability and natural mortality (*M*) (de la Mare, 1994a, 1994b).

The KYM-attached decision rules use a 75% krill escapement level as the midpoint between making no allowance for krill predator needs (i.e., treating krill as a single-species fishery with 50% escapement) or providing complete protection for predators (i.e., no fishery) (Miller and Agnew, 2000). Exploring the functional relationships between krill and its predators thus remains high on CCAMLR's agenda with respect to direct, and indirect, interactions between the krill fishery, krill, and other species. Only with more complete knowledge of such functional relationships will it be possible to define krill escapement more precisely.

Generalised Management of Fisheries

Building on the KYM approach, Constable and de la Mare (1996) recognised that it was specifically tailored to assumptions concerning krill growth, fishing seasons, and the timing of spawning. Furthermore, yield could only be determined as a proportion of the estimated B_0. Therefore, Constable and de la Mare developed a more generally structured model (general yield model [GYM]) (Table 2) to allow flexibility in assessment of krill growth patterns, natural mortality, spawning, and fishing. The decision rules outlined in Table 1 were thus recast as general principles indicating that (1) escapement of the spawning stock is sufficient to avoid the likelihood of declining recruitment and (2) reserves of exploited harvest stock abundance are sufficient to fulfil dependent species (usually predators) needs. Stock trajectories can then be calculated from estimated levels of absolute recruitment (*R*) in relation to fishing mortality (*F*).

Although the GYM was specifically tailored for finfish assessments, its outputs for krill were remarkably similar to those of the KYM (Constable and de la Mare, 1996). Therefore, from 1994 onward, CCAMLR has used the GYM to determine long-term annual yields for harvested stocks in absolute terms rather than as a proportion of B_0. Examples of CMs formulated using the generalised approach include CM 51-01 (krill fishing in CCAMLR Statistical Area 48) as well as CMs 41-20 and 41-03 for toothfish (*Dissostichus eleginoides*) fishing in the same area.[8]

The CCAMLR continues to refine the scientific basis of its finfish fishery management approach. More recently, it has sought to integrate diverse data sets within a generalised stock assessment "package" (Hillary et al., 2006; Candy and Constable, 2008). Such data include multiple fisheries catch-at-age proportions, fisheries-independent research survey data, and mark-recapture data from different fisheries. These techniques will undoubtedly improve future management efforts. Similarly, advances in determination of krill age, growth, and maturation (Brown et al., 2010; Virtue et al., 2010) have again raised interest in exploring age-based assessments of the species' annual productivity and yield.

Illegal, Unreported, and Unregulated Fishing

Illegal, unreported, and unregulated (IUU) fishing has seriously undermined CCAMLR's efforts to manage the Patagonian toothfish (*Dissostichus eleginoides*) fishery in the Indian Ocean (Agnew, 1999; Miller, 2007). As a result, total toothfish removals and fishery-related mortality (*F*) from the CCAMLR area are largely uncertain. In response, CCAMLR began to develop a standard methodology to estimate IUU catches in the Convention area (CCAMLR, 2005: pars. 8.3, 8.4) in 2005. In 2007, CCAMLR agreed to continue using the traditional method developed by SC-CAMLR for estimating IUU catches, which is based on

TABLE 2. Variation of the krill yield model and its later modification into the general yield model (after Miller, 2002).

Formula	Key features	Source
$Y = 0.5MB_0$	0.5 too high due to uncertainties in estimating natural mortality (*M*) and recruitment (*R*)	Gulland (1971) formulation
$Y = \lambda B_0$	Used for determining CCAMLR krill precautionary catch limits with λ applied as a single proportionality constant	Butterworth et al. (1994)
$Y = \gamma B_0$	Refinement of above with absolute recruitment (*R*) and natural mortality (*M*) being subsumed into a single calculated constant γ. The stock is tracked stochastically over a 20-year period with an appropriate yield level being selected by a three-part, conservatively applied decision rule to designate the γ value (see Table 1)	Constable and de la Mare (1996)

vessel sightings and other information (CCAMLR, 2007: paragraph 10.51). More recently, CCAMLR has agreed to continue development of other methods, such as an index to determine the density of licensed vessels fishing on particular grounds. Clearly, procedures are needed to refine IUU vessel identification as well as systematically and objectively determining breakdowns in compliance with CCAMLR CMs.

Ecosystem Effects

General Effects

The SC-CAMLR recognised that krill fishing may cause intolerable variations in the trophic dynamics of Antarctic marine ecosystems (SC-CAMLR, 1995: Annex 4; Constable et al., 2000). Although the KYM approach implicitly accounted for this possibility, CEMP was predicated on the assumption that the information it obtained could be used to predict the impact of different harvesting strategies and thereby provide an opportunity to avoid any serious deterioration in ecosystem health. To that end, CEMP would seek to improve understanding of relationships between fisheries, target species, and target species predators.

Over the past decade, the CCAMLR scientific community has sought to develop predictive models of such relationships to refine the decision rules used in conjunction with the KYM and GYM. These predictive models have provided a new basis for setting catch limits that do not pose significant risks to ecosystem predators (e.g., Constable, 2001, 2005; Hill et al., 2007). Such efforts are ongoing and important physical and biological interactions have been identified (SC-CAMLR, 1995, Annex 4). However, models estimating krill availability to predators remain limited (e.g., Murphy et al., 1988; Murphy, 1995), and those examining the consequences of different levels of such availability are rare (e.g., Butterworth and Thomson, 1995; Mangel and Switzer, 1998). One notable advance has been the development of a framework (e.g., Constable, 2005) to evaluate krill management procedures in an ecosystem context. The framework is particularly noteworthy because it allows and, indeed, facilitates explicit assessment of uncertainty in the modelled systems.

Despite such advances, the explicit linkage of CEMP-derived predator information, krill availability, and fishing activity remains elusive in the formulation of CCAMLR CMs aimed at fully addressing all the objectives of Convention Article II. As highlighted by Reid et al. (2008), work is still required to

- detect the effects of fishing on any process/ecosystem component in an operationally useful way and with respect to an agreed reference point(s),
- remain cognisant of appropriate trade-offs between CEMP aims and prevailing uncertainty about ecosystem function, and
- promote a realistic appreciation of CEMP's ability to provide data relevant to a specific management objective for the krill fishery or krill-associated predators.

Small-Scale Management Units

The CCAMLR krill CMs require precautionary catch limits to be subdivided into smaller spatial management units known as SSMUs (Figure 5).[9] A set of candidate options have been proposed for such subdivision in CCAMLR Area 48 (West Atlantic; Constable and Nicol, 2002; Hewitt et al., 2004). Hill et al. (2007) have compiled parameters for various available krill ecosystem dynamic models to assess options based on plausible limits for parameter values. This complex work continues despite the perception that the krill fishery is expanding now and will continue to expand in the future. The studies involved may help resolve some of the concerns identified by Everson (2002) regarding fishery, krill, and predator interactions, as well as a reduction in krill availability due to shifts in the species' distribution (SC-CAMLR, 1990, 1994; Murphy, 1995).

Once krill catches reach a "trigger," the total allowable catch set in CCAMLR CM 51-01 is to be subdivided into smaller areas (including SSMUs). Anticipating growth in the krill fishery, SC-CAMLR and the Committee advised that the 620,000 tonne trigger in CM 51-01 could be concentrated in a single area (SC-CAMLR, 2009: pars. 4.26, 4.28). However, this would increase the risk of significant adverse impacts on krill-dependant predators, especially those that are land based (SC-CAMLR, 2009: pars. 3.126–3.132). With that concern in mind, SC-CAMLR and the Committee have advised the Commission to spatially distribute krill fishing effort to avoid large catches in restricted areas as the trigger level is approached. Five models have been provided to distribute the krill trigger level over CCAMLR Statistical Area 48 (SC-CAMLR, 2009: table 1). Drawing on this approach, the Commission agreed to an interim measure (CM 51-09) to distribute the trigger level proportionately between Statistical Subareas 48.1 and 48.4 (CCAMLR, 2009: pars. 12.60, 12.61). This interim measure will lapse at the end of the 2010/2011 fishing season but will be kept under review by SC-CAMLR and the Commission.

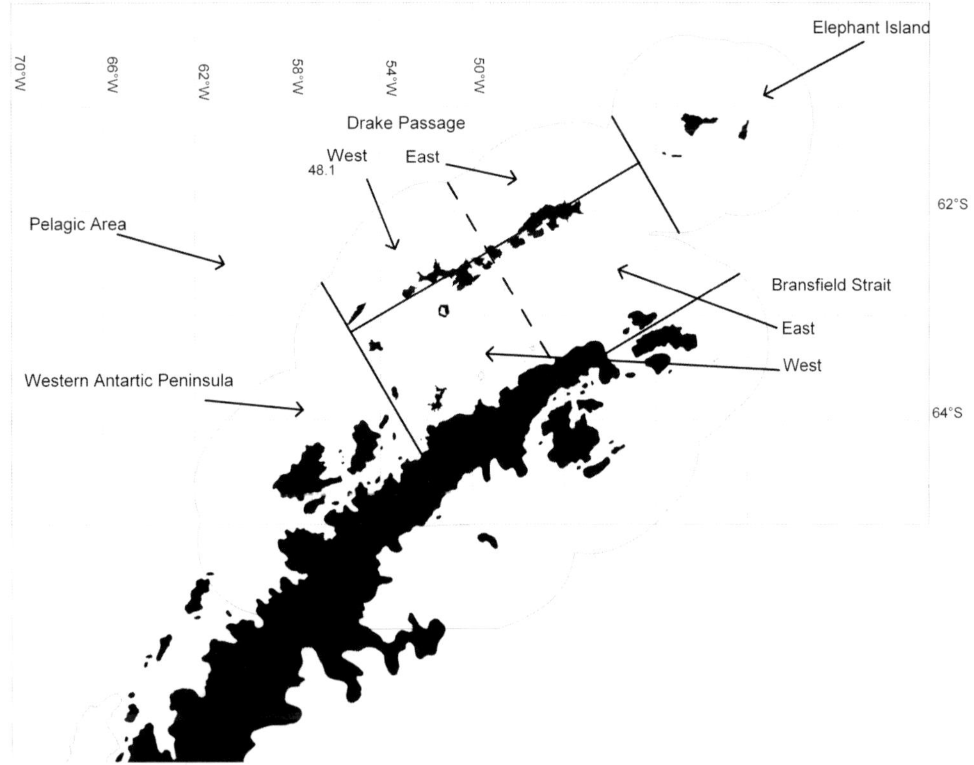

FIGURE 5. Small-scale management units (SSMUs) in CCAMLR Statistical Area 48.1. From SC-CAMLR (2002: Annex 4, Appendix D, fig. 37).

Bycatch

The SC-CAMLR and the Commission also have been concerned about fisheries bycatch. Fortunately, CCAMLR's management of seabird bycatch during toothfish longline fishing (CM 25-02) has been a notable success (Miller, 2007). The number of seabirds incidentally caught has been dramatically reduced from tens of thousands in the CCAMLR area a decade and a half ago to a few individual birds. Similar measures have reduced the entanglement of seals and other animals (CCAMLR, 2009: paragraph 6.4) in fishing devices (e.g., nets and pots) as well as marine debris. Scientific observers appointed under the CCAMLR International Scheme of Scientific Observation play an important role in monitoring incidental seabird bycatch, deploying mitigation devices, and educating fishers to the dangers of fisheries-induced mortality caused by the direct effects of fishing activity on nontarget species.[10]

A notable exception to the above has been in the French exclusive economic zone around Kerguelen and the Crozet Islands, where more than 1,000 birds were taken annually (SC-CAMLR, 2008: paragraph 5.3) until a dramatic improvement in the application of mitigation measures over the past two years (CCAMLR, 2009: paragraphs 6.5–6.8).

Other measures to monitor and mitigate fishery bycatch include reporting procedures (e.g., CM 41-08, Annex 41-08A, paragraph iv), bycatch limits or proportions (CM 41-02, paragraphs 6 and 7), and "move-on" rules when bycatch is encountered (CM 41-02, paragraph 8). One of SC-CAMLR's scientific working groups evaluates these measures periodically to provide appropriate advice as needed. Directed scientific studies continue to assess the species that are, or may be, taken as fisheries bycatch (e.g., the 2009 "Year of the Skate"; CCAMLR, 2008: paragraph 4.55).

Spatial Management

General Management

Apart from SSMUs, CCAMLR is considering, or has initiated, a number of spatially bound measures to address the precautionary and ecosystem-directed elements of Article II. One such measure (CM 26-01), applied to the entire CCAMLR area, aims to minimise the risks of alien-species contamination and marine pollution from fishing vessels. This measure has established specific controls on dumping, or discharge, and the translocation of poultry in the Convention area south of 60°S, where the effects of such events are likely to be most acutely felt. The measure has been recently modified to refine definitions of "offal," "discards," "releases," and "benthic" organisms (CCAMLR, 2009: paragraph 12.28).

Additional measures (e.g., CM 91-01) protect CEMP sites, and others set ice-strengthening requirements for fishing vessels at high latitude (Resolution 20/XXII), general vessel safety standards (Resolution 23/XXIII), and ballast-water exchange restrictions (Resolution 28/XXVII). Most recently, Resolution 29/XXVIII urges CCAMLR members to ratify the 1989 International Convention on Salvage, or any other measures deemed appropriate, to facilitate the recovery of reasonable expenses incurred by vessel operators assisting other vessels, or other property in danger, in the CCAMLR area (CCAMLR, 2009: paragraph 12.87). All such measures have drawn on advice from SC-CAMLR and the Committee in terms of mitigating potential dangers to the Antarctic marine environment.

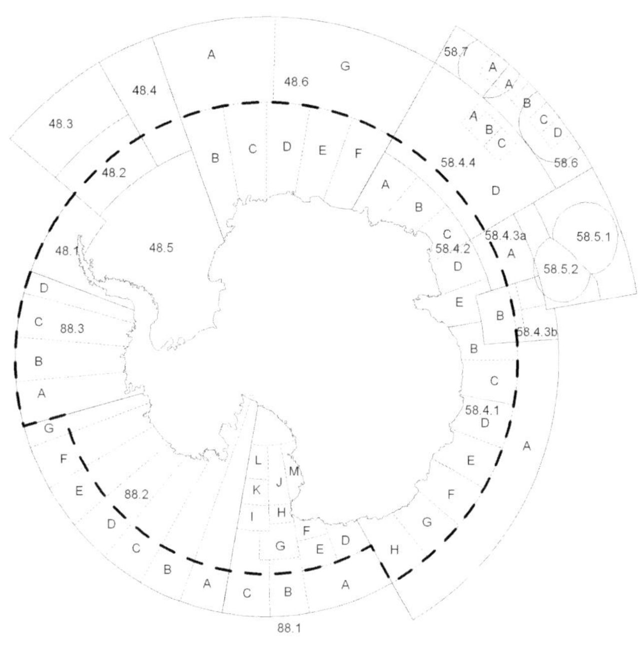

FIGURE 6. Small-scale research units (SSRUs) in the CCAMLR area. From CCAMLR CM 41-01.

Small-Scale Research Units

The CCAMLR has developed small-scale research units (SSRUs) to spread the risk of spatially concentrated fishing when scientific knowledge of the stock(s) concerned is limited (e.g., CM 41-09, paragraph 3). Such units were initially applied to experimental crab fisheries (CCAMLR: 1993, paragraph 8.36, CM 75/XII; Watters, 1997) but have since been expanded to various exploratory toothfish fisheries (CM 41-05, fig. 1; Figure 6). They not only impose a degree of precaution but also promote collection of essential operational data from the fishery, often a responsibility of the CCAMLR scientific observers aboard the vessels involved. In these terms, the use of SSRUs may be viewed as an inexpensive alternative to research vessel surveys as data may be consistently gathered from wide areas, with scientific observers providing the necessary scientific objectivity to render such data worthwhile.

Marine Protected Areas

Over the past decade, CCAMLR has considered implementing spatial management measures to facilitate biodiversity conservation consistent with targets set by the 2002 World Summit on Sustainable Development (WSSD). The CCAMLR and the Committee for Environmental Protection (CEP) have afforded high priority to the designation of Southern Ocean marine areas for biodiversity conservation (CCAMLR, 2004: paragraph 4.13; CEP, 2006: paragraphs 94–101).[11] In 2007 CCAMLR sponsored a workshop to develop benthic and pelagic bioregionalisations (CCAMLR, 2007: paragraphs 7.3–7.19) based on the results of a World Wildlife Fund–Peregrine Travel sponsored meeting of experts in 2006 (Grant et al., 2006).[12] These bioregionalisations are being used to design a representative network of CCAMLR marine protected areas (MPAs).

In 2007, CCAMLR also agreed to continue consolidating the scientific rationale for the above MPA network (CCAMLR, 2007: paragraph 7.18). It agreed that the network should focus on, but not be limited to, 11 priority areas identified by SC-CAMLR and the Committee (CCAMLR, 2008: paragraph 7.2(vi); SC-CAMLR, 2008: Annex 4, fig. 12; Figure 7a). Development of the network is ongoing and draws on a work plan outlined by SC-CAMLR (2008: paragraph 3.55). The network also is an important topic in the ongoing dialogue between SC-CAMLR and the Committee, and the CEP (CEP, 2009a; 2009b). Most significantly, the 2009 CCAMLR meeting adopted CM 91-03 (Figure 7b), which will contribute to

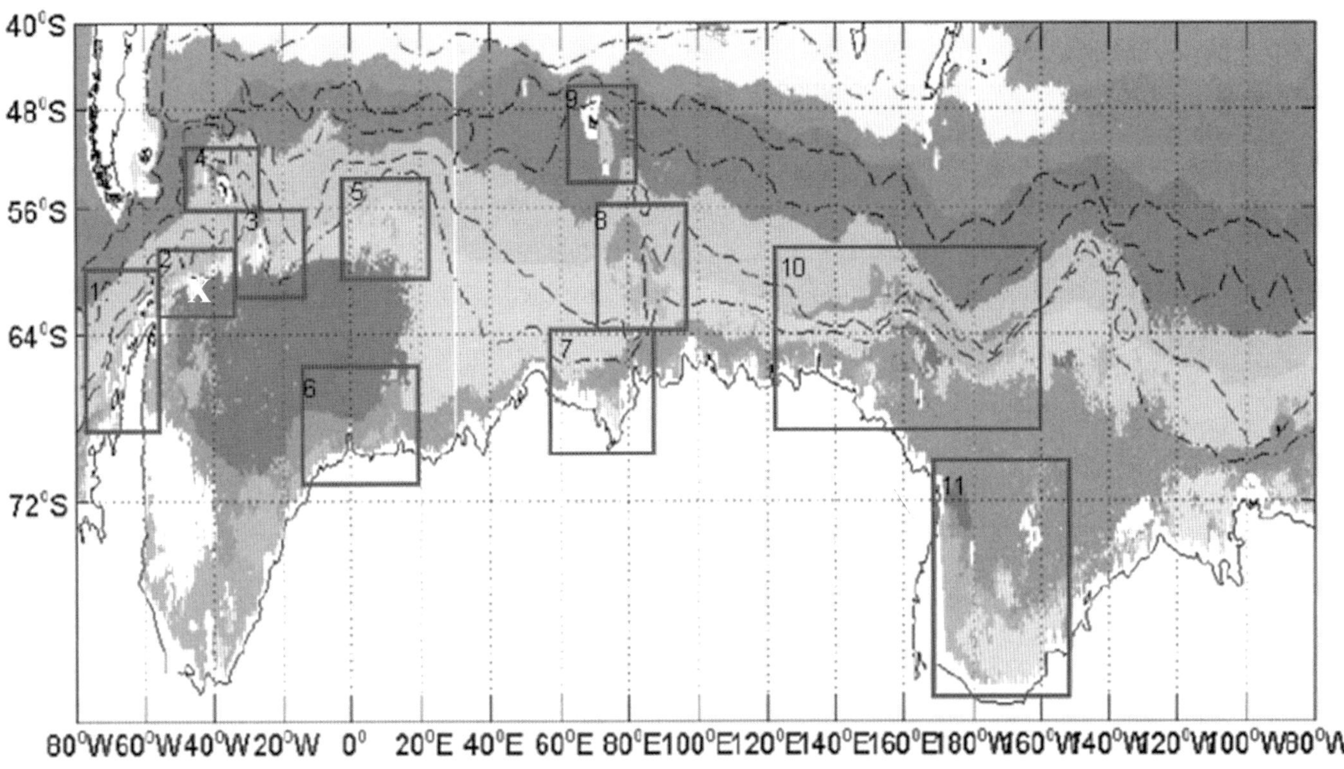

FIGURE 7a. The CCAMLR priority areas for identifying marine protected areas (MPAs) as part of a representative network of such sites (CCAMLR, 2008). Numbers refer to area and are not in priority order. 1, Western Antarctic Peninsula; 2, South Orkney Islands; 3, South Sandwich Islands; 4, South Georgia; 5, Maud Rise; 6, eastern Weddell Sea; 7, Prydz Bay; 8, Banzare Bank; 9, Kerguelen; 10, northern Ross Sea/East Antarctica; 11, Ross Sea Shelf. From SC-CAMLR (2008: Annex 4, fig. 12). X—South Orkney Islands MPA (see Figure 7b and text for details).

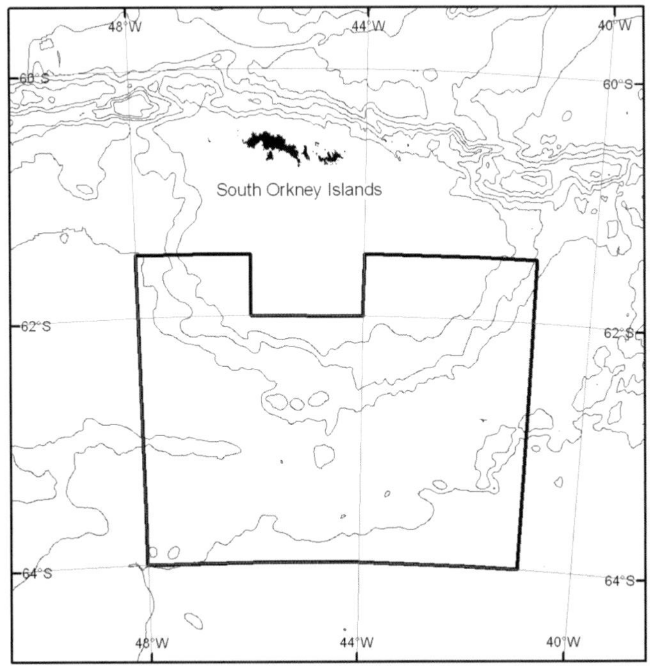

FIGURE 7b. The CCAMLR South Orkney Islands Southern Shelf Marine Protected Area. Depth contours are at 1000 m intervals (CCAMLR CM 91-03).

biodiversity conservation in Subarea 48.2 (South Orkney Islands), as well as to a network of protected areas across the CCAMLR area (SC-CAMLR, 2009: pars. 3.14–3.19; CCAMLR, 2009: paragraph 12.86). The biodiversity conservation area in Subarea 48.2 is one of the first of its kind to be adopted for the high seas and illustrates the value of science in the conservation of marine living resources. Conversely, some view CM 91-03 as little more than a compromise arrangement which required the originally proposed area to be reduced to avoid the inclusion of potential fishing grounds (CCAMLR, 2009: paragraph 7.17). Nevertheless, there is general agreement that the measure itself is an important milestone toward the achievement of a representative system of MPAs within the Convention area by 2012 (CCAMLR, 2009: paragraph 7.19).

Vulnerable Marine Ecosystems

United Nations General Assembly (UNGA) Resolution 61/105 (UNGA, 2007) calls upon Regional Fisheries Management Organizations or Arrangements (RFMO/As) to close areas to bottom fishing until appropriate measures are in place to prevent significant adverse impacts on vulnerable marine ecosystems (VMEs). The resolution (UNGA, 2007: paragraph 83) urged RFMO/As to implement relevant VME measures by 31 December 2008. Despite a recent increase in research (Brandt et al., 2007), the data available for managing benthic fauna in the Southern Ocean remains sparse.

The CCAMLR responded to the UNGA resolution by formulating CMs 22-06 and 22-07. The CM 22-06 freezes the current bottom fishing footprint to areas approved for such fisheries in the 2006/2007 fishing season. The CM 22-07 provides a format for identifying VMEs encountered during scientific research cruises, defines a VME "encounter" during fishing operations, and describes the resulting action to be taken by a vessel. Two such notifications were made in 2008 (CCAMLR, 2008).

To determine when a VME has been encountered under CM 22-06, vessels are required to monitor the catch of agreed VME indicator organisms in an identified sampling segment. When 10 or more VME indicator units are recovered in one segment, the area is considered a "VME risk area," and vessels are required to complete hauling in the area and immediately communicate its location to CCAMLR and their flag state. On receiving this information, CCAMLR then notifies all fishing vessels in the fishery (and their flag states) that the area is closed to fishing.

Longline fishing targeting toothfish under CM 22-07 took place in seven CCAMLR subareas/divisions between December 2008 and February 2009. The highest fishing effort occurred in Subareas 88.1 and 88.2 in the Ross Sea, and seven VME risk areas (five in Subarea 88.1 and two in Subarea 88.2) were closed to fishing (Table 3). During the same period, eight notifications were received from a single "near-miss" area in Subarea 88.2.[13] In the five Subarea 88.1 VME risk areas, sponges (*Porifera*) were the dominant VME indicators, with lesser amounts of stony corals (*Scleractinia*) being present in three areas. In the two Subarea 88.2 VME risk areas, hydrocorals (*Anthoathecatae*) were the dominant VME indicator organisms, with sea fans/sea whips (*Gorgonacea*) also occurring.

At its 2009 meeting SC-CAMLR reviewed these data, as well as application of CM 22-07, to provide the Commission with relevant advice. It noted that CCAMLR scientific observers played a key role in implementing the CMs concerned. In addition to the information outlined in the previous paragraph, it was recognised that the CCAMLR Secretariat had received 30 VME indicator notifications, of which seven notifications consisted of at least 10 VME indicator units. This had resulted in seven risk areas being declared in Subareas 88.1 and 88.2 (SC-CAMLR, 2009: Annex 5, paragraph 10.29). In taking this information into account, CCAMLR urged the Scientific Committee and its working groups to carefully consider the practical aspects of implementing recommendations arising from its work (CCAMLR, 2009: paragraph 5.10). It therefore seems prudent to conclude that CCAMLR's approach to VME's remains under development and that care needs to

TABLE 3. CCAMLR vulnerable marine ecosystems (VME) risk areas for longline fisheries in 2008/2009.

Subarea/division	Date notified	Risk area midpoint		Number of VME indicator units	VME indicator taxa
		Latitude	Longitude		
88.1[a]	7 January 2009	75° 08.70′S	176° 04.98′W	60	*Porifera, Scleractinia*
	7 January 2009	75° 08.52′S	176° 07.14′W	69	*Porifera, Scleractinia*
	7 January 2009	75° 12.10′S	175° 55.10′W	25	*Porifera, Scleractinia, Actinaria*
	15 January 2009	71° 34.90′S	172° 11.40′E	11	*Porifera, Anthoathecatea, Gorgonacea*
	15 January 2009	71° 40.60′S	172° 15.40′E	13	*Porifera, Anthoathecatea*
88.2[b]	19 January 2009	69° 07.98′S	123° 41.34′W	10	*Anthoathecatea, Gorgonacea*
	19 January 2009	69° 08.04′S	123° 43.86′W	10	*Anthoathecatea, Gorgonacea*

[a] Longline fishing effort reflected as the number of hooks deployed = 5749982.
[b] Longline fishing effort reflected as the number of hooks deployed = 2751260.

be taken to ensure that that the current CMs (CMs 22-06 and 22-07) are not viewed as "having done the job." In these terms, CM 22-07 is truly an interim measure.

Ecosystem Status

CEMP Indices

As indicated, ecosystem assessments of krill predators have been on CCAMLR's agenda since 1997. These entail examining trends in the predator parameters collected by CEMP and then applying various models to explain the trends. Key parameters are those that provide information on target species (i.e., notably krill), the physical environment (e.g., sea surface temperature and sea ice extent), and predators of the target species (i.e., CEMP-measured parameters).

While de la Mare and Constable (2000) have developed ways to summarise many CEMP parameters into a single metric, deciding what action to take in response to changes in parameter values or the single metric remains a challenge. For this purpose, the detection of extreme values in a naturally varying system is as important as detecting anomalous trends caused by fishing (Constable et al., 2000; Constable, 2001). The ongoing development of more-objective approaches to scaling CCAMLR management decisions thus remains under consideration. As Reid et al. (2008) have emphasised, some evaluation of risk in terms of identifying the consequence of type I and type II errors is essential, as illustrated by Field et al. (2004). Unfortunately, a clear strategy for applying such evaluations remains elusive in terms of selecting an appropriate level of statistical significance (α) and power to categorise any detected change in CEMP indices as a function of fishing.

Climate Change

The CCAMLR has recently tasked SC-CAMLR with addressing the issue of climate change in relation to conservation of Antarctic marine living resources (CCAMLR, 2007: paragraph 15.36). To that end, SC-CAMLR (SC-CAMLR, 2008: paragraph 7.13) has indicated that it should examine (1) the robustness of its advice and stock assessments, particularly with regard to predicting future population responses to climate change, (2) the need to improve current monitoring programs for harvested and other species to provide timely, robust indicators of climate change impacts, and (3) whether CCAMLR's management objectives and performance indicators should be modified to reflect the uncertainty regarding climate change effects. The matter remains a high priority for CCAMLR, and Resolution 30/XXVIII, adopted in late 2009, urges consideration of climate change impacts in the Southern Ocean to better inform CCAMLR management decisions.

CONCLUSIONS

Within the ATS, science may be viewed as the observation, identification, description, experimental investigation, and theoretical explanation of phenomena. This paper illustrates the essential value of science to sustainable management, and the case studies provide a number of important lessons.

First, and in CCAMLR terms, "the best scientific evidence available" and "sustainable management" are essentially equivalent in that the latter will fail in the absence of the former. Second, at an organizational level CCAMLR has developed a way of doing business that not only promotes consensus but also serves to underpin its status as a successful "new generation" agreement (Miller et al., 2004). While its many advances owe their existence to the strong spirit of cooperation between the CCAMLR members, these advances have been hard-won and have required a coherent, adaptable, and decision-driven management approach over the years (Miller et al., 2004). The work of SC-CAMLR has had a major role to play in this regard.

Third, many of the Convention's objectives have been addressed and met, even when there is very little supporting information available and knowledge of ecosystem functioning is limited. Fourth, fisheries within the CCAMLR area can be managed using a precautionary, ecosystem-based approach, the krill fishery being the most notable example. Fifth, CCAMLR has been able to develop scientifically based management despite uncertainty about important parameters and ecosystem behaviour; the VME approach is a clear example of this.

Sixth, science provides an iterative and robust framework for developing and implementing rigorously defined, management action. As stipulated in Convention Article XV, SC-CAMLR constitutes "a forum for consultation and co-operation concerning the collection, study and exchange of information with respect to the marine living resources to which the Convention applies." The Committee has also encouraged and promoted scientific cooperation to expand knowledge about Antarctic marine living resources and the associated ecosystem.

However, there is still work to be done! Plausible models are needed to guide management procedures in the face of the Antarctic marine ecosystem's "unknown and uncertain behaviors" (Constable et al., 2000). Expansion of the krill fishery is a very real possibility, and finalization of SSMUs has become a matter of growing urgency (Gascón and Werner, 2009). Equally, the majority of CCAMLR members have recognised the urgent need to subdivide krill areal catch limits within CCAMLR Statistical Area 48 (West Atlantic) to minimise risks associated with localised overfishing and associated ecosystem effects. Although this is a key concern, only an interim measure (CM 51-09) has been agreed by CCAMLR to date.

The CCAMLR further needs to articulate and set operational objectives for predators (Constable, 2002). This requires assessing the plausibility and furthering the development of ecosystem and food web models (Constable, 2005). Most importantly, the management procedures already in place must be evaluated prior to any appreciable increase in the krill fishery (Gascón and Werner, 2009). At the same time, decision rules associated with these and any new procedures should be tested and improved as needed. Such rules need to be robust to uncertainty and consistent, with objectively defined and clearly articulated operational criteria.

Despite the clear need for adaptability, CCAMLR has proven itself successful in addressing many of the ecological issues facing fisheries in other parts of the world's oceans. It has used science to overcome many challenges in ways consistent with the Antarctic Treaty's aspirations. As an innovative global leader in marine ecosystem management, CCAMLR warrants its status as an organization based on best practices in science and management (Lodge et al., 2007). The extensive research documented in the journal *CCAMLR Science* attests to the vast contribution that science has made to the formulation of the organization's conservation policies and management measures.[14] As De Cesari (1996:455) maintains, "The regulation of circumpolar waters falls under the legal ambit of the Antarctic Treaty System which aims to preserve and protect the right of Contracting Parties to conduct marine scientific research in the Southern Ocean".

The recently adopted CCAMLR Resolution 31/XXVIII (CCAMLR, 2009: pars. 12.90–12.93) highlights the role of science as fundamental to CCAMLR's work. This role is consistent with the vision espoused in Convention Article IX, which was renewed by the 1990 CCAMLR Working Group for the Development of Approaches to Conservation of Antarctic Marine Living Resources. In Resolution 31/XXVIII, formal recognition of the value of science in CCAMLR's day-to-day activities comes of age, as does its inclusion in the very fabric of the commission's policy decisions. Coupled with CCAMLR's clearly stated policy to enhance cooperation with Non-Contracting Parties,[15] the recent innovative, and far-reaching, steps taken by the commission to build scientific capacity within the organization (CCAMLR, 2009: pars. 16.8–16.11) stand out as a clear indication of science's inestimable value to the organization's work.

Acknowledgments

The views expressed in this chapter are those of the author and do not reflect the official views or decisions of the Commission for the Conservation of Antarctic Marine Living Resources (CCAMLR). The author thanks Natasha Slicer for her constructive comments during the chapter's development.

NOTES

1. In this chapter the Southern Ocean is the area defined in CAMLR Convention Article I. The Convention also applies to the Antarctic Treaty area south of 60°S; see CCAMLR Web site, Basic Documents section, http://www.ccamlr.org/pu/e/e_pubs/bd/toc.htm (accessed 17 November 2010).

2. The Antarctic Treaty System comprises the international arrangements underpinning relations among states in the Antarctic.

3. Unless otherwise qualified, specific Articles of the Convention will be referred to by number as "Article [X]."

4. The Commission (CCAMLR) is established under Article VII of the CAMLR Convention. It is the Convention's executive arm (see note 5) and has legal personality under Article VIII. The Commission's functions and responsibilities are outlined in Article IX, with a key function being to promulgate conservation measures (CMs).

5. The CCAMLR CMs are outlined in Convention Article IX, paragraphs 1 and 2. Their adoption by consensus (Article XII) follows procedures in Convention Article IX, paragraph 3. They are found on the CCAMLR Web site, http://www.ccamlr.org/pu/e/e_pubs/cm/drt.htm (accessed 17 November 2010).

6. The CAMLR Scientific Committee (SC-CAMLR) was established under Article XIV of the Convention. It functions (Article XV) as a "forum for consultation and co-operation concerning the collection, study and exchange of information" on the resources to which the Convention applies.

7. "Ecosystem health" in CCAMLR is taken to be the provision of adequate safeguards for harvested species so that harvesting does not prejudice the long-term future of dependent species. An "ecosystem assessment" is necessary to ensure that all the management requirements of Convention Article II are met in an operational sense (Everson, 2002).

8. The CCAMLR CMs in force for any year may be found on the CCAMLR Web site, http://www.ccamlr.org/pu/e/e_pubs/cm/drt.htm (accessed 17 November 2010).

9. Small-scale management units (SSMUs) are defined in CCAMLR (2002: paragraph 4.5) using an agreed and scientifically objective approach (SC-CAMLR, 2002: Annex 4, Appendix D).

10. See CCAMLR, "Text of the CCAMLR Scheme of International Scientific Observation," http://www.ccamlr.org/pu/e/e_pubs/cm/08-09/obs.pdf (accessed 17 November 2010).

11. The CEP was set up under Article 11 of the 1991 Protocol on Environmental Protection to the Antarctic Treaty.

12. "Bioregionalisation" is an objective, usually scientific, process that identifies the spatial boundaries of bioregions on the basis of ecological attributes, such as geology, ocean currents, and biota (National Oceans Office, 2002).

13. A "near-miss" area is considered to be an area where five or more VME indicator units are recovered within one line segment, within a single fine-scale rectangle as per paragraphs 5 and 7 of CM 22-07.

14. Despite a specialised, CCAMLR-centric content, *CCAMLR Science* has an impact factor of 1.389. It is ranked 19th out of 40 fisheries journals in Thomson's Journal Citation Reports Science Edition. This ranking compares with the *ICES Journal of Marine Science*'s 10th ranking and impact factor of 1.661.

15. See CCAMLR, "Policy to Enhance Cooperation between CCAMLR and Non-Contracting Parties," http://www.ccamlr.org/pu/e/e_pubs/cm/09-10/coop.pdf (accessed 19 November 2010).

LITERATURE CITED

Agnew, D. J. 1997. Review: The CCAMLR Ecosystem Monitoring Programme. *Antarctic Science*, 9:235–242.

———. 1999. The Illegal and Unregulated Fishery for Toothfish in the Southern Ocean and the CCAMLR Catch Documentation Scheme. *Marine Policy*, 24:361–374.

Beddington, J. R., and J. G. Cooke. 1983. The Potential Yield of Fish Stocks. *FAO Fisheries Technical Paper* 242. Rome: Food and Agricultural Organisation.

Beddington, J. R., and R. M. May. 1980. Maximum Sustainable Yields in Systems Subject to Harvesting at More Than One Trophic Level. *Mathematical Biosciences*, 51:261–281.

Beverton, R. J. H., and S. J. Holt. 1957. On the Dynamics of Exploited Fish Stocks. *Fishery Investigation Series* 19. London: Ministry of Agriculture Fisheries and Food.

Brandt, A., A. J. Gooday, S. N. Brandão, S. Brix, W. Brökeland, T. Cedhagen, M. Choudhury, N. Cornelius, B. Danis, I. G. De Mesel, R. J. Diaz, D. C. Gillan, B. Ebbe, J. A. Howe, D. Janussen, S. Kaiser, K. Linse, M. Malyutina, J. Pawlowski, M. Raupach, and A. Vanreusel. 2007. First Insights into the Biodiversity and Biogeography of the Southern Ocean Deep Sea. *Nature*, 447(7142):307–311.

Brown, M., S. Kawaguchi, S. G. Candy, and P. Virtue. 2010. Temperature Effects on the Growth and Maturation of Antarctic Krill (*Euphausia superba*). *Deep Sea Research, Part II, Topical Studies in Oceanography*, 57(7–8):672–682.

Butterworth, D. S. 1986. Antarctic Ecosystem Management. *Polar Record*, 37–47.

Butterworth, D. S., G. R. Gluckman, R. B. Thomson, S. Chalis, K. Hiramatsu, and D. J. Agnew. 1994. Further Computations of the Consequences of Setting the Annual Krill Catch Limit to a Fixed Fraction of the Estimate of Krill Biomass from a Survey. *CCAMLR Science*, 1:81–106.

Butterworth, D. S., A. E. Punt, and M. Basson. 1991. A Simple Approach for Calculating the Potential Yield of Krill from Biomass Survey Results. *CCAMLR Selected Scientific Papers*, 8:207–217.

Butterworth, D. S., and R. B. Thomson. 1995. Possible Effects of Different Levels of Krill Fishing on Predators—Some Initial Modelling Attempts. *CCAMLR Science*, 2:79–97.

Candy, S. G., and A. J. Constable. 2008. An Integrated Stock Assessment for the Patagonian Toothfish (*Dissostichus eleginoides*) for Heard and McDonald Islands Using CASAL. *CCAMLR Science*, 15:1–34.

Commission for the Conservation of Antarctic Marine Living Resources (CCAMLR). 1990. Report of the Ninth Meeting of the Commission (CCAMLR-IX). Hobart, Australia.

———. 1993. Report of the Twelfth Meeting of the Commission (CCAMLR-XII). Hobart, Australia: CCAMLR.

———. 2002. Report of the Twenty-First Meeting of the Commission (CCAMLR-XXI). Hobart, Australia: CCAMLR.

———. 2004. Report of the Twenty-Third Meeting of the Commission (CCAMLR-XXIII). Hobart, Australia: CCAMLR.

———. 2005. Report of the Twenty-Fourth Meeting of the Commission (CCAMLR-XXIV). Hobart, Australia: CCAMLR.

———. 2007. Report of the Twenty-Sixth Meeting of the Commission (CCAMLR-XXVI). Hobart, Australia: CCAMLR.

———. 2008. Report of the Twenty-Seventh Meeting of the Commission (CCAMLR-XXVII). Hobart, Australia: CCAMLR.

———. 2009. Report of the Twenty-Eighth Meeting of the Commission (CCAMLR-XXVIII). Hobart, Australia: CCAMLR.

Committee for Environmental Protection (CEP). 2006. Report of the Committee for Environmental Protection CEP-IX. Buenos Aires, Argentina: Antarctic Treaty Secretariat. http://www.ats.aq/documents/cep/cep%20documents/atcm29_cepix_e.pdf, (accessed 17 November 2010).

———. 2009a. Report of the Committee for Environmental Protection CEP-XII–Section 7 (Paragraphs 159–170). Buenos Aires, Argentina: Antarctic Treaty Secretariat. http://www.ats.aq/documents/ATCM32/att/atcm32_att084_rev2_e.doc (accessed 17 November 2010).

———. 2009b. Towards a Representative System of Marine Spatial Protection for the Orkney Islands. ATCM-XXXIII Working Paper 29. Buenos Aires, Argentina: Antarctic Treaty Secretariat. http://www.ats.aq/documents/ATCM32/wp/ATCM32/wp/ATCM32_wp029_e.doc (accessed 17 November 2010).

Constable. A. J. 2001. The Ecosystem Approach to Managing Fisheries: Achieving Conservation Objectives for Predators of Fished Species. *CCAMLR Science*, 8:37–64.

———. 2002. CCAMLR Ecosystem Monitoring and Management: Future Work. *CCAMLR Science*, 9:233–253.

———. 2005. A Possible Framework in Which to Consider Plausible Models of the Antarctic Marine Ecosystem for Evaluating Krill Management Procedures. *CCAMLR Science*, 12:99–117.

Constable, A. J., and W. K. de la Mare. 1996. A Generalized Model for Evaluating Yield and the Long-Term Status of Fish Stocks under Conditions of Uncertainty. *CCAMLR Science*, 3:31–54.

Constable, A. J., W. K. de la Mare, D. J. Agnew, I. Everson, and D. G. M. Miller. 2000. Managing Fisheries to Conserve the Antarctic Marine Ecosystem: Practical Implementation of the Convention on the Conservation of Antarctic Marine Living Resources. *ICES Journal of Marine Science*, 57:778–791.

Constable, A. J., and S. Nicol. 2002. Defining Smaller-Scale Management Units to Further Develop the Ecosystem Approach in Managing Large-Scale Pelagic Krill Fisheries in Antarctica. *CCAMLR Science*, 9:117–131.

De Cesari, P. 1996. "Scientific Research in Antarctica: New Developments." In *International Law for Antarctica*, 2nd ed., ed.

F. Franconi and T. Scovazzi, pp. 413–455. The Hague: Kluwer International.

de la Mare, W. K. 1994a. Modelling Krill Recruitment. *CCAMLR Science,* 1:49–54.

———. 1994b, Estimating Krill Recruitment and Its Variability. *CCAMLR Science,* 1:55–69.

de la Mare, W. K., and A. J. Constable. 2000. Utilising Data from Ecosystem Monitoring for Managing Fisheries: Development of Statistical Summaries of Indices Arising from the CCAMLR Ecosystem Monitoring Programme. *CCAMLR Science,* 7:101–117.

Eddie, G. C. 1977. *The Harvesting of Krill.* Southern Ocean Fisheries Survey Programme GLO/SO/77/2. Rome: Food and Agricultural Organisation.

El-Sayed, S. Z. 1994. "History, Organization and Accomplishments of the BIOMASS Programme." In *Southern Ocean Ecology: The BIOMASS Perspective,* ed. S. Z. El-Sayed, pp. 1–8. Cambridge: Cambridge University Press.

Everson, I. 1977. *Antarctic Fisheries.* Southern Ocean Fisheries Survey Programme, GLO/SO/77/1. Rome: Food and Agricultural Organisation.

———. 2002. Consideration of Major Issues in Ecosystem Monitoring and Management. *CCAMLR Science,* 9:213–232.

Field, J., A. J. Tyre, N. Jonzen, J. R. Rhodes, and H. P. Possingham. 2004. Minimizing the Cost of Environmental Management Decisions by Optimizing Statistical Thresholds. *Ecology Letters,* 7:669–675.

Gascón, V. G., and R. K. Werner. 2009. Preserving the Antarctic Food Web: Achievements and Challenges in Antarctic Krill Fisheries Management. *Ocean Yearbook,* 23:279–307.

Grant, S., A. J. Constable, B. Raymond, and S. Doust. 2006. Bioregionalisation of the Southern Ocean: Report of Experts Workshop (Hobart, Australia, September 2006). Sydney: WWF-Australia. http://www.wwf.org.au/publications/bioregionalization-southern-ocean.pdf (accessed 17 November 2010).

Grantham, G. J. 1977. *The Utilization of Krill.* Southern Ocean Fisheries Survey Programme GLO/SO/77/3. Rome: Food and Agricultural Organisation.

Gulland, J. 1971. *The Fish Resources of the Ocean.* West Byfleet, UK: Fishing News (Books).

Hewitt, R. P., and E. H. Linen Low. 2000. The Fishery on Antarctic Krill: Defining an Ecosystem Approach to Management. *Reviews in Fisheries Science,* 8:235–298.

Hewitt, R. P., G. Watters, P. N. Trathan, J. P. Croxall, M. E. Goebel, D. Ramm, K. Reid, W. Z. Trivelpiece, and J. L. Watkins. 2004. Options for Allocating the Precautionary Catch Limit for Krill among Small-Scale Management Units in the Scotia Sea. *CCAMLR Science,* 11:81–97.

Hilborn, R., and C. J. Walters. 1992. *Quantitative Fisheries Stock Assessment: Choice, Dynamics and Uncertainty.* London: Chapman and Hall Inc.

Hillary, R. M., G. P. Kirkwod, and D. J. Agnew. 2006. An Assessment of Toothfish in Subarea 48.3 Using CASAL. *CCAMLR Science,* 13:65–96.

Hill, S. L, K. Reid, S. E. Thorpe, J. Hinke, and G. M. Watters. 2007. A Compilation of Parameters for Ecosystem Dynamics Models of the Scotia Sea—Antarctic Peninsula Region. *CCAMLR Science,* 14:1–25.

Kock, K.-H. 1992. *Antarctic Fish and Fisheries.* Cambridge: Cambridge University Press.

———, ed. 2000. *Understanding CCAMLR's Approach to Management.* Hobart, Australia: CCAMLR. http://www.ccamlr.org/pu/E/e_pubs/am/toc.htm (accessed 17 November 2010).

Lodge, M., D. Anderson, T. Løbach, G. Munro, K. Sainsbury, and A. Willock. 2007. *Recommended Best Practices for Regional Fisheries Management Organizations.* London: Chatham House. http://www.chathamhouse.org.uk/files/10301_rfmo0807.pdf (accessed 17 November 2010).

Mangel, M., and P. V. Switzer. 1998. A Model at the Level of the Foraging Trip for the Indirect Effects of Krill (*Euphausia superba*) Fisheries on Krill Predators. *Ecological Modelling,* 105:235–256.

Miller, D. G. M. 1991. Exploitation of Antarctic Marine Living Resources: A Brief History and a Possible Approach to Managing the Krill Fishery. *South African Journal of Marine Science,* 10:321–339.

———. 2000. The Southern Ocean: A Global View. *Ocean Yearbook,* 14:468–513.

———. 2002. Antarctic Krill and Ecosystem Management—From Seattle to Siena. *CCAMLR Science,* 9:175–212.

———. 2007. Managing Fishing in the Sub-Antarctic. *Papers and Proceedings of the Royal Society of Tasmania,* 141:121–140.

Miller, D. G. M., and D. J. Agnew. 2000. "Krill Fisheries in the Southern Ocean." In *Krill: Biology, Ecology and Fisheries,* ed. I. Everson, pp. 300–337. Fisheries and Aquatic Resources Series 6. Oxford: Blackwell Science.

Miller, D. G. M., and I. Hampton. 1988. Biology and Ecology of the Antarctic Krill (*Euphausia superba* Dana). *BIOMASS Scientific Series* 9. Cambridge: SCAR and SCOR.

Miller, D. G. M., E. N. Sabourenkov, and D. C. Ramm. 2004. Managing Antarctic Marine Living Resources: The CCAMLR Approach. *International Journal of Marine and Coastal Law,* 19:317 363.

Mitchell, B., and R. Sandbrook. 1980. *The Management of the Southern Ocean.* London: International Institute for Environmental Development.

Murphy, E. J. 1995. Spatial Structure of the Southern Ocean Ecosystem: Predator-Prey Linkages in Southern Ocean Food Webs. *Journal of Animal Ecology,* 64:333–347.

Murphy, E. J., D. J. Morris, J. L. Watkins, and J. Priddle. 1988. "Scales of Interaction between Antarctic Krill and the Environment." In *Antarctic Oceans and Resources Variability,* ed. D. Sahrhage, pp. 120–130. Berlin: Springer-Verlag.

National Oceans Office. 2002. Ecosystems: Nature's Diversity—The South-east Regional Marine Plan. Hobart, Australia. http://www.environment.gov.au/coasts/mbp/publications/south-east/pubs/natures-diversity.pdf (accessed 17 November 2010).

Reid, K., J. P. Croxall, and E. J. Murphy. 2008. The Power of Ecosystem Monitoring. *Aquatic Conservation: Marine and Freshwater Ecosystems,* 17:S79–S92.

Sabourenkov, E. N., and D. G. M. Miller. 2004. "The Management of Transboundary Stocks of Toothfish, *Dissostichus* spp. under the Convention on the Conservation of Antarctic Marine Living Resources." In *Management of Shared Fish Stocks,* ed. A. I. L. Payne, C. M. O'Brien, and S. I. Rogers, pp. 68–94. Oxford: Blackwell.

Scientific Committee for the Conservation of Antarctic Marine Living Resources (SC-CAMLR). 1987. Report of the Sixth Meeting of the Scientific Committee (SC-CAMLR-VI). Hobart, Australia: CCAMLR.

———. 1990. Report of the Ninth Meeting of the Scientific Committee (SC-CAMLR-IX). Hobart, Australia: CCAMLR.

———. 1994. Report of the Thirteenth Meeting of the Scientific Committee (SC-CAMLR-XIII). Hobart, Australia: CCAMLR.

———. 1995. Report of the Fourteenth Meeting of the Scientific Committee (SC-CAMLR-XIV). Hobart, Australia: CCAMLR.

———. 2002. Report of the Twenty First Meeting of the Scientific Committee (SC-CAMLR-XXI). Hobart, Australia: CCAMLR.

———. 2008. Report of the Twenty-Seventh Meeting of the Scientific Committee (SC-CAMLR-XXVII). Hobart, Australia: CCAMLR.

———. 2009. Report of the Twenty-Eighth Meeting of the Scientific Committee (SC-CAMLR-XXVIII). Hobart, Australia: CCAMLR.

United Nations General Assembly (UNGA). 2007. *Sustainable Fisheries, Including through the 1995 Agreement for the Implementation of the Provisions of the United Nations Convention on the Law of the Sea of 10 December 1982 relating to the Conservation and Management of Straddling Fish Stocks and Highly Migratory Fish Stocks, and Related Instruments.* Resolution A/Res/61/105. 61st sess. 6 March. http://daccess-dds-ny.un.org/doc/UNDOC/GEN/N06/500/73/PDF/N0650073.pdf?OpenElement (accessed 17 November 2010).

Virtue, P., S. Kawaguchi, J. McIvor, S. Nicol, S. Wotherspoon, M. Brown, R. Casper, S. Davenport, L. Finley, J. Foster, T. Yoshida, and T. Yoshiki. 2010. Krill Growth and Condition in Western Indian Ocean Sector of the Southern Ocean 30–80°E in Austral Summer 2006. *Deep Sea Research, Part II, Topical Studies in Oceanography,* 57(7–8):948–955.

Watters, G. 1997. Preliminary Analyses of Data Collected during Experimental Phases of the 1994/95 and 1995/96 Antarctic Crab Fishing Seasons. *CCAMLR Science,* 141–159.

Willock, A., and M. Lack. 2006. *Follow the Leader: Learning from Experience and Best Practice in Regional Fisheries Management Organizations.* London: WWF International and TRAFFIC International.

Zumberge, J. H., and L. A. Kimball. 1986. "Workshop on the Antarctic Treaty System: Overview." In *Antarctic Treaty System: An Assessment*, pp. 3–12. Washington, D.C.: National Academies Press.

Science and Diplomacy: Montreal Protocol on Substances that Deplete the Ozone Layer

K. Madhava Sarma and Stephen O. Andersen

ABSTRACT. The ozone layer forms a thin shield in the stratosphere, protecting life on Earth from harmful ultraviolet radiation. Emissions of ozone-depleting substances (ODS) used in many sectors (such as refrigeration, air-conditioning, foams, and firefighting) destroy stratospheric ozone. Increased ultraviolet radiation from major depletion of stratospheric ozone can cause increases in skin cancer and cataracts, weaken the human immune systems, damage some agricultural crops, impact natural ecosystems, and degrade materials such as plastic. The Montreal Protocol on Substances that Deplete the Ozone Layer seeks worldwide phaseout of the production and consumption of ODS. Scientists confirmed that the protocol is working and that the ozone layer is on its way to recovery around the year 2050. Science and technology, including research at Antarctic stations proving that manufactured chemicals destroy stratospheric ozone and cause the Antarctic ozone hole, played important roles in the evolution and success of the protocol. Scientists provided early warning about the issue, discovered the Antarctic ozone hole, and linked it to CFC emissions and, along with nongovernmental organizations and the media, informed the public. The United Nations Environment Programme facilitated negotiations by governments. Science and technology panels of the protocol verified the performance of and facilitated periodical strengthening of the protocol. The scientific findings stimulated and motivated industry to innovation of alternatives to ODS. The protocol promoted universal participation, early action, continuous learning, and progressively tougher action. The protocol's Multilateral Fund and its implementing agencies assisted developing countries through technology transfer, creation of national focal points and networks, training, and introduction of regulations and policies.

INTRODUCTION

The Antarctic Treaty of 1959, one of the first treaties to protect global commons, formalized scientific cooperation, set aside Antarctica as a scientific preserve, established freedom of scientific investigation, and banned military activity on the Antarctic continent.

The Vienna Convention for the Protection of the Ozone Layer, 1985, and its Montreal Protocol on Substances that Deplete the Ozone Layer, 1987, promote global cooperation to meet the global threat of stratospheric ozone depletion. The Antarctic Treaty was a research platform for the science that later proved essential for the protection of the ozone layer. The Antarctic is (1) the

K. Madhava Sarma (deceased), United Nations Environment Programme and Montreal Protocol Technology and Economic Assessment Panel, Chennai, India. Stephen. O. Andersen, Montreal Protocol Technology and Economic Assessment Panel, 2317 North Road, Barnard, Vermont 05031-0257, USA. Correspondence: Anderson, soliverandersen@aol.com.

first place on Earth were ozone depletion was observed to be depleted at alarming rates, (2) the location of an alarming "ozone hole" that inspired the global action, (3) the place where scientists established the link between CFCs and ozone depletion, and (4) the place from where important data will continue to be generated on the expected recovery of the ozone layer.

The ozone layer forms a thin shield in the stratosphere, protecting life on Earth from the harmful effects of excessive ultraviolet radiation (UV). Emissions of human-made ozone-depleting substances (ODS) transported by the wind to the stratosphere release chlorine and bromine atoms that destroy ozone. Excessive UV radiation increases the risk of skin cancer, weakens human immune systems, damages crops and natural ecosystems, and degrades paint and plastic.[1] Most of these ODS are also greenhouse gases that contribute to climate change, causing glacier melting and sea level rise, and changes in precipitation and temperature.[2]

Ozone-depleting CFCs were invented in 1928 by a technologist working for General Motors and were marketed by DuPont to replace ammonia, sulphur dioxide, and other flammable and toxic refrigerants. CFCs are nonreactive and nonflammable, have low toxicity, and have a long atmospheric life. They were considered wonder gases and quickly became favored as in many applications.

By the late 1980s, more than 250 separate product categories were made with, or contained, ODS. Many of these products had become vital to society.

The more critical uses of ODSs included medical applications (metered-dose medicine inhalers and sterilisation); refrigeration; air-conditioning; foam; solvents for cleaning of electronic and mechanical components; soil, building, and commodity fumigation; and fire protection.

The Montreal Protocol on Substances that Deplete the Ozone Layer (Montreal Protocol) of 1987, as amended from time to time, has been hailed as the most successful environmental agreement ever. This is the only international agreement with participation of all 196 countries of the world. A pattern of fruitful collaboration has been established between scientists, governments, nongovernmental organizations (NGOs), media, and UN organizations: science leading to understanding, understanding leading to policy, policy leading to implementation, and implementation leading to global environmental protection.

If there were no Montreal Protocol, the chlorine and bromine in the atmosphere would be, by the year 2065, 40 times higher than its natural level. Total ozone would have decreased by two-thirds, which would have ultimately resulted in many more millions of cases of skin cancer and cataracts and would have irreparably damaged agriculture and ecosystems. The reasons for the success of the protocol may be summarized as

- the strong role played by scientists and technologists in the foundation and evolution of the protocol,
- the development and deployment of ozone-safe technologies by industry, and
- the protocol regime facilitating universal participation and transferring ozone-safe technologies expeditiously to developing countries on fair terms.

SCIENCE AS A SOURCE OF EARLY WARNING

Scientists have known the importance of the ozone layer from 1930, and some countries regularly monitored the atmospheric ozone. In preparation for the International Geophysical Year in 1957–1958, a worldwide network of scientific stations was developed to measure ozone profiles and the total column abundance of ozone using a scientific instrument and procedure pioneered by Gordon M. B. Dobson. The World Meteorological Organization (WMO) established the framework for ozone-observing projects, related research, and publications; this network eventually became the Global Ozone Observing System, with approximately 140 monitoring stations. The British, Japanese, and North American scientific stations in Antarctica in 1957 installed ozone monitors, which eventually recorded the high depletion of the stratospheric ozone that is called the Antarctic ozone hole.

In 1970, Paul Crutzen of the Netherlands demonstrated the importance of catalytic loss of ozone by the reaction of nitrogen oxides and theorized that chemical processes that affect atmospheric ozone can begin on the surface of the Earth.[3] Nitrogen oxide emissions result from industrial and medical processes and, to a small extent, from use of NO_2-propelled aerosol products. They are also formed in the atmosphere through chemical reactions involving nitrous oxide (N_2O), which originates from microbiological transformations on the ground. Therefore, Crutzen theorized increasing atmospheric concentration of nitrous oxide from the use of agricultural fertilizers might lead to reduced ozone levels. At the same time, James Lovelock of the United Kingdom measured air samples in the North and South Atlantic and reported in 1973 that CFCs had been detected in every one of his samples, wherever and whenever they were sought.[4]

In 1971, Harold Johnston of the United States showed that the nitrogen oxides produced in the high-temperature exhaust of the proposed fleet of SSTs could contribute significantly to ozone loss by releasing the nitrogen oxides directly into the stratospheric ozone layer.[5] In 1972, Crutzen elaborated on this theory with a paper that explained the process by which ozone is destroyed in the stratosphere, and presented estimates of the ozone reduction that could result from the operation of supersonic aircraft.[6]

Another American, James McDonald, theorized in 1971 that even a small change in the abundance of stratospheric ozone could have significant effects in transmitting more ultraviolet radiation to the surface of the Earth, affecting the incidence of skin cancer. In March 1971, the U.S. House of Representatives voted not to continue funding development of the American SST. Subsequently, in 1974, the U.S. Department of Transportation completed the first comprehensive scientific assessment of stratospheric ozone depletion called the "Climatic Impact Assessment Program—CIAP." In 1973, Pan Am and TWA cancelled their orders for Concorde SSTs. Only British Airways and Air France purchased Concorde aircraft for routes across the Atlantic Ocean. Recently, for reasons of safety, all Concorde flights have been discontinued.

Mario J. Molina and F. Sherwood Rowland, two chemists at the University of California at Irvine, were the first to study CFCs as a possible source of chlorine in the stratosphere. CFCs refer to all fully halogenated compounds containing chlorine, fluorine, and carbon. In a paper published in the 28 June 1974 issue of *Nature*, Molina and Rowland hypothesized that when CFCs reach the stratosphere, ultraviolet radiation causes them to decompose and release chlorine atoms, which, in turn, become part of a chain reaction; as a result of the chain reaction, a single chlorine atom would destroy as many as 100,000 molecules of ozone.[7] Rowland and Molina estimated that "if industry continued to release a million tons of CFCs into the atmosphere each year, atmospheric ozone would eventually drop by 7 to 13 percent."

SCIENCE AS A FORCE FOR CHANGE

Rowland and Molina did not rest with their theoretical discoveries. They foresaw the danger to the planet and, with the encouragement of the Natural Resources Defense Council (NRDC), an NGO, presented their findings and held a press conference at a meeting of the American Chemical Society in 1974. Rowland reported that if CFC production rose at the then-current rate of 10 percent a year until 1990, and then levelled off, up to 50 percent of the ozone layer would be destroyed by the year 2050. Even a 10 percent depletion, he said, could cause as many as 80,000 additional cases of skin cancer each year in the United States alone, along with genetic mutations, crop damage, and possibly even drastic changes in the world's climate.

In January 1975, a report of the U.S. National Academy of Sciences and Department of Transportation confirmed similar findings. These reports laid the foundation for widespread public concern and forced the governments to consider regulatory action.

The significant media coverage of Molina and Rowland's press conference at the meeting of the American Chemical Society in 1974 resulted in headlines in the U.S. media such as "Aerosol Spray Cans May Hold Doomsday Threat." The U.S. environmentalists were galvanized. Many consumer groups demanded a ban on the use of CFCs in aerosols, a "frivolous use." The NRDC petitioned the U.S. Consumer Product Safety Commission to ban the use of CFCs in aerosols. The media exposure motivated several governments, including Canada, Sweden, and the United States, to take measures to reduce the ODS consumption wherever alternatives were readily available.

SCIENCE AS A SOURCE OF ISSUES ON THE POLICY AGENDA

The U.S. National Academy of Science, in a 1976 report, confirmed the earlier findings and further noted that CFCs were produced and used around the world, advising, "Clearly, although any action taken by the United States to regulate the production and use of CFMs [CFCs] would have a proportionate effect on the reduction in stratospheric ozone, such action must become worldwide to be effective in the long run." Thus, was born the concept of a global stratospheric ozone depletion problem that needs action by the entire world for it to be solved.

SCIENCE AS A CONFIDENCE-BUILDING ACTIVITY

Since individual scientists of a few countries came up with ozone depletion discoveries, the challenge was convincing the governments of the world of the threat to the ozone layer. Hence, many countries felt it was necessary for the UN to organize scientists from many countries in a collaborative effort.

The UN organized the Conference on Human Environment in Stockholm, Sweden, in June 1972, the first of such global environment conferences. The institutional arrangements set out in the conference report led to the establishment of the UN Environment Programme (UNEP). The "Pollutants" paper of the conference called for research on how human activities influenced the stratospheric transport and distribution of ozone.

In April 1975, the UNEP Governing Council backed the Outer Limits Programme to protect stratospheric ozone and other vulnerable global commons.[8] At its meeting in April 1976,[9] the council requested the executive director to convene a meeting to review all aspects of the ozone layer, identify related ongoing activities and future plans, and agree on a division of labor and a coordinating mechanism for the compilation of research activities and future plans and the collection of related industrial and commercial information.

In March 1977 a meeting convened by UNEP in Washington, D.C., in accordance with this mandate agreed a World Plan of Action on the Ozone Layer and established the UNEP Coordinating Committee on the Ozone Layer. The basic components of the action plan were

- coordinate atmospheric research (WMO);
- study the impact of changes in the ozone layer/biosphere (World Health Organization [WHO], WMO/UNEP, and Food and Agriculture Organization [FAO]);
- assess the impacts on human health (WHO);
- investigate other biological effects (FAO);
- develop computational climate models (WMO) and study regional climate effects (FAO);
- research socioeconomic aspects (UNEP, International Chamber of Commerce [ICC], Organization for Economic Cooperation and Development [OECD], and International Civil Aviation Organization);
- evaluate aircraft emissions, nitrogen fertilizers, and other potential modifiers of the stratosphere (UN Department of Economic and Social Affairs and OECD); and
- identify institutions to implement the action plan: UN bodies, specialized agencies, international, national, intergovernmental, and nongovernmental organizations, and scientific institutions.

The many reports of the UNEP Coordinating Committee on the Ozone Layer and National Academy of Sciences convinced many governments of the danger to the ozone layer. However, some countries of Europe and the companies that manufactured the CFCs were not convinced that CFC emissions were the primary cause of ozone depletion. They wanted more studies. To develop a world consensus, UNEP initiated diplomatic negotiations in 1982. The negotiations went on for three years, resulting in the Vienna Convention for the Protection of the Ozone Layer, 1985 (Vienna Convention), which agreed on further research but no steps for curbing the emissions of CFCs, in view of the scepticism of some countries. The labors of the scientists continued, and governments agreed to continue negotiations.

Seven international agencies teamed up to write a three-volume assessment of the state of the ozone layer in 1985. The report calculated the predicted magnitude of ozone perturbations for a variety of emission scenarios involving a number of substances. As early as October 1981, Dobson instrument measurements from Japanese, British, and other research stations recorded reductions in ozone levels above Antarctica. In 1984, Shigeru Chubachi of the Japanese Meteorological Research Institute reported his findings on declining ozone amounts over Antarctica but did not suggest that there was anything unusual about these data.[10] By May 1985, Farman, Gardiner, and Shanklin of the British Antarctic Survey had realized the scientific significance of the widespread measurements that ozone levels above Antarctica were significantly depleted every Antarctic spring. Unlike Chubachi, they chose to publish their findings in *Nature*, where the policy significance would be appreciated, and to suggest a connection between ozone depletion and chlorofluorocarbons.[11] The phenomenon of ozone depletion over Antarctica became known as the "ozone hole." Another International Ozone Trends Panel in 1988 confirmed and expanded these findings.

SCIENCE AS A BEACON TO INDUSTRY

In early 1986, representatives of the companies DuPont, Allied, and ICI separately reported that between 1975 and 1980, they had identified compounds meeting environmental, safety, and performance criteria for some CFC applications but had terminated research and development when they concluded that none were as inexpensive as CFCs and there would be no market for the alternatives.[12] The U.S. Environmental Protection Agency quickly organized a team of international experts, who confirmed, by consensus, that a wide range of chemical alternatives with no or low ozone depletion potential (ODP) could be commercialized at just three to five times the price of the ODSs they would replace. Since ODSs are typically a very small part of total cost of products, the higher ODS price was considered insignificant and well worth the benefits of ozone layer protection.

Industry attitudes had changed considerably by December 1986. Previously, producers and users of CFCs argued that further regulations were uncalled for until science proved the ozone depletion theory. The industry coalition Alliance for a Responsible CFC Policy changed its position in 1986 and said that it would support a reasonable global limit on the future rate of growth of fully halogenated CFC production capacity.

Warnings by scientists that large unrestrained growth in CFC usage would lead to future ozone depletion caused industry to fear that the growth in demand of CFCs was bound to concern governments. Further, the Vienna Convention had served notice that the ozone depletion issue was being taken seriously. The negotiations under the auspices of UNEP on a protocol under the Vienna Convention further confirmed this feeling. The U.S. producers, from that point, added to the pressure for an international protocol, wanting to avoid a situation in which the United States regulated CFCs domestically while the rest of the world did not. Thus, after a decade of industry opposition to regulation, industry claimed that it was the lack of regulation that prevented it from introducing products to protect the ozone layer.

In 1986, scientists provided the first evidence that chlorine chemistry was, indeed, the cause of the ozone hole on the basis of ground-based experiments.[13] In 1987, the internationally sponsored Airborne Antarctic Ozone Experiment confirmed the key role of chlorine in chemical reactions associated with ozone hole formation.[14] The experiment's "smoking gun" data showed an inverse correlation between ozone and chlorine monoxide from CFCs.

On 16 September 1987 the UNEP conference of the governments agreed on the Montreal Protocol on Substances that Deplete the Ozone Layer. Only mild control measures were agreed upon to ensure that all countries could come aboard. In Article 6 of the protocol, the governments agreed that there will be periodic scientific, technological, and economic assessment of the issues concerning the CFCs and that the protocol will be revised on the basis of the results of the assessment. In October 1988, in compliance with Article 6 of the Montreal Protocol, the scientific, environmental, technology, and economic assessment processes were initiated.

SCIENCE AS A TOOL OF DIPLOMACY

In November 1989, four Montreal Protocol assessment panels reported their findings: The Scientific Assessment Panel (SAP) reported that "Even if the control measures of the Montreal Protocol (of 1987) were to be implemented by all nations, today's atmospheric abundance of chlorine (about 3 parts per billion by volume) will at least double to triple during the next century. If the atmospheric abundance of chlorine reaches about 9 parts per billion by volume by about 2050, ozone depletions of 0–4 percent in the tropics and 4–12 percent at high latitudes would be predicted. To return the Antarctic ozone layer to levels of the pre-1970s, and hence to avoid the possible ozone dilution effect that the Antarctic ozone hole could have at other latitudes, one of a limited number of approaches to reduce the atmospheric abundance of chlorine and bromine is a complete elimination of emissions of all fully halogenated CFCs, halons, carbon tetrachloride, and methyl chloroform, as well as careful considerations of the HCFC substitutes." The Environmental Effects Assessment Panel (EEAP) confirmed the adverse impacts of ozone depletion on human health and environment. The Technology Assessment Panel (TAP) concluded that it was technically feasible to phase down the production and consumption of the five controlled CFCs by at least 95%, phase out production and consumption of carbon tetrachloride, and phase down the production and consumption of methyl chloroform by at least 90 percent. The Economic Assessment Panel (EAP) noted that many companies already started phasing out the CFCs and the costs were much less than was originally feared.

The synthesis of the four assessment panels' reports provided many policy options to governments for phasing out CFCs. It also concluded that

> Protection of the ozone layer will require a full partnership between developed countries that have caused the problem and those in developing countries who would now like to improve their standard of living by using these chemicals for uses such as refrigeration. The lack of technical knowledge and financial resources of developing countries inhibits the adoption of certain CFC/halon replacement technologies and the definition and implementation of the best national options for the transition to CFC-free technologies. Funding is needed to assist the transfer of technology to developing countries during the transition period because currently available resources are already strained as a result of the world debt problem and the dire economic situation of many countries.

It is this report that led to more negotiations and an agreement in the second Meeting of the Parties in London in 1990 to completely phase out CFCs by the year 2000, with a 10-year grace period for developing countries, and to assist the developing countries with technologies and financial assistance through a Multilateral Fund (MLF) contributed by the developed countries. At the second meeting, the parties merged the TAP and EAP into the Technology and Economics Panel (TEAP) and asked the all the assessment panels to submit another comprehensive assessment in November 1991. The 1991 TEAP report found that

> It is technically feasible to eliminate virtually all consumption of controlled substances in developed countries by 1995–1997, if commercial quantities of transitional substances are available . . . As a result of rapid development of technology, the costs of eliminating controlled substances are lower than estimated in 1989 and will decline further.

The parties to the protocol approved the Copenhagen Adjustment and Amendment of 1992. They brought into the protocol HCFCs, HBFCs, and methyl bromide as controlled substances, each with a specific control schedule. The phaseout of CFCs, carbon tetrachloride, and methyl chloroform by the developed countries was advanced from the year 2000 to 1996, and the phaseout of halons was advanced to 1994.

The assessment panels' 1994 report put forward further options to strengthen the protocol.[15] As a result of this assessment, the 1995 meeting of the parties further strengthened the protocol, and in 1997 and 1998 the protocol was further strengthened. In 2007, the protocol was further adjusted to advance the phaseout of the HCFCs, the low-ODP substances used to replace the ODS.

SCIENCE FOR MONITORING, REPORTING, AND VERIFICATION

Since 1957, the WMO has provided the backbone of the global ozone monitoring network. In 1960, it established the World Ozone Data Centre in Toronto, Canada. Many countries measure ozone and abundance of ODS in the atmosphere through satellites, aircraft, balloons, and ground measurements. The scientific assessment panel of the protocol collates this information and studies the consistency of the scientific observations with the data on production and consumption of ODS reported by the parties to the protocol annually to the secretariat of the protocol. Any anomalies are investigated and causes found. Science thus provides a check on the reports of governments to the protocol secretariat. Following the measurements of the Antarctic ozone hole in 1984–1985, WMO initiated the public release of Antarctic ozone bulletins, which are issued every 10–14 days, beginning in mid-August. Springtime bulletins are issued for northern midlatitudes and the Arctic regions when conditions warrant.

SCIENCE TO MEASURE REGULATORY PERFORMANCE

The 2006 UNEP/WMO SAP report synthesized all the scientific observations of the ozone layer and concluded that the Montreal Protocol was a success:[16]

> The total combined abundances of anthropogenic ozone-depleting gases in the troposphere continue to decline from the peak values reached in the 1992–1994 time period.
>
> The combined stratospheric abundances of the ozone-depleting gases show a downward trend from their peak values of the late 1990s, which is consistent with surface observations of these gases and a time lag for transport to the stratosphere.
>
> The Montreal Protocol is working: There is clear evidence of a decrease in the atmospheric burden of ozone-depleting substances and some early signs of stratospheric ozone recovery.

Economic analyses of the Montreal Protocol's control measures have found that the speed of the phaseout has been faster, the costs have been lower, and the alternatives and substitutes have been more environmentally acceptable than the parties anticipated at the protocol's initial and ongoing negotiations.[17]

The HFCs that replaced CFCs were zero ODP and had generally much lower global warming potentials (GWP), and the HCFCs that replace CFCs were generally low ODP and had equal or lower GWP. However, in some cases alternatives to ODSs had comparable GWPs that were too high to be environmentally sustainable. Overall, national regulations, voluntary actions, and compliance with the Montreal Protocol have protected the climate in the past and can add to climate protection in the future. Over the Kyoto Protocol to the United Nations Framework Convention on Climate Change (Kyoto Protocol) period (1990–2010), the reduction in GWP-weighted ODS emissions from compliance to control measures of the Montreal Protocol was about 8 Gt CO_2 equivalents per year. This reduction is substantially greater than the first Kyoto reduction target (2 Gt CO_2 equivalents per year), even after accounting for the climate impact of ozone depletion and HFC emissions. And now, there are proposals before the parties to the Montreal Protocol to control the HFCs that were once necessary to replace the ODSs.

DEVELOPMENT OF OZONE-SAFE TECHNOLOGIES

From 1988, many companies proactively innovated and introduced many ozone-safe technologies. Industry leadership was an important ingredient in the accelerated and cost-effective phaseout of ODSs. The industry had many sources of motivation: respect for science, social motivation, desire for reputation and good will, motivation to avoid excessive regulation by governments, economic and strategic motivation, public relations, and employee motivation.

GLOBAL INDUSTRY COOPERATION

To accelerate the pace of toxicity testing and reduce costs, in 1988, 14 global chemical manufacturers with an interest in commercialising new substitutes to the most damaging ozone-depleting substances formed the Program for Alternative Fluorocarbon Toxicity Testing (PAFT). Another significant response was the creation of the Alternative Fluorocarbon Environmental Acceptability Study (AFEAS) consortium formed in 1989 to determine the environmental fate and investigate any potential impacts of alternatives in cooperation with government agencies and academic scientists. This unprecedented scientific cooperation shortened the time to commercialisation of new HCFC and HFC chemical substitutes by three to five years.

At least six industry associations based on science and engineering were started with the express goals of speeding the elimination of ODSs: AFEAS, the Halon Alternatives Research Corporation (HARC), Halon Users National Consortium (HUNC), the Industry Cooperative for Ozone Layer Protection (ICOLP), the Japan Industrial Conference for Ozone Layer Protection (JICOP), and PAFT. At least two other industry organizations, the U.S. Alliance for Responsible Atmosphere Policy (ARAP) and the Australian Association of Fluorocarbon Consumers and Manufacturers (AFCAM), transformed themselves from questioning to supporting regulations to protect the ozone layer. Several dozen other existing organizations created substantial internal subcommittees on ozone layer protection.

TECHNOLOGY AND ECONOMIC ASSESSMENT

The parties to the Montreal Protocol benefit from annual, up-to-date technical assessments from its TEAP and its Technical Options Committees (TOCs) for the six sectors of ODS use. The TOC reports are consolidated by the TEAP, and the results are synthesized with findings of the SAP and the EEAP.

The TEAP consists of the cochairs of the TOCs and a few other experts. Each TOC has cochairs from both developing and developed countries and 20–35 members from all parts of the world. Members of the TEAP are appointed by Meetings of the Parties (MOPs). Governments may propose members to TOCs. The cochairs of the TOCs have the full freedom to choose whom they want in consultation with the TEAP, depending on the expertise needed, which may vary from time to time. The membership is from government environment ministries, industries, academia, and a few professional consultants.

The presence of industry on the TOCs and the TEAP provides access to cutting-edge data that are often not yet published in scientific or technical journals since industry rarely publishes about emerging technologies it has developed for commercial purposes. As a result, reports from the TOCs and the TEAP often provide the parties with the first public disclosure of the latest developments. A code of conduct for TEAP and TOCs ensures that membership does not lead to taking undue advantage by the members.

Whereas the TEAP and TOCs were originally constituted to advise the parties at least once in four years on strengthening the protocol, the MOPs have actually used the TEAP and TOCs to spearhead more aggressive phaseout and to solve the many problems faced by the parties. For example, every three years the TEAP and the TOCs are asked to recommend the replenishment requirements of the MLF.

The reports of the TEAP or TOCs are presented to the parties as they are written, without any editing by policy makers. Parties are free to disagree with the reports but cannot amend them. The panels can present information that is relevant for policy making but do not recommend specific policies.

ROLE OF THE PROTOCOL REGIME

Regime Encouraging Involvement of all the Stakeholders

All developing countries became parties to the protocol because of the concessions given to them, including a grace period for implementation of the control measures and a fund to meet their incremental costs. Every party to the Montreal Protocol has engaged in stakeholder dialogue and collaboration, and most operate national steering committees comprised of representatives from government ministries (e.g., agriculture, defence, environment, finance, and industry), industry associations, technical experts, NGOs, and others, such as from international implementing organizations or bilateral donor agencies.

Multilateral Fund and Implementing Agencies

The financial mechanism of the Montreal Protocol, the MLF, is based on the recognition that many developing countries lack the capacity to comply with treaty obligations and that developed countries that are often disproportionately responsible for causing the ozone depletion, should provide technologies and financial assistance to developing countries to ensure compliance. The developing and developed parties are equally represented in the executive committee of the fund. The contributions of the MLF have been critical to the success of the Montreal Protocol. The Global Environment Facility (GEF), though not a financial mechanism of the protocol, provided financial assistance to countries with economies in transition, which were not eligible to receive financial assistance from the MLF.

The MLF is also the focus of all the activities to assist the developing countries. Donor countries can have their own bilateral Montreal Protocol programmes (up to 20% of their contribution due to the MLF) in developing countries, but such programmes have to be approved by the executive committee. This requirement avoids confusion and duplication of activities.

Another reason for the success of the MLF is the replenishment process, which occurs every three years. The TEAP estimates the funding required for each replenishment period, taking into account the obligations of the developing countries, the projects already approved, and the lead time for completion of projects. The TEAP report is reviewed and decided upon by the parties at the MOP.

National Focal Points and Networks

The MLF financed creation of an office, or "focal point," within each developing country's government with financial assistance. This office coordinates the country activities for the phaseout, consults with industry and other interested organizations on the steps to be taken for the phaseout, prepares a country programme, designs and implements the national law and the financial measures to facilitate phaseout, organizes awareness and training programmes for the industry and public, and creates a system for monitoring and reporting on national production and consumption of ODSs.

The focal points of each country, along with interested developed countries, are organized into nine regional networks to facilitate the exchange of information, best practices, and technology transfer. These networks facilitate feedback to the MLF and to other parties, allowing parties to learn from each other and transfer expertise and technology from one country to another.

National Regulations and Policies

All the parties to the Montreal Protocol established regulations that included outright bans on production and imports. Many countries have taxes or fees on ODSs to discourage use and raise revenue. Other mechanisms included auctioning the right to the permitted ODSs. Labelling programmes help inform consumers which products and processes are ozone safe. The labelling programmes encourage product manufacturers to halt ODS use to satisfy customers and avoid administrative expenses and penalties.

CONCLUSION

The Montreal Protocol on Substances that Deplete the Ozone Layer is the most successful environmental agreement ever, and the Antarctic Treaty was a research platform for the science that was instrumental in protecting the ozone layer. The Montreal Protocol is the only international agreement with participation of all 196 countries of the world, and it is the only environmental agreement to be on track to achieve all of its goals. The foundation of its success is science and technology, including the science discovered in Antarctica. Collaboration has been established between scientists, governments, NGOs, media, and UN organizations: science leading to understanding, understanding leading to policy, policy leading to implementation, and implementation leading to global environmental protection. If there were no Montreal Protocol, stratospheric ozone would have decreased by two-thirds, ultimately resulting in death and disability from tens of millions of cases of skin cancer, cataracts, and suppression of the human immune system, and would have irreparably damaged agriculture and ecosystems, which would have resulted in even more misery.

NOTES

1. Ultraviolet radiation can reach components of the immune system present in the skin. Experiments on animals show that UV exposure decreases the immune response to skin cancers, infectious agents, and other antigens and can lead to unresponsiveness upon repeated challenges, and studies of human subjects also indicate that UVB exposure can suppress some immune system functions. The risk of these immune

effects for humans is uncertain but may be significant where infectious diseases already challenge human health and in persons with impaired immune function. See A. Jeevan and M. L. Kripke, "Impact of Ozone Depletion on Immune Function," *World Resource Review* 5 (2001): 2; and Janice D. Longstreth, Frank R. de Gruijl, and Margaret L. Kripke, "Effects of Increased Solar Ultraviolet Radiation on Human Health" *Ambio* 24, no. 3 (1995): 153–165. See also the Columbia University Center for International Earth Science Information Network (CIESIN) thematic guide to the impact of stratospheric ozone depletion on suppression of the human immune system, http://www.ciesin.org/TG/HH/ozimmun.html (accessed 7 December 2010).

2. Because ozone-depleting substances were already scheduled for phaseout under the Montreal Protocol, they are not included in the Kyoto Protocol. However, SF_6, PFCs, and, particularly, HFCs that are substitutes for ozone-depleting substances in some applications are controlled by the Kyoto Protocol. The HFCs controlled under the Kyoto Protocol have global warming potentials (GWPs) that are generally lower than the CFCs they replaced. For example, the GWP of HFC-134a is about one-sixth the GWP of the CFC-12 it replaces as a refrigerant. See UNEP Ozone Secretariat, "The Implications to the Montreal Protocol of the Inclusion of HFCs and PFCs in the Kyoto Protocol," report of the HFC and PFC Task Force of the Technology and Economic Assessment Panel, 1999, http://www.ozone.unep.org/Assessment_Panels/TEAP (accessed 7 December 2010).

3. P. Crutzen, "The Influence of Nitrogen Oxides on the Atmospheric Ozone Content," *Quarterly Journal of the Royal Meteorological Society*, 96, no. 408 (1970): 320–325.

4. J. E. Lovelock, R. J. Maggi, and R. J. Wade, "Halogenated Hydrocarbons in and over the Atlantic," *Nature*, 241 (1973): 195, as discussed in M. Kowalok, "Common Threads: Research Lessons from Acid Rain, Ozone Depletion, and Global Warming," *Environment* 35, no. 6 (1993): 12–20, 35–38, http://www.ciesin.org/docs/011-464/011-464.html (accessed 7 December 2010).

5. H. S. Johnston, "Reduction of Stratospheric Ozone by Nitrogen Oxide Catalysts from Supersonic Transport Exhaust," *Science* 173 (1971): 517–522.

6. P. Crutzen, "SST's: A Threat to the Earth's Ozone Shield," *Ambio* 1, no. 2 (1972): 41–51.

7. M. Molina and F. S. Rowland, "Stratospheric Sink for Chlorofluoromethanes: Chlorine Atom-Catalyzed Destruction of Ozone," *Nature* 249, no. 5460 (1974): 810–812.

8. UN Environment Programme Governing Council, Decision 29(III), April 1975.

9. UN Environment Programme Governing Council, Decision 65(IV), April 1976.

10. S. Chubachi, "Preliminary Result of Ozone Observations at Syoma Station from February 1982 to January 1983," *Memoirs of National Institute of Polar Research* 34 (1984): 13–19.

11. J. S. Farman, B. G. Gardiner, and J. D. Shanklin, "Large Losses of Total Ozone in Antarctica Reveal Seasonal ClO_x/NO_x Interaction," *Nature*, 315 (1985): 207–210.

12. See Robert S. Orfeo, "Response to questions to the panel from Senator John H. Chafee," *Ozone Depletion, the Greenhouse Effect, and Climate Change, Hearings before the Senate Subcommittee on Environmental Pollution of the Committee on Environment and Public Works* (Washington, D.C.: GPO, 1986), pp. 189–192; and Donald Strobach, "A Search for Alternatives to the Current Commercial Chlorofluorocarbons," in *Protecting the Ozone Layer: Workshop on Demand and Control Technologies* (U.S. Environmental Protection Agency: Washington, D.C., 1986).

13. S. Solomon, G. H. Mount, R. W. Sanders, and A. L. Schemltekopf, "Visible Spectroscopy at McMurdo Station, Antarctica: 2. Observation of OClO," *Journal of Geophysical Research* 92 (1987): 8329–8338.

14. NASA, "Airborne Antarctic Ozone Experiment," http://geo.arc.nasa.gov/sge/jskiles/fliers/all_flier_prose/antarcticO3_condon/antarcticO3_condon.html (accessed 7 December 2010).

15. World Meteorological Organization, *Scientific Assessment of Ozone Depletion: 1994; Executive Summary,* World Meteorological Organization Global Ozone Research and Monitoring Project Report 37, World Meteorological Organization, Geneva, 1995.

16. World Meteorological Organization, Scientific Assessment of Ozone Depletion*: 2006; Executive Summary*, World Meteorological Organization Global Ozone Research and Monitoring Project Report 50, World Meteorological Organization, Geneva, 2007, http://ozone.unep.org/Assessment_Panels/SAP/Scientific_Assessment_2006_Exec_Summary.pdf (accessed 7 December 2010).

17. Economic Options Committee, 1991, 1994, 1998; and Stephen O. Andersen and K. Madhava Sarma, *Protecting the Ozone Layer: The United Nations History* (London: Earthscan, 2002), pp. 187–233.

Outer Space as International Space: Lessons from Antarctica

Armel Kerrest

INTRODUCTION

Antarctica and outer space have a lot in common. Like Antarctica, outer space is dangerous for humans; like Antarctica, outer space has a high strategic value; like Antarctica, outer space is quite interesting for research purposes. This means a lot for lawyers because the nature of a space has a great impact on its legal status.

Nevertheless, for historical reasons Antarctica and outer space are rather different as far as their legal statuses are concerned. In fact, despite the existing claims by some states on Antarctica, on the one hand, and the acceptance of the nonappropriation principle of outer space, on the other, the common natural, strategic, and scientific aspects of both spaces make a comparison of their legal framework and governance very efficient.

In 1959 activities in Antarctica were already important, and the Antarctic Treaty succeeded in breaking the vicious circle that impeded scientific activities on this disputed territory.[1] The freezing of the claims and refusal of new claims made possible efficient scientific activities on the cold continent. Outer space activities were at their very beginning, and the cold war and a significant balance between both superpowers made possible the recognition of a legal status that in many ways was copied from the Antarctic Treaty.

Both Antarctic and outer space activities were boosted by the International Geophysical Year, 1957–1958. Sputnik, the first artificial satellite of the Earth, was launched on 4 October 1957; Explorer 1 launched on 1 February 1958, opening the way to the discovery of the Van Allen belt.

Fifty years later, it is interesting to go on comparing both regimes. Doing so, we must keep in mind that outer space is much more sensitive for strategy and defence than Antarctica; the vision of a dominance of the Earth through space dominance is commonplace in geostrategic theories. Economically, outer space is also quite important, for instance, in telecommunications and remote sensing. Still, on many issues, this comparison may be quite useful. For a lawyer and a specialist in space law the hypothesis for this paper is that we have a rather evolved legal framework for outer space, but we have too few cooperation mechanisms. For the time being, the treaties governing outer space are

Armel Kerrest, Faculté de droit, l'Université Européenne de Bretagne, 12 rue de Kergoat, F-29000 Brest, France, and European Centre for Space Law, European Space Agency, 8/10 rue Mario-Nikis, F-75738 Paris Cedex 15. Correspondence: Armel.Kerrest@univ-brest.fr.

rather good for setting important principles regulating outer space activities, but cooperation between interested states is too limited to manage this common space and to improve the current legal framework without destroying it. Many problems are now before us that need concrete international cooperation to be solved. It seems that the cooperation in Antarctica may be a good example of what should be done in outer space.

This paper will present the current legal status of outer space, keeping in mind a comparison with the legal status of Antarctica, and will consider the necessity of a common international governance, taking advantage of the experience of Antarctica, which is more advanced but quite comparable in many ways.

THE LEGAL FRAMEWORK: PRINCIPLES OF OUTER SPACE LAW

Outer space is ruled by treaties setting precise and accepted legal principles. Because of the cold war, the two superpowers supported and accepted treaties organising outer space activities. Both wanted a rather precise legal framework in order to block the other's activities. A good example of this is Article II of the 1967 Treaty on Principles Governing the Activities of States in the Exploration and Use of Outer Space (also called the Outer Space Treaty [OST]), which establishes the nonappropriation principle.[2] Given the balance between them, especially in the race to the Moon, both were interested in preventing the other one from claiming any possession in outer space and especially on the Moon. Both states also accepted the provision to limit military activities in outer space and on the Moon and other celestial bodies. Both accepted their responsibility and liability for space activities. These rather progressive provisions were proposed by the two powers and accepted by other states years before practical activities made it a necessity.

The main rules regulating outer space activities will now be considered. Like in Antarctica, but certainly more clearly and precisely, states play a very central role in outer space activities.

CONTROL OF ACTIVITIES IN OUTER SPACE

States are responsible for "national activities in Outer Space." This important provision of Article VI of the Outer Space Treaty, the "Magna Charta of Outer Space," was the interesting result of a compromise between the Union of Soviet Socialist Republics (USSR) and the United States. In their proposal for a "Draft Declaration of the Basic Principles Governing the Activities of States Pertaining to the Exploration and Use of Outer Space" to the Committee on the Peaceful Uses of Outer Space (COPUOS) in 1962, the USSR wanted to block any private activity in outer space.[3] Despite the fact that no private activity was conducted there at the time, the United States refused this limitation. A compromise was finally found that accepts private activities under the strict control of a state. Point 5 of the Declaration of Legal Principles Governing the Activities of States in the Exploration and Use of Outer Space and Article VI of the Outer Space Treaty consider states to be responsible for "national activities in Outer Spaces."[4] Those texts specify that these activities include "nongovernmental" ones: "whether such activities are carried on by governmental agencies or by non-governmental entities."

Thanks to this compromise, private activities are allowed, but are clearly under the control of a state, which is responsible for their adherence to international law, including space law.[5] Moreover, Article VI goes on to specify that "the activities of non-governmental entities in outer space, including the moon and other celestial bodies, shall require authorization and continuing supervision by the appropriate State Party to the Treaty." These rules make clear that any activity in outer space and on the Moon and other celestial bodies must be carried out "in accordance with international law, including the Charter of the United Nations."[6] For this reason many states involved in space activities are currently enacting domestic space legislation to control any space activity from their territory and also any activity of their nationals from international territory or even from the territory of a foreign state.

This principle goes further than the usual international law obligations of a state because of its personal jurisdiction. It creates a responsibility for states on behalf of their private entities, which is the only such case in international law and, therefore, is particularly important for spaces that are out of territorial jurisdiction of states. Like many other provisions of the Outer Space Treaty, the 1968 Rescue Agreement,[7] the 1972 Liability Convention,[8] and the 1975 Registration Convention[9] have been widely accepted and may be considered as customary law and therefore are applicable to every state whether it is a party to the Outer Space Treaty or not.

LIABILITY FOR DAMAGE CAUSED BY A SPACE OBJECT

The other main provision of space law is the liability set by Article VII of the Outer Space Treaty and the

Liability Convention. It seems that this very "victim-oriented" rule was the counterpart favoured by nonspace-faring countries for accepting the freedom of use of outer space by other countries. Given the sovereignty of states over their territory recognised in the Paris Convention of 1919 and that this freedom was not obvious at the time, the guarantee given by the United States and USSR that damage on Earth would be indemnified was a good way to limit the concerns of states not taking part but at risk to be damaged by the fall of space objects.

This liability is rather broad as relating to damage caused on Earth or to an aircraft in flight. It is much less efficient for damage caused in orbit when another space-faring state is involved.

The liability for damage on Earth is very protective. It lies with the launching state, defined as a state launching, a state procuring the launch, or a state whose facilities or territory are used for the launch. If there is more than one launching state, which is currently very often the case, they are jointly and severally liable; that means that the victim may sue any of them for the whole indemnification. There are no possible exceptions; neither an act of God nor the fault of a third person may be used by the liable launching state, not even the fault of the victim if not gross negligence or willful misconduct. Contrary to the liability of ship owners according to the Brussels International Convention on Civil Liability for Oil Pollution Damage,[10] the liability of the launching state is unlimited in amount or in time. Moreover, the victim is not prevented from seeking compensation through other ways, for instance, before a domestic judge under a domestic law.[11] As such, the 1972 Liability Convention mechanism may be seen as a safety net provided by the launching state to potential victims. It also has the advantage of motivating states to exercise a strict and efficient control over the activities that might cause them to be considered as a liable launching state.

The responsibility of states for national activities in outer space, including the obligation to authorise and supervise private ones, and the liability of the launching states are a strong incentive for states to exert efficient control over every outer space activities.

There are nevertheless some important shortcomings of the 1972 Liability Convention. The most important is related to damage. As usual in law, damage to the environment as such is not taken into consideration. This general problem does not come from the nature of the damage but from the fact that we need a victim to ask for and to get compensation. If the environmental damage is caused on the territory of a state, like in 1978 with the fall of the Soviet satellite Cosmos 954 on the territory of Canada, the state can ask for compensation.[12] If the damage is caused to an international space like the high seas or outer space and at least some parts of Antarctica, that would not be the case; basically, no state would be entitled to ask for compensation for this damage.

There are currently some proposals in the legal subcommittee of the COPUOS to envisage the negotiation of a general convention on space activities following the example of the Montego Bay Convention on the Law of the Sea. Russia and China propose to enter into discussion in a "holistic approach." Despite the interest to enter into discussions, such a project appears extremely dangerous to currently accepted rules, especially on responsibility and liability. For the time being it is very doubtful that any state would accept such a heavy burden. It is true that the situations are rather different; the risk of damage is much higher in Antarctica than damage from a space object falling on the Earth, but we can see from the negotiations on Annex VI to the Protocol on Environmental Protection to the Antarctic Treaty regarding liability that it would be quite difficult to make states accept now, in a different context, the rules of the 1972 Liability Convention.

APPROPRIATION AND NONAPPROPRIATION OF INTERNATIONAL SPACES

Regarding appropriation and sovereignty, the legal situation of outer space is much clearer than Antarctica's.[13] Article II of the Outer Space Treaty clearly sets a nonappropriation principle.[14] Despite some interpretations which are often close to bad faith, the rule is wide, clear, and indisputable: "Outer space, including the moon and other celestial bodies, is not subject to national appropriation by claim of sovereignty, by means of use or occupation, or by any other means." It applies not only to the bodies but also to the orbits, the "void space," as Bin Cheng named it.[15]

Despite this clear wording, some try to dispute this principle. In our time of general private appropriation, they cannot accept a common domain for humanity. Some argue that the limitation is for "national appropriation" and thus does not apply to private persons. It is a misunderstanding of the word "national," which is not synonym with "state". If we consider the context, i.e., Article VI of the same treaty, "national activities" expressly include governmental and nongovernmental entities.[16] In American English the word "nation" is often used instead of "state," but, in fact, the "nation" is both the government and the people having the nationality of a state.[17]

Even if some claims are far from serious, they appear so interesting to the world's media that they are widely spread and enable some to make a lot of money to the detriment of not only consenting victims but also, and more seriously, of the principle itself. The well-known claims made by the "Head Cheese," Dennis Hope, for the Moon and every planet of the solar system are a good example of this distortion of the law and of the evolution of a fanciful project turning into a money making enterprise.[18] Another claim is more interesting from a legal perspective. A U.S. citizen, Gregory W. Nemitz, knowing about a project by NASA to land a space probe on the asteroid Eros, decided to claim it as his property. When NASA landed its spacecraft on the asteroid, he asked for a rent before federal courts of justice.[19] The decisions of the courts dismissed this claim but are not quite decisive on the nonappropriation principle itself. On the other hand, the U.S. Department of State had the opportunity to fully clarify the point of claims on asteroids. Responding to Mr. Nemitz's letters, Ralph L. Braibanti, Director of the Space and Advanced Technology, U.S. Department of State, clearly stated, "Dear Mr. Nemitz. We have reviewed the 'notice' dated February 13, 2003, that you sent to the U.S. Department of State. In the view of the Department, private ownership of an asteroid is precluded by article II of the Treaty on Principles Governing the Activities of States in the Exploration and Use of Outer Space, including the Moon and Other Celestial Bodies. Accordingly, we have concluded that your claim is without legal basis."[20]

The problem is more serious and practical when orbits are concerned, especially the geostationary orbit. As is well known, the satellites that are placed on a circular and equatorial orbit at an altitude of 35,786 km (22,236 miles) are turning quite fast but remain in view of the same position of the Earth.[21] By nature, such orbital positions are limited, and so are the radio frequencies needed for communication from and to the Earth. The International Telecommunication Union is in charge of administering these limited resources for states, with their cooperation. The application of the "first come, first served" principle was criticized by less-developed countries who disliked the attribution of some orbital positions and radio frequencies on an a priori basis. The evolution of a scientific technique eased the way for a solution. The colocalisation of many satellites on the same position and the digitalisation of the emissions enabled the useful capacity of orbits and number of frequencies to be greatly increased. The issue is still present, and need an efficient international cooperation, but having the issue considered in a technical way where practical solutions are needed is helpful.

PEACEFUL USE OF OUTER SPACE

The provisions on military uses of outer space are globally much less ambitious than the one accepted in the Antarctic Treaty. Military activities were envisaged from the beginning of space activities by both the United States and the USSR. We have to remember that at that time, both states were conducting large spying activities, with the USSR mostly on the ground and the United States overflying the Soviet territory with the U2.[22] The launch of the first satellite by the USSR was perhaps an opportunity for the United States and western countries because it opened the way for freedom of use and, consequently, satellite intelligence. The USSR tried to outlaw the use of satellites for intelligence purposes,[23] but this prohibition was not considered further. The laws of physics and the practical impossibility of preventing this use necessarily overrule the legal rules.

According to the OST, outer space is divided into two different parts as far as military activities are concerned: the orbits around the Earth, on the one hand, and the Moon and other celestial bodies and their orbits, on the other. International customary law, the OST, and, in fact, general international law prescribe peaceful use of outer space. Article IV of the OST also prohibits placing "in orbit around the earth any objects carrying nuclear weapons or any other kinds of weapons of mass destruction." The Treaty Banning Nuclear Weapon Tests in the Atmosphere, in Outer Space and Under Water also applies.[24] Any other military activities are not prohibited on the orbit around the Earth. The meaning of *peaceful use* may be disputed; given the common practice of states, it is difficult to see there a ban of any military activity and anything more than the obligation not to be aggressive. Currently, satellites, whether civilian or military, are used by the military for remote sensing/intelligence, communication, and positioning. Many of these activities are dual use. It may also be considered that remote sensing/intelligence satellites may help tracking every activity and are therefore a necessity to preserve peace.

A much less acceptable evolution is what is called "weaponisation," which is the act of putting weapons in outer space whether they are directed to targets in space or on the Earth. This sensitive point will be examined later in the light of the Antarctica Treaty System.

On the Moon and other celestial bodies, the legal situation is very close to the Antarctic one. The wording of

Article IV of the Outer Space Treaty duplicates nearly exactly Article I of the Antarctic Treaty.

> The moon and other celestial bodies shall be used by all States Parties to the Treaty exclusively for peaceful purposes. The establishment of military bases, installations and fortifications, the testing of any type of weapons and the conduct of military manoeuvres on celestial bodies shall be forbidden.

There are two differences that seem to weaken the OST compared to the Atlantic Treaty: The words "for peaceful purposes only" are changed into an apparently stronger "exclusively for peaceful purposes." This wording may have been used in order to make a clearer distinction between the "peaceful use" that is required everywhere in outer space and "exclusively peaceful use" only compulsory for celestial bodies. The second difference is quite significant of the more-limited outline of the OST; it is the removal of the words "inter alia," which are so important in legal texts. It transforms an open list into a limited one. In addition, a useful precision is added in the more modern text, including installations along with military bases and fortifications.

In both texts, the last precision, under a slightly different wording, is quite useful to enlighten the meaning of "peaceful purposes only" and "exclusively for peaceful purposes," respectively. If there is a case where military personnel or equipment may be used when they are not conducting military activity, this wording clarifies that in Antarctica and on celestial bodies military activities as such are prohibited.

THE PROTECTION OF SPACE ENVIRONMENT

At the time of the adoption of the Outer Space Treaty, environmental issues were not paramount. Article IX of the OST deals with "harmful contamination" of outer space and celestial bodies and "adverse changes of the environment of the Earth." It was the follow up of the consideration by the Committee on Space Research (COSPAR) when OST considered the possible contamination from outer space and established in 1958 the Committee on Contamination by Extra-terrestrial Exploration and in 1959 the Consultative Group on Potentially Harmful Effects of Space Experiments. The draft of Article IX of the Outer Space Treaty was very much influenced by the cold war. The USSR complained against the U.S. West Ford Experiment, which consisted of placing millions of copper needles in outer space,[25] and the United States criticized the USSR for nuclear testing in the high atmosphere. Article IX set some obligations to cooperate which, for the time being, remained mostly theoretical. They will be presented later in connection with the lessons that may be learned from the activities in Antarctica.

The framework set for outer space by the UN treaties and resolutions had been established during the cold war by a consensus between the two superpowers. For the time being, the normative process is at a standstill. We need to evolve to a more-efficient cooperation between interested states. The work of the COPUOS is currently nearly blocked. The practice of the Antarctic Treaty System may be a good example to give a new start to real cooperation driven by scientists and engineers if political, military, and strategic issues can be set aside, at least in part.

THE NEED FOR INTERNATIONAL COOPERATION

There are many cooperations in outer space, both multilateral, for example, the activities of the International Space Station, and bilateral. Even during the cold war, some cooperations between the two superpowers took place. These cooperations are mostly performing some task together and are not targeted at jointly regulating outer space itself and the activities conducted there.

Over the last few years, it has appeared more and more obvious that some kind of international regulations are necessary. The increase in the number of spacefaring states, the danger coming from space debris, the necessity to rationalise space traffic on some overcrowded orbits, the trend to weaponize outer space, and the projects aimed at the Moon, Mars, and other celestial bodies increase the necessity to enter into cooperation, especially if the use of the resources of theses bodies is concerned.

The cooperation of states in Antarctica within the Antarctic Treaty System seems to be quite a good example to follow. The two spaces have some important differences. The main one seems to be legal; paradoxically, in practice, it is not. The existence of claims in Antarctica and the undisputed nonappropriation of outer space seem to have few consequences. Article IV of the Antarctic Treaty regarding "freezing of the claims" seems sufficient to push aside most difficulties.

The main difference comes, perhaps, from the uses of both spaces. A strategic and even military use of outer space is not abandoned; it is even very much increasing. Even if some commercial activities take place in Antarctica like tourism, they are still much less important than the scientific activities. This is not the case of outer space, where commercial activities are important. Some, like telecommunication, are already very profitable. Generally speaking, the role of scientists in outer space activities is much less than what they are in Antarctica.[26]

Still some characteristics of outer space are close to Antarctica's. If states really want to commonly organise outer space as an international common, the example of the cooperation in Antarctica seems to be quite relevant. Given the strategic and economical importance of outer space, it will certainly be more difficult than in Antarctica. Three major issues will be discussed: spatial environment, reduction and control of military activities, and the management of resources of outer space and celestial bodies.

REGULATING ACTIVITIES AND PROTECTING SPACE ENVIRONMENT

For the time being, we have some rules for outer space that are rather general and imprecise, and in any case, they are applied by states without any international intergovernmental control or even international cooperation. No specialized intergovernmental organisation exists for regulating outer space activities. The COPUOS is only a subsidiary of the UN General Assembly, with very little autonomy and small technical and administrative capacity. Some organisations are dealing with space activities as a part of their attributions, like the International Telecommunication Union, which is in charge of allocating radio frequencies and geostationary orbital positions. Other organisations, like UNESCO, intervene in outer space activities but have little real effects. In Geneva the UN Conference on Disarmament is competent for military activities in outer space, but despite some proposals, discussions on these issues are currently at a standstill because some major states do not want any discussions on these issues. As far as nongovernmental organisations are concerned, COSPAR has an important role in some precise and limited fields of space activities, especially those that do not yet have major strategic or economical impact, such as the study of potentially environmentally detrimental activities or planetary protection.[27] The Interagency Debris Coordination Committee has been created by space agencies to cooperate on space debris mitigation. In any case, this cooperation is limited by the reluctance of some states to enter into discussions that may lead to any legal constraint.

Article IX of the OST sets a general obligation to "conduct all their activities in outer space . . . with due regard to the corresponding interests of all other States Parties to the Treaty." It deals with possible harmful contamination of celestial bodies and "adverse changes in the environment of the Earth resulting from the introduction of extraterrestrial matter." Cooperation between states is required "if a State Party to the Treaty has reason to believe that an activity or experiment . . . would cause potentially harmful interference with activities of other States Parties in the peaceful exploration and use of outer space."

It would be of major interest to have some organised discussions after the establishment of a mechanism of environmental impact assessment. In this matter, the sophisticated mechanism applicable to Antarctica could be transformed for space activities.

In the field of planetary protection, even if it is a relatively limited activity compared with other more strategic and commercial spatial endeavours, we have a good example of what could be done. It is the most comparable issue with cooperation and scientific influence within the Antarctic system. The COSPAR's Panel on Potentially Environmentally Detrimental Activities in Space (PEDAS) and Panel on Planetary Protection (PPP) are active in this limited but important field.[28]

The graduation of requirements according to possible impact would be major progress. Even if, at the end of the process, states would have the last word, the necessity to discuss their projects would be quite interesting. Some controversial projects were already proposed for outer space. Fortunately, they were partially stopped. Let me refer, for example, to the Project West Ford to put a ring of copper needles around Earth's orbit in order to communicate using the needles as a reflector. This project contributed to space debris and was criticized by scientists.[29] The system was abandoned when satellite communication became efficient.[30] Another project was also set and abandoned: Russian scientists launched *Znamya,* a mirror reflecting the Sun and able to illuminate places during the night, with illumination about two times the glow of a full moon. This mirror would conserve electricity but would create significant light pollution. Exploration and use of the Moon, Mars, and other celestial bodies open the way to discussions on the impact of these activities on the celestial bodies, such as contamination by terrestrial organisms (forward contamination), and also the impact on the Earth as a result of materials returned from outer space carrying potential extraterrestrial organisms (backward contamination). A comparison may be made between this issue and the activities of the Scientific Committee on Antarctic Research and, for instance, its Subglacial Antarctic Lake Exploration Group of Specialists.[31]

Many other programs have been or may be envisaged; publicly available environmental impact assessments are necessary before they are launched, especially, but not only, when nuclear power sources are involved or for activities on celestial bodies that appear to have more than a "minor or transitory impact on the environment." The rules of Annex I of the Protocol on Environmental Protection to the Antarctic Treaty and the way they are implemented would be very a good example to follow. Most of them can be directly transposed and used for outer space activities.[32] The rules will work if the strategic or economical pressures are not too strong. If they are, a stronger and compulsory legal framework should be decided and generally accepted, a difficult work in perspective.

On a more regularly basis the protection of outer space against space debris is much needed. Some orbits are already dangerous. The recent creation of much debris[33] in very useful orbits shows the necessity to organise a kind of "space traffic management."[34]

MILITARY ACTIVITIES IN OUTER SPACE

As discussed, military activities are not prohibited in orbits around the Earth as far as they are nonaggressive and do not use weapons of mass destruction. It is now a necessity to avoid an arm race in outer space. The so-called weaponisation would be extremely costly. It must be emphasised that weapons would also be mostly useless for security purposes. Satellites are very fragile; it is quite easy to destroy them, either one by one with appropriate rockets or laser beams or all at once with nuclear bombs. Satellites for military activities are useful for low- or middle-level conflicts.[35] In case of a high-level conflict involving spacefaring countries, the destruction of satellites could be very quickly done as a "Spatial Pearl Harbor."[36] Such destruction with the related creation of a lot of debris would prevent any activity, whether military or civilian, for years or even centuries. The solution is not to increase the space dominance of one state or another or to try without success to harden satellites but to limit militarisation and to forbid weaponisation of outer space.

If agreements may be negotiated and accepted, it would be necessary to set an efficient international control, the condition of this acceptation by any state. The example of the current practice in Antarctica would, mutatis mutandis, be quite interesting. Of course, the practical situation is rather different as theses activities are conducted in outer space, where it is not technically possible to make any inspection. On the other hand, no space activity can be really secretly conducted, launching a spacecraft is so "noisy" that every state with some technical capabilities is immediately aware of each of them.[37] A control on Earth is needed and should be accepted. The argument that the possible use of many apparently civilian satellites for military or even aggressive purposes prevents any efficient control is not acceptable. It would be like refusing to control the commerce on heavy weapons because crimes might be committed with kitchen knives.[38] Of course, it is obvious that it would be a more difficult task to have this limitation accepted for outer space than for Antarctica, where military activities seems much less "useful."

The situation is, of course, different for military activities on the Moon or other celestial bodies. The current legal situation is very comparable to Antarctica's: no military activity is permitted. Inspection of installations is feasible as far as the states have the technical capability to do so. Article XII of the Outer Space Treaty opens the possibility of such a visit:[39]

> All stations, installations, equipment and space vehicles on the moon and other celestial bodies shall be open to representatives of other States Parties to the Treaty on a basis of reciprocity. Such representatives shall give reasonable advance notice of a projected visit, in order that appropriate consultations may be held and that maximum precautions may be taken to assure safety and to avoid interference with normal operations in the facility to be visited.

EXPLOITING THE MINERAL RESOURCES OF THE MOON AND OTHER CELESTIAL BODIES

Given the technical and financial difficulties of exploiting the Moon or any other celestial bodies, this activity seems to be rather futuristic. Here also it may be quite interesting to compare with the situation of Antarctica. For a nonscientist, It is difficult to have a precise opinion of whether a ban of any mining activity should be supported for the Moon as it was for Antarctica; it may be.

If not, it may be quite useful to have a look at the former Convention on the Regulation of Antarctic Mineral Resource Activities (CRAMRA). First of all, this text was proposed before any mining activity took place in Antarctica; the supportive states expressed their will to discuss this issue before it would be necessary to act in a hurry. We are perhaps in the same situation for celestial bodies.

The mechanism created by CRAMRA succeeded at an apparently impossible task: to organise a mining activity on a territory where states do not agree on sovereignty. It would be much easier task for the Moon and celestial bodies, where the principle of nonappropriation is accepted by treaties and even by international customary law.

For the time being, we do have a treaty: the Moon Agreement.[40] It was mostly proposed by the U.S. delegation to COPUOS and accepted by consensus in the COPUOS and by the UN General Assembly.[41] Later, because of political changes in the United States, strong lobbying of some space activists, and the necessity to obtain the authorisation of the U.S. Senate for ratification, the project was set aside, and many states are no longer considering its ratification. The agreement was only accepted by 13 states.[42] None of them has or even considers having the capability to go to the Moon. Nevertheless, as shown by its acceptation by consensus in the COPUOS and UN General Assembly, this agreement is quite acceptable if ideology can be set aside. In Article 11, it declares "the moon and its natural resources are the common heritage of mankind." States have the right to explore and use the moon without discrimination. Exploitation would need an agreement establishing an international regime "to govern the exploitation of the natural resources of the moon." Such a regime should be negotiated "when such exploitation is about to become feasible." Article 11, paragraph 7, indicates the main purpose of such a regime.

Despite its limited ambitions, for reasons that are more ideological than practical, this agreement is currently demonised. If we want to have a legal regime for exploiting the resources of the Moon, it may be necessary to draft a new instrument. Both the Montego Bay Convention on the Law of the Sea (as modified by the New York Agreement) and CRAMRA may be used by analogy to build the future regime.

As is currently the case for the resources of the bottom of the sea, if there is some possibility to mine the Moon, it will be necessary to adopt a clear international agreement. The concept of the common heritage of mankind is the logical consequence of the nonappropriation and *res communis*, the common province of mankind principles when consumable goods (i.e., goods destroyed by first use) are to be exploited. This is already the case for sea resources. The refusal of this principle has more to do with ideology than pragmatism. The Moon Agreement, as accepted by every delegation to the COPUOS, envisages "an equitable sharing by all States Parties in the benefits derived from those resources, whereby the interests and needs of the developing countries, as well as the efforts of those countries which have contributed either directly or indirectly to the exploration of the moon, shall be given special consideration." In any case, it will be a long time before such exploitation becomes financially profitable. Like for Antarctica, it may be useful to enter into discussion before the activity begins. The existence of a clear and undisputed legal regime is always a necessity before considering important investments. Here they promise to be huge. The CRAMRA was very much oriented toward a protection of the environment; on that issue, it may be quite useful for comparison.

CONCLUSIONS

The current status of Antarctica is generally well accepted; efficient cooperation is occurring. In outer space it should be quite useful to try, mutatis mutandis, to use the lessons from the Antarctic Treaty System. First, world scientists should be given a more important role when issues are not too strategic; groups of experts within the framework of the United Nations could be created in related scientific areas, including space law. They should range from particular domains, like planetary protection, to more general uses, including mitigation of space debris, space traffic management, and even limitation of military uses.

In a longer perspective, the creation of an international organisation may be envisaged, but it is not a priority for the time being. A real international intergovernmental cooperation should be largely improved, especially among states interested in space activities. The specificities of every state may be taken into consideration.[43]

Finally, the issue of demilitarisation with the necessary control should be seriously considered. Nonmilitarisation of outer space, like accepted for Antarctica, is certainly not possible in the foreseeable future for the orbit around the Earth, but international agreements to block weaponisation are necessary and feasible. The example of Antarctica is quite interesting in that regard.

NOTES

1. Armel Kerrest, L'Antarctique, un statut juridique extraordinaire, *Revue "Accès,"* 2003 tome II.

2. "Treaty on Principles Governing the Activities of States in the Exploration and Use of Outer Space, including the Moon and Other Celestial Bodies," opened for signature on 27 January 1967, entered into force on 10 October 1967, XXX *United Nations Treaty Series* (UNTS) XXX, XX *United States Treaties and Other International Agreements* (UST) XXX, *Treaties and Other International Acts Series* (TIAS) No. XXXX; adopted by the General Assembly in Resolution 2222 (XXI), with 98 ratifications and 27 signatures as of 1 January 2008; also referred to as the Outer Space Treaty (OST).

3. UN General Assembly, COPUOS, "Draft Declaration of the Basic Principles Governing the Activities of States Pertaining to the Exploration and Use of Outer Space," UN Doc. A/AC.105/L.2, 10 September 1962, at point 7: "All activities on any kind pertaining to the exploration and use of outer space shall be carried out solely and exclusively by States."

4. UN General Assembly, Plenary Meeting, "Declaration of Legal Principles Governing the Activities of States in the Exploration and Use of Outer Space," 13 December 1963; Resolution 1962 (XVIII).

5. Outer Space Treaty, Article III.

6. Outer Space Treaty, Article III.

7. "Agreement on the Rescue of Astronauts, the Return of Astronauts and the Return of Objects Launched into Outer Space," opened for signature on 22 April 1968, entered into force on 3 December 1968, 672 UNTS 199, 19 UST 7570, TIAS No. 6599; adopted by the UN General Assembly in Resolution 2345 (XXII), with 90 ratifications, 24 signatures, and 1 acceptance of rights and obligations as of 1 January 2008; also referred to as the Rescue Agreement.

8. "Convention on International Liability for Damage Caused by Space Objects," opened for signature on 29 March 1972, entered into force on 1 September 1972, 961 UBTS 187, 24 UST 2389, TIAS No. 7762; adopted by the General Assembly in Resolution 2777 (XXVI), with 86 ratifications, 24 signatures, and 3 acceptances of rights and obligations as of 1 January 2008; also referred to as the Liability Convention.

9. "Convention on Registration of Objects Launched into Outer Space," opened for signature on 14 January 1975, entered into force on 15 September 1976, 1023 UNTS 15, 28 UST 695, TIAS 8480; adopted by the General Assembly in Resolution 3235 (XXIX), with 51 ratifications, 4 signatures, and 2 acceptances of rights and obligations as of 1 January 2008; also called the Registration Convention.

10. "International Convention on Civil Liability for Oil Pollution Damage," 29 November 1969, UNTS 973, p. 3, 9 *International Legal Materials* (ILM) 45.

11. Liability Convention, Article 10.

12. The claim between both states was finally settled by an agreement: "Protocol between the Government of Canada and the Government of the Union of Soviet Socialist Republics." done on April 2, 1981, http://www.oosa.unvienna.org/oosa/SpaceLaw/multi_bi/can_ussr_001.html (accessed 7 December 2010).

13. Armel Kerrest, "L'appropriation de la lune et des corps célestes," in *Droit de l'Espace*, ed. Philippe Achilleas (Brussels: Larcier, 2009), pp. 342–358.

14. See also the "Declaration of Legal Principles Governing the Activities of States in the Exploration and Use of Outer Space," Resolution 1962 (XVIII), 13 December1963, at point 3.

15. The expression was used by one of the finest space law lawyers, Bin Cheng, when he wanted to make a clearer distinction from the difference between the 1963 phrase "outer space and celestial bodies" and the 1967 phrase "outer space, including the moon and other celestial bodies." Bin Cheng, *Studies in International Space Law* (Oxford: Clarendon Press, 1997), p. 517, note 13.

16. See Freeland and Jakhu on Article II, *Cologne Commentary on Space Law*, ed. Hobe, Smiddt-Tedd, and Schrogl (Cologne: Carl Heymanns Verlag, 2009), p. 52.

17. The redactors of the U.S. code took this point into consideration and decided to change the word "Nation" to "Country," which is quite right: "In this chapter, the word 'Country' is substituted for 'Nation' for consistency in the revised title and with other titles of the United States Code" (*U.S. Code* 49), subtitle IX, chapter 701, Commercial Space Launch Activities, footnote).

18. The text of his claim (22 November 1980) is by itself quite revealing of this fanciful character: "This is to inform the sovereign planet of Earth, that, Dennis M. Hope is now and shall ever be known as, 'THE OMNIPITANT RULER OF THE LIGHTED LUNAR SURFACE,' [sic] . . . [and to] inform the world that the ownership of the Moon, of Earth, is hereby claimed by me, Dennis Hope. Said property shall remain in my possession until such time as I declare differently. Let it also be known to all mankind that I subsequently claim ownership of the remaining known eight planets and their respective moons from this day forward . . ." It is amusing to see that despite the obviously far from serious characteristics of this proclamation, many people are taking these claims seriously.

19. U.S.District Court, District of Nevada, 6 November 2003; U.S. Court of Appeals for the Ninth Circuit in San Francisco, California, 20 July 2004; as discussed on The Eros Project for Space Law Web site, http://www.erosproject.com (accessed 20 November 2009).

20. Letter from Ralph L. Braibanti, Director of Space and Advanced Technology, U.S. Department of State, Washington, D.C., to Gregory William Nemitz, 15 August 2003, reproduced on the Web site of Mr. Nemitz, http://www.erosproject.com/exhibit01.html (accessed 20 November 2009)

21. This orbit, also known as the Clarke Orbit, has orbital velocity of 3.07 km/s (1.91 miles/s) with a period of 1436 minutes.

22. "The U-2 Incident," http://www.eisenhowermemorial.org/stories/U2.pdf (accessed 20 November 2009).

23. UN General Assembly, COPUOS, "Draft Declaration of the Basic Principles Governing the Activities of States Pertaining to the Exploration and Use of Outer Space," UN Doc. A/AC.105/L.2, 10 September 1962, at point 8: "The use of artificial satellites for the collection of intelligence information in the territory of foreign States is incompatible with the objectives of mankind in its conquest of outer space."

24. "Treaty Banning Nuclear Tests in the Atmosphere, in Outer Space and Under Water 5," August 1963, in force 10 October 1963, 480 UNTS 43.

25. On this issue, especially on the history of drafting of Article IX, see Sergio Marchisio in *Cologne Commentary on Space Law*, pp. 169–182

26. This lack of involvement may be the reason why COSPAR, which is an observer to COPUOS, despite the fact that it is the main intergovernmental body for regulating outer space, does not attend (at least since 2000) any meeting of the Main Committee or of the Legal Subcommittee and not always the meeting of the Scientific and Technical Subcommittee. Since 2000, COSPAR was not represented at the 2010, 2009, and 2006 meetings; UN COPUOS Report A/AC/105/869, at point 6.

27. The COSPAR Panel on Potentially Environmentally Detrimental Activities in Space (PEDAS), H. Klinkrad (European Space Operations Centre, European Space Agency), chair, and N. L. Johnson (United States), vice-chair; the COSPAR Panel on Planetary Protection (PPP), J. D. Rummel (United States), chair, and G. Kminek (European Space Research and Technology Centre, European Space Agency), vice-chair.

28. A workshop of the COSPAR PPP was scheduled to take place in Princeton in June 2010.

29. On 20 May 1964 the executive council of the Committee of Space Research (COSPAR) adopted a resolution on "no harmful interference from Westford experiment." See Marchisio, p. 173, on Article IX.

30. See Marchisio, p. 172.

31. See the interesting comparison made between the PPP and the Subglacial Antarctic Lake Exploration Group of Specialists in "Antarctic Governance and Implications for Exploration of Subglacial Aquatic Environment," in *Exploration of Antarctic Subglacial Aquatic Environments environmental and Scientific Stewardship* (Washington, D.C.:

National Academies Press, 2007), pp. 104–113, especially a table of comparison on pp. 107–109.

32. Secretariat of the Antarctic Treaty, "Guidelines for Environmental Impact Assessment in Antarctica," http://www.ats.aq/documents/recatt/Att266_e.pdf, (accessed 21 November 2009).

33. China's destruction of one of its weather satellite (Fengyun-1C, 11 January 2007) as a demonstration of its capacity to destroy a satellite created much debris in a rather high and very useful orbit, creating around 2630 catalogued fragments. In 2008 the accidental collision between Iridium 33 and Cosmos 2251 created more than 1,500 debris fragments larger than 10 cm on a range from 200 to 1700 km. Some fragments will fall to Earth many will stay until the end of the century. See *Orbital Debris Quarterly News* 13, no. 3 (2009): 2–3, http://www.orbitaldebris.jsc.nasa.gov/newsletter/pdfs/ODQNv13i3.pdf (accessed 20 November 2009).

34. International Academy of Astronautics, *Cosmic Study on Space Traffic Management* (Paris: International Academy of Astronautics, 2006), http://iaaweb.org/iaa/Studies/spacetraffic.pdf (accessed 21 November 2009).

35. Testimony of Michael Krepon of the Henry L. Stimson Center before the House Committee on Armed Services, Subcommittee on Strategic Forces, 18 March 2009, http://www.fas.org/irp/congress/2009_hr/space.pdf (accessed 7 December 2010).

36. According to the wording used by the Commission to Assess United States National Security Space Management and Organization (Rumsfeld Commission) in 2001.

37. For the current position of the United States against the Chinese and Russian proposal to limit weaponisation of outer space, see "Contemporary Practice of the United States," *American Journal of Intentional Law* 102: 667–669; and Paula A. DeSutter, "Is an Outer Space Arms Control Treaty Verifiable?" (remarks to the George C. Marshall Institute Roundtable at the National Press Club, Washington, D.C., 4 March 2008), http://www.nti.org/e_research/official_docs/dos/dos030408.pdf (accessed 22 November 2009). For quite a different philosophy, see "Outline of Basic Provisions of a Treaty on General and Complete Disarmament in a Peaceful World (submitted by the US Delegation to the UN Committee on Disarmament Geneva April 18 1962)," *American Journal of International Law* 56, no. 3 (1962): 899–925

38. DeSutter, "Is an Outer Space Arms Control Treaty Verifiable?".

39. Cf. Antarctic Treaty, Article VII, paragraph 3.

40. "The Agreement Governing the Activities of States on the Moon and Other Celestial Bodies," opened for signature on 18 December 1979, entered into force on 11 July 1984, 1363 UNTS 3, 18 ILM 1434–1979, http://www.unoosa.org/oosa/en/SpaceLaw/moon.html (accessed 7 December 2010); adopted by the General Assembly in Resolution 34/68, with 13 ratifications and 4 signatures as of 1 January 2008; also called the Moon Agreement.

41. Carl Q. Christol, "The Moon Treaty Enters into Force: Current Developments," *American Journal of International Law* 79, no. 1 (1985): 163–168.

42. As of 1 January 2008, 13 states have ratified, 4 have signed; http://www.unoosa.org/oosa/en/SpaceLaw/moon.html (accessed 21 November 2009).

43. States with launch pads, strong satellites operators, remote sensing capabilities, etc.

Policies for Scientific Exploration and Environmental Protection: Comparison of the Antarctic and Outer Space Treaties

Margaret S. Race

INTRODUCTION

The Antarctic Treaty (AT) has been successful by almost any measure. It has dealt effectively with military challenges posed by nuclear weapons, political tensions of sovereignty claims, and the scientific desire for shared access to research sites across vast, unexplored expanses. Over the past 50 years the AT has contributed to global stability, cooperative scientific exploration, and international management for peaceful purposes of nearly 10% of the Earth (Grimaldi, 2009). In similar ways, the UN Outer Space Treaty (OST),[1] which was, in part, modeled on the Antarctic Treaty, has also withstood the test of time, designating outer space as a resource for peaceful uses in the interest of all mankind. In addition to its role in cold war diplomacy and preventing a nuclear space race, the Outer Space Treaty has contributed to productive scientific exploration, international cooperation, and the protection of planets from biological contamination ("planetary protection") for more than four decades.

Although both treaties shared similar priority goals in their early stages, each has responded to quite different challenges, both social and technological, over the last 50 years. As a result, they have diverged over that time, particularly with respect to environmental protection and management. As a guide to the future and to understand the environmental and management challenges of an increased human presence in outer space, it may be instructive to examine the key features of each treaty at the time of negotiation and compare how each was modified over the decades. As both environments will likely face increasing demands for access and use of their relatively hostile, yet fragile, environments, lessons learned from the comparisons can provide insights on how the treaties can respond to future challenges like increased exploration and increased tourism, as well as the more complex decisions about resource management and use brought about by the increased presence of humans in these environments.

For both treaties, sound scientific information has been essential for the establishment and revision of management plans and regulatory guidelines. Looking ahead, ongoing research and new scientific understanding of both Antarctica and outer space will be important to effectively address the challenges posed by increased human activities, whether they result from government, scientific, commercial, and industrial or private sector pursuits.

Margaret S. Race, SETI Institute, 189 Bernardo Avenue, Mountain View, California 94043, USA.

INITIAL TREATY FRAMEWORKS

As noted by Kerrest (this volume), Antarctica and outer space have a lot in common. Both are hostile environments for humans, both are viewed with the potential for extensive and valuable resources of different types, and both are of intense interest for scientific research and exploration. Likewise, both Antarctica and outer space have potentially high strategic value and were the focus of significant political and military interest during the cold war.

Both treaties were products of the cold war era, developed on the heels of the very successful International Geophysical Year (IGY; 1957–1958) that reflected international scientific cooperation in the post–World War II era. At that time, the Antarctic Treaty deliberations served as a framework to address concerns over possible cold war military expansion as well as conflicting sovereignty claims on Antarctic areas that had been put forward by a handful of nations. Although subsequent discussions about the Outer Space Treaty likewise centered on potential military expansion and national security, they were coupled with a desire to establish the precedent of "freedom of international space," thereby heading off tensions over legal restrictions aimed at orbiting satellites and spacecraft. From a historical perspective, one could argue that scientific activities served as peacekeeping surrogates and cooperative ventures that ensured internationalization and diffused political tensions, that the "political exploitation of scientific goodwill" was used to "achieve essentially political objectives" (Launius, 2009). Regardless, for both treaties, scientific exploration legitimized international control by creating mechanisms for management and goals for continued rational use that continue to this day.

The 17 articles of the Outer Space Treaty have considerable overlap and similarity with the 14 articles of the original Antarctic Treaty. As shown in Table 1, both stipulate exclusively peaceful uses and strict limitations on military activities and the use of nuclear weapons and materials. Both prohibit governments from extending national sovereignty or making new resource claims, and each indicates that states parties are responsible for authorization, supervision, and responsibility over their national activities, whether those activities are undertaken by governmental or nongovernmental entities. Both declare the expectation of freedom of scientific investigations, exchanges of information and personnel, access for observers, and peaceful dispute settlements. In addition, both have provisions for amending, interpreting, and upholding the treaty as well as mechanisms to allow other states to become signatories. Notable differences have to do with the nature of space exploration and the potential for astronauts to come back to the Earth in unplanned ways to unplanned locations. In the Outer Space Treaty, states agree to provide assistance to astronauts in the event of accidents or emergencies; to retain jurisdiction, control, and ownership of their launched objects; and to accept liability for damages caused by objects in their control, whether on Earth or other planets, in air space or outer space.

Although discussions of both treaties began around the same time, the Antarctic Treaty was developed by a group of just 12 countries, led by the United States and the United Kingdom.[2] Treaty deliberations and modifications occur through Antarctic Treaty Consultative Meetings (ATCM), which are now held annually. In contrast, the Outer Space Treaty was negotiated as a United Nations treaty.[3] The UN Committee on the Peaceful Uses of Outer Space (COPUOS), which was established by the General Assembly in 1959, was designated as the focal point of international cooperation and deliberations regarding peaceful exploration and use of outer space. Originally, COPUOS had 24 members but has since grown to 69 members, making it one of the largest committees in the United Nations.

Interestingly, both treaties are supported by strong, active, international scientific panels that grew out of IGY research efforts and which predate the signing of their respective treaties. The Scientific Committee for Antarctic Research (SCAR) and the Committee on Space Research (COSPAR) were established by the International Council of Scientific Unions (now the International Council for Science, ICSU) in 1957 and 1958, respectively, to provide independent scientific advice on matters related to their respective treaties, as well as information on emerging issues. The COSPAR, as a nongovernmental organization, was granted permanent observer status to the UN COPUOS in 1962.[4] The SCAR is similarly a third-party, nongovernmental organization that functions as a permanent observer and advisor to the Antarctic Treaty through the ATCM.[5]

In considering the initial makeup of the treaties, two features are linked to later expansion in areas of environmental and science management.

1. *Science reserves for exploration versus science and use*: Although both treaties stipulate scientific exploration for peaceful purposes for the benefit of mankind, the Antarctic Treaty designated the continent as a natural reserve devoted to science, whereas the Outer Space Treaty specifically mentioned science, cooperation, and use for mankind, keeping the door open for all types of activities, not just scientific exploration on celestial bodies and in outer space.

TABLE 1. Key features of the Antarctic and Outer Space treaties at ratification.

Features	Antarctic Treaty[a] Article	Outer Space Treaty[b] Article
Peaceful Uses for Mankind	I	I, III, IV
No Military Activities or Bases	I	IV
Science Investigation and Cooperation	II	Science Exploration, Cooperation and Use I
No Sovereign Claims	IV	II
No Nuclear Explosives/Waste Disposal	V	No Nuclear Weapons or WMDs in Orbit IV
Jurisdiction and Responsibility for National Activities	VIII	VI
Freedom of Access	III	I
Share Information on Science/Activities	III	XI
Freedom of Personnel and Observers	III	I, X, XII
Peaceful Settlement of Issues and Discourage Contrary Activities	X, XI	Practical Questions Resolved by Consultations XIII, IX
Procedures for Accession	XIII	XIV
Amendment Provisions	XII	XV
Consultative Meetings	IX	—
	—	Avoid Harmful Contamination of Celestial Bodies and Adverse Changes to Earth IX
	—	Assist Astronauts V
	—	Liability for Launched Items VII
	—	Retain Jurisdiction, Ownership of Items VIII
Scientific Advisory Group (independent, 3rd party NGOs)	Sci. Committee on Antarctic Research (SCAR) (1958)	Committee on Space Research (COSPAR) (1958)

[a]Signed in 1959; in force 1961.
[b]Signed in 1967; in force 1967.

2. *Environmental oversight*: The Outer Space Treaty stipulates that states should conduct exploration of celestial bodies in ways "so as to avoid their harmful contamination and also adverse changes in the environment of the Earth caused by the introduction of extraterrestrial matter." The initial version of the Antarctic Treaty made no specific mention of contamination, biological or otherwise, although it does indicate that preservation and conservation of living resources are within the scope of its Consultative Meetings.

In hindsight, neither treaty provided much in the way of initial guidance for later expansion into regimes that would address concerns about environmental management and protection. Over time, each has dealt with these issues quite differently, as described below.

EVOLUTION AND IMPLEMENTATION OF THE TREATIES OVER THE DECADES

Antarctic Treaty System

When the Antarctic Treaty went into force in 1961, it was a mere shadow of what it is today regarding environmental and science protection. It is now a treaty system, comprising ~200 agreements and measures that have been developed and ratified via the ATCM process, with considerable multidisciplinary input through SCAR. The system's extensive environmental oversight and protections are an outgrowth of international deliberations and sound science that have been translated incrementally into precautionary, multispecies, and ecosystem-based approaches

TABLE 2. Comparison of the Antarctic Treaty (after 50 years) and the Outer Space Treaty (after 40 years).

Features	Antarctic Treaty, 1959	Outer Space Treaty, 1967
Agreements/legal instruments	Conservation of Antarctic Fauna and Flora (1964; in force 1982) Conservation of Antarctic Seals (1972; in force 1978) Conservation of Antarctic Marine Living Resources (1980; in force 1982) Protocol on Environmental Protection (1991; in force 1998) Regulation of Antarctic Mineral Resource Activities (1988; later rejected)	Agreement on the Rescue and Return of Astronauts and Objects (1968) Convention on International Liability for Damage by Space Objects (1972) Convention on Registration of Objects Launched into Outer Space (1975; in force1976) Agreement Governing Activities of States on the Moon and Other Celestial Bodies (1979; in force 1984) Guidelines on Space Debris Mitigation (COPUOS- IADC; 2010)
Annexes	Environmental Impact Assessments 1991 (1998) Fauna and Flora 1991 (1998) Waste Management 1991 (1998) Marine Pollution 1991 (1998) Special Protected Areas (& moratorium on mineral activities 1991 (2002) Liability arising for environmental emergencies (2005) (not in force yet)	Declaration on Activities in Exploration and Uses of Outer Space (adopted 1963) Use of Artificial Earth Satellites for International Direct TV Broadcasting (1982) Remote Sensing of Earth from Outer Space (1986) Use of Nuclear Power Sources in Outer Space (1992) International Cooperation in Exploration and Use for the Benefit of all States, and Needs of Developing Countries (1996)
Governance framework	AT Consultative Meetings (ATCM), 1961 AT Secretariat, 2004 Scientific Committee for Antarctic Research (SCAR), 1958	Governance framework UN Committee on Peaceful Uses of Outer Space (COPUOS), 1959 UN Office for Outer Space Affairs (UNOOSA), 1958 Committee On Space Research (COSPAR), 1958

to management. As summarized in Table 2, the Antarctic Treaty System is now an amalgam of five main agreements, six annexes, and various legally binding measures relating to protection of Antarctic environments and resources. Most additions to the original treaty were developed from the 1970s through the 1990s, but changes are continuing. As a treaty system, the Antarctic Treaty System is a dynamic entity, considerably more effective and stronger than when originally ratified. What began as a treaty built around cold war diplomacy, military and nuclear limitations, and peaceful science exploration has evolved into a remarkable instrument of environmental protection, international science cooperation, and stewardship for the benefit of humankind, all the while maintaining its important geopolitical and security objectives.

Although the early conventions and agreements on flora and fauna, living resources, and seals were noteworthy, perhaps the most important elements of the Antarctic Treaty for protection of the environment and dependent ecosystems were developed in the 1990s with the Protocol on Environmental Protection and its associated annexes. In addition to preventing development and providing protection for the Antarctic environment, this protocol established a set of binding mandates related to prevention of marine pollution, conservation of flora and fauna, waste disposal and management, special area protection and management, and environmental impact assessments. The result is a clear, comprehensive framework that outlines a code of conduct for expeditions and station activities, along with procedures for international review in advance of proposals likely to have significant environmental impacts. Activities with anticipated minor or transitory impacts fall under the oversight and jurisdiction of national authorities. Ongoing participation and input by SCAR to the ATCM, as well as to the Committee for Environmental Protection (CEP), provide opportunities to update relevant scientific information, identify emerging issues or concerns, and make recommendations for revisions related to stewardship or those intending to minimize the adverse impacts of human activities.[6]

Outer Space Treaty

In contrast to the dynamically evolving Antarctic Treaty System, the Outer Space Treaty has remained unchanged over the decades. As shown in Table 2, the OST has been joined by four additional international treaties. Three of these (rescue and return of astronauts, liability, and registration) elaborate on principles included in the original treaty. The fourth, The Agreement Governing the Activities of States on the Moon and Other Celestial Bodies (also called the Moon Agreement; accepted by the General Assembly in 1973; nominally in force in 1984) designated "the Moon and its natural resources as the common heritage of mankind." The Moon Agreegment has been ratified by only 13 States and signed by only 4 others,[7] despite repeated calls by the General Assembly (Tuerk, 2009). Among other things, the Moon Agreement embraces nonappropriation of property while asserting the right of states to collect and remove samples of the Moon's minerals and other substances in quantities appropriate for the support of their missions. In addition to these four legal instruments, there is a fifth document that complements the Outer Space Treaty. Recently, after more than a decade of deliberative work by the Inter-Agency Space Debris Coordination Committee (IADC),[8] both COPOUS (2007) and the General Assembly (2008) endorsed the set of voluntary space debris mitigation guidelines and encouraged their implementation through national mechanisms.[9]

During the past four decades, neither the OST nor any of the subsequent agreements have established specific regulations for activities related to the commercialization, exploitation, or use of any natural resources of the Moon or other celestial bodies by either public or private entities. Deliberations by COPUOS have focused largely on activities in Earth orbit or those that might impact Earth (e.g., missions with astronauts, space debris, satellites, liability for damages, ownership of objects, launch registration, nuclear power sources in space, remote sensing of Earth, defense against hazardous asteroids, etc.).[10] Only one article of the OST addresses protection of the Earth and contamination avoidance in space. In Article IX, the OST stipulates avoidance of harmful contamination, protection of exploration, and prevention of "adverse" changes on Earth from the return of extraterrestrial materials.

Despite the lack of development of other OST provisions, the implementation of Article IX has resulted in a long and successful history of planetary protection (from living or organic contamination) of celestial bodies during space exploration. True to its consultative role with COPUOS, COSPAR has played a strong role in developing international policies and guidelines to avoid forward contamination (transport of hitchhiker organisms on spacecraft launched from Earth) and back contamination (uncontained return of extraterrestrial samples or materials that could be biohazardous to Earth). Early efforts in spacecraft decontamination began during the first decade of space exploration beyond Earth, and planetary protection controls have been updated repeatedly to reflect advances in science and technology ever since.[11]

In recent years, the increasing pace of astrobiology research and space missions has contributed to a new understanding of planetary environments, cosmological processes, biological potential, and life in extreme environments. Accordingly, COSPAR and the scientific community have continued to refine planetary protection policies associated with one-way, round-trip, robotic and human missions to solar system bodies.[12] The focus on *biological* and *organic* contamination means there are no specific policies addressing other sorts of environmental management or protection needed to protect physical environments and natural resources beyond the Earth. As a nongovernmental organization without institutional authority, COSPAR's recommendations are not internationally legally binding, except through consultation with and interpretation by COPUOS and the voluntary adoption of COSPAR standards by spacefaring nations in separate, multiparty agreements. Nonetheless, planetary protection provisions have been voluntarily adopted by launching nations over the decades, thereby affording indirect environmental protection to target bodies with possible habitable conditions.

For a variety of reasons, the OST has not developed a comprehensive framework of mandated environmental protections similar to that afforded by the Antarctic Treaty System. Part of the difference is based on the nature and extent of scientific information available about Earth versus outer space, and this lack of knowledge (of the environments, of the capabilities of Earth organisms in those environments, and of the possible existence of extraterrestrial life) has meant that the implementation of the OST's "no harmful contamination" article has focused on biological contamination avoidance, rather than on environmental protection, per se. Although an understanding of Antarctic microbes and ecosystems has only recently developed, our understanding about flora, fauna, and environments on Earth is extensive and can be applied to Antarctica for developing environmental and resource protections. In contrast, our knowledge about planetary environments and the uncertainty about possible associated biota and dependent ecosystems in outer space make it more difficult to establish appropriate levels of protection drawn directly from scientific analogies or legal precedents on Earth. When one celestial body is deemed to be lifeless (like the Moon or some asteroids) compared to another that could potentially harbor extraterrestrial life (like Mars or Europa), one can debate the merits and justifications for developing varied environmental management and planetary protection policies for each, but such designations are subject to change as new knowledge becomes available. Scientists are continuing to deliberate on how to update planetary protection policies and control measures that will protect the various bodies of the solar system even as new launching nations add to a growing number of science missions to diverse target bodies.

Although voluntary adherence to biological contamination controls has translated into protection of science exploration over the years, there is still nothing that provides a framework around the OST similar to the AT's protocol of environmental protection, code of conduct, special area designations,[13] or environmental impact assessments for proposed activities. This lack of a framework has implications for space missions both now and in the future. For example, a number of missions have deliberately impacted the Moon with spacecraft to detect and analyze subsurface ice (e.g., Lunar Prospector, Lunar Crater Observation and Sensing Satellite [LCROSS], etc.), yielding significant information for researchers interested in potential water reserves on the Moon. Nonetheless, other researchers interested in studying the lunar atmosphere or who might want to study the record of past cometary impact on the Moon have expressed concerns that repeated landings, deliberate impacts, or other volatile-rich lunar surface activities could contaminate the fragile atmosphere in ways that could interfere with future scientific study and interpretation of the lunar record. Unlike the Antarctic Treaty, the Outer Space Treaty has no internationally accepted framework or process that requires states parties to assess, in advance, the effects of various science mission proposals or to evaluate their relative merits or cumulative impacts on other science efforts. Concerns about this lack of a review process are likely to grow and become more complicated in the future, with the anticipated increase of commercial, industrial, and private sector activities on the Moon and other planetary surfaces.

LOOKING AHEAD

The Antarctic and Outer Space treaties have each performed well for many decades and, barring any unfortunate geopolitical crises, will presumably maintain their important roles in cooperative science exploration, nonappropriation, prevention of military and nuclear activities, and peaceful uses of their respective territories. However, when it comes to environmental protection and resource management, the Antarctic Treaty framework is currently better prepared to tackle likely future challenges, as detailed in the following comparison.

Antarctic Treaty

On the basis of the original treaty and subsequent revisions, the Antarctic Treaty System outlines clear statements about its prohibitions, regulations, and objectives and has evolved regulatory and procedural frameworks effective for environmental management and changing scenarios. It is a streamlined legal instrument, overseen by a relatively limited number of acceding states whose highly involved user communities rely on the ATCM and up-to-date information to manage the continent as a reserve for scientific research. The existing framework provides an established means to tackle emerging challenges such as the growing interest in bioprospecting, increasing demand for tourism, and continued interest in mineral exploitation, oil and gas extraction, and expansion of economic activities.[14] Other complications may arise from tensions between science preservation and perceived national interests, particularly in regard to pollution control, marine resources, or rights at the intersection of other treaties (e.g., the UN Convention on the Law of the Sea). All in all, the Antarctic Treaty has grown into a strong environmental treaty over time and has contributed to five decades of peaceful scientific exploration and cooperative stewardship, even though historians suggest that science was manipulated in the beginning to achieve Western geopolitical aims during the cold war era (cf. Launius, 2009). From today's perspective, the treaty can provide valuable lessons and useful analogues on how to approach the management of sensitive international resources for the benefit of humankind.

Outer Space Treaty

Although the original Outer Space Treaty and its subsequent agreements likewise outline clear statements about prohibitions, guidelines, and objectives, its implementation through COPUOS over the past four decades has focused predominantly on launches and activities in Earth orbit (issues related to astronauts, ownership, liability, sustainability and protection of orbital assets, handling of space debris, and equipment at end-of-life, etc.). At the same time, COSPAR and the international scientific community have concentrated on the only element of the treaty that specifically mentions contamination or protection beyond Earth orbit. So far, COSPAR has incrementally developed planetary protection "rules of the road" that represent "detailed and very specific non-binding, standards and guidelines that amount to soft law instruments applicable to extraterrestrial space exploration" (Bohlmann, 2009:192. According to Bohlmann (2009:193), this evolution of policies and law governing space protection reflects the increased influence of the science community and a shift of political motivations for space exploration initiatives away from "the early hard power arguments to the quest for scientific knowledge perceived as a cultural imperative."

Already, we can anticipate the kinds of pressures likely to arise in the coming decades. For example, planned human activities may contribute to a variety of direct, indirect, and cumulative impacts, including base infrastructure construction, waste handling and disposal, exploration, road building, mining, in situ resource utilization, traffic management of orbital assets, end-of-mission debris handling, placement of large radio telescopes, use and disposal of nuclear power sources, and eventual settlement and associated development. Concerns about potential impacts on historical sites or special areas have been raised by proposals for novel private or commercial activities like aerospace prize competitions, space tourism, and even astroburials on the lunar surface. Although many of these scenarios have analogues on Earth or in Earth orbit, they present unusual complications as the pace of activities increases.

Although a predominantly science-based approach has worked well in Antarctica to develop a framework for environmental protection, resource management, and prevention of harmful contamination, there are some distinctively different issues associated with this type of approach in space.[15] Given the wide variety of different environments found in outer space, even the conceptual basis for such a framework will need reconsideration. Notions like environmental stewardship, sustainability, preservation, resource use, exploitation, or adverse impacts on, under, or above celestial bodies have yet to be defined and discussed in detail because in many cases hostile space environments are incapable of sustaining life. Accordingly, there are no general guidelines for how to address the protection of lifeless environments in the solar system.

Other possibly unique complications could arise if and when verified extraterrestrial life is discovered since all legal and ethical systems on Earth are based on life as we know it. Recently, scientists have even suggested the need to discuss whether ethical considerations should be integrated into planetary protection policy along with protection of science (National Research Council [NRC], 2006:111–114). The recommendation for an international workshop on the topic was endorsed by COSPAR in 2008, and a workshop on ethical issues in planetary protection was held in June 2010 and discussed at the COSPAR General Assembly in Bremen, Germany (July 2010). With so many different environmental situations possible in "outer space," some of which are distinctly different from those encountered in terrestrial situations, questions about a treaty regime that will ensure the appropriate protection of unique natural and physical systems are sure to persist. Clearly, there is a long road ahead before we can develop a consensus system for balancing science exploration, environmental protection, and diverse, peaceful uses of outer space for human benefit (to say nothing about benefiting "all mankind").

The good news is that research and analysis during the past 10–15 years have already identified various issues and gaps or inadequacies in outer space policy (e.g., Hargrove, 1986; Lupisella and Logsdon, 1997; Almar, 2002; Race and Randolph, 2002; Tennen, 2003; Cockell and Horneck, 2004; Williamson, 2006; Sterns and Tennen, 2007; Masson-Zwann, 2008), and the COSPAR planetary protection policy has been updated and expanded every two years (at biannual COSPAR Assemblies) since 2002. In addition, recently a number of interdisciplinary groups have begun organized discussions on how to develop environmental management agreements in ways that effectively integrate scientific exploration with potentially expanding commercial and private sector activities. For example, the International Academy of Astronautics (IAA) "Cosmic Study" on Protecting the Environment of Celestial Bodies (PECB) was formed under the auspices of IAA Commission V (Space Policy, Law, and Economy) to examine current planetary protection controls for avoiding biological contamination and consider whether and how protection might extend to geophysical, industrial, and cultural realms. The PECB study report (Hoffman et al., In press) identified a variety of problems related to environmental protection, including the lack of suitable detection methodologies and an insufficient legal framework, a paucity of economic analytical tools, and a shortage of the political will to address the issues ahead. COSPAR's Panel on Exploration (PEX) (COSPAR, In press) undertook a study to provide independent input to support the development of worldwide space exploration programs while safeguarding the scientific assets of solar system objects. The PEX report also outlines how to protect the lunar and Martian environments for scientific research under various legal frameworks. Elsewhere, the European Space Foundation (ESF) co-organized a transdisciplinary conference and dialogue with the European Space Agency (ESA) and the European Space Policy Institute (ESPI) in 2007 to assess issues at different phases in human exploration, first in Earth orbit, then on other bodies, and finally as colonizers off Earth (Codignola and Schrogl, 2009). A subsequent ESF scoping conference (2009) extended discussions to even broader considerations, from philosophy and religion to culture, education, legal, ethical, political, and social frameworks. Ultimately, the conference output will lead to publication of a multidisciplinary research roadmap (ESF, 2011). Finally, COSPAR's Planetary Protection Panel has begun planning a symposium for 2011 that will examine planetary protection policy and environmental protection in outer space as a continuum and determine what revisions in COSPAR policy, if any, may be needed to adapt to the changing face of space exploration.

Viewed collectively, many of the ideas identified as ways to move forward in outer space bear striking similarities to elements of the Antarctic Treaty's framework for environmental management. For example, tentative suggestions have included the need to consider

- designation of special management areas or protected zones to avoid or mitigate impacts in advance (e.g., special scientific regions, historical/cultural/aesthetic reserves, planetary parks, special natural features or formations, developable regions, etc.);
- development of a comprehensive environmental protection protocol (for scientific and other proposals) that outlines procedural approaches for review and assessment of proposed activities that have the potential for significant direct or indirect contamination or exploitation impacts;
- establishment of code(s) of conduct appropriate for different types of celestial bodies and environments (including subsurface and orbital) and an elaboration of how these may apply to various categories of activities and different sectors (scientific, commercial, industrial, private, etc.); and
- development of workable analytical tools and criteria for evaluating considerations such as costs, benefits, reversibility, and varying degrees of impacts from proposed activities, including cumulative impacts.

Although the underlying concepts and principles for environmental management and stewardship will necessarily be drawn from terrestrial analogues and experiences, some issues may require innovative approaches or consideration. For example, there is need to anticipate what complications could arise if and when extraterrestrial life is discovered and verified. Since all current ethical and legal systems are based on life as we know it, such a discovery will likely challenge the bases for management and stewardship in outer space. Likewise, questions about how to determine the balance between scientific exploration and the use of an environment for the benefit of humankind will require discussions of issues like "fair" access and equity among different current users, as well as issues like the long-term sustainability of resources and environments in outer space and consideration of obligations to nonspacefaring nations and future generations. In light of these unusual complications, some observers have suggested the need for a new international consultative body to engage in more coordinated and informed consideration of the complex issues ahead.

Once these discussions start in earnest, multiple "user" communities can enter into deliberations about environmental management that have previously been overseen largely by COSPAR and the rest of the scientific community. It is important to continue the application of existing planetary protection controls and policies as working guidelines for scientific and other users, even as we evaluate how to transition to a more comprehensive set of mandates and regulations covering more than biological and organic contamination. Planetary protection policies, even today, incorporate echoes of the notion of a "period of biological exploration" (set at 50 years), which once suggested that when we know more about planets like Mars and had determined whether extraterrestrial life exists, then we might transition to a more active period of human activity and development. In some ways, this period could function like the moratorium on mineral exploration in Antarctica and provide a suitable cushion of time for a conservative or precautionary approach in the face of scientific uncertainty.

Both the Antarctic and space communities are involved in explorations aimed at understanding extreme environments of interest and importance to humankind. Both communities recognize the need to devise workable plans for environmental stewardship and management that can respond to new challenges posed by human presence, yet which will continue to sustain the resources of these vast areas, now and in the future. It is too early to say what a suitable framework for environmental management in outer space should be, particularly in the face of increasing pressures by diverse user groups. Although these communities continue to protect and sustain science exploration and discovery through existing treaties and policies, we must find ways to allow appropriate technological development and expansion of human activities beyond Earth, presumably borrowing from successful analogues and precedents on Earth. On the basis of lessons learned from the Antarctic experiences, it is clear that the space community has considerable work ahead. Fortunately, the Antarctic Treaty System provides a workable model that may be emulated with some confidence as the exploration of outer space moves ahead.

Acknowledgments

The author extends special thanks to John Rummel, Patricia Sterns, Leslie Tennen, Mark Williamson, Mahlon Kennicutt, and Roger Launius for their helpful reviews and suggestions during the preparation of this paper.

NOTES

1. The Treaty on Principles Governing the Exploration and Use of Outer Space, including the Moon and Other Celestial Bodies.

2. The Antarctic Treaty was originally signed by 12 parties and now has been ratified by 47 parties, 28 of which are Consultative Parties eligible to vote at ATCMs.

3. The Outer Space Treaty was signed initially by 27 parties; as of 2008, the treaty had been signed and ratified by 98 signatory states (plus 27 additional states not fully ratified).

4. Many other nongovernmental organizations have been granted observer status with the COPUOS in the subsequent decades, including the International Astronautical Federation (IAF), the International Institute of Space Law (IISL), and the International Academy of Astronautics (IAA).

5. Mahlon Kennicutt II, Department of Oceanography, Texas A&M University, personal communication, 2010.

6. For example, questions about the advisability of drilling into pristine subglacial aquatic lakes and environments like Lake Vostok became the subject of extensive discussions by SCAR and the scientific community for over a decade in efforts to minimize harmful contamination. These discussions were undertaken largely within the context of the treaty structure. See NRC (2007) for a historical review of deliberations to develop a sound scientific basis for contamination and cleanliness standards aimed at managing future research and exploration in these sensitive environments.

7. At the time of signing, all 13 were nonspacefaring nations; subsequently, France and India have become launching nations.

8. For information on IADC, see http://www.iadc-online.org/index.cgi?item=home (accessed 18 November 2010).

9. UN Office for Outer Space Affairs, "Space Debris Mitigation Guidelines of COPUOS," (United Nations, Vienna, 2010), http://www.unoosa.org/pdf/publications/st_space_49E.pdf (accessed 18 November 2010).

10. Additional agreements that relate to outer space issues but are not considered part of the treaty include the Nuclear Test Ban Treaty (1963) and the International Telecommunication Union Constitution and Convention (1992) (geostationary orbits) (Williamson, 2006).

11. For historical reviews of planetary protection policies, see NRC (2006: pp. 11–35) and Williamson (2006: pp. 91–148). Depending on the target body and the type of science activities planned for a mission, general planetary protection requirements may include a combination of clean room assembly of parts and spacecraft; cleaning and sterilization of components, subsystems, and whole spacecraft; microbiological reduction and control via use of standard cleaning procedures and assays on hardware; methods to prevent recontamination before launch; calculation of impact probabilities to minimize accidental contamination; and inventories of organic compounds on spacecraft for certain missions categories.

12. See "COSPAR Planetary Protection Policy," http://cosparhq.cnes.fr/Scistr/PPPolicy(20-July-08).pdf (accessed 18 November 2010); and NASA planetary protection Web site, http://www.planetaryprotection.nasa.gov (accessed 18 November 2010).

13. The Moon Treaty, Article 7, par. 3, mentions areas of special scientific interest, but it has never been implemented.

14. Mahlon Kennicutt II, personal communication, March 2010.

15. The interpretation of harmful contamination has been suggested to mean harmful to humans rather than harmful to the environment, especially because Article IX of the Outer Space Treaty mentions causing harmful interference with activities in the peaceful exploration and use of outer space. Some suggest that it relates to avoiding harm to human activities, rather than harm to space environments (Cypser, 1993; Williamson, 2006:160).

LITERATURE CITED

Almar, I., 2002. What Could COSPAR Do to Protect the Planetary and Space Environment? *Advances in Space Research*, 30(6):1577–1581.

Bohlmann, U. M. 2009. "The Need of a Legal Framework for Space Exploration." In *Humans in Outer Space: Interdisciplinary Odysseys*, ed. L. Codignola and K.-U. Schrogl, pp. 182–195. NewYork: Springer.

Cockell, C., and G. Horneck. 2004. A Planetary Park System for Mars. *Space Policy*, 20(4):291–295.

Codignola, L., and K.-U. Schroegel, eds. 2009. *Humans in Outer Space: Interdisciplinary Odysseys*. New York: Springer.

Committee on Space Research (COSPAR) Panel on Exploration Report (PEX), 2010. Toward a Global Space Exploration Program: A Stepping Stone Approach. 80 pp. COSPAR: Paris. http://cosparhq.cnes.fr/PEX_Report2010_June22a.pdf (Accessed 19 Novevmber 2010).

Cypser, D. A. 1993. International Law and Policy of Extraterrestrial Planetary Protection. *Jurimetrics: Journal of Law, Science and Technology*, 33:315–339.

European Space Foundation (ESF). 2011. *Humans in Outer Space: Interdisciplinary Perspective*. Studies in Space Policy, Vol. 5, ed. Ulrike Landfester, Nina-Louisa Remuss, Kai-Uwe Schrogl, and Jean-Claude Worms. Vienna: Springer-Verlag.

Grimaldi, A., 2009. Governance of Both Poles. *Science*, 326:1042.

Hargrove, E. C., ed. 1986. *Beyond Spaceship Earth: Environmental Ethics and the Solar System*. San Francisco: Sierra Club Books.

Hofmann, M., P. Rettberg, and M. Williamson, eds. 2010. *Protecting the Environment of Celestial Bodies (PECB Cosmic Study)*. Paris: International Academy of Astronautics. http://law.leiden.edu/organisation/publiclaw/iiasl/staff/masson-zwaan.html#publications-2008 (Accessed 22 November 2010).

Kerrest, A. 2011 (this volume). "Outer Space as International Space: Lessons from Antarctica." In *Science Diplomacy: Antarctica, Science, and the Governance of International Spaces*, ed. P. A. Berkman, M. A. Lang, D. W. H. Walton, and O. R. Young, pp. 133–142. Washington, D.C.: Smithsonian Institution Scholarly Press.

Launius, R. 2009. "Comments on Origins of the Antarctic Treaty of 1959." Paper presented at the Antarctic Treaty Summit, Washington, D.C., 30 November.

Lupisella, M., and J. Logsdon. 1997. Do We Need a Cosmocentric Ethic? Paper IAA-97-IAA.9.2.09. Presented at the International Astronautical Federation Congress, American Institute of Aeronautics and Astronautics, Turin, Italy.

Masson-Zwann, T. 2008. "Lunar Exploration and Exploitation as a Special Case of Planetary Exploration-Legal Issues." In *The Contemporary Problems of International Space Law*, ed. A. Kapustin and G. Zhukov, pp. 159–169. Moscow: Peoples' Friendship University of Russia. https://openaccess.leidenuniv.nl/dspace/bitstream/1887/13925/2/TMZ+russian+book.pdf (Accessed 22 November 2010).

National Research Council (NRC). 2006. *Preventing the Forward Contamination of Mars*. Washington, D.C.: National Academies Press.

———. 2007. *Exploration of Antarctic Subglacial Aquatic Environments: Environmental and Scientific Stewardship*. Washington, D.C.: National Academies Press.

Race, M. S., and R. Randolph. 2002. The Need for Operating Guidelines and a Decision Making Framework Applicable to the Discovery of Non-intelligent Extraterrestrial Life. *Advances in Space Research*, 30(6):1583–1591.

Sterns, P. M., and L. I. Tennen. 2007. Ethics and the Conquest of Space: From Peenemunde to Mars and Beyond. IAF Paper IAC-07-E6.5.08. In *Proceedings of the 50th Colloquium on the Law of Outer Space*. Reston, Va.: AIAA.

Tennen, L. I. 2003. Evolution of the Planetary Protection Policy: Conflict of Science and Jurisprudence? *Advances in Space Research*, 34:2354.

Tuerk, H. 2009. "The Negotiation of the 'Moon Agreement.'" Paper presented at UN 30th Anniversary of the "Moon Agreement": Retrospect and Prospects, Vienna, 23 March 2009. http://www.unoosa.org/pdf/pres/lsc2009/symp00.pdf (accessed 18 November 2010).

Williamson, M., 2006. *Space: The Fragile Frontier*. Reston, Va.: AIAA.

New Frontiers and Future Directions in Antarctic Science

Mahlon Kennicutt II

ABSTRACT. The study of Antarctica and the Southern Ocean, and their role in the Earth system, has never been more important as the region experiences change that has global implications. The Antarctic region is a "natural laboratory" for scientific research of importance in its own right and impossible to achieve elsewhere on the planet. Understanding the Earth system, its components, connections and feedbacks is a major endeavour of contemporary Antarctic science. The following on-going and emerging research activities will be a continued focus of Antarctic research in the coming years: past, current and future climate change; the systematic response of Antarctica to change; understanding Antarctic biodiversity, evolution and ecology; exploration and modelling of ice dynamics and sub-ice environments; ocean, ice, atmospheric and cryospheric observing and modelling; linkages and teleconnections between polar regions and the Earth system; and the poles as a vantage point to observe Earth, near-Earth space, the Solar System and beyond. The Scientific Committee on Antarctic Research (SCAR) is a leader in facilitating international, interdisciplinary science in Antarctica, and through its portfolio of scientific projects, committees, and programs provides a venue for partnerships and exchange of the latest findings. The SCAR accomplishes its scientific mission in close partnership with a wide range of organizations, including the Council of Managers of National Antarctic Programs, the Convention for the Conservation of Antarctic Marine Living Resources, the Scientific Committee on Oceanic Research, the Association of Polar Early Career Scientists, and the International Arctic Science Committee. The SCAR works to ensure that maximum value is derived from the Antarctic research. Emerging frontiers and new directions in Antarctic science continue the historical recognition of the value of the Antarctic as a reserve for science and peace.

INTRODUCTION

As we celebrate on the 50th anniversary of the signing of the Antarctic Treaty and the successes of the International Polar Year, it is an opportune time to reflect on emerging themes in Antarctic science. This is one of the most, if not the most, exciting times for Antarctic science in history. The study of Antarctica and the Southern Ocean, and their role in the Earth system, has never been more important as the region experiences change that has global implications. The Antarctic region is a "natural laboratory" for scientific research of importance in its own right and impossible to achieve elsewhere on the planet. In addition, sound science and knowledge-based advice have never been more critical

Mahlon Kennicutt II, Scientific Committee on Antarctic Research and Department of Oceanography, Texas A&M University, Room 608 O&M Building, 3146 TAMU, College Station, Texas 77843-3146, USA. Correspondence: m-kennicutt@tamu.edu.

to the policy community to inform decision making and to support complex environmental stewardship and conservation efforts in Antarctica. The Scientific Committee on Antarctic Research (SCAR), as an interdisciplinary, international scientific body of the International Council of Science (ICSU), has been a facilitator and champion of Antarctic science for more than 50 years, dating back to the beginnings of the Antarctic Treaty (Walton, this volume).

PREDICTING FUTURE TRENDS IN ANTARCTIC SCIENCES

Predicting future directions in Antarctic science is difficult as investments in science are decided individually by each nation in different ways:

- investments in science are national enterprises,
- processes for setting scientific priorities are highly variable among nations,
- future directions are dependent on the outcome of "in progress" research,
- trajectories can be non-linear or discontinuous, and
- technology and science can be decoupled.

Indeed, science can drive technology and technology can drive science.

Looking at the broad sweep of Antarctic science, several trends are discernable. Antarctica, as a geographic focus for science, is unique in that the community of scientists that conduct research in the region come from almost all scientific disciplines. In the twenty-first century, Antarctic science will be increasingly called upon to address complex questions that require sophisticated and diverse technologies. In the twenty-first century, an Earth system science approach is fundamental to understanding Antarctica's past, present, and future, and in most instances, Antarctic science will be pursued within an interdisciplinary framework. Understanding the Earth system, its components, connections and feedbacks is a major endeavor of contemporary Antarctic science and research. Antarctic research will generate large and complex volumes of diverse data and information, require transcontinental or at least region-wide investigations to address scientific questions, and entail greater access to all areas of the continent.

On the basis of a review of the International Polar Year (IPY) project database, a wide range of planning documents, and conferring with leaders in Antarctic science, several major scientific themes are apparent:

- Antarctica and global climate;
- deciphering paleoclimate;
- organisms, ecosystems, and biodiversity;
- subglacial aquatic environments;
- exploration beneath the ice;
- cryospheric observing and modeling;
- ice sheet dynamics and sea level;
- Southern Ocean observing and modeling; and
- the poles as a vantage point.

Life Sciences. Although thought of as a cold and isolated environment, Antarctica is undergoing significant change due to regional climate warming, ozone depletion, non-native species introductions, global transport of contaminants, increased scientific and tourist visits, and natural resource exploitation and extraction. Biologically, Antarctica and the Southern Ocean are centers of evolutionary divergence and adaptation to environmental extremes. Antarctic life sciences research focuses on understanding the effect of past, current, and predicted environmental change on biodiversity, adaptation, organism functioning, ecosystem structure/function and the effects of cold, darkness, and isolation on organisms and ecosystems, both on the continent and in the Southern Ocean.

Geosciences. The Antarctic continent and surrounding oceans have been key elements of the Earth system throughout the history of the planet. The basement of Antarctica is built of a suite of crustal blocks that were parts of various supercontinents and the continent contains outcrops that provide insight into Earth processes in the distant past. Sedimentary records on and around Antarctica provide glimpses of paleohistory and variations in the Earth's environment over the eons, harboring clues to the evolution of Antarctica. Geodetic and geophysical observatories document the geodynamics of the continent. Antarctic geosciences research focuses on continental crustal structure and composition, geodynamical processes, the record of life in a warmer Antarctica, the effects of geological processes on Antarctic biota and understanding the controls on ice sheet evolution and stability.

Physical Sciences. Processes at the interfaces between ice, ocean, land and atmosphere are key to understanding climate dynamics and predicting future climate. The nearly pole centered continent of Antarctica gives it a unique place in the global climate system. The role of, and the impact upon, the polar regions in climate processes are a focus of Antarctic physical sciences research. This research aims to understand ice sheet dynamics, climate records from ice cores, changes in sea ice distribution and ocean circulation, atmospheric dynamics and chemistry, oceanic upwelling and melting ice shelves and the impact of the ozone hole on Antarctic climate. The Antarctic continent is also a unique place for astronomical and solar-terrestrial observations of phenomena such as interactions between the Sun and the Earth.

This chapter reviews these major themes and highlights some of the ongoing programs and projects illustrative of future directions. Reflective of the truly integrated nature of modern Antarctic science, many scientific programs crosscut interdisciplinary scientific themes. This chapter can only provide a partial glimpse of the complex web of science programs that link thousands of scientists in more than 30 countries collectively forming modern Antarctic science.

ANTARCTICA AND GLOBAL CLIMATE

By far the most pervasive theme in Antarctic science is climate change. The study of climate change in the region and linkages with the global climate system will occupy Antarctic scientists for many years to come.

The Antarctic is a critically important part of the Earth system. The climate, physical, and biological properties of the continent and the surrounding ocean are closely coupled to other parts of the global environment by the ocean and the atmosphere. Antarctica contains approximately 90% of the world's ice and approximately 70% of the world's freshwater, which is enough to raise sea level by 63 m. It also holds high-resolution records of past climate change and sensitive biological indicators of contemporary change. For example, the Antarctic ozone hole was one of the most significant scientific discoveries of the last century and resulted in major changes in environmental management throughout the world (Benedick, 1998). For the last 30 years the ozone hole has shielded the Antarctic from the effects of "global warming." The western coast of the Antarctic Peninsula is experiencing one of the most rapid rises in mean temperature anywhere on Earth. The Southern Ocean warming causes change in both terrestrial and marine ecosystems. There has been a rapid expansion of the area covered by the two flowering plants on the Antarctic Peninsula. Parts of the Antarctic are losing ice at a rapid rate. Paleoclimate studies in Antarctica show the current changes in global climate are unusual. Assuming a doubling of greenhouse gas concentrations over the next century, Antarctica is predicted to warm significantly, with the largest increases experienced by West Antarctica.

The instrumental records from the research stations and automatic weather stations are valuable but are generally too short to provide enough data for climate trend analyses where changes need to be looked at over decades, centuries, or even longer. When these records are integrated with proxy records of change from ice and sediment cores, they offer a powerful tool for climate analyses. The SCAR has released a comprehensive synthesis of current understanding of Antarctic climate science, *Antarctic Climate Change and the Environment* (Turner et al., 2009; this report has been widely distributed and is available from the SCAR Web site, http://www.scar.org). The report concludes that a key objective for future Antarctic climate studies is to improve representations of polar processes in models so that more-accurate predictions are produced. Higher-resolution global models, regional climate models, and ecosystem and ice sheet models are required. Climate models require better simulations of polar-specific processes, such as sea ice and the atmospheric boundary layer.

Climate variability in the polar regions is greater than in other parts of the world, and improved monitoring and more detailed understanding of past climate are needed in order to discriminate natural variability from anthropogenic influences. There is an urgent need to establish marine and terrestrial biological baseline monitoring programs in order to understand past change and to establish the links between physical and biological variability. There is a requirement for greater cross- and interdisciplinary observational efforts linked to modeling studies that will be discussed later.

In order to better understand climate variability a detailed understanding of past climate is essential. Gaps in records of past climate archived in ice and sedimentary cores must be filled. This objective is accomplished by several differing approaches that increase the spatial and temporal coverage of climate records. Because of the remoteness of the continent, Antarctica is an ideal location to study local- to global-scale climate change. However, this remoteness has also prevented the collection of instrumental records, similar to those collected in the Northern Hemisphere, that are required to assess Antarctica's role in and response to environmental and climate change.

The continued study of surface and near-surface ice core records is essential. High-resolution ice core records are the most direct way to document climate with resolutions as fine as seasonal and, potentially, on time scales as long as a million years. Fundamental issues of spatial and temporal climatic and environmental variability still need to be addressed by determining the spatial variability of Antarctic climate over the last 200 years, and where the data are available, the last 1000 years. High-resolution ice core records are also critical for establishing spatial gradients in ice core properties as a complement to deep ice core records that support the objective of obtaining the oldest ice core record in Antarctica. The search for a 1.5 million year record of climate and greenhouse gases from Antarctica will extend knowledge of past climate change, much as the European Project for Ice Coring in Antarctica (EPICA) ice core supplemented the Vostok ice core climate record.

Complementary to ice core records are climate records contained in sedimentary sequences. Recovery and interpretation of sedimentary records of climate change are the objectives of several major programs including Antarctic Geological Drilling (ANDRILL; http://www.andrill.org/), Shallow Drilling on the Antarctic Continental Margin (SHALDRILL; http://www.shaldril.rice.edu), the Integrated Ocean Drilling Program (IODP; http://www.iodp.org/), and integrative synthesis programs such as SCAR's Antarctic Climate Evolution (ACE) program. Studies of the greenhouse world 50 MYA imply a higher "climate sensitivity" than currently accepted, suggesting the potential for additional positive feedbacks not currently represented in climate models.

Knowledge of the behavior of Polar Regions in a high-CO_2 world still remains one of the greatest uncertainties in predicting future climate response. There is a continuing need to recover Antarctic geological records beyond the age range of ice cores, dating as far back as 30–50 MYA when Earth's atmospheric CO_2 was two to four times higher than at present, the high end of the Intergovernmental Panel on Climate Change (IPCC) projections for 2100. Major scientific objectives in the geosciences include obtaining geological records that sample past Antarctic ice sheet dynamics and integrate climate and ice sheet proxy data with the latest generation of coupled ice sheet–climate models. Much remains to be accomplished in these research areas.

Finally, it will be essential to integrate sedimentary, ice, and instrumental records of climate change with climate and ice sheet models to constrain predictions of future change. Each type of climate record contributes differing spatial and temporal records of past climate change that together provide a comprehensive picture of climate forcings.

ANTARCTIC ORGANISMS, ECOSYSTEM, AND BIODIVERSITY

Research directions in the life sciences will build on current research being conducted by programs such as SCAR's Scientific Research Program Evolution and Biodiversity in Antarctica (EBA). Although significant advances have been made in recent years, Antarctica's biological and ecological domains remain, to a large extent, unexplored. Antarctic life scientists strive to understand the evolution and diversity of life in Antarctica to determine how evolution and biodiversity have produced Antarctic ecosystems. Understanding of ecosystem functioning is fundamental.

One of the most important recent developments in life sciences in the Antarctic is the increase in knowledge of biodiversity in the terrestrial and marine settings, especially the deep sea. We also know that organisms and biodiversity are beginning to change in response to climate change. There is a great need to describe the living residents of Antarctica and to better understand their origins. There is also a critical need to document nonendemic species as climate change affects floral and faunal ranges worldwide and the probability of alien introductions increases (Frenot et al., 2005).

Life sciences research in the Antarctic focuses on three main ecological topics that are important worldwide: changes in habitats, loss of biodiversity, and the effect of climate change. A first step in improving our basic understanding is to document what organisms are present. An excellent example of one such program is the Census of Antarctic Marine Life (CAML). The CAML investigated the distribution and abundance of Antarctica's marine biodiversity to develop a benchmark (http://www.caml.aq).

Life sciences research in Antarctica has a long history of studying adaptations, ecosystem function and structure, and the physiology of the unique organisms that inhabit Antarctica. Much research on these topics is expected to continue to address basic questions about life in the cold and dark, life in subglacial aquatic environments (which I will return to), and life at the extremes of our planet. Research objectives will require extension of observations beyond the traditional summer season and the application of modern methods in molecular genomics and proteomics.

Antarctic biodiversity and biogeography will remain a topic of high interest for years to come. An exemplary program is the SCAR Marine Biodiversity Information Network (SCAR-MarBIN; http://www.scarmarbin.be), which is the Antarctic node for the Ocean Biogeographic Information System (OBIS) and a companion project of CAML. The SCAR-MarBIN is a distributed system of interoperable databases that compiles and manages existing and new information on Antarctic marine biodiversity.

Subsequent to the Larsen Ice Shelf collapse, the first observations of cold seep communities in Antarctic were recorded. These unique communities and possibly hydrothermal vent communities are being considered as possible vulnerable marine areas in need of special protection. These sites also present opportunities to study unusual ecosystems that have only recently been identified in Antarctica.

The success of the Convention for the Conservation of Marine Living Resources (CCAMLR) in promoting an ecosystem management approach to Southern Ocean fisheries relies, to a considerable extent, on the marine biology undertaken by SCAR scientists. The changes in the Southern Ocean food webs attributable to recent fish, squid, and krill harvesting suggest that this research will be even more important in the future, especially in the establishment of marine protected areas and the monitoring of secondary effects of fishing on higher predators.

Today, Antarctica is almost 99.7% covered by permanent ice and snow, and evidence suggests that as recently as the Last Glacial Maximum, ice sheets were both thicker and much more extensive than they are now. Most, if not all, of the currently ice-free ground would have been overridden by ice during previous glaciations, suggesting that Antarctic preglacial terrestrial life was wiped out by successive glacial events. This, in turn, suggests that most, possibly all, contemporary terrestrial life has colonized the continent during subsequent periods of glacial retreat. A combination of recent biological and geological data compiled by Convey et al. (2008) challenges this paradigm. New and complex conclusions about terrestrial Antarctic biogeography suggest greater regionalization and evolutionary isolation than previously suspected for circum-Antarctic marine fauna. These findings require the adoption of a new biological paradigm within Antarctica and challenge current understanding of Antarctic glacial history. Future research that will flow from these investigations will have major implications for understanding the key role of Antarctica in the Earth system.

SUBGLACIAL AQUATIC ENVIRONMENTS

The study and exploration of subglacial aquatic environments is at its beginnings. Subglacial aquatic environment research by its nature is highly interdisciplinary and is poised to fundamentally change our view of how Antarctica responds as part of the Earth system. The study of these environments will contribute to a wide range of Antarctic scientific topics, including the tectonic evolution and history of the continent, the importance of subglacial hydrology in ice sheet and ice stream dynamics, and the adaptation of microbial life in these unique environments. It is also conjectured that these environments may hold records of the past climate of the interior of the continent and that outbursts of subglacial waters have been important processes over geologic time.

There are three major subglacial lake exploration programs projecting lake entry and sampling in 2011–2012. These projects include the long-term studies at Lake Vostok, the studies of subglacial Lake Ellsworth, and coordinated studies of the Whillans Ice Stream. International, field-intensive programs are exploring the Antarctic continent hidden beneath kilometers of ice in East and West Antarctica. These studies use a range of technologies and are providing a view of the basement beneath the Antarctic ice sheet never before seen. International coordination of the science is through a SCAR Group of Specialists (http://www.sale.scar.org/).

EXPLORATION BENEATH THE ICE

Three projects highlight future directions in Antarctic geosciences: Antarctica's Gamburtsev Province Project (AGAP), Ice and Climate Evolution of the Central Antarctic Plate (ICECAP), and Polar Earth Observing Network (POLENET). The AGAP is exploring the history of the East Antarctic ice sheet and lithospheric structure of the Gamburtsev subglacial mountains, a major mountain range buried by the East Antarctica Ice Sheet, which includes numerous subglacial lakes. AGAP is a multinational and multidisciplinary program that includes aerogeophysics, traverse programs, passive seismic experiments, and ice core and bedrock drilling.

The objective is to better understand the tectonic origin of the Gamburtsev Mountains, providing crucial new data for ice sheet and climate models (Bo et al., 2009). Fundamental questions to be addressed include

- What role does topography play in the nucleation of continental ice sheets?
- How are major elevated continental massifs formed within intraplate settings but without a straightforward plate tectonic mechanism?
- How do tectonic processes control the formation, distribution, and stability of subglacial lakes?
- Where is the oldest climate record in the Antarctic ice sheet?

The ICECAP is a collaborative program between the United States, the United Kingdom, and Australia to use a multi-instrumented long-range aircraft over three austral summers to survey portions of the East Antarctic Ice Sheet. The ICECAP is acquiring aerogeophysical observations to determine ice thickness and date internal layers in support of ice sheet modeling, observing flow regime change recorded in the internal layers. and studying crustal geology and subglacial hydrological systems from the perspective of processes controlling past and future change in the East Antarctic Ice Sheet.

The POLENET is a collaborative, international project to understand how the Earth's surface responds to changes in polar ice sheets. The POLENET project is collecting GPS and seismic data from stations at remote sites spanning much of Antarctica. Integrated GPS and seismic measurements are used to model how much ice has been lost over the past 10,000 years. A combination of ground-based and satellite data is used to determine where, and at what rate, the ice sheets are changing in response to recent climate change.

CRYOSPHERIC OBSERVATIONS AND MODELING

The Global Inter-agency IPY Polar Snapshot Year (GIIPSY) project collects data to understand the role of polar processes in climate change, the contribution of the polar ice sheet to sea level, and ice sheet and ocean interactions. An ambitious schedule of missions over the next several years is already planned. Satellite observations support a wide range of research efforts.

Some regions of Antarctica, particularly the peninsula, have warmed rapidly in recent years, contributing to the disintegration of ice shelves and accelerating the sliding of glaciers. These events have focused attention on the stability of the West Antarctic Ice Sheet (WAIS) as much of it is grounded below sea level. The WAIS Divide ice core will provide Southern Hemisphere climate and greenhouse gas records comparable in time resolution and duration to the Greenland ice cores. The WAIS Divide ice core will also be used to test models of WAIS history and stability.

Recent findings suggest that from 1957 through 2006, temperatures across Antarctica rose an average of 0.2°F (0.1°C) per decade, comparable to global warming rates. In East Antarctica, where temperatures had been thought to be falling, researchers have found a slight warming over the last 50 years.

There is growing consensus that the Antarctic ice sheet is experiencing net mass loss. The long-term trends in these data will be of interest for years to come. Sea level has risen in recent years, mostly because of thermal expansion of the world's ocean, glacier melt, and losses of mass from the Greenland ice sheet. However, as previously noted, the ice sheets of Antarctica are the major global reservoir of freshwater and represent by far the greatest potential for sea level rise in the future. The status of and trends in the Antarctic cryosphere will be of high interest for years to come (Rohling et al., 2009).

SOUTHERN OCEAN OBSERVING AND MODELING

As for Antarctica's cryosphere, a better understanding of the Southern Ocean is critical to anticipating and predicting response to climate change. The Southern Ocean has a global influence with the potential for significant feedbacks. There is evidence that changes in the Southern Ocean are underway, but sparse observations make interpretations difficult.

System-scale observations of the Southern Ocean are critical. Integrated multidisciplinary observations are necessary to understand and ultimately predict the response of biota to changes in physical drivers. An integrated, coordinated, and broadly multidisciplinary approach to a Southern Ocean observing system is being developed. Some elements are already in place, such as (1) repeat hydrography, (2) ships of opportunity, (3) Argo floats (http://www.argo.ucsd.edu/newsletter.html), (4) tagging of marine mammals (http://biology.st-andrews.ac.uk/seaos), (5) SCAR continuous plankton recorder, and (6) satellites (e.g., Sea-viewing Wide Field-of-view Sensor [SeaWiFS]; http://oceancolor.gsfc.nasa.gov/SeaWiFS).

Ocean acidification due to uptake of atmospheric carbon dioxide can be deleterious to many marine organisms and ecosystems. Predicted ocean acidification (McNeil and Matear, 2008) is expected to cause major changes in nutrients, phytoplankton diversity, biodiversity, biogeochemical cycles, marine community structure and robustness, and calcification rates while reducing behavioral capacity, growth, production, life span, and tolerance to environmental fluctuations. Following this growing problem will be a focus of research for years to come.

THE POLES AS A VANTAGE POINT

Antarctica possesses special advantages for astronomers with its clear skies, high plateau, low humidity, and stable atmosphere (Storey, 2005). Increasing investment in a range of telescopes at the South Pole and Dome C has provided major new facilities for the international community. Antarctic astronomy and astrophysics will address fundamental questions in the next decade, including

- locating first stars, first galaxies, and reionization tomography;
- defining the nature of the dark universe;
- detecting gravity waves;
- identifying exoplanets and the formation of exo-solar systems;
- exploring variations in fundamental constants;
- searching for extra dimensions; and
- defining the transient universe.

One program, IceCube (http://icecube.lbl.gov), is searching for neutrinos from the most violent astrophysical sources, events like exploding stars, gamma ray bursts, and cataclysmic phenomena involving black holes and neutron stars. The IceCube telescope could reveal the physical processes associated with the enigmatic origin of the highest-energy particles in nature.

Near-Earth space (geospace) is an integral part of the Earth system, providing the material link between the Sun and Earth, primarily through the polar regions. Research in this area will create an integrated, quantitative description of the upper atmosphere over Antarctica and its coupling to the geospace environment. The Super Dual Auroral Radar Network (SuperDARN; http://superdarn.jhuapl.edu/), an international radar network, studies the Earth's upper atmosphere, ionosphere, and connection into space.

CONCLUSIONS

The realities of conducting research in the southern polar regions bring with it great challenges but also great opportunities. The questions being asked by those with interests in Antarctica, the Southern Ocean and the Earth system are more complex and demanding than ever before. The critical role of scientific knowledge developed from the study of Antarctica and the Southern Ocean has never been more important in discerning the future of our planet. Antarctica and the Southern Ocean are a natural laboratories where global forces play out in ways not experienced or observable elsewhere on the planet. Antarctica also serves as a unique vantage point to look outwards from our planet to observe near-Earth space, our solar system and beyond. In a time of economic stress, it is important that resources be used to optimum affect, that investments in science in Antarctica be justified, and that the community develops and shares a collective vision of future scientific directions. A well-conceived strategy is not only essential but critical. This partial review of major themes in Antarctic science over the next 10–20 years illustrates what an exciting and productive time is in store for Antarctic scientists. A combination of scientific ideas and societal issues will drive future research directions. Twenty-first century Antarctic science and research will address complex questions that require holistic, interdisciplinary, international, and technologically intensive experiments that will require access to all of Antarctica. The need for access to data and data sharing will increase along with the necessity for ever-more-sophisticated data and information infrastructure to collect, store, archive, and synthesize the vast amounts of data that will be generated.

Antarctica evokes a sense of discovery as a location of unexplored places and the origin of surprising findings that inspire unconventional thinking. In the next few decades the Antarctic science community will build on its history of accomplishment and elevate the presence and importance of Antarctic science in the global conversation. There are opportunities for coordination, partnerships, and synergy that build on the historical international partnerships that epitomize Antarctic science. Where our community will be in 10 or 20 years is only limited by our imagination, as the future is in our hands!

LITERATURE CITED

Benedick, R. 1998. *Ozone Diplomacy*. Cambridge, Mass.: Harvard University Press.

Bo, S., M. J. Siegert, S. M. Mudd, D. Sugden, S. Fujita, C. Xiangbin, J. Yunyun, T. Xueyuan, and L. Yuansheng. 2009. The Gamburtsev Mountains and the Origin and Early Evolution of the Antarctic Ice Sheet. *Nature,* 459:690–693.

Convey, P., J. A. E. Gibson, C. D. Hillenbrand, D. A. Hodgson, P. J. A. Pugh, J. L. Smellie, and M. I. Stevens. 2008. Antarctic Terrestrial Life: Challenging the History of the Frozen Continent? *Biological Reviews,* 83:103–117.

Frenot, Y., S. L. Chown, J. Whinam, P. M. Selkirk, P. Convey, M. Skotnicki, and D. M. Bergstrom. 2005. Biological Invasions in the Antarctic: Extent, Impacts and Implications. *Biological Reviews,* 80:45–72.

McNeil, B. I., and R. J. Matear. 2008. Southern Ocean Acidification: A Tipping Point at 450-ppm Atmospheric CO_2. *Proceedings of the National Academy of Sciences of the United States,* 105(48):18,860–18,864.

Retamales, J., and M. Rogan-Finnemore. 2011 (this volume). "The Role of the Council of Managers of National Antarctic Programs." In

Science Diplomacy: Antarctica, Science, and the Governance of International Spaces, ed. P. A. Berkman, M. A. Lang, D. W. H. Walton, and O Young, pp. 231–239. Washington, D.C.: Smithsonian Institution Scholarly Press.

Rohling, E. J., K. Grant, M. Bolshaw, A. P. Roberts, M. Siddall, C. Hemleben, and M. Kucera. 2009. Antarctic Temperature and Global Sea Level Closely Coupled over the Past Five Glacial Cycles. *Nature Geoscience*, 2(7):500–504

Storey, J. W. V. 2005. Astronomy from Antarctica. *Antarctic Science*, 17(4):555–560.

Turner, J., R. A. Bindschadler, P. Convey, G. Di Prisco, E. Fahrbach, J. Gutt, D. A. Hodgson, P. A. Mayewski, and C. P. Summerhayes, eds. 2009. *Antarctic Climate Change and the Environment*. Cambridge: Scientific Committee on Antarctic Research.

Walton, D. W. H. 2011 (this volume). "The Scientific Committee on Antarctic Research and the Antarctic Treaty." In *Science Diplomacy: Antarctica, Science, and the Governance of International Spaces*, ed. P. A. Berkman, M. A. Lang, D. W. H. Walton, and O Young, pp. 75–88. Washington, D.C.: Smithsonian Institution Scholarly Press.

Modern Research in Polar Regions

Jörn Thiede

Jörn Thiede, Alfred Wegener Institute, Am Handelshafen 12, D-27570 Bremerhaven, Germany. Correspondence, jt@geo.ku.dk.

Research in the polar regions, in particular in Antarctica and the Southern Ocean, is demanding on scientists, equipment, and financial resources. However, it is also urgently needed by governments, not only because of the sensitivity of the polar regions to global change in real time but also because of the role of the polar regions as major drivers for global climate and environmental changes (e.g., sea level, ocean circulation through the "conveyor belt," etc.). As highlighted by the present president of the Scientific Committee on Antarctic Research (SCAR), Antarctic research is research at the "frontiers to the unknown" (subglacial geology, subglacial lakes, ice older than 1 million years, etc.), and the topics selected for the Antarctic Treaty Summit (the ozone hole, the ice core story, cosmology from Antarctica, and the Southern Ocean) not only cover an enormous range of scales in time and space but also demonstrate the excellence and relevance of Antarctic research.

Research in Antarctica and the Southern Ocean is challenging and also dangerous because the environment is hostile to mankind, and thus, it is exceptionally important that we have the right tools. Are we properly equipped and are our methods robust and safe? During the last International Polar Year (IPY) many traverses were organised using nonspecialist vehicles, but frequent breakdowns of vehicles illustrated how dangerous they could be; luckily, no lives were lost. Over the past 50 years many stations have been established in Antarctica, probably too many in some places (i.e., the situation on King George Island). Some are now outdated and little used, and yet the international exchange of scientists that could use these station is really in its infancy. The hypermodern French-Italian station on Dome Concordia is an extraordinary exception and shows that at least at the bilateral level international stations are possible (compare with the Argentine-German station at Jubany). The leading nations in Antarctic research should be more forthcoming with their support to the emerging polar research nations, certainly much more than they have been so far, through sharing their infrastructure, both on land and at sea, as well as developing their scientific programs jointly with their "younger" partners.

There have been remarkable political changes in the attitude of nations with interests in Antarctic research. First, there are a remarkable number of new nations that have joined SCAR, adding strength to all of the scientific efforts in and around Antarctica. Second, we have seen the emergence of regional groups of nations that found value in coordinating their polar research with the aim of supporting and strengthening their scientific efforts. For example, the European Polar Board of the European Science Foundation has succeeded in raising enough interest with the political authorities of the European Union to generate substantial European funding for some aspects of Antarctic research (e.g., the European Project for Ice Coring in Antarctica [EPICA] project). The same applies to nations in the Far East (PAG), where nations now coordinate their Arctic and Antarctic research efforts.

The Council of Managers of National Antarctic Programs (COMNAP), with the help of SCAR, has established new systems to relieve precious polar research vessels from logistical obligations in East Antarctica, thus giving them more cruise time for science, and an increased transport efficiency more like that in New Zealand and Australia. The Dronning Maud Land Air Network (DROMLAN) serves blue ice runways close to the Russian Novolazarevskaja and the Norwegian Troll stations directly from Cape Town, thus allowing many researchers much more rapid access to their Antarctic laboratories and, again, saving substantial amounts of precious research time. The shipping network Dronning Maud Land Shipment (DROMSHIP) employs an ice-strengthened freighter (also from Cape Town) with the aim of conserving ship time of dedicated polar research vessels that would otherwise have to be used for logistical purposes. More sharing of transport systems must be adopted as operators look for ways of reducing costs while increasing efficiencies.

Dedicated ice-breaking polar research vessels are rare and are usually not in the Southern Ocean during the unfavourable seasons of the year. There is a pressing demand for research ships that can master Antarctic winter sea ice and the storms of the Southern Ocean. The capacities of large modern research ice breakers will probably also require a system of international consortia to run such vessels.

Progress in the internationalisation of Antarctic and Southern Ocean research has been slow, despite the IPYs, and I relate this to the fragmented nature of the organisations supporting science-related activities in high southern latitudes. The Antarctic Treaty (AT) with its recently established office in Buenos Aires, SCAR and the Convention for the Conservation of Marine Living Resources (CCAMLR) with their separate offices, and the loose link between COMNAP and SCAR are all examples of this fragmentation. The linkage to the International Arctic Science Committee (IASC) in the north is only growing slowly and needs to be much better developed in the future because the two polar regions share many interesting attributes. The 50th Anniversary of the AT offered a wonderful opportunity to consider these problems, and one would hope that the coming years will be used to promote the internationalisation of research in Antarctica and the Southern Ocean. One important feature is that scientific data are deposited in internationally accessible data banks and hence open to the international science community. There is so much to be done and space for everybody to contribute to sustainable scientific exploration. The momentum of polar research gained during the Fourth IPY should not be lost but used to keep a young and motivated generation of researchers engaged in the polar regions, while more new countries join the relevant international organisations.

ANTARCTIC AND GLOBAL STEWARDSHIP: TIMES OF CHANGE IN THE NATURE OF POLAR RESEARCH

I have had the privilege to be involved in polar research both in high northern and southern latitudes for the past 30 years. My first exposure to the Arctic Ocean was the famous Swedish YMER-80 expedition, which was organised to commemorate the 100th anniversary of Nordenskjöld's first crossing of the Northern Sea Route on *Vega*. Political problems with the Soviet government prevented the *Ymer* from following Nordenskjöld's course. The *Ymer* therefore visited the deep waters around Svalbard and demonstrated for the first time that research could be done from conventional ice breakers in these difficult and ice-infested waters. Now, research icebreakers routinely plow the Arctic Ocean and are able to visit the North Pole. As chairman of European Polar Board (EPB) of the European Science Foundation (ESF) and president of SCAR as well as director of the German Alfred Wegener Institute, I have been able to have some influence on research in high southern latitudes and to contribute to their activities myself. I am extremely happy that the methods of doing polar research are experiencing a phase of rapid change, which is needed both to keep the attention and interest of politicians and to ensure the attraction of this type of research for the young generation of polar scientists who are appearing in a growing number of polar and nonpolar countries. An increasing number of smaller nonpolar countries are now entering the polar research arena, and the big "players" would be well advised to offer any assistance possible both to ensure a broadening of the constituency of interests and to underpin the quality of all polar research.

The SCAR has played a central role in this development, and it continuously has to make sure that it remains the central and most qualified scientific organization in Antarctic research. Only in this way will it remain the best source for scientific advice to the Antarctic Treaty System (ATS). The membership of SCAR therefore has to be recruited from the best and most experienced scientists in its member countries. There is no monopoly in Antarctic sciences, and SCAR will be wise to play its role in close collaboration with other relevant international science organisations. It must promote excellence in Antarctic and Southern Ocean research, but providing scientific leadership also requires focus because nobody can do everything. The scheme of strategic research themes developed by SCAR represents an attempt at defining the most challenging scientific problems in Antarctica and the Southern Ocean as well as providing a series of umbrellas to gather in and focus research from rich and poorer countries alike.

The SCAR has changed greatly over the past 10 years from an almost "closed shop" into an open science organisation. The introduction of the Open Science Conferences since 2004 has attracted many established as well as numerous young polar scientists. They have provided an important base for the large efforts of the Fourth IPY, which brought more than 50,000 scientists into the polar regions.

In its role advising the ATS, SCAR has to strive to provide independent, high-quality advice, and it also has to critically evaluate the methods and ethics of the conduct of Antarctic research. To retain its position as the major scientific advisory body, SCAR has to express informed opinions on Antarctic research, be proactive in flagging important new developments for the ATS, and respond as far as possible to requests from the ATS; the recent publication of a major report on the impact of climate change in the Antarctic is an excellent example of this change in SCAR's attitude. The SCAR has succeeded in regaining the attention of the ATS and can look with confidence into the future in this area of science diplomacy.

However, the future is not without dangers, and I am extremely happy that the Forever Declaration of Antarctic Treaty Summit clearly highlights the importance of science and research for the ATS. There may be a problem in the future with the filtering effect of the Committee for Environmental Protection (CEP) in the consideration of SCAR's advice to the ATS, but SCAR has the opportunity to raise serious matters in the plenary. The separation of SCAR from COMNAP (in the south) and IASC from the Forum of Arctic Research Operators (FARO; in the north) weakens the impact of the polar sciences, and bipolar research topics gain momentum only slowly under the influence of the SCAR-IASC Bipolar Action Group (BipAG). The IASC and SCAR should find a common roof for the benefit of both and improve the impact of the research conducted under their auspices, maybe under a new "International Union of Polar Sciences."

In considering the past 50 years of Antarctic science we can conclude that much has been achieved, but even more is left to be done. I am certain that Antarctic science will have a bright future and it will continue to have a major role to play in the future of the AT.

The Vostok Venture: An Outcome of the Antarctic Treaty

Jean Robert Petit

Jean Robert Petit, Laboratoire de Glaciologie et Géophysique de l'Environnement, Centre National de la Recherche Scientifique, Université Joseph Fourier BP96, F-38402 Saint-Martin-d'Hères CEDEX, France. Correspondence: petit @lgge.obs.ujf-grenoble.fr.

INTRODUCTION

Polar ice sheets and glaciers contain well-ordered archives of ancient ice that fell as snow, years to millions of years ago. With an ice blanket of more than 3 km thick and an annual precipitation rate comparable to that from hyperarid regions (equivalent to 2–5 cm water annually), the slow-moving East Antarctic plateau has considerable potential for providing a long-undisturbed ice sequence. Because of the remoteness of inland sites along with the harsh weather conditions, exploration and deployment of scientific traverses or deep ice core drilling operations require coordination of considerable logistic support, technical, and scientific skills.

Vostok station was settled at the time of the International Geophysical Year (IGY) by the Soviet Union and is a location 1,400 km from the coast at 3,488 m above sea level altitude, with an annual temperature of –55°C. Thanks to the Antarctic Treaty, which promoted the international collaboration, the study of a 2-km-deep ice core revealed the close link between temperature and atmospheric CO_2 over the last 150,000 years. This fact soon revealed the climate issues caused by increasing anthropogenic emissions of greenhouse gases.

The ice composition and impurities and the gases trapped in air bubbles provide a unique history of the past climate change and environmental and atmospheric composition. By reaching 3.4 km depth, the climate record was extended back 400,000 years, confirming the close climate–greenhouse gas relationship. This link is now further extended over 800,000 years.

At the base of the ice sheets the geothermal flux warms the ice, up to the melting point in some places. The water produced accumulates at the interface with the bedrock to form a lake. This is the case in the region of Vostok, where a giant lake lies under the station. Ice core drilling penetrated an ice massif of refrozen lake water at 3.6 km depth. The recovery of frozen lake samples opens new fields for research, especially for the search for life in this very extreme environment, which may help the search for life elsewhere.

THE HISTORICAL CONTEXT

Vostok station was settled during the IGY on the East Antarctic plateau by the Soviet Antarctic Expedition and was opened on 16 December 1957 (Figure 1). For the image and prestige of this complex operation, the site needed to be located at a pole, and the geomagnetic South Pole was chosen. The geomagnetic South Pole is where the axis of a virtual magnetic dipole at the center of Earth, producing the major part of the observed Earth magnetic field, crosses the surface. This location was expected to be favorable for studying the ionosphere and the effects of magnetic storms. It is situated at 79°S, 105°E, and the place is known to be the coldest on Earth (–89.3°C in July 1983). Since its founding, the station, manned by approximately a dozen persons, has been operating almost continuously as an observatory for ionospheric studies, meteorology, magnetism, aerology, geophysics, glaciology, geodesy, etc. For supply and maintenance, over the last 50 years Vostok station has required the deployment of significant logistics (airplanes, ships, tractors, etc.) and personnel (e.g., Lukin et al., 2006). Since the mid-1960s, drilling has been conducted by dedicated and resourceful wintering teams (Vassilev et al., 2007) with the aim of geophysical studies (e.g., study of the ice sheet temperature in relation to ice sheet dynamics), glaciology, and, more recently, paleoclimatology as laboratory structures and techniques dedicated to ice core geochemistry evolved (e.g., water isotope mass spectrometry, gas and liquid chromatography, clean rooms, etc.).

Following IGY, the signature of the Antarctic Treaty alleviated administrative boundaries between nations, and despite the political context of the cold war, it gave scientists a structure for pursuing the IGY scientific endeavor. Scientists from Eastern and Western countries were able to travel abroad to meet regularly at annual colloquia. New ambitious exploration projects grew and became feasible through international collaborations. The bipartite Soviet-French collaboration began by the 1980s and then became a tripartite Soviet-U.S.-French venture (Figure 1), aiming to

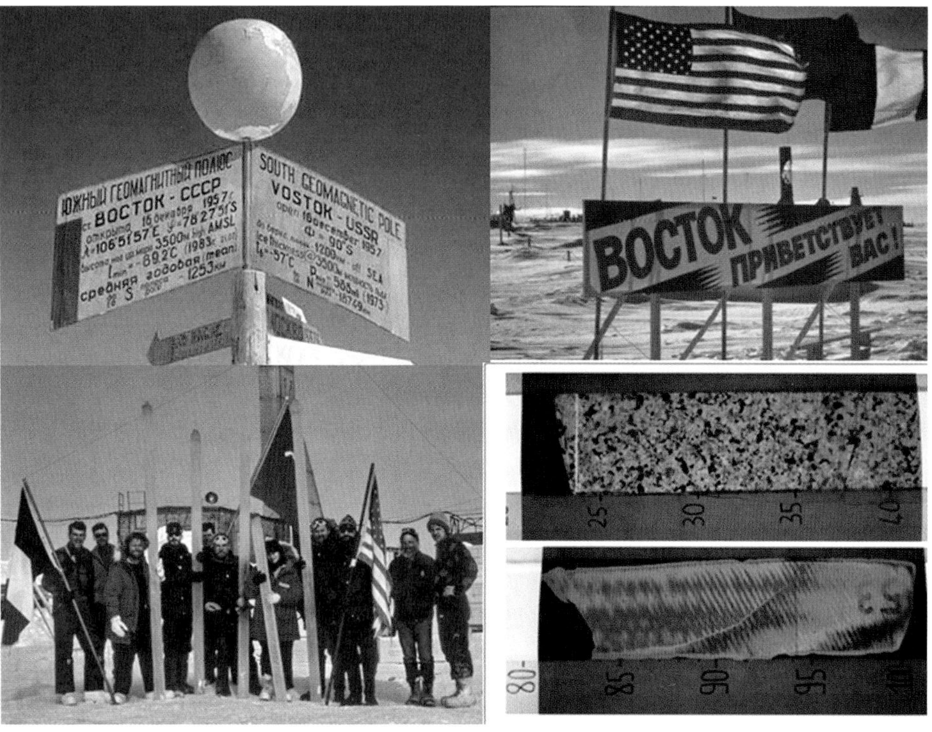

FIGURE 1. Vostok Station and the 1990s tripartite collaboration for ice core studies. (top) Geomagnetic South Pole memorial and welcome signs. (bottom) Ice core "festival" and view of thin sections of glacier (small crystals) and lake ice (single large crystal) between crossed polarizers. The scale is in centimeters, and irregular thickness makes the color iridescence for the lake ice crystal (Photos ® Extra-Pol).

collaborate on the Vostok ice cores. This collaboration represents one of these emblematic projects that were set up independently from political considerations and that continued to exist despite the political context and difficulties.

THE 400,000-YEAR CLIMATE RECORD

At Vostok the ice thickness is 3,750 m, and the snow accumulation is only an equivalent of 2 cm annually. Such conditions offer a rare opportunity to obtain a long climatic record with relatively high time resolution. In the 1980s, ice core drilling reached 2,000 m depth. A first 150,000-year record of Antarctic temperature (Lorius et al., 1985; Jouzel et al., 1987) and CO_2 was published (Barnola et al., 1987). In January 1996, the drill reached 3,350 m depth. The climate record was extended back to 420,000 years (Petit et al., 1999). From the stable isotope composition of the ice, the gases trapped in air bubbles, the atmospheric dust particles, and the soluble chemicals, which are kept frozen, together provide a unique history of past changes of the climate, the atmospheric composition, and the environmental conditions over oceans and continents.

The climate record (Figure 2) displays a complete natural cycle of the temperature, which oscillates by about 12°C amplitude between the warm conditions of the present climate and the three previous interglacial periods (circa 120,000 BP, 220,000 BP, 330,000 BP, and 400,000

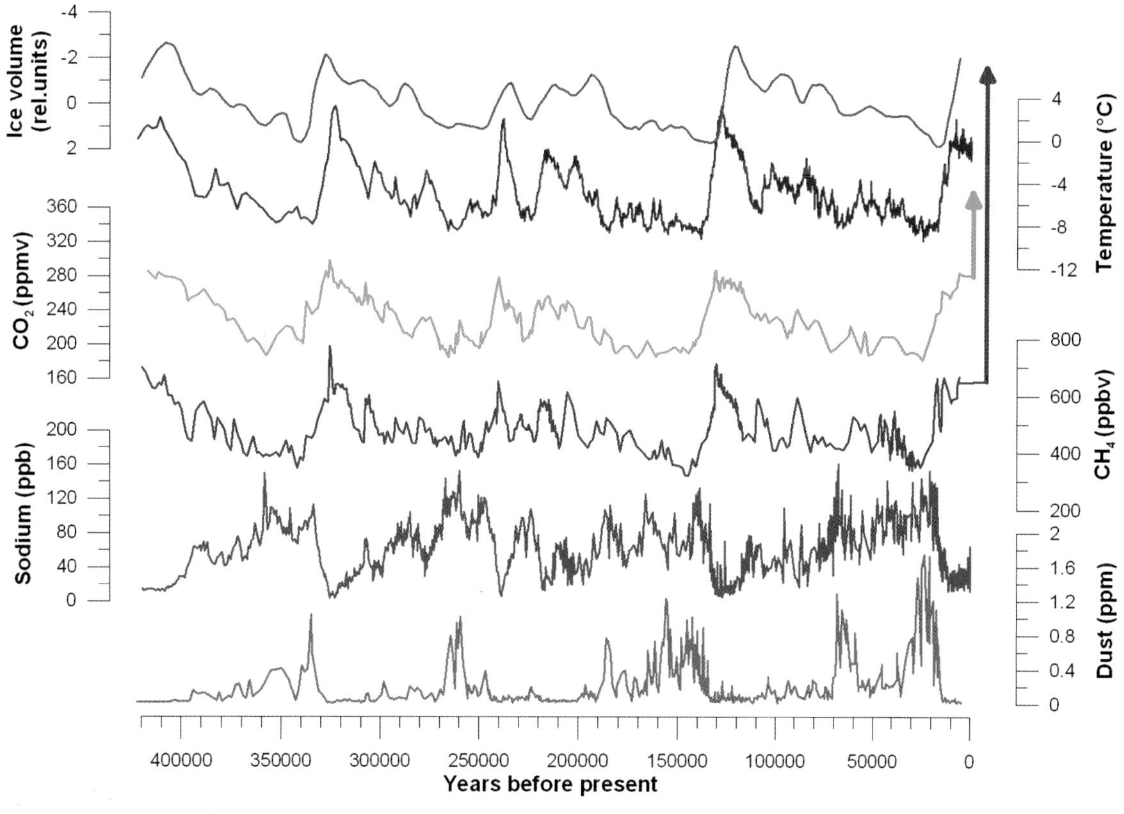

FIGURE 2. The climatic record over the last 400,000 years deduced from the first 3,310 m of the Vostok ice core (adapted from Petit et al., 1999). From top to bottom: Global ice volume (in relative units) as deduced from the marine sediment record; temperature (difference with the present surface temperature) deduced from the stable isotope composition of the ice; records of greenhouse gases CO_2 (ppmv: parts per million in volume) and CH_4 (ppbv: parts per billion in volume) as deduced from entrapped air bubbles; record of sodium concentration (ppb: parts per billion in mass), representative of sea spray aerosols; and record of dust concentration (ppm: parts per million in mass), representative of emissions from continental arid areas. Note that the recent increase up to the present levels for CO_2 (388 ppmv, http://co2now.org/) and CH_4 (~1800 ppbv, http://cdiac.ornl.gov/pns/current_ghg.html) are a consequence of anthropogenic activity since the 1850s.

BP), on the one hand, and the cold conditions of the glacial periods in between (e.g., between 80,000 BP and 20,000 BP to for the last glacial period), on the other. Most of this natural climate variability during glacial-interglacial changes occurs with periodicities corresponding to that of the precession, obliquity, and eccentricity of the Earth's orbit, with a larger concentration of variance in the 100,000-year band.

The "sawtooth" pattern of the Vostok temperature record roughly mimics the sea level changes deduced from marine sediment studies. The CO_2 concentrations deduced from analyses of the air bubbles also oscillate between high values of about 280 parts per million in volume (ppmv) for the preindustrial times (prior to circa AD 1850) and the warm interglacial periods and lower values of about 190 ppmv for the glacial periods. Indeed, the CO_2 record mimics the temperature record over the four climatic cycles, and the record in Petit et al. (1999) extended the one published 12 years before (Barnola et al., 1987) by three more climatic cycles. In the late 1980s, a set of three papers dedicated to Vostok ice core published by *Nature* magazine (Jouzel et al., 1987; Barnola et al., 1987; Genthon et al., 1987) made a large impact and generated much interest, with someone calling it a "big bang" for the scientific community. The link between the climate and the carbon cycle was clearly established, and polar ice became the indisputable complementary archive to marine sediments. More importantly, ice core records provided a natural record of climate and atmospheric changes from which the sensitivity of the surface temperature to variations of the global atmospheric composition could be deduced (Lorius et al., 1990). Looking ahead, the question of the potential impact of the rising CO_2 concentration (388 ppmv today) due to anthropogenic activities on the climate was clearly opened. The close linkage between climate and CO_2 throughout the four climatic cycles is now extended over 800,000 years with the ice core at Dome C by the European Project for Ice Coring in Antarctica (EPICA) (EPICA Community Members, 2004; Luthi et al., 2008) and supports the role of the greenhouse gases as amplifiers of initial orbital forcing.

OTHER ENVIRONMENTAL INFORMATION AND BRIDGING WITH GREENLAND RECORDS

In addition to the past temperature and atmospheric composition, other climatic indicators extracted from the ice core depicted complementary features of environmental changes (De Angelis et al., 1987; Legrand et al., 1988; Petit et al., 1990, 1999). The much higher concentration (factor of ~50) of atmospheric dust particles during full glacial periods than during interglacials (Figure 2) observed over the last 800,000 years (Wolff et al., 2006; Lambert et al., 2008) is interpreted as indicating more-extensive deserts and arid areas due to the deep cold climate and the very dry atmosphere. The reduced hydrological cycle caused the continental aridity, and the lower atmospheric cleansing induced a more-efficient aerosol transport to polar regions. This transport efficiency may also explain the higher input (factor of 5) observed for sea spray aerosols (sodium, Figure 2), although the role of sea ice extent and higher winds remains to be determined (Wolff et al., 2006; Petit and Delmonte, 2009).

The methane (CH_4) was also extracted and measured from the air bubbles. Methane is produced mostly by the biological activity of soils and wetlands and therefore is sensitive to the temperature, and at first order it follows the temperature (Figure 2). Indeed, methane is sensitive to temperature over the continents in the Northern Hemisphere (Chappellaz et al., 1993) and has a higher variability spectrum. On the other hand, methane atmospheric concentration changes at a global scale and represents a useful stratigraphic marker as a proxy of the Northern Hemisphere temperature, which is preserved within Antarctic ice. This has been used for matching the high-resolution EPICA Droning Maud Land ice core to the Greenland record over the last 100,000 years. During the last glacial period, the high-amplitude wiggles of the temperature (so-called Dansgaard-Oeschger events) recorded in the Greenland ice core result from changes in the meridional ocean circulation and the switch of advection of heat from the tropics, sometimes coincident with the northern ice cap discharge of armadas of icebergs. The comparison between Greenland and Antarctic ice core records revealed companion events in Antarctica (EPICA Community Members, 2006). The Greenland sudden warming is out of phase by a few hundred years with a warm phase occurring in Antarctica, and the amplitude of Greenland warming appears to be proportional to the duration of the preceding Antarctic warm phase (Figure 3). Such a seesaw phenomenon suggests heat storage in the Southern Ocean and its distribution to the north through the Atlantic Ocean, a phenomenon reflecting millennial-scale temperature variability that persisted during the glacial periods of the past eight glacial cycles. (Loulergue et al., 2008).

Reconstructions of past environments are now recognized as important information for climatic and environmental studies. They allow assessing the degree of natural variability and place current observed changes in

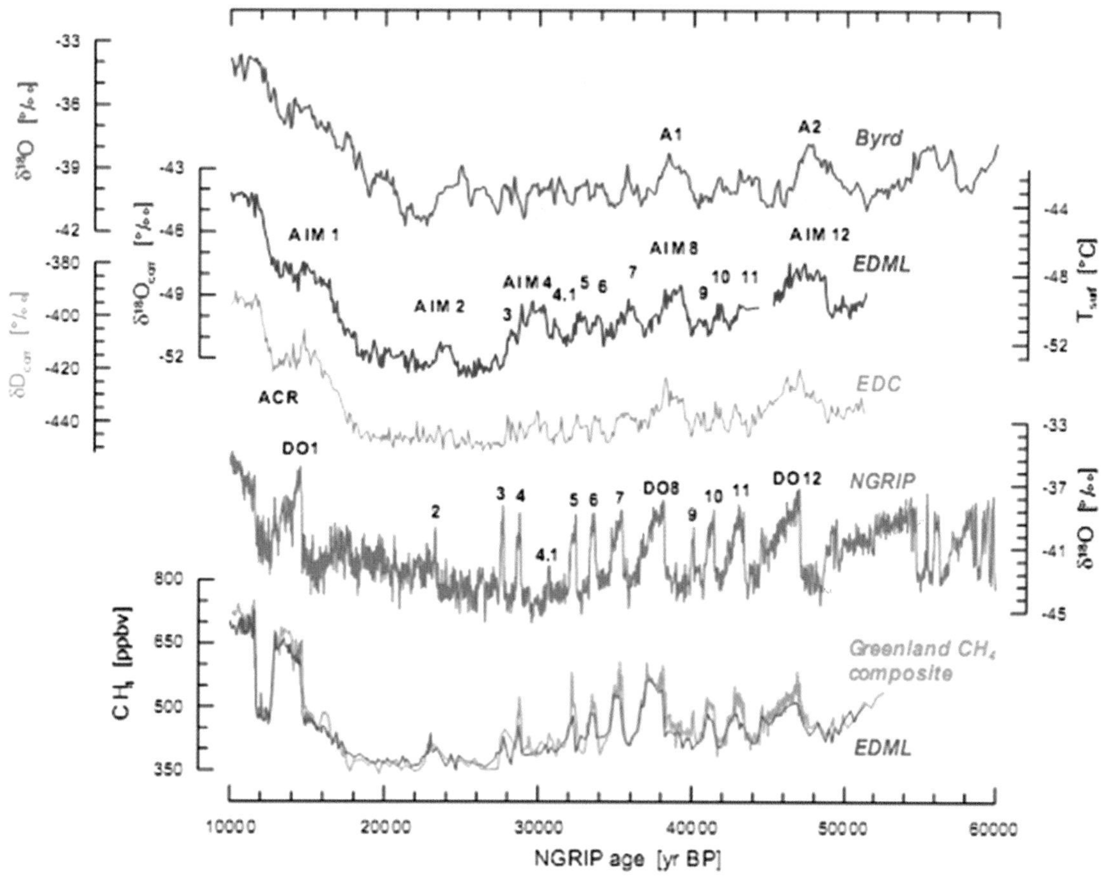

FIGURE 3. North-south connections: one-to-one Greenland and Antarctic climate variability during the last glacial period (adapted from EPICA Community Members, 2006). Stable isotope variations (100-year averages) in the EDML (Epica Dronning Maud Land), EDC (Epica Dome C), and Byrd ice core are compared with the NGRIP (North Greenland Ice Project) $\delta^{18}O$ record from northern Greenland. Temperature estimates for EDML are shown on the right axis. The EDML, EDC, and Byrd have been CH_4 synchronized with NGRIP. Yellow bars indicate the Greenland stadial (cold) periods related to respective Antarctic temperature increases.

a broader perspective (Jansen et al., 2007). They help us to understand causes and mechanisms of the changes and contribute to validating models by comparison of output with empirical data. The last few hundred thousand years are an appropriate context in which we can learn how the Earth system works.

SURPRISES FROM THE DEEP ICE

In January 1998, the tripartite Russian-French-U.S. collaboration got new highlights from deep drilling by reaching 3,623 m depth, which was the deepest ice core ever recovered (3,667 m was then reached in 2008). The drilling stopped 130 m above Lake Vostok, a deep subglacial water body discovered and mapped earlier from satellite observations (Ridley et al., 1993). The lake extends below the ice sheet over an area of 15,000 km^2, similar to Lake Ontario today. With water depth up to 1,200 m, its total volume represents 5,000 km^3, suggesting it has been present a very long time (Kapitsa et al., 1996; Siegert et al., 2001).

The recovery of ice refrozen from lake water (accretion ice) at the bottom of the ice core opens an unexpected window to this unknown environment. The accretion ice formed by large ice crystals (Figure 4) as the result of a very slow freezing process represents the best analogue for lake water composition and biological content. The high pressure, the low temperature, the absence of solar energy, the nutriment supply from the very clean overlaying ice, and the isolation from our environment for thousands

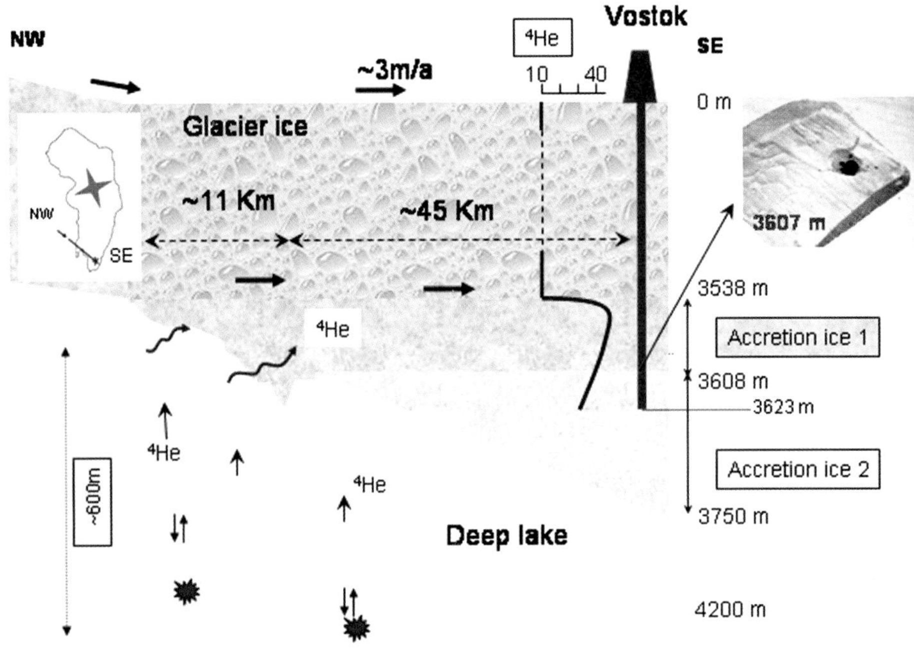

FIGURE 4. Sketch of the glacier and lake basement along the Vostok ice flow line (adapted from Bulat et al., 2004). On the 3,623 m Vostok ice core, the accreted ice interval from 3,538 to 3,608 m depth (accretion ice 1) contains visible sediment inclusions (insert on the right). Deeper ice and likely that down to the glacier-water interface (accretion ice 2) are clean. A glacier flows at about 3 m per year from the northwest to southeast (insert on the left). A rise in relief is located at about 11 km, enfolding a shallow-depth embayment where sediments could be trapped into accreted ice. Then the glacier floats over a ~600 m deep lake. The rock basement is characterized by escarpments where deep faults allow water to seep in depth and to circulate. Fault activity (explosion symbols) may fuel hydrothermal circulation and activate ^4He degassing from the rocks. Also represented is a sketch of down-core ^4He concentration (Jean Baptiste et al., 2001) showing a constant value for glacier ice and the change, by a factor of 3, at the glacier-accretion ice boundary. In accretion ice a ^4He maximum concentration suggests contribution from a shallow-depth area upstream from Vostok (adapted from Bulat et al., 2004).

(maybe millions) of years make the subglacial lakes one of the most extreme environments on Earth and a probable limit for life.

Ongoing studies of Lake Vostok accretion ice core show that because of the low biomass, the forward contamination of samples is a substantial problem and the main cause of diverse chemical and biological results (Priscu et al., 1999; Karl et al., 1999; Christner et al., 2001; Bulat et al., 2004), the drilling fluid coming in contact with the ice being one source of contamination (Alekhina et al., 2007). From repeated independent investigations, the accretion ice is now found to be essentially carbon- and germ-free, indicating that the water body (at least the upper layer) beneath the ice sheet should support only a highly sparse life, if any. In recent studies, a phylotype representing the extant thermophilic facultative chemolithoautotrophic bacterium *Hydrogenophilus thermoluteolus* gave a reliable molecular biology signature and is the single print of life found to date in the Lake Vostok ice horizons (Bulat et al., 2004; Lavire et al., 2006). Such thermophilic organisms are unlikely to thrive in the open lake, where the temperature is a little above zero and the high concentration of dissolved oxygen is expected to be a significant constraint for any bacterial life. Rather, they live at great depths in "hot" basement faults filled with sediments that may have been colonized soon after their formation and possibly before the onset of the Antarctic glaciation around 30 MYA. According to a scenario built from the available geophysical and geochemical information, some niches have been suggested within deep faults or sediments close to fault mouths where chemolithoautotrophic microorganisms are likely to be protected and fed by hydrothermal fluids. The way they are integrated into the accretion ice, likely boosted by sporadic local or distant seisms, would be the result of the contact between the mouth of bedrock faults with the base of the glacier upstream from Vostok (Bulat et al., 2004). The helium concentration (^4He), which is found in excess in the accretion ice, supports the suggestion of a modest but persistent tectonic activity, although the absence of ^3He rules out the presence of hydrothermal vents like the black smokers observed in deep oceans that are associated with magma ascending into crustal fractures (Jean Baptiste et al., 2001).

At the bottom of Lake Vostok a deep biosphere within a "biotectonic environment" is likely, which represents an interesting alternative scenario for primary production consistent with the extreme environment of the lake. Finally, the multidisciplinary approach that has been developed for searching for life in the Lake Vostok ice leads to some guiding principles that could be applicable for searching life in other extreme environments or for the study of extraterrestrial samples (Petit et al., 2005).

TALES FROM THE FIELD AND HIGHLIGHTS FROM THE VOSTOK VENTURE

Drilling operations are never simple, and at Vostok drillers overcame many technical issues (Vassilev et al., 2007), and unexpected events are the rule of the exploration. As an example, at the time (during the 1990s) of the dramatic and economical changes that occurred in connection with the collapse of the Soviet Union, Vostok station endured a critical epoch and had to close for winter. The tripartite Soviet then Russian-U.S.-French collaboration (1989–1998) remained in effect, however. This collaboration allowed several issues regarding providing more technical help and logistic support to be solved. In 1995, the situation improved, and drilling operations were soon resumed. The ice core reached 3,109 m depth, establishing a new world record.

The long-lasting Vostok venture is one of the fortunate outcomes from the Antarctic Treaty. The climate record and the relationship with CO_2 in the past as revealed by the deep ice core soon became a reference curve. This salient result also highlighted the potential of the ice cores for climate studies and promoted other projects (e.g., EPICA and Dome Fuji) for obtaining longer climate records (EPICA Community Members, 2004; Watanabe et al., 2003). At time of the IGY more than 50 years ago, by choosing the south geomagnetic pole for the settlement of Vostok station, nobody envisaged the presence of a huge subglacial lake there. Even more, once the subglacial body was known, no one expected an ice massif of frozen lake water at the drilling spot. As a result, a unique window to a subglacial environment has been offered.

Under the influence of anthropogenic activities, recent climate change creates a real concern about the future of human societies on our planet The present-day atmospheric CO_2 concentration and its rapid increase are likely to be unprecedented over the history of the past 800,000 years (Luthi et al., 2008). Climate scientists are trying to provide realistic assessments of how our climate will change in the future (Jansen et al., 2007). International collaboration helped to decipher the dynamics of the climate and pacing of the ice ages. The Vostok CO_2-climate correlation was and is still greatly impacting the ongoing research on the carbon cycle and its evolution in relation to climate changes. In this sense, the Vostok record has been one of the "iconic records" used throughout the various Intergovernmental Panel on Climate Change (IPCC) assessments dealing with the fate of the anthropogenic CO_2.

The discovery of more than 200 subglacial lakes in Antarctica generates a great deal of scientific and public discussion and speculation about the origin, nature, and fate of the subglacial lakes. For example, the numerous lakes raise questions on their possible contribution to the ice sheet dynamics as well as on the stability and evolution of the ice caps (Wingham et al., 2006). Also, the discovery of imprints of water on Mars and icy Europa, a Jovian satellite, is promoting the ever-asked question of extraterrestrial life. In this context the subglacial Antarctic lakes buried under more than 3,000 m of ice, representing an extreme environment and a limit for potential life, were soon taken as a possible analogue of the hydrosphere of such icy environments. Finally, the subglacial lakes attracted technological experiments that led to projects for robotic exploration promoted within Scientific Committee on Antarctic Research (SCAR) committees, and Vostok, its ice core, and its giant subglacial lake are still being studied is a tribute to the Antarctic Treaty.

ACKNOWLEDGMENTS

This work is dedicated to the memory of colleagues from the Vostok community who have passed away. Acknowledged with gratitude are researchers, engineers, technicians, administrative personnel, and field participants from Institutes, Universities, and Academies from Russia, USA, and France. Field operations were supported by Russian Antarctic Expeditions (RAE), US National Science Foundation (NSF), and the French Polar Institute (IPEV).

LITERATURE CITED

Alekhina, I., D. Marie, J. R. Petit, et al. 2007. Molecular Analysis of Bacterial Diversity in Kerosene-Based Drilling Fluid from the Deep Ice Borehole at Vostok, East Antarctica. *FEMS Microbiology Ecology*, 59:289–299.

Barnola, J. M., D. Raynaud, Y. S. Korotkevich, and C. Lorius. 1987. Vostok Ice Core Provides 160,000-Year Record of Atmospheric CO_2. *Nature*, 329:408–414.

Bulat, S., I. A. Alekhina, M. Blot J. R. Petit , M. de Angelis , D. Wagenbach, V. Y. Lipenkov , L. Vasilyeva, D. Wloch, R. D., and V. V. Lukin. 2004. DNA Signature of Thermophilic Bacteria from the Aged Accretion Ice of Lake Vostok: Implications for Searching Life in Extreme Icy Environments. *International Journal of Astrobiology*, 3(1):1–12, doi:10.1017/s147355040400189.

Chappellaz, J., T. Blunier, D. Raynaud, J. M. Barnola, J. Schwander, and B. Stauffer. 1993. Synchronous Changes in Atmospheric CH_4 and Greenland Climate between 40 and 8 kyr BP. *Nature*, 366:443–445.

Christner, B., E. Mosley-Thompson, L. Thompson, and J. Reeve. 2001. Isolation of Bacteria and 16S rDNAs from Lake Vostok Accretion Ice. *Environmental Microbiology*, 3:570–577.

De Angelis, M., N. I. Barkov, and V. N. Petrov. 1987. Aerosol Concentrations over the Last Climatic Cycle (160 kyr) from an Antarctic Ice Core. *Nature*, 325:318–321.

EPICA Community Members. 2004. Eight Glacial Cycles from an Antarctic Ice Core. *Nature*, 429:623–628.

———. 2006. One-to-One Coupling of Polar Climate Variability. *Nature*, 444:195–198.

Genthon, G., J. M. Barnola, D. Raynaud, C. Lorius, J. Jouzel, N. I. Barkov, Y. S. Korotkevich, and V. M. Kotlyakov. 1987. Vostok Ice Core: Climatic Response to CO_2 and Orbital Forcing Changes over the Last Climatic Cycle. *Nature*, 329:414–418.

Jansen, E., J. Overpeck, K. R. Briffa, J-C Duplessy, F. Joos, V. Masson-Delmotte, D. Olago, B. Otto-Bliesner, W. R. Peltier, S. Rahmstorf, R. Ramesh, D. Raynaud, D. Rind, O. Solomina, R. Villalba, and D. Zhang. 2007. "Palaeoclimate." In *Climate Change 2007: The Physical Science Basis. Contribution of Working Group I to the Fourth Assessment Report of the Intergovernmental Panel on Climate Change*, ed. S. Solomon, D. Qin, M. Manning, Z. Chen, M. Marquis, K. B. Averyt, M. Tignor, and H. L. Miller, 399 p. Cambridge: Cambridge University Press.

Jean Baptiste, P., J. R. Petit, V. Y. Lipenkov, D. Raynaud, and N. I. Barkov. 2001. Constraints on Hydrothermal Processes and Water Exchange in Lake Vostok from Helium Isotopes. *Nature*, 411:460–462.

Jouzel, J., C. Lorius, J. R. Petit, C. Genthon, N. I. Barkov, V. M. Kotlyakov, and V.M. Petrov. 1987. Vostok Ice Core: A Continuous Isotope Temperature Record over the Last Climatic Cycle (160,000 years). *Nature*, 329:403–408.

Kapitsa, A., J. F. Ridley, G. d. Q. Robin, M. J. Siegert, and I. Zotikov. 1996. Large Deep Freshwater Lake beneath the Ice of Central Antarctica. *Nature*, 381:684–686.

Karl, D. M., D. F. Bird, K. Bjökman, T. Houlihan, R. Shakelford, and L. Tupas. 1999. Microorganisms in the Accreted Ice of Lake Vostok, Antarctica. *Science*, 286:2144–2147.

Lambert, F., B. Delmonte, J. R. Petit, M. Bigler, P. R. Kaufmann, M. A. Hutterli, T .F. Stocker, U. Ruth, J. P. Steffensen, and V. Maggi. 2008. Dust-Climate Couplings over the Past 800,000 Years from the EPICA Dome C Ice Core. *Nature*, 452:616–619.

Lavire, C., P. Normand, I. Alekhina, S. Bulat, D. Prieur, J. L. Birrien, P. Fournier, C. Hänni, and J. R. Petit. 2006. Presence of Hydrogenophylus Thermoluteolus DNA in Accretion Ice in the Subglacial Lake Vostok, Antarctica, Assessed Using rrs, cbb and hox. *Environmental Microbiology*, 8:2106–2114.

Legrand, M., C. Lorius, N. I. Barkov, and V. N. Petrov. 1988. Atmospheric Chemistry Changes over the Last Climatic Cycle (160,000 yr) from Antarctic Ice. *Atmospheric Environment*, 22:317–331.

Lorius, C., J. Jouzel, C. Ritz, L. Merlivat, M. Pourchet, V. M. Kotlyakov, and Y .S. Korotkevich. 1985. A 150,000-Years Climatic Record from Antarctic Ice. *Nature*, 316:591–596.

Lorius, C., J. Jouzel, D. Raynaud, J. Hansen, and H. Le Treut. 1990. Greenhouse Warming, Climate Sensitivity and Ice Core Data. *Nature*, 347:139–145.

Loulergue, L., A. Schilt, R. Spahni, V. Masson-Delmotte, T. Blunier, B. Lemieux, J.-M. Barnola, D. Raynaud, T. F. Stocker, and J. Chappellaz. 2008. Orbital and Millennial-Scale Features of Atmospheric CH4 over the Past 800,000 Years, 453(7193):383–386.

Lukin V. V., N. A. Kornilov, and N. K. Dmitriev. 2006. *Sovietskie i Rossiiskie Antarktichskie Ekspeditsii v Tsifrakh I Faktakh (1955–2005 GG)* [Soviet and Russian expeditions in numeral and facts (1955–2005)]. St. Petersburg, Russia: AARI.

Luthi, D., M. Le Floch, B. Bereiter, T. Blunier, J.-M. Barnola, U. Siegenthaler, D. Raynaud, J. Jouzel, H. Fischer, K. Kawamura, and T. F. Stocker. 2008. High-Resolution Carbon Dioxide Concentration Record 650,000–800,000 Years before Present. *Nature*, 453:379–382.

Petit, J. R., L. Mounier, J. Jouzel, Y. S. Korotkevich, V. I. Kotlyakov, and C. Lorius. 1990. Palaeoclimatological and Chronological Implications of the Vostok Core Dust Record. *Nature*, 343:56–58.

Petit, J. R., I. Alekhina, and S. Bulat. 2005. "Lake Vostok, Antarctica: Exploring a Subglacial Lake and Searching for Life in an Extreme Environment." In *Advances in Astrobiology and Biogeophysics, Lectures in Astrobiology*, edited by M. Gargaud, B. Barbier, H. Martin, and J. Reisse, pp. 227–288. Berlin: Springer.

Petit, J. R., J. Jouzel, D. Raynaud, N. I. Barkov, J. M. Barnola, I. Basile, M. Bender, J. Chappellaz, M. Davis, G. Delaygue, M. Delmotte, V. M. Kotlyakov, M. Legrand, V. Y. Lipenkov, C. Lorius, L. Pepin, C. Ritz, E. Saltzman, and M. Stievenard. 1999. Climate and Atmospheric History of the Past 420,000 Years from the Vostok Ice Core, Antarctica. *Nature*, 399:429–436.

Petit, J. R., and B. Delmonte. 2009. A Model for Large Glacial-Interglacial Climate-Induced Changes in Dust and Sea Salt Concentrations in Deep Ice Cores (Central Antarctica): Paleoclimatic Implications and Prospects for Refining Ice Core Chronologies. *Tellus, Series B*, 61:768–790.

Priscu, J. C., E. E. Adams, B. Lyons, M .A. Voytek, D. W. Mogk, R. L. Brown, C. P. McKay, C. D. Takacs, K. A. Welch, C. F. Wolf, J. D.

Kirshtein, and R. Avci. 1999. Geomicrobiology of Subglacial Ice above Lake Vostok, Antarctica. *Science,* 286:2141–2143.

Ridley, J. F., W. Cudlip, and S. Laxon. 1993. Identification of Subglacial Lakes Using ERS-1 Radar Altimeter. *Journal of Glaciology,* 39(133):625–634.

Siegert, M. J., C. Ellis-Evans, M. Tranter, C. Mayer, J. R. Petit, A. Salamatin, and J. Priscu. 2001. Physical, Chemical and Biological Processes in Lake Vostok and Other Antarctic Subglacial Lakes. *Nature*, 414:603–609.

Vassilev, N. I., P. G. Talalay, N. E. Bobin, V. K. Chistyakov, V. M. Zubkov, A. V. Krasilev, A .N. Dmitriev, S. V. Yankilevich, and V. Y. Lipenkov. 2007. Deep Drilling at Vostok Station, Antarctica: History and Recent Events. *Annals of Glaciology*, 47:10–23.

Watanabe, O., J. Jouzel, S. Johnsen, F. Parrenin, H. Shoji, and N. Yoshida. 2003. Homogeneous Climate Variability across East Antarctica over the Past Three Glacial Cycles. *Nature*, 422:509–512.

Wingham, D., M. Siegert, A. Shepherd, and A. Muir. 2006. Rapid Discharge Connects Antarctic Subglacial Lakes. *Nature*, 440:1033–1036.

Wolff, E. W., H. Fischer, F. Fundel, U. Ruth, B. Twarloh, G. C. Littot, R. Mulvaney, R. Rothlisberger, M. D. Angelis, C. F. Boutron, M. Hansson, U. Jonsell, M. A. Hutterli, F. Lambert, P. Kaufmann, B. Stauffer, T. F. Stocker, J. P. Steffensen, M. Bigler, M. L. Siggaard-Andersen, R. Udisti, S. Becagli, E. Castellano, M. Severi, D. Wagenbach, C. Barbante, P. Gabrielli,V. Gaspari. 2006. Southern Ocean Sea-Ice Extent, Productivity and Iron Flux over the Past Eight Glacial Cycles. *Nature*, doi:10.1038/nature04614.

The Southern Ocean in the Earth System

Stephen R. Rintoul

ABSTRACT. Southern Ocean processes influence climate and biogeochemical cycles on global scales. The Southern Ocean connects the ocean basins and links the shallow and deep limbs of the overturning circulation, a global-scale system of ocean currents that determines how much heat and carbon the ocean can store. The upwelling of deep waters releases carbon and returns nutrients that support biological productivity in the surface ocean; the compensating sinking of surface waters into the ocean interior sequesters carbon and heat and renews oxygen levels. The capacity of the ocean to moderate the pace of climate change is therefore controlled strongly by the circulation of the Southern Ocean. The future of the Antarctic ice sheet, and hence sea level rise, is increasingly understood to be determined by the rate at which the relatively warm ocean can melt floating glacial ice around the margin of Antarctica. Given the significance of the Southern Ocean to the Earth system, any change in the region would have impacts that extend well beyond the high southern latitudes. Recent studies suggest change is underway: the Southern Ocean is warming and freshening throughout most of the ocean depth; major currents are shifting to the south, causing regional changes in sea level and the distribution of organisms and supplying additional heat to melt ice around the rim of Antarctica; and the future of the Southern Ocean carbon sink is a topic of vigorous debate. Many of these discoveries are the result of the concerted multidisciplinary effort during the International Polar Year, which has provided an unprecedented view of the status of the Southern Ocean, a baseline for assessing change, and a demonstration of the feasibility, value, and timeliness of a Southern Ocean Observing System. The sustained observations of the Southern Ocean provided by such an observing system are essential to provide the knowledge needed to inform policy decisions and wise stewardship of the region.

THE ROLE OF THE SOUTHERN OCEAN IN THE EARTH SYSTEM

For many years, studies of the Southern Ocean were somewhat neglected by the Antarctic science community. The "real" Antarctic science took place on the continent itself; the rough ocean crossing was the uncomfortable prelude and postscript to a season of excitement in the last great wilderness on Earth. However, growing recognition of the global influence of Southern Ocean processes has heightened interest in oceanographic studies of the region.

Stephen R. Rintoul, Centre for Australian Weather and Climate Research, and Antarctic Climate and Ecosystem Cooperative Research Centre, Wealth from Oceans National Research Flagship, GPO Box 1538, Hobart, Tasmania 7001, Australia. Correspondence: steve.rintoul@csiro.au.

Southern Ocean oceanography, in fact, got off to an early start, and many important oceanographic discoveries had been made even before the continent itself was discovered. James Cook noted the strange fact that water temperatures increased with depth in some parts of the region, counter to the tendency everywhere else they had made measurements. James Clark Ross noticed that his ship was consistently set to the east and inferred there was a strong west-to-east flow circling Antarctica, a current system we now know as the Antarctic Circumpolar Current (ACC). Many later Antarctic explorers made measurements in the surrounding ocean, and those measurements provide a baseline to which comparisons of recent measurements are made to detect changes in the Southern Ocean.

The definition of the Southern Ocean is somewhat fuzzy and varies from author to author. From an oceanographic perspective, it makes most sense to consider the Southern Ocean as encompassing those waters that surround Antarctica and participate in the circumpolar circulation around the continent. These waters have physical, chemical, and biological distributions that distinguish them from waters at lower latitudes but that vary only slowly along the path of the flow around Antarctica. Here we define the Southern Ocean to include waters between the Antarctic continent and the Subtropical Front, an oceanographic feature that marks the transition between warm and salty subtropical waters and cooler, fresher waters to the south (Deacon, 1937, 1982). The latitude of the Subtropical Front varies with longitude, but generally lies between 35°S and 45°S (Orsi et al., 1995). The purpose of this paper is to provide an overview of recent progress in understanding how the circulation of the Southern Ocean influences the Earth system. Further background on the history of Southern Ocean exploration and the results of earlier work can be found in Deacon (1982) and Nowlin and Klinck (1986).

The profound influence of the Southern Ocean on the rest of globe can ultimately be traced to the unique continental geometry at high southern latitudes (Rintoul et al., 2001). The Drake Passage is the only latitude band where ocean waters circle the Earth. The lack of continental boundaries means that a circumpolar flow can connect the ocean basins and transfer climate anomalies between them (Figure 1). A dynamical consequence of the lack of land boundaries is that there can be no net north-south flow above the height of the shallowest bathymetry (north-south flows are possible, but must average to zero); this dynamical barrier to north-south exchange of heat contributes to the present glacial climate of the Antarctic continent. The ACC is the largest current in the world ocean, carrying roughly 135–147 $\times 10^6$ m^3 s^{-1} of water around Antarctica (Cunningham et al., 2003; Rintoul and Sokolov, 2001). The absence of land masses in the latitude band of the Drake Passage also means that the dynamics of the ACC differ from those of low-latitude currents, with small-scale eddies playing a prominent role.

The strong eastward flow of the ACC is in dynamical balance with density layers that shoal steeply to the south. Waters found at depths greater than 3,000 m north of the current can reach the sea surface near Antarctica. In this sense, the Southern Ocean provides a window to the deep sea. Where these dense waters outcrop at the sea surface, the exchange of heat and moisture between the ocean and the atmosphere acts to transform water from one density class to another. The net result is an overturning circulation consisting of two cells (Figure 2): deep water that upwells near Antarctica is converted to denser Antarctic Bottom Water that sinks to great depth and ventilates the abyssal ocean; deep water that upwells farther north is converted by warming, precipitation, and melt of sea ice to less-dense waters that ventilate the intermediate layers of the Southern Hemisphere oceans (Speer et al., 2000).

The Southern Ocean overturning circulation has a number of significant implications for the Earth system. The sinking of water from the surface of the Southern Ocean carries oxygen, heat, and carbon dioxide into the ocean interior. These water masses then spread throughout much of the ocean. In this way, the Southern Ocean renews the oxygen levels in the deep ocean and sets the capacity of the Southern Hemisphere oceans to store heat and carbon. When we talk about global warming over the last 50 years, we really mean ocean warming: more than 85% of the total increase in heat stored by the Earth system has gone into warming the ocean, with much smaller amounts of energy going into warming the atmosphere and land surface or into melting of ice (Levitus et al., 2005). The overturning circulation efficiently transports heat from the surface into the ocean interior, and as a result, the warming of the Southern Ocean extends far below the sea surface. Integrated around the globe, the Southern Ocean stores more of the excess heat trapped by the Earth system than any other latitude band. The Southern Ocean also absorbs a large amount of the carbon dioxide released by human activities, with about 40% of the total ocean inventory of anthropogenic CO_2 found south of 30°S (Figure 3; Sabine et al., 2004). The accumulation of anthropogenic CO_2 on the northern side of the Southern Ocean reflects the efficiency with which the upper cell of the overturning circulation transfers water from the surface, where the ocean absorbs CO_2 from the atmosphere, to the interior of

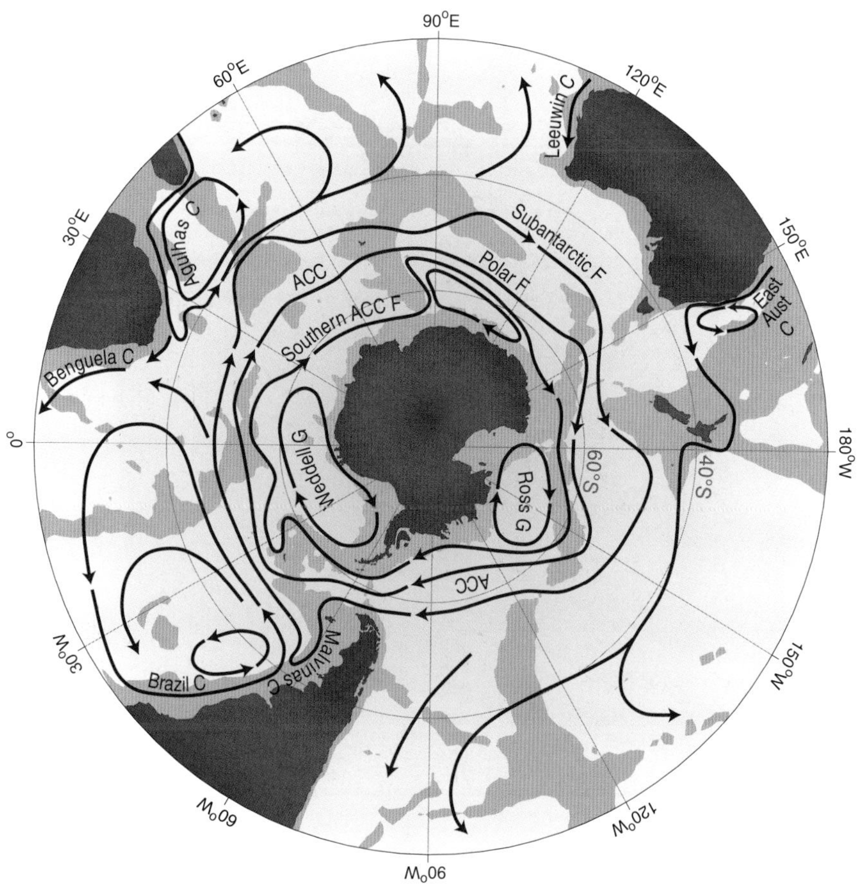

FIGURE 1. A schematic representation of the current systems in the Southern Ocean. The Antarctic Circumpolar Current (ACC) flows from west to east around Antarctica in two major branches, the Polar Front and Subantarctic Front. Clockwise gyres fill the deep basins between the Antarctic continent and the ACC. Adapted from Rintoul et al. (2001).

the ocean. Cooling and sinking of subtropical waters also contribute to the high inventory of anthropogenic CO_2 in this region.

The Southern Ocean overturning also has implications for the biology and chemistry of the global ocean. The upwelling of deep water returns nutrients to the surface ocean, where they can be used by phytoplankton. In model simulations, if the export of nutrients by the Southern Ocean overturning circulation is set to zero, the primary production in the rest of the ocean is reduced by 75% (Sarmiento et al., 2004). Deep water is also very rich in carbon; when deep water upwells, carbon is lost to the atmosphere (Le Quéré et al., 2007). The sinking of intermediate and bottom waters, on the other hand, tends to remove anthropogenic carbon dioxide from the atmosphere and sequester it in the ocean. The balance between the upwelling and downwelling limbs of the Southern Ocean overturning circulation plays a large part in determining how much carbon dioxide is absorbed and stored by the ocean. Biological production also plays a role in sequestering carbon as organic material sinks from the surface ocean and decomposes in the deep sea.

Climate and sea level rise are influenced strongly by interactions between the Southern Ocean and the cryosphere. Freezing of the ocean surface in winter forms sea ice covering about 16 million km^2, larger than the area of the Antarctic continent itself (Figure 4). Changes in sea ice extent or volume in the future may result in changes in the Earth's albedo, oceanic water mass formation rates, and air-sea exchange of gases such as carbon dioxide and affect the habitat of oceanic organisms from microbes to whales. Melting of floating glacial ice by ocean waters

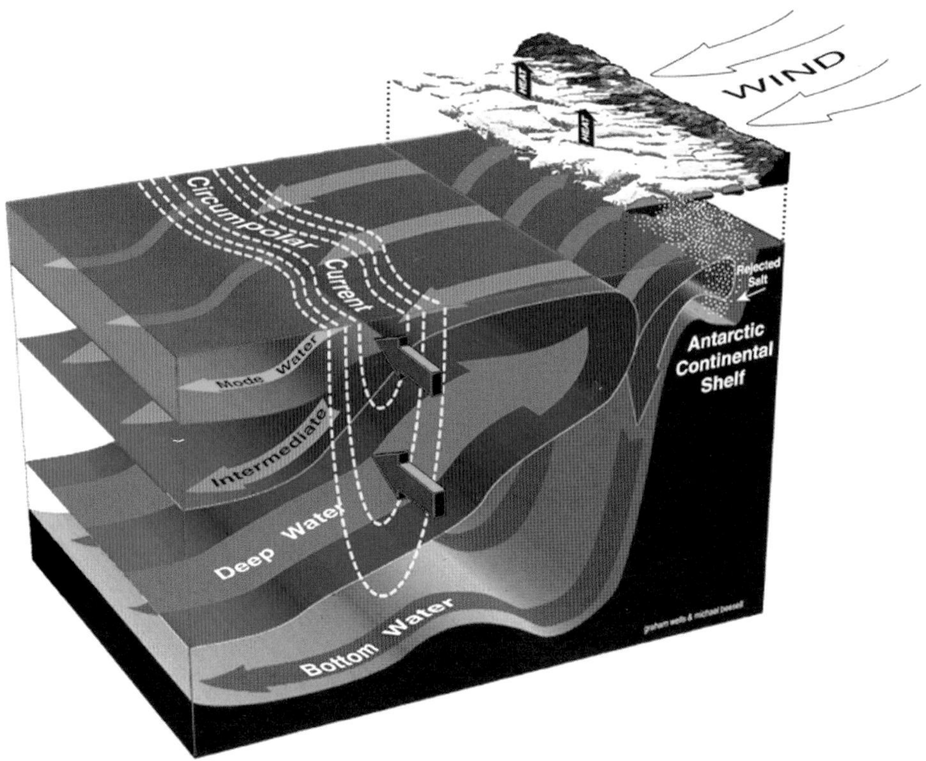

FIGURE 2. A schematic representation of the Southern Ocean overturning circulation. The figure shows the two cells contributing to the overturning: deep water upwelling to the surface of the Southern Ocean either moves toward Antarctica and sinks to form dense Antarctic Bottom Water or moves north and ultimately sinks to depths of 500–1,500 m on the northern flank of the ACC. From Rintoul (2000); used with permission.

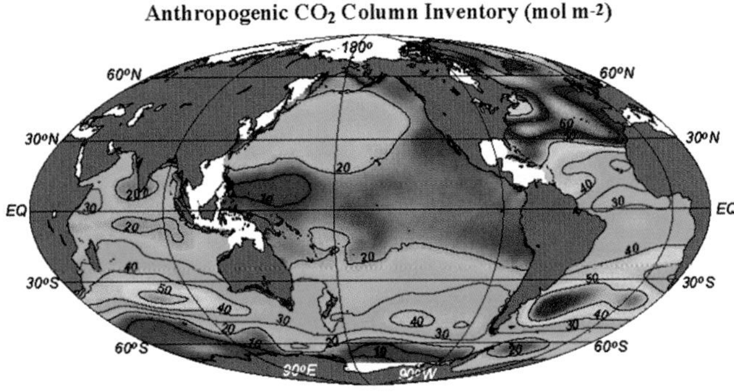

FIGURE 3. The inventory of anthropogenic carbon dioxide in the ocean. High values (shown in yellow and red) are located in regions where water masses sink from the sea surface to the interior of the ocean, in the North Atlantic and between 30°S and 50°S in the Southern Hemisphere oceans. From Sabine et al. (2004); used with permission.

at temperatures above the local freezing point influences the high-latitude freshwater budget and stratification and affects the mass balance of the Antarctic ice sheet and the rate at which glacial ice flows into the sea (Rignot et al., 2004).

The Southern Ocean therefore has a significant influence on global climate, biogeochemical cycles, biological productivity, and the Antarctic ice sheet. By connecting the ocean basins, the Southern Ocean allows a global-scale overturning circulation to exist. This system of alternating flows in the shallow and deep ocean transports heat and carbon efficiently around the Earth and establishes mean climate patterns. The uptake and storage of heat and carbon by the Southern Ocean act to slow the rate of atmospheric warming caused by increases in greenhouse gases. The Southern Ocean also connects the deep and shallow layers of the ocean, providing a return path for nutrients and maintaining global ocean productivity at levels that

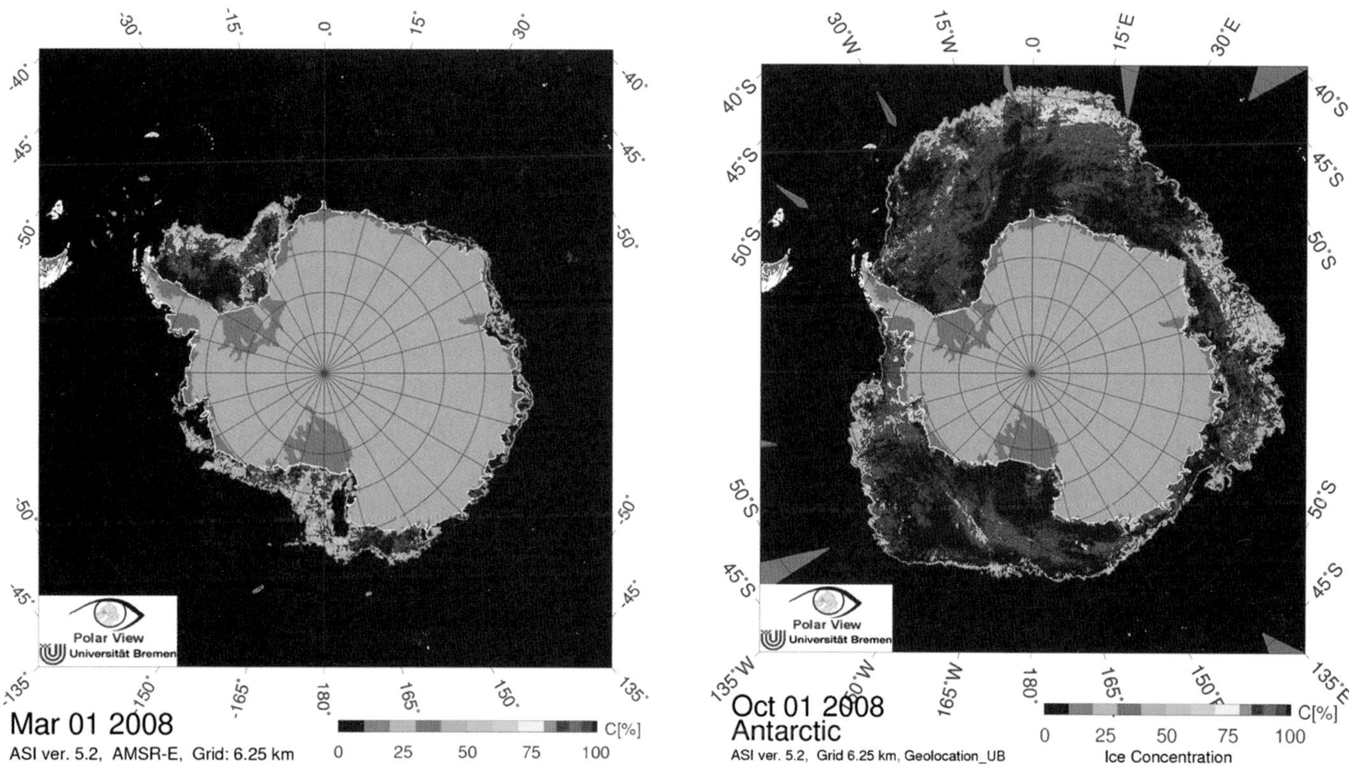

FIGURE 4. (left) Summer (1 March) and (right) winter (1 October) distribution of Antarctic sea ice in 2008. The sea ice extents reaches a maximum value of about 16 million km^2 in winter. From AMSR-E (http://www.iup.uni-bremen.de:8084/amsr/amsre.html).

are much higher than would be the case in the absence of this connection.

EVIDENCE FOR A CHANGING SOUTHERN OCEAN

Given the global influence of the Southern Ocean, any changes in the region would have widespread consequences. In particular, coupling between ocean circulation, sea ice, and biogeochemical cycles can result in positive feedbacks that drive further climate change. Changes to the freshwater balance as a result of changes in sea ice, precipitation, or ocean–ice shelf interaction may influence the strength of the overturning circulation. Reductions in sea ice extent would drive further warming through the ice-albedo feedback. Models suggest that the ability of the Southern Ocean to absorb carbon dioxide will decline with climate change, providing another positive feedback (Sarmiento et al., 2004; Le Quéré et al., 2007).

Changes in the physical and biogeochemical state of the Southern Ocean are, in fact, already underway (Turner et al., 2010). The Southern Ocean is warming (Figure 5) more rapidly than the global ocean average (Gille, 2002, 2008; Böning et al., 2008). The upper layers of the Southern Ocean have freshened as the result of an increase in precipitation and possibly melting of ice (Curry et al., 2003; Jacobs et al., 2002). The dense water that sinks near Antarctica to form the deep branch of the overturning circulation, known as Antarctic Bottom Water (AABW), has become less salty and less dense in recent decades in the Indian and Pacific sectors of the Southern Ocean (Figure 6) (Jacobs, 2004, 2006; Aoki et al., 2005; Rintoul, 2007). The freshening likely reflects an increase in basal melt of floating glacial ice, particularly in the southeast Pacific, with increased melt caused by warmer ocean temperatures (Shepherd et al., 2004; Rignot et al., 2008). Widespread warming of AABW has also been observed (e.g., Johnson and Doney, 2006).

Since 1992, satellite measurements show an overall increase in sea level and strong regional trends linked to shifts in fronts of the ACC (Sokolov and Rintoul, 2009). The sea surface is higher on the equatorward side of the ACC, so a southward shift of the current results in a

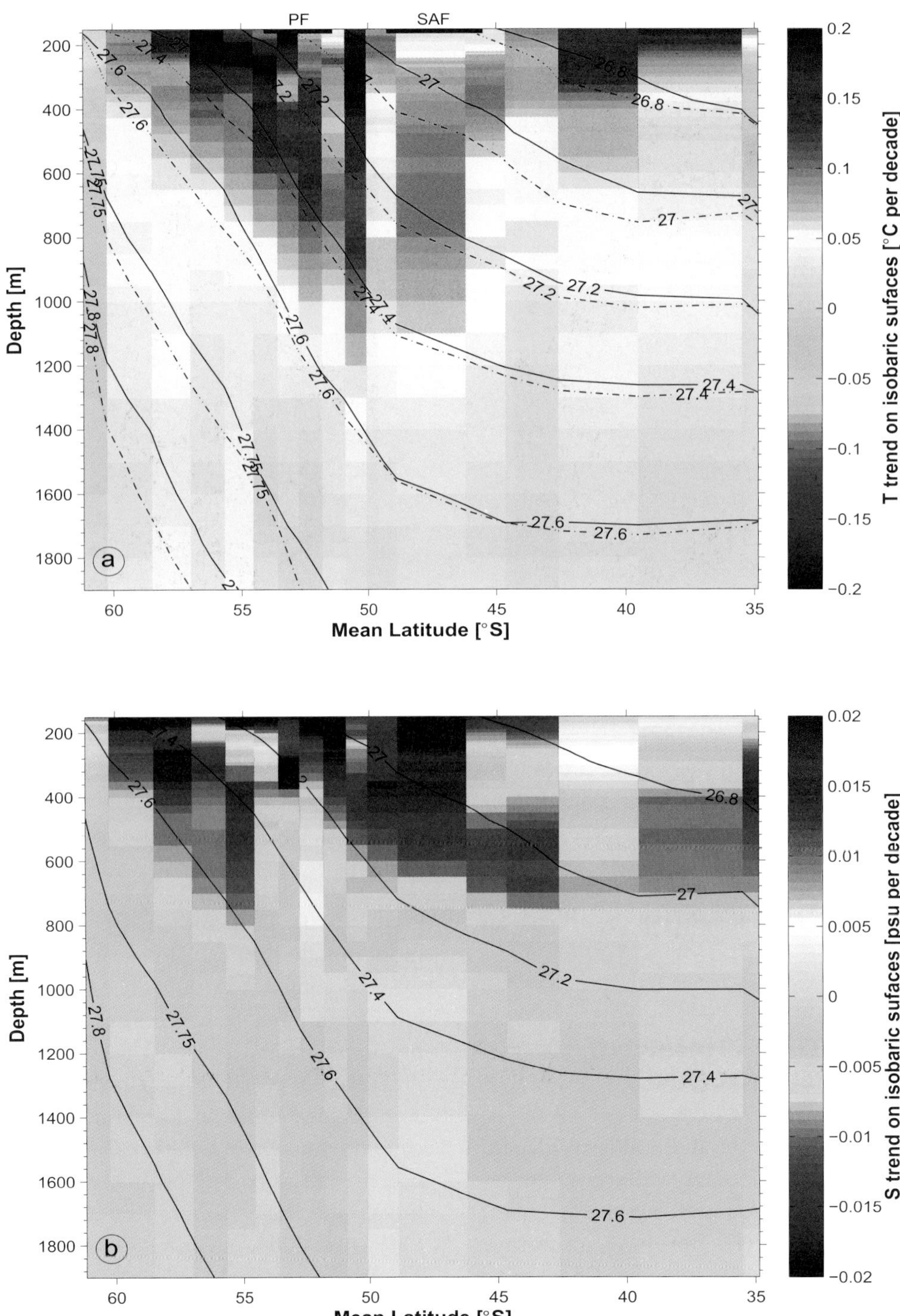

FIGURE 5. Decadal trends in (top) temperature and (bottom) salinity between 35°S and 60°S, estimated by subtracting recent measurements from ships and Argo floats from a long-term mean climatology (color). Differences are taken on surfaces of constant pressure (similar to depth) and along the mean streamlines of the ACC. The black lines on the plot indicate surfaces of constant density anomaly (in kg m^{-3},–1,000). The density surfaces shift south with time, but with little change in slope, indicating the transport of the ACC does not change much with time. From Böning et al. (2008); used with permission.

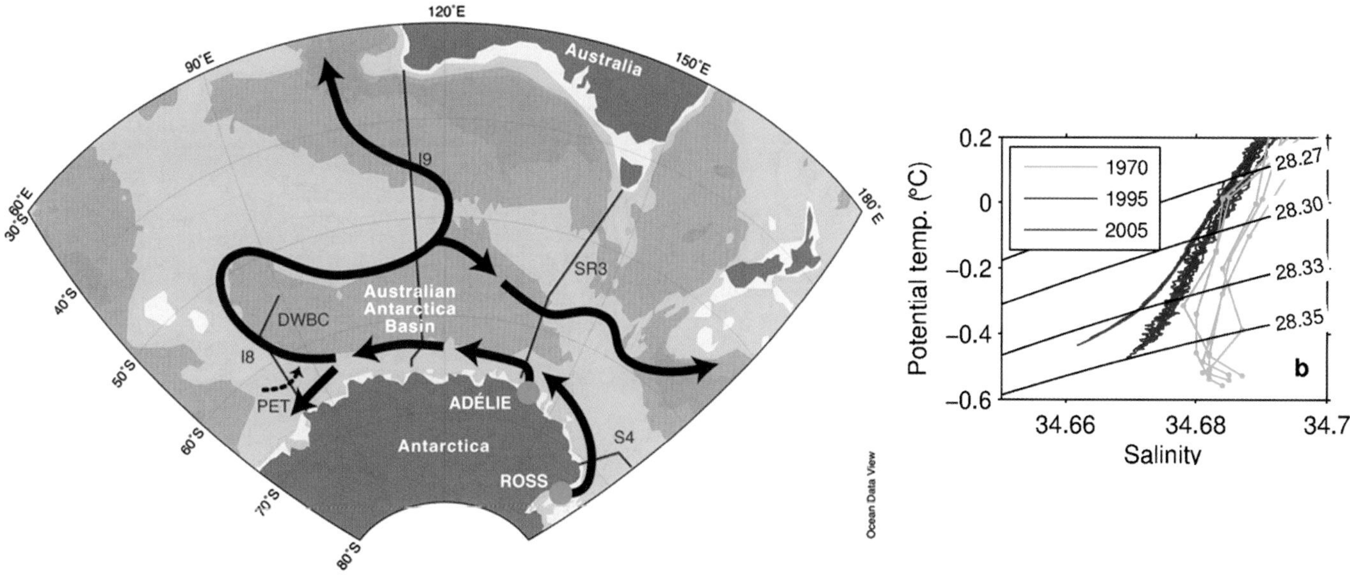

FIGURE 6. Freshening of Antarctic Bottom Water in the Australian Antarctic Basin. (left) Comparison of observations from the early 1970s, mid-1990s, and mid-2000s shows a shift toward less-salty and less-dense bottom water formed in the Indian and Pacific oceans at each of the sections indicated by red lines on the map. (right) An example of the changes in potential temperature and salinity observed near 115°E is also shown. (Potential temperature is the temperature of the water corrected for pressure effects.) The solid black lines indicate surfaces of constant density anomaly. From Rintoul (2007); used with permission.

regional increase in sea level. Changes in the location of ocean currents will also affect the distribution of organisms, and there are some early indications that species are also shifting south (Cubillos et al., 2007).

In contrast to the Arctic, where large decreases in sea ice extent and thickness have occurred, the overall extent of Antarctic sea ice has slightly increased in recent decades (the trend is not statistically significant) (Zwally et al., 2002; Parkinson, 2004). However, strong regional changes in sea ice extent and the seasonality of advance and retreat have been recorded in the Pacific sector (Stammerjohn et al., 2008), with substantial impacts on the marine ecosystem (Wilson et al., 2001).

The most dramatic changes observed in recent decades in Antarctica and the Southern Ocean have occurred along the Antarctic Peninsula. The peninsula has warmed more rapidly than anywhere else in the Southern Hemisphere, with the largest warming trend observed at Faraday/Vernadsky station (+0.53°C per decade for the period 1951–2006; the station is located at 65°15′S, 64°16′W). Ocean temperatures have also increased (Meredith and King, 2005), and the extent and duration of the winter sea ice cover have declined in the northern peninsula (Stammerjohn et al., 2008). Significant changes have also taken place in the marine ecosystem. Phytoplankton production has declined in the northern and increased in the southern part of the waters west of the Antarctic Peninsula (Montes-Hugo et al., 2009), as the result of changes in the sea ice regime. Gentoo penguins are extending their range farther south along the peninsula into regions previously dominated by Adelie penguins, and shifts in penguin diets have been observed (Ducklow et al., 2007).

Many of these changes observed in Antarctica and the Southern Ocean in recent decades are likely caused by the changes in winds over this time period (Turner et al., 2010). Changes in winds, in turn, drive changes in ocean circulation and temperature patterns and in the distribution and seasonality of sea ice (Figure 7). The primary mode of variability of the Southern Hemisphere winds is known as the Southern Annular Mode (SAM), which refers to a ring or vortex of winds that circles Antarctica from west to east and reaches from the stratosphere to the sea surface. In recent decades, there has been a tendency for this wind pattern to strengthen and contract closer to the Antarctic continent (Marshall, 2003). The changes observed to date in the SAM wind pattern are likely caused by a reduction in ozone in the stratosphere (Figure 8; Thompson and Solomon, 2002), but climate models suggest that increases in

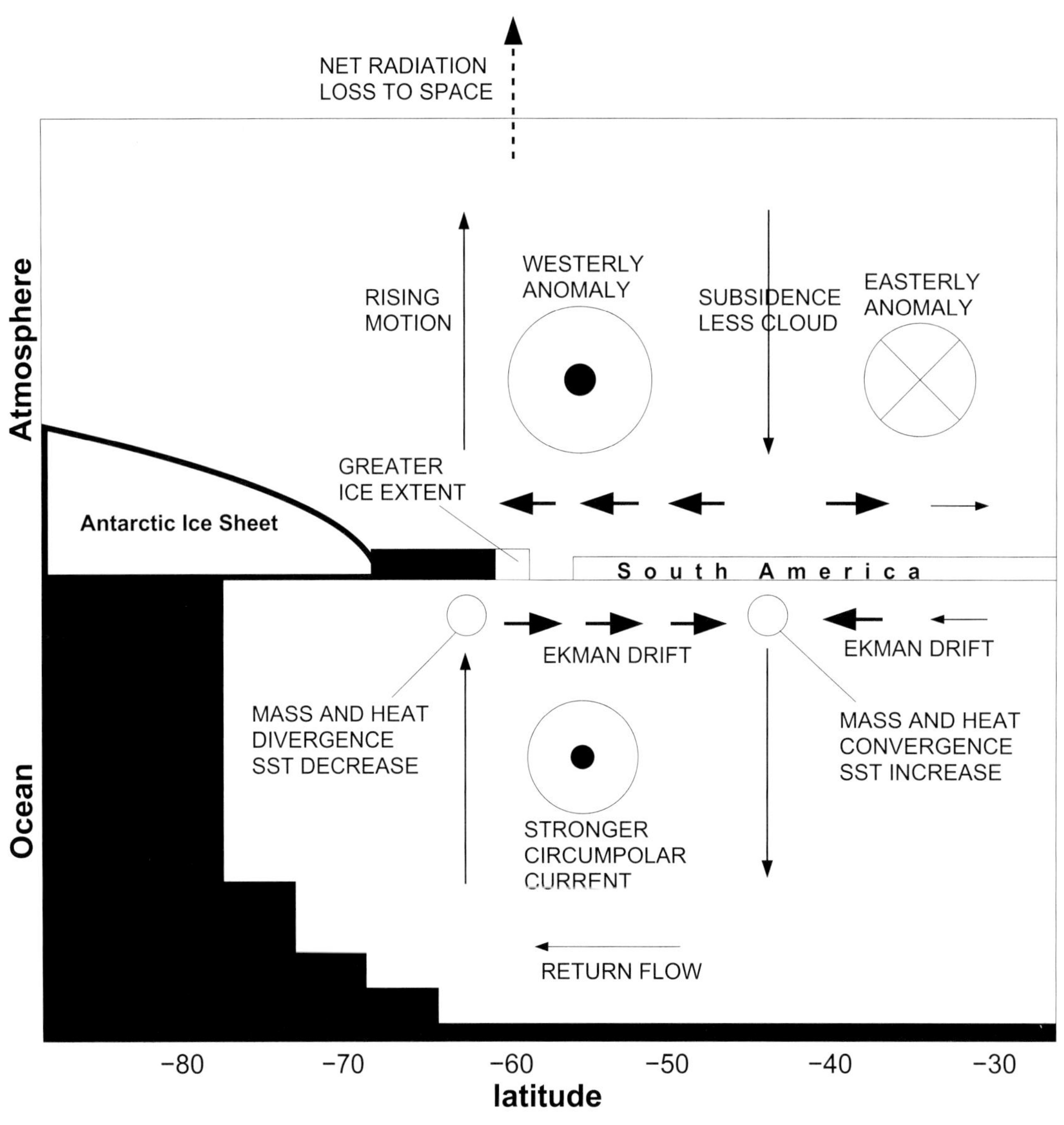

FIGURE 7. A representation of the changes in the atmosphere and ocean associated with variations in the Southern Annular Mode (SAM), the primary mode of variability of the Southern Hemisphere atmosphere. A strengthening of the winds drives stronger upwelling on the southern side of the Southern Ocean and stronger downwelling on the northern side. The stronger winds also tend to drive sea ice farther offshore. From Hall and Visbeck (2002); used with permission.

greenhouse gases will, in the future, drive similar changes in Southern Ocean winds (Schindell et al., 1998).

Although the fact that the Southern Ocean absorbs large amounts of anthropogenic carbon dioxide is a positive in the sense of slowing the rate of climate change, the additional carbon dioxide is also changing the chemistry of the ocean in ways that are likely to affect marine life. The uptake of CO_2 by the ocean is increasing the total inorganic carbon concentration, increasing the acidity, and reducing the amount of carbonate ion (Vazquez-Rodriguez et al., 2009). Because of the temperature dependence of the saturation state of aragonite (a form of calcium carbonate used by many organisms to make shells or other hard structures), the saturation threshold will be crossed first in the polar regions (Orr et al., 2005; McNeil and Matear, 2008). Indeed, there is some evidence that the changes are already causing a reduction in calcification of the shells of some organisms (Moy et al., 2009). Changes

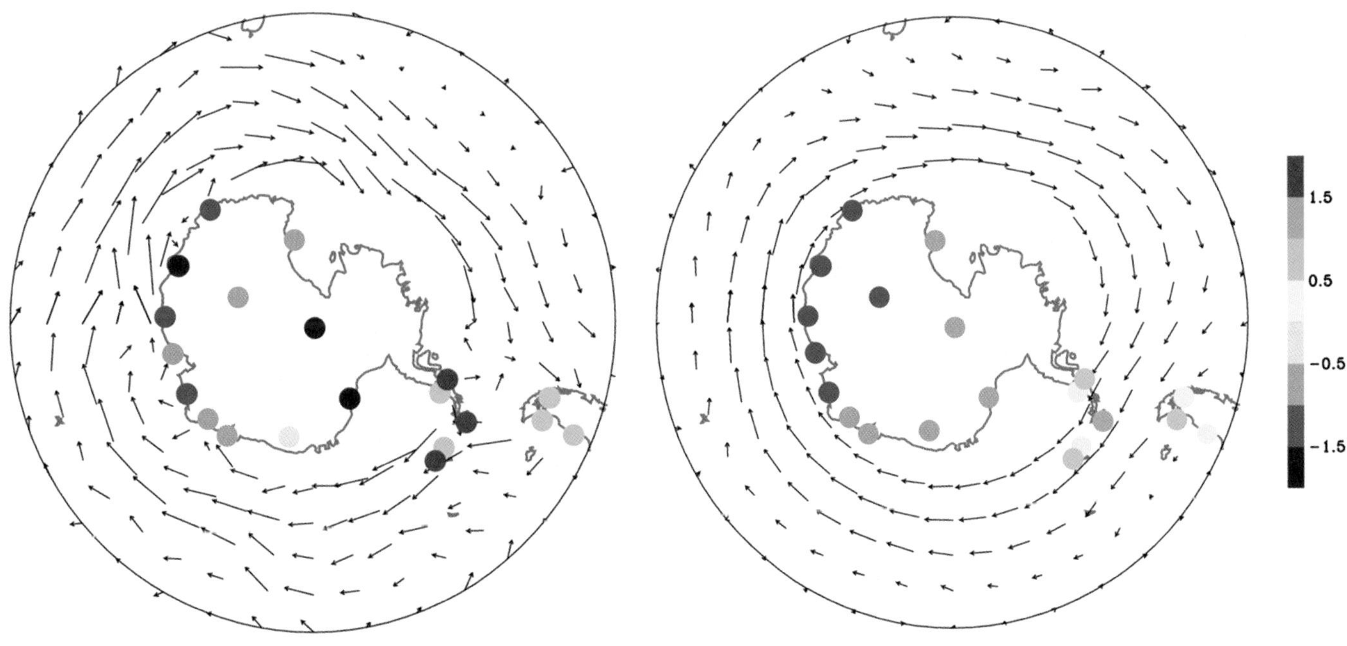

FIGURE 8. (left) Observed trends in surface wind over the Southern Ocean (arrows) and surface air temperature at Antarctic stations (colored dots) and (right) the part of the pattern that is congruent with the Southern Annular Mode. The wind data are from the NCAR/NCEP Reanalysis, for the period 1979–2000. From Thompson and Solomon (2002); used with permission.

in the quantity and nutritional quality of primary production will have consequences for secondary production, food web carbon and energy flows, and biogeochemical cycling, but the impact of changes in ocean chemistry on the Southern Ocean food web is largely unknown.

PROJECTIONS OF FUTURE CHANGE

Predicting future change in the Southern Ocean is particularly challenging. Small-scale phenomena like ocean eddies, which are unresolved by climate models, play a particularly important role in the Southern Ocean. Observations are scarce for testing of ocean models and for developing improved parameterisations. Existing models often do not perform well in the Southern Ocean. For example, an ocean carbon model intercomparison study found that the models diverged most dramatically in the Southern Ocean, primarily because of differences in how the models simulated the stratification and circulation (Orr et al., 2005).

Faced with a set of divergent model projections, one approach is to form a "weighted average" of a number of models, in which higher weight is placed on results from models that do a better job of simulating high-latitude climate (Bracegirdle et al., 2008). Using output from a large number of climate models used in the Intergovernmental Panel on Climate Change (IPCC) assessment reports, the weighted-mean model results predict further warming of the Southern Ocean over the next century, a 25% reduction in sea ice production, and a continued increase in strength of the westerly winds.

A particularly important issue is the response of the Southern Ocean overturning circulation to climate change. As discussed above, the overturning circulation influences strongly the ability of the Southern Ocean to absorb heat and carbon dioxide, as well as the supply of nutrients. A key question is how the overturning circulation responds to a change in winds blowing over the Southern Ocean. Coarse-resolution models, like those used to project future changes in response to increasing greenhouse gas concentrations, tend to show that stronger winds mean a stronger overturning circulation (as well as a stronger ACC) and a larger release of carbon dioxide from upwelling deep waters. High-resolution models that resolve the effects of small-scale eddies tend to show that the overturning and ACC transport are less sensitive to wind changes because a change in the eddies acts to compensate the change in wind forcing. Observations of the response to past changes in the winds are so far inconclusive, with atmospheric measurements favoring the former scenario (i.e., the Southern Ocean is becoming less effective at soaking up CO_2; Le Quéré et al., 2007) whereas eddy-resolving ocean model simulations and ocean measurements have been interpreted as evidence of the latter view (Hallberg and Gnanadesikan, 2006; Meredith and Hogg, 2006; Böning et al., 2008). Resolution of this issue will be an important step toward increasing certainty in projections of future climate change.

It is likely that warming and freshening of the surface layer will increase the stratification of the upper ocean, reducing nutrient inputs to the euphotic zone. Biological productivity and ecosystem function are also likely to be affected by a reduction in sea ice. Climate models using a business-as-usual scenario for CO_2 emissions predict that surface waters will become undersaturated with respect to aragonite by 2050, extending through the entire Southern Ocean by 2100 (Orr et al., 2005). When seasonal variations in carbonate ion concentration are taken into account, surface waters become undersaturated for aragonite as early as 2030 (McNeil and Matear, 2008).

A REVOLUTION IN SOUTHERN OCEAN OBSERVATIONS

Understanding of the influence of the Southern Ocean on the Earth system has increased rapidly in recent years. Much of the recent progress has relied on the ongoing revolution in ocean observations: tools are now available that enable scientists to really measure the Southern Ocean for the first time. Autonomous platforms like Argo profiling floats are allowing year-round measurements of remote regions like the Southern Ocean (Figure 9). In the last six years the Argo program has already provided more temperature and salinity profiles than obtained in the entire history of ship-based oceanography in the Southern Hemisphere. A variety of satellite sensors are delivering year-round, regular, circumpolar measurements of key variables, including sea surface temperature, sea ice, wind

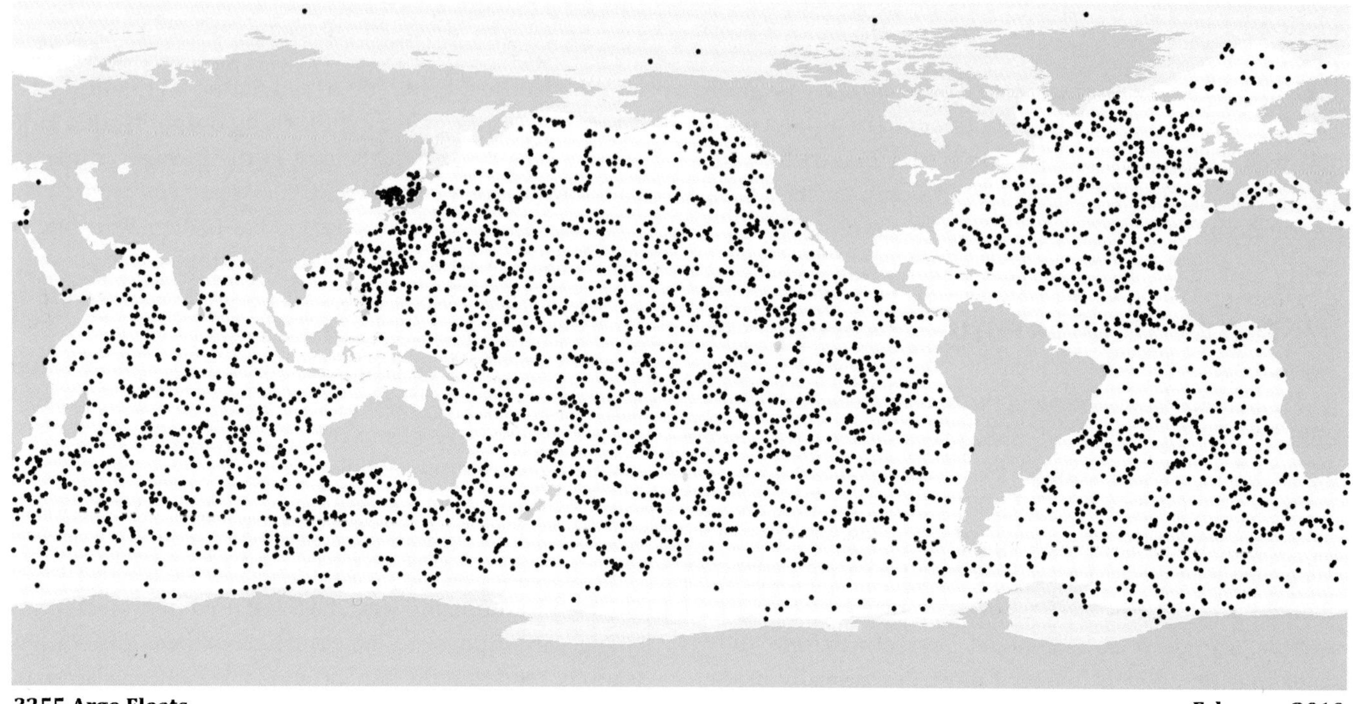

FIGURE 9. Distribution of Argo floats as of February 2010. Each float acquires and transmits a vertical profile of temperature and salinity as a function of pressure (equivalent to depth), from 2,000 m to the sea surface, every 10 days. From the JCOMMOPS Web site (http://www.jcommops.org).

stress, ocean color (a measure of phytoplankton biomass), sea surface height, and the mass balance of the Antarctic ice sheet. Deep measurements collected by ships have revealed changes in the ocean inventory of heat, freshwater, and carbon. Sensors mounted on elephant seals and ice-capable floats have provided the first broad-scale profiles of the ocean beneath the sea ice in winter (Klatt et al., 2007; Charrassin et al., 2008). By providing simultaneous observations of seal behaviour and oceanographic conditions, the seal observations have provided new insights into the foraging behaviour and population dynamics of the seals (Biuw et al., 2007).

Many of these achievements have relied on the international cooperation and coordination established by the International Polar Year (IPY) and other programs. A legacy of the IPY is the demonstration that a Southern Ocean Observing System (SOOS) is feasible, cost-effective, needed, and timely. The SOOS will provide the sustained observations needed to detect, interpret, and respond to change in the Southern Ocean. During IPY, the community obtained a circumpolar snapshot of the Southern Ocean that has provided new insights into the coupling between physical, chemical, and biological systems and their sensitivity to change. This was achieved with a level of investment only slightly greater than the "business as usual" support of Southern Ocean science. Key to the achievements of the IPY was broad international support and the focus on multidisciplinary science.

SOUTHERN OCEAN SCIENCE INFORMING POLICY

Southern Ocean science contributes to several dimensions of policy. Perhaps the most important contribution is to educate, to inspire, and to raise awareness of the deep and intimate connection between Antarctica and the Southern Ocean and the rest of the globe. The influence of Antarctica on the Earth system is largely mediated through the surrounding oceans. Changes in the Southern Ocean will have significant implications for the Earth system, through feedbacks involving the overturning circulation, the carbon cycle, and ocean-ice interactions. Observations of the Southern Ocean help define what climate trajectory we are on, are essential for testing models used to make climate projections, and may provide an early warning of impending shifts in the climate system. Models that incorporate a better representation of Southern Ocean processes will deliver more skilful climate projections, providing better information to guide mitigation and adaptation strategies. Knowledge of the response of the Southern Ocean to change will help manage the risks of a changing climate.

Human pressures on the Southern Ocean are increasing and will continue to grow. The growth in Antarctic tourism has implications for the safety of both human lives and the environment (e.g., Enzenbacher, 1992; Fraser and Patterson, 1997; Frenot et al., 2005). Further exploitation of marine resources is likely as more traditional sources of protein decline or increase in cost, either for direct human consumption or as feed for aquaculture. Geoengineering approaches to enhancing carbon sequestration (e.g., iron fertilisation of the Southern Ocean; see Watson et al., 2008, and accompanying articles) are being considered. As the use of the Southern Ocean increases, so will the demand for knowledge required to manage marine resources and to inform decisions by policy makers, industry, and the community. To deliver the understanding of the Southern Ocean on which sound policy depends, a sustained, multidisciplinary Southern Ocean Observing System is essential.

LITERATURE CITED

Aoki, S., S. R. Rintoul, S. Ushio, S. Watanabe, and N. L. Bindoff. 2005. Freshening of the Adélie Land Bottom Water near 140°E. *Geophysical Research Letters*, 32:L23601, doi:10.1029/2005GL024246.

Biuw, M., L. Boehme, C. Guinet, M. Hindell, D. Costa, J. B. Charrassin, F. Roquet, F. Bailleul, M. Meredith, S. Thorpe, Y. Tremblay, B. McDonald, Y. H. Park, S. R. Rintoul, N. Bindoff, M. Goebel, D. Crocker, P. Lovell, J. Nicholson, F. Monks, and M. A. Fedak. 2007. Variations in Behavior and Condition of a Southern Ocean Top Predator in Relation to *in situ* Oceanographic Conditions. *Proceedings of the National Academy of Sciences of the United States of America*, 104:13,705–13,710.

Böning, C. W., A. Dispert, M. Visbeck, S. R. Rintoul, and F. Schwarzkopf. 2008. The Response of the Antarctic Circumpolar Current to Recent Climate Change. *Nature Geoscience*, 1:864–869, doi:10.1038/ngeo362.

Bracegirdle, T. J., W. M. Connolley, and J. Turner. 2008. Antarctic Climate Change over the Twenty First Century. *Journal of Geophysical Research*, 113:D03103, doi:10.1029/2007JD008933.

Charrassin, J. B., M. Hindell, S. R. Rintoul, F. Roquet, S. Sokolov, M. Biuw, D. Costa, L. Boehme, P. Lovell, R. Coleman, R. Timmermann, A. Meijers, M. Meredith, Y. H. Park, F. Bailleul, M. Goebel, Y. Tremblay, C. A. Bost, C. R. McMahon, I. C. Field, M. A. Fedak, and C. Guinet. 2008. Southern Ocean Frontal Structure and Sea-Ice Formation Rates Revealed by Elephant Seals. *Proceedings of the National Academy of Sciences of the United States of America*, 105:11,634–11,639, doi:11610.11073/pnas.0800790105.

Cubillos, J. C., S. W. Wright, G. Nash, M. F. de Salas, B. Griffiths, B. Tilbrook, A. Poisson, and G. M. Hallegraeff. 2007. Calcification Morphotypes of the Coccolithophorid *Emiliania huxleyi* in the

Southern Ocean: Changes in 2001 to 2006 Compared to Historical Data. *Marine Ecology Progress Series,* 348:47–54.

Cunningham, S. A., S. G. Alderson, B. A. King, and M. A. Brandon. 2003. Transport and Variability of the Antarctic Circumpolar Current in Drake Passage. *Journal of Geophysical Research,* 108(C5):8084, doi:10.1029/2001JC001147.

Curry, R., B. Dickson, and I. Yashayaev. 2003. A Change in the Freshwater Balance of the Atlantic Ocean over the Past Four Decades. *Nature,* 426: 826–829.

Deacon, G. E. R. 1937. The Hydrology of the Southern Ocean. *Discovery Reports,* 15:1–24.

———. 1982. Physical and Biological Zonation in the Southern Ocean. *Deep-Sea Research,* 29:1–15.

Ducklow, H. W., K. Baker, D. G. Martinson, L. B. Quetin, R. M. Ross, R. C. Smith, S. E. Stammerjohn, M. Vernet and W. Fraser, 2007. Marine Pelagic Ecosystems: The West Antarctic Peninsula. *Philosophical Transactions of the Royal Society B: Biological Sciences,* 362:67–94.

Enzenbacher, D. J. 1992. Antarctic Tourism and Environmental Concerns. *Marine Pollution Bulletin,* 25:9–12.

Fraser, W. R., and D. L. Patterson. 1997. "Human Disturbance and Long-Term Changes in Adelie Penguin Populations: A Natural Experiment at Palmer Station, Antarctic Peninsula." In *Antarctic Communities: Species, Structure and Survival, Scientific Committee for Antarctic Research (SCAR), Sixth Biological Symposium,* eds. B. Battaglia, J. Valencia and D. W. H. Walton, pp. 445–452. New York, N.Y.: Cambridge University Press.

Frenot, Y., S. L. Chown, J. Whinam, P. M., Selkirk, P. Convey, M. Skotnicki, and D. M. Bergstrom. 2005. Biological Invasions in the Antarctic: Extent, Impacts and Implications. *Biological Reviews,* 80:45–72.

Gille, S. T. 2002. Warming of the Southern Ocean since the 1950s. *Science,* 295:1275–1277.

———. 2008. Decadal-Scale Temperature Trends in the Southern Hemisphere Ocean. *Journal of Climate,* 21:4749–4765.

Hall, A. and M. Visbeck, 2002. Synchronous Variability in the Southern Hemisphere Atmosphere, Sea Ice and Ocean Resulting from the Annular Mode. *Journal of Climate,* 15, 3043–3057.

Hallberg, R., and A. Gnanadesikan. 2006. The Role of Eddies in Determining the Structure and Response of the Wind-Driven Southern Hemisphere Overturning: Results from the Modeling Eddies in the Southern Ocean (MESO) Project. *Journal of Physical Oceanography,* 36:2232–2252.

Jacobs, S. S. 2004. Bottom Water Production and Its Links with the Thermohaline Circulation. *Antarctic Science,* 16(4):427–437.

———. 2006. Observations of Change in the Southern Ocean. *Philosophical Transactions of the Royal Society A,* 364:1657–1681, doi:10.1098/rsta.2006.1794.

Jacobs, S. S., C. F. Giulivi, and P. A. Mele. 2002. Freshening of the Ross Sea during the Late 20th Century. *Science,* 297:386–389.

Johnson, G. C., and S. C. Doney. 2006. Recent Western South Atlantic Bottom Water Warming. *Geophysical Research Letters,* 33:L14614, doi:10.1029/2006GL026769.

Klatt, O., O. Boebel, and E. Fahrbach. 2007. A Profiling Float's Sense of Ice. *Journal of Atmospheric and Oceanic Technology,* 24(7):1301–1308, doi:10.1175/JTECH2026.1.

Le Quéré, C., C. Rödenbeck, E. T. Buitenhuis, T. J. Conway, R. Langenfelds, A. Gomez, C. Labuschagne, M. Ramonet, T. Nakazawa, N. Metzl, N. Gillett, and M. Heimann. 2007. Saturation of the Southern Ocean CO_2 Sink due to Recent Climate Change. *Science,* 316:1735–1738, doi:10.1126/science.1136188

Levitus, S., J. Antonov, and T. Boyer. 2005. Warming of the World Ocean, 1955–2003. *Geophysical Research Letters,* 32(2):L02604, doi:10.1029/2004GL021592.

Montes-Hugo, M., S. C. Doney, H. W. Ducklow, W. Fraser, D. Martinson, S. E. Stammerjohn, and O. Schofield. 2009. Recent Changes in Phytoplankton Communities Associated with Rapid Regional Climate Change Along the Western Antarctic Peninsula. *Science,* 323:1470–1473.

Marshall, G. J. 2003. Trends in the Southern Annular Mode from Observations and Reanalyses. *Journal of Climate,* 16:4134–4143.

McNeil, B. I., and R. J. Matear. 2008. Southern Ocean Acidification: A Tipping Point at 450-ppm Atmospheric CO_2. *Proceedings of the National Academy of Sciences of the United States of America,* 105:18,860–18,864.

Meredith, M. P., and A. M. Hogg. 2006. Circumpolar Response of Southern Ocean Eddy Activity to Changes in the Southern Annular Mode. *Geophysical Research Letters,* 33:L16608, doi:10.1029/2006GL026499.

Meredith, M. P., and J. C. King. 2005. Rapid Climate Change in the Ocean to the West of the Antarctic Peninsula during the Second Half of the Twentieth Century. *Geophysical Research Letters,* 32:L19604, doi:10.1029/2005GL024042.

Moy, A. D., W. R. Howard, S. G. Bray, and T. W. Trull. 2009. Reduced Calcification in Modern Southern Ocean Planktonic Foraminifera. *Nature Geoscience,* 2:276–280, doi:10.1038/ngeo460.

Nowlin, W. D., and J. M. Klinck. 1986. The Physics of the Antarctic Circumpolar Current. *Reviews of Geophysics,* 24:469–491.

Orr, J. C., V. J. Fabry, O. Aumont, L. Bopp, S. C. Doney, R. A. Feely, A. Gnanadesikan, N. Gruber, A. Ishida, F. Joos, R. M. Key, K. Lindsay, E. Maier-Reimer, R. Matear, P. Monfray. A. Mouchet, R. G. Najjar, G. K. Plattner, K. B. Rodgers, C. L. Sabine, J. L. Sarmiento, R. Schlitzer, R. D. Slater, J. J. Totterdell, M. F. Weirig, Y. Yamanaka, A. Yool, 2005 Anthropogenic Ocean Acidification over the Twenty-First Century and Its Impact on Calcifying Organisms. *Nature,* 437:681–686.

Orsi, A. H., T. W. Whitworth III, and W. D. Nowlin Jr. 1995. On the Meridional Extent and Fronts of the Antarctic Circumpolar Current. *Deep-Sea Research, Part I,* 42, 641–673.

Parkinson, C. L. 2004. Southern Ocean Sea Ice and Its Wider Linkages: Insights Revealed from Models and Observations. *Antarctic Science,* 16:387–400.

Rignot, E., J. L. Bamber, M. R. Van Den Broeke, C. Davis, Y. Li, W. J. van de Berg and E. van Meijgaard, 2008. Recent Antarctic Ice Mass Loss from Radar Interferometry and Regional Climate Modelling. *Nature Geoscience,* 1:106–110.

Rignot, E., G. Casassa, P. Gogineni, W. Krabill, A. Rivera, and R. Thomas. 2004. Accelerated Ice Discharge from the Antarctic Peninsula Following the Collapse of Larsen B Ice Shelf. *Geophysical Research Letters,* 31:L18401, doi:10.1029/2004GL020697.

Rintoul, S. R. 2000. Southern Ocean Currents and Climate. *Papers and Proceedings of the Royal Society of Tasmania,* 133:41–50.

———. 2007. Rapid Freshening of Antarctic Bottom Water Formed in the Indian and Pacific Oceans. *Geophysical Research Letters,* 34:L06606, doi:10.1029/2006GL028550.

Rintoul, S. R., C. Hughes, and D. Olbers. 2001. "The Antarctic Circumpolar System." In *Ocean Circulation and Climate, International*

Geophysics Series Vol. 77, eds. G. Siedler, J. Church, and J. Gould, pp. 271–302. London: Academic Press.

Rintoul, S. R., and S. Sokolov. 2001. Baroclinic Transport Variability of the Antarctic Circumpolar Current South of Australia (WOCE repeat section SR3). *Journal of Geophysical Research*, 106:2795–2814.

Sabine, C. L., R. A. Feely, N. Gruber, R. M. Key, K. Lee, J. L. Bullister, R. Wanninkhof, C. S. Wong, D. W. R. Wallace, B. Tilbrook, F. J. Millero, T. H. Peng, A. Kozyr, T. Ono, A. F. Rios, 2004. The Oceanic Sink for Anthropogenic CO_2. *Science,* 305:367–371.

Sarmiento, J. L., N. Gruber, M. A. Brzezinski, J. P. Dunne, 2004. High-Latitude Controls of Thermocline Nutrients and Low Latitude Biological Productivity. *Nature,* 427:56–60.

Schindell, D. T., D. Rind, and P. Lonergan. 1998. Increased Polar Stratospheric Ozone Losses and Delayed Eventual Recovery Owing to Increasing Greenhouse-Gas Concentrations. *Nature*, 392:589–592, doi:10.1038/33385.

Shepherd, A., D., Wingham, and E. Rignot. 2004. Warm Ocean Is Eroding West Antarctic Ice Sheet. *Geophysical Research Letters,* 31:L23402, doi:10.1029/2004GL021106.

Sokolov, S., and S. R. Rintoul. 2009. The Circumpolar Structure and Distribution of the Antarctic Circumpolar Current Fronts: 2. Variability and Relationship to Sea Surface Height. *Journal of Geophysical Research*, 114:C11019, doi:10.1029/2008JC005248.

Speer, K., S. R. Rintoul, and B. Sloyan. 2000. The Diabatic Deacon Cell. *Journal of Physical Oceanography*, 30:3212–3222.

Stammerjohn, S. E., D. G. Martinson, R. C. Smith, X. Yuan, and D. Rind. 2008. Trends in Antarctic Annual Sea Ice Retreat and Advance and Their Relation to El Nino–Southern Oscillation and Southern Annular Mode Variability. *Journal of Geophysical Research,* 113:C03S90, doi:10.1029/2007JC004269.

Thompson, D. W. J., and S. Solomon. 2002. Interpretation of Recent Southern Hemisphere Climate Change. *Science*, 296:895–899.

Turner, J., R. A. Bindschadler, P. Convey, G. Di Prisco, E. Fahrbach, J. Gutt, D. A. Hodgson, P. A. Mayewski, and C. P. Summerhayes, 2010. *Antarctic Climate Change and the Environment,* 526 pp. Cambridge, UK: SCAR.

Vázquez-Rodríguez, M., F. Touratier, C. Lo Monaco, D. Waugh, X. A. Padin, R. G. J. Bellerby, C. Goyet, N. Metzl, A. F. Ríos, and F. F. Pérez. 2009. Anthropogenic Carbon in the Atlantic Ocean: Comparison of Four Data-Based Calculation Methods. *Biogeosciences*, 6:439–451.

Watson, A. J., P. W. Boyd, S. M. Turner, T. D. Jickells, and P. S. Liss. 2008. Designing the Next Generation of Ocean Ice Fertilization Experiments. *Marine Ecology Progress Series,* 364:303–309.

Wilson, P. R., D. G. Ainley, N. Nur, S. S. Jacobs, K. J. Barton, G. Ballard, J. C. Comiso, 2001. Adelie Penguin Population Change in the Pacific Sector of Antarctica: Relation to Sea Ice Extent and the Antarctic Circumpolar Current. *Marine Ecology Progress Series,* 213:301–330, doi:10.3354/MEPS213301.

Zwally, H. J., J. C. Comiso, C. L. Parkinson, D. J. Cavalieri, and P. Gloersen. 2002. Variability of Antarctic Sea Ice 1979–1998. *Journal of Geophysical Research,* 107:3041, doi:10.1029/2000JC000733.

The Antarctic Ozone Hole: A Unique Example of the Science and Policy Interface

Susan Solomon and Marie-Lise Chanin

ABSTRACT. The discovery of an unexpected large depletion of the Antarctic ozone layer in the 1980s attracted the attention of scientists, policymakers, and the public. The phenomenon quickly became known as the "ozone hole." Observations established that the ozone losses were driven primarily by human-made compounds, chlorofluorocarbons and bromocarbons, whose chemistry is particularly enhanced for ozone loss under the extreme cold conditions of the Antarctic. Systematic long-term data of Antarctic total ozone date back to the 1950s at several international stations, and these key records owe their existence to the International Geophysical Year in 1957–1958 as well as to the Antarctic Treaty System. Although ozone depletion is greatest in the Antarctic, significant depletion has also been observed in the Arctic and at midlatitudes in both hemispheres. Ozone depletion enhances the ultraviolet light at the planet surface and thereby can damage ecosystems and some crops as well as increasing the incidence of human eye cataracts and skin cancer. These concerns led policymakers to agree to the Montreal Protocol on Substances that Deplete the Ozone Layer (Montreal Protocol) in 1987, and progressive advances in understanding the Antarctic ozone hole were important for the considerations by policy over the next 10 years that ultimately led to controls that have essentially phased out the production of chlorofluorocarbons and bromocarbons. Chlorofluorocarbons not only deplete ozone, but they are also greenhouse gases that contribute to climate change. It is not widely appreciated that the phaseout of the chlorofluorocarbons under the Montreal Protocol has probably contributed about five times more to mitigation of climate change than has occurred due to the Kyoto Protocol to the United Nations Framework Convention on Climate Change (Kyoto Protocol) to date. Thus, the Antarctic ozone hole and the subsequent scientific understanding and policy process have played key roles not only for ozone protection but also for climate protection.

INTRODUCTION

A distinguishing feature of the twentieth century was the recognition of the fact that human activities are changing the Earth's atmosphere. Carbon dioxide, methane, and chlorofluorocarbon concentrations have increased, causing people around the world to come to a new realization: the atmosphere is vast but finite. There are now so many people on this planet that some of the gases we release are affecting the composition of our atmosphere. The most striking illustration of the concurrent development of scientific theory, observation, and

Susan Solomon, NOAA Earth System Research Laboratory, 325 S. Broadway, Boulder, Colorado 80305, USA. Marie-Lise Chanin, Laboratoire Atmosphères (LATMOS), Centre National de la Recherche Scientifique, (CNRS), Université de Versailles Saint Quentin, F-91370 Verrières-le-Buisson, France. Correspondence: susan.solomon@noaa.gov; chanin@latmos.ipsl.fr.

societal implications of atmospheric change has been the depletion of the Earth's protective ozone layer, and this remarkable change has been most pronounced in the most remote place on the planet: Antarctica.

ANTARCTIC OBSERVATIONS OF OZONE: A BELLWETHER FOR THE PLANET

The first identification of a human impact on the ozone layer was possible as a result of the commitment to long-term monitoring of Antarctica that began in the International Geophysical Year (IGY) in 1957–1958, when continuous, year-round observations of ozone were begun at multiple sites around the continent. The IGY was a cornerstone in global monitoring of the atmosphere not only in Antarctica but worldwide, and the establishment of this baseline system of scientific study was among the factors that bolstered both the success of the Antarctic Treaty dialogue at that time and the attraction of many young scientists into their careers. Among the key scientists who participated in the revision of the Antarctic Treaty in the 1980s was Jacques Cousteau, who argued for a treaty that would continue to consider Antarctica as a continent devoted to science and preservation of nature. These elements combined to produce the scientific capabilities that led to many advances, among them the discovery of the ozone hole.

In 1985, scientists from the British Antarctic Survey reported that the October Antarctic ozone content had decreased by almost half compared, e.g., to the measurements taken there in the first two decades after the IGY (Farman et al., 1985). This change was far greater than the natural variations observed at Halley in monthly averaged ozone. Data from three key stations are shown in Figure 1, illustrating how the international research programs in Antarctica undertaken by numerous nations around the time of the IGY complemented one another in jointly providing independent evidence of an unprecedented change in Antarctic total ozone.

Chlorofluorocarbons and bromocarbons produced by man were suspected as a possible cause. Ozone depletion leads to more ultraviolet light falling on the planet surface, which can cause damage to the DNA of plants and animals. The Antarctic ozone hole therefore raised the important question of whether or not similar processes could occur in other locations, particularly middle and low latitudes. Among other impacts, damage to certain ecosystems, crops, and human health (including cataracts and some types of skin cancers) are enhanced when ozone is reduced, making global ozone losses a matter of societal concern (see, e.g., United Nations Environment Programme, 1999).

Within a few years, aircraft and ground-based observations were carried out that measured not just Antarctic ozone but also a broad suite of chemicals, both manmade and natural, that can affect it (de Zafra et al., 1987; Solomon et al., 1987; Anderson et al., 1989; Waters et al., 1993). As a result of the work of hundreds of researchers, it is now well established that ozone depletion is pronounced in Antarctica because it is, indeed, the coldest place on Earth, which gives rise to chemical processes profoundly different from those occurring in warmer environments.

The extreme coldness of the Antarctic stratosphere allows chemical reactions to occur on and in the surfaces of polar stratospheric clouds that rapidly liberate reactive chlorine from chemically inert reservoirs, making the chlorine from chlorofluorocarbons much more damaging to ozone than it would otherwise be (Solomon et al., 1986). The most rapid ozone loss occurs in Antarctica during September because both cold temperatures and sunlight are involved in the chemistry of Antarctic ozone depletion. The depletion occurs over a particular range of altitudes from about 12 to 25 km because this is the height range where the polar stratospheric clouds occur. The structure of this depletion is shown in Figure 2, and it is one of the important pieces of evidence showing a "fingerprint" of the ozone hole that provides the evidence supporting the understanding that the depletion is driven by chlorofluorocarbon chemistry (see the review by Solomon, 1999, and references therein).

Ups and downs in the depth and size of the ozone hole from one year to another depend mainly on how cold or warm it is each year (see, e.g., World Meteorological Organization (WMO), 2007). Loss of ozone affects the temperature in the stratosphere too: less ozone leads to a colder stratosphere (Ramaswamy et al., 2001, and references therein). Strong cooling in Antarctica in turn affects the wind pattern in the troposphere and even at the ground and is one of the factors that has caused some parts of Antarctica to get colder while other parts have gotten warmer over about the past three decades (Gillett and Thompson, 2003). Thus, ozone depletion also affects the pattern of Antarctic surface climate change. Indeed, the discovery that Antarctic ozone depletion could couple to surface climate via circulation changes is a new process in chemistry-climate linkages. In addition, it has long been known that stratospheric ozone depletion could introduce a cooling effect on global surface climate. However, the

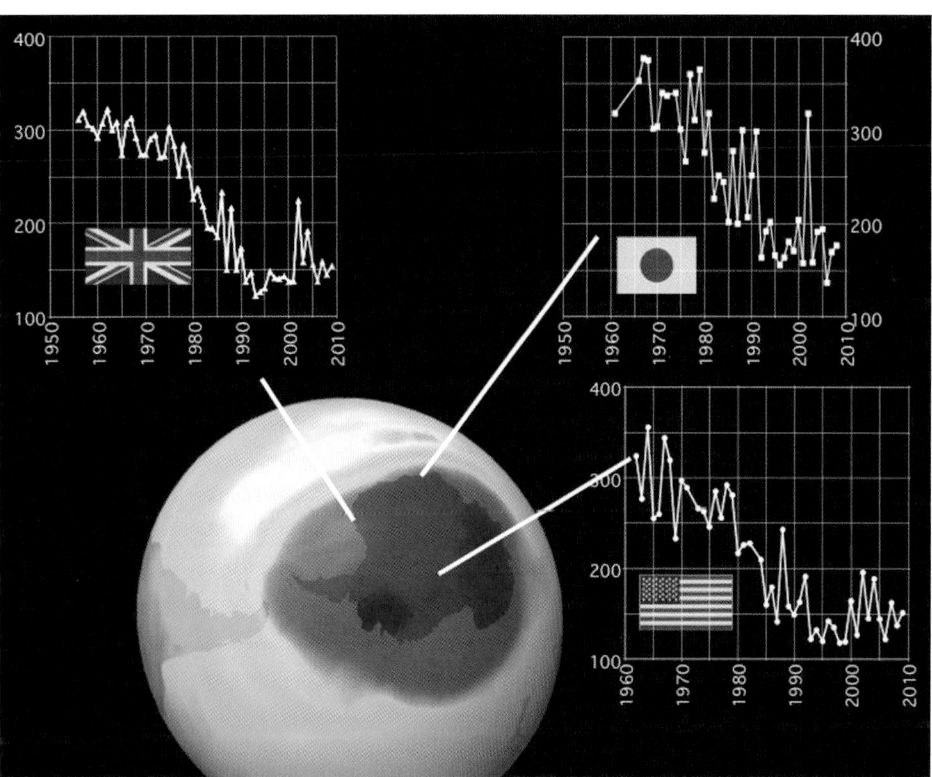

FIGURE 1. October monthly mean total ozone records (in dobson units) from (top left) Halley, (top right) Syowa, and (bottom right) South Pole stations, with the latter being the mean of the second half of the month only because of the limited availability of sunlight needed to make measurements there. Data for Syowa are available at the World Ozone and Ultraviolet Data Center (WOUDC), and those for the South Pole are available at the NOAA Earth System Research Laboratory, Global Monitoring Division, ftp archive; the Halley data are courtesy of J. D. Shanklin, available at the British Antarctic Survey Web site (http://www.antarctica.ac.uk). A satellite ozone map for 6 September 2000 is also shown (courtesy of NASA).

halocarbons that cause ozone depletion are also potent greenhouse gases that contribute importantly to warming along with other compounds including carbon dioxide, methane, and nitrous oxide; see Figure 4 and the discussion below.

CONTRASTS BETWEEN THE ARCTIC AND ANTARCTIC

A logical next question is whether or not ozone depletion is also occurring in the Arctic. The answer is yes, but the changes are smaller there, primarily because the Arctic stratosphere is warmer than the Antarctic, particularly in spring. Most important is that the Arctic stratosphere generally warms up sooner than the Antarctic does. This in turn means that the overlap between the cold temperatures that cause clouds to form and the sunlight that returns to the polar regions in spring is less effective in the north than in the south. However, some studies have highlighted an important aspect of natural variability: the spring Arctic stratosphere can sometimes be very cold. In unusually cold years, more Arctic ozone depletion is, indeed, observed. Figure 3 shows that the ozone losses in the Arctic were most pronounced in the mid- to late 1990s (which were colder than average in the Arctic), but these Arctic ozone depletions were still considerably smaller than those found in the Antarctic. Figure 3 also underscores the fact that whereas there are many sites where some Arctic ozone data have been taken for shorter periods, there is only one station in the High Arctic (Resolute, Canada) where a continuous record extends back to the IGY. In contrast, there

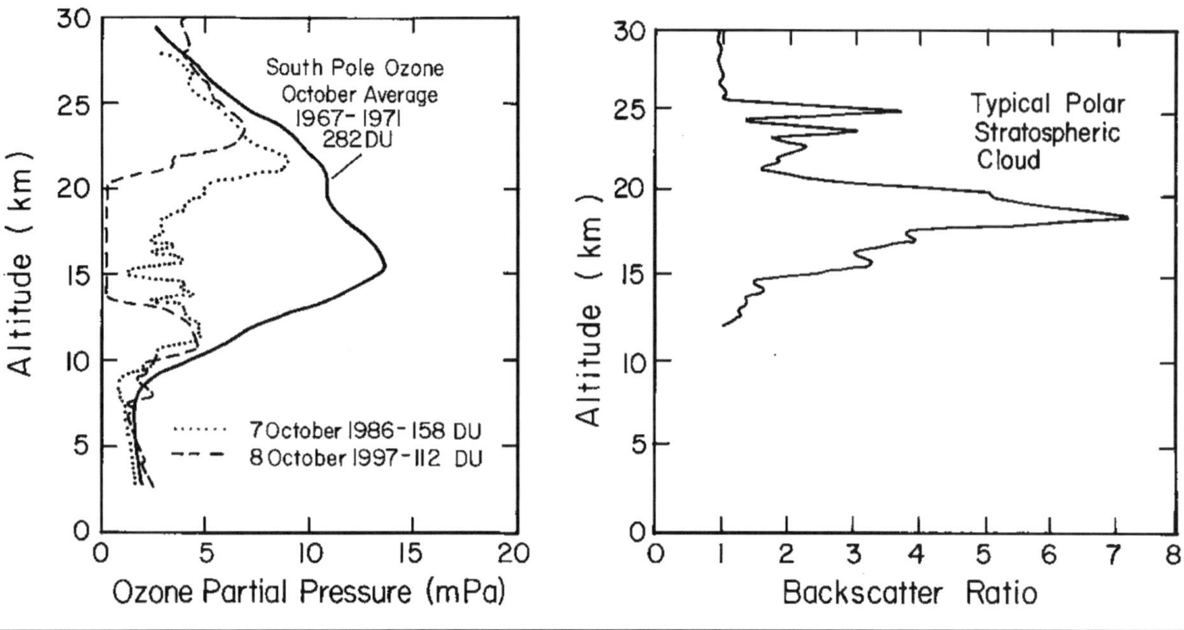

FIGURE 2. (left) Observations of the vertical profile of ozone observed at the South Pole during October in the late 1960s and early 1970s, contrasted with those of 1986 and 1997. Total ozone (dobson units) is indicated for each profile. (right) Typical polar stratospheric clouds observed at the South Pole are shown. From Solomon (1999).

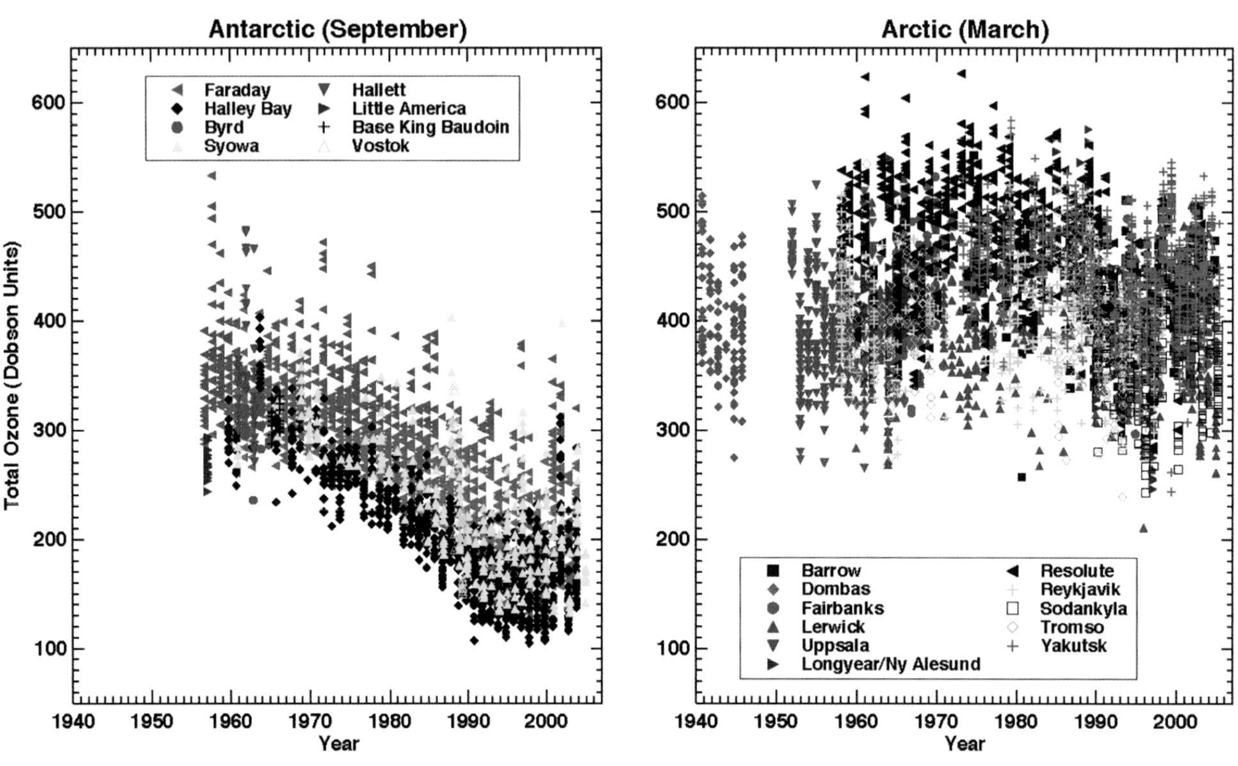

FIGURE 3. Observations of daily total column ozone (left) in Antarctica in September and (right) in the Arctic in March. Some records have been offset in time slightly for clarity. From Solomon et al. (2007).

are four sites with such records in the Antarctic, again attesting to the importance of the IGY and to the way in which the interface of science and policy in protecting the Antarctic also facilitated Antarctic science, especially systematic monitoring. Indeed, as the world looks forward to the future of the ozone layer and its interactions with climate change, the Antarctic Treaty can serve as model in preserving required data records, but no such international provisions fully cover the Arctic at present. Further, the question of whether the Arctic stratosphere might become colder or warmer in the future due to climate changes has been raised (see WMO, 2007), introducing the issue of whether or not Arctic ozone depletion could worsen in coming decades, at least in some years.

GLOBAL OZONE CHANGES AND GLOBAL POLICY AGREEMENT: THE MONTREAL PROTOCOL

Ozone changes are happening at midlatitudes too. Here again, there is evidence that these ozone changes are not natural. Observations suggest that human use of chlorofluorocarbons and other ozone depleting substances is the fundamental cause of the midlatitude ozone depletions and that reactions on surfaces are also significant in enhancing these ozone losses, albeit less so than in the polar regions (WMO, 2007).

As a result of concerns about our changing ozone layer, a handful of governments agreed the landmark 1987 Montreal Protocol, which started with modest controls on chlorofluorocarbons and bromocarbons but over the next two decades was joined by nearly every country in the world (the only UN treaty with full participation) and strengthened by amendments and adjustments to phase out dozens of additional ozone-depleting substances worldwide (Andersen and Sarma, 2002). The chief U.S. negotiator of the Montreal Protocol has written a memoir that discusses the key factors in the negotiation of the agreement (Benedick, 1998) and has emphasized a leading role played by the United States along with others, including Canada, Norway, and Sweden. Benedick (1998) suggests that the Montreal Protocol would likely have been agreed in 1987 even if the Antarctic ozone hole had not been discovered. It is, however, useful to note that the original Montreal Protocol required only that global chlorofluorocarbon production and consumption be reduced by 50% and that bromocarbon production and consumption not exceed the rates prevailing in the 1980s (i.e., emissions were to remain frozen at the rates occurring at that time). If that had been the only policy action taken, these gases would have continued to increase in the atmosphere, and massive amounts of ozone depletion would eventually have occurred in the Arctic; indeed, even the tropical ozone layer would have exhibited dramatic depletion at certain altitudes by about the 2050s (Newman et al., 2009).

The Montreal Protocol's precepts included a provision calling for review of the science, technology, and economics of the ozone depletion issue and revision over time, and it is evident that the subsequent amendments and adjustments to the Montreal Protocol that were agreed, e.g., in 1990 and 1992 were influenced by advances in understanding the science, in particular the science of the Antarctic ozone hole (see WMO, 2007; Newman et al., 2009). These revisions to the Montreal Protocol took the form of successive advancements of phaseout dates of production and consumption of ozone-depleting chemicals used in various sectors (e.g., solvents, refrigeration, airconditioning, fire extinguishing, etc.) as substitute chemicals and processes were found. Global emissions of chlorofluorocarbons today are near zero, and the concentrations of the chlorofluorocarbons already in the atmosphere are starting to decrease in response to this unprecedented global agreement. But the chlorofluorocarbon that is already in our atmosphere is very stable; it is destroyed only by very slow processes and lives for 50–100 years. This means that although the ozone layer is expected to eventually recover, the chlorofluorocarbon that is already present will continue to destroy ozone from one pole to the other well into the middle of the twenty-first century (WMO, 2007).

INTERACTIONS BETWEEN THE MONTREAL AND KYOTO PROTOCOLS

Observations of chlorofluorocarbons attest to the fact that global compliance with the Montreal Protocol has been highly successful (WMO, 2007). Although efforts are continuing to ensure a full understanding of residual emissions, it is clear that these are extremely small compared to the large amounts annually released prior to the protocol.

The chlorofluorocarbons that effectively deplete the ozone layer are also potent greenhouse gases and thereby contribute to global climate change. Emissions of greenhouse gases are considered under another global protocol, the Kyoto Protocol, but ozone-depleting substances are not included in its provisions because they are covered separately under the Montreal Protocol. Recent studies have drawn attention to the fact that the emissions of chlorofluorocarbons have made surprisingly important contributions to warming of the Earth's climate (see Intergovernmental Panel on Climate Change, 2005; Velders et al., 2007). By the late 1980s, just before the Montreal Protocol was signed, the emission of chlorofluorocarbons was equivalent to about 7.5 gigatonnes (Gt) of CO_2, and the emission of CO_2 itself from fossil fuel burning was about 22 Gt in that year, as shown in Figure 4. If there had not been a Montreal Protocol, continued growth in chlorofluorocarbons at the rates prevailing in the late 1980s would have led to a warming contribution of more than 10 Gt of CO_2 equivalent emission by 2009 (Figure 4); offsets due to cooling from ozone depletion and increased emissions of substitute gases (such as hydrochlorofluorocarbons) are included in this best estimate and amount to a few gigatonnes of CO_2 equivalent. But because of the Montreal Protocol, emissions of chlorofluorocarbon in 2009 were near zero, implying that the Montreal Protocol has already averted the emission of about 10 Gt per year of CO_2 equivalent (see Figure 4 and Velders et al., 2007). In contrast, the Kyoto Protocol calls for a global reduction of emissions of CO_2 and other greenhouse gases of about 2 Gt per year. Thus, the Montreal Protocol and the underlying science of Antarctic ozone depletion have not only protected the ozone layer but also made a contribution to protection of the climate that is about five times larger than the current provisions of the Kyoto Protocol. In closing, we emphasize that the Antarctic ozone hole serves as a remarkable example of the many ways in which the research conducted because of the Antarctic Treaty System has had far-reaching effects on science, on the environment, and on the global formulation of policy.

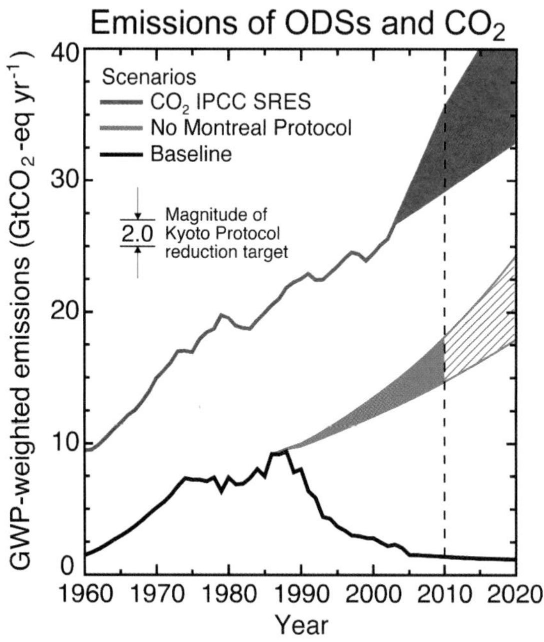

FIGURE 4. Global warming potential (GWP)–weighted emissions for the period 1960–2020. Calculated GWP-weighted emissions (100-year time horizon) are shown (see WMO, 2007). All emissions are normalized by their direct GWPs to equivalent Gt CO_2. The indirect contribution to the GWP due to ozone depletion, which is thought to be ≈20% (see text), is not included in these figures. The shaded blue region reflects a range of 2%–3% for assumed annual production increases in ozone-depleting substances in the absence of the Montreal Protocol after 1987. The CO_2 emissions for 1960–2003 are from global fossil fuel and cement production. Shown for reference is the magnitude of the reduction target of the first commitment period of the Kyoto Protocol, which is based on a 1990–2010 projection of global greenhouse gas emission increases and the average reduction target for participating countries. Adapted from Velders et al. (2007), kindly provided by the authors.

LITERATURE CITED

Andersen, S. O., and K. M. Sarma. 2002. *Protecting the Ozone Layer: The United Nations History*. London: Earthscan.

Anderson, J. G., W. H. Brune, and M. H. Proffitt. 1989. Ozone Destruction by Chlorine Radicals within the Antarctic Vortex: The Spatial and Temporal Evolution of ClO-O_3 Anticorrelation Based on In Situ ER-2 Data. *Journal of Geophysical Research*, 94:11,465–11,479.

Benedick, R. 1998. *Ozone Diplomacy*. Cambridge, Mass.: Harvard University Press.

de Zafra, R. L., M. Jaramillo, A. Parrish, P. Solomon, B. Connor, and J. Barnett. 1987. High Concentrations of Chlorine Monoxide at Low Altitudes in the Antarctic Spring Stratosphere: Diurnal Variation. *Nature*, 328:408–411.

Farman, J. C., B. G. Gardiner, and J. D. Shanklin. 1985. Large Losses of Total Ozone in Antarctica Reveal Seasonal ClO_x/NO_x Interaction. *Nature*, 315:207–210.

Gillett, N. P., and D. W. J. Thompson. 2003. Simulation of Recent Southern Hemisphere Climate Change. *Science*, 302:273–275.

Intergovernmental Panel on Climate Change. 2005. *IPCC/TEAP Special Report: Safeguarding the Ozone Layer and the Global Climate System: Issues related to Hydrofluorocarbons and Perfluorocarbons*. New York: Cambridge University Press.

Newman, P. A., L. D. Oman, A. R. Douglass, E. L. Fleming, S. M. Frith, M. M. Hurwitz, S. R. Kawa, C. H. Jackman, N. A. Krotkov, E. R. Nash, J. E. Nielsen, S. Pawson, R. S. Stolarski, and G. J. M. Velders. 2009. What Would Have Happened to the Ozone Layer If Chlorofluorocarbons (CFCs) Had Not Been Regulated? *Atmospheric Chemistry and Physics*, 9:2113–2128.

Ramaswamy, V., M. L. Chanin, J. Angell, J. Barnett, D. Gaffen, M. E. Gelman, P. Keckhut, Y. Koshelkov, K. Labitzke, J. J. R. Lin, A. O'Neill, J. Nash, W. Randel, R. Rood, K. Shine, M. Shiotani, and R. Swinbank. 2001. Stratospheric Temperature Trends: Observations and Model Simulations. *Reviews of Geophysics*, 39:71–122.

Solomon, S. 1999. Stratospheric Ozone Depletion: A Review of Concepts and History. *Reviews of Geophysics*, 37:275–316.

Solomon, S., R. R. Garcia, F. S. Rowland, and D. J. Wuebbles. 1986. On the Depletion of Antarctic Ozone. *Nature*, 321:755–758.

Solomon, S., G. H. Mount, R. W. Sanders, and A. L. Schemltekopf. 1987. Visible Spectroscopy at McMurdo Station, Antarctica: 2. Observation of OClO. *Journal of Geophysical Research*, 92:8329–8338.

Solomon, S., R. W. Portmann, and D. W. J. Thompson. 2007. Contrasts Between Arctic and Antarctic Ozone Depletion. *Proceedings of the National Academy of Sciences of the United States of America*, 104:445–449.

Velders, G. J. M., S. O. Andersen, J. S. Daniel, D. W. Fahey, and M. McFarland. 2007. The Importance of the Montreal Protocol in Protecting Climate. *Proceedings of the National Academy of Sciences of the United States of America*, 104:4814–4819.

Waters, J. W., L. Froidevaux, W. G. Read, G. L. Manney, L. S. Elson, D. A. Flower, R. F. Jarnot, and R. S. Harwood. 1993. Stratospheric ClO and Ozone from the Microwave Limb Sounder on the Upper Atmosphere Research Satellite. *Nature*, 362:597–602.

United Nations Environment Programme. 1999. *Synthesis of the Reports of the Scientific, Environmental Effects, and Technology and Economic Assessment Panels of the Montreal Protocol, A Decade of Assessments for Decision Makers Regarding the Protection of the Ozone Layer: 1988–1999*. Nairobi: United Nations Environment Programme.

World Meteorological Organization (WMO). 2007. *Scientific Assessment of Ozone Depletion: 2006*. Global Ozone, Research and Monitoring Project Report 50. Geneva, Switzerland: WMO.

Cosmology from Antarctica

Antony A. Stark

ABSTRACT. We are in a golden age of observational cosmology, where measurements of the universe have progressed from crude estimates to precise knowledge. Many of these observations are made from the Antarctic, where conditions are particularly favorable. When we use telescopes to look out at the distant universe, we are also looking back in time because the speed of light is finite. Looking out 13.7 billion years, the cosmic microwave background (CMB) comes from a time shortly after the big bang. The first attempt at CMB observations from the Antarctic plateau was an expedition to the South Pole in December 1986 by the Radio Physics Research group at Bell Laboratories. The measured sky noise and opacity were highly encouraging. In the austral summer of 1988–1989, three CMB groups participated in the "Cucumber" campaign, where a temporary summer-only site dedicated to CMB anisotropy measurements was set up 2 km from South Pole Station. Winter observations became possible with the establishment in 1990 of the Center for Astrophysical Research in Antarctica (CARA), a U.S. National Science Foundation Science and Technology Center, which developed year-round observing facilities in the "Dark Sector," a section of Amundsen-Scott South Pole Station dedicated to astronomical observations. Scientists at CARA fielded several astronomical instruments: Antarctic Submillimeter Telescope and Remote Observatory (AST/RO), South Pole Infrared Explorer (SPIREX), White Dish, Python, Viper, Arcminute Cosmology Bolometer Array Receiver (ACBAR), and Degree-Angular Scale Interferometer (DASI). By 2001, data from CARA, together with Balloon Observations of Millimetric Extragalactic Radiation and Geophysics (BOOMERANG), a CMB experiment on a long-duration balloon launched from McMurdo Station on the coast of Antarctica, showed clear evidence that the overall geometry of the universe is flat, as opposed to being open or closed. This indicates that the total energy content of the universe is near zero, so that the energy needed to originate the material of the universe is balanced by negative gravitational energy. In 2002, the DASI group reported the detection of polarization in the CMB. These observations strongly support a "concordance model" of cosmology, where the dynamics of a flat universe are dominated by forces exerted by the mysterious dark energy and dark matter. The CMB observations continue on the Antarctic plateau. The South Pole Telescope (SPT) is a 10-m-diameter offset telescope that is beginning to measure anisotropies on scales much smaller than 1°, as well as discovering new protogalaxies and clusters of galaxies. Plans are in progress to measure CMB polarization in detail, observations that will yield insights to phenomena in the first second of time.

Antony A. Stark, Smithsonian Astrophysical Observatory, 60 Garden Street, Cambridge, Massachusetts 02138, USA. Correspondence: aas@cfa.harvard.edu. *Portions of this paper are excerpted and updated from Wilson and Stark, "Cosmology from Antarctica," in Smithsonian at the Poles: Contributions to International Polar Year Science, ed. I. Krupnik, M. A. Lang, and S. E. Miller, pp. 359–368 (Smithsonian Institution Scholarly Press, 2009).*

INTRODUCTION

Observations of the deep universe have driven the development of Antarctic astronomy. The speed of light is finite, so as we look out in distance, we are also looking back in time. We see the Sun as it was 8 minutes ago, we see the Andromeda galaxy as it was 2.5 million years ago, and we see the most distant galaxies as they were billions of years ago. The farthest we can see is 13.7 billion light years distant, to a time that was only 350,000 years after the big bang, the "surface of last scattering." Before that time, the universe was opaque because photons could travel only a short distance before encountering a free electron. But at that time, the universe had just cooled enough that electrons could be captured into atoms. Space became transparent as a result of the disappearance of free electrons. Most of the photons released have travelled unimpeded to the present day; this is the cosmic microwave background (CMB) radiation (Penzias and Wilson, 1965). At present, the wavelength of the CMB radiation is a factor of 1,000 longer than it was when it was emitted, as a result of the universal expansion. Those wavelengths now lie in the millimeter-wave band, wavelengths that interact with water vapor in the Earth's atmosphere, subtracting signal and adding noise. In order to get the best possible view of the early universe, we need to go to into space or to sites like the Antarctic plateau that have very little water vapor.

This is an account of the history of Antarctic astronomy, the decades-long effort by many people within the Antarctic program to study the CMB from the South Pole. One result of these observations is the solution to one of the great metaphysical problems: the origin of matter. Other results include definitive confirmations of big bang cosmology and insights into the formation of the first galaxies. Still to come in the decades ahead may be insights to major unsolved problems in modern physics.

OBSERVATIONS OF THE COSMIC MICROWAVE BACKGROUND

Cosmology has become a precise observational science in past two decades. Cosmologists describe the universe by a model with roughly a dozen parameters, for example, the Hubble constant, H_0, and the density parameter, Ω. These constants describe and determine the mathematical model of the universe used in cosmology. A decade ago, typical errors on these parameters were 30% or greater; now, most are known within 10%. We can honestly discriminate for and against cosmological hypotheses on the basis of quantitative data. The current concordance model, Lambda–Cold Dark Matter (Ostriker and Steinhardt, 1995), is both highly detailed and consistent with observations. Many of those observations have come from the Antarctic.

The CMB radiation is highly isotropic, meaning that it is almost the same from all directions on the sky. From the first, it was understood that deviations from perfect isotropy would advance our understanding of cosmology (Peebles and Yu, 1970; Harrison, 1970): small deviations from smoothness in the early universe are the seeds from which subsequent structure grows, and these small irregularities in the surface of last scattering appear as small differences, or anisotropies, in the brightness of the CMB in different directions on the sky. Anisotropies in the CMB radiation indicate slight variations in density and temperature that eventually evolve into stars, galaxies, and clusters of galaxies. The physical size of the irregularities in the surface of last scattering can be calculated from the cosmological models, and these predictions can be compared to observations, as we shall see below.

Observations at progressively higher sensitivity by many groups of scientists from the 1970s through the 1990s failed to detect the anisotropy (cf. the review by Lasenby et al., 1999). In the course of these experiments, better observing techniques were developed, detector sensitivities were improved by orders of magnitude, and the effects of atmospheric noise became better understood. The techniques and detectors were so improved that the sensitivity of experiments came to be dominated by atmospheric noise at most observatory sites. Researchers moved their instruments to orbit, to balloons, and to high, dry observatory sites in the Andes and Antarctica. Eventually, CMB anisotropies were detected by the Cosmic Background Explorer satellite (COBE; Fixsen et al., 1996). Ground-based experiments at remote sites also met with success.

After the detection of CMB anisotropy, the next step was to measure its power spectrum. Individual spots on the sky that are slightly brighter or slightly dimmer in the CMB are not of significance in themselves. What matters are the statistics about the angular size and intensity of the anisotropies over large swaths of sky. The power spectrum, which is brightness as a function of spatial frequency, captures this information. The power spectrum was measured by a series of ground-based and balloon-borne experiments, many of them located in the Antarctic. The data were then vastly improved upon by the Wilkinson Microwave Anisotropy Probe (WMAP; Spergel et al.,

2003) and the South Pole Telescope. The Planck satellite mission (Tauber, 2005), launched in May 2009, will provide high signal-to-noise data on CMB anisotropy and polarization that will reduce the error on some cosmological parameters to the level of 1%.

DEVELOPMENT OF ASTRONOMY IN THE ANTARCTIC

The principal source of atmospheric noise in radio observations is water vapor. Because it is exceptionally cold, the climate at the South Pole implies exceptionally dry observing conditions. As air becomes colder, the amount of water vapor it can hold is dramatically reduced. At 0°C, the freezing point of water, air can hold 83 times more water vapor than saturated air at the South Pole's average annual temperature of –49°C (Goff and Gratch, 1946). Together with the relatively high altitude of the pole (2,850 m), this means the water vapor content of the atmosphere above the South Pole is two or three orders of magnitude smaller than it is at most places on the Earth's surface. This has long been known (Smythe and Jackson, 1977), but many years of hard work were needed to realize the potential in the form of new astronomical knowledge (cf. the review by Indermuehle et al., 2006).

A French experiment, Emission Millimetrique (EMILIE; Pajot et al., 1989), made the first astronomical observations of submillimeter waves from the South Pole during the austral summer of 1984–1985. It was a ground-based single-pixel bolometer dewar operating at $\lambda 900 \mu$m and fed by a 45 cm off-axis mirror and it had successfully measured the diffuse galactic emission while operating on Mauna Kea in Hawaii in 1982, but the accuracy of that result had been limited by sky noise (Pajot et al., 1986). Martin A. Pomerantz, a cosmic ray researcher at Bartol Research Institute, encouraged the EMILIE group to relocate their experiment to the South Pole (Lynch, 1998). There they found better observing conditions and were able to make improved measurements of galactic emission.

Pomerantz also enabled Mark Dragovan, then a researcher at Bell Laboratories, to attempt CMB anisotropy measurements from the pole. Dragovan et al. (1990) built a lightweight 1.2-m-diameter offset telescope and were able to get it working at the pole with a single-pixel helium-4 bolometer during several weeks in January 1987 (Figure 1). No CMB anisotropies were seen, but the atmospheric calibration results were sufficiently encouraging that several CMB groups (Dragovan et al., 1989; Gaier et al., 1989; Meinhold et al., 1989; Peterson, 1989) participated in the "Cucumber" campaign in the austral summer of 1988–1989. Three Jamesway tents and a generator were set up at a temporary site dedicated to CMB anisotropy 2 km from South Pole Station in the direction of the international date line. These were summer-only campaigns, where instruments were shipped in, assembled, tested, used, disassembled, and shipped out in a single three-month-long summer season. Considerable time and effort were expended in establishing and then demolishing observatory facilities, with little return in observing time. What little observing time was available occurred during the warmest and wettest days of midsummer.

Permanent, year-round facilities were needed. The Antarctic Submillimeter Telescope and Remote Observatory (AST/RO; Stark et al., 1997, 2001) was a 1.7-m-diameter offset Gregorian telescope mounted on a dedicated, permanent observatory building. It was the first radio telescope to operate year-round at South Pole. The AST/RO was started in 1989 as an independent project, but in 1991 it became part of a newly founded National Science Foundation Science and Technology Center, the Center for Astrophysical Research in Antarctica (CARA, http://astro.uchicago.edu/cara; cf. Novak and Landsberg, 1998). The CARA fielded several telescopes: White Dish (Tucker et al., 1993), Python (Dragovan et al., 1994; Alvarez, 1995; Ruhl et al., 1995; Platt et al., 1997; Coble et al., 1999), Viper (Peterson et al., 2000), the Degree-Angular Scale Interferometer (DASI; Leitch et al., 2002a), and the South Pole Infrared Explorer (SPIREX; Nguyen et al., 1996), a 60 cm telescope operating primarily in the near-infrared K band. These facilities were housed in the "Dark Sector," a grouping of buildings that includes the AST/RO building, the Martin A. Pomerantz Observatory building (MAPO) and a new "Dark Sector Laboratory" (DSL), all located 1 km away from the main base across the aircraft runway in a radio quiet zone at a longitude of approximately 90°W.

The combination of White Dish, Python, and UCSB South Pole 1994 (Ganga et al., 1997) data gave the first indication, by 1997, that the spectrum of spatial anisotropy in the CMB was consistent with a flat cosmology. Figure 2 shows the state of CMB anisotropy measurements in May 1999. The early South Pole experiments, shown in green, clearly delineate a peak in CMB anisotropy at a scale $\ell = 200$, or 1°, consistent with a flat universe ($\Omega_0 = 1$). Shortly thereafter, the Balloon Observation of Millimetric Extragalactic Radiation and Geophysics (BOOMERANG)-98 long-duration balloon experiment (de Bernardis et al., 2000; Masi et al., 2006, 2007; Piacentini et al., 2007) and the first year of DASI (Leitch et

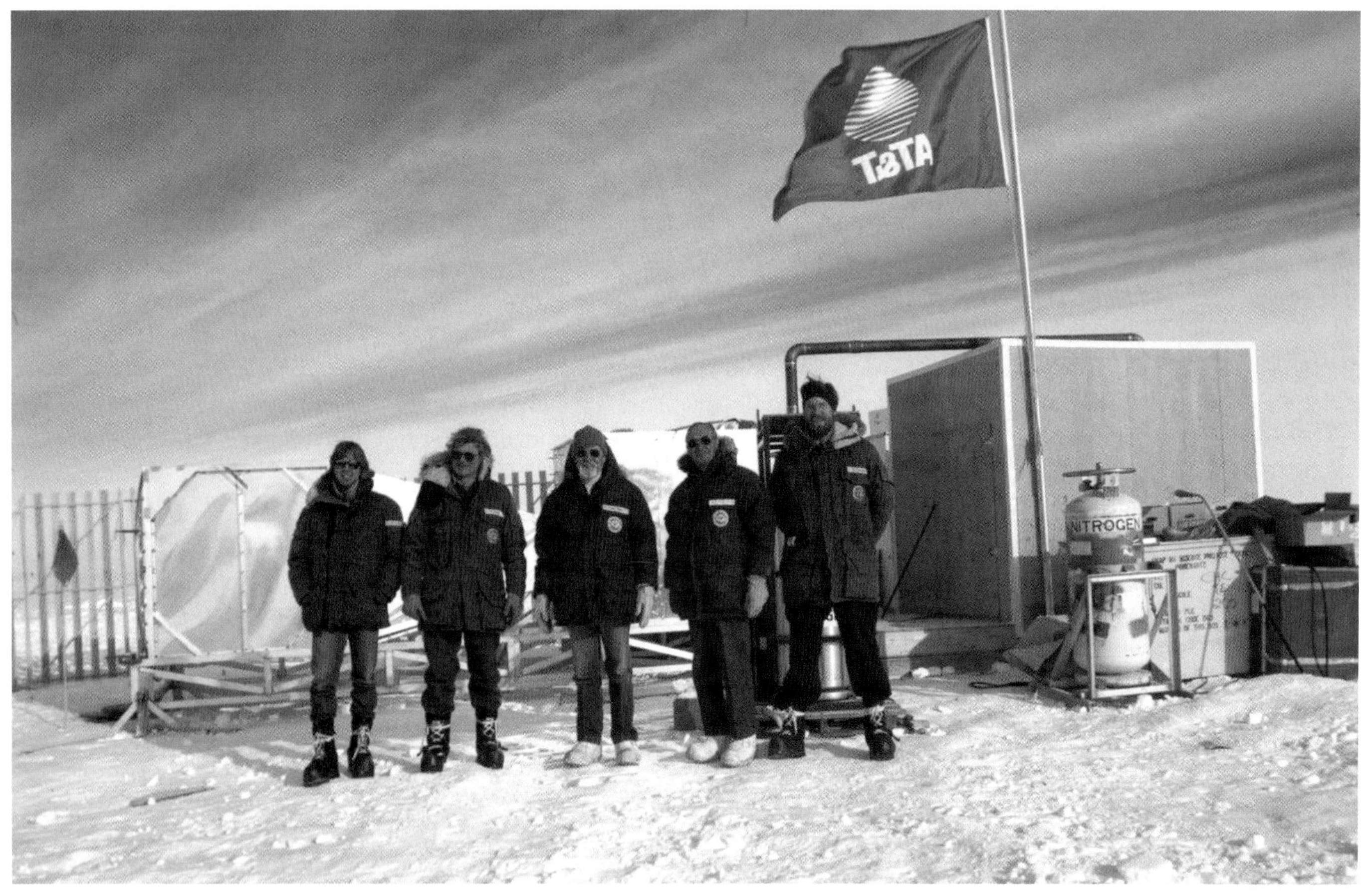

FIGURE 1. Mark Dragovan, Robert Pernic, Martin Pomerantz, Robert Pfeiffer, and Tony Stark, with the AT&T Bell Laboratories 1.2 m horn antenna at the South Pole in January 1987. This was the first attempt at a CMB measurement from the South Pole.

al., 2002b) provided significantly higher signal-to-noise data, yielding $\Omega_0 = 1$ with errors less than 5%. This was a stunning achievement, definitive observations of a flat universe balanced between open and closed Friedmann solutions. In its second year, a modified DASI made the first measurement of polarization in the CMB (Leitch et al., 2002c; Kovac et al., 2002). The observed relationship between polarization and anisotropy amplitude provided a detailed confirmation of the acoustic oscillation model of CMB anisotropy (Hu and White, 1997) and strong support for the standard model. The demonstration that the geometry of the universe is flat is a major scientific result from the Antarctic.

SITE TESTING

One of the primary tasks for the CARA collaboration was the characterization of the South Pole as an observatory site (Lane, 1998). It proved unique among observatory sites for unusually low wind speeds, the complete absence of rain, and the consistent clarity of the submillimeter sky. Schwerdtfeger (1984) and Warren (1996) have comprehensively reviewed the climate of the Antarctic plateau and the records of the South Pole meteorology office. Chamberlin (2001) analyzed weather data to determine the precipitable water vapor (PWV), a measure of total water vapor content in a vertical column through the atmosphere. He found median wintertime PWV values of 0.3 mm over a 37-year period, with little annual variation. The PWV values at the South Pole are small, stable, and well understood.

Submillimeter-wave atmospheric opacity at South Pole has been measured using skydip techniques. Chamberlin et al. (1997) made over 1,100 skydip observations at 492 GHz ($\lambda 609 \mu$m) with AST/RO during the 1995 observing season. Even though this frequency is near a strong oxygen line, the opacity was below 0.70 half of the time

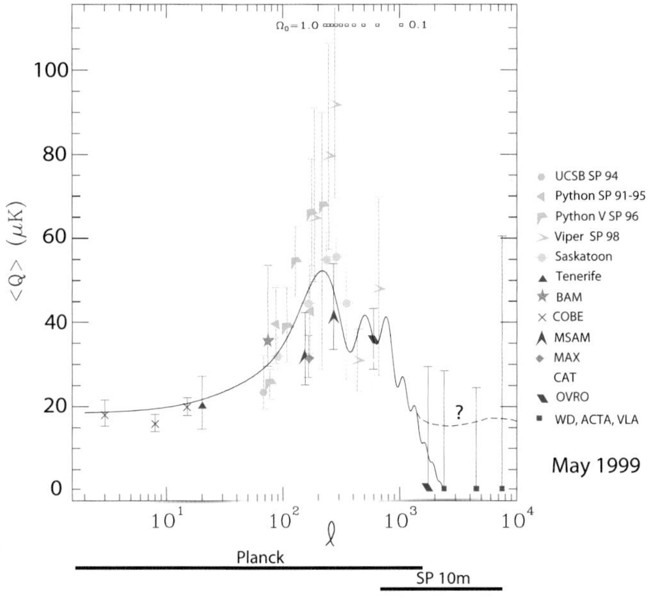

FIGURE 2. Microwave background anisotropy measurements as of May 1999. This was prior to the launch of BOOMERANG, the deployment of DASI, and the launch of WMAP, all of which significantly improved the data. South Pole experimental results are shown in green. Note that the peak at $\ell = 200$ is clearly defined, indicating a flat universe ($\Omega_0 = 1$). Abbreviations are as follows: UCSB SP 94 = a campaign at the South Pole in 1994 by the University of California, Santa Barbara, sponsored by NSF; BAM = Balloon-borne Anisotropy Measurement; COBE = Cosmic Background Explorer; MSAM = Medium-Scale Anisotropy Measurement experiment; MAX = Millimeter Anisotropy Experiment; CAT = Cosmic Anisotropy Telescope; OVRO = Owens Valley Radio Observatory; WD = White Dish; ACTA = Australia Telescope Compact Array; VLA = Very Large Array.

during the austral winter and reached values as low as 0.34, better than ever measured at any other ground-based site. From early 1998, the $\lambda 350 \mu m$ band has been continuously monitored at Mauna Kea, Chajnantor, and the South Pole by identical tipper instruments developed by S. Radford of the National Radio Astronomy Observatory and J. Peterson of Carnegie-Mellon University and CARA. The 350 μm opacity at the South Pole is consistently better than at Mauna Kea or Chajnantor.

Sky noise is caused by fluctuations in total power or phase of a detector caused by variations in atmospheric emissivity and path length on timescales of order 1 s. Sky noise causes systematic errors in the measurement of astronomical sources. This is especially important at the millimeter wavelengths for observations of the CMB: at millimeter wavelengths, the opacity of the atmosphere is at most a few percent, and the contribution to the receiver noise is at most a few tens of degrees, but sky noise may still set limits on observational sensitivity. Lay and Halverson (2000) show analytically how sky noise causes observational techniques to fail: fluctuations in a component of the data due to sky noise integrate down more slowly than $t^{-1/2}$ and will come to dominate the error during long observations. Sky noise at the South Pole is considerably smaller than at other sites, even comparing conditions of the same opacity. The PWV at the South Pole is often so low that the opacity is dominated by the dry air component (Chamberlin and Bally, 1995; Chamberlin, 2001); the dry air emissivity and phase error do not vary as strongly or rapidly as the emissivity and phase error due to water vapor. Lay and Halverson (2000) compared the Python experiment at the South Pole (Dragovan et al., 1994; Alvarez, 1995; Ruhl et al., 1995; Platt et al., 1997; Coble et al., 1999) with the Site Testing Interferometer at Chajnantor (Holdaway et al., 1995; Radford et al., 1996) and found that the amplitude of the sky noise at the South Pole is 10 to 50 times less than that at Chajnantor (Bussmann et al., 2004).

The best observing conditions occur only at high elevation angles, and at the South Pole this means that only the southernmost third of the celestial sphere is accessible with the South Pole's uniquely low sky noise, but this portion of sky includes millions of galaxies and cosmological sources, the Magellanic Clouds, and most of the fourth quadrant of the galaxy. The strength of the South Pole as a millimeter and submillimeter site lies in the low sky noise levels routinely obtainable for sources around the south celestial pole.

LOGISTICS

South Pole Station provides logistical support for astronomical experiments: room and board for on-site scientific staff, electrical power, network and telephone connections, heavy equipment support, and cargo and personnel transport. The station power plant provides about 200 kW of power to astronomical projects out of a total generating capacity of about 1200 kW. Heavy equipment at South Pole Station includes cranes, forklifts, and bulldozers; these can be requisitioned for scientific use as needed. The station is supplied by over 200 flights each year of LC-130 ski-equipped cargo aircraft. Annual cargo capacity is about 3,500 tons. Aircraft flights are scheduled only during the period from late October to early February, so the station is inaccessible nine months of the year. All engineering operations for equipment installation and maintenance are tied to the annual cycle of physical access to the instruments. For quick repairs and upgrades during the austral summer season, it is possible to send equipment between the South Pole and anywhere serviced by commercial express delivery in about five days. During the winter, however, no transport is possible, and projects must be designed and managed accordingly.

In summer, there are about 20 astronomers at the pole at any given time. Each person stays at the pole for a few weeks or months in order to carry out their planned tasks as well as circumstances allow; then they depart, to be replaced by another astronomer. Each year there are four or five winter-over astronomers who remain at the South Pole for a year.

Experiments at the pole use about 20 L of liquid helium per day. Helium also escapes from the station in one or two weather balloons launched each day. The National Science Foundation and its support contractors must supply helium to the South Pole, and the most efficient way to transport and supply helium is in liquid form. Before the winter-over period, one or more (4,000–12,000 L) storage dewars are brought to the South Pole for winter use. The supply of liquid helium has been a chronic problem for South Pole astronomy, but improved facilities in the new South Pole Station eliminate single points of failure and provide a more-certain supply.

Internet and telephone service to the South Pole is provided by a combination of two low-bandwidth satellites, LES-9 and GOES-3, and the high-bandwidth (3 Mbps) NASA Tracking and Data Relay Satellite System TDRS-F1. These satellites are geosynchronous but not geostationary since their orbits are inclined. Geostationary satellites are always below the horizon and cannot be used. Internet service is intermittent through each 24-hour period because each satellite is visible only during the southernmost part of its orbit; the combination of the three satellites provides an Internet connection for approximately 12 hours within the period 1 to16 hours Greenwich local sidereal time. The TDRS link helps provide a store-and-forward automatic transfer service for large computer files. The total data communications capability is about 100 gigabytes per day.

TELESCOPES AND INSTRUMENTS AT THE SOUTH POLE

The Antarctic Submillimeter Telescope and Remote Observatory (AST/RO) was the first radio telescope to be operated year-round on the Antarctic plateau. It was designed as a demonstration of feasibility and a prototype for the telescopes to follow. It was a general-purpose 1.7-m-diameter Gregorian (Stark et al., 1997, 2001) for astronomy and aeronomy studies at wavelengths between 200 and 2000 μm. The AST/RO was located in the Dark Sector in a dedicated building and was operational from 1995 through 2005. It was used primarily for spectroscopic studies of neutral atomic carbon and carbon monoxide in the interstellar medium of the Milky Way and the Magellanic Clouds. Six heterodyne receivers and a bolometer array were used on AST/RO: (1) a 230 GHz receiver (Kooi et al., 1992), (2) a 450–495 GHz quasi-optical receiver (Zmuidzinas and LeDuc, 1992; Engargiola et al., 1994), (3) a 450–495 GHz waveguide receiver (Walker et al., 1992; Kooi et al., 1995), which could be used simultaneously with (4) a 800–820 GHz fixed-tuned superconductor-insulator-superconductor (SIS) waveguide mixer receiver (Honingh et al., 1997), (5) the PoleSTAR array, which deployed four 810 GHz fixed-tuned SIS waveguide mixer receivers (Groppi et al., 2000; Walker et al., 2001), (6) Terahertz Receiver with NbN HEB Device (TREND), a 1.5 THz heterodyne receiver (Gerecht et al., 1999; Yngvesson et al., 2001), and (7) the South Pole Imaging Fabry-Perot Interferometer (SPIFI; Swain et al., 1998). There were four acousto-optical spectrometers (AOS; Schieder et al., 1989): two low-resolution spectrometers with a bandwidth of 1 GHz, an array AOS having four low-resolution spectrometer channels with a bandwidth of 1 GHz for the PoleSTAR array, and one high-resolution AOS with 60 MHz bandwidth. The AST/RO produced data for over a hundred scientific papers relating to star formation and the dynamics of cold interstellar gas in the Milky Way and the Magellanic Clouds. Among the more significant are a submillimeter-wave spectral line survey of the galactic center region (Martin et al., 2004) that showed the episodic nature of starburst and black hole activity in the center of our galaxy (Stark et al., 2004).

Viper was a 2.1 m off-axis telescope designed to allow measurements of low-contrast millimeter-wave sources. It was mounted on a tower at the opposite end of the MAPO from DASI. Viper was used with a variety of instruments: Dos Equis, a CMB polarization receiver operating at 7 mm; Submillimeter Polarimeter for Antarctic Remote Observing (SPARO), a bolometric array polarimeter operating at $\lambda 450$ μm; and the Arcminute Cosmology Bolometer Array Receiver (ACBAR), a multiwavelength bolometer array used to map the CMB. The ACBAR is a 16-element bolometer array operating at 300 mK. It was designed specifically for observations of CMB anisotropy and the Sunyaev-Zel'dovich effect (SZE). It was installed on the Viper telescope early in 2001, and was successfully operated until 2005. The ACBAR has made high-quality maps of SZE in several nearby clusters of galaxies and has made significant measurements of anisotropy on the scale of degrees to arcminutes (Runyan et al., 2003; Reichardt et al., 2009).

The SPARO was a nine-pixel polarimetric imager operating at $\lambda 450 \mu m$. It was operational on the Viper telescope during the early austral winter of 2000. Novak et al. (2000) mapped the polarization of a region of the sky (~0.25 square degrees) centered approximately on the galactic center. Their results imply that within the galactic center molecular gas complex, the toroidal component of the magnetic field is dominant. The data show that all of the existing observations of large-scale magnetic fields in the galactic center are basically consistent with the "magnetic outflow" model of Uchida et al. (1985). This magnetodynamic model was developed in order to explain the galactic center radio lobe, a limb-brightened radio structure that extends up to 1° above the plane and may represent a gas outflow from the galactic center.

The DASI (Leitch et al., 2002a) was a compact centimeter-wave interferometer designed to image the CMB primary anisotropy and measure its angular power spectrum and polarization at angular scales ranging from 2° to several arcminutes. As an interferometer, DASI measured CMB power by simultaneous differencing on several scales, measuring the CMB power spectrum directly. The DASI was installed on a tower adjacent to the MAPO during the 1999–2000 austral summer and had four successful winter seasons. In its first season, DASI made measurements of CMB anisotropy that confirmed with high accuracy the "concordance" cosmological model, which has a flat geometry and significant contributions to the total stress energy from dark matter and dark energy (Halverson et al., 2002; Pryke et al., 2002). In its second year, DASI made the first measurements of "E-mode" polarization of the CMB (Leitch et al., 2002c; Kovac et al., 2002).

Q and U Extra-Galactic Sub-mm Telescope (QUEST) at DASI (QUaD; Church et al. 2003) is a CMB polarization experiment that placed a highly symmetric antenna feeding a bolometer array on the former DASI mount at MAPO, becoming operational in 2005. It is capable of measuring amplitude and polarization of the CMB on angular scales as small as 0.07°. The QUaD has sufficient sensitivity to detect the conversion of E-mode CMB polarization to B-mode polarization caused by gravitational lensing in concentrations of dark matter.

BICEP2/SPUD (Keating et al., 2003; Yoon et al., 2006; Nguyen et al., 2008) is a millimeter-wave receiver designed to measure polarization and amplitude of the CMB over a 20° field of view with 1° resolution. It is mounted on the roof of the Dark Sector Laboratory and has been operational since early 2006. The design of BICEP2 is optimized to eliminate systematic background effects and thereby achieve sufficient polarization sensitivity to detect the component of CMB polarization caused by primordial gravitational waves. These measurements test the hypothesis of inflation during the first fraction of a second after the big bang.

The South Pole Telescope (SPT) is a 10-m-diameter off-axis telescope that was installed during the 2006–2007 season (Ruhl et al., 2004; Carlstrom et al., in press). It is equipped with a large field of view (Stark, 2000) that feeds a state-of-the-art 960-element bolometer array receiver. The initial science goal is a large SZE survey covering 4,000 square degrees at 1.3¢ resolution with 10 μK sensitivity at a wavelength of 2 mm. This survey will find all clusters of galaxies more massive than 3.5×10^{14} $M_\odot$ regardless of redshift. It is expected that an unbiased sample of approximately 3,000 clusters will be found, with over 700 at redshifts greater than 1. The sample will provide sufficient statistics to use the density of clusters to determine the equation of state of the dark energy component of the universe as a function of time. The SPT has made a first detection of galaxy clusters using the SZE (Staniszewski et al., 2009) and a first measurement of arcminute-scale CMB anisotropy (Lueker et al., 2010). The SPT has also discovered new class of galaxies that are unusually bright at millimeter wavelengths (Vieira et al., 2010).

THE ORIGIN OF MATTER IN A FLAT UNIVERSE

The discovery by Antarctic telescopes that the universe has a flat geometry was the final step in solving one of the great problems in metaphysics: the origin of matter. The Friedmann metric is the solution to the Einstein field equations that describes the big bang. The Einstein equations describe gravity as a non-Euclidean geometry, where space is a manifold with an intrinsic curvature, so that the sum of the angles of a triangle between three points in space-time do not necessarily add up to 180°. The force of gravity on a freely falling body is manifested in a trajectory that follows a geodesic curve in a curved space. In the Friedmann solution, all of space is uniformly filled with material, whose density changes as the universe expands and evolves. (The Friedmann metric is fundamentally different from the Schwarzschild metric that describes black holes: the Schwarzschild metric describes a static space that is a vacuum everywhere except at a single singular point where all the mass is concentrated.) Three different spatial geometries are possible in Friedmann models: closed, flat, and open.

The closed geometry is, at any given instant in time, a three-dimensional hypersphere. That means that if you instantly draw a straight line in any direction, it will circle around the hypersphere and come back at you from the opposite direction. The sum of the angles of a triangle are more than 180° (bigger triangles more than little ones), and the circumference of a circle is less than 2π times the radius (bigger circles to a greater extent than little ones). The volume of the hypersphere is finite at all times, and so the universe is finite at all times. A Friedmann model that is finite in space must also be finite in time: the hypersphere starts small, expands to a finite maximum extent, and then shrinks back to zero size after a finite lifetime.

The open geometry is, at any given instant, an infinite three-dimensional hyperboloid. That means that given a line and a plane in that space, there exists more than one other plane (in fact, an infinite number) that pass through that point but nowhere intersect the first plane. The sum of the angles of a triangle is less than 180°, and the circumference of a circle is more than 2π times the radius. The volume of the hyperboloid is infinite at all times, and so the universe is infinite at all times, except at the singular instant of the big bang. A Friedmann model that is infinite in space must also be future-eternal: the hyperboloid expands forever.

The flat geometry is, at any given instant, an infinite three-dimensional Euclidean space that follows Euclidean rules for geometric entities. With time, however, the entire space expands or contracts homogeneously, perhaps at a variable rate. It is an intermediate case between closed and open and can be thought of as a closed geometry with an extremely large radius of curvature or an open geometry with an extremely flat hyperboloid. The flat Friedmann model just barely expands forever, which means that it recollapses only after an infinite time has gone by.

The difference in the geometry of triangles in the three cases provides an observational test that is sensitive to the geometry. The physical size of the anisotropies on the surface of last scattering can be calculated. The angular size that they appear to us depends on the geometry since the angles of the 13.7 billion light-year-long triangle between us and the two sides of a feature are distorted by the geometry. Figure 3 shows actual BOOMERANG data, in comparison to computer simulations of the appearance of CMB anisotropies in the three cases. The geometry of our universe is very nearly flat.

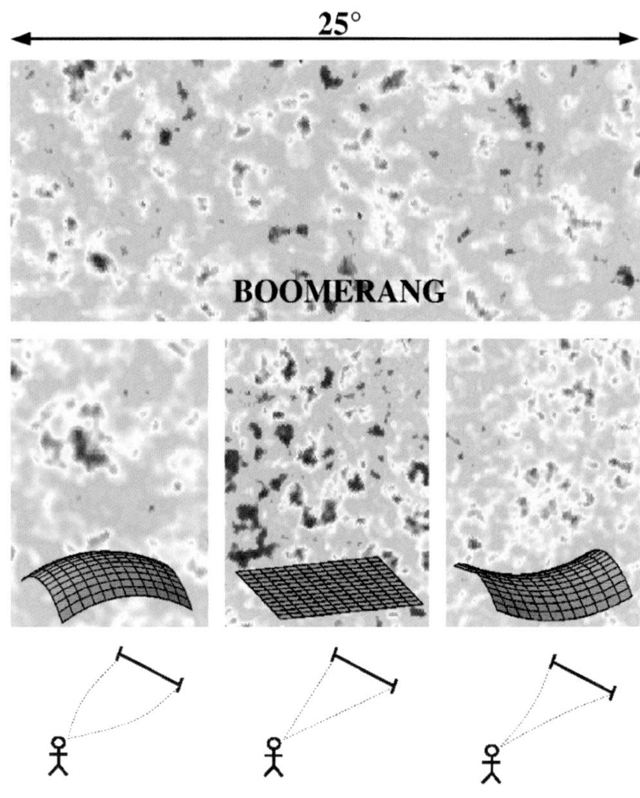

FIGURE 3. Data from the BOOMERANG experiment, showing a picture of CMB anisotropies in an actual map of the sky in the top panel. The middle three panels show computer simulations of the expected anisotropies in three cases: (left) a closed universe, (middle) a flat universe, and (right) an open universe. The drawings at the bottom illustrate how features on the surface of last scattering would appear to have different angular sizes, depending on the effect of geometry on the photon paths. The flat model clearly fits the data best.

This result is highly significant because the energy content of the universe is different in the different geometries. As Einstein showed, energy and matter can be converted, one into the other. All the material of the universe has positive energy. The gravitational field, however, has negative energy. Consider, for example, a weight attached to a rope that has been hauled up to the ceiling. The weight plus the Earth has a particular gravitational field strength. If we lower the weight to the floor, we find that the gravitational field has increased. But in the process of lowering the weight, we can extract energy, for example, by attaching the rope to run a pulley on an electrical generator. By increasing the gravitational field, we can extract energy: the gravitational field must therefore have negative energy. Landau and Lifshitz (1962) show that in the closed and flat cases, the gravitational energy of the universe as a whole exactly balances the positive energy of all the material, so that the total energy content of the universe is zero. This is not true in the open universe case, where the positive energy of the matter exceeds the negative energy of the gravitational field. At the start of our universe, no material and no energy were needed; matter is created by the separation of positive and negative energies.

CONCLUSIONS

Even in the era of CMB satellites, ground-based CMB observations are still essential for reasons of fundamental physics. The CMB radiation occurs only at wavelengths longer than 1 mm. The resolution of a telescope (in radians) is equal to the observed wavelength divided by the telescope diameter. To work properly, the overall accuracy of the telescope optics must be a small fraction of a wavelength. Observing the CMB at resolutions of a minute of arc or smaller therefore requires a telescope like the SPT that is 10 m in diameter or even larger, with an overall accuracy of 0.1 mm or better. There are no prospects for an orbital or airborne telescope of this size and accuracy in the foreseeable future. There is, however, important science to be done at high resolution, work that can only be done with a large ground-based telescope at the best possible ground-based sites.

Observations from the Antarctic have brought remarkable advances in cosmology. Antarctic observations have definitively demonstrated that the geometry of the universe is flat. These observations were made possible by excellent logistical support offered for the pursuit of science at the Antarctic bases. Cold climate and lack of water vapor provide atmospheric conditions that for some purposes is nearly as good as space, but at greatly reduced cost. Antarctica provides a platform for innovative, small instruments operated by small groups of scientists as well as telescopes that are too large to be lifted into orbit. In future, Antarctica will continue to be an important site for observational cosmology.

LITERATURE CITED

Alvarez, D. L. 1995. Measurements of the Anisotropy in the Microwave Background on Multiple Angular Scales with the Python Telescope. Ph.D. thesis, Princeton University, Princeton, N. J.

Bussmann, R. S., W. L. Holzapfel, and C. L. Kuo. 2004. Millimeter Wavelength Brightness Fluctuations of the Atmosphere above the South Pole. *Astrophysical Journal,* 622:1343–1355.

Carlstrom, J. E., P. A. R. Ade, K. A. Aird, B. A. Benson, L. E. Bleem, S. Busetti, C. L. Chang, E. Chauvin, H.-M. Cho, T. M. Crawford, A. T. Crites, M. A. Dobbs, N. W. Halverson, S. Heimsath, W. L. Holzapfel, J. D. Hrubes, M. Joy, R. Keisler, T. M. Lanting, A. T. Lee, E. M. Leitch, J. Leong, W. Lu, M. Lueker, J. J. McMahon, J. Mehl, S. S. Meyer, J. J. Mohr, T. E. Montroy, S. Padin, T. Plagge, C. Pryke, J. E. Ruhl, K. K. Schaffer, D. Schwan, E. Shirokoff, H. G. Spieler, Z. Staniszewski, A. A. Stark, K. Vieira, and J. D. Vanderlinde. In press. "The 10 meter South Pole Telescope." *Publications of the Astronomical Society of the Pacific.*

Chamberlin, R. A. 2001. "Comparisons of Saturated Water Vapor Column from Radiosonde, and mm and submm Radiometric Opacities at the South Pole." In *Astronomical Site Evaluation in the Visible and Radio Range,* ed. J. Vernin, Z. Benkhaldoun, and C. Muñoz-Tuñón, p. 172– 178. ASP Conference Proceedings, No. 266. San Francisco: Astronomical Society of the Pacific.

Chamberlin, R. A., and J. Bally. 1995. The Observed Relationship between the South Pole 225 GHz Atmospheric Opacity and the Water Vapor Column Density. *International Journal of Infrared and Millimeter Waves,* 16:907–920.

Chamberlin, R. A., A. P. Lane, and A. A. Stark. 1997. The 492 GHz Atmospheric Opacity at the Geographic South Pole. *Astrophysical Journal,* 476:428–433.

Church, S., P. Ade, J. Bock, M. Bowden, J. Carlstrom, K. Ganga, W. Gear, J. Hinderks, W. Hu, B. Keating, J. Kovac, A. Lange, E. Leitch, O. Mallie, S. Melhuish, A. Murphy, B. Rusholme, C. O'Sullivan, L. Piccirillo, C. Pryke, A. Taylor, and K. Thompson. 2003. QUEST on DASI: A South Pole CMB Polarization Experiment. *New Astronomy Review,* 47:1083–1089.

Coble, K., M. Dragovan, J. Kovac, N. W. Halverson, W. L. Holzapfel, L. Knox, S. Dodelson, K. Ganga, D. Alvarez, J. B. Peterson, G. Griffin, M. Newcomb, K. Miller, S. R. Platt, and G. Novak. 1999. Anisotropy in the Cosmic Microwave Background at Degree Angular Scales: Python V Results. *Astrophysical Journal Letters,* 519:L5–L8.

de Bernardis, P., P. A. R. Ade, J. J. Bock, J. R. Bond, J. Borrill, A. Boscaleri, K. Coble, B. P. Crill, G. De Gasperis, P. C. Farese, P. G. Ferreira, K. Ganga, M. Giacometti, E. Hivon, V. V. Hristov, A. Iacoangeli, A. H. Jaffe, A. E. Lange, L. Martinis, S. Masi, P. V. Mason, P. D. Mauskopf, A. Melchiorri, L. Miglio, T. Montroy, C. B. Netterfield, E. Pascale, F. Piacentini, D. Pogosyan, S. Prunet, S. Rao, G. Romeo, J. E. Ruhl, F. Scaramuzzi, D. Sforna, and N. Vittorio. 2000. A Flat Universe from High-Resolution Maps of the Cosmic Microwave Background Radiation. *Nature,* 404:955–959.

Dragovan, M., S. R. Platt, R. J. Pernic, and A. A. Stark. 1989. "South Pole Submillimeter Isotropy Measurements of the Cosmic Microwave Background." In *Astrophysics in Antarctica,* ed. D. J. Mullan, M. A. Pomerantz, and T. Stanev, p. 97. New York: AIP Press.

Dragovan, M., A. A. Stark, R. Pernic, and M. A. Pomerantz. 1990. Millimetric Sky Opacity Measurements from the South Pole. *Applied Optics,* 29:463.

Dragovan, M., J. Ruhl, G. Novak, S. R. Platt, B. Crone, R. Pernic, and J. Peterson. 1994. Anisotropy in the Microwave Sky at Intermediate Angular Scales. *Astrophysical Journal L.,* 427:L67.

Engargiola, G., J. Zmuidzinas, and K.-Y. Lo. 1994. 492 GHz Quasioptical SIS Receiver for Submillimeter Astronomy. *Review of Scientific Instruments,* 65:1833.

Fixsen, D. J., E. S. Chang, J. M. Gales, J. C. Mather, R. A. Shafer, and E. L. Wright. 1996. The Cosmic Microwave Background Spectrum from the Full COBE FIRAS Data Set. *Astrophysical Journal,* 473:576–587.

Gaier, T., J. Schuster, and P. Lubin. 1989. "Cosmic Background Anisotropy Studies at 10° Angular Scales with a HEMT Radiometer." In *Astrophysics in Antarctica*, ed. D. J. Mullan, M. A. Pomerantz, and T. Stanev, p. 84. New York: AIP Press.

Ganga, K., B. Ratra, J. O. Gundersen, and N. Sugiyama. 1997. UCSB South Pole 1994 Cosmic Microwave Background Anisotropy Measurement Constraints on Open and Flat-Lambda Cold Dark Matter Cosmogonies. *Astrophysical Journal*, 484:7–30.

Gerecht, E., C. F. Musante, Y. Zhuang, K. S. Yngvesson, T. Goyette, J. Dickinson, J. Waldman, P. A. Yagoubov, G. N. Gol'tsman, B. M. Voronov, and E. M. Gershenzon. 1999. NbN Hot Electron Bolometric Mixers—A New Technology for Low Noise THz Receivers. *IEEE Transactions on Microwave Theory and Techniques*, 47:2519–2527.

Goff, J. A., and S. Gratch. 1946. Low-Pressure Properties of Water from −160 to 212 F. *Transactions of the American Society of Heating and Ventilating Engineers*, 52:95–121.

Groppi, C., C. Walker, A. Hungerford, C. Kulesa, K. Jacobs, and J. Kooi. 2000. "PoleSTAR: An 810 GHz Array Receiver for AST/RO." In *Imaging Radio through Submillimeter Wavelengths*, ed. J. G. Mangum and S. J. E. Radford, p. 48. ASP Conference Series, No. 217. San Francisco: Astronomical Society of the Pacific.

Halverson, N. W., E. M. Leitch, C. Pryke, J. Kovac, J. E. Carlstrom, W. L. Holzapfel, M. Dragovan, J. K. Cartwright, B. S. Mason, S. Padin, T. J. Pearson, A. C. S. Readhead, and M. C. Shepherd. 2002. Degree Angular Scale Interferometer First Results: A Measurement of the Cosmic Microwave Background Angular Power Spectrum. *Astrophysical Journal*, 568:38–45.

Harrison, E. R. 1970. Fluctuations at the Threshold of Classical Cosmology. *Physical Review D*, 1:2726–2730.

Holdaway, M. A., S. J. E. Radford, F. N. Owen, and S. M. Foster. 1995. Fast Switching Phase Calibration: Effectiveness at Mauna Kea and Chajnantor. Millimeter Array Technical Memorandum 139. Charlottesville, Va.: National Radio Astronomy Observatory.

Honingh, C. E., S. Hass, K. Hottgenroth, J. Jacobs, and J. Stutzki. 1997. Low-Noise Broadband Fixed-Tuned SIS Waveguide Mixers at 660 and 800 GHz. *IEEE Transactions on Applied Superconductivity*, 7:2582–2586.

Hu, W., and M. White. 1997. A CMB Polarization Primer. *New Astronomy*, 2:323–334.

Indermuehle, B. T., M. G. Burton, and S. T. Maddison. 2006. A History of Astronomy in Antarctica. *Publications of the Astronomical Society of Australia*, 22:73–90.

Keating, B. G., P. A. R. Ade, J. J. Bock, E. Hivon, W. L. Holzapfel, and A. E. Lange, H. Nguyen, and K. W. Yoon. 2003. "BICEP: A Large Angular Scale CMB Polarimeter." In *Polarimetry in Astronomy*, ed. S. Fineschi. *Proceedings of SPIE*, 4843:284–295.

Kooi, J. W., M. S. Chan, B. Bumble, H. G. LeDuc, P. L. Schaffer, and T. G. Phillips. 1995. 230 and 492 GHz Low-Noise SIS Waveguide Receivers Employing Tuned Nb/ALO_x/Nb Tunnel Junctions. *International Journal of Infrared and Millimeter Waves*, 16:2049–2068.

Kooi, J. W., M. Chan, T. G. Phillips, B. Bumble, and H. G. LeDuc. 1992. A Low-Noise 230 GHz Heterodyne Receiver Employing a 0.25-μm^2 Area Nb/AlO_x/Nb Tunnel Junction. *IEEE Transactions on Microwaves Theory and Techniques*, 40:812–815.

Kovac, J. M., E. M. Leitch, C. Pryke, J. E. Carlstrom, N. W. Halverson, and W. L. Holzapfel. 2002. Detection of Polarization in the Cosmic Microwave Background Using DASI. *Nature*. 420:772–787.

Landau, L. D., and E. M. Lifshitz. 1962. *The Classical Theory of Fields*. Cambridge, Mass.: Addison-Wesley Press.

Lane, A. P. 1998. "Submillimeter Transmission at South Pole." In *Astrophysics from Antarctica*, ed. G. Novak and R. H. Landsberg, p. 289. ASP Conference Series, No. 141. San Francisco: Astronomical Society of the Pacific.

Lasenby, A. N., A. W. Jones, and Y. Dabrowski. 1999. "Observations of the Cosmic Microwave Background and Implications for Cosmology and Large-Scale Structure" *Royal Society of London Philosophical Transactions Series A*, 357:35–57.

Lay, O. P., and N. W. Halverson. 2000. The Impact of Atmospheric Fluctuations on Degree-Scale Imaging of the Cosmic Microwave Background. *Astrophysical Journal*, 543:787–798.

Leitch, E. M., C. Pryke, N. W. Halverson, J. Kovac, G. Davidson, S. LaRoque, E. Schartman, J. Yamasaki, J. E. Carlstrom, W. L. Holzapfel, M. Dragovan, J. K. Cartwright, B. S. Mason, S. Padin, T. J. Pearson, A. C. S. Readhead, and M. C. Shepherd. 2002a. Experiment Design and First Season Observations with the Degree Angular Scale Interferometer. *Astrophysical Journal*, 568:28–37.

Leitch, E. M., J. E. Carlstrom, N. W. Halverson, J. Kovac, C. Pryke, W. L. Holzapfel, and M. Dragovan. 2002b. "First Season Observations with the Degree Angular Scale Interferometer (DASI)." In *Experimental Cosmology at Millimetre Wavelengths*, ed. de M. Petris and M. Gervasi, pp. 65–71. AIP Conference Series, No. 616. Melville, N.Y.: American Institute of Physics.

Leitch, E. M., J. M. Kovac, C. Pryke, J. E. Carlstrom, N. W. Halverson, W. L. Holzapfel, M. Dragovan, B. Reddall, and E. S. Sandberg. 2002c. Measurement of Polarization with the Degree Angular Scale Interferometer. *Nature*, 420:763–771.

Lueker, M., C. L. Reichardt, K. K. Schaffer, O. Zahn, P. A. R. Ade, K. A. Aird, B. A. Benson, L. E. Bleem, J. E. Carlstrom, C. L. Chang, H.-M. Cho, T. M. Crawford, A. T. Crites, T. de Haan, M. A. Dobbs, E. M. George, N. R. Hall, N. W. Halverson, G. P. Holder, W. L. Holzapfel, J. D. Hrubes, M. Joy, R. Keisler, L. Knox, A. T. Lee, E. M. Leitch, J. J. McMahon, J. Mehl, S. S. Meyer, J. J. Mohr, T. E. Montroy, S. Padin, T. Plagge, C. Pryke, J. E. Ruhl, L. Shaw, E. Shirokoff, H. G. Spieler, B. Stalder, Z. Staniszewski, A. A. Stark, K. Vanderlinde, J. D. Vieira, and R. Williamson. 2010. Measurements of Secondary Cosmic Microwave Background Anisotropies with the South Pole Telescope. *Astrophysical Journal*, 719:1045–1066.

Lynch, J. T. 1998. "Astronomy & Astrophysics in the U. S. Antarctic Program." In *Astrophysics from Antarctica*, ed. G. Novak and R. H. Landsberg, p. 54. ASP Conference Series, No. 141. San Francisco: Astronomical Society of the Pacific.

Martin, C. L., W. M. Walsh, K. Xiao, A. P. Lane, C. K. Walker, and A. A. Stark. 2004. The AST/RO Survey of the Galactic Center Region. I. The Inner 3 Degrees. *Astrophysical Journal, Supplement Series*, 150:239–262.

Masi, S., P. A. R. Ade, J. J. Bock, J. R. Bond, J. Borrill, A. Boscaleri, P. Cabella, C. R. Contaldi, B. P. Crill, P. de Bernardis, G. de Gasperis, A. de Oliveira-Costa, G. de Troia, G. di Stefano, P. Ehlers, E. Hivon, V. Hristov, A. Iacoangeli, A. H. Jaffe, W. C. Jones, T. S. Kisner, A. E. Lange, C. J. MacTavish, C. Marini Bettolo, P. D. Mason, P. Mauskopf, T. E. Montroy, F. Nati, L. Nati, P. Natoli, C. B. Netterfield, E. Pascale, F. Piacentini, D. Pogosyan, G. Polenta, S. Prunet, S. Ricciardi, G. Romeo, J. E. Ruhl, P. Santini, M. Tegmark, E. Torbet, M. Veneziani, and N. Vittorio. 2006. Instrument, Method, Brightness, and Polarization Maps from the 2003 Flight of BOOMERanG. *Astronomy and Astrophysics*, 458:687–716.

Masi, S., P. A. R. Ade, J. J. Bock, J. R. Bond, J. Borrill, A. Boscaleri, P. Cabella, C. R. Contaldi, B. P. Crill, P. de Bernardis, G. de Gasperis,

A. de Oliveira-Costa, G. de Troia, G. di Stefano, P. Ehlers, E. Hivon, V. Hristov, A. Iacoangeli, A. H. Jaffe, W. C. Jones, T. S. Kisner, A. E. Lange, C. J. MacTavish, C. Marini Bettolo, P. Mason, P. D. Mauskopf, T. E. Montroy, F. Nati, L. Nati, P. Natoli, C. B. Netterfield, E. Pascale, F. Piacentini, D. Pogosyan, G. Polenta, S. Prunet, S. Ricciardi, G. Romeo, J. E. Ruhl, P. Santini, M. Tegmark, E. Torbet, M. Veneziani, and N. Vittorio. 2007. The Millimeter Sky as Seen with BOOMERanG. *New Astronomy Review*, 51:236–243.

Meinhold, P. R., P. M. Lubin, A. O. Chingcuanco, J. A. Schuster, and M. Seiffert. 1989. "South Pole Studies of the Anisotropy of the Cosmic Microwave Background at One Degree." In *Astrophysics in Antarctica*, ed. D. J. Mullan, M. A. Pomerantz, and T. Stanev, p. 88. New York: AIP Press.

Nguyen, H. T., J. Kovac, P. Ade, R. Aikin, S. Benton, J. Bock, J. Brevik, J. Carlstrom, D. Dowell, L. Duband, S. Golwala, M. Halpern, M. Hasslefield, K. Irwin, W. Jones, J. Kaufman, B. Keating, C.-L. Kuo, A. Lange, T. Matsumura, B. Netterfield, C. Pryke, J. Ruhl, C. Sheehy, and R. Sudiwala. 2008. BICEP2/SPUD: Searching for Inflation with Degree Scale Polarimetry from the South Pole. *Proceedings of SPIE,* 7020:36–45.

Nguyen, H. T., B. J. Rauscher, S. A. Severson, M. Hereld, D. A. Harper, R. F. Lowenstein, F. Morozek, and R. J. Pernic. 1996. The South Pole Near-Infrared Sky Brightness. *Publications of the Astronomical Society of the Pacific,* 108:718–720.

Novak, G., and R. H. Landsberg. 1998 Astrophysics from Antarctica. ASP Conference Series, No. 141. San Francisco: Astronomical Society of the Pacific.

Novak, G., J. L. Dotson, C. D. Dowell, R. H. Hildebrand, T. Renbarger, and D. A. Schleuning. 2000. Submillimeter Polarimetric Observations of the Galactic Center. *Astrophysical Journal,* 529:241–250.

Ostriker, J. P., and P. J. Steinhardt. 1995. The Observational Case for a Low Density Universe with a Non-Zero Cosmological Constant. *Nature*, 377:600–602.

Pajot, F., R. Gispert, J. M. Lamarre, R. Peyturaux, J.-L. Puget, G. Serra, N. Coron, G. Dambier, J. Leblanc, J. P. Moalic, J. C. Renault, and R. Vitry. 1986. Submillimetric Photometry of the Integrated Galactic Emission. *Astronomy and Astrophysics,* 154:55–60.

Pajot, F., R. Gispert, J. M. Lamarre, R. Peyturaux, M. A. Pomerantz, J.-L. Puget, G. Serra, C. Maurel, R. Pfeiffer, and J. C Renault. 1989. Observations of the Submillimetre Integrated Galactic Emission from the South Pole. *Astronomy and Astrophysics,* 223:107–111.

Peebles, P. J. E., and J. T. Yu. 1970. Primeval Adiabatic Perturbation in an Expanding Universe. *Astrophysical Journal,* 162:815–836.

Penzias, A. A., and R. W. Wilson. 1965. A Measurement of Excess Antenna Temperature at 4080 Mc/s. *Astrophysical Journal*, 142:419–421.

Peterson, J. 1989. "Millimeter and Sub-millimeter Photometry from Antarctica." In *Astrophysics in Antarctica*, ed. D. J. Mullan, M. A. Pomerantz, and T. Stanev, p. 116. New York: AIP Press.

Peterson, J. B., G. S. Griffin, M. G. Newcomb, D. L. Alvarez, C. M. Cantalupo, D. Morgan, K. W. Miller, K. Ganga, D. Pernic, and M. Thoma. 2000. First Results from Viper: Detection of Small-Scale Anisotropy at 40 GHz. *Astrophysical Journal Letters,* 532:L83–L86.

Piacentini, F., P. A. R. Ade, J. J. Bock, J. R. Bond, J. Borrill, A. Boscaleri, P. Cabella, C. R. Contaldi, B. P. Crill, P. de Bernardis, G. de Gasperis, A. de Oliveira-Costa, G. de Troia, G. di Stefano, E. Hivon, A. H. Jaffe, T. S. Kisner, W. C. Jones, A. E. Lange, C. Marini-Bettolo, S. Masi, P. D. Mauskopf, C. J. MacTavish, A. Melchiorri, T. E. Montroy, F. Nati, L. Nati, P. Natoli, C. B. Netterfield, E. Pascale, D. Pogosyan, G. Polenta, S. Prunet, S. Ricciardi, G. Romeo, J. E. Ruhl, P. Santini, M. Tegmark, M. Veneziani, and N. Vittorio. 2007. CMB Polarization with BOOMERanG 2003. *New Astronomy Review,* 51:244–249.

Platt, S. R., J. Kovac, M. Dragovan, J. B. Peterson, and J. E. Ruhl. 1997. Anisotropy in the Microwave Sky at 90 GHz: Results from Python III. *Astrophysical Journal Letters,* 475:L1–L4.

Pryke, C., N. W. Halverson, E. M. Leitch, J. Kovac, J. E. Carlstrom, W. L. Holzapfel, and M. Dragovan. 2002. Cosmological Parameter Extraction from the First Season of Observations with the Degree Angular Scale Interferometer. *Astrophysical Journal,* 568:46–51.

Radford, S. J. E., G. Reiland, and B. Shillue. 1996. Site Test Interferometer. *Publications of the Astronomical Society of the Pacific,* 108:441–445.

Reichardt, C. L., P. A. R. Ade, J. J. Bock, J. R. Bond, J. A. Brevik, C. R. Contaldi, M. D. Daub, J. T. Dempsey, J. H. Goldstein, W. L. Holzapfel, C. L. Kuo, A. E. Lange, M. Lueker, M. Newcomb, J. B. Peterson, J. Ruhl, M. C. Runyan, and Z. Staniszewski. 2009. High Resolution CMB Power Spectrum from the Complete ACBAR Data Set. *Astrophysical Journal,* 694:1200–1219

Ruhl, J. E., P. A. R. Ade, J. E. Carlstrom, H. M. Cho, T. Crawford, T. M. Dobbs, C. H. Greer, N. W. Halverson, W. L. Holzapfel, T. M. Lantin, A. T. Lee, J. Leong, E. M. Leitch, W. Lu, M. Lueker, J. Mehl, S. S. Meyer, J. J. Mohr, S. Padin, T. Plagge, C. Pryke, D. Schwan, M. K. Sharp, M. C. Runyan, H. Spieler, Z. Staniszewski, and A. A. Stark. 2004. The South Pole Telescope. *Proceedings of SPIE,* 5498:11–29.

Ruhl, J. E., M. Dragovan, S. R. Platt, J. Kovac, and G. Novak. 1995. Anisotropy in the Microwave Sky at 90 GHz: Results from Python II. *Astrophysical Journal*, 453:L1–L4.

Runyan, M. C., P. A. R. Ade, J. J. Bock, J. R. Bond, C. Cantalupo, C. R. Contaldi, M. D. Daub, J. H. Goldstein, P. L. Gomez, W. L. Holzapfel, C. L. Kuo, A. E. Lange, M. Lueker, M. Newcomb, J. B. Peterson, D. Pogosyan, A. K. Romer, J. Ruhl, E. Torbet, and D. Woolsey. 2003. First Results from the Arcminute cosmology Bolometer Array Receiver. *New Astronomy Reviews,* 47:915–923.

Schieder, R., V. Tolls, and G. Winnewisser. 1989. The Cologne Acousto Optical Spectrometers. *Experimental Astronomy,* 1:101.

Schwerdtfeger, W. 1984. *Weather and Climate of the Antarctic.* Amsterdam: Elsevier.

Smythe, W. D., and B. V. Jackson. 1977. Atmospheric Water Vapor at South Pole. *Applied Optics*, 16:2041–2042.

Spergel, D. N., L. Verde, V. Hiranya, E. Peiris, M. R. Komatsu, C. L. Nolta, M. Bennett, G. Halpern, N. Hinshaw, A. Jarosik, M. Kogut, S. S. Limon, L. Meyer, G. S. Page, J. L. Tucker, E. Weiland, E. Wollack, and E. L. Wright. 2003. First-Year Wilkinson Microwave Anisotropy Probe (WMAP) Observations: Determination of Cosmological Parameters. *Astrophysical Journal, Supplement Series,* 148:175–194.

Staniszewski, Z., P. A. R. Ade, K. A. Aird, B. A. Benson, L. E. Bleem, J. E. Carlstrom, C. L. Chang, H.-M. Cho, T. M. Crawford, A. T. Crites, T. de Haan, M. A. Dobbs, N. W. Halverson, G. P. Holder, W. L. Holzapfel, J. D. Hrubes, M. Joy, R. Keisler, T. M. Lanting, A. T. Lee, E. M. Leitch, A. Loehr, M. Lueker, J. J. McMahon, J. Mehl, S. S. Meyer, J. J. Mohr, T. E. Montroy, C.-C. Ngeow, S. Padin, T. Plagge, C. Pryke, C. L. Reichardt, J. E. Ruhl, K. K. Schaffer, L. Shaw, E. Shirokoff, H. G. Spieler, B. Stalder, A. A. Stark, K. Vanderlinde, J. D. Vieira, O. Zahn and A. Zenteno. 2009. Galaxy Clusters Discovered with a Sunyaev-Zel'dovich Effect Survey. *Astrophysical Journal,* 701:32–41.

Stark, A. A. 2000. "Design Considerations for Large Detector Arrays on Submillimeter-Wave Telescopes." In *Radio Telescopes*, ed. by H. R. Butcher, *Proceedings of SPIE*, 4015:434–445.

Stark, A. A., J. Bally, S. P. Balm, T. M. Bania, A. D. Bolatto, R. A. Chamberlin, G. Engargiola, M. Huang, J. G. Ingalls, K. Jacobs, J. M. Jackson, J. W. Kooi, A. P. Lane, K.-Y. Lo, R. D. Marks, C. L. Martin, D. Mumma, R. Ojha, R. Schieder, J. Staguhn, J. Stutzki, C. K. Walker, R. W. Wilson, G. A. Wright, X. Zhang, P. Zimmermann, and R. Zimmermann. 2001. The Antarctic Submillimeter Telescope and Remote Observatory (AST/RO). *Publications of the Astronomical Society of the Pacific*, 113:567–585.

Stark, A. A., R. A. Chamberlin, J. Cheng, J. Ingalls, and G. Wright. 1997. Optical and Mechanical Design of the Antarctic Submillimeter Telescope and Remote Observatory (AST/RO). *Review of Scientific Instruments*, 68:2200–2213.

Stark, A. A., C. L. Martin, W. M. Walsh, K. Xiao, A. P. Lane, and C. K. Walker. 2004. Gas Density, Stability, and Starbursts near the Inner Lindblad Resonance of the Milky Way. *Astrophysical Journal Letters*, 614:L41–L45.

Swain, M. R., C. M. Bradford, G. J. Stacey, A. D. Bolatto, J. M. Jackson, M. Savage, and J. A. Davidson. 1998. Design of the South Pole Imaging Fabry-Perot Interferometer (SPIFI). *Proceedings of SPIE*, 3354:480–492.

Tauber, J. A. 2005. "The Planck Mission." In *New Cosmological Data and the Values of the Fundamental Parameters*, ed. A. Lasenby and D. A. Wilkinson, p. 86. IAU Symposium and Colloquium Proceedings Series, No. 201. San Francisco: Astronomical Society of the Pacific.

Tucker, G. S., G. S. Griffin, H. T. Nguyen, and J. S. Peterson. 1993. A Search for Small-Scale Anisotropy in the Cosmic Microwave Background. *Astrophysical Journal Letters*, 419:L45–L48.

Uchida, Y., Y. Sofue, and K. Shibata. 1985. Origin of the Galactic Center Lobes. *Nature*, 317:699–701.

Vieira, J. D., T. M. Crawford, E. R. Switzer, P. A. R. Ade, K. A. Aird, M. L. N. Ashby, B. A. Benson, L. E. Bleem, M. Brodwin, J. E. Carlstrom, C. L. Chang, H.-M. Cho, A. T. Crites, T. de Haan, M. A. Dobbs, W. Everett, E. M. George, M. Gladders, N. R. Hall, N. W. Halverson, F. W. High, G. P. Holder, W. L. Holzapfel, J. D. Hrubes, M. Joy, R. Keisler, L. Knox, A. T. Lee, E. M. Leitch, M. Lueker, D. P. Marrone, V. McIntyre, J. J. McMahon, J. Mehl, S. S. Meyer, J. J. Mohr, T. E. Montroy, S. Padin, T. Plagge, C. Pryke, C. L. Reichardt, J. E. Ruhl, K. K. Schaffer, L. Shaw, E. Shirokoff, H. G. Spieler, B. Stalder, Z. Staniszewski, A. A. Stark, K. Vanderlinde, W. Walsh, R. Williamson, Y. Yang, O. Zahn and A. Zenteno. 2010. Extragalactic Millimeter-Wave Sources in South Pole Telescope Survey Data: Source Counts, Catalog, and Statistics for an 87 Square-Degree Field. *Astrophysical Journal*, 719:763–783.

Walker, C. K., J. W. Kooi, W. Chan, H. G. LeDuc, P. L. Schaffer, J. E. Carlstrom, and T. G. Phillips. 1992. A Low-Noise 492 GHz SIS Waveguide Receiver. *International Journal of Infrared and Millimeter Waves*, 13:785–787.

Walker, C., C. Groppi, A. Hungerford, K. Kulesa, C. Jacobs, U. Graf, R. Schieder, C. Martin, and J. Kooi. 2001. "PoleSTAR: A 4-channel 810 GHz Array Receiver for AST/RO." Paper presented at Twelfth International Symposium on Space THz Technology, NASA Jet Propulsion Laboratory, Pasadena, Calif.

Warren, S. G. 1996. "Antarctica." In *Encyclopedia of Weather and Climate*, ed. S. H. Schneider, p. 32. New York: Oxford Univ. Press.

Yngvesson, K. S., C. F. Musante, M. Ji, F. Rodriguez, Y. Zhuang, E. Gerecht, M. Coulombe, J. Dickinson, T. Goyette, J. Waldman, C. K. Walker, A. A. Stark, and A. P. Lane. 2001. "Terahertz Receiver with NbN HEB Device (TREND)—A Low-Noise Receiver User Instrument for AST/RO at the South Pole." Paper presented at the Twelfth International Symposium on Space THz Technology, NASA Jet Propulsion Laboratory, Pasadena, Calif.

Yoon, K. W., P. A. R. Ade, D. Barkats, J. O. Battle, E. M. Bierman, J. J. Bock, J. A. Brevik, H. C. Chiang, A. Crites, C. D. Dowell, L. Duband, G. S. Griffin, E. F. Hivon, W. L. Holzapfel, V. V. Hristov, B. G. Keating, J. M. Kovac, C. L. Kuo, A. E. Lange, E. M. Leitch, P. V. Mason, H. T. Nguyen, N. Ponthieu, Y. D. Takahashi, T. Renbarger, L. C. Weintraub, and D. Woolsey. 2006. "The Robinson Gravitational Wave Background Telescope (BICEP): A Bolometric Large Angular Scale CMB Polarimeter." In *Millimeter and Submillimeter Detectors and Instrumentation for Astronomy III*, ed. J. Zmuidzinas, W. S. Holland, S. Withington, and W. D. Duncan. *Proceedings of SPIE*, 6275:62751K.

Zmuidzinas, J., and H. G. LeDuc. 1992. Quasi-Optical Slot Antenna SIS Mixers. *IEEE Transactions on Microwave Theory and Techniques*, 40:1797–1804.

Managing the Antarctic Environment: The Evolving Role of the Committee for Environmental Protection

Olav Orheim, Anthony Press, and Neil Gilbert

ABSTRACT. In this paper we discuss the evolution of Antarctic environmental management, seen from our perspective as the first three chairs of the Committee for Environmental Protection (CEP). This body was established under the Protocol on Environmental Protection to the Antarctic Treaty adopted by the Antarctic Treaty Consultative Parties (ATCPs) in 1991. The ATCPs have over time placed considerable emphasis on managing the Antarctic environment. The protocol followed years of developing environmental standards and practices and set out tough new rules on environmental protection. The concomitant establishment of the CEP demonstrated the high ambitions of the parties for protecting the Antarctic environment. Following the entry in to force of the protocol in 1998, the CEP needed to put in place procedures and practices to enable it to fulfil its mandate effectively and efficiently. In the 12 years that have passed since then, the context in which the CEP is undertaking its work has changed. The Antarctic environment has been subject to various pressures, including climate change, which has resulted in regional rises in temperature and loss of ice shelves; introduction of nonnative species; and rapidly increasing numbers of tourists. National program activities have also increased markedly. Air access to Antarctica has become more prevalent with many new ice runways giving access to parts of Antarctica that had previously been logistically difficult to access. The role that the CEP plays and its capacity to deal with such challenges now merits close attention. If the CEP is to continue to meet its mandate of providing timely and defensible advice to the Treaty Parties on environmental protection in the Antarctic Treaty area, it needs to address two key issues: managing a burgeoning workload and timely access to data and information.

CONSIDERATION OF ENVIRONMENTAL ISSUES PRIOR TO THE ENVIRONMENTAL PROTOCOL

The Washington discussions, culminating in the signing of the Antarctic Treaty in 1959, did not spend much time on environmental issues.[1] This lack of consideration was inevitable as the negotiators had their focus firmly on the difficult political issues of the time, there was little environmental awareness in the general public, and there were no environmental lobby groups as we see them today. The Antarctic environment is only obliquely referred to in the text of the Antarctic Treaty (but disposal of radioactive wastes is prohibited). The most important environmental reference is in Article IX, paragraph 1(f),

Olav Orheim, Research Council of Norway, P.O. Box 2700, St. Hanshaugen, N-0131 Oslo, Norway. Anthony Press, Antarctic Climate and Ecosystems Cooperative Research Centre, University of Tasmania, Private Bag 80, Hobart, Tasmania 7001, Australia. Neil Gilbert, Antarctica New Zealand, Private Bag 4745, Christchurch, New Zealand. Correspondence: oo@rcn.no

which states that the Antarctic Treaty Consultative Meetings (ATCM) can consider "preservation and conservation of living resources."[2]

Gradually the Treaty Parties' attention to the Antarctic environment would change. Landmark work was done in 1964 when, within just three years of the Antarctic Treaty entering in to force, the ATCM adopted the Agreed Measures for the Conservation of Antarctic Fauna and Flora (Agreed Measures).[3]

The Agreed Measures consisted of 14 articles that recognised the scientific importance and unique nature of the region's fauna and flora and noted the parties' desire to achieve protection, facilitate scientific study, and (notably) ensure rational use of Antarctic fauna and flora. The Agreed Measures established the need for permits to be issued for any killing, wounding, capturing, or molesting of any native mammals or birds (including for scientific purposes), as well as for the designation of "specially protected species."[4] They also provided for the establishment of "specially protected areas" for places of outstanding scientific interest, as well as controls on the importation of nonnative species in to Antarctica.[5]

The Agreed Measures provided the foundation for managing the Antarctic environment for almost 30 years. Under the provisions of the Agreed Measures numerous specially protected areas were established in Antarctica. It was not until 1991 that the Agreed Measures were superseded by the more comprehensive Protocol on Environmental Protection to the Antarctic Treaty.[6]

Once the Agreed Measures were in place, the delegates from the 12 original signatory nations seem to have felt that this part of the management of Antarctica now was adequately covered. Until the negotiations started in 1978 on the Convention on the Conservation of Antarctic Marine Living Resources (CCAMLR) there were no major new environmental initiatives from the ATCM.[7] Admittedly, the Convention for the Conservation of Antarctic Seals was signed in 1972, but at that time there was no sealing industry in the Antarctic (indeed, there has never been commercial sealing since the adoption of that convention).[8]

It was, however, a major new development when CCAMLR entered into force in 1980. This convention, which has at its core "the Conservation of Antarctic marine living resources . . . [where] the term 'conservation' includes rational use" was groundbreaking in that it took an ecosystem approach to managing fisheries.[9] This was far ahead of such conventions elsewhere in the world. It is a great credit to those involved in the negotiations that the convention was agreed: the commercial krill fishery was well established at the time by vessels from Eastern Europe.

At the same time that CCAMLR was established, interest was growing around how to regulate any future exploitation of Antarctic mineral resources. Mineral resources had been considered during the negotiation of the Antarctic Treaty but were not specifically addressed in 1959 for practical and political reasons. The subject of mining was on the agenda for the ATCM in 1972, and thereafter several expert meetings were held. The Scientific Committee for Antarctic Research (SCAR) established its Environmental Impact Assessment of Mineral Resource Exploration and Exploitation in Antarctica (EAMREA) group to provide advice to the ATCM on environmental, scientific, and technical issues related to mineral activities in Antarctica.[10] The EAMREA would evolve in 1981 to become the group of specialists on Antarctic Environmental Implications of Possible Mineral Exploration and Exploitation (AEIMEE).[11]

Right from the early stages of these discussions, environmental considerations were explicitly enunciated, and the ATCM in 1972 agreed to Recommendation VII-6, which paired "protection of the environment" with the "wise use of resources."[12] Even though there was general agreement that no commercial mining activity would take place in Antarctica in the foreseeable future, the Antarctic Treaty Consultative Parties formally agreed in 1981 to negotiate a convention to regulate mining activities. Indeed, the motivation for starting this difficult process was to solve a potential future problem before it materialised as a concrete political issue.

The Fourth Special Antarctic Treaty Consultative Meeting to discuss what would eventually become the Convention on the Regulation of Antarctic Mineral Resource Activities (CRAMRA) met for the first time in Wellington in 1982 and concluded its work in 1988, after 12 formal meetings. During the 1980s the number of Antarctic Treaty Consultative Parties grew significantly. It is arguable that the main driver for this growth was the perception from those not active in Antarctica that there were riches in the Antarctic that a few select nations (the original 12 Antarctic Treaty Parties) were preparing to distribute among themselves. In the United Nations "The Question of Antarctica" was placed on the agenda and remained a periodic agenda item in the UN until the mid-2000s. Other nations became active in the Antarctic, carrying out scientific research programs and achieving the status of Consultative Parties (Figure 1).

The discussions of mining in the Antarctic also provoked the interest of environmental nongovernmental organizations (NGOs), which began to place Antarctica higher on their agendas. An umbrella organization of many NGOs, the Antarctic and Southern Ocean Coalition

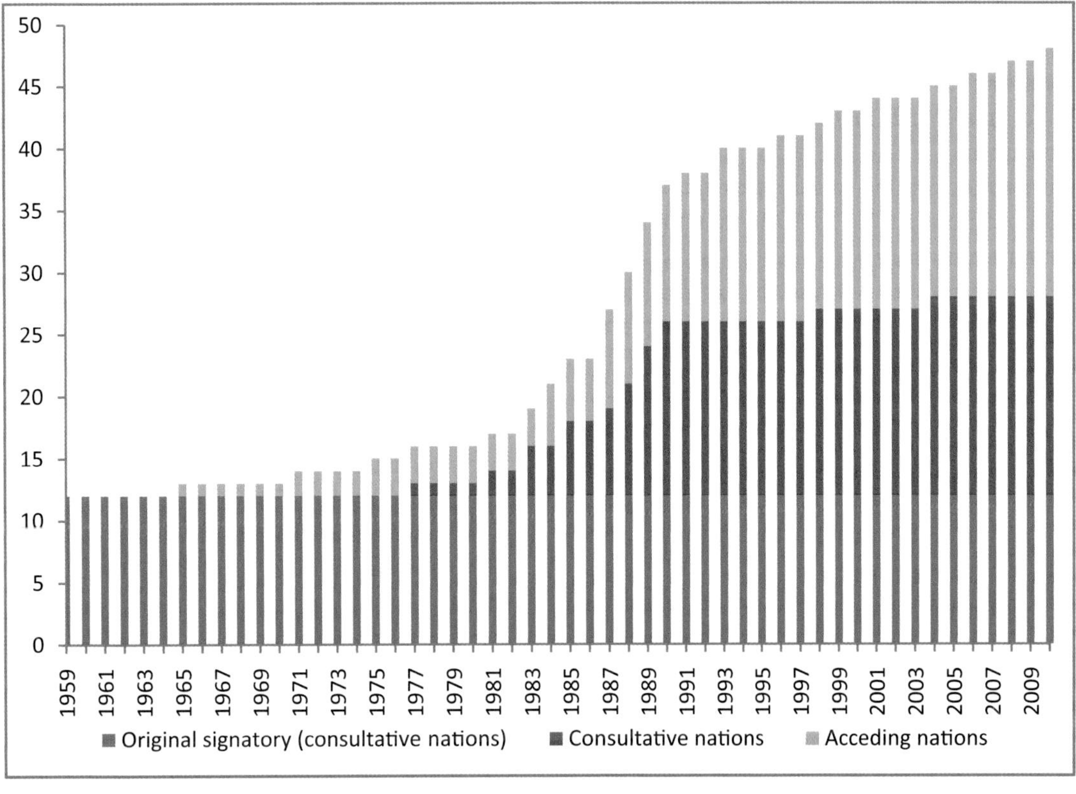

FIGURE 1. The number of Treaty Parties over time, divided into original signatory nations, consultative nations, and acceding (nonconsultative) nations. Note the growth in membership of the Antarctic Treaty during the 1980s.

(ASOC), was formed in 1978. As an observer to Antarctic Treaty Consultative Meetings, ASOC became increasingly active as the CRAMRA negotiations proceeded. The discussions provoked considerable passion, and on occasion, delegates to the ATCM had to pass lines of protesters on their way to meetings, a sight not seen before or after the CRAMRA negotiations.

The final negotiated text on CRAMRA was necessarily a compromise, and it raised difficulties for some Antarctic Treaty Parties.[13] One major challenge was how to balance the political interests of claimants and nonclaimants. Another, which became the most strongly voiced criticism in the end, was that the convention would open Antarctica up for mineral activities which, in turn, would harm the environment.

In 1989 Australia and France announced that they would not sign CRAMRA, an announcement that would herald the most critical period in the history of the Antarctic Treaty. In 1977 the Antarctic Treaty Consultative Parties had agreed to a voluntary moratorium on mineral activity, as long as progress was being made on an agreement to regulate such activities. The announcement by Australia and France had now disrupted this process, and the voluntary moratorium on mineral activities no longer applied. In theory, any party could now start such activities, a situation that would likely lead to conflict among the ATCPs. There was also a great deal of concern that the treaty itself could collapse.

There was much uncertainty about how nations would proceed in relation to Article XII, paragraph 2, of the Antarctic Treaty, which provided that 30 years after its entry into force (that is, in 1991), a party could ask for a meeting to review the operation of the treaty and thereby provide the opportunity for withdrawal from the treaty. How the parties would view the options provided by Article XII was not clear in 1989, and in the UN, there was much pressure on the Antarctic Treaty Parties from those countries not within the "Antarctic club."

ESTABLISHMENT OF THE PROTOCOL ON ENVIRONMENTAL PROTECTION TO THE ANTARCTIC TREATY AND THE COMMITTEE FOR ENVIRONMENTAL PROTECTION

With all of these issues in the background, the 15th ATCM in Paris in 1989 was a difficult meeting. Nonetheless, it started a process that led to the successful adoption in Madrid only two years later of the Protocol on Environmental Protection to the Antarctic Treaty (Madrid Protocol). The Antarctic Treaty Consultative Parties were conscious of the need to quickly find a way back to consensus, and it became clear that the only way to achieve this was by agreeing to legally binding rules for preserving the Antarctic environment and a ban on mineral activities.[14] It is probable that the political pressures that had developed sped up the process of negotiating the Madrid Protocol.

The protocol itself is quite simple in its form. It set down a number of environmental principles governing all activity in the Antarctic, and it established a new institutional body, the Committee for Environmental Protection (CEP). The protocol built on the 1964 Agreed Measures, and it picked up environmental management concepts that had been developed during the CRAMRA negotiations, such as the requirement for environmental impact assessments of proposed activities.

The protocol designates Antarctica as a natural reserve, devoted to peace and science, and sets forth legally binding environmental protection principles applicable to human activities in Antarctica, including obligations to accord priority to scientific research. The protocol prohibits all activities relating to Antarctic mineral resources, except for scientific research, and provides that this prohibition cannot be amended by less than unanimous agreement for at least 50 years following the entry into force of the protocol. The protocol requires parties to protect Antarctic fauna and flora and imposes strict limitation on disposal of waste in Antarctica and discharge of pollutants into Antarctic waters. It also requires application of environmental impact assessment procedures to activities undertaken in Antarctica, including nongovernmental activities, for which advance notice is required under the Antarctic Treaty. Parties are further required to provide for response to environmental emergencies, including the development of joint contingency plans.

Detailed mandatory rules for environmental protection pursuant to these requirements are incorporated in a system of annexes, forming an integral part of the protocol. Specific annexes on environmental impact assessment, conservation of Antarctic fauna and flora, waste disposal and waste management, and the prevention of marine pollution were adopted with the protocol. A fifth annex on area protection and management was adopted later in 1991 by the Antarctic Treaty Consultative Parties at the 16th Antarctic Treaty Consultative Meeting. Provision is also made for additional annexes to be incorporated following entry into force of the protocol. Accordingly the parties added in 2005 a sixth annex, "Liability for Environmental Damage."

Tensions within the Antarctic Treaty System eased in 1991 when the negotiations of the Madrid Protocol were concluded. In the ensuing years, however, there was an increasing sense of impatience among many parties with the drawn out process of ratification. In the three Antarctic Treaty Consultative Meetings from 1995 to 1997, prior to the entry into force of the protocol in 1998, a weeklong meeting was set aside for what was termed the Transitional Environmental Working Group (TEWG). These meetings were held so that the provisions of the protocol could be informally implemented prior to its entry into force and to prepare the way for the CEP to start its work efficiently. Thus, the development of draft rules of procedure at the 1997 TEWG meeting in Christchurch allowed the CEP to start its work effectively in 1998 without a focus on procedural issues.

When the protocol finally entered into force in 1998, the first meeting of CEP was then held in Tromsø. At this meeting the parties demonstrated considerable will to make progress on substantial environmental issues. Procedurally, a number of matters relating to the rules of procedure also had to be clarified, such as which invited experts and observers were able to attend CEP meetings, the establishment of CEP subsidiary bodies, and submission of documents to the CEP.[15] The committee had also to establish its own modes of work, and the ATCM and the CEP had to fine-tune their relationship. Both of these issues are discussed further below.

The arrival of CEP as a new body within the Antarctic Treaty System also meant clarifying its role in relation to other already established bodies, such as SCAR, the Scientific Committee for the Conservation of Antarctic Marine Living Resources (SC-CAMLR) established under CCAMLR, and the Council of Managers of National Antarctic Programs (COMNAP).

The SCAR was—and still is—the primary body for providing scientific advice to the ATCM. Over the years SCAR had also established a role of giving advice on environmental management issues through one of its groups of specialists, the Group of Specialists on Environmental

Affairs and Conservation (GOSEAC). Initially, there were some difficulties in the relationship between SCAR and the CEP, especially over the role of GOSEAC, but the rapid development of environmental management competence within the CEP saw SCAR gradually withdraw from its practice of providing environmental advice, and its role has become more focused on scientific advice.

The relationship between the CEP and COMNAP evolved more smoothly, aided by the considerable overlap between delegations to CEP meetings and staff employed by national Antarctic programs with environmental management responsibility. Over the past 12 years this has often seen the CEP and COMNAP develop common approaches to problem solving. The relationship between the CEP and SC-CAMLR is discussed below.

THE GROWTH OF WORK OF THE CEP

As the CEP matured over the first decade of the twenty-first century, its workload increased significantly (and continues to do so). It had become standard practice by then for the annual ATCM to be held over two weeks, with the CEP meeting in the first week, adopting its report on the last day, compiling, translating, and printing it over the weekend and reporting to the plenary of the ATCM at the beginning of the second week.

The number of working papers and information papers presented to the committee has grown significantly over the period of its operation, with just 12 working papers considered at its first meeting and some 48 at its most recent (Figure 2). The number of information papers

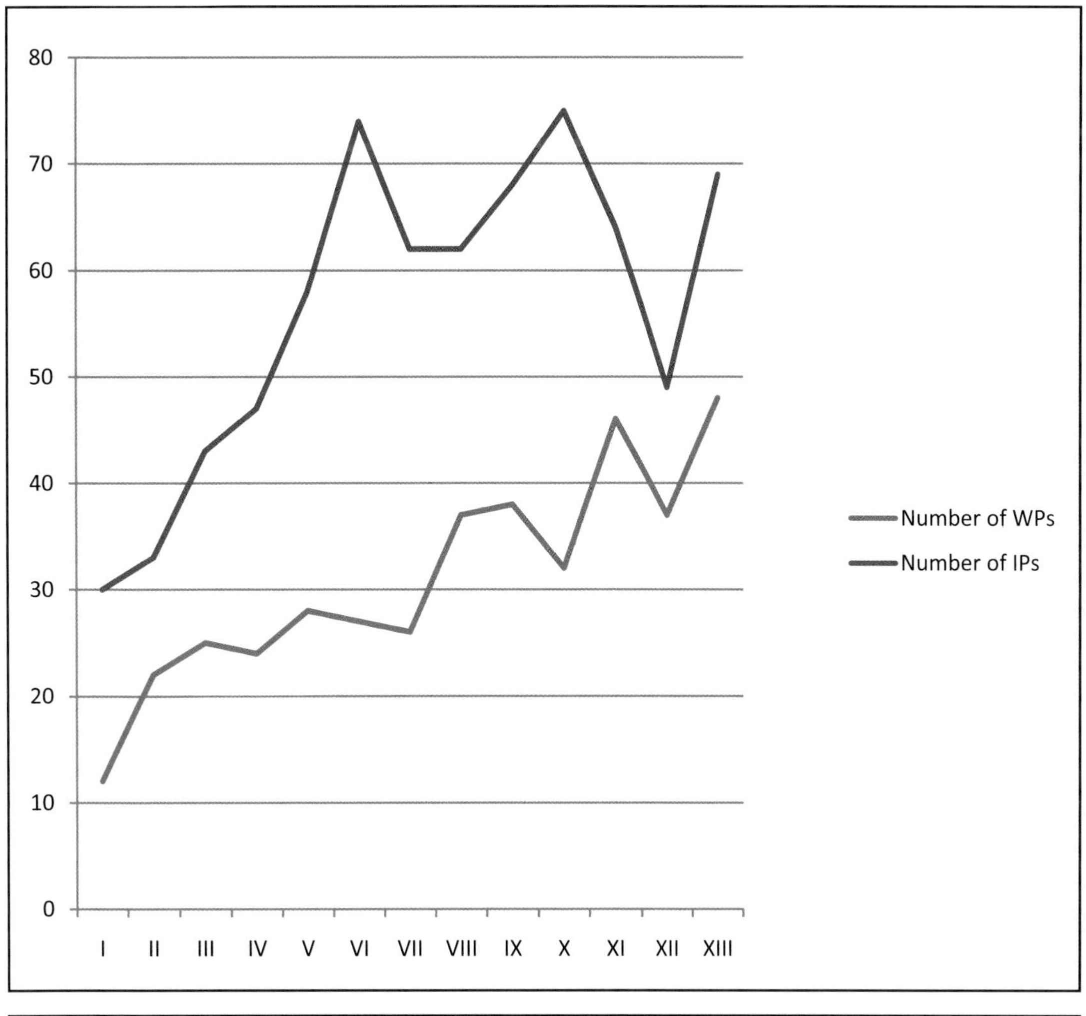

FIGURE 2. The number of working papers (WPs) and information papers (IPs) presented to each meeting of the CEP.

has always exceeded the number of working papers, but these too have grown in number. The committee's practice has been to consider all working papers because they contain matters of substance on the committee's agenda or required discussion on issues on which the committee was able to provide recommendations to the ATCM. Although the committee was not necessarily required to do more than "note" information papers, the practice of many members and committee observers remains to introduce and speak to most (if not quite all) of their submitted papers.

This growth in the number of papers has also affected the scale of the CEP report. The number of paragraphs in its report might be taken as a simple measure of the amount of work undertaken by the committee at its annual meetings (Figure 3). This in itself takes up time in that each of the paragraphs of the CEP's report has to be agreed by the committee before it closes its business each year. Adoption of the CEP's report now takes close to one full day of its weeklong meeting.

As a result, managing the business of CEP meetings has become increasingly complex and, to an extent, has limited the committee's ability to make progress on intractable issues or provide adequate time for discussion of high-priority issues (see below for discussion of the CEP's informal workshop in 2006 in Edinburgh, which, among other things, recommended streamlining the business of CEP meetings and prioritising matters for its future consideration).

Environmental Impact Assessments

A significant area of work for the committee emerged as parties began to fulfil their obligations under Article 8 and Annex 1 of the protocol, and the CEP established its practice for consideration of draft comprehensive environmental evaluations (CEEs; and other matters related to environmental impact assessment).

Article 8 of the protocol requires parties to ensure that "activities [to be undertaken in Antarctica] . . . shall be subject to the procedures set out in Annex I for prior assessment of the impacts of those activities on the Antarctic environment or on dependent or associated ecosystems according to whether those activities are identified as having: (a) less than a minor or transitory impact; (b) a minor or transitory impact; or (c) more than a minor or transitory

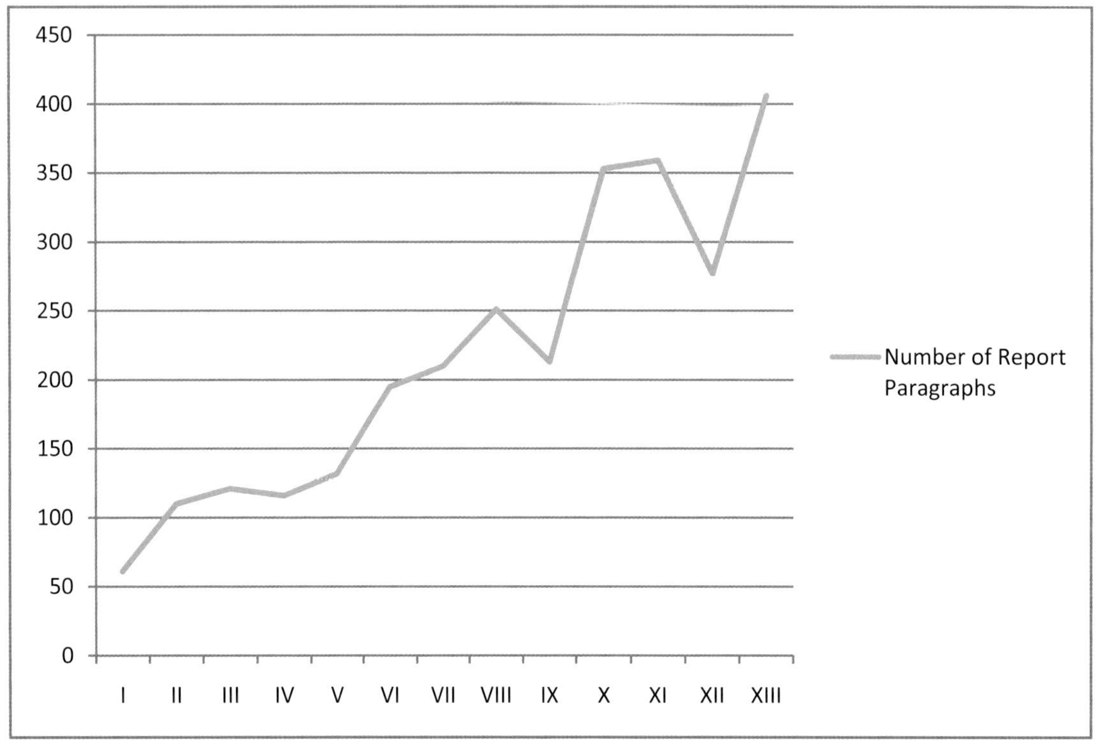

FIGURE 3. The total number of paragraphs in each of the CEP's annual reports.

impact." If an activity is determined to have "more than a minor or transitory impact," the party is required to prepare a draft CEE, which is to be circulated to all parties and at the same time forwarded to the CEP. Annex I provides that "no final decision shall be taken to proceed with the proposed activity in the Antarctic Treaty area unless there has been an opportunity for consideration of the draft Comprehensive Environmental Evaluation by the Antarctic Treaty Consultative Meeting on the advice of the Committee."

This provision is (like other elements of the protocol) open to interpretation. Having the "opportunity for consideration" does not *necessarily* mean that the committee must spend time at its meeting discussing a draft CEE that has been circulated.

At its first meeting in Tromsø in 1998, one of the significant issues discussed was the role of the CEP in considering CEEs and the interplay between the party providing the draft CEE, the CEP, and the ATCM. The report of the committee's first meeting records at paragraph 25 the following:

> The majority of delegations expressed the view that given the potential environmental significance of major activities the CEP should provide advice to the ATCM on all draft CEEs. The US was of the view that the CEP should take the opportunity to review draft CEEs only when a member of the Committee believed that there was a particular scientific, technical, or procedural matter requiring consideration. Chile was concerned with the need for the future practice of the CEP in this matter to conform strictly with the provisions of the Protocol and its Annex I. The Committee agreed that the Protocol gives the CEP the opportunity to consider and give advice on scientific, technical or procedural issues on draft CEEs. Furthermore, as laid down in Article 3(4) of Annex I, the Committee recognized that draft CEEs are to be forwarded to the CEP at the same time as they are circulated to the Parties, and at least 120 days before the next ATCM for consideration as appropriate.[16]

At the second meeting of the CEP in Lima in 1999 the committee agreed to formalise an agenda item: "Consideration of Draft CEEs forwarded to the CEP in accordance with Paragraph 4 of Article 3 of Annex I to the Protocol." From these early deliberations arose the standard practice of the CEP considering all draft CEEs provided by parties and then preparing formal advice to the ATCM on these draft CEEs. Thus, the CEP began its process of formal evaluation of the environmental impacts of activities in Antarctica subject to a CEE, and at its third meeting in The Hague in 2000, the CEP provided formal advice to the Special ATCM on a draft CEE from Germany for "recovering a deep ice core in Dronning Maud Land, Antarctica."[17]

We note in passing that there was no regular ATCM in The Hague in 2000, so this was a time when there were two years between regular ATCMs, a situation that existed in the past and could exist again in the future. Instead of the regular ATCM, a Special ATCM, the 12th, was arranged to follow the end of CEP meeting to consider the CEP report and the draft CEE. In this way a practice was instituted that overcame the problem of a year without a regular ATCM, which could have caused corresponding delays in planning Antarctic activities. Since 2000 there have been annual regular ATCMs, so this situation has not arisen again.

Consideration of the German CEE was followed by the more controversial proposal of the Russian Federation to penetrate Lake Vostok by drilling more than 3,500 m below the surface of the ice in East Antarctica. At the 2002 meeting in Warsaw the Russian Federation presented a working paper containing a draft CEE for their proposed drilling, but it had not been circulated in conformity with Annex 1 of the protocol. Although discussion on the proposal took place at CEP V, formal consideration was deferred until the following meeting in 2003 in Madrid, where the CEP considered not only the draft CEE of the Russian Federation but also a draft CEE from New Zealand for sedimentary rock drilling at Cape Roberts in the Ross Sea region and a draft CEE for a new station to be built by the Czech Republic (which had not yet ratified the protocol, and was therefore not legally bound to comply with its provisions).

The requirement of the protocol for the CEP to give advice on a draft CEE is one of the core functions of the committee. Consideration of draft CEEs took a considerable portion of the time allocated to the CEP's agenda, and concern continued to grow about the workload of the CEP. As the procedures of the CEP evolved, it instituted mechanisms that allowed for initial consideration of draft CEEs between meetings, through the formation of an Intersessional Contact Group, with formal consideration in the annual committee meeting.[18] By the time of the Baltimore meeting in 2009 (CEP XII), nine draft CEEs had been formally considered by the CEP.

Although consideration of CEEs provided the highest level of scrutiny by the CEP of proposed activities in Antarctica, parties began the practice of also submitting initial environmental evaluations to the committee as a means of providing information and guidance on environmental impact procedures and evaluation. Annex I of the protocol provides that "unless it has been determined that an activity will have less than a minor or transitory impact, or unless a Comprehensive Environmental Evaluation is being prepared . . . , an Initial Environmental Evaluation shall be prepared. It shall contain sufficient detail to assess whether a proposed activity may have more than a minor or transitory impact . . . If an Initial Environmental Evaluation indicates that a proposed activity is likely to have no more than a minor or transitory impact, the activity may proceed." At its first meeting in Tromsø in 1998, the CEP considered a number of papers providing guidance on preparing environmental impact assessments under the protocol. In its second meeting in 1999 the CEP recommended, and the ATCM adopted, "Guidelines for Environmental Impact Assessment in Antarctica," and these were revised by the CEP in 2005.[19]

Management Plans for Protected Areas

Another significant area of "statutory" work conducted by the CEP, which also grew significantly during the first decade of the twenty-first century, was the consideration of management plans under Annex V, "Area Protection and Management." Management plans are required for all Antarctic Specially Protected Areas (ASPAs; Article 3 of Annex V of the protocol) and Antarctic Specially Managed Areas (ASMAs; Article 4 of Annex V of the protocol), and all management plans are required to be reviewed every five years. By the end of 2009 there were 71 ASPAs and 7 ASMAs declared under the provisions of the protocol.

In 2000 the parties adopted "Guidelines for the Implementation of the Framework for Protected Areas Set Forth in Article 3, Annex V of the Environmental Protocol" to assist parties in developing management plans for the CEP's consideration.[20] With the growing maturity of the CEP and the parties' compliance with the provisions of the protocol, interest grew in designating ASMAs and developing management plans for them.

The first ASMAs to be formally designated by the ATCM (in 2004) were for the Dry Valleys in Southern Victoria Land and at Cape Denison, Commonwealth Bay (although the designation "ASMA 1" was reserved for the proposed ASMA at Admiralty Bay, which had been under development for almost a decade and which was eventually designated in 2006). With this increased interest in designating ASMAs and the need to refine the CEP's consideration of protected area management plans, the parties adopted in 2008 the "Guide to the Presentation of Working Papers Containing Proposals for Antarctic Specially Protected Areas, Antarctic Specially Managed Areas or Historic Sites and Monuments."[21]

The requirement to not only consider plans of management for new protected areas but also to review all management plans every five years resulted in a significant growth in work for the CEP. Ultimately, this led to the CEP developing its first formal subsidiary body tasked with the consideration of management plans developed under Annex V to the protocol (see discussion below).

A ROLLING REVIEW OF THE ANNEXES TO THE PROTOCOL

At the CEP's fourth meeting in Saint Petersburg in 2002, 11 years after the adoption of the protocol, the CEP decided to conduct a rolling review of the annexes to the protocol: "The CEP noted that its work, most recently the intersessional considerations of Specially Protected Species, had shown that improvements could be made to the Annexes of the protocol. The Committee therefore decided to conduct a rolling review of the Annexes, starting at CEP V with Annex II."[22] This was endorsed by the ATCM. Article 12 of the protocol outlines the functions of the committee, and Article 9 provides the framework for amendments to the annexes to the protocol. In good faith, the CEP set out to instigate a process whereby the annex would be reviewed by the committee and recommendations forwarded to the ATCM to amend the annex and improve the operation of the annexes in light of new information or experience in implementation or changes in best practice approaches to environmental management. It was initially thought that each review would take two years.[23]

The reality of amending the annexes is borne out by the fact that it was not until 2009 in Baltimore that the parties finally accepted the CEP's recommendations to amend Annex II to the protocol (Measure 16 [2009], "Amendment of Annex II to the Protocol on Environmental Protection to the Antarctic Treaty: Conservation of Antarctic Fauna and Flora").[24] What was accepted in Baltimore was a much-refined and reduced set of proposed amendments to the annex than had originally been presented by the CEP to the ATCM in 2004.

What had been envisaged as a practical look at how the CEP and the Antarctic Treaty Parties could meet their obligations under the protocol became a very highly politicised and complex negotiation over the scope not only of the annex but of the protocol itself. The most intense discussions and negotiations were over the name of the annex and definitions of flora and fauna for the purposes of the annex.

How marine species were to be dealt with, whether microbes should be covered and how, and what was covered by accidental or deliberate introduction (and many other matters), all became the subject of intense and long deliberation, first in the CEP (to 2004) and subsequently in the ATCM (to 2009). Some parties felt that reviewing the annexes amounted to a renegotiation of the protocol itself (despite its explicit facility for review), and others were concerned that amendments to the annexes required complicated domestic legal actions, which they felt were not warranted. Perhaps, in hindsight, it was unwise to begin the rolling review with Annex II, which intersects with other parts of the Antarctic Treaty System and with other international instruments.

Sanchez and McIvor considered that after the conclusion of deliberations on Annex II the most likely candidates for further review would be Annex I ("Environmental Impact Assessment") or Annex V ("Area Protection and Management"), for which a considerable amount of practice has developed among parties and within the CEP. [25] Although this suggestion remains apposite, at the time of writing this paper, the CEP had not discussed the issue of making any further amendments to the protocol's annexes. Although there are several elements of the annexes that might merit attention and improvement, the political appetite to begin amending another annex is unlikely to return for some time.

A GROWING MATURITY

After more than a decade of operation, the role of the CEP, and to an extent the importance of the role it plays, is worthy of some attention. As has been noted in this paper, the Antarctic Treaty Parties have, over time, placed considerable emphasis on managing the Antarctic environment. Negotiation of and agreement on the Environmental Protocol could be regarded as a zenith in this regard: the culmination of years of development of environmental standards and practices synthesised into a single agreement that set out tough new rules on environmental protection. The concomitant establishment of the CEP with its advisory role to the Treaty Parties on the effectiveness of implementation of the protocol was also a clear demonstration of the importance that the parties place on setting high standards of protection for the Antarctic environment.

As a new body, it was important for the CEP to establish itself and put in place procedures and practices that allowed it to fulfil its mandate effectively and efficiently. The means and the success by which the CEP has established itself have been covered earlier in this paper.

However, since the Environmental Protocol was agreed in 1991 and even since the CEP first met in 1998, the context in which the CEP has undertaken its work has changed. The Antarctic environment has experienced significant change and has been subject to additional pressures. Such pressures are becoming more evident and arguably more urgent in their need for attention.

Since 1991 shipborne tourists making landings in Antarctica have increased from 6,704 to 32,198.[26] The average annual mean temperature on the Antarctic Peninsula has increased by more than 2.5°C over the past 50 years.[27] There has been a significant loss of ice shelves,[28] and nonnative species have been identified in Antarctica.[29] National program activities have also increased, with eight new bases being established around the continent.[30] Air access to Antarctica has become more prevalent, with approximately 11 new ice runways (permanent and temporary) constructed.[31]

These environmental pressures are very real and likely only to become more intense over time. As a result, the role that the CEP plays and its capacity to deal with the challenges being faced by the Antarctic environment merit close attention. If the CEP is to continue to meet its mandate of providing timely and defensible advice to the ATCM, it must continue to address two key issues: the capacity of the committee to manage a burgeoning workload and its access to timely and defensible data and information.

PRIORITISING THE CEP'S WORKLOAD

Over the decade or so of the CEP's operation, it has evolved a number of means to facilitate its work. These include establishing ad hoc informal discussion groups among those parties wishing to be involved that communicate by e-mail between meetings (these are known as Intersessional Contact Groups), the holding of workshops (usually immediately ahead of annual CEP meetings to ensure maximum attendance), and the development of an online discussion forum. The Intersessional Contact Groups and online discussion forums have provided useful mechanisms to progress the work of the CEP. However, having no formal status, their recommendations and deliberations still require the committee's endorsement, a fact that sometime leads to prolonged and often repetitious discussion.

In June 2006, immediately prior to its ninth meeting in Edinburgh, the committee held an informal Workshop on Antarctica's Future Environmental Challenges.[32] Informal workshops such as these have provided useful and productive mechanisms for exchanging ideas and generating initiatives for the committee's further consideration.

A central issue of the Edinburgh workshop was the CEP's workload and the committee's ability to address high-priority and emerging environmental issues. A number of potential options for managing this issue were proposed, including means to prioritise the CEP's work and making better use of the CEP's informal subsidiary bodies.

Although it seemed clear to participants in the workshop that there was a need to manage the burgeoning workload of the CEP and provide focus on priority environmental issues, the adoption of a clear prioritised work plan has taken time to emerge. In its consideration of the outcome of the workshop, CEP IX agreed to develop a prioritised five-year work plan. Following intersessional consultation, a draft prioritised work plan was presented to CEP X, at which the committee agreed to implement it on a trial basis.

An important principle that emerged during the development of the CEP's work plan was that prioritising issues on the CEP's agenda needed to be based on the severity of actual or perceived threats to the Antarctic environment and its biota. Although this would appear to be an obvious approach to take, it did require a deliberate shift in the approach to the work being taken by the committee. Up to that point the committee had simply been adding new issues to its meeting agendas as they arose, an approach that resulted in the CEP attempting to address a growing raft of issues at every meeting, irrespective of the actual threat posed to the Antarctic environment.

The act of recognising that some issues demanded more immediate attention than others has had two results. First, the higher-priority issues have received greater and more focussed attention, including greater discussion time at the CEP's annual meetings. Second, issues considered to be of a lesser threat to the environment (for example, waste management, which national Antarctic programs largely have in hand) have been removed from the CEP's agenda (though they can be reinstated as required).

The CEP's prioritised five year work plan should provide two additional benefits. First, it allows the CEP's observers and invited experts to see in advance when the CEP is likely to tackle issues in which they have an interest and thus plan their own contributions to the CEP's work. The work plan should also allow the ATCM to anticipate when it might receive advice from the committee on key issues. Concomitantly, such an approach should also provide the ATCM with an opportunity to comment on and influence the prioritisation of the CEP's work in accordance with the ATCM's own interests and priorities. The interaction between the CEP and the ATCM will be discussed later in this paper.

To date, the five-year work plan has been used somewhat tentatively by the CEP, and options for a more rigorous approach to setting the CEP's work priorities through the five-year plan need to be explored. These might include allocating more time to discussing the matter of work prioritisation at the CEP's annual meeting and making the work plan more widely available to CEP members and observers through the CEP's Web site (rather than the current practice of simply appending the work plan to the CEP's annual report).

The second option for tackling the CEP's workload, on which some action has recently been taken, involves the establishment of topic-related working groups. The CEP's rules of procedure provide for the establishment of subsidiary bodies with the ATCM's approval, though there has been an element of reluctance to do so.[33] Arguably, the principle reason for the CEP and ATCM being reluctant to establish formal subsidiary bodies has been the requirement in the CEP's rules of procedure for such bodies to operate in the four official languages of the Antarctic Treaty.[34] The perceived impediment has been the substantial costs involved in having interpretation and translation facilities available for intersessional meetings of these subsidiary bodies.

In somewhat characteristic fashion, albeit after a few years of consideration, the CEP found a practical solution to this challenge. In 2009 the CEP recommended to the ATCM the establishment of a subsidiary body to manage the consideration of protected and managed area management plans (Subsidiary Group on Management Plans, SGMP). As discussed above, consideration of management plans for such areas had for some time dominated meetings of the committee. By delegating this work to a permanently established subgroup with a dedicated convenor, the CEP anticipated freeing up a substantial amount of time at its annual meeting for other discussions. In presenting this case to the ATCM, the CEP overcame the issue of interpretation and translation by suggesting that all intersessional work be conducted by e-mail and use of the CEP online discussion forum in one common language (English), with the product of its work, i.e., its report to the CEP, being translated into the four languages of the treaty sufficiently well in advance so that all participants had the opportunity to view it in their preferred language, prior to its consideration by the CEP. The SGMP has been in operation for the last two years, and the anticipated benefits have already been realised in the committee's work.

These are perhaps the most substantive examples of how the CEP has had to adapt in order to ensure it is giving adequate attention to issues of high priority for the Antarctic environment. But in the opinion of the authors the CEP cannot afford to rest there. Additional measures need to be pursued, including the establishment of additional subsidiary bodies or experts groups on issues considered to be a high priority.

AVAILABILITY OF DATA AND INFORMATION

Although the prioritisation of its agenda will hopefully continue to ensure that the CEP is addressing those matters most critical to the Antarctic environment, there remain additional constraints that the CEP has recognised need further attention. Unlike the SC-CAMLR established under the Convention on the Conservation of Antarctic Marine Living Resources (arguably the CEP's "sister committee" within the Antarctic Treaty System), the CEP does not have dedicated resources that it can draw on. The SC-CAMLR can seek, with the commission's endorsement, dedicated funding for intersessional work, such as the holding of workshops and subsidiary scientific meetings. The SC-CAMLR also has dedicated support within the CCAMLR Secretariat, including a science officer and data management support. The CEP has no access to such resources. There is no "environmental officer" within the Antarctic Treaty Secretariat's staff and no dedicated data management resources (although secretariat staff spend a considerable proportion of their effort on CEP business). Yet the expectation remains (appropriately) that the CEP provide the ATCM with timely, scientifically defensible advice on the management of the Antarctic environment.

At present, the CEP does not routinely review or consider a prescribed set of data or information or summary reports on aspects that would support its policy advisory role. It would be expected of a fully functioning committee that it routinely have access to a range of environmental information for its review and on which it can base its advice. This might include, for example, status and trends of key species, trends in tourism numbers (e.g., at key locations), nonnative species data, and climate change reports (e.g., regional climate trends and environmental responses). At present, no mechanisms exist for the CEP routinely to have such information made available to it.

Perhaps part of this problem lies more in the fact that the CEP has not yet been able to agree on what its information requirements are, rather than the means of accessing it. This has been and remains to a large extent a fundamental challenge for the CEP and is a matter deserving of priority attention by the committee.

In the absence of its own data and information management resources, the CEP has been required to seek the advice of, as well as data from, other sources and organisations. Key among the organisations with which the CEP has needed to forge a relationship is SCAR. The Protocol on Environmental Protection to the Antarctic Treaty recognises SCAR's expertise and advisory role (to both the CEP and the ATCM) in a number of its articles.[35] The SCAR has played a significant advisory role to the ATCM since the early 1960s, including in the development of the Agreed Measures of 1964, the negotiations of CCAMLR, and the development of other ATCM recommendations and initiatives.[36]

Notwithstanding this central role played by SCAR for several decades, the establishment of the CEP in 1998 has forced a reassessment of the various relationships within the ATS. The establishment of the CEP usurped much of the advisory position that SCAR had maintained since the entry in to force of the Antarctic Treaty. It has been necessary for both the CEP and SCAR to adjust to a new way of working. This has been in large part tempered by the time it has taken for the CEP to establish itself and begin to stand on its own feet.

However, SCAR also has limited resources and relies on its membership to provide their support to SCAR's work mostly on a voluntary basis. The SCAR's ability to respond to and support the CEP's needs is limited and needs to be carefully managed, and it is far from ideal for the CEP to be wholly dependent upon others for making progress on its work. It remains important for the CEP to continue to examine its own data and information needs and how these might be met.

EMERGING OPPORTUNITIES

Opportunities are emerging that may help improve the situation. Over the last few years there has been a proliferation of online Antarctic databases and information. Examples include the SCAR-Marine Biodiversity Information Network (SCAR-MarBIN),[37] SCAR's biodiversity database (maintained by the Australian Antarctic Division),[38] and the Agreement on the Conservation of Albatross and Petrels' species summary reports.[39] Such resources have so far been underutilised by the CEP and need to be more routinely used to support the CEP's work, both at its annual meetings and in its intersessional work.

The SCAR's *Antarctic Climate Change and the Environment* (ACCE) report also represents a further opportunity for the CEP to have access to rigorous information on climate change in the Antarctic region (as do, of course, the reports of the Intergovernmental Panel on Climate Change and other scientific reports on the Antarctic region).[40] The CEP needs to use this as a basis for consideration of where its own effort should be placed. But regular updates on elements of the ACCE (for example, by means of a "report card" approach) would be useful for the CEP.

Furthermore, the component parts of the treaty system also need to give consideration to how they interact with regard to data and information gathering and sharing. The two key bodies in this regard are SC-CAMLR and the CEP. The effective scope of both these bodies overlap, particularly on species protection, protected area management, and environmental monitoring. Greater cooperation and joint effort in areas of common interest can only be of benefit to both the CEP and SC-CAMLR. The recent joint workshop between the CEP and the SC-CAMLR (held in Baltimore in April 2009) was a significant achievement and successful in sharing information and ideas, clarifying lead roles on key matters, and clarifying what is and what is not of shared interest.

Other organisations with which the CEP has established good working relationships include the International Union for the Conservation of Nature (IUCN), the United Nations Environment Programme (UNEP), ASOC, and the International Association of Antarctica Tour Operators (IAATO). Good progress has been made in these relationships, but further effort is required to make information and data exchange between these bodies and the CEP effective and useful.

THE RELATIONSHIP BETWEEN THE CEP AND THE ATCM

It is self-evident that the CEP has an important relationship with the ATCM. That relationship merits closer scrutiny.

In its Article 10, the protocol makes it clear that the primary decision- and policy-making role in respect of managing the Antarctic environment remains squarely with the ATCM. Article 10 also states that the ATCM, in making its decisions, shall review the work of the committee and draw upon its advice. Article 11 of the protocol requires the CEP to report to the ATCM, and Article 12 states that "the functions of the Committee shall be to provide advice and formulate recommendations to the Parties in connection with the implementation of this Protocol, including the operation of its Annexes, for consideration at Antarctic Treaty Consultative Meetings, and to perform such other functions as may be referred to it by the Antarctic Treaty Consultative Meetings." Article 12, paragraph 1(j), specifically requires the CEP to advise the ATCM on the state of the Antarctic environment.

It is therefore clear that the committee is an advisory body to the ATCM and subservient to it. This then places a responsibility upon both bodies. The CEP needs to ensure that it is providing timely, relevant, and scientifically based advice to the ATCM. In turn, the ATCM needs to be responsive to the advice of the committee and provide adequate direction to the committee to ensure that it is working on issues that are important and of benefit to the ATCM. Our experience shows that this is a role that not always has been given priority by the ATCM.

FUTURE CHALLENGES

The point of suggesting improvements and highlighting the issues in this paper is that managing the Antarctic environment has arguably never been more pressing. Significant challenges remain with a changing Antarctic climate, most immediately on the Antarctic Peninsula, affected species, and the implications of increasing human activity (both through tourism and the activities of national programs).

Although it is up to the parties to appoint their representatives and experts to the CEP, the work load and diversity of issues at considered by the CEP has become larger and more complex, and the burden on those attending CEP has increased. More than ever, the CEP needs a broad range of skills and competence, and representatives need to be well prepared for the agenda of the meetings. There is, unfortunately, a tendency to allow some parties to carry a disproportionate share of the work load of the CEP. This trend is probably not sustainable in the long term.

The pace of change in Antarctica is beginning to demand a more responsive and proactive system of management. To that end, the CEP is likely to play an increasingly important advisory role to the ATCM. The CEP needs to be adequately supported and resourced, and it needs to develop and maintain strong partnerships with key organisations to ensure it fulfils its mandate in the future.

NOTES

1. The Antarctic Treaty, http://www.ats.aq/documents/ats/treaty_original.pdf (accessed 1 December 2010).

2. Antarctic Treaty.

3. Report of the Third Antarctic Treaty Consultative Meeting (ATCM), http://www.ats.aq/devAS/ats_meetings_meeting.aspx?lang=e (accessed 1 December 2010).

4. Report of the Third ATCM.

5. Report of the Third ATCM.

6. The Protocol on Environmental Protection to the Antarctic Treaty, http://www.ats.aq//e/ats_protocol.htm (accessed 1 December 2010).

7. Convention on the Conservation of Antarctic Marine Living Resources, http://www.ccamlr.org (accessed 1 December 2010).

8. Convention for the Conservation of Antarctic Seals, http://www.ats.aq/documents/recatt/Att076_e.pdf (1 December 2010).

9. Convention on the Conservation of Antarctic Marine Living Resources, Article 2.

10. P. J. Beck, *The International Politics of Antarctica* (London: Croom Helm, 1986), pp. 246–247.

11. Beck, *International Politics.*

12. Beck, *International Politics,* p. 245

13. Convention on the Regulation of Antarctic Mineral Resource Activity; and the Final Act of the Fourth Special Antarctic Treaty Consultative Meeting on Antarctic Mineral Resources, http://www.ats.aq/devAS/ats_meetings_meeting.aspx?lang=e (accessed 1 December 2010).

14. T. Andersen, "Resource Management and the Protection of the Environment," in *Norway in the Antarctic* (Oslo: Schibsted, 2008), pp. 108–129.

15. O. Orheim, "The Committee for Environmental Protection: Its Establishment, Operation and Role within the Antarctic Treaty System," in *Implementing the Environmental Protection Regime for the Antarctic,* ed. D. Vidas (Dordrecht, the Netherlands: Kluwer Academic Publishers, 2000), pp. 107–124.

16. Report of the Committee for Environmental Protection (CEP I), http://www.ats.aq//documents/cep/atcm22_cepi_e.pdf (accessed 1 December 2010).

17. Report of the Committee for Environmental Protection (CEP III), http://www.ats.aq//documents/cep/cep%20documents/ml_376356825578704_finalReportE.pdf (accessed 1 December 2010).

18. R. Sanchez and E. McIvor, "The Antarctic Committee for Environmental Protection: Past, Present, and Future," *Polar Record* 43 (2007): 239–246.

19. "Guidelines for Environmental Impact Assessment in Antarctica," http://www.ats.aq/documents/recatt/Att266_e.pdf (accessed 1 December 2010).

20. "Guidelines for the Implementation of the Framework for Protected Areas Set Forth in Article 3, Annex V of the Environmental Protocol," http://www.ats.aq/documents/recatt/att081_e.pdf (accessed 1 December 2010).

21. "Guide to the Presentation of Working Papers Containing Proposals for Antarctic Specially Protected Areas, Antarctic Specially Managed Areas or Historic Sites and Monuments," http://www.ats.aq/documents/recatt/Att406_e.pdf (accessed 1 December 2010).

22. Report of the Committee for Environmental Protection (CEP IV), http://www.ats.aq//documents/cep/cep%20documents/ml_376374591319444_finalReportE.pdf (accessed 1 December 2010).

23. All three authors had leading roles in this process, and all initially expected that the process would be straight forward.

24. Final report of the Thirty-Second Antarctic Treaty Consultative Meeting, http://www.ats.aq//documents/ATCM32/fr/ATCM32_fr002_e.pdf (accessed 1 December 2010).

25. Sanchez and McIvor, "The Antarctic Committee for Environmental Protection," 239–246.

26. International Association of Antarctica Tour Operators, "IAATO Overview of Antarctic Tourism: 2008–2009: Antarctic Season and Preliminary Estimates for 2009–2010 Antarctic Season," ATCM XXXII Information Paper 86 (IAATO, 2009), http://www.ats.aq/documents/ATCM32/ip/ATCM32_ip086_rev1_e.doc (accessed 1 December 2010).

27. J. Turner, R. A. Bindschadler, P. Convey, G. Di Prisco, E. Fahrbach, J. Gutt, D. A. Hodgson, P. A. Mayewski, and C. P. Summerhayes, *Antarctic Climate Change and the Environment* (Cambridge: Scientific Committee for Antarctic Research, 2009).

28. Turner et al., *Antarctic Climate Change.*

29. Y. Frenot, S. L. Chown, J. Whinam, P. M. Selkirk, P. Convey, M. Skotniki, and D. M. Bergstrom, "Biological Invasions in the Antarctic: Extent, Impacts and Implications," *Biological Reviews* 80 (2005): 45–72.

30. Source: Council of Managers of National Antarctic Programmes, http://www.comnap.aq/facilities (accessed 1 December 2010).

31. Council of Managers of National Antarctic Programmes Web site.

32. "Antarctica's Future Environmental Challenges: A Summary Report of the CEP Workshop, Edinburgh, United Kingdom, 9–10 June 2006," CEP IX Working Paper 42 http://www.ats.aq//devAS/ats_meetings_documents.aspx?lang=e&id=60 (accessed 1 December 2010).

33. CEP, "Rules of Procedure," http://www.ats.aq/e/cep_rop.htm (accessed 1 December 2010).

34. CEP, "Rules of Procedure."

35. See, for example, Articles 10, paragraph 2, and 12, paragraph 2, of the Protocol on Environmental Protection to the Antarctic Treaty; Article 3, paragraph 1, of Annex III to the protocol; and Articles 5, paragraph 1, and 6 of Annex V to the protocol.

36. J. H. Zumberge, "The Antarctic Treaty as a Scientific Mechanism—The Scientific Committee on Antarctic Research and the Antarctic Treaty System," in *Antarctic Treaty System: An Assessment. Proceedings of a Workshop Held at Beardmore South Field Camp, Antarctica, January 7–13, 1985* (Washington, D.C.: National Academies Press, 1986), pp. 153–168.

37. The SCAR-Marine Biodiversity Information Network, http://www.scarmarbin.be (accessed 1 December 2010).

38. SCAR's Biodiversity Database, http://data.aad.gov.au/aadc/biodiversity (accessed 1 December 2010).

39. The Agreement on the Conservation of Albatross and Petrels' species summary reports, http://www.acap.aq/publications-acap-species (accessed 1 December 2010).

40. Turner et al., *Antarctic Climate Change.*

The ANTOSTRAT Legacy: Science Collaboration and International Transparency in Potential Marine Mineral Resource Exploitation of Antarctica

Alan Cooper, Peter Barker, Peter Barrett, John Behrendt, Giuliano Brancolini, Jonathan Childs, Carlota Escutia, Wilfried Jokat, Yngve Kristoffersen, German Leitchenkov, Howard Stagg, Manabu Tanahashi, Nigel Wardell, and Peter Webb

ABSTRACT. The Antarctic Offshore Stratigraphy project (ANTOSTRAT; 1989–2002) was an extremely successful collaboration in international marine geological science that also lifted the perceived "veil of secrecy" from studies of potential exploitation of Antarctic marine mineral resources. The project laid the groundwork for circum-Antarctic seismic, drilling, and rock coring programs designed to decipher Antarctica's tectonic, stratigraphic, and climate histories. In 2002, ANTOSTRAT evolved into the equally successful and currently active Antarctic Climate Evolution research program. The need for, and evolution of, ANTOSTRAT was based on two simple tenets within SCAR and the Antarctic Treaty: international science collaboration and open access to data. The ANTOSTRAT project may be a helpful analog for other regions of strong international science and geopolitical interests, such as the Arctic. This is the ANTOSTRAT story.

ANTARCTIC OFFSHORE STRATIGRAPHY PROJECT: THE EARLY YEARS

In 1986, the science community established the Scientific Committee on Antarctic Research (SCAR) Group of Specialists on Cenozoic Paleoenvironments in Southern High Latitudes to study and assess geologic sample and core data as well as geophysical remote sensing data to better comprehend Antarctica's geologic history and its impact on global sea level and climate change (Figure 1). Recognizing that Antarctica is 98% ice covered, the Antarctic

Alan Cooper (emeritus), U.S. Geological Survey, and Department of Geological and Environmental Sciences, Stanford University. Peter Barker (retired), British Antarctic Survey, and Earth and Environmental Sciences, University of Birmingham. Peter Barrett, Antarctic Research Centre and New Zealand Climate Change Research Institute, Victoria University of Wellington. John Behrendt, Institute of Arctic and Alpine Research, University of Colorado, and (emeritus) U.S. Geological Survey. Giuliano Brancolini (retired), Istituto Nazionale di Oceanografia e di Geofisica Sperimentale. Jonathan Childs, U.S. Geological Survey. Carlota Escutia, Instituto Andaluz de Ciencias de la Tierra, Consejo Superior de Investigaciones Científicas–Universidad de Granada. Wilfried Jokat, Alfred Wegener Institute. Yngve Kristoffersen, Department of Earth Science, University of Bergen. German Leitchenkov, Research Institute for Geology and Mineral Resources of the World Ocean, VNIIOkeangeologia. Howard Stagg (retired), Geoscience Australia. Manabu Tanahashi, Geological Survey of Japan. Nigel Wardell, Istituto Nazionale di Oceanografia e di Geofisica Sperimentale. Peter Webb, School of Earth Sciences, Ohio State University.

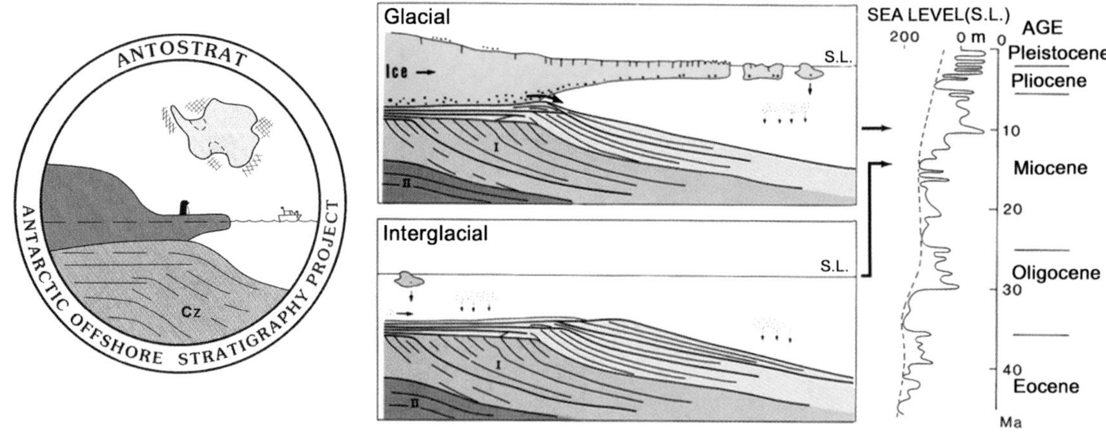

FIGURE 1. The ANTOSTRAT logo and an early 1990s ANTOSTRAT model linking global sea levels to Antarctic ice sheet history (modified from Cooper and Webb, 1992).

Offshore Stratigraphy project (ANTOSTRAT) was established under the aegis of the Group of Specialists to focus geoscience investigations on Antarctica's offshore regions (Cooper and Webb, 1992). The stated objective of ANTOSTRAT was to bring together all research groups responsible for collecting offshore geological and geophysical data, to collaborate in field and laboratory studies directed toward understanding Cenozoic paleoenvironments, to plan future offshore geologic studies, and to promote scientific deep drilling.

Prelude to Potential Marine Minerals

Data relevant to ANTOSTRAT had been collected in Antarctica since the early 1970s, but these were commonly unavailable to anyone except the data collectors (or to collaborators via private data exchange agreements). The geologic and geophysical data collected during the pre-ANTOSTRAT years were also being used for assessments of offshore mineral resources by national, academic, and corporate research groups. Because many of the offshore geologic and geophysical data, especially the seismic reflection data, were not openly accessible, there was a perceived "veil of secrecy" on the eventual uses of ongoing geoscientific studies. Many beyond the Antarctic community were asking whether these studies were for research purposes or for mineral exploration.

In the decade preceding the establishment of ANTOSTRAT, interest in Antarctica's potential mineral resources was increasing (e.g., Behrendt, 1983; Splettstoesser and Dreschhoff, 1990), with the escalating price and demand for such resources. The most important of these resources were hydrocarbons.

Collaboration in Science

With the implementation of ANTOSTRAT in 1989 and the first ANTOSTRAT symposium in April 1990 (Cooper and Webb, 1990), at which the emphasis was on offshore geoscience data, the level of interest in the science and geopolitics of the offshore areas blossomed. At the 1990 symposium, the groundwork for collaboration in studying the offshore data was laid down with the formation of working groups for the five principal marine regions around the Antarctic continent accessible by surface vessels (i.e., Ross Sea, Wilkes Land, Prydz Bay, Weddell Sea, and Antarctic Peninsula). The working groups were tasked to collate, analyze, and publish collaborative research papers on the geoscience data from each region. The first tenet of ANTOSTRAT (i.e., collaboration in science) was now in place, and the interest in, and support for, ANTOSTRAT gained momentum among all countries engaged in conducting marine surveys of the Antarctic margin.

THE ANTARCTIC SEISMIC DATA LIBRARY SYSTEM FOR COOPERATIVE RESEARCH: OPEN ACCESS TO DATA—A LINK TO THE ANTARCTIC TREATY

There was, however, still no mechanism in place for open access to the most valuable of all Earth science data

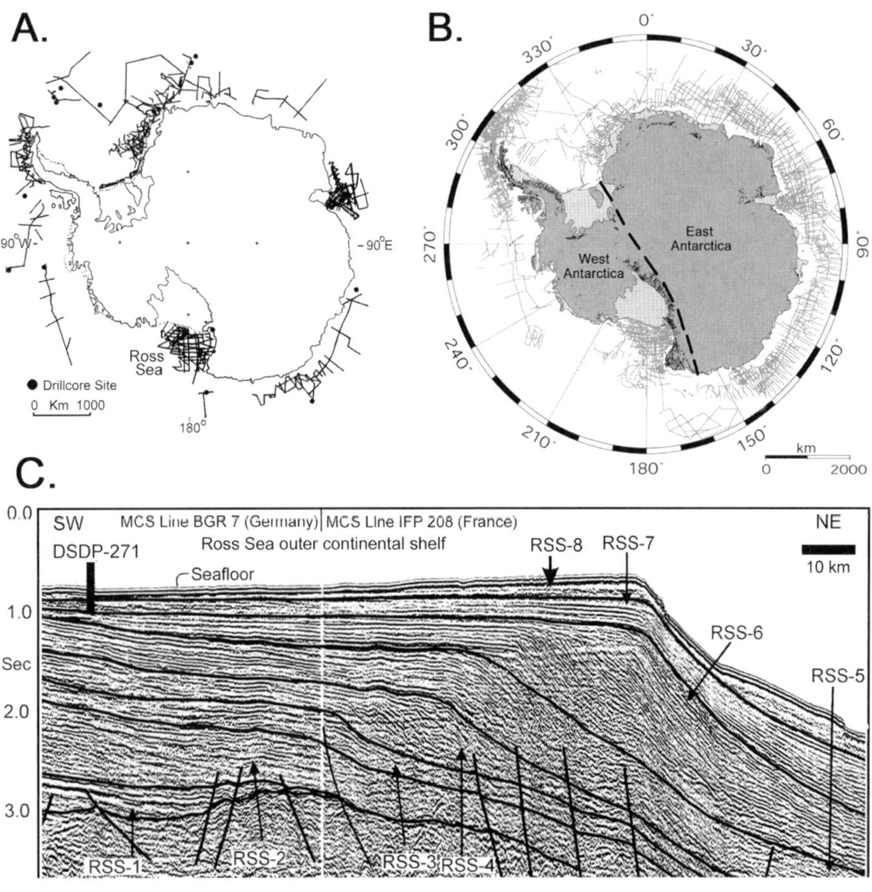

FIGURE 2. Multichannel seismic reflection (MCS) data. Maps showing track lines of data: (A) collected before 1988 (modified from Behrendt, 1990) and (B) collected as of late 2009 (about 350,000 km). (C) Example MCS profile across the Ross Sea with seismic stratigraphic units (RSS) and Deep Sea Drilling Project site noted (modified from Cooper et al. 2009). About 275,000 km of MCS data are now in the SDLS.

for research and hydrocarbon exploration: multichannel seismic reflection (MCS) data (Figure 2). The MCS data are used to image the structure of the Earth, from the seafloor down to 10 km or more below the sea floor. Such information is needed to decipher how continents and their margins formed. They also help to identify where hydrocarbons may be present. The MCS data are therefore both a powerful research tool and a basic and widely used tool in the exploration for petroleum. A key criterion for establishing their intended use is the level of access to the data. MCS data used for research purposes will be openly accessible to others (via publication and later release), but data collected for commercial exploration purposes will rarely be made accessible.

In late 1990, with the level of debate on Antarctica's mineral resources increasing, it was clear to members of the ANTOSTRAT steering committee that the second tenet of ANTOSTRAT (i.e., open access to data in accord with Article III of the Antarctic Treaty) needed to be addressed promptly to clearly demonstrate that ANTOSTRAT was truly a science project and not mineral exploration of Antarctica undertaken under another name. In April 1991, ANTOSTRAT convened a special workshop in Oslo, Norway, to develop and agree to a system by which the highly valued MCS data would be made openly accessible. This would help ANTOSTRAT move forward faster with its collaborative science agenda of making circum-Antarctic maps needed for understanding Antarctica's geologic and climate history.

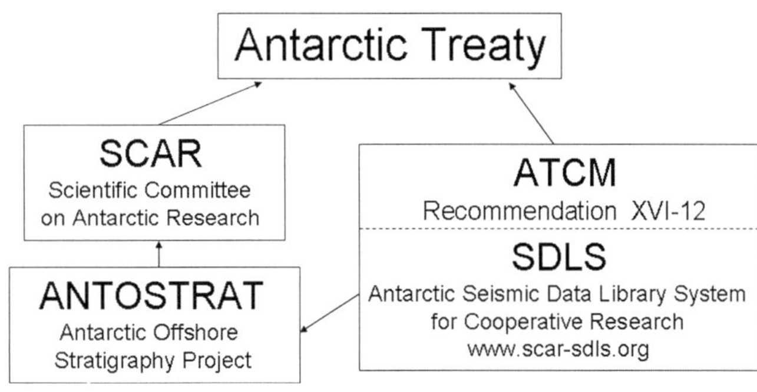

FIGURE 3. Generalized organizational diagram showing the former relationships of SCAR, ANTOSTRAT (now ACE), SDLS, and the Antarctic Treaty. The SDLS is now under ACE.

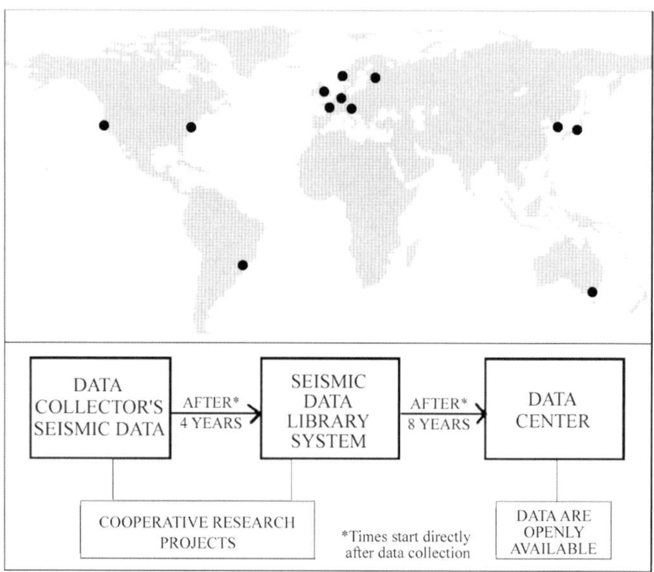

FIGURE 4. (top) Locations of SDLS branches and(bottom) concepts of the SDLS (modified from Cooper and the ANTOSTRAT Steering Committee, 1991, and SDLS, http://www.scar-sdls.org, accessed January 2010). The SDLS provides open access worldwide to Antarctic seismic reflection data for use in cooperative research projects.

The Oslo workshop included lead scientists from groups in the 11 countries that had collected MCS data (Cooper and the ANTOSTRAT Steering Committee, 1991; Figure 2A,C).[1] The participants developed a plan for a new science data library. All participants agreed to the plan and forwarded an outline of it to the XVI Antarctic Treaty Consultative Meeting (October 1991). There the outline statement was discussed and adopted as Recommendation XVI-12, thereby formalizing the SCAR Antarctic Seismic Data Library System for Cooperative Research (SDLS) as part of the Antarctic Treaty System (Figure 3). The second tenet of ANTOSTRAT (i.e., open access to data) was now in place.

In the same year, 1991, the Madrid Protocol on Antarctic Environmental Protection to the Antarctic Treaty (Antarctic Treaty System, 1991) was signed establishing a 50-year moratorium on resource exploration and exploitation. The MCS data can be used for both exploration and basic research, yet the adoption of the SDLS into the treaty opened access to these data and removed the perceived veil of secrecy about how they were being used. Because MCS data are critical for understanding Earth history and paleoclimates, they continue to be collected and made openly available for research purposes.

A Unique Approach

The SDLS is unique in its approach to resolving the difficult issue of open access to highly valued data. The SDLS is a research library system under SCAR and the treaty and not an international data bank linked to national or other agencies. The focus is on promoting collaboration and data sharing for research purposes, while respecting and preserving intellectual property rights. The World Data Center (http://www.ngdc.noaa.gov/wdc/) has primary responsibility for archival of data.

The SDLS operates under clearly defined guidelines in SCAR Report 9 (Cooper et al., 1991; Childs et al., 1994). These guidelines apply to all MCS data collected in Antarctic regions.

A key guideline of the SDLS is that the restrictions on use and access to MCS data decrease with time after the data are collected (Figure 4):

- For an initial period (zero to four years after collection), data collectors retain full intellectual property rights to their data.
- For the succeeding period (four to eight years), MCS data go into the SDLS, where they can only be used for collaborative research purposes with the data collector. The data collector cannot deny the collaborative efforts unless another research group is already working on the same proposed project.
- In the final period (after eight years), the MCS data then become openly accessible to anyone, with the only restriction being that persons who use the data cite the data collector. The open access is via the

World Data Center, other unrestricted data centers, and/or the SDLS Web site (http://www.scar-sdls.org).

A key hurdle in organizing the SDLS was how it was to be funded. Summarizing from SCAR Report 9 (Cooper et al., 1991), SCAR provides no funds for the SDLS. Funding for library branches is the responsibility of the host organization. Data are currently sent to branches on CD-ROM and DVD-ROM; hence, a room and computer system that is supervised by a senior Antarctic researcher (to ensure SDLS guidelines are followed) is sufficient. Funds for the data standardization and preparation of the CDs and DVDs containing the MCS data are the responsibility of the data collector, via National Antarctic Programs and/or institutional funds. The funds are submitted to the group producing the CDs and DVDs when the MCS data are submitted. Currently, the CDs and DVDs are produced by the Istituto Nazionale di Oceanografia e di Geofisica Sperimentale (OGS) in Trieste, Italy. Oversight and management of the SDLS is done by a three-member executive committee, currently with two members at the U.S. Geological Survey and one member at OGS.

Achievements in Transparency and Collaboration

The implementation of the SDLS under ANTOSTRAT purview has provided an acceptable and rational mechanism for graduated open access to seismic data (Figure 4) and has removed the secrecy of data collection for mineral exploration. The eventual use of MCS data is not guided by SDLS guidelines. Yet the SDLS has, since 1991 (i.e., for 19 years as of the time of this report), facilitated and promoted a culture of geoscience collaboration on large-scale (i.e., more than 10 countries) international projects in Antarctica's offshore regions, projects that would not otherwise be possible.

The SDLS has further helped encourage a greater willingness to cooperate in sharing of expensive and difficult-to-collect MCS data. The reality is, however, that each organization's practice in their data submissions to the SDLS is influenced by many factors, including funds available to submit data, national agency policies, protecting students and others undertaking research projects, and incomplete data processing. Hence, data submissions are frequently behind the SDLS schedule and vary between countries. Patience and persistence has been required to achieve the SDLS-stipulated and Antarctic Treaty Consultative Meeting (ATCM)-approved data submissions. Nevertheless, over the years, the SDLS, initially under ANTOSTRAT and more recently under the Antarctic Climate Evolution program (ACE), has gradually incorporated about 275,000 km of MCS data, which is 85% of the MCS data due at the SDLS and 79% of all data collected (Figure 2B). A majority of those data are older than 8 years and are therefore openly accessible (Cooper et al., 2009).

The SDLS, like the Antarctic Treaty, is a dynamic body that requires constant attention and participation of the science community for its success, and to achieve this, the SDLS holds yearly to biyearly workshops. The SDLS now has 13 branches in 11 countries (http://www.scar-sdls.org).

ANTOSTRAT: LATER YEARS AND SUCCESSES

The history of ANTOSTRAT and its principal research findings (see Cooper et al., 2008) would not be complete without listing some of the successes achieved under its two principal tenets of science collaboration and open access to data. The ANTOSTRAT project has spawned and helped a generation of young researchers to learn how science is accomplished in Antarctica, under SCAR and the Antarctic Treaty, and to promote their science and the greater collaborative interests within the science community. It has also inspired and promoted a generation of major offshore Antarctic drilling projects and currently, under ACE, a project to create circum-Antarctic stratigraphic and paleobathymetry maps for climate history. Scientists working under ANTOSTRAT collaborations have

- published hundreds of individual research papers (see the 54-page bibliography in Cooper et al. [2008]);
- held numerous international ANTOSTRAT symposia and workshops to disseminate research results and SDLS workshops to assess SDLS operations and plans;
- compiled and published several geoscience map atlases of offshore regions based on multinational data sets from areas around Antarctica;
- promoted, designed, and conducted many offshore drilling operations for climate history (e.g., Ocean Drilling Project Legs 178, 188, and 318 (2010), Cape Roberts Project drilling [http://www.victoria.ac.nz/geo/croberts/], and others);
- submitted to the SDLS about 275,000 km of MCS data estimated at more than $300 million to collect and process; and
- carried the valued tenets of ANTOSTRAT into the next generation as significant elements in the ACE program (Florindo and Siegert, 2008; ACE, 2010).

ANTOSTRAT was one of many successful long-term international science projects under the leadership of SCAR. Unlike all other geoscience projects, ANTOSTRAT was directly linked to the Antarctic Treaty System, a link that has continued, now under ACE, for 19 years, via the SDLS and ATCM Recommendation XVI-12. In a small way, ANTOSTRAT and the SDLS helped carry the treaty through one of its most challenging periods during the search for a solution to the Antarctic minerals exploration problem.

As with all dynamic institutions, the continuing success of the SDLS relies on the proactive determinations of its constituents, the scientists and their national Antarctic programs, to keep it vibrant with their creative ideas, active science participation, and funding for data submissions. We see long-term value for these endeavors and urge continued support of the SDLS.

ANTOSTRAT: FUTURE ANALOGS

Can ANTOSTRAT, with its successes in facilitating international collaboration and open access to valuable data for marine geologic studies of the Antarctic continental margin, be adopted as a template for studies of other continental margins with potential mineral resources and inherent scientific value in paleoenvironment and climate histories? As an example, could the ANTOSTRAT template be applied in the other polar region, the Arctic?

The Arctic Ocean and its continental margin is an area of great international and economic interest, but there is yet no established guiding treaty for the region as there is for Antarctica. With regard to mineral resources and geoscience research (i.e., ANTOSTRAT analog), the Arctic region is now governed by laws of the encircling nations and further subject to the tenets of the United Nations Convention on the Law of the Sea. Yet these laws and guidelines do not promote or achieve the greater goal of open access to data to facilitate scientific studies of benefit to all. Although large geoscience data sets, including a growing amount of seismic reflection data (e.g., Kristofferson and Mikkelsen, 2004), already exist for the Arctic Ocean region and many of these have been published, there are still many such data sets that are not yet openly accessible to the international science community. Furthermore, there is currently no internationally adopted mechanism by which future data sets would be made openly accessible.

In the Arctic example, as in other regions of international interest, adopting the straightforward tenets of ANTOSTRAT (and the SDLS) could facilitate greater geopolitical harmony by promoting scientific research over national and commercial interests. Such research is needed to answer fundamental questions about Earth processes that are key to our survival.

Acknowledgments

We thank the editors for the invitation to relate the ANTOSTRAT success story, one in which the real "heroes" to be thanked are the hundreds of geoscience investigators and managers from research institutions in more than 20 countries, people whose dedicated collaborations within SCAR and under treaty guidelines provide a role model for Antarctic science endeavors. We thank Jerry Mullins and Ginger Barth for their helpful reviews.

Expanded Author Information

Alan Cooper (emeritus), U.S. Geological Survey, 345 Middlefield Road, Menlo Park, California 94301, USA, and Department of Geological and Environmental Sciences, Stanford University, Stanford, California 94306, USA. Peter Barker (retired), British Antarctic Survey, Cambridge, UK, and Earth and Environmental Sciences, University of Birmingham, Birmingham B15 2TT, UK. Peter Barrett, Antarctic Research Centre and New Zealand Climate Change Research Institute, Victoria University of Wellington, Kelburn Parade, Wellington 6012, New Zealand. John Behrendt, Institute of Arctic and Alpine Research, University of Colorado, Boulder, Colorado 80309, USA, and (emeritus) U.S. Geological Survey, Federal Center, Denver, Colorado 80225, USA. Giuliano Brancolini (retired), Istituto Nazionale di Oceanografia e di Geofisica Sperimentale, Borgo Grotta Gigante 42/c, I-34010 Sgonico, Trieste, Italy. Jonathan Childs, U.S. Geological Survey, 345 Middlefield Road, Menlo Park, California 94301, USA. Carlota Escutia, Instituto Andaluz de Ciencias de la Tierra, Consejo Superior de Investigaciones Científicas–Universidad de Granada, Campus de Fuentenueva s/n, E-18002 Granada, Spain. Wilfried Jokat, Alfred Wegener Institute, Am Handelshafen 12, D-27570 Bremerhaven, Germany. Yngve Kristoffersen, Department of Earth Science, University of Bergen, Allegaten 41, N-5007 Bergen, Norway. German Leitchenkov, Research Institute for Geology and Mineral Resources of the World Ocean, VNIIOkeangeologia, 1 Angliysky Avenue, 190 121 St. Petersburg, Russia. Howard Stagg (retired), Geoscience Australia, GPO Box 378, ACT 2609, Australia. Manabu Tanahashi, Geological Survey of Japan, AIST C-7, Tsukuba 305-8567, Japan. Nigel Wardell, Istituto Nazionale di Oceanografia e di Geofisica Sperimentale, Borgo Grotta Gigante 42/c, I-34010 Sgonico, Trieste, Italy. Peter Webb, School of Earth Sciences, Ohio State University, Columbus, Ohio 43210, USA. Correspondence: acooper@usgs.gov; akcooper@pacbell.net; peter@pnjbarker.co.uk; peter.barrett@vuw.ac.nz; john.behrendt@colorado.edu; giuliano.brancolini@libero.it; jchilds@usgs.gov; cescutia@ugr.es; wilfried.jokat@awi.de; yngve.kristoffersen@geo.uib.no; german_l@mail.ru; hstagg@apex.net.au; tanahashi-m@aist.go.jp; nwardell@ogs.trieste.it; webb.3@osu.edu.

NOTE

1. The People's Republic of China was not represented at the workshop because no one was aware that they had collected MCS data in 1990–1991 until they reported this fact at ATCM XVI.

LITERATURE CITED

ACE. 2010. Antarctic Climate Evolution. http://www.csam.montclair.edu/earth/eesweb/scar_ace/ (accessed January 2010).

Antarctic Treaty System. 1991. Protocol on Environmental Protection to the Antarctic Treaty. http://www.antarctica.ac.uk/about_antarctica/geopolitical/treaty/update_1991.php (accessed January 2010).

Behrendt, J. C., ed. 1983. *Petroleum and Mineral Resources of Antarctica. U.S. Geological Survey Circular* 909. Reston, Va.: U.S. Geological Survey.

———. 1990. "Recent Geophysical and Geological Research in Antarctica Related to the Assessment of Petroleum Resources and Potential Environmental Hazards to Their Development." In *Mineral Resources Potential of Antarctica*, ed. J. F. Splettstoesser and G.A. Dreschhoff, pp. 163–174. Antarctic Research Series, No. 51. Washington, D.C.: American Geophysical Union.

Childs, J. R., R. W. Sliter, and A. K. Cooper. 1994. A Progress Report on the Antarctic Seismic Data Library System for Cooperative Research (SDLS). *Terra Antarctica*, 1(2):243–246.

Cooper, A. K., and the ANTOSTRAT Steering Committee. 1991. A SCAR Seismic Data Library System for Cooperative Research (SDLS): Summary Report of the International Workshop on Antarctic Seismic Data Oslo, Norway, April 11–15, 1991. *SCAR Report* 9. Scientific Committee on Antarctic Research. http://www.scar.org/publications/reports/9/#summary1 (accessed January 2010)

Cooper, A. K., P. Barrett, R. DeConto, R. Dunbar, C. Escutia, M. Siegert, N. Wardell, and J. Childs. 2009. Harmonies of Ice and Past Climate Change: Antarctic Paleoclimate, SCAR and Treaty Successes, Abs., *Abstract Book for Antarctic Treaty Summit*, p.45.

Cooper, A. K., G. Brancolini, C. Escutia, Y. Kristoffersen, R. Larter, G. Leitchenkov, P. O'Brien, and W. Jokat. 2008. "Cenozoic Climate History from Seismic-Reflection and Drilling Studies on the Antarctic Continental Margin." In *Antarctic Climate Evolution*, ed. F. Florindo and M. Siegert, pp. 115–228. Developments in Earth and Environmental Sciences, No. 8. Amsterdam: Elsevier.

Cooper, A. K., and P. N. Webb, eds. 1990, *International Workshop on Antarctic Offshore Acoustic Stratigraphy (ANTOSTRAT): Overview and Extended Abstracts, Pacific Grove, California, June 1990. U.S. Geological Survey Open-File Report* 90-309. Menlo Park, Calif.: U.S. Geological Survey.

———. 1992. "International Offshore Studies on Antarctic Cenozoic History, Glaciation and Sea-Level Change: The ANTOSTRAT Project." In *Recent Progress in Antarctic Earth Science*, ed. Y. Yoshida, pp. 655–659. Tokyo: Terra Scientific Publishing Company.

Florindo, F., and M. Siegert, eds. 2008. *Antarctic Climate Evolution.* Developments in Earth and Environmental Sciences, No. 8. Amsterdam: Elsevier.

Kristofferson, Y., and N. Mikkelsen, eds. 2004. Scientific Drilling in the Arctic Ocean and the Site Survey Challenge: Tectonic, Paleoceanographic and Climatic Evolution of the Polar Basin. JEODI Workshop, Copenhagen, 2003. Geological Survey of Denmark and Greenland, Special Publication. Copenhagen: Geological Survey of Denmark and Greenland. http://www.geus.dk/program-areas/nature-environment/international/reports/geus_special_publ_nov_2004.pdf (accessed January 2010).

Splettstoesser, J. F., and G. A. Dreschhoff, eds. 1990. *Mineral Resources Potential of Antarctica.* Antarctic Research Series, No. 51. Washington, D.C.: American Geophysical Union.

The Role of the Council of Managers of National Antarctic Programs

José Retamales and Michelle Rogan-Finnemore

INTRODUCTION

The Antarctic Treaty of 1959 built on the scientific successes of the International Geophysical Year (IGY) and proposed that the Antarctic Treaty area would be used for peaceful purposes only and for scientific cooperation (Antarctic Treaty, Articles I, paragraph 1, and II). The Antarctic Treaty did not, however, specify how such objectives would be met, except in its Article IX, paragraph 2, where it provides an example of activity that could represent substantial scientific research activity in Antarctica. The example, as we all know, has come to be interpreted as meaning that substantial scientific research activity of a party to the Antarctic Treaty area can be demonstrated by the country establishing a scientific research station there.

This is exactly what has happened since 1959. As participating countries in the Antarctic Treaty System grew from the initial 12 original signatories to the Antarctic Treaty to the present-day membership of 48 parties, the Antarctic Treaty Consultative countries have, individually, established approximately 65 research stations in the Antarctic Treaty area.

Over the course of the 50 years since IGY, many things have changed in regard to the Antarctic, but a number of things have also remained the same. For example, it was clear from the experiences of countries involved in the IGY that organizing scientific expeditions to Antarctica was an expensive and complex activity. This is still the case today.

What has changed is that then, in order to facilitate the science of the IGY, many countries relied at least in part on assistance from their military, who alone had aircraft and logistics experience and capability to transport people and their equipment to and from the Antarctic. They also often possessed the necessary engineering skills that were essential in building Antarctic stations and required infrastructure. This aspect of Antarctic activity has changed. Although some national Antarctic programs continue to operate in partnership with their military organizations, many do not, opting to develop the necessary logistics and engineering capabilities within their National Antarctic Programs.

In 1958, the Scientific Committee for Antarctic Research (SCAR) was established to "further international organization of scientific activity in Antarctica."[1]

José Retamales, Instituto Antártico Chileno and Council of Managers of National Antarctic Programs, Plaza Munoz Gamero 1055, Punta Arenas, Chile. Michelle Rogan-Finnemore, Council of Managers of National Antarctic Programs, COMNAP Secretariat, Private Bag 4800, Christchurch, New Zealand. Correspondence: jretamales@inach.cl; michelle.finnemore@comnap.aq.

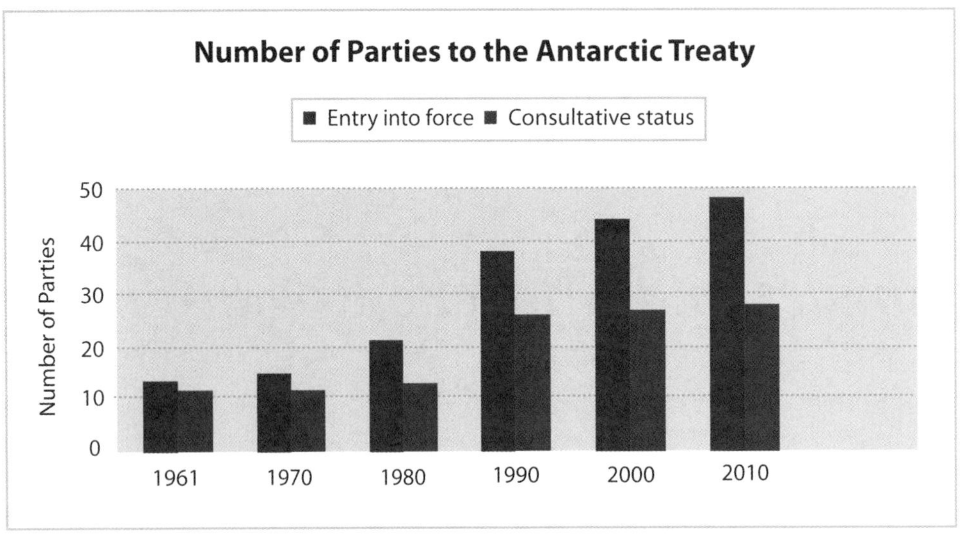

FIGURE 1. Chart showing the number of countries that are signatories to the Antarctic Treaty, cumulative by decade. It also shows the number of countries who have obtained Consultative State status over the years.

Recognizing that good science required more than good scientists, SCAR established within its framework the Working Group on Logistics (WGL). The WGL existed within SCAR until 1988. During the 1980s, there was significant interest from countries to join the Antarctic Treaty System (Figure 1). A total of 18 countries acceded to the Antarctic Treaty during that decade.[2] Many of these acceding nations were readying themselves to fully participate in the Antarctic Treaty System by obtaining Consultative State status within that system. Furthermore, in order to do this, many were preparing to establish an Antarctic research station and/or launch an Antarctic expedition. In many cases this was achieved through a national Antarctic program. The managers of these national Antarctic programs had much in common, yet they did not have a formal mechanism in place for discussions or meetings concerning items of common interest. Finally, in 1988, the decision to create a separate organization for the managers of national Antarctic programs was implemented. This independent organization would be known as the Council of Managers of National Antarctic Programs (COMNAP).

Today, 22 years on from its inception, COMNAP remains an independent organization for managers of national Antarctic programs. All 28 current Consultative State's national Antarctic programs are COMNAP members. The COMNAP provides a forum for supporting international collaboration in the Antarctic Treaty System. Whereas national Antarctic programs are governmental organizations, COMNAP is a nonpolitical organization where best practice and advice is shared among members, regardless of a country's political view of the Antarctic.

This chapter explores the role of COMNAP by discussing its inception, the last 20 years, and its recently adopted new objectives. The COMNAP is an organization whose members are very diverse organizations but who share the common goal of supporting and delivering the science that is so fundamental to the success of the Antarctic Treaty.

THE BIRTH OF COMNAP

Referring to the managers of National Antarctic Programs, Al Fowler, the first executive secretary of COMNAP, noted "it is surprising that these particular individuals had never, prior to 1986, organized themselves into an appropriate regular forum for discussion of their common interests."[3] Many of the issues that were the responsibility of the managers of national Antarctic programs had been formally discussed within the confines of SCAR. From 1972 to 1987 the SCAR WGL met on a regular basis. But, by 1986, there were calls from national Antarctic program managers for their own separate forum for regular and direct formal contact. Discussion of such a forum took place over several years. By 1987, terms of reference for the meetings of managers of national Antarctic programs were created and agreed to by the then 22 managers of national Antarctic programs that were in existence. The COMNAP was formally created on 15 September 1988 to bring together the officials responsible for carrying out national activity in the Antarctic on behalf of their governments, all of them parties to the Antarctic Treaty.

The Standing Committee on Antarctic Logistics and Operations (SCALOP) was also created at that time to replace the WGL. The SCALOP would be composed of one member from each country as nominated by the respective manager of a national Antarctic program and would usually be the program's logistics and operations person. The SCALOP remained in existence until 2008, when COMNAP restructured its organization. Even though a formal standing committee no longer exists, discussions on logistics and operations still take place and are still important aspects of COMNAP that are now considered by a number of Expert Groups.

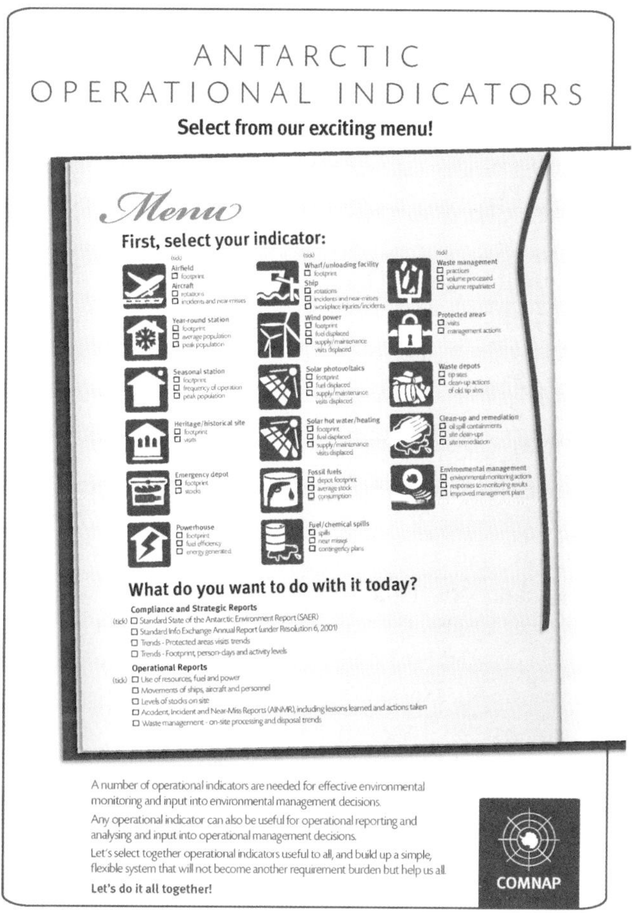

FIGURE 2. An example of outreach material developed by COMNAP in 2006.

COMNAP 1988–2008

Two of the topics that preoccupied the managers of national Antarctic programs in 1988 were air operations and telecommunications. They are topics that are still of concern to COMNAP members today. Matters such as these generally became the subject of consideration by SCALOP until it was formally disbanded by COMNAP at its Annual General Meeting (AGM) XX in 2008 in St. Petersburg, Russia. Over the course of its 20 years of existence SCALOP convened 10 symposia that provided an opportunity for members and others to present, orally and via posters, information on a range of topics broadly related to logistics and operations in Antarctica. The topics included innovation, infrastructure and logistics, human resource management, transportation, environmental issues, emergency response, and medical concerns (Figure 2). In addition to the opportunity these symposia provided to those able to attend in person, another result is the published volumes of proceedings from each of these events, which, taken together, provide a valuable source of information on these topics for the future and provide an insight into the evolution of national Antarctic program activity over the past 20 years.

In 1991 at the Antarctic Treaty Consultative Meeting (ATCM) XVI in Bonn, Germany, COMNAP was granted observer status, thereby joining only SCAR and the Commission of the Convention on Antarctic Marine Living Resources (CCAMLR) with this status at ATCMs. Having observer status is important, given that only formally designated observer organizations and the Consultative Parties to the Antarctic Treaty may prepare and present working papers at the annual ATCMs. Thus, COMNAP was given the ability to influence the political side of the system by delivering working papers at meetings that included recommendations to Antarctic Treaty Parties. In the 20 year period from 1988 to 2008, COMNAP prepared and presented a total of 18 working papers and almost 50 information papers, covering a range of topics from education and training to contingency planning and waste management.

The COMNAP also responds to requests from the ATCM. This is especially evident in the number of recommendations and measures of an operational nature which have requested COMNAP action or response that have been adopted by the ATCM over the past two decades.

The recommendations categorized as having an operational nature currently number 47.[4] Many of these are no longer valid given there have been significant changes to the operation environment and capabilities in Antarctica. Some of these recommendations required COMNAP to prepare a product or tool as guidance on matters or in support of the information exchange policy of the Antarctic Treaty System. Two such tools are the Antarctic Telecommunications Operational Manual (ATOM)[5] and the Antarctic Flight Information Manual (AFIM),[6] both of which remain in use, are updated on a regular basis, and are distributed widely.

For the 20th anniversary of the establishment of COMNAP, the members agreed to a proposal prepared by the executive committee to reconsider the role and purpose of COMNAP and to refocus much of COMNAP's efforts on managing the support of science. The change was a reflection of the diversity amongst the role of the managers of national Antarctic programs, most of whom are now assisted by a logistic manager who is in charge of many of the operational areas that were the previous focus of the SCAR WGL and SCALOP.

THE ROLE OF COMNAP TODAY

The council is still the primary forum for managers of national Antarctic programs. However, the purpose of COMNAP has evolved, reflecting the growing responsibilities of managers of national Antarctic programs. For example, many of the managers are involved in or often lead the development of their countries' Antarctic science strategy. More often than not, the national Antarctic program manager is responsible for the preparation and defense of their countries' Antarctic budget. The nature of national Antarctic program activity in Antarctica means that planning often takes place years before the actual season that is being planned. This requires not only an understanding of the national policy and strategy regarding Antarctica but also an understanding of the international considerations and an understanding of the science that is being proposed. So although there is often the misconception that managers are solely concerned with logistics, many of the managers never deal directly with logistics problems but, of course, need the ability to understand the requirements of logistics and operations since logistics and operations are what physically allow the delivery of scientific observations and results from Antarctica and international cooperation in scientific investigation there.

Even the COMNAP of 1988 recognized these as "matters of top priority and greatest management concern," listing the "establishment of scientific priorities and long term scientific goals" as its number one objective on the list from inaugural COMNAP discussions in 1987.[7]

The purpose of COMNAP as stated in its present constitution is to develop and promote best practices in managing the support of scientific research in Antarctica. The COMNAP achieves this purpose by

- serving as a forum to improve effectiveness of activities in an environmentally responsible manner;
- facilitating and promoting international partnerships;
- providing opportunities and systems for information exchange; and
- providing the Antarctic Treaty System with objective, practical, technical, and nonpolitical advice drawn from the national Antarctic programs' pool of expertise.

This is much broader than the role that the SCAR WGL and SCALOP played within the Antarctic Treaty System. Yet the misconception that COMNAP is only about logistics persists. The managers of national Antarctic programs control more than the logistics of their respective programs.

Managers of national Antarctic programs organize and fund the support to research (scientific and wider) that has been evaluated and approved at a national level, usually through a peer-review process, on the basis of the quality of the research and, of course, what they can actually physically support. Therefore, the managers are not just organizing support.

At the national level, the managers of national Antarctic programs are part of the strategic decision-making process about which Antarctic projects that will actually be supported. They are responsible for implementing their national scientific policies in Antarctica, and also, at the international level, they are the officers responsible for promoting and facilitating international partnerships in the spirit of the Antarctic Treaty, enabling scientists to fully participate and operate in the Antarctic as, when, and where their research requires.

The COMNAP is the organization that brings together national Antarctic programs. However, like the managers themselves, national Antarctic programs are diverse organizations with national reporting lines that vary, usually across a range of government ministries and departments. The physical assets of the 28 national Antarctic programs represented by COMNAP vary considerably as well. These assets include a range of aircraft, over 40 vessels, around 30 Antarctic airfields, over 37 year-round stations, equipment that sustains telecommunications and IT capabilities around the continent, and equipment required in support of deep field operations. Human capacity involves more than 1,100 people in the Antarctic in winter time and over 4,000 in summer time. These people, scientists and support staff, are themselves supported by a network of highly skilled people based in national Antarctic programs' home countries. In some cases the network includes support from military agencies and military personnel. In other cases, the network includes contracts with and support from nongovernmental organizations, charitable foundations, and commercial operators.

The roles that COMNAP plays and the tasks it undertakes reflect the diverse nature of its membership. Examples of the diversity of managers' work include

- reviewing scientific proposals and being part of the decision-making process of which projects should get approved every year;
- allocating funds for every scientific project;
- providing logistics in support of scientific research (requires expertise in management, field operations, transport, etc.);
- support in the event of an incident/accident involving human life (search and rescue);
- protecting the environment, which requires expertise in environmental management practices and an understanding of the legal obligations within the Antarctic Treaty System;
- outreach and education as it is often the national Antarctic program personnel who are requested to inform the media of issues related to Antarctica, prepare information for schools, and provide public presentations and displays; and
- data management and coordination (scientific data and other data related to more technical issues and information on vessels and stations).

The COMNAP's objectives to serve as a forum to support best practices and facilitate international partnerships stretch across all these categories.

Increasingly, regional, as opposed to bilateral, alliances are developing. Two examples are the Dronning Maud Land Air Network (DROMLAN) and the coordination of science in King George Island (Figure 3).

The DROMLAN air network facilitates communication and the transportation of scientists and equipment between Cape Town and Dronning Maud Land and between

FIGURE 3. Researchers on the Brazil-Chile–U.S. Climate of Antarctica and South America Deep Ice Core Drilling in the Antarctic Peninsula (CASA) project.

the scientific stations and field locations within Dronning Maud Land. Formally established as an international project at the XIV COMNAP Meeting in Shanghai during July 2002, it is supported by a consortium of the 11 national programs that have stations or operations in Dronning Maud Land. The network connects the 3,000 m ice runway at Novo Air Base, close to the Russian Novolazarevskaya Station, to Cape Town International Airport by an intercontinental flight. The Novo runway acts as a hub from which feeder flights by ski-equipped aircraft can connect to other stations and field locations within Dronning Maud Land. The DROMLAN is available to any member organization of COMNAP and any SCAR country for science-related activities, including logistics. The DROMLAN cooperation includes maintaining, improving, and operating two airfields in Dronning Maud Land close to the Novolazarevskaya (Russia) and Troll (Norway) stations for intercontinental flights from Cape Town; organizing intercontinental flights with appropriate aircraft to transport personnel and cargo between Cape Town and the airfields at Novolazarevskaya and Troll; organizing connecting flights with small ski-equipped aircraft to all stations and field destinations in Dronning Maud Land, including further options such as Vostok, South Pole, and the stations of the East Antarctic coastal region; and organizing the necessary support services, such as weather forecasting, provision of fuel, and accommodation at stations in Dronning Maud Land.

The second example, the King George Island project,[8] involves 10 countries and the collection and analysis of information from each of those countries regarding their activities on King George Island. The goal is to better coordinate science and logistics activities on the island in order to reduce duplication of activities. The project establishes a database that is simply a tool that includes information on research projects proposed, locations of each project, and principle investigators and their contact details. Geographic coordinates for each entry are also included so that the data and information can be analyzed via a GIS interface. This is a new project agreed to at the 2009 COMNAP AGM in Punta Arenas, Chile. Such a tool relies on the goodwill of the staff of national Antarctic programs, who will be responsible for input of data and information in a timely manner.

SCIENCE–POLICY INTERACTIONS

Aspects of all of these programs are of particular interest as we focus on science-policy interactions. Those aspects are as follows.

- Improving the effectiveness of national activities leads to increased efficiencies, so that we can carry out more science within the budget we get from our governments.
- More international collaboration means more and even better science with the same global budget and less duplication of efforts, that is, similar science output with fewer projects in the field.
- The nature of Antarctic science has evolved from cartographers drawing maps to interdisciplinary research activities that require expertise in foreword planning of complicated Antarctic research programs.[9]
- The decision-making process for the science to be supported has changed enormously in the last 50 years. Now the standard is to have a competitive peer-review system in which the managers and staff of national Antarctic programs are usually involved.

The COMNAP is in the process of becoming a project-oriented organization, more focused and strategic, concentrating on what COMNAP members, policy makers, and even the global general public might expect from such an organization. Presently, the development of a five-year work plan is underway. The work plan attempts to consider the national Antarctic program priorities in the near future and also addresses the key issues that are being considered in both the ATCM and at the Committee for Environmental Protection (CEP). Problems such as the prevention of the introduction of nonnative species into the Antarctic region require a collective response from the various organizations within the Antarctic Treaty System.

Antarctic science is generally more expensive than science in other parts of the world. Undoubtedly, all high-quality science projects deserve to be supported, but neither the money nor the infrastructure will always be available to support them as costs increase. Therefore, unless we can successfully communicate the value of Antarctic science to policy makers and to the general public, we may all have to cancel or defer some important projects until we can dedicate to them some of the limited time and money available. However, COMNAP can assist in this task by looking at what resources can be pooled and/or shared with others and looking at projects to see if they can be modified or associated with similar projects in other countries. The COMNAP has recognized a greater need for collaborative support.

DEVELOPING STRATEGIC PARTNERSHIPS

Perhaps because of the nature of COMNAP's birth, COMNAP has historically been an organization that has been inward looking, providing its membership with the framework they need to develop their own, usually bilateral, partnerships but shying away from the formal development of partnerships with other Antarctic organizations. It has also generally been slow to develop and promote strategic relationships with external organizations with goals that also support the spirit of the Antarctic Treaty System or that perform similar roles in the Arctic.

This behavior is changing, with COMNAP actively looking to strengthen its strategic partnerships with other Antarctic Treaty System bodies. Those strategic partnerships include SCAR, the CEP, and the International Association of Antarctica Tour Operators. This change is a reflection of the importance of identifying issues that require common action such as outreach, education, capacity building, data management, sustainability, and supporting the goals of peaceful use of and scientific cooperation in Antarctica.

COMNAP'S CONTRIBUTION TO THE SCIENCE–POLICY INTERFACE

Today, more than ever, COMNAP can be seen to be of value given the complex nature of Antarctic science questions being posed. Science programs often address key research questions, such as how the Antarctic system as a whole is responding to change. Such complex queries are increasingly becoming the norm. Complex science often requires multidisciplinary, multinational science teams and often demands reaching into new parts of the Antarctic, where those parts could be new surface, subsurface, atmosphere, or marine depths. The physical extent of Antarctic science is further than was ever previously possible.

Fifty years ago, Antarctic science was Antarctic presence. Although there is no denying that this is still the case, the ability for a nation to engage in Antarctic research activities is much more than that.

The COMNAP, as an organization, assists its members to successfully deliver their national Antarctic research programs and projects. Such programs are, generally, becoming bigger, are reaching out into previously unexplored areas of the Antarctic region (including into subglacial aquatic environments), and usually involve multinational and often interdisciplinary teams of researchers, support staff, IT/communications experts, health and safety practitioners, environmental consultants, outreach staff, and medical staff.

Member national Antarctic programs and COMNAP, with their wealth of firsthand Antarctic expertise, are well placed to face the Antarctic challenges of the future as they have in the past. National Antarctic programs discovered the ozone hole over Antarctica,[10] have drilled for the oldest ice core ever extracted,[11] have gathered data on the Census of Antarctic Marine Life covering millions of nautical miles,[12] and have plans to explore Antarctic subglacial lakes.[13] The diversity of activity reflects the diversity of the science questions that require exploration and support.

It seems the challenges of isolation and extreme environmental conditions are no longer an adequate barrier to the Antarctic region. We continue to see an increase in human activity in the Antarctic, whether from tourists, fishing industry personnel, or members of national Antarctic programs. Recognizing and responding to the increase is important not only from an environmental perspective but from the need to protect human life in the Antarctic.

The COMNAP, as one of its recent projects, convened two workshops on improving cooperation in regards to search and rescue (SAR) in the Antarctic. Even collectively, our capacity to respond to a large-scale accident or incident in the Antarctic region, on land and in the maritime environment, is extremely limited. Five marine rescue coordination centers, one each based in Australia, Argentina, Chile, New Zealand, and South Africa, have International Maritime Organization (IMO) responsibility for SAR activities over different areas of the marine area south of 60°S latitude (Figure 4).

However, even given that those SAR authorities had responsibility for certain parts of the maritime area around Antarctica, there was the perception that such authorities did little in the way of developing strategic relationships among themselves and even less between themselves and national Antarctic programs who, along with the fishing and tourist industry, were the primary operators in the waters.

The COMNAP presented the results of its most recent workshop on Antarctic search and rescue to the Antarctic Treaty Meeting of Experts on the Management of Shipborne Tourism in the Antarctic Treaty Area (ATME, December 2009, Wellington, New Zealand) and to ATCM XXXIII (2010, Punta del Este, Uruguay) in support of the COMNAP objective to provide practical and nonpolitical advice to the Antarctic Treaty System. This workshop is in addition to the Ship Position Reporting System (SPRS) that COMNAP developed and introduced. It is simply another example of the range of issues that COMNAP has played a lead role in for the development of guidance and policy on Antarctic issues and concerns.

CONCLUSION

Demonstrating a country's interest in Antarctica has become the role assigned to the national Antarctic

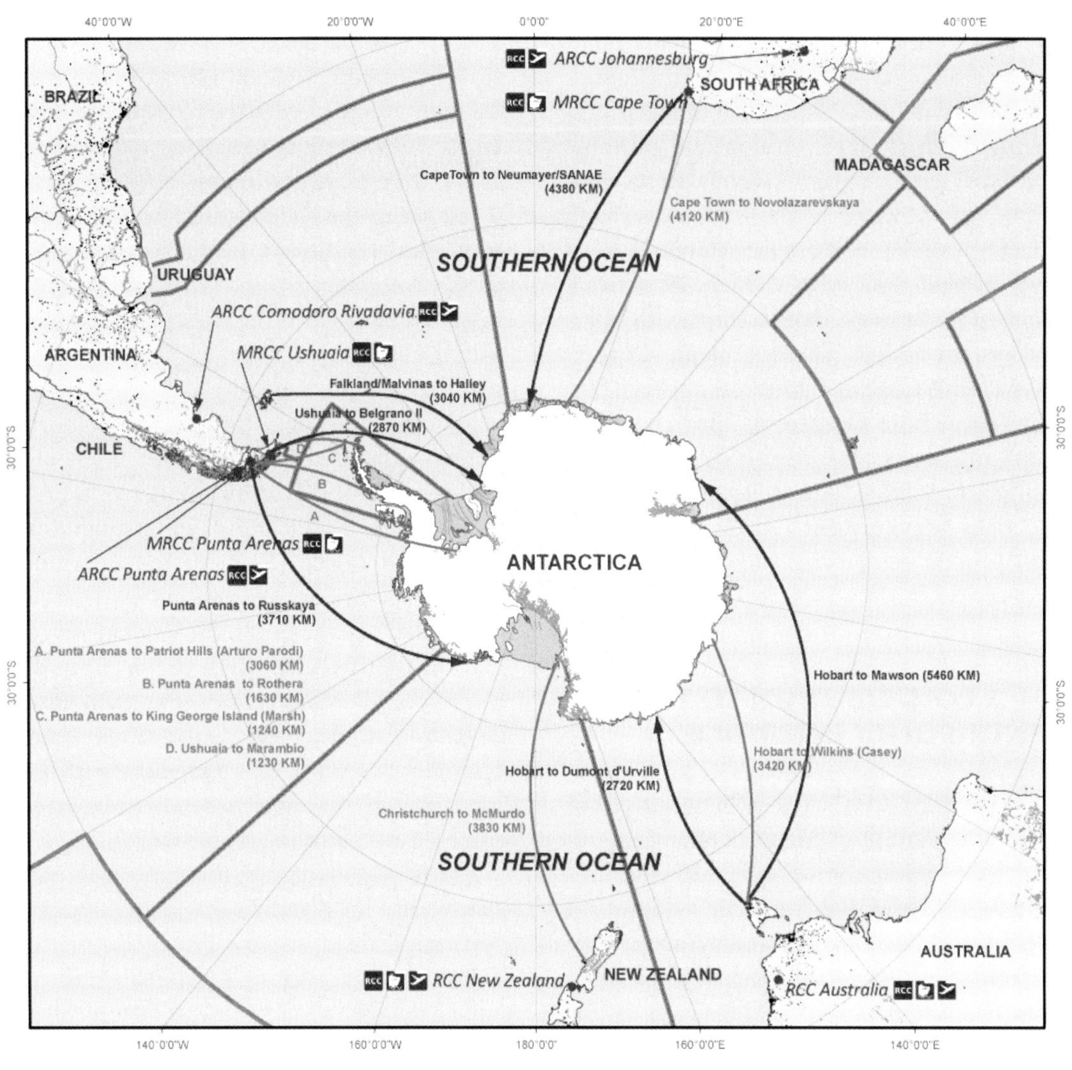

FIGURE 4. Map developed by COMNAP to assist rescue centers with search and rescue operations in the region.

programs of each Antarctic Treaty Consultative State. Many of these national Antarctic programs are broader than the scientific mandates that were the principle Consultative States when the Antarctic Treaty first entered into force. National Antarctic programs often contribute to outreach and education activities, provide input into science strategies and the funding that supports such strategic direction, contribute significantly to the environmental management of the area, and are often the greatest source of information on how the Antarctic is responding to change since their staff spend more time in the Antarctic region than anyone else does. This fundamental understanding of Antarctica from a practical and nonpolitical perspective will continue to be a strength of national Antarctic programs individually and a strength of COMNAP as an assembly of those programs. It is an understanding that is required of an area currently devoted to peaceful and scientific use and will also be of value in the future should the values we associate with the area be changed.

NOTES

1. See "History of the Institutionalisation of Antarctic Research," www.scar.org/about/history/, accessed May 2010.

2. A. N. Fowler, *COMNAP: The National Managers in Antarctica* (Baltimore, Md.: American Literary Press, 2000), p. 29.

3. Fowler, *COMNAP*, p. 8.

4. Antarctic Treaty Secretariat, "Review of the Status of ATCM Recommendations on Operational Matters," ATCM XXXIII Paper SP06 (Buenos Aires: Antarctic Treaty Secretariat, 2010).

5. ATCM Recommendation X-3 (1977) "Improvement of Telecommunications in the Antarctic." Note that the original request was for SCAR action since COMNAP did not exist in 1977. The COMNAP now takes responsibility for this publication.

6. ATCM Recommendation XV-20 (1989) "Air Safety in Antarctica."

7. Fowler, *COMNAP*, p. 44.

8. The working title of this project is Antarctic Peninsula Advanced Science Information System (APASI).

9. Antarctica's Gamburtsev Province Project (AGAP), Antarctic Drilling Project (ANDRILL), and the European Project for Ice Coring in Antarctica (EPICA) are only a few such recent projects. The establishment of multinational research stations in the Antarctic is another example of greater international cooperation.

10. See "The Ozone Hole: Science Briefing 2009", British Antarctic Survey, http://www.antarctica.ac.uk/press/journalists/resources/science/the_ozone_hole_2009.pdf (accessed 22 November 2010).

11. EPICA, 1996–2006, supported by the European Commission and national contributions from Belgium, Denmark, France, Germany, Italy, the Netherlands, Norway, Sweden, Switzerland, and the United Kingdom.

12. Census of Antarctic Marine Life (CAML), 2006–2009.

13. Including Lake Vostok, Lake Ellsworth, and Whillans Ice Stream (Whillans Ice Stream Subglacial Access Research Drilling, WISSARD).

International Cooperation and Management of Tourism: A World within a World

Denise Landau

Denise Landau, Associates Inc. 25 Dakota Meadows Dr. Carbondale, CO 81623 USA. Former Executive Director, International Association of Antarctica Tour Operators, iaato@iaato.org.

INTRODUCTION

Human activities in Antarctica have notably created a microcosm, a world within a world. Enthusiasts from more than 50 countries work in collaboration toward common objectives in the fields of science, logistics, tourism, policy, and law. Antarctic tourism exemplifies international cooperation, as science did beginning with the International Geophysical Year (IGY) of 1957–1958. Cooperation within the tourism industry and interaction with Antarctic Treaty Parties has successfully transcended political boundaries. The foresight in the development of the Antarctic Treaty in 1959 and the subsequent Antarctic Treaty System (ATS), their recommendations, resolutions, measures, and decisions for environmental protection and peaceful usage has shown its value. However, the management of tourism has essentially been left to the industry to operate responsibly. The tourism industry, meanwhile, has developed its own standards for over 40 years (International Association of Antarctica Tour Operators [IAATO], 2009, 2010a, 2010b), sometimes working in conjunction with the ATS, though more often than not advancing more rapidly because they were directly involved in on-site operations and less fettered by the requirements of a wider political consensus.

The tour operators, through the IAATO, observed firsthand what policies and procedures had to be introduced to protect the integrity of the wilderness and physical environment in Antarctica. Through industry interaction with the scientific community, protection of Antarctic ecosystems was possible by the development of numerous operational procedures to mitigate for potential impacts to historic sites, scientific study sites, and flora and fauna even prior to the adoption of the Protocol on Environmental Protection to the Antarctic Treaty in 1991 and subsequent policies linked to it. The IAATO was also formed in 1991, and since its inception, the tourism industry has grown. The concern toward environmental protection and safety grew in response, and subsequently, the industry developed over 45 voluntary procedures to proactively manage the complexities of industry growth, such as mandatory briefing to implement ATCM Recommendation XVIII-1 “Guidance for Those Organising and Conducting Tourism and Non-Governmental Activities in the Antarctic,” wildlife watching guidelines; site-specific guidelines; boot, clothing, and equipment decontamination guidelines; ship scheduling and communication requirements and procedures; emergency contingency planning; and many more (IAATO, 2009).

Procedures established for vessel operations through the vessels' flag states, ship classification societies, and international bodies such as the International Maritime Organization (IMO) have evolved to provide for safe operation of vessels and protection of human life in polar waters. The recent adoption of the Polar Shipping Guidelines by the IMO may also serve to enhance the safety of all vessels operating in polar regions. The future success of the industry group to effectively manage tourism will depend on its vigilance to enforce its own guidelines and work in close cooperation with groups such as the IMO and the ATS in order to assure that the most effective processes are in place and implemented. Can the industry continue to effectively regulate and manage its own activities as it has done in the past and what roles do the Antarctic Treaty Parties, national governments, and other regulatory bodies need to undertake in the future?

COOPERATION

Since the early 1960s, an unexpected element of human activity has arisen in Antarctica. The founders of the Antarctic Treaty did not anticipate tourism as a likely activity in Antarctica, nor could they have foreseen how rapidly it would thereafter develop. Upward of 40,000 tourists now visit Antarctica each year, compared with a small fraction of that number 40 years ago. A single commercial tour vessel in the early 1970s, MS *Lindblad Explorer*, led to the development of an industry that presently encompasses small, six-person yachts to 3000-passenger-capacity cruise ships and numerous aircraft as well as a diversification of both ship- and land-based activities, plus kayaking, camping, skiing, and climbing. Tour operators, crew, and expedition staff work together to operate safe and responsible voyages. Tourism development in the Antarctic and subantarctic islands (Landau, 2007) has since led to expeditioners exploring the Arctic, Amazon, and a myriad of coastlines worldwide with tourists. Multiple languages are spoken on nearly every Antarctic departure. Many of the expedition staff have migrated from science, policy, and logistics sectors within national program operations to extend their Antarctic careers by sharing their knowledge with tourists. Scientists, station staff, and accompanying research equipment are transported on tourist ships to and from the Antarctic. Numerous research projects have been initiated by scientists on the basis of their experience with tourist ships, and the funding for various environmental projects has come from donations from tour companies, suppliers, foundations, and tourists.

REGULATION AND MANAGEMENT

Yet in many ways, regulation of tourism remains an enormous challenge. Because the Antarctic tourism industry has established selected standards and procedures ahead of government regulation, a quandary has developed for regulators. Antarctic Treaty Parties (ATPS) spend considerable time in discussions involving tourism practices and whether they are acceptable. The ATPS are the decision makers for Antarctica, but time-consuming hurdles of discussion and mutual agreement become obstacles because of the consensus requirement. The consensus process has both pros and cons relative to tourism. From the tourism standpoint, the operators have steamed ahead at a remarkable pace, developing the noted operational procedures to manage tourism. Conversely, the ATPS are lagging behind in either adopting the industry standards or creating their own because of the difficulty in reaching a consensus on whether or not a procedure is effective. In order to match the uneven pace of development, it has now reached a point where a new way forward could be forged, creating an innovative partnership between law, science, and tourism, consistent with the spirit of the Antarctic Treaty. Since Antarctica is not owned by any one country, the sheer diversification of countries' legal processes, tour operators, and tourists representing over 60 countries from around the world calls for a robust cooperative process to assure the long-term protection of Antarctica. The industry group IAATO needs to maintain its global outreach program and to not be seen as too attached to any one ATP, and the ATPs could look more realistically at officially adopting important operational procedures to even out the fast-paced guidelines developed by the industry.

The industry believes that tourism has been successfully managed and regulated by voluntary guidelines or best practices since the 1960s, well before the formation of the IAATO in 1991 (Splettstoesser, 1999, 2000). From the point of view of environmental protection, this modus operandi is a precarious situation. Is good will enough? Laws passed by governments or operational requirements set forth by shipping-related organizations such as the

IMO, ship classification societies, ship registries, etc., or aviation authorities are more rigorously being considered, as tourism numbers and vessel incidents have increased. The industry currently has little ability or authority to impose legal restrictions or limit the operations of any company active in Antarctica. Yet it has achieved remarkable success in working with industry competitors to develop agreed management techniques thus far.

The makeup of the tourism industry has changed dramatically from single-family-owned businesses to large, globalized corporations. The strong sense of stewardship and environmental protection now relies primarily on the expedition staff, whereas in the past it was the policy of the company owners, many of whom were also the expedition leaders. Some critics claim that without legal oversight and jurisdiction, the self-regulatory nature of the industry must change so that the ATPS can resolve situations by stronger action.

Since 2005, there has been an annual increase in incidents involving tourist vessels in Antarctica. One specific incident ignited the interest of the international shipping regulators and the ATPs: the sinking of the MS *Explorer* on 23 November 2007. The vessel sank in the Bransfield Strait 40.23 km southeast of King George Island in the Antarctic Peninsula. All 91 passengers, 9 expedition staff, and 54 crew were safely rescued by another tourist vessel that was sailing nearby. There were no human casualties, no major injuries, and only one minor injury. The vessel hit ice, resulting in a 3.1 m hole in the hull of the ship (Bureau of Maritime Affairs, 2009). This sole example served as a sort of wake-up call. The close cooperation within the industry itself, their computerized ship-scheduling program, the master contact list of all tourist vessels and air operators, and the ability to produce timely information on the vessel's progress (IAATO, 2009), as well as favorable weather averted a disaster. Passengers, crew, and expedition staff were rescued from the MS *Explorer*'s Zodiacs and lifeboats and transferred to another tourist vessel, the MV *Nordnorge*. In addition, the MS *Endeavour* remained in regular contact in case another vessel was required to assist. The MV *Nordnorge* sailed directly to King George Island and disembarked all rescued persons from the MS *Explorer* at the Chilean Base Presidente Frei. Airplanes were chartered from Uruguay and Chile, and everyone was flown to Punta Arenas, Chile, to connect with onward flights home. The industry demonstrated that the operating practices that IAATO had in place proved to be effective. From the time the ship's captain issued a Mayday call, all vessels operating in Antarctica were on standby and ready to assist. The IAATO office personnel kept all its members, vessels, governments, stakeholders, and the press from around the world advised of developments. Potential environmental impacts (e.g., fuel, hardware being washed ashore, etc.) were monitored for the remainder of the Antarctic season by industry operators. It was a monumental effort by industry and some governments and national program operators. The sinking of the MS *Explorer* served to illustrate the grave importance of the industry group working closely together and with the ATPs.

Recently, the IMO and the ATPs have emphasized the need for the international acceptance of the Polar Shipping Code, a document that has been in draft form for nearly 10 years. The IMO has banned the use of heavy fuels in Antarctica, posing challenges to both large cruise ships and expedition ships, which prefer to burn the less-expensive, sulfur-laden heavy fuel. The tourism industry has responded by collaborating on a tiered risk assessment approach, intended to provide tour operators with a framework for voyage planning and risk assessment and also a structure for governments to use in their permitting and authorization of tourism activities in Antarctica.

CONCLUSION

The continuing efforts of the tourist industry and the ATPs to achieve a high level of protection of the environment, its marine and terrestrial ecosystems, and human life in Antarctica have shown success in resolving issues as they arise. An acceptable working solution, tourism self-regulation, remains until the ATPs and the industry reach a mutual agreement on a process that satisfies both. In 1959, the signatories of the Antarctic Treaty boldly agreed one of the most powerful strategies the world had ever seen. As human activities have increased in Antarctica, we have reached yet another crossroad. How do we manage the increase of our human footprint in Antarctica? Keeping with the spirit of the Antarctic Treaty, a holistic approach to the management and regulation of not just tourism but all human activities is needed. What better gift can we give future generations than new management tools to protect one of the greatest marine and terrestrial wildernesses on Earth?

LITERATURE CITED

Bureau of Maritime Affairs. 2009. Decision of the Commissioner of Maritime Affairs R.L. and the Report of Investigation in the Matter of Sinking of the Passenger Vessel Explorer (O.N. 8495) 23 November 2007 in the Bransfield Strait and South Shetland Islands. Monrovia, Liberia.

International Association of Antarctica Tour Operators (IAATO). 2008. Regulation of Antarctic Tourism: A Marine Perspective. ATCM XXXI Information Paper IP 83. Providence, R.I.: IAATO. http://www.iaato.org/info.html (accessed June 2008).

———. 2009. IAATO Field Operations Manual. ATCM XXXII Information Paper IP 87. Providence, R.I.: IAATO. http://www.iaato.org/info.html (accessed July 2009).

———. 2010a. IAATO Bylaws. http://www.iaato.org/bylaws.html (accessed July 2010).

———. 2010b. Guidelines: Tour Operators. http://www.iaato.org/guidelines.html (accessed July 1994).

International Maritime Organization (IMO). 2010. Ships Operating in Polar Regions. London: IMO. http://www.imo.org/OurWork/Safety/SafetyTopics/Pages/PolarShippingSafety.aspx (accessed June 2009).

Landau, D. 2007. Tourism in Polar Regions and the Sub-Antarctic Islands. *Papers and Proceedings of the Royal Society of Tasmania*, 141(1):173–179.

Splettstoesser, J. 1999. "Antarctica Tourism: Successful Management of a Vulnerable Environment." In *Development of Tourism in Critical Environments,* ed. T. V. Singh and S. Singh, pp. 137–148. New York: Cognizant Communications Corporation.

———. 2000. IAATO's Stewardship of the Antarctic Environment. *International Journal of Tourism Research*, 2(1):47–55.

Ocean Dumping and Fertilization in the Antarctic: Tangled Legal Currents, Sea of Challenges

David L. VanderZwaag

ABSTRACT. The law and policy framework governing potential ocean disposals in the Antarctic is surveyed using two nautical images. First, the "tangle of legal currents" is described with a focus on six global agreements relevant to ocean dumping and the 1991 Protocol on Environmental Protection to the Antarctic Treaty (Madrid Protocol). The Madrid Protocol strictly controls the disposal of wastes generated in the Antarctic region through various removal obligations. Second, the "sea of challenges" surrounding effective control of ocean dumping is highlighted. Those challenges include ensuring full adoption and implementation of international agreements relevant to ocean dumping, getting an effective governance grip on ocean fertilization projects, and securing strong compliance with the two key global agreements targeting ocean dumping, the Convention on the Prevention of Marine Pollution by Dumping of Wastes and Other Matter, 1972 (London Convention) and the 1996 Protocol to the London Convention.

INTRODUCTION

Two nautical images help capture the international governance of potential ocean dumping and ocean fertilization activities in the Antarctic. First is "tangled legal currents." A complex mix of global and regional agreements may interact to control ocean disposals in the Southern Ocean. Second is a "sea of challenges." Effective control of ocean dumping faces numerous constraints, including ensuring full adoption and implementation by states of key international agreements, getting a firm international grip on ocean fertilization projects, and securing compliance with ocean-dumping-related instruments.

A two-part "cruise" follows. The tangle of international agreements addressing ocean dumping is first surveyed, followed by a tour of three major challenges being faced in implementation practice. A particular focus is given to the law and policy challenges raised by proposed ocean fertilization experiments in the Southern Ocean. Does ocean fertilization constitute dumping? What international law and policy responses have occurred? What can be learned from a recent ocean fertilization experiment in the Atlantic sector of the Southern Ocean, the LOHAFEX experiment[1], led by the Alfred Wegener Institute for Polar and Marine Research?

David L. VanderZwaag, Schulich School of Law, Marine & Environmental, Law Institute, Dalhousie University, 6061 University Avenue, Halifax, Nova Scotia B3H 4H9, Canada. Correspondence: david.vanderzwaag@dal.ca. This chpater attempts to be accurate as of 1 December 2009.

TANGLED LEGAL CURRENTS

The tangle of international legal currents relevant to potential ocean disposals in the Southern Ocean involves six global and two regional agreements. At the global level, the 1982 UN Law of the Sea Convention[2] might be viewed as a major foundational "undercurrent," and two agreements, the 1972 London (Dumping) Convention[3] and the 1996 Protocol to the London Convention,[4] might be described as the "mainstreams" for ocean dumping control. Three other global agreements might be characterized as "side currents" as they more tangentally address potential ocean disposals. Those agreements are the Convention on Biological Diversity (1992),[5] the Basel Convention on the Transboundary Movement of Hazardous Wastes and Their Disposal (1989),[6] and the Joint Convention on the Safety of Spent Fuel Management and on the Safety of Radioactive Waste Management (1997).[7] Two "regional gyres" complete the regulatory current picture, namely, the Antarctic Treaty (1959)[8] and the Madrid Protocol on Environmental Protection to the Antarctic Treaty (1991).[9] A synopsis of these key global and regional agreements follows. This paper does not address the regulation of discharges from ships, such as sewage and garbage, covered by the International Convention for the Prevention of Pollution from Ships (MARPOL 73/78) (IMO, 2006).

Six Key Global Agreements

The Major "Undercurrent"

The 1982 UN Law of the Sea Convention (LOSC) sets out various general marine environmental protection responsibilities of states, e.g., the obligation to protect and preserve the marine environment (Article 192) and the duty to minimize the release of toxic, harmful, or noxious substances into the marine environment (Article 194, paragraph 3(a)). The LOSC also provides environmental impact assessment (EIA) requirements such as undertaking EIAs for planned activities under the jurisdiction or control of states that may cause substantial pollution or significant and harmful changes to the marine environment (Article 206) and reporting of results (Article 205). The LOSC specifically targets ocean dumping (Article 210) by requiring states to adopt national ocean dumping laws no less effective than global standards, urging states to establish global and regional rules/standards for controlling pollution by dumping and mandating the express prior consent of the coastal state for any dumping within national zones of jurisdiction

A major potential limitation in the control of potential ocean dumping off the Antarctic continent is the lack of generally recognized coastal states with authority to legislate and enforce national laws against foreign vessels (Vigni, 2001) that might engage in ocean disposals. A sector of the Antarctic remains unclaimed (Watts, 1992). The historic territorial claims by seven states (Argentina, Australia, Chile, France, New Zealand, Norway, and the United Kingdom) remain "frozen" pursuant to Article 4 of the Antarctic Treaty (Gautier, 1992; Joyner, 1992, 1998), and thus, flag state not coastal state jurisdiction stands as the prime means of legal control (Zovko, 2007).

"Mainstreams"

The 1972 London Convention represents a permissive approach to ocean dumping (VanderZwaag and Daniel, 2009). Almost anything can be dumped at sea if a permit is granted by a state party. General permits for most types of waste are covered in Annex III of the convention, which sets out various factors decision makers must carefully consider before issuing a permit, such as characteristics of the waste (e.g., toxicity, persistence, oxygen demand, and nutrients) and characteristics of the dumping site and method of deposit (e.g., distance from the coast and resource exploitation areas, dispersal potentialities, and existing pollutant loads). General considerations include possible effects on marine living resources, possible effects on other uses of the sea (such as fishing, shipping, and marine conservation areas), and practical availability of alternative land-based methods of disposal or treatment. Special permits may be granted for Annex II–listed wastes (the "grey list") which include, for example, wastes containing arsenic, chromium, copper, lead, nickel, zinc, cyanides, and fluorides, but particular care in disposal must be taken. Only a limited prohibited list of wastes are listed in Annex I where ocean dumping is generally not allowed: organohalogen compounds, mercury and mercury compounds, cadmium and cadmium compounds, persistent plastics, crude oil and its wastes, radioactive wastes, biological and chemical warfare materials, industrial waste, and incineration at sea of industrial waste and sewage sludge.

The 1996 Protocol to the London Convention shifts toward a precautionary approach (VanderZwaag and Daniel, 2009). The protocol explicitly recognizes the need for a precautionary approach in Article 3, paragraph 1: "In implementing this Protocol, Contracting Parties shall apply a precautionary approach to environmental protection from dumping of wastes or other matter whereby appropriate preventative measures are taken when there is reason to believe that wastes or other matter introduced into the marine environment are likely to cause harm even where there is no conclusive evidence to prove a causal relation between impacts and their effects."

The protocol also adopts a "reverse listing" approach where listing favours the environment and is precautionary. Nothing can be dumped unless it is listed on a "safe list," i.e., dredged material; sewage sludge; fish wastes; vessels and platforms or other man-made structures; inert, inorganic geological material; organic materials of natural origin; and bulky items primarily comprising iron, steel, concrete, and similarly unharmful materials for which concern is physical impact (limited to where wastes are generated at locations having no practicable access to disposal options other than dumping). Sequestration of carbon dioxide under the seabed has also been added to the "safe list" through an amendment adopted 2 November 2006 and in force 10 February 2007.

Even for wastes on the safe list, Annex 2 of the protocol further encourages a precautionary approach through the permitting process (de La Fayette, 1998). The permitting authority is encouraged to require ocean dumping applicants to undertake waste prevention audits, i.e., whether waste reduction or prevention at source is feasible, for example, through product reformulation or clean production technologies. If so, applicants should be required to formulate a waste prevention strategy, and waste reduction and prevention requirements should be included as permit conditions. The permitting authority is obligated to refuse issuing a permit if appropriate opportunities exist to reuse, recycle, or treat the waste without undue risks to human health or the environment or disproportionate costs. The permitting authority is also urged to deny an ocean dumping permit if an environmental assessment does not include adequate information to determine the likely effects of the proposed disposal.

"Side Currents"

The 1992 Convention on Biological Diversity (CBD), although not dealing directly with ocean dumping, might be described as "side venue" on various counts. The convention may be relevant to EIA of proposed ocean disposal activities as the convention requires parties to ensure their EIA procedures address project impacts on biological diversity with a view to avoiding or minimizing significant adverse effects (Article 14, paragraph 1(a)). Voluntary guidelines on biodiversity-inclusive impact assessment have been developed (CBD, 2006), and further guidance for the implementation of EIA for activities that may have significant impacts on marine biological diversity beyond national jurisdiction was provided through an Expert Workshop on Scientific and Technical Aspects Relevant to EIA in Areas Beyond National Jurisdiction held in November 2009 (CBD, 2009). The convention has also become a forum discussing the scientific and governance challenges posed by ocean fertilization projects. A *Scientific Synthesis of the Impacts of Ocean Fertilization on Marine Biodiversity* was published in 2009 (Secretariat of the Convention on Biological Diversity, 2009), and the Conference of the Parties has advocated a precautionary approach be taken toward proposed ocean fertilization activities, as discussed further below.

The 1989 Basel Convention on the Transboundary Movement of Hazardous Wastes and Their Disposal prohibits the export of hazardous wastes for disposal within the area south of 60°S latitude (Article 4, paragraph 6). The convention leaves implementation of the prohibition to each party through national legislation.

The 1997 Joint Convention on the Safety of Spent Nuclear Fuel Management and on the Safety of Radioactive Waste Management represents a parallel current to the Basel Convention, but with a focus on preventing the disposal of radioactive wastes in the Antarctic. Article 27, paragraph 2, of the convention requires contracting parties not to licence the shipment of spent fuel or radioactive waste to a destination south of latitude 60°S for storage or disposal.

Regional Gyres

The 1959 Antarctic Treaty, which mainly encourages scientific cooperation, is relevant to potential ocean dumping in two main ways. Article V prohibits radioactive waste disposal in the area south of 60°S latitude. Article VII, paragraph 5, requires each contracting party to give notice to other contracting parties of all proposed expeditions to and within Antarctica on the part of ships or nationals. This provision could cover future proposed ocean disposal activities, such as ocean fertilization, a topic further discussed below.

The 1991 Madrid Protocol on Environmental Protection to the Antarctic Treaty contains three main "legal eddies" relevant to ocean disposal. First, Annex III specifically addresses wastes generated in the Antarctic in four main ways (minimization, removal, disposal, and planning requirements). The protocol urges minimizing the amount of wastes produced in the Antarctic as far as practicable (Article 1, paragraph 2). Article 2, paragraph 1, requires the removal of many generated wastes.

Generators of many wastes produced after entry into force of the annex must remove them from the Antarctic Treaty area, e.g., radioactive materials; electrical batteries; fuels; wastes with harmful levels of heavy metals or acutely toxic compounds; various products that could produce harmful emissions if incinerated such as rubber, lubricating oils, treated timbers, and polyvinyl chloride materials; plastic wastes; and fuel drums and other solid, noncombustible wastes (unless greater adverse environmental impacts would result than leaving them in their existing locations). Article 3, paragraph 1, imposes disposal obligations by incineration for combustible wastes, other than those wastes listed in Article 2, paragraph 1 (such as plastics, batteries, rubber, and treated timbers), not removed from the Antarctic. Solid residues of incineration also must be removed from the treaty area. Sea disposal of sewage and domestic liquid wastes is allowed subject to various conditions (Article 5): taking into account the assimilative capacity of the receiving environment, locating discharge areas where rapid dispersal occurs, and treating large quantities of waste (generated in stations having an average weekly occupancy over the austral summer of approximately 30 individuals or more) at least by maceration. The protocol further mandates parties carrying out activities in the Antarctic Treaty area to prepare waste management plans (Article 8) to be annually reviewed and updated and shared with other parties and sent to the Committee for Environmental Protection, which may review and offer comments (Article 9).

A second eddy is stirred by Article 3 of the protocol, which sets out principles to be followed for proposed activities in the Antarctic (which could include ocean disposals). Activities should avoid significant adverse effects on air or water quality, avoid further jeopardy to endangered or threatened species, and be based on sufficient information for prior environmental impact assessment.

The third eddy is the establishment of three levels of EIA for activities in the treaty area (Article 8 and Annex I). Those levels are preliminary assessment (if an activity is determined to have less than a minor or transitory impact it may proceed), initial environmental evaluation (IEE; if an activity is determined as likely to have a minor or transitory impact), and comprehensive environmental evaluation (CEE; if an IEE indicates the potential for more than a minor or transitory impact or that determination is otherwise made). The draft CEE is subject to review/comment through the Committee for Environmental Protection and Antarctic Treaty Consultative Meeting (ATCM). The final CEE must address comments received.

SEA OF CHALLENGES

An array of challenges surrounds the governance of ocean dumping. Three major challenges are highlighted below: ensuring full adaption of key international agreements relevant to ocean dumping, getting a firm legal grip on ocean fertilization projects, and securing compliance with ocean dumping related treaty obligations. Other constraints beyond the scope of this paper but discussed elsewhere (VanderZwaag and Daniel, 2009) include keeping up with the numerous guidelines surrounding ocean dumping, sorting out the boundaries of the London Convention/Protocol with other international agreements, such as MARPOL 73/78, providing adequate financial and technical assistance, addressing liability and compensation, and ensuring adequate enforcement.

Ensuring Full Adoption of Key International Agreements

An ongoing concern in relation to potential ocean disposals in the Southern Ocean is the limited adoption by states of the key global and regional agreements aimed at preventing and controlling ocean dumping activities. As of 31 October 2009 there were only 86 parties to the 1972 London Convention, comprising 67.09% of world tonnage, and only 37 parties to the 1996 Protocol to the London Convention (hereafter referred to as the 1996 Protocol), comprising 32.22% of world tonnage.[10] There are limited parties (47) to the Antarctic Treaty (28 consultative and 19 nonconsultative), and only 34 parties to the Madrid Protocol.[11]

Thus, the window remains open for vessels not flagged by state parties to the relevant conventions to sidestep the various legal obligations. The effectiveness of the Antarctic Treaty System in light of vessels flagged to nonparties has been especially worrisome in relation to tourist vessels (New Zealand, 2007), but the range of concerns is much broader than tourism activities and could extend to ocean dumping.

Getting a Firm International Legal Grip on Ocean Fertilization Projects

The international control of proposed ocean fertilization projects, exemplified by adding iron to increase phytoplankton blooms and the fixation of CO_2 from the atmosphere, might be described as slippery. Controversy has arisen over application of the ocean dumping regime to ocean fertilization projects with considerable fragmentation and uncertainties in international responses to date (Sagarin et al., 2007; Freestone and Rayfuse, 2008; Rayfuse et al., 2008). The limited international "grip" is exemplified by the 2009 LOHAFEX ocean fertilization experiment in the Atlantic sector of the Southern Ocean.

A first slippery aspect is how proposed ocean fertilization activities relate to the two global ocean dumping agreements. Differing views have emerged over whether ocean fertilization projects constitute ocean dumping as defined in the 1972 London Convention and 1996 Protocol as "any deliberate disposal at [into the] sea of wastes or other matter from vessels, aircraft, platforms or other man-made structures at sea." "Yes" views argue iron does constitute dumping as the "iron matter" is deposited deliberately and is abandoned, whereas "no" views posit that deliberate iron deposits are not undertaken for disposal purposes but for constructive purposes such as marine scientific research (IMO, 2008a, 2008b).

Perspectives have also differed on whether ocean fertilization projects might fall under a major exception found in both 1972 London Convention and the 1996 Protocol as "'dumping' does not include . . . placement of matter for a [the] purpose other than the mere disposal thereof, provided that such placement is not contrary to the aims of this convention [protocol]." Disagreements exist over whether ocean fertilizations are placements (with a possible restricted meaning of placing with the ability to retrieve), and a lack of clarity surrounds what placements would be contrary to the aims of the convention (IMO, 2008a, 2008b).

Even if ocean fertilization is deemed subject to the ocean dumping regime, questions of prohibition or permitting requirements arise. Under the 1972 London Convention, could iron be an industrial waste listed on Annex 1 and thus be prohibited from disposal at sea? Or would the special or general permitting requirement apply? Under the 1996 Protocol, is iron an inert, inorganic, geological material that is allowed to be dumped? The fact that adding iron to marine waters is meant to catalyze growth of phytoplankton supports a conclusion against inertness (IMO, 2008c).[12]

A second slippery aspect is the considerable fragmentation and uncertainties in international responses to ocean fertilization proposals to date. A fragmented array of international bodies/institutions have offered statements/decisions regarding ocean fertilization, e.g., the Conference of the Parties to the CBD at their ninth meeting, scientific groups and meetings of the parties to the London Convention and 1996 Protocol, the International Oceanographic Commission ad hoc Consultative Group on Ocean Fertilization, and the Intergovernmental Panel on Climate Change (IMO, 2008e).

Considerable uncertainties remain in the wake of two of the most important international pronouncements/processes. In 2008 the Ninth Conference of the Parties to the CBD adopted Decision IX/16 on biodiversity and climate change, which urged parties and other governments to adopt a precautionary approach to ocean fertilization. The text called upon parties and other governments:

> [I]n accordance with the precautionary approach, to ensure that ocean fertilization activities do not take place until there is an adequate scientific basis on which to justify such activities, including assessing associated risks, and a global, transparent and effective control and regulatory mechanism is in place for these activities; with the exception of *small scale scientific research studies within coastal waters*. Such studies should only be authorized if justified by the need to gather specific scientific data, and should also be subject to a thorough prior assessment of the potential impacts of the research studies on the marine environment, and be strictly controlled, and not be used for generating and selling carbon offsets or any other commercial purposes. (emphasis added)[13]

The text left major questions outstanding regarding what ocean fertilization projects were allowable. What are small-scale scientific studies? What are coastal waters?

Key uncertainties also surround the numerous efforts to address ocean fertilization under the London Convention and 1996 Protocol. In June 2007, the Scientific Groups to the London Convention and Protocol issued a statement of concern regarding iron fertilization to sequester CO_2 and took the view that knowledge about the effectiveness and potential environmental impacts of ocean fertilization currently was insufficient to justify large-scale operations (IMO, 2007a). The statement of concern, subsequently endorsed by the governing bodies at their meeting in November 2007 (IMO, 2007b), was not clear regarding what would constitute "large-scale operations."

In October 2008, the governing bodies issued Resolution LC-LP.1 on the "Regulation of Ocean Fertilization," which also raised various uncertainties. The parties agreed that in order to provide for legitimate scientific research, such research should be regarded as placement of matter for a purpose other than mere disposal thereof; scientific research proposals should be assessed on a case-by-case basis using an assessment framework to be developed by the scientific groups; until specific assessment guidance is available, parties should be urged to use utmost caution and the best available guidance to evaluate scientific research proposals to ensure marine environmental protection consistent with the convention/protocol; and given the present state of knowledge, ocean fertilization activities other than legitimate scientific research should not be allowed and such other activities should be considered as contrary to the aims of the convention/protocol (IMO, 2008d).

What precisely constitutes legitimate scientific research remained hazy. This was especially the case since the "assessment framework for scientific research involving ocean fertilization" had yet to be finalized.

The Intersessional Legal and Related Issues Working Group on Ocean Fertilization, established in 2008, developed at its meeting in February 2009 eight decision options for further addressing ocean fertilization (IMO, 2009a). Options ran from nonbinding (e.g., a further statement concern or resolution) to binding (e.g., a stand-alone article on ocean fertilization or an amendment of Annex I to the 1996 Protocol). Australia and New Zealand considered the simplest and most effective way of regulating legitimate scientific research involving ocean fertilization would be to add a new paragraph to Annex I (the global safe list): "material or substances for which the principal intention is ocean fertilization for legitimate scientific research" (IMO, 2009b). At the time of writing, there was no consensus yet on the best option, and the Intersessional Working Group on Ocean Fertilization was tasked with continuing the discussions with a meeting proposed for March 2010 (IMO, 2009c).

The limited "international grip" reality is exemplified by the 2009 LOHAFEX experiment, the joint iron fertilization experiment carried out in January–March 2009 by the Alfred Wegener Institute for Polar and Marine Research (AWI) and the National Institute of Oceanography (India). Approximately 6 tonnes of dissolved iron were applied to a 300 km^2 area outside the Antarctic Treaty area in an eddy around 48°S, 16°W (AWI, 2009a). Considerable criticisms emanated from environmental nongovernmental organizations as an alleged violation of the CBD's moratorium (only small-scale scientific research studies in coastal waters allowed). No international EIA process was applicable. The project fell outside the Madrid Protocol's EIA provisions since it took place outside the Antarctic Treaty area. A scientific risk assessment was conducted by AWI and the National Institute of Oceanography (AWI, 2009b), and on behalf of the Federal Ministry of Education and Science (Germany) further reviews of the risk assessment were solicited from various institutions (including from the British Antarctic Survey, University of Heidelberg, and University of Kiel).[14] The risk assessment interpreted the CBD criteria broadly. The project was a spatial small-scale experiment covering just 300 km^2 compared to the 50 million km^2 covered by the Antarctic Circumpolar Current and involved coastal waters as coastal plankton species inhabit the offshore fertilized waters (AWI, 2009b).

Securing Compliance

One of the greatest compliance challenges is the failure by many parties to the London Convention and the 1996 Protocol to report on the nature and quantity of wastes permitted to be dumped at sea (as required by Article VI, paragraph 4, of the convention and Article 9, paragraph 4, of the protocol). For 2007 (latest year for which annual reporting was available) only 35 contracting parties provided a national report, and 53 contracting parties did not report (IMO, 2009d). Thirty-three contracting parties had not submitted reports in the last five years (IMO, 2009e)!

It remains to be seen how effectively a Compliance Group, established in 2007, will facilitate compliance with reporting requirements. The Compliance Group's questionnaire asking parties to explain reasons for not reporting received only 18 protocol parties' responses, and only two convention parties answered (IMO, 2009f). The Compliance Group, at its second meeting in October 2009, recommended as a first step establishing or reestablishing contact with parties not reporting and suggested as a second step developing a comprehensive database on parties having national implementing legislation in order to ascertain whether national permitting requirements exist for which reporting would be mandatory (IMO, 2009f). The Compliance Group has authority to address noncompliance by individual parties, but the noncompliance procedure has not been invoked yet.

CONCLUSION

Ocean dumping in the Southern Ocean from outside the region is not reportedly occurring.[15] This is likely for two main reasons: preference by disposers to dispose of wastes in areas within national 200 nautical mile zones because of cost savings and hazardous and radioactive waste export prohibitions to the Antarctic Treaty area pursuant to the Basel Convention and Joint Convention on Spent Nuclear Fuel and Radioactive Waste Management, respectively.

The Madrid Protocol has substantially curtailed the ocean disposal of wastes generated within the Antarctic region with the exception of sewage and domestic liquid wastes. Although the protocol requires cleanups of waste sites located on land (Article 1, paragraph 5), the protocol does not impose a parallel requirement to address past dumping of wastes in the ocean. Thus, the need to clean up historical offshore dumping sites could become a future issue.[16]

The greatest challenge on the law and policy horizon relating to ocean dumping appears to be possible future ocean fertilization experiments in the Antarctic region. Six iron enrichment experiments have already occurred in the Southern Ocean (Strong et al., 2009), and potential negative effects of large-scale fertilizations, such as creating anoxic regions, altering marine food webs, and increasing ocean acidity, remain a concern (Cullen and Boyd, 2008; Denman, 2008) as does the potential for substantial nitrous oxide production (Law, 2008). Although considerable uncertainty surrounds the future scale and numbers of ocean fertilization initiatives, in light of experiments like LOHAFEX, where carbon sequestration was smaller than expected, and because of the serious difficulty in verifying net greenhouse gas reduction (Strong et al., 2009), one thing is certain. Getting a firm international governance grip on ocean fertilization proposals remains an "unfinished voyage."

NOTES

1. "LOHA" is the Hindi word for iron, and "FEX" refers to fertilization experiment.

2. "United Nations Convention on the Law of the Sea," 10 December 1982, 21 *International Legal Materials* (ILM) 1261.

3. "Convention on the Prevention of Marine Pollution by Dumping of Wastes and Other Matter," 29 December 1972, 11 ILM 1291.

4. "Protocol to the Convention on the Prevention of Marine Pollution by Dumping of Wastes and Other Matter," 7 November 1996, 36 ILM 1 (1997).

5. "Convention on Biological Diversity," 5 June 1992, 31 ILM 818.

6. "Basel Convention on the Control of Transboundary Movements of Hazardous Wastes and Their Disposal," 22 March 1989, http://www.basel.int/text/documents.html (accessed 27 November 2009).

7. "Joint Convention on the Safety of Spent Fuel Management and on the Safety of Radioactive Waste Management," 29 September 1997, International Atomic Energy Agency INFCIRC/546 (24 December 1997).

8. "Antarctic Treaty," 1 December 1959, 402 *United Nations Treaty Series* 71.

9. "Protocol on Environmental Protection to the Antarctic Treaty," 4 October 1991, 30 ILM 1455.

10. IMO, "Summary of Status of Conventions," http://www.imo.org/Conventions/mainframe.asp?topic_id=247 (accessed 20 November 2009).

11. Secretariat of the Antarctic Treaty, "Parties," http://www.ats.aq/devAS/ats_parties.aspx?lang=e (accessed 8 November 2009).

12. "Revised Specific Guidelines for the Assessment of Inert, Inorganic Geological Material," adopted in 2008, further clarify that the term "inert" is intended to ensure that the only impacts of concern following dumping are restricted to physical effects (IMO, 2008d: Annex 4).

13. Convention on Biological Diversity, "COP 9 Decisions," Decision IX/16, Section c(4), http://www.cbd.int/decisions/cop/?m=cop-09 (accessed 27 November 2009).

14. The reviews are on the AWI Web site, http://www.awi.de/en/news/selected_news/2009/lohafex/experiment (accessed 27 November 2009).

15. For example, ocean dumping activities reported by contracting parties for the year 2006 overwhelmingly constituted dredged materials, which were disposed of in coastal waters, and no dumping permits were reported as issued for the Southern Ocean. See IMO, Final draft summary report on dumping permits issued in 2006, Report LC 31/INF.3 London: IMO, 2009.

16. An example of a marine area being subject to at least limited past ocean disposals and contamination by heavy metals from a land-based disposal site is provided by Brown Bay near Australia's Casey Station. See "Initial Environmental Evaluation for Clean-up of Thala Valley Waste Disposal Site at Casey Station, Antarctica (2003)," http://www.ats.aq/documents/EIA/7041enThala%20Valley%20IEE(2003).pdf (accessed 27 November 2009).

LITERATURE CITED

Alfred Wegener Institute for Polar and Marine Research (AWI). 2009a. Lohafex Provides New Insights on Plankton Ecology—Only Small Amounts of Atmospheric Carbon Dioxide Fixed. Press release 23 March. Bremnerhaven, Germany: AWI.

———. 2009b. Risk Assessment for LOHAFEX. Bremnerhaven, Germany: AWI.

Convention on Biological Diversity (CBD). 2006. "Impact Assessment: Voluntary Guidelines on Biodiversity-Inclusive Impact Assessment." COP 8 Decision VIII/28. http://www.cbd.int/decision/cop/?id=11042 (accessed 27 November 2009).

———. 2009. Report of the Expert Workshop on Scientific and Technical Aspects Relevant to Environmental Impact Assessment in Marine Areas Beyond National Jurisdiction. UNEP/CBD/EW-EIAMA/2. Montreal: Secretariat of the Convention on Biological Diversity.

Cullen, J. J., and P. W. Boyd. 2008. Predicting and Verifying the Intended and Unintended Consequences of Large-Scale Ocean Iron Fertilization. *Marine Ecology Progress Series*, 364:295–301.

de La Fayette, L. 1998. The London Convention 1972: Preparing for the Future. *The International Journal of Marine and Coastal Law*, 13:515–536.

Denman, K. L. 2008. Climate Change, Ocean Processes and Ocean Iron Fertilization. *Marine Ecology Progress Series*, 364:219–225.

Freestone, D., and R. Rayfuse. 2008. Ocean Iron Fertilization and International Law. *Marine Ecology Progress Series*, 364:227–233.

Gautier, P. 1992. "The Maritime Area of the Antarctic and the New Law of the Sea." In *The Antarctic Environment and International Law*, ed. J. Verhoeven, P. Sands and M. Bruce, pp. 121–137. London: Graham & Trotman.

International Maritime Organization (IMO). 2006. *MARPOL Consolidated Edition 2006*. London: IMO.

———. 2007a. Statement of Concern Regarding Fertilization of the Ocean to Sequester CO_2. Circular LC-LP.1/Cir.14. London: IMO.

———. 2007b. Report of the Twenty-Ninth Consultative Meeting and the Second Meeting of Contracting Parties. Report LC 29/17. London: IMO.

———. 2008a. Report of the Legal and Intersessional Correspondence Group on Ocean Fertilization (LICG), Submitted by the United Kingdom. Report LC 30/4. London: IMO.

———. 2008b. Report of the Legal and Intersessional Correspondence Group on Ocean Fertilization (LICG)—Breakdown of Comments, Submitted by the United Kingdom. Report LC 30/INF.2. London: IMO.

———. 2008c. Report of the Working Group on Ocean Fertilization. Report LC/SG-31/WP.3/Rev.1. London: IMO.

———. 2008d. Report of the Thirtieth Consultative Meeting and the Third Meeting of Contracting Parties. Report LC 30/16. London: IMO.

———. 2008e. A Compilation of Recent International Statements, Agreements and Recommendations Regarding Ocean Fertilization, Submitted by the United Nations Environment Programme (UNEP). Report LC/30/INF.4. London: IMO.

———. 2009a. Report of the 1st Meeting of the LP Intersessional Legal and Related Issues Working Group on Ocean Fertilization. Report LP/CO2 2/5. London: IMO.

———. 2009b. Regulating Ocean Fertilization Experiments under the London Protocol and Convention: Submitted by Australia and New Zealand. Report LC 31/4/1. London: IMO.

———. 2009c. Report of the Thirty-First Consultative Meeting and the Fourth Meeting of Contracting Parties. Report LC 3/15. London: IMO.

———. 2009d. First Draft Summary Report on Dumping Permits Issued in 2007. Report LC 31/INF.7. London: IMO.

———. 2009e. Status of Compliance with the Notification and Reporting Requirements under Article VI(4) of the London Convention 1972 and Article 9.4 of the London Protocol. Report LC 31/6. London: IMO.

———. 2009f. Report of the Second Meeting of the Compliance Group under the London Protocol. Report LC 31/WP.1. London: IMO.

Joyner, C. C. 1992. *Antarctica and the Law of Sea*. Dordrecht, the Netherlands: Martinus Nijhoff Publishers.

———. 1998. *Governing the Frozen Commons: The Antarctic Regime and Environmental Protection*. Columbia, S.C.: University of South Carolina Press.

Law, C. S. 2008. Predicting and Monitoring the Effects of Large-Scale Ocean Iron Fertilization on Marine Trace Gas Emissions. *Marine Ecology Progress Series*. 364:283–288.

New Zealand. 2007. Tourist Vessels Flagged to Non Parties: Implications for the Effectiveness of the Antarctic Treaty System. WP 14 rev. 1, XXX Antarctic Treaty Consultative Meeting, New Delhi, 30 April 10 to 11 May.

Rayfuse, R., M. G. Lawrence, and K. M. Gjerde. 2008. Ocean Fertilization and Climate Change: the Need to Regulate Emerging High Seas Uses. *The International Journal of Marine and Coastal Law*, 23:297–326.

Sagarin, R., M. Dawson, D. Karl, A. Michael, B. Murray, M. Orbach, and N. St. Clair. 2007. Iron Fertilization in the Ocean for Climate Mitigation: Legal, Economic and Environmental Challenges. Nicholas Institute Working Paper 07-07. Durham, N.C.: Duke University.

Secretariat of the Convention on Biological Diversity. 2009. *Scientific Synthesis of the Impacts of Ocean Fertilization on Marine Biodiversity*. CBD Technical Series, No. 45. Montreal: Secretariat of the Convention on Biological Diversity.

Strong, A. L., J. J. Cullen, and S. W. Chisholm. 2009. Ocean Fertilization: Science, Policy, and Commerce. *Oceanography*, 22(3):236–261.

VanderZwaag, D. L., and A. Daniel. 2009. "International Law and Ocean Dumping: Steering a Precautionary Course Aboard the 1996 London Protocol; but Still an Unfinished Voyage." In *The Future of Ocean Regime-building: Essays in Tribute to Douglas M. Johnston*, ed. A. Chircop, T. L. McDorman, and S. J. Rolston, pp. 515–550. Leiden, the Netherlands: Martinus Nijhoff Publishers.

Vigni, P. 2001. "Antarctic Maritime Claims: 'Frozen Sovereignty' and the Law of the Sea." In *The Law of the Sea and Polar Maritime Delimitation and Jurisdiction*, ed. A. G. Oude Elferink and D. R. Rothwell, pp. 85–104. The Hague: Martinus Nijhoff Publishers.

Watts, A. 1992. *International Law and the Antarctic Treaty System*. Cambridge: Grotius Publications Ltd.

Zovko, I. 2007. "Vessel-Sourced Pollution in the Southern Ocean: Benefits and Shortcomings of Regional Regulation." In *Antarctica: Legal and Environmental Challenges for the Future*, ed. G. Triggs and A. Riddell, pp. 191–222. London: British Institute of International and Comparative Law.

Parallel Precedents for the Antarctic Treaty

Cornelia Lüdecke

INTRODUCTION

Uninhabited and remote regions were claimed by a nation when their economic, political, or military values were realized. Examples from the Northern and Southern hemispheres show various approaches on how to treat claims among rivaling states. The archipelago of Svalbard in the High Arctic and Antarctica are very good examples for managing uninhabited spaces. Whereas the exploration of Svalbard comprises about 300 years of development, Antarctica was not entered before the end of the nineteenth century. Obviously, it took much more time to settle the ownership of the archipelago in the so-called Svalbard Treaty of 1920 than to find a solution for Antarctica and the existence of overlapping territorial claims by adopting the Antarctic Treaty of 1959. Why was the development at the southern continent so much faster? What is the essential difference between the situations obtaining in the two hemispheres? Was there a transposition of experiences from north to south? And did the Svalbard Treaty help to construct the Antarctic Treaty? Answers to these questions will be given by the analysis of single periods in the history of polar research, scientific networks, and special intergovernmental and nongovernmental organizations with concomitant scientific or economic interests that merged in the twentieth century to arrange exploration and exploitation of polar regions on an international basis.

EXPLORATION AND SCIENCE BEFORE WORLD WAR I

Svalbard

After the era of whaling around the archipelago of Svalbard, the Norwegians were the only ones to exploit the area economically, including fishing, since the 1850s, whereas Swedish expeditions starting in the same decade were the first to explore the interior of the islands (Liljequist, 1993; Holland, 1994; Magnússon, 2000). Names were given to discoveries, therewith inscribing on maps the idea of occupation and claims (Wråkberg, 2002; Norwegian Polar

Cornelia Lüdecke, SCAR History Action Group, Fernpaßstraße 3, D-81373 Munich, Germany. Correspondence: c.luedecke@lrz.uni-muenchen.de.

Institute, 2003). However, at the end of the nineteenth century, the archipelago of Svalbard still was a *terra nullius,* or "no-man's land." This situation changed when coal mining began on West Spitsbergen, the main island of the archipelago (hereafter called Spitsbergen) in 1898. The British were the first to open a coal mine in Advent Bay. From then on, the land around a mine was claimed by Americans, Norwegians, Swedes, and Russians or by companies from those countries. Coal from Svalbard tends to be purer and burns much more efficiently than coal from other mines, thus making it a desirable resource, especially for Norway and Russia.

When Norway separated from Sweden and became an independent kingdom in 1905, it led to a Norwegianization policy, especially relating to Svalbard with its important resources (Ericson, 2000; Barr, 2003). Thus, Svalbard should become Norwegian, a claim that led to serious disputes about ownership. A joint Norwegian, Swedish, and Russian administration could have been one of the options to solve the problem, and a lot of effort was spent to satisfy all needs, but all negotiations came to an end because of the outbreak of World War I (Wråkberg, 2002; Barr, 2003).

In 1910 Ferdinand Graf von Zeppelin of Germany led an expedition to the west coast of Spitsbergen to examine the feasibility of using his airships for exploration of the Arctic from the air (Lüdecke, 2008). The results of the expedition showed that there was far too little meteorological information available to realize safe zeppelin flights in the unknown Arctic. Consequently, in 1911, a German geophysical observatory was established on a private base for the investigation of the upper air (Dege, 1962; Lüdecke, 2008). It was the first permanent manned scientific station functioning in Spitsbergen until the outbreak of World War I. Then the station was closed permanently, but the published data became a valuable source for later climatological analysis.

The establishment of coal mines and the German meteorological station to support further exploration by aircraft both hinged on a geopolitical motive in their permanent maintenance as an underlying and tacit mode of effective occupation (Wråkberg, 2002; Hacquebord and Avango, 2009).

Antarctica

Throughout the eighteenth century sealing only took place at peri-Antarctic islands (Riffenburgh, 2007; Headland, 2009). The scientific intermezzo of the "magnetic crusade" to discover the magnetic pole on the Southern Hemisphere by competing British, French, and American expeditions around 1840 laid the foundation for later British and French claims in Antarctica on the basis of the principle of "discovery." When whaling in the Arctic declined, new whaling grounds were found in Antarctic waters at the end of the nineteenth century, but at that time, there was no need to sail farther south for exploration of the terra incognita.

In contrast to private or national initiatives to explore Spitsbergen, the first exploration period of the Antarctic continent was organized on an international level by the VIth International Geographical Congress at London in 1895. The General Assembly recommended that scientific societies throughout the world should urge the exploration of the still unknown South Pole region (Lüdecke, 2003). The rival political great powers, Great Britain and Germany, were especially interested in this project. They established their own national commissions involving the most knowledgeable persons available to prepare an Antarctic expedition for exploration and discovery. However, it was the Belgian naval officer Adrien de Gerlache who most immediately followed and realized the *Belgica* expedition (1897–1899), which not only comprised an international crew of seamen and scientists but was also the first expedition ever to overwinter in Antarctic waters.

During the VIIth International Geographical Congress in Berlin in 1899, Clements Markham, president of the Royal Geographical Society in London, defined the fields of work of the planned German and British expeditions. He divided a map with the outline of Antarctica into four quadrants starting at the 0° Greenwich meridian. The Weddell and Enderby quadrants were designated as the working area of the German expedition, whereas the Ross and Victoria quadrants were designated as British owing to earlier British exploration and early scientific work in that region.

Additionally, an international cooperative effort around meteorological and magnetic measurements evolved in the period 1901–1904, largely designed along the lines of the program of the first International Polar Year (IPY, 1882–1883). The secretariat of the congress at Berlin functioned as coordinating agency. Thus, in spite of the political rivalry between Great Britain and Germany, a scientifically driven agreement was obtained with no governmental influence. After the return of the British (leader: Robert Falcon Scott), German (leader: Erich von Drygalski), Scotch (leader: William Speirs Bruce), and Swedish (leader: Otto Nordenskjöld) expeditions, all meteorological data of the participants were collected, analyzed, and published in Germany.

Although not mentioned explicitly, imperialistic interests were the backstage driving force of this period. The political evaluation of the expedition brought shame to the German emperor Wilhelm II. He felt beaten because Scott had reached 82°S, while Drygalski's ship was trapped by ice at the polar circle. A side effect of this period was the foundation of an Argentine-Norwegian whaling company and the first whaling station in Grytviken on South Georgia by Nordenskjöld's expedition captain, Carl Anton Larsen, in 1904 (Fogg, 1992; Riffenburgh, 2007). His initiative triggered the onset of a very successful and lucrative whaling business in Antarctic waters.

Ten years later conditions had changed, and the South Pole became the object of political and personal interests. After his first expedition, it was well known that Scott planned to conquer the South Pole for the British empire. At the same time Wilhelm Filchner of Germany raised money for a private expedition to investigate whether west and east Antarctica were connected by land or separated by an inlet filled with ice (Filchner, 1994). His original plan was to perform a trans-Antarctic expedition in cooperation with the British expedition (Lüdecke, 1995). Instead, Antarctica obviously had become a place of imperialism, where scientific collaboration had lost its base. There was an uproar when Roald Amundsen, who had gained Antarctic experience as second mate during the *Belgica* expedition, headed south to win the race to the pole. This was regarded as an affront and an act of trespassing in the eyes of Scott's compatriots (Fogg, 1992; Headland, 2009). Additionally, a private Japanese expedition appeared at the Bay of Whales close to Amundsen's wintering station, but without appropriate equipment and lacking experience, it could only perform limited research.

International Polar Organization

When the first wave of Antarctic expeditions returned after the successful period of international cooperation in the beginning of the century, their achievements were discussed during the International Congress on World Economy in Mons (Belgium) in 1905 (Lüdecke, 2001). A resolution was passed that the Belgian government should be requested to organize an "International Congress for the Study of Polar Regions" in the following year. The initiative came from the director of the observatory at Uccle, Georges Lecointe, the former navigation officer of the *Belgica* expedition. He planned to establish an "International Association of Polar Research" with the following objectives (Lüdecke, 2001:162):

1. an international agreement on open questions of polar geography,
2. a general effort to reach the poles of the Earth,
3. expeditions to increase our knowledge of the polar regions, and
4. a specific program of scientific work to be carried out by different countries during their international expeditions.

It was quite obvious that governmental support was needed to institutionalize polar research in the participating countries, but this support was unlikely because serious questions of power already threatened to shake the political balance at that time. However, Lecointe's proposal was signed by most Antarctic expedition leaders present at Mons. After the congress, the Polish member of the *Belgica* expedition, Henryk Arctowski, published a proposal for the planned meeting in 1906, in which he suggested purely geographical research expeditions in Antarctica as a first step, to be followed by fixed circumpolar overwintering stations to facilitate systematic scientific investigation as the next step, supplemented by extended overland journeys for geological investigations of the continent (Arctowski, 1905). During the subsequent congress in Brussels in 1906, when the draft of the statutes of the planned polar organization was discussed (Beernaert, 1906), Nordenskjöld was the only acting delegate present who had participated in the first international cooperative effort of Antarctic expeditions (Lecointe, 1908a). The goals of the association were (Lüdecke, 2001:164):

1. systematization of polar research,
2. support and publishing of the results of polar research, and
3. support of enterprises with respect to the scientific investigation of polar regions through material and advisory support.

Some scientists supported the idea of setting up this kind of international polar commission, one that would only give advice to expeditions. However, polar research seemed not yet to be ripe for this type of organization without some national polar institute to back it up. Others criticized the planned composition of the commission favoring polar explorers above scientists as the main participants at a time when a combination of station observation and geographical exploration was still essential. Finally, a polar commission was established as an intergovernmental organization with official delegates representing participating states. In addition, persons without a mandate from governments were allowed to contribute to the polar conferences in their individual capacities. Participants regretted that the original intention of an International Polar Association to firmly organize polar expeditions was not achieved.

When the next conference took place in 1908, only 12 countries participated. Notably missing were leading states in polar research, like the United Kingdom, Germany, and Norway, a gap that indicated the waning interest in this internationalist project. However, the statutes of the International Polar Commission contain nine significant articles that were approved. The objects of the commission were

1. establishment of closer scientific relation between polar explorers,
2. securing methods and coordination of scientific observation,
3. discussion of scientific results of expeditions, and
4. assistance to enterprises to study polar regions.

Nordenskjöld was elected vice president and Lecointe became secretary of the commission. During the conference Arctowski presented a plan for international cooperation, and Lecointe gave an outline of the establishment of an international polar institute and library (Arctowski, 1908; Lecointe, 1908b).

It took five years to organize the third polar congress, which was held in Rome during the Xth International Geographical Congress in 1913 (Lecointe, 1913). Both poles, one of the major goals of the commission, were reached twice in the meantime. In Rome, Nordenskjöld was reelected vice president, and Robert Edwin Peary, who stood at the North Pole a year earlier, was made secretary general. The International Polar Commission was a farsighted attempt to organize bipolar research on an international basis, but polar research still was not institutionalized in any country. This failure, finally, contributed to the commission being dissolved during World War I.

INTERWAR PERIOD (1918–1939)

Svalbard Treaty

World War I interrupted the negotiations about the fate of Svalbard and, luckily, also offered a solution in the course of the Versailles negotiations. Finally, the Treaty Concerning the Archipelago of Spitsbergen (later called Svalbard Treaty; available at http://www.jus.uio.no/treaties/01/1-11/svalbard-treaty.xml, accessed 29 October 2009) between Norway, the United States, Denmark, France, Italy, Japan, the Netherlands, Great Britain and Ireland and the British overseas dominions, and Sweden was signed on 9 February 1920. One hundred-twenty claims existed at that time (Sysselmannen, 2008). The treaty established Norway's full sovereignty over Svalbard, including the obligation to protect Svalbard's natural environment. Other important points were demilitarization, free communication, and equal rights regarding economic exploitation by citizens of other treaty nations for the development and peaceful utilization of the archipelago. It also made a commitment toward the management of research in Svalbard as well as regulation of the same. Above all, an international meteorological station was to be established, referring to the earlier permanent observatory that had been briefly maintained by Germany. A mining code was added in 1923, defining claims up to 120 km^2, which were to be based on "geological indications," primarily from aerial photographs (Barr, 2003).

It took more than five years to gather the most important signatures for the treaty. Among them, Germany, with its scientific work, and Russia, with its coal mining industry, were seen to be crucially important actors in view of claims that might be raised later. The treaty entered into force as Svalbard Act on 14 August 1925. When the claims were finally settled, interest turned toward international cooperation in research. Not only were grants for expeditions to Svalbard given by the Norwegian government, but also the Norwegian Polar Institute was founded in 1928, a way of achieving further Norwegian influence. The Svalbard Treaty, giving sovereignty to Norway and granting exploitation rights to all treaty nations, showed how claims of an originally uninhabited polar region could be handled.

Antarctic Claims

After World War I whaling in Antarctic waters increased again. The British income from whaling licenses and later from taxes on whale oil were used to purchase the *Discovery* and refit it for oceanographic research in 1923 (Savours, 1992). The American Antarctic policy at the time was inconsistent, with the United States, on the one hand, sometimes unofficially indicating that a claim was to be laid but, on the other hand, officially denying "discovery" as a valid principle for claims, replacing it with the principle of "effective occupation" entrenched in the Hughes Doctrine of 1924, which entailed a criterion more difficult to fulfill (Hall, 1989; Riffenburgh, 2007).

Toward the end of the 1920s, aerial flight reconnaissance was introduced in Antarctic research, strongly promoted and exemplified by the American polar researcher and navy officer Richard Evelyn Byrd, who flew to the South Pole on 29 November 1929 (Headland, 2009). In addition, many discoveries were made by whalers, namely, by the Norwegians, who charted the coast of Lars Christensen Land in the 1930–1931 season. Parallel to the growing whaling industry, scientific expeditions were funded for the preparation of national claims. Byrd's second expedition to the Bay of Whales (1933–1935) led to extensive geological survey and reconnaissance flights to the interior of the Antarctic continent. And the third German Antarctic Expedition 1938/1939 performed an extensive aerial mapping with the aim of occupation between 14°W and 20°E to secure German whaling interests (Lüdecke and Summerhayes, In press). Antarctic mineral resources like coal did not play any role until the mid 1970s (Fifield, 1987).

At the same time, neighboring states like Argentina and Chile, as part of their self-interest, developed the concept that parts of the Antarctic Peninsula belonged to their countries. In the course of the discoveries of the seventh continent as well as the fishing and whaling grounds in the adjacent Antarctic Ocean interested parties promoted their wish to foster their claims of the uninhabited area. Cutting the continent into big cakelike slices similar to what Markham had done was one option. But both South American countries had overlapping claims that interfered with British claims made in 1908 and 1917, including the Malvinas (Falkland Islands). These overlapping claims complicated the issues that had to be handled (Howkins, 2006). Then, in 1937 Argentine claimed a right to all British dependencies because that area was defined as included under the scope of the Treaty of Tordesillas of 1494 (Fuchs, 1983; Howkins, 2006). In 1940 Chile also put forward similar claims with the geological argument that the peninsula is a natural continuation of the Andes and thus part of the motherland. This dispute became the so-called "ABC Problem" between Argentina, Britain, and Chile. In 1943 the British reacted and started the naval expedition Operation Tabarin (1943–1945) to "preserve the country's existing rights by occupying and re-occupying various sites within the Falkland Island Dependencies" (Fuchs, 1983:31). The first two permanent bases were established on Deception Island and at Port Lockroy, both claimed by Argentina. Continuous meteorological and other scientific investigations, including biology, geology, and survey, were performed to strengthen the British claim (Headland, 2009).

International Society for the Exploration of the Arctic Regions by Means of Aircraft (Aeroarctic)

Rapid development of airships during World War I provided a new means of transport, with airships that could fly over great distances and carry heavy loads. In the future they would offer the first suitable means for trans-Arctic traffic routes from Europe to Tokyo or San Francisco, at least according to a much-discussed suggestion emerging in commercial circles in Germany in 1919.

For further planning, more meteorological information than already provided by the German observatory in Spitsbergen was needed. A German initiative promoted a feasibility study, i.e., an airship expedition (Lüdecke, 1995). This study led to the foundation of the International Society for the Exploration of the Arctic Regions by Means of Aircraft (Aeroarctic) under the presidency of Fridtjof Nansen and incorporated in Berlin in 1924 as a nongovernmental organization (Studiengesellschaft, 1924). It was the first international scientific organization with German and Russian members after World War I. At that time both countries were still excluded from the International Research Council (IRC) founded after the war by the scientific academies of the major Allied nations, with the rationale that excluding the former Central Powers was necessary to prevent a new rise of German scientific dominance (Cock, 1983). The inclusion of Russia in Aeroarctic was essential since cooperation in the Russian Arctic was crucial for the exploration of trans-Arctic air routes. In the end the society consisted of 21 national committees with 394 individual members and 42 bodies (Lüdecke, 1995, 1999). Aeroarctic was managed by the Council of the Society, the Exploration Council, and the Ordinary General Assembly of the members (Anonymous, 1931); see Figure 1. An editorial board for the journal *Arktis* was also installed (Nansen, 1928–1929; Berson et al., 1930–1931). The journal came out for four years and terminated in 1931 as a result of the economic crisis.

The president of the International Meteorological Organization (IMO) Ewoud van Everdingen concurrently became the Dutch member of the Council of Aeroarctic. He was the ideal person to promote the exploratory study expedition within the most appropriate organization (Cannegieter, 1963). In addition, the Danish Aeroarctic member, Dan LaCour, became president of the Commission for the Second International Polar Year (1932–1933) of the IMO. Six more scientists were members of both groups, four of them even on the council of Aeroarctic. This overlap underlines the successful international networking of

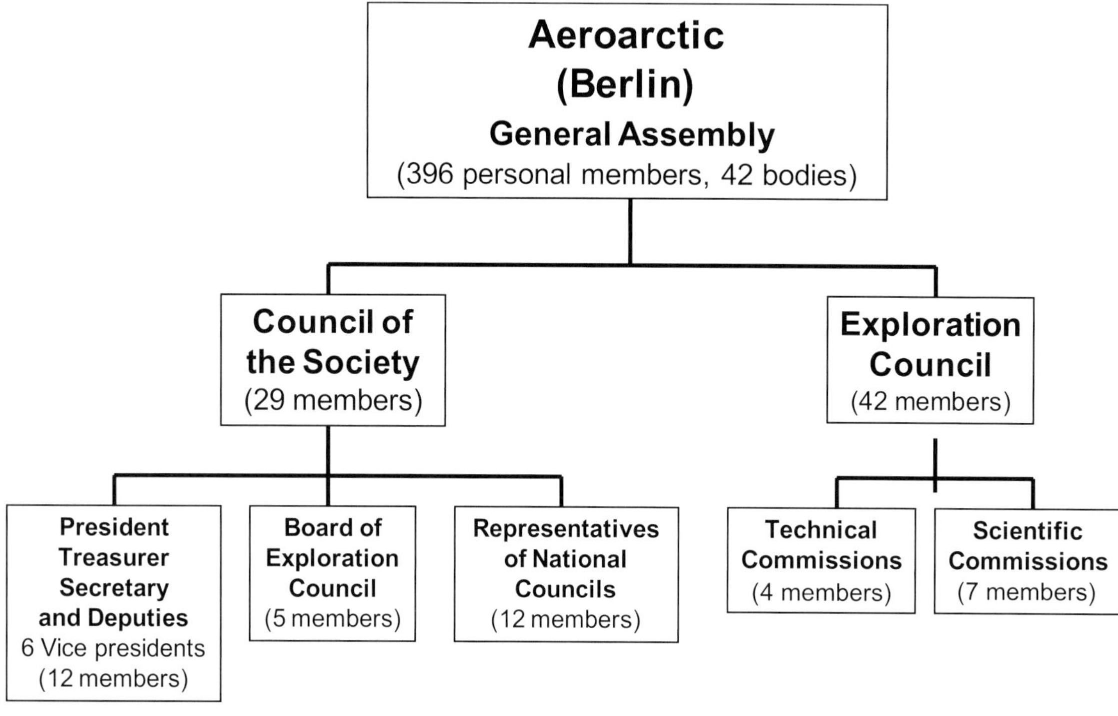

FIGURE 1. Organization chart of Aeroarctic in 1931 according to Berson et al. 1931.

Aeroarctic. Moreover, it is interesting to note that Everdingen and the Polish member Arctowski were also familiar with the early attempts of the International Polar Commission. Everdingen had been one of the Dutch deputies delegated, and Arctowski was a Belgian deputy delegate and, of course, one of the driving forces of the prewar International Polar Commission (Lecointe, 1908a).

Membership in Aeroarctic was dominated by 32% Germans, 20% Russians, and 12% Americans. During the meteorological planning for the expedition with the airship LZ 127 *Graf Zeppelin* to the Russian Arctic, more meteorological data were needed. Such data, it was held, might be supplied by a new International Polar Year (Second IPY, 1932–1933), a notion originally suggested by a member of Aeroarctic: "The permanent monitoring of the [Russian] Arctic is, so to speak, thought to be a permanent repetition of the International Polar Year 1882/83, only with the difference that the airship as means of transport would be introduced" (Berson and Breitfuß, 1927:112, my translation).

In the first volume of the journal *Arktis*, Nansen described the proposed working program of the society, including a network of observing stations on islands in the Arctic Ocean and additional radio weather stations on the drift ice of the inner Arctic installed with the help of airships or aircraft for monitoring of the geophysical conditions (Nansen, 1928). Later, drift stations became part of the Russian Second IPY program. After the return of the successful zeppelin expedition with LZ 127 *Graf Zeppelin* in 1931, data were analyzed and the results published. With the ill-fated crash of the airship LZ 129 *Hindenburg* on 6 May 1937, the futuristic vision of global airlines with airships had to be abandoned.

Aeroarctic had pooled members living in countries neighboring the Arctic and interested in polar research for a single purpose. It provides a fascinating example of how an international nongovernmental organization managed a joint scientific program during the interwar period. However, it failed to continue when political and economical conditions of the principal actor, Germany, changed and airships disappeared from the sky.

POST–WORLD WAR II

Politics and Science in Svalbard

By November 1944, when Soviet troops were in northern Norway, the Soviet Union wanted to expand its influence on the archipelago of Svalbard and proposed to repeal the Treaty of Spitsbergen and to replace it by a Soviet-Norwegian administration (Barr, 2003). A Norwegian counterproposal of April 1945 allowed for a Soviet-Norwegian defense system with military installations on Svalbard instead of joint possession. The election of a new Labour Party government in Norway changed the political situation after the war, resulting in a cessation of further discussions in early 1947. The Soviets realized that the "status quo in Svalbard was the best policy" (Barr, 2003:247). Strategic interest in the Arctic grew, and the cold war became the dominant feature of the period. Consequently, Norway was among the first states that became signatories to the North Atlantic Treaty Organization (NATO) in 1949 "to keep the Russians out, the Americans in, and the Germans down" (Reynolds, 1994:13).

In 1963 the Norwegian mine in Ny-Ålesund was closed due to an accident in which 21 miners were killed. Geopolitical considerations to inhabit the abandoned village again led to the establishment of the first scientific station by the Norwegian Polar Institute. Focus was on the investigation the ionosphere and Earth magnetism as well as cosmic physics. In addition, in 1967 a telemetry station was established by the European Space Research Organization (ESRO), in which the Soviet Union was not represented as member, connecting Svalbard with space. The gradual change from a mining village to an international science village was crucial for Norway; otherwise, the Soviet Union might have settled in Ny-Ålesund as an additional location for manifesting its presence.

Politics and Science in Antarctica

After World War II management of the Antarctic stations of the Falkland Island Dependencies was turned over to the Falkland Island Dependencies Survey within the Colonial Office (1945–1961), and the number of Antarctic stations increased from five in 1946 to ten. When the survey was renamed the British Antarctic Survey in 1962, the number of stations was reduced to eight (Fuchs, 1983).

The United States embarked on a different strategy. The largest exploratory venture was organized primarily as a naval training exercise under the name United States Antarctic Development Project (Operation High Jump, 1946/1947) (Riffenburgh, 2007). Some 4,700 men were given polar experience, which would be useful in the event of a war with the Soviet Union in the far north. This operation was followed by Operation Windmill in 1947/1948, with objectives including "re-enforcing, through continuity in 'occupation and use' the validity of possibly United States claims in the Antarctic regions." (Headland, 2009:320). However, the United States did not put forward any such claim (Moore, 2004).

In contrast to this military operation the Norwegian-British-Swedish Expedition (NBSX, 1949–1952) to the Norwegian Dronning Maud Land and overlapping German discovery of Neuschwabenland proved that a small international project under the auspices of Norwegian scientists and organized as a tripartite consortium could be very successful, and it delivered interesting results in meteorology, geophysics, and air photography (Lewander, 2007). International cooperation seemed fruitful for future investigations. Although foreign policy and security were the prime concerns, the NBSX served the "emerging need for increased knowledge of weather systems by defense organizations worldwide," i.e., the western alliance (Lewander, 2007:137).

Antarctic Commission

After 1945, various nations sent out expeditions and established permanent scientific stations to explore the interior of Antarctica preparatory to advancing territorial claims. Also, further steps were taken to solve the unsettled status of the continent. At first, Argentina and Chile agreed upon their position against the United Kingdom in a declaration "on the rights of both countries over parts in Antarctica and . . . their desire to arrive as soon as possible at the conclusion of a Treaty" signed on 12 July 1947 (Headland, 2009:314). Parallel to this attempt the United States was searching for a solution to unite the claimant states with the main aim of excluding Soviet influence on Antarctica. A secret American aide-memoire and draft agreement on Antarctica was handed to the embassies of Argentina, Chile, the United Kingdom, Australia, New Zealand, France, and Norway on 9 August 1948 (Department of State, 1948). The United States had come to the conclusion that "an international status for the Antarctic area is the most practicable and preferable method of solving the problem of conflicting and potentially conflicting claims" (Department of State, 1948:36). The foreseeable values of the South Pole region were held to be "predominantly scientific rather than strategic or economic." However, internationalization would help to preserve control of the possible strategic use and economic value in the hands of nations interested. This is different from the approach of the Svalbard Treaty in which Norway, the United Kingdom, and the United States were involved. An international administration would take care of

1. systematic exploration and investigation of Antarctic phenomena,
2. meteorological observation important to long-range weather forecasting (as in Svalbard),
3. removal from present or future conflict,
4. preserving control over any actual or potential values, and
5. widening the sphere of friendly, cooperative international endeavor to all islands of 60°S except the South Shetland Islands and South Orkney Islands.

The plan for an international administration was summed up in eight articles. The main aspect was to freeze all territorial claims and to create an Antarctic Commission involving one representative from each participating state, which, in turn, would constitute the actual government. The commission would work together with the United Nations and international scientific bodies. Article V described the formation of a scientific board, which would "draw up plans for exploration, investigation and scientific and technical development . . . The Commission shall prescribe appropriate procedures and conditions under which states, and privately sponsored expeditions, may conduct scientific investigations, [and] develop resources" (Department of State, 1948:40). The "establishment of facilities and the conduct of scientific investigation" were to be fostered as well as "free access to, and freedom of transit through or over the area." The signatory states were asked to take all measures necessary to maintain international peace and security. This was, on the whole, the background to the American suggestion, predicated on consensus around the conviction that the Soviet Union should *not* be allowed to step onto the white continent, which should be under the influence of the Western Hemisphere only. The idea was revisited and modified a decade later in the context of the International Geophysical Year (IGY), planning for which started in 1950 (see Berkman, this volume).

In the wake of the IGY, naming of Antarctic features was addressed in German newspapers (Lüdecke, 2009). When the German *Schwabenland* expedition (1938/39) had discovered and investigated Neuschwabenland by extensive aerial survey, one of the prerequisites of "effective" occupation had been achieved (Wråkberg, 2002). As German claims were never made, German names, the newspapers maintained, should at least be highlighted on the map. Visible signs of German footprints were important to underline geopolitical desires at a time when the fate of Antarctica was still unknown.

OUTLOOK

The extensive IGY program initiated during a dinner conversation in Silver Spring (Maryland) in 1950 was the biggest scientific experiment ever (Korsmo, 2007). It was carried through in parallel in both polar regions from 1 July 1957 until 31 December 1958. A dense network of stations was set up along the Antarctic coast and at points on the continent, including the American Amundsen-Scott South Pole Station; the name of this station indicated that no national preference was given for this special location, in which all longitudes defining Antarctic sectors come together. Peaceful cooperation, especially of American and Soviet scientists during the cold war, finally prompted the Antarctic Treaty in 1959 (Belanger, 2006), which incorporated some salient ideas of the Svalbard Treaty like demilitarization, free communications, and equal rights of all members.

Besides the treaty a Scientific Committee of Antarctic Research (SCAR) emerged from the Comité Speciale de l'Année Geophysique Internationale (CSAGI) and was established within the International Council of Scientific Unions (ICSU) to guide coordination in research and provide scientific advice to the Antarctic Treaty Parties. (Fifield, 1987; Fogg, 1992; Jabour and Haward, 2009). It resembled the organizational structure of Aeroarctic (see Figure 2).

The function of SCAR, which consists of one representative from each member country, is similar to the function of the General Assembly of Aeroarctic, with personal members representing their countries; the SCAR Executive Committee corresponds to the Council of Aeroarctic, and the SCAR Working Groups correspond to the Aeroarctic Exploration Council.

It is amazing to realize that it took about three centuries from the discovery of Svalbard until the Svalbard Treaty, whereas in Antarctica the process of arriving at a treaty, historically speaking, went much faster. After the decline of living resources in Arctic waters, interest shifted to Antarctic waters, where sealing and whaling became highly profitable. However, the first scientists entered the southern continent in 1899. They set the scene for geopolitical discussions, occupation, and claims. However, there were no aspirations to gain a permanent settlement at that stage, and Antarctica continued to be a no-man's land until a greater appetite for matters of sovereignty came up, essentially starting in the 1930s. During the cold war the IGY provided the first possibility for all participating countries as equal partners to establish a permanent presence on the southern continent. This was achieved as a first step by the continuation of scientific work for another

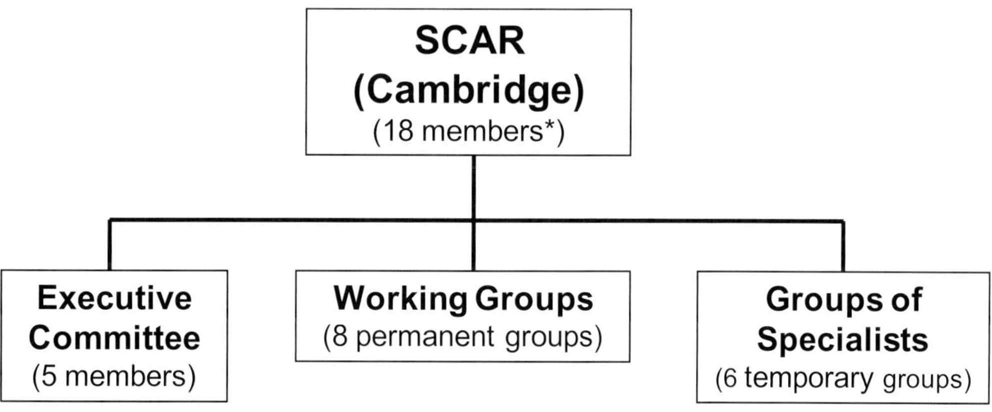

FIGURE 2. Organization chart of SCAR in 1987 according to Fifield (1987).

year. Logically, the parties involved at that time became the exclusive 12 nations to sign the Antarctic Treaty and become members of SCAR; they were the only ones to do so until Poland and the Federal Republic of Germany joined in 1978 (Headland, 2009).

Although the IGY also had an Arctic program, questions of sovereignty made it difficult for scientific cooperation, especially in respect to the Soviet Arctic, which was more or less closed to foreigners (Magnússon, 2000). In consequence, no organization similar to SCAR developed after the IGY for the North Pole region. In 1987, SCAR initiated a first meeting of representatives of the so-called Arctic countries (Canada, Denmark/Greenland, Finland, Iceland, Norway, Soviet Union, Sweden, and United States) that finally led in 1990 to the foundation of the International Arctic Science Committee (IASC) in Resolute (Canada), a body that is associated with ICSU.

Currently, we are facing negotiations about the economic use of the northwest and northeast passages in the Arctic and the political implications attending this prospect. It will be interesting to see if experiences gathered in the south will be transposed back to the north and how the Antarctic Treaty can offer guidance to establish a possible Arctic Treaty.

Acknowledgments

First, I have to thank Paul Berkman for his invitation to give the historical talk during the Antarctic Treaty Summit in Washington, D.C., on 30 November 2009. I also want to thank two anonymous reviewers for their constructive remarks and Aant Elzinga (Gothenburg) for his comments and the correction of my English text.

LITERATURE CITED

Anonymous. 1931. Statutes of the Aeroarctic. *Arktis,* 1931(4):42–45.

Arctowski, H. 1905. *Projet d'une exploration systématique des régions polaires.* Brussels: Vander Auwera & Cie. Reprint in Beernaert, M., 1906. *Congrès International pour l'Étude de Régions polaires tenue à Bruxelles du 7 au 11 septembre 1906,* vol. 1. Brussels: Hayez.

———. 1908. "Note sur la coopération internationale pour l'étude des régions polaires." In *Commission Polaire Internationale, Session de 1908. Procès-verbaux des scéances,* ed. G. Lecointe, pp. XXVI–XXVIII. Brussels: Hayez.

Barr, S. 2003. *Norway: A Consistent Polar Nation? Analysis of an Image Seen through the History of the Norwegian Polar Institute.* Oslo: Kolofon AS.

Beernaert, M. 1906. *Congrès International pour l'Étude de Régions polaires tenue à Bruxelles du 7 au 11 septembre 1906.* 2 vols. Brussels: Hayez.

Belanger, D. O., 2006. *Deep Freeze: The United States, the International Geophysical Year, and the Origins of Antarctica's Age of Science.* Boulder, Colo.: University Press of Colorado.

Berkman, P. A. 2011 (this volume). "President Eisenhower, the Antarctic Treaty, and the Origin of International Spaces." In *Science Diplomacy: Antarctica, Science, and the Governance of International Spaces,* ed. P. A. Berkman, M. A. Lang, D. W. H. Walton, and O. R. Young, pp. 17–27. Washington, D.C.: Smithsonian Institution Scholarly Press.

Berson, A., and L. Breitfuß. 1927. Sitzung des Sonderausschusses am 16.11.1926. *Petermanns Geographische Mitteilungen, Ergänzungsheft,* 191:110–113.

Berson, A., L. Breitfuß, and W. Bruns, eds. 1930–1931. *Arktis, Vierteljahreszeitschrift der internationalen Gesellschaft zur Erforschung der Arktis mit Luftfahrzeugen.*

Cannegieter, H. G. 1963. The History of the International Meteorological Organization 1872–1951. *Annalen der Meteorologie,* 1:1–280.

Cock, A. G. 1983. Chauvinism and Internationalism in Science: The International Research Council, 1919–1926. *Notes and Records of the Royal Society,* 37:249–288.

Dege, W. 1962. Deutsches Observatorium Ebeltofthafen-Spitzbergen. Zur 50. Wiederkehr der 1. Überwinterung 1912/13. *Polarforschung,* 32(1/2):136–140.

Department of State. 1948. U.S. Aide-Memoire and Draft Agreement on Antarctica. August 9, 1948. In *National Security Council.* 1958. Antarctica. NSC 5804. February 25, 1958. Eisenhower Library, National Archives, Abilene, Kans.

Ericson, L. 2000. "Exploration and Strategy: The Swedish Military and the Arctic and Sub-Arctic Region, from 1880s to the 1980s." In *Aspects of Arctic and Sub-Arctic History. Proceedings of the International Congress on the History of the Arctic and Sub-Arctic Region Reykjavik, 18–21 June, 1998,* ed. I. Sigurðssen and Jón Skaptason, pp. 431–440. Reykjavik: University of Iceland Press.

Fifield, R. 1987. *International Research in the Antarctic.* Oxford: ICSU Press.

Filchner, W. 1994. *To the Sixth Continent: The Second German South Polar Expeditions,* trans. W. Barr. Bluntisham, UK: Bluntisham Books.

Fogg, G. E. 1992. *History of Antarctic Science.* Studies in Polar Research. Cambridge: Cambridge University Press.

Fuchs, V. 1983. *Of Ice and Men. The Story of the British Antarctic Survey 1943–1973.* Oswestry, Shopshire, UK: Anthony Nelson.

Hacquebord, L., and D. Avango. 2009. Settlements in an Arctic Resource Region. *Arctic Anthropology,* 46(1/2):25–39.

Hall, H. R. 1989. The "Open Door" into Antarctica: An Explanation of the Hughes Doctrine. *Polar Record,* 25(153):137–140.

Headland, R. K. 2009. *A Chronology of Antarctic Exploration: A Synopsis of Events and Activities from the Earliest Times until the International Polar Years.* London: Quaritch.

Holland, C. 1994. *Arctic Exploration and Development, c. 500 B.C. to 1915: An Encyclopedia.* New York: Garland Pub.

Howkins, A. 2006. Icy Relations: The Emergence of South American Antarctica during the Second World War. *Polar Record,* 42(221):153–165.

Jabour, J., and M. Haward. 2009. "Antarctic Science, Politics and IPY Legacies." In *Legacies and Change in Polar Sciences: Historical, Legal and Political Reflections on the International Polar Year,* ed. J. M. Shadian and M. Tennberg, pp. 101–124. Global Interdisciplinary Studies Series. Farnham, UK: Ashgate.

Korsmo, F. 2007. The International Geophysical Year of 1957 to 1958. An analysis of why both the executive and legislative branches of the US Government funded the IGY of 1957 to 1958. *Science, People and Politics* 2:1.1.07, 01.15 GMT. http://www.gavaghan communications.com/sppkorsmoigy.html (accessed 19 November 2010).

Lecointe, G., ed. 1908a. *Commission Polaire Internationale. Session de 1908. Procès-verbaux des séances.* Brussels: Hayez.

———. 1908b. "L'Institut Polaire International." In *Commission Polaire Internationale. Session de 1908. Procès-verbaux des séances,* ed. G. Lecointe, pp. CXLVI–CLX. Brussels: Hayez.

———. 1913. *Commission Polaire Internationale. Session de 1913. Procès-verbaux de la Session. Tenue à Rome en 1913.* Brussels: Hayez.

Lewander, L. 2007. "The Norwegian-British-Swedish Expedition (NBSX) to Antarctica 1949–1952: Science and Security." In *Steps of Foundation of Institutionalized Antarctic Research. Proceedings of the1st SCAR Workshop on the History of Antarctic Research, Munich 2–3 June 2005,* ed. C. Lüdecke. *Berichte zur Polar- und Meeresforschung,* 560:123–141.

Liljequist, G. H. 1993. *High Latitudes: A History of Swedish Polar Travels and Research.* Stockholm: Swedish Polar Research Secretariat.

Lüdecke, C. 1995. Die deutsche Polarforschung seit der Jahrhundertwende und der Einfluß Erich von Drygalskis. *Berichte zur Polarforschung,* 158:340pp, 72 pp Appendix.

———. 1999. "Problems for Further Research on the History of Science of the Polar Regions." In *The Centennial of S.A. Andrée's North Pole Expedition. Proceedings of a Conference on S.A. Andrée and the Agenda for Social Science Research of the Polar Regions,* ed. U. Wrakberg, pp. 154–177. Bidrag till Kungl. Svenska Vetenskapsakademiens Historia, No. 29. Stockholm: Royal Swedish Academy of Sciences, Center for History of Science.

———. 2001. "The Belgian Attempt to Institutionalize Polar Research (1905–1915) and the German Point of View." In *The BELGICA Expedition Centennial: Perspectives on Antarctic Science and History,* ed. H. Decleir and C. de Broyer, pp. 161–169. Brussels: VUB Brussels University Press.

———. 2003. Scientific Collaboration in Antarctica (1901–1903): A Challenge in Times of Political Rivalry. *Polar Record,* 39(208):25–48.

———. 2008. "From the Bottom to the Stratosphere-Arctic Climate as Seen from the 1st International Polar Year (1882–1883) until the end of World War II." In *Climate Variability and Extremes During the Past 100 Years,* ed. S. Brönnimann, J. Luterbacher, T. Ewen, H. F. Diaz, R. S. Stolarsky, and Q. Neu, pp. 29–45. Heidelberg: Springer.

———. 2009. "Expanding to Antarctica—Discussions about German Naming and a New Map of Antarctica in the Early 1950s". In *2nd SCAR Workshop on the History of Antarctic Research. Multidimensional Exploration of Antarctica Around the 1950s,* ed. C. Lüdecke. *Boletín Antártico Chileno,* 45–52. Punta Arenas, Chile: Instituto Antártico Chileno. http://www.inach.cl/InachWeb Neo/Controls/Neochannels/Neo_CH6231/deploy/boletin%20 historico.pdf (accessed 19 November 2010).

Lüdecke, C., and C. Summerhayes. In press. *The Third Reich in Antarctica: The Story of the German Antarctic Expedition of 1938/9.* Norfolk, UK: Erskine Press.

Magnússon, M. 2000. "International Co-operation in Arctic Science." In *Aspects of Arctic and Sub-Arctic History. Proceedings of the International Congress on the History of the Arctic and Sub-Arctic Region Reykjavik, 18–21 June, 1998,* ed. I. Sigurðssen and Jón Skaptason, pp. 563–573. Reykjavik: University of Iceland Press.

Moore, J. K. 2004. Bungled Publicity: Little America, Big America and the Rationale for Non-claimancy, 1946–1961. *Polar Record,* 40(212): 19–30.

Nansen, F., ed. 1928–1929. *Arktis, Vierteljahreszeitschrift der internationalen Gesellschaft zur Erforschung der Arktis mit Luftfahrzeugen.*

———. 1928. Geleitwort zum Arbeitsprogramm der Aeroarctic. *Arktis,* 1(1/2):45–52.

Norwegian Polar Institute. 2003. The Place Names of Svalbard. Rapportserie 122. Tromsø: Norwegian Polar Institute.

Reynolds, D. 1994. *The origins of the Cold War in Europe. International perspectives.* New Haven, Yale University Press.

Riffenburgh, B., ed. 2007. *Encyclopedia of the Antarctic.* 2 vols. New York: Routledge.

Savours, A. 1992. *The Voyages of the Discovery. The illustrated History of Scott's Ship*. Frome, Summerset, UK: Butler and Tunner.

Studiengesellschaft. 1924. *Das Luftschiff als Forschungsmittel in der Arktis. Eine Denkschrift*, Berlin: Internationale Studiengesellschaft zur Erforschung der Arktis mit dem Luftschiff.

Sysselmannen. 2008. The Svalbard Treaty. http://www.sysselmannen.no/hovedEnkel.aspx?m=45301 (accessed 29 October 2009).

Wråkberg, U. 2002. "The Politics of Naming: Contested Observations and Shaping of Geographical Knowledge." In *Narrating the Arctic: A Cultural History of Nordic Scientific Practices*, ed. M. Bravo and S. Sörlin, pp. 155–197. Canton, Mass.: Science History.

International Collaboration in the Antarctic for Global Science

Karl A. Erb

ABSTRACT. Article III of the Antarctic Treaty outlines the way in which international cooperation, established during the International Geophysical Year, should be continued. Exchanges of scientists have occurred among many nations over the last 50 years, but increasing planning and logistics collaboration have marked the achievement of many major scientific goals possible only through multinational activity. The recently completed International Polar Year provides clear evidence of how well this is succeeding in Antarctic science for the twenty-first century, and the publication record clearly reflects this pooling of talent.

INTRODUCTION

The International Geophysical Year of 1957–1958 was a major milestone in many ways. Not only did it provide an opportunity for wide-scale international cooperation in physical sciences, but its Antarctic activities provided motivation for an international treaty setting the continent aside for peace and science. In negotiating the treaty the diplomats were at pains to ensure that the requirement for international collaboration was written into the text. Articles II and III of the Antarctic Treaty lay out the principles of freedom of scientific investigation, international cooperation, and the free availability of results and data.

This paper highlights several recent exemplars of the international research in Antarctica that, in practical terms, a single nation could not have undertaken on its own. Much of this science is currently helping to explain the Antarctic region's involvement in global change, a central research question of our age. This research echoes the themes of the Antarctic Treaty Summit: science interacting with diplomacy, science as a source of policy issues, science as an early warning, and science as a quest for fundamental knowledge.

Researchers themselves are attentive to these broad points. On a recent visit to the National Science Foundation a polar ecologist remarked "we are ethically obligated to stay ahead on climate change." She is looking beyond her science to the broader communities' need to understand the science and to take action based on those scientific findings.

Karl A. Erb, Office of Polar Programs, National Science Foundation, 4201 Wilson Boulevard, Arlington, Virginia 22230, USA. Correspondence: kerb@nsf.gov.

INTERNATIONAL RESEARCH COLLABORATION

The Antarctic Treaty did not invent international science, but its provisions have fostered international science in powerful ways. During the Cold War in the 1950s and later, the United States and the Soviet Union exchanged scientists in the Antarctic. At first they simply traded personnel. But international projects now involve detailed planning, shared logistics, and interactive science.

In 1981 the Soviet icebreaker *Mikhail Somov* was the research platform for 13 Soviet scientists and 13 U.S. scientists. The ship went far into ice-infested regions of the Weddell Sea, the first deep penetration since Shackleton's famous voyage on *Endurance* in 1915–1916. The result was the first comprehensive data set obtained in winter sea ice. A decade later, the Russian icebreaker *Akademik Federov* and the U.S. icebreaker *Nathaniel B. Palmer* collaborated in the same region to establish a drifting camp on the sea ice. Seventeen American and 15 Russian scientists collected data for four months regarding the Weddell Gyre, which is a key constituent of the global climate system, sending cold, dense Antarctic waters throughout the world's ocean. The Soviet Union transformed itself into the Russian Federation while the ship was deployed, but the Antarctic research was completed as planned.

Experience and the ever-present Antarctic Treaty gave its member nations the confidence to do complex international projects like these, requiring the full commitment of each partner for project success. The achievements for science are irrefutable. As the number of Treaty Consultative Parties roughly doubled from the original 12 to 28 nations, Dastidar and Ramachandran (2008) showed that published international Antarctic papers with coauthors from two or more nations increased from 15 papers in 1980 to 190 international papers in 2004 (Figure 1). This accomplishment is significantly greater than for world science as a whole. The bibliographic record also shows that other scientists cite the international papers more than they cite the single-nation papers, proof that international cooperation increases the progress of science and enables research that otherwise would be expensive or infeasible.

INTERNATIONAL POLAR YEAR PROGRESS

In the years since 2004, my counterparts heading Antarctic programs in the other treaty nations will likely agree

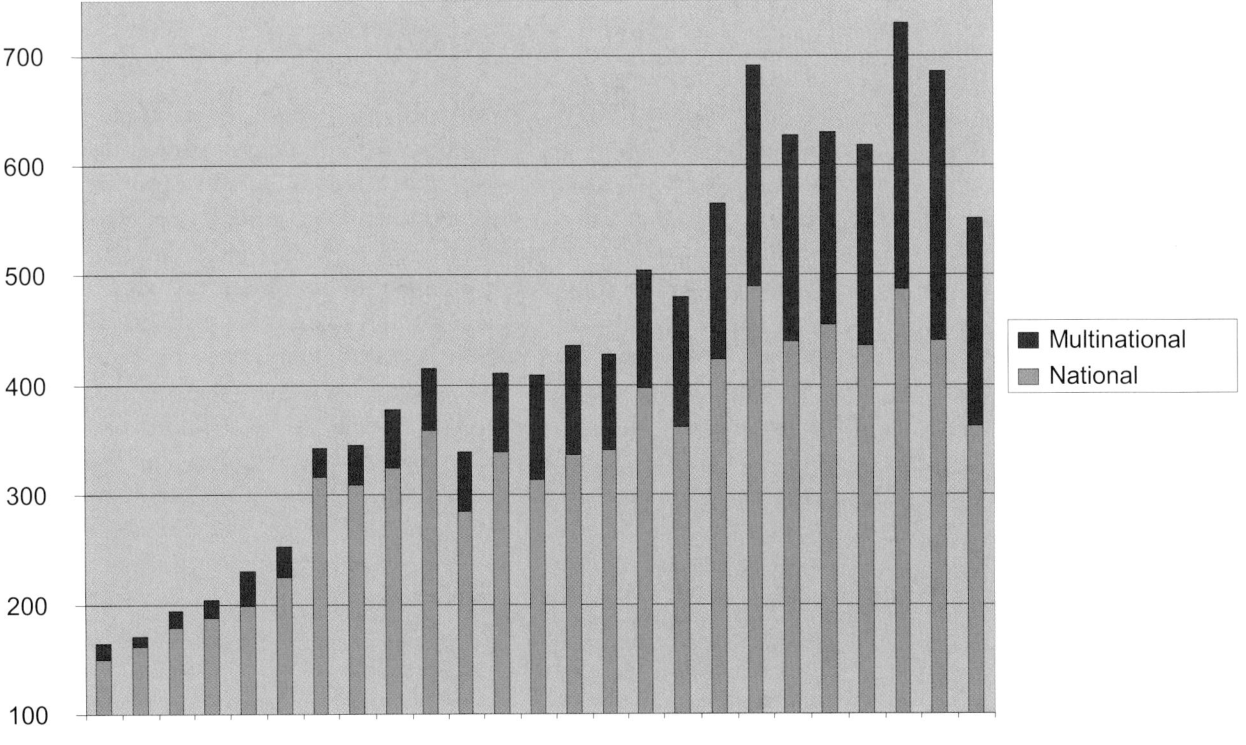

FIGURE 1. Antarctic paper publications from 1980 to 2004.

that the recently concluded field phase of the International Polar Year of 2007–2008 is resulting in dramatic advances in understanding this important part of the world. The rise in polar climate papers has been particularly steep.

Countries are working together to describe current and potential future events impacting the Antarctic ice sheet. Only through such a broad effort involving China, the United Kingdom, France, the United States, and other countries can we hope to reduce uncertainties in the Intergovernmental Panel on Climate Change (IPCC) estimates of long-term global sea level rise. The goal is to determine the rates of loss of ice from the main drainage basins (Figure 2) and how the rates depend on bed lubrication, topography, and ocean temperature.

The Antarctica's Gamburtsev Province (AGAP) project is an IPY effort involving the United States, the United Kingdom, Russia, Germany, China, and Australia that discovered river valleys in the Gamburtsev Mountains under the Antarctic ice sheet. This is the location of the first Antarctic ice sheet (~34 MYA) and thus represents potentially very old ice and a tectonic enigma. The effort gave us a first detailed look at what that part of the continent, as big as the Alps, might have been like before it was covered in ice. This project involved close international collaboration in science, technology, and logistics.

An IPY signature project, the Larsen Ice Shelf System, Antarctica (LARISSA; Figure 3), is a collaboration by Argentina, Belgium, South Korea, Ukraine, and the United States to study a regional problem with global change implications. The abrupt environmental change in Antarctica's Larsen Ice Shelf system was investigated using marine and Quaternary geosciences, cryosphere and ocean studies, and research into marine ecosystems. In an example of IPY's education and legacy roles, a two-week course in the United States in July 2010 under the auspices of the Australia-based International Antarctic Institute used recently acquired marine data, sediment cores, and imagery.

Twenty-eight countries are collaborating in the Polar Earth Observing Network (POLENET) to map uplift of the Antarctic crust resulting from a decreased mass of the

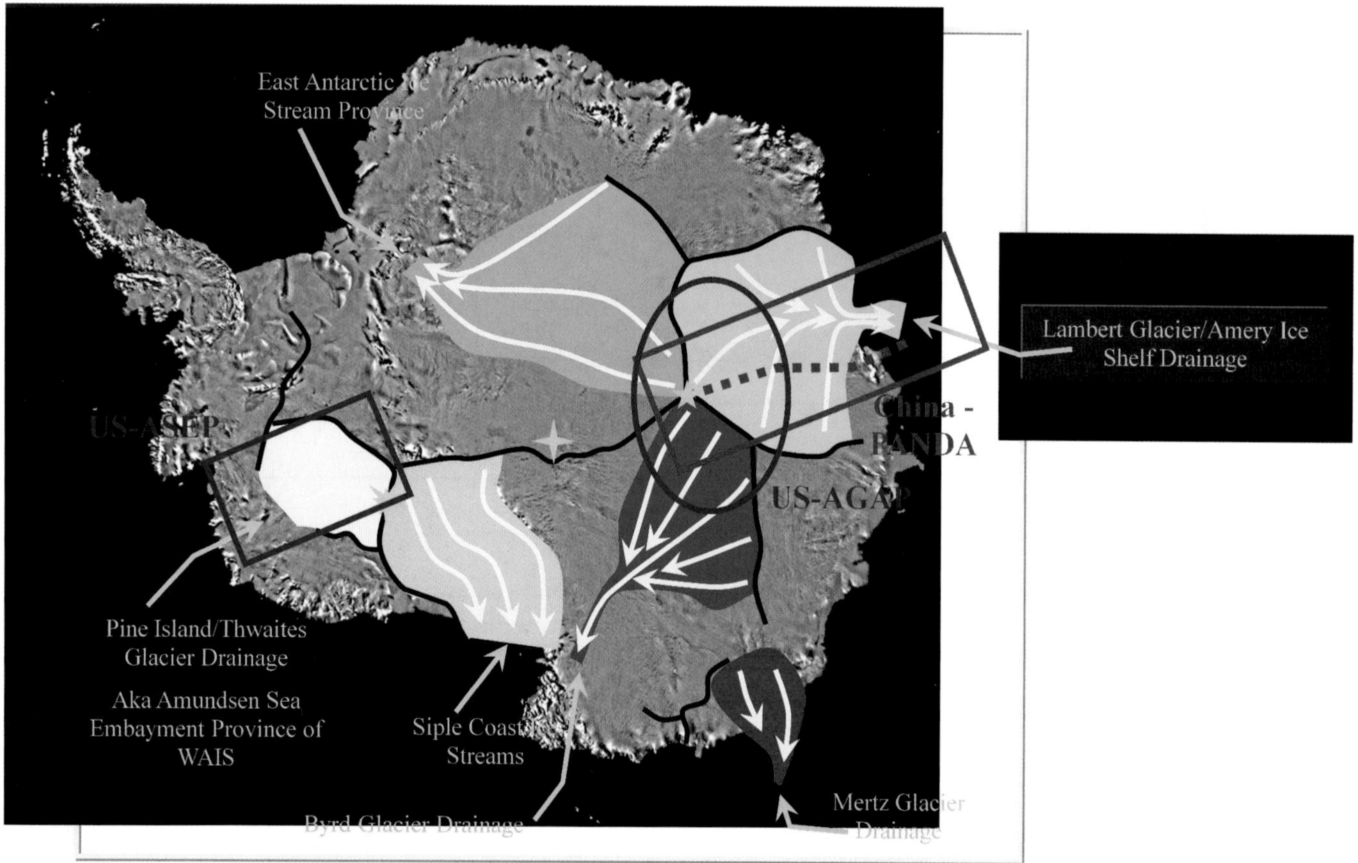

FIGURE 2. Antarctic ice sheet drainage.

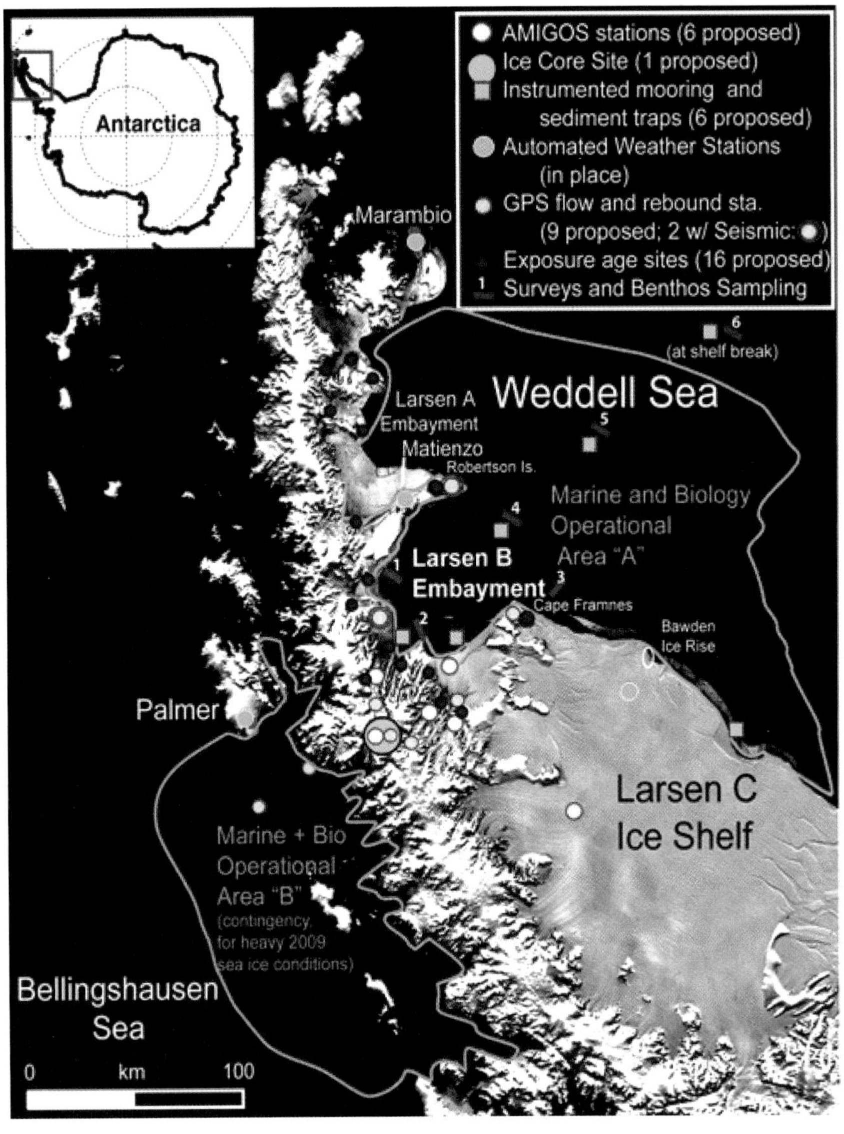

FIGURE 3. LARISSA study area.

covering ice sheet. Data from new GPS and seismic stations spanning much of the Antarctic and Greenland ice sheets are used to model how much ice was lost over the 10,000 years since the last major ice age. These data, taken with information gathered by satellites, help in determining where, and at what rate, the ice sheets are changing in response to recent climate change. The measurements are critical in refining estimates of future global sea level rise. The collaborations have led to new technology for continuous measurement at autonomous observatories operating in polar conditions and have provided a legacy framework for ongoing international geophysical observations.

Thirteen countries are participating in the International Trans-Antarctic Scientific Expedition (ITASE), which is collecting ice core samples that provide signatures of how constituents of the atmosphere have changed since the beginning of the industrial revolution. The ITASE is an existing project (begun in 1990) that matches IPY goals and that flourished during the IPY period. Like the ice sheet drainage collaborations shown in Figure 2, ITASE has tended to distribute its goals geographically among the involved nations. A workshop identified tasks for national participants, and the Scientific Committee on Antarctic Research (SCAR) Global Change Program provides coordination.

Germany, Italy, New Zealand, the United Kingdom, and the United States contributed to the Antarctic Geological Drilling Program (ANDRILL) and obtained deep sediment cores from the sea bed that show Earth's climate 15–30 MYA. These paleoclimate perspectives increase confidence in the ability to predict future change. Using the McMurdo Ice Shelf as a drilling platform, the project found new evidence that even a slight rise in atmospheric carbon dioxide affects the stability of the West Antarctic Ice Sheet.

France and the United States combined their capabilities in the Concordiasi project to develop a new way of measuring the constituents of the atmosphere, layer by layer, from top to bottom with new instruments that are dropped from long-duration stratospheric superpressure balloons deployed from McMurdo. Their data are coupled with surface observations at a number of Antarctic locations. This Concordiasi project is intended to reduce uncertainties in aspects of climate change that could change the mass balance of the Antarctic ice sheet. Figure 4 shows an instrument (dropsonde) launched on demand under a parachute to measure atmospheric parameters on the way down over Antarctica.

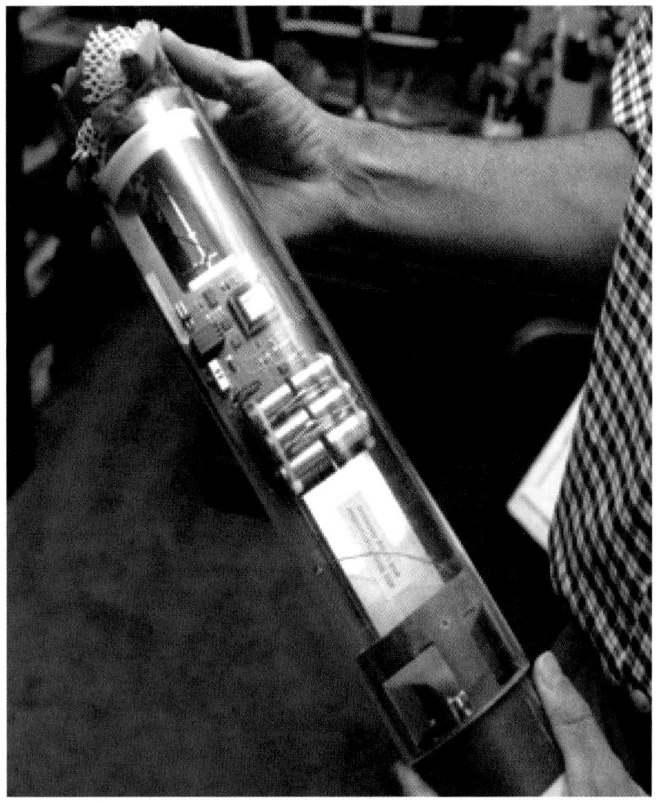

FIGURE 4. Dropsonde.

In biology a major impetus has been provided to marine scientists by the Census of Antarctic Marine Life (CAML). The Southern Ocean is around 10% of the world's oceans, and together with the Arctic Ocean, it is the least studied. It is a major carbon sink, and one of the globe's major ecosystems. This five-year CAML program involved 27 cruises on research vessels from the United States, United Kingdom, Australia, New Zealand, France, Russia, Belgium, Germany, Spain, Italy, Brazil, Chile, Uruguay, Peru, and Japan searching both the seafloor and the water column for new species, of which hundreds have already been identified.

These multinational research programs are conceived through a variety of mechanisms that include scientific workshops, meetings convened under science and technology agreements between and among nations, and, increasingly, electronic access to data of common interest. For over 50 years SCAR has provided a broadly international forum for identifying and building on common interests among scientists and building collaborations and plans for achieving them. Its major new programs on Antarctic climate evolution, biodiversity, subglacial lakes, and solar-terrestrial physics now involve more than 30 nations.

INFRASTRUCTURE AND LOGISTICS

Implementing these multinational projects is possible only because nations share access to their national infrastructures and logistics in Antarctica. The Council of Managers of National Antarctic Programs (COMNAP), which brings operational expertise to bear in all aspects of Antarctic support, is of particular importance in facilitating the range of logistic support needed in Antarctica to carry out these studies in a safe and environmentally responsible manner. The COMNAP members work closely with each other, with other governmental agencies in their nations, and with SCAR to match international logistic infrastructure to the needs of these international science collaborations.

The following are just a few examples of shared infrastructure:

- the French-Italian station at Dome C that hosts, among many other projects, a significant portion of the Concordiasi project;
- the Airbus A319 that is operated by the Australian Antarctic Program as an important component of the logistics pool, as are the wheeled and ski-equipped

C-130s that New Zealand and the United States operate; and

- the Swedish icebreaker *Oden* that hosts joint U.S.-Swedish research in the Southern Ocean and opens the channel through the sea ice that enables annual resupply of the U.S. research stations at McMurdo and the South Pole.

The flags of the 12 nations that brought the Antarctic Treaty into being are proudly arranged in front of the new Amundsen-Scott South Pole Station of the U.S. Antarctic Program that was dedicated in 2009 (Figure 5). This station hosts researchers from around the world in the tradition of partnership that so characterizes Antarctica. Clearly, Antarctica, with its unique treaty and its long heritage of scientific research, remains a model of international cooperation, one with lessons for international science everywhere.

FIGURE 5. The new Amundsen-Scott South Pole Station of the U.S. Antarctic Program that was dedicated in 2009. Flags of the 12 original signatory nations of the Antarctic Treaty are arranged in front.

SUMMARY

Research at the frontier of science certainly can be performed and organized solely by individual scientists in two or more nations. But when complicated logistics partnerships are required, as are needed in supporting research in the huge and distant Antarctic, the legal framework provided by the Antarctic Treaty and the intellectual framework provided by the International Polar Year enable partnerships to develop and flourish over the several years required for planning, fieldwork, and follow-through in laboratories back home. The scientific value of the Antarctic will continue to increase as its role in Earth system science is more fully realized, and it is only through international collaboration that many of these pressing questions will be answered.

Acknowledgment

I am pleased to have this opportunity to thank and congratulate the International Council of Science and the World Meteorological Organization, together with the national IPY programs, for shouldering the critically needed responsibilities that made this fourth IPY a success.

LITERATURE CITED

Dastidar, P., and S. Ramachandran. 2008. Intellectual Structure of Antarctic Science: A 25-Years Analysis. *Scientometrics,* 77(3):389–414.

Public Participation in Antarctica: The Role of Nongovernmental and Intergovernmental Organizations

Harlan Cohen

Article III of the Antarctic Treaty provides, inter alia, that "to the greatest extent feasible and practicable" information regarding plans for scientific programs and scientific observations and results from Antarctica are to be exchanged and made freely available. In implementation of this article, every encouragement is to be given to establishing cooperative working relations with United Nations specialized agencies and other international organizations having a scientific or technical interest in Antarctica.[1]

Thus, from the beginning, and anchored in the treaty itself, was the concept that there was a role for international organizations having a scientific or technical interest in Antarctica, both nongovernmental and intergovernmental organizations. Nongovernmental organizations are generally created by private persons or groups with no participation or representation by governments. They may raise funds privately and may also receive funds from governments, often for specific projects. Intergovernmental organizations generally include as members sovereign states or other intergovernmental organizations. National academies of science are often chartered, and largely funded, by governments but operate as and are considered nongovernmental. The Scientific Committee on Antarctic Research (SCAR) is an interdisciplinary committee of the International Council for Science (ICSU), which, in turn, is a nongovernmental body made up of national scientific members (often national academies of science) and international scientific unions.

At the First Antarctic Treaty Consultative Meeting (ATCM) in Canberra in 1961, the parties adopted two measures that confirmed this role. Recommendation I-IV recognized that SCAR's recommendations concerning scientific programs and cooperation were "a most valuable contribution" to international scientific cooperation in Antarctica" and that SCAR should be encouraged to continue its advisory work. Recommendation I-V recommended that governments encourage the work of international organizations having a scientific or technical interest in Antarctica and was not limited in its reference only to intergovernmental bodies.

Nevertheless, the Antarctic Treaty System (ATS) could not be considered open to outside bodies during its first years, although SCAR's advice and influence continued to play a prominent role.[2] The first opening of Antarctic Treaty

Harlan Cohen, International Union for Conservation of Nature, Suite 300, 1630 Connecticut Avenue NW, Washington, DC 20009.

meetings to intergovernmental organizations came in the 1970s. The Food and Agriculture Organization of the United Nations (FAO) participated as an observer delegation to the Conference on the Conservation of Antarctic Seals in London in February 1972 at which the Convention for the Conservation of Antarctic Seals was adopted.

Following the adoption of this convention, work within the treaty system focused on marine living resources. This led to growing involvement by both intergovernmental and nongovernmental organizations in providing expert analyses, participating as observers in ATS meetings, and participating as members of national delegations to Antarctic Treaty meetings. At the Eighth Consultative Meeting in 1975, Recommendation VIII-10 put certain questions to SCAR, which led to a meeting of scientists in 1976 to develop a research program on the Biological Investigation of Marine Antarctic Systems and Stocks (known as BIOMASS). The FAO prepared three reports in 1977 on the importance of krill to Antarctic marine ecosystems and their health.

The negotiation of the Convention on the Conservation of Antarctic Marine Living Resources (CCAMLR) represented a significant milestone in opening up the Antarctic Treaty System. In the United States, the National Environmental Policy Act (NEPA) became law in 1970. It provided for public consultation on the environmental effects of certain U.S. federal activities and alternatives thereto. The United Nations Conference on the Human Environment in Stockholm in 1972 also served as a stimulus for an expectation for public participation in environmental consultations. As early as 1977 at IX ATCM the U.S. delegation included an advisor from the nongovernmental organization The American Committee on International Conservation and the British delegation included an advisor from British Petroleum.

In Washington the Center for Law and Social Policy focused on Antarctica following the announcement by the 1972–1973 Deep Sea Drilling Project of the discovery of hydrocarbons in the Ross Sea. In London, the International Institute for Environment and Development began an Antarctica project in 1975–1976. Both urged the International Union for Conservation of Nature (IUCN) to become more involved in Antarctic issues, and members of the IUCN adopted resolutions with respect to Antarctica at IUCN general assemblies starting in 1977. The Antarctic and Southern Ocean Coalition (ASOC) was established in 1978. The 1981 IUCN resolution called, inter alia, for Antarctic Treaty Consultative Parties (ATCPs) to invite qualified nongovernmental organization representatives, including IUCN and ASOC, to participate in ATCMs. The IUCN Council in 1981 called for the preparation of a conservation strategy for Antarctica and the Southern Ocean.

The conference adopting CCAMLR held in Canberra in May 1980 included a variety of international organizations, both intergovernmental and nongovernmental. These organizations included the European Community, the FAO, the Intergovernmental Oceanographic Commission (IOC) of the United Nations Educational, Scientific and Cultural Organization (UNESCO), the International Whaling Commission (IWC), IUCN, SCAR, and the Scientific Committee on Oceanic Research (SCOR). Through the adoption of ATCM Recommendation IX-2 in 1977 it had been decided to include participation on an observer basis of "appropriate international organizations" "actively engaged in research and exploitation of Antarctic Marine Living Resources."

Interest from outside of the Antarctic Treaty System continued. With the adoption of CCAMLR, Consultative Parties turned their attention to the potential for the exploitation of mineral resources. At XI ATCM in 1981 in Buenos Aires it was agreed to consider a legal instrument with respect to mineral resources. The United Nations Convention on the Law of the Sea, adopted in 1982, provided that the resources, referred to as minerals, on the seabed beyond national jurisdiction were the "common heritage of mankind." Several developing states were of the view that mineral resources in Antarctica should be subject to a similar regime and raised the issue within the United Nations. In 1983, the question of Antarctica was discussed as an agenda item within the United Nations General Assembly. The Antarctic Treaty System was criticized because of its closed nature. This criticism served as a catalyst for opening the Antarctic Treaty meetings to Non-Consultative Parties and to international organizations, including nongovernmental ones. It also served to encourage greater public availability of papers and reports from Consultative Meetings.

Thus, over time participation in its meetings and processes was opened to observers from the outside. These changes were reflected in the Rules of Procedure, which were amended at XIV ATCM in Rio de Janeiro in 1987 to provide for participation by representatives of SCAR and the CCAMLR Secretariat as observers and representatives of several international organizations as experts. Observers were viewed as permanent components of the Antarctic Treaty System, whereas experts were to be invited only for specific agenda items on which they had expertise. Invited to XIV ATCM were the World Meteorological Organization (WMO) with respect to agenda items 13 and 15 on Antarctic meteorology and telecommunications and an international system of marine hydrometeorological services to navigation in the Southern Ocean, SCAR with respect to agenda item 14 on air safety in Antarctica, and IUCN with respect to agenda item 9 on human impact on the Antarctic Environment.[3]

These organizations provide important information and advice without which the Antarctic Treaty Parties could not effectively or efficiently manage Antarctica. In other words, if these organizations did not provide certain necessary information, the parties would have to develop that information themselves. I refer to the scientific advice that is received, for example, from SCAR, ASOC, the International Hydrographic Organization (IHO), IOC, IUCN, SCAR, the United Nations Environment Programme (UNEP), and WMO. From the earliest days of the treaty system, SCAR provided advice and information that informed key decisions, including the adoption of the Agreed Measures for the Conservation of Antarctic Fauna and Flora, the Convention for the Conservation of Antarctic Seals, and CCAMLR.

The IUCN members maintained a focused interest in the conservation of Antarctica and its environment.[4] As early as 1972 it had been recommended at the Second World Conference on National Parks that Antarctica be designated as a world park. Following a 1984 IUCN resolution on Antarctica and consultations with SCAR and a joint IUCN-SCAR symposium on the scientific requirements for Antarctic conservation in 1985, a joint IUCN-SCAR working group was established to consider a long-term conservation plan for Antarctica. An interim report was prepared in 1986. The IUCN had prepared a report on "Conservation and Development of Antarctic Ecosystems" in 1984, and SCAR had published a report on "Man's Impact on the Antarctic Environment" in 1985. The IUCN has sent a delegation to ATCMs in most years since 1987 and to CCAMLR Commission meetings in most years since the first one in 1982. In 1991 IUCN published "A Strategy for Antarctic Conservation." In 1994 IUCN published "Developing the Antarctic Protected Area System: Proceedings of the SCAR/IUCN Workshop on Antarctic Protected Areas" following a workshop held in 1992 in Cambridge, and in 1996 it published "Opportunities for Antarctic Environmental Education and Training: Proceedings of the SCAR/IUCN Workshop on Environmental Education and Training" following a workshop held in 1993 in Gorizia. The IUCN also published the "Proceedings of the IUCN Workshop on Cumulative Impacts in Antarctica: Minimisation and Management" following a workshop held in 1996 in Washington, D.C.

The ASOC provides key information on a variety of issues. For example, ASOC submitted nine information papers to the most recent Consultative Meeting in Baltimore, including ones on marine protection, tourism, and climate change. The coalition submitted seven papers to the CCAMLR meetings in 2009. The Oceanites Project, a nongovernmental nonprofit science and education foundation, has participated for some years at Consultative Meetings as advisers on a national delegation and has provided invaluable information through the Antarctic Site Inventory on visitor sites. The UNEP has provided advice on bioprospecting and on other topics, sometimes in collaboration with other UN family bodies. Conservation trusts that do not necessarily participate directly in meetings provide information for the management of certain historic sites and monuments.

The International Association of Antarctica Tour Operators (IAATO) was founded as an industry group in 1991 to promote and practice safe and environmentally responsible private travel to Antarctica. The IAATO has acted as a conduit from Consultative Meetings to its members to provide the industry with up-to-date information about safety and environmental protection requirements adopted at Consultative Meetings. The IAATO also provides Consultative Meetings with data about tourists, their numbers, their site visits, and their management. Consultative Parties need these data to manage and would have to collate them directly if IAATO did not provide them.

The various nongovernmental and intergovernmental organizations that attend Antarctic Treaty meetings also serve their members and the general public by providing information on actions taken with respect to the governance of Antarctica and developments on and around the continent, especially including those with respect to the environment. This, in turn, encourages interest in Antarctica and helps to build constituencies within different countries in support of programs in Antarctica, both for science and for conservation. It also requires care, as organizations must be careful to address or avoid the claimant/nonclaimant issue in such a way as to help the parties without offending any. Sometimes, an effective approach can be to provide scientific and technical advice to national delegations in a discrete and diplomatic way. At other times, a public approach may be more effective.

The IUCN has an additional complexity in that its members include both governments and nongovernmental organizations. Over half of the Treaty Parties are state members of IUCN, and many of the others have agencies that are also IUCN members. The IUCN's mission is to influence, encourage, and assist societies throughout the world to conserve the integrity and diversity of nature and to ensure that any use of natural resources is equitable and ecologically sustainable. In some countries IUCN is recognized under private law; in others it is an international organization. In addition, the IUCN family includes six commissions, which are made up of individual volunteers, some with a private, academic, conservation, or industry nongovernmental background and others who work for government agencies. There are, at times, members of commissions who also serve on national delegations. These individuals may provide advice directly through IUCN or as part of a national delegation. The IUCN thus must provide its advice in such a way that it reflects resolutions passed at its governing meeting while at the same time reflecting its diverse membership and ensuring that it is true to its mission to influence, encourage, and assist societies to conserve the integrity and diversity of nature and to ensure that any use of natural resources is equitable and ecologically sustainable.

I would like to turn to the issue of public availability of information, which is clearly and directly related to the issue of public participation. Looking back, the Antarctic Treaty grew out of the International Geophysical Year of 1957–1958 and was developed as a way to reserve Antarctica from cold war tensions that troubled the world at the time. It represented an innovative way to use scientific exchanges to promote disarmament, but in many ways the impetus for the Antarctic Treaty was disarmament. Thus, the treaty grew out of a disarmament (and therefore an arms) background. This set the stage for a culture in which governments of the time operated in relative secrecy, and early ATCMs were conducted in that atmosphere (though from the beginning the advice of SCAR and other international organizations was sought). As developments in the United Nations and several international treaty processes increasingly noted, the closed nature of the Antarctic Treaty System became more and more of an anomaly, and the debates on Antarctica in the United Nations General Assembly beginning in 1983 also played a major role in promoting more open information policies.

At the preparatory meeting for XII ATCM in April 1983 it was agreed to invite Non-Consultative Parties for the first time. At the Twelfth Consultative Meeting in September 1983 in Canberra Recommendation XII-6 was adopted and referred to the Antarctic Treaty as based on the principles of the United Nations Charter, acknowledging "the value of increasing public knowledge of the achievements and operation of the Antarctic Treaty system." This recommendation included a call to send certified copies of the final report of the meeting to the Secretary-General of the United Nations and to draw the attention, when ATCPs through it appropriate, of any United Nations specialized agency or any other international organization having a scientific or technical interest in Antarctica. The *Antarctic Treaty Handbook* was to be renamed and brought up to date. Starting with the Thirteenth Consultative Meeting, delegates were to indicate when submitting information documents if these were intended to be publicly available. After the closure of the meeting and provided no Consultative Party objected, any party could make the information document publicly available. The United States, as Depositary Government for the Antarctic Treaty, was invited to identify and catalog publicly available information about the treaty system.

At the Thirteenth Consultative Meeting in October 1985 in Brussels, through Recommendation XIII-1, it was agreed that efforts should continue to ensure full and accurate records of Consultative Meetings and that to the extent allowable under national law the reports of Consultative Meetings, the *Antarctic Treaty Handbook*, and annual exchanges of information under the Antarctic Treaty should be made available to the public upon request. At XIV ATCM in October 1987 in Rio de Janeiro, Recommendation XVI-1 was adopted, amending Recommendation XIII-1 to read that all information documents would be considered public at the close of the Consultative Meeting unless the submitting party notified otherwise in advance.

With the opening of Consultative Meetings to Non-Consultative Parties, to observers, and to experts, reports of the meetings and documents submitted to it became available to those groups. The practice still remained to consider documents as not public, though the Internet has, to a large extent, changed this practice. Documents remain password protected until after the Consultative Meeting, though parties and all interested international organizations, both intergovernmental and nongovernmental, have access to the password.

From the very beginning the role and expertise of nongovernmental organizations, and here I refer to SCAR, and of some other international organizations was recognized. The FAO and WMO, for example, were both recognized early on as important to Antarctic management.

Nongovernmental and intergovernmental organizations provide information and advice that is essential to good governance by Antarctic Treaty Parties. If information and advice from these organizations were not available, the system would have to compile this on its own and at considerable expense to itself, or it would not be able to fulfill properly its mandate. Participation by these organizations assists the parties; indeed, it is necessary for the management of Antarctica. These organizations also make better known to the general public the importance of Antarctica with its special role for peace and science. A number of organizations have helped to bring to public attention the effects of climate change that are now causing lasting and worrisome changes to the environment of Antarctica and the Southern Ocean.

Although the system has opened to nongovernmental and intergovernmental organizations over the years and recently has been fully open, the Rules of Procedure do not fully reflect this. Although Article IX of the Antarctic Treaty provides that Consultative Parties alone are entitled to appoint representatives to Consultative Meetings, the Rules of Procedure rightly provide that representatives of Non-Consultative Parties and of observers and experts may be invited. Some areas for consideration for change in the Rules of Procedure when they are next reviewed by the parties could include the following:

- Rules 3 and 27 should be amended to reflect that Non-Consultative Parties should always be invited (in practice, this has been the case in recent decades).
- Rules 32 and 42 should be amended to reflect that observers and invited experts are normally welcome at all sessions of the Consultative Meeting (in practice, this has been the case in recent years).
- Though not reflected in the Rules of Procedure, the handling of documents for meetings should be changed to make them publicly available ab initio and to eliminate the password protection procedures on the secretariat web site.[5]

Recalling the key role of science in Antarctica and with respect to Antarctic governance from the beginning of the Antarctic Treaty System, an increase in funding for science, including for basic research, would support continued public participation in the diffusion of knowledge about Antarctica and its role in global physical processes, including biological, geochemical, and environmental processes. The promotion of science would thus promote both public participation and the objectives of the Antarctic Treaty, especially Article III.

Acknowledgments

I thank the organizers and the Smithsonian Institution for making the Antarctic Treaty Summit: Science-Policy Interactions in International Governance possible and for inviting me to provide some comments on the historical role that nongovernmental and intergovernmental organizations have played in the treaty system. On the 50th anniversary of the signing of the Antarctic Treaty, I think it important to acknowledge those who crafted this elegant treaty that reserved a continent for peace and science, ensuring that this special place would remain free of military fortifications and activities while promoting international cooperation in scientific investigation. The remarks given herein belong solely to the author and do not necessarily represent the views or policies of IUCN.

NOTES

1. Sources for information incorporated in these remarks include the Web site of the Antarctic Treaty Secretariat, http://www.ats.aq/index_e.htm; Harlan K. Cohen, ed., *Handbook of the Antarctic Treaty System*, 9th ed. (Washington, D.C.: U.S. Department of State, 2002), http://www.state.gov/g/oes/rls/rpts/ant/; Christopher C. Joyner and Sudhir K. Chopra, eds., *The Antarctic Legal Regime* (Dordrecht, the Netherlands: Martinus Nijhoff Publishers, 1988); Philippe Sand, ed., *Greening International Law* (New York: The New Press, 1994); the ASOC Web site, http://www.asoc.org/AboutUs/tabid/163/Default.aspx; the IAATO Web site, http://www.iaato.org/about.html; the Oceanites Web site, http://www.oceanites.org/; the SCAR Web site, http://www.scar.org/; and Lee Kimball, personal communication. All web sites cited here were accessed in December 2009

2. The SCAR's advice was sought with respect to conservation of Antarctic fauna and flora (The Agreed Measures for the Conservation of Antarctic Fauna and Flora) and again two years later specifically with respect to seals, and this advice was recognized through recommendations adopted at the Third and Fourth Consultative Meetings in Brussels in June 1964 and Santiago in November 1966, respectively. The SCAR's influence was recognized in a preambular paragraph of the Agreed Measures for the Conservation of Antarctic Fauna and Flora as adopted through Recommendation III-VIII.

3. The SCAR, CCAMLR, and COMNAP now participate as observers, and at recent meetings experts who were invited included those from the Interim Secretariat of ACAP, ASOC, IAATO, IHO, IMO, IOC, the IPY International Programme Office, IUCN, UNEP, WMO, and WTO. Thus, the observers include one nongovernmental organization, one intergovernmental organization, and one international association of government employees. The experts include three nongovernmental organizations, seven intergovernmental organizations (including three that are UN specialized agency related), and several that are independent of the United Nations. However, the Rules of Procedure provided that experts would not necessarily be invited to observe the whole of the meeting, and indeed, until the late 1990s experts were asked to leave the meeting during discussion of at least one agenda item.

4. Founded in 1948 as the world's first global environmental organization, IUCN is the world's largest professional global conservation network, whose membership includes over 200 government and over 800 nongovernment organizations; thus, it is a unique intergovernmental and nongovernmental organization.

5. There would appear to be no real reason to protect working, information, or secretariat papers before the meeting. All parties and

interested observers and experts who assist the meeting have access to the documents. It is unlikely that representatives of a state that is not a party to the treaty could not find a friendly country to share papers, and it is doubtful that there are large numbers of unaffiliated persons who might seek access. But even if persons unaffiliated with the system obtained access to papers in advance, no obvious harm would be done. Public availability of documents reflects modern best practice and would ease access for delegates and simplify work for the secretariat.

The Antarctic Treaty System: Perspectives of Environmental Nongovernmental Organizations on Addressing Key Issues

James N. Barnes

INTRODUCTION

The overriding objective of the Antarctic and Southern Ocean Coalition (ASOC) is to ensure that the world's last unspoiled wilderness, Antarctica and the Southern Ocean, survives intact as a global commons for the heritage of future generations of humans and wildlife. The ASOC is the only nongovernmental organization with expert observer status to the Antarctic Treaty System (ATS). The ASOC sends teams of scientists and policy experts to key international treaty meetings around the world where Antarctica's future is decided: the Antarctic Treaty Consultative Meeting (ATCM), Commission on the Conservation of Antarctic Marine Living Resources (CCAMLR), International Maritime Organization (IMO), International Whaling Commission (IWC), and Agreement on Conservation of Albatrosses and Petrels (ACAP). We also follow closely other international fora of importance to Antarctica, including the Convention on Biological Diversity (CBD).

A VISION OF ANTARCTICA IN 2060: ASOC'S ASPIRATIONS

Drawing on the presentations at the Antarctic Treaty Summit, it is clear that as we look ahead 50 years and ask what kind of Antarctica we hope will exist then, the ATS faces some significant challenges. Drawing on ASOC's experiences over the past 30 years and recent surveys of Antarctic Treaty Parties, scientists, and the public, there are some bedrock truths to keep in mind.

- There is strong support for using Antarctica to carry out globally significant science for which it is the only, or the best, platform and maintaining in perpetuity the open science regime of the Antarctic Treaty.
- There is strong public support for maintaining the "wilderness and esthetic values" of the Antarctic and for the region to be kept as pristine as possible and emerging awareness among Antarctic Treaty Parties of the desirability of minimizing the "human footprint" of activities in the region. There is increasing support in the ATS for taking more steps to minimize the

James N. Barnes, Antarctic and Southern Ocean Coalition, 1630 Connecticut Ave. NW, 3rd Fl., Washington DC 20009, USA. Correspondence: james.barnes@asoc.org.

human footprint by sharing logistics and infrastructure, avoiding duplication of activities, and generating more of the energy needed for science and logistics from sustainable sources. The ASOC sponsored a resolution on wilderness values at the World Parks Congress in Mexico in December 2009, which was agreed to unanimously.

- There is broad public support for creating more protected areas on land and in the Southern Ocean, including developing a representative network of marine reserves. This has become a priority of CCAMLR and Antarctic Treaty Parties over the past two years. The CCAMLR has set a target date of 2012 for establishing an initial network of marine protected areas (MPAs), and the Atlantic Treaty Consultative Parties (ATCPs) are moving forward to develop a more comprehensive system of Antarctic Specially Protected Areas and Antarctic Specially Managed Areas under Annex V to the Protocol on Environmental Protection to the Antarctic Treaty (Environmental Protocol).
- There is no support for Antarctica becoming a mass tourism destination, with hotels and other infrastructure on land and large vessels carrying thousands of passengers. The Antarctic Treaty Parties have been moving steadily the past few years to control commercial tourism and establish rules to minimize the impacts of tourism.

RECOMMENDATIONS FOR IMPROVEMENTS OF THE ANTARCTIC TREATY SYSTEM

On the basis of views expressed and papers presented at the summit and ASOC's experiences within the ATS during the past 30 years, I have the following suggestions on process and substance issues of importance to the continuing health of the ATS.

Process

- Bringing measures, annexes, and recommendations into force promptly is very important for the credibility and legitimacy of the ATS and also has practical implications. Too many legally binding requirements from past Antarctic Treaty Consultative Meetings are not in force because one or more states have not ratified them. The case of the liability annex (Annex VI to the Environmental Protocol), so far ratified by only four states, is illustrative.
- The information exchange system that lies at the heart of the AT is in some disarray, with around 50% of parties not providing this crucial information either ever or an a timely basis. There needs to be serious commitment by all parties to meet those basic obligations, on time.
- Although the inspection regimes of the Antarctic Treaty and Environmental Protocol are not mandatory, it is important for the credibility of the ATS that regular inspections are undertaken by a wide range of parties working jointly or individually. That step will help improve compliance and promote best practices.
- Promoting positive synergies among the various international agreements with pertinence and/or competence in the Southern Ocean is very important, particularly with the IMO, ACAP, the IWC, and the CBD.
- Giving the ATCM some form of continuing "personality" rather than it having just a two-week life each year would help provide better continuity and follow-up and allow the ATCM to have a "voice" at other international fora. It would also be helpful to have a standing committee for key subjects, rather than the ad hoc intersessional contact groups utilized now.
- The ATS could take further steps toward fuller transparency, including following the precedent of the Edinburgh ATCM to include the media and civil society in the meetings. Most ATCMs are eerily quiet places from the standpoint of the media, which is unsurprising since the press are not invited save for a token opening ceremony photo opportunity and all the working and information papers are embargoed until after the meeting ends. At least these papers are eventually made publicly available on the ATS Web site, but CCAMLR papers are never made public. Even accredited experts such as ASOC cannot regularly access the documents of past CCAMLR meetings. Being more transparent will help build greater public support for the money needed to finance research and logistics in Antarctica. It would also likely speed up the pace of gaining full agreement on important new steps and on bringing into legal force past commitments.
- More countries need to participate actively in the key intersessional working groups established with varying degrees of formality by the ATCM and CCAMLR. Since decisions ultimately are by consensus, the process of building that consensus is crucial. When so many CCAMLR Parties do not participate at the key Working Group on Environmental Monitoring and Management (WG-EMM), for example, that means

the dialogue and discussion take much longer and that often decision makers at the commission level have not been well briefed by their scientists since they were not at the EMM. Hence, it is harder to come to a decision.

Substance

- Developing a regulatory system for commercial tourism remains a high priority. Although some initial steps have been taken, so far there is no agreement on a comprehensive, legally-binding system that will prevent mass tourism, land-based infrastructure such as hotels, and use of larger, riskier vessels.
- Working closely with the IMO on a legally binding Polar Code for all vessels operating in Antarctica is a high priority, and although linked to the first point on tourism to a certain degree, it is far broader in its scope. There are major concerns about vessel accidents causing loss of human life and pollution of the marine environment, which would be a tragedy and also give the ATS a black eye in terms of its management of the region. These fears were enhanced by the sinking of the MV *Explorer*. The Polar Code negotiations began in February 2010 at the IMO. The initial discussions show good support for appropriate ice-strengthening standards and other vessel- and crew-related rules to better protect the environment and human life. The ATCPs support negotiation of a mandatory Polar Code by the IMO and are participating actively, through their national representatives.
- Creating a representative system of large marine reserves and more land-based protected areas using the tools of the protocol and CCAMLR is a major priority and opportunity. It is very positive that the ATCPs, working through the Committee for Environmental Protection (CEP), and CCAMLR Parties have endorsed a target of 2012 for achieving the first phase of an MPA system, focusing on the list of 11 areas that have been identified so far. In this context, the first joint meeting of the CEP and CCAMLR Scientific Committee took place in April 2009, which engendered substantial progress toward a representative network. On the MPA list is the Ross Sea, which is a particular priority for ASOC and scientists around the world. Having more regular joint meetings of the CEP and Scientific Committee of CCAMLR would build on this good precedent and help ensure a harmonized approach within the ATS.
- Illegal fishing—a large, valuable international business involving many companies and vessels, including some from ATS Parties—is estimated to be 15% to 25% of the legal fisheries. All Antarctic Treaty and CCAMLR Parties ritually condemn illegal fishing in the Southern Ocean, and the public wants it stopped. The question is how to use the available assets and tools cooperatively to do this. We should take note of the new Port States Agreement, which offers new tools. I hope it is ratified and brought into force quickly. At the same time, there are many steps parties can take both individually and collectively to bring to a halt the pirate fishing, which is focused on Antarctic and Patagonian toothfish. These steps include better use of sophisticated imaging and tracking devices, ideally on a cooperative basis, and more robust enforcement within the ATS area.
- Completing an ecosystem-based, small-scale management unit system for the krill fishery, the base of the marine food chain, will constitute an important step forward for CCAMLR as well as providing a model for other regional fishery management organizations. Although this has been under discussion at CCAMLR for several years regarding Area 48, the focus of the krill fishery, so far it has not been possible to reach agreement on the precise methodology to follow. This is partly because of lack of adequate data about impacts on predators.
- Developing a framework to cover commercial biological prospecting, which is developing into a major commercial activity, is an important task. This has been on the agenda of the ATCM for several years, but so far without agreement on any form of regulatory structure. Although substantively this should be a joint task of the ATCM and CCAMLR, so far only the ATCM has discussed it. One key problem goes back to a procedural issue referred to above: the poor response of ATCPs to providing the information required by Recommendation 2 of Resolution 7 (2005), which requires parties to provide detailed information on biological prospecting by its scientists and companies as well as details on patents and products utilizing Antarctic organisms. Shared information about scientific research and expeditions lies at the heart of the ATS and is a key obligation of all parties. Failure to comply with this obligation risks undermining the Antarctic Treaty over time.
- Antarctica provides a preeminent platform for carrying out scientific research on climate change of

global importance. Over the past 50 years, the Antarctic Peninsula has warmed four times faster than the global average, making it one of the most rapidly warming regions on the planet. Dramatic changes to terrestrial and marine ecosystems are occurring in areas of warming. The southward retreat of the High Antarctic Zone and successful invasions of nonindigenous species on subantarctic islands are among the trends in biotic change brought by increasing human activity and increasing temperatures. In the past few years the ATCM and CCAMLR have begun elevating climate change to a mainstream and crucial item of discussion at their meetings, and the first special meeting of experts on climate change took place in April 2010 in Norway. Those experts conveyed 30 recommendations to the 2010 ATCM in Punta del Este, Uruguay, which were endorsed by the ATCM. Taking account of climate change impacts through management decisions about fisheries and protected areas, taking actions in Antarctica to mitigate impacts, and utilizing Antarctic science in international negotiations to help avoid dangerous climate change are priorities for the ATS.

CONCLUDING REMARKS

The Southern Ocean is a commons of immense value to the world for science, wildlife, wilderness, and sustainable use of its marine resources. Antarctica helps to regulate the planet's climate by acting as a heat sink, and the Antarctic Circumpolar Current links the world's major oceans, driving global ocean circulation. The Antarctic merits protection for its uniqueness, beauty, biological diversity, and scientific value. It as an exceptional platform for carrying out globally significant science and recording the environmental health of the planet. Protecting the Antarctic region as a whole is important to ensuring a sustainable future for the global environment. The ASOC plays an important role in these efforts and looks forward to working with Antarctic Treaty System Parties, other ATS experts and observers, and scientists in the coming decades.

Common Interests in the Ocean

Rüdiger Wolfrum

INTRODUCTION

Oceans (the high seas, the deep-ocean floor, and its subsoil) differ fundamentally from territories or spaces under national jurisdiction. Whereas the management of the latter rests in the responsibility of a given state, activities in the former are governed by international law, implemented and enforced by individual states or organs of the community of states as the case may be. It is to be assumed from this very fact that community interests in the proper management and preservation of the oceans are prevailing. In this chapter, I address the legal regime for common interests in the oceans focusing on the lessons learned from Antarctica.

STATUS OF THE AREA

The most evident expression of common interests in the oceans is to be found in the common heritage principle. The term was formally introduced by Malta in a note verbale on 18 August 1967 (UN Doc. A/6695) requesting the introduction of an agenda item into the agenda of the UN General Assembly: "Declaration and treaty concerning the reservation exclusively for peaceful purposes of the sea-bed and the ocean floor, underlying the seas beyond the limits of present national jurisdiction, and the use of their resources in the interests of mankind."

The common heritage principle is an essential element, even the basis, of Part XI of the UN Convention on the Law of the Sea (1982) concerning the deep seabed, from where it has found its way into national legislation relating to seabed activities. It was also introduced in 1967 into the then beginning discussion on a legal regime for outer space and, to a lesser extent, later into the legal framework for Antarctica. The Agreement Relating to the Implementation of Part XI of the United Nations Convention on the Law of the Sea of 10 December 1982 (Implementation Agreement) has, in fact, modified the deep-seabed regime somewhat, but without sacrificing the core of the principle.

Rüdiger Wolfrum, Max Planck Institute for Comparative Public Law and International Law, Im Neuenheimer Feld 535/69120 Heidelberg, Germany. Correspondence: wolfrum@mpil.de.

In the UN Convention on the Law of the Sea the common heritage of mankind is set forth under different provisions. The Preamble refers to UN General Assembly Resolution 2749 (XXV) of 17 December 1970 (A/RES/25/2749) in which the UN General Assembly solemnly declared, inter alia, that the area of the "sea-bed and ocean floor, and the subsoil thereof, beyond the limits of national jurisdiction . . . as well as the resources of the area, are the common heritage of mankind." The principle is highlighted in Article 136 of the UN Convention on the Law of the Sea, according to which this area and its resources are the common heritage of mankind. The significance of this principle to the UN Convention on the Law of the Sea becomes evident through its Article 311, paragraph 6, which provides that there will be no amendments to the basic principle relating to the common heritage of mankind set forth in Article 136 of the UN Convention on the Law of the Sea. This attributes to Article 136 of the UN Convention on the Law of the Sea a special status above treaty law without qualifying it as *jus cogens* (i.e. peremptory international law). The common heritage principle as established by the UN Convention on the Law of the Sea contains several core elements, which will be discussed in the remainder of this chapter.

NONOCCUPATION/NONAPPROPRIATION

According to Article 137 of the UN Convention on the Law of the Sea, no state shall claim or exercise sovereignty or sovereign rights over any part of the seabed and the ocean floor or its resources, nor shall any state or natural or juridical person appropriate any part thereof. No such claim or exercise of either sovereignty rights or such appropriation shall be recognized.

The legal significance of the nonoccupation and the nonappropriation element of the common heritage principle concerning the high seas was minimal, as Article 2 of the Geneva Convention on the High Seas already prohibited any occupation of the high seas. Equally, an appropriation by private entities is excluded.

This element of nonoccupation is also inherent in Article IV of the Antarctic Treaty, which excludes new territorial claims. It is a matter to be looked into as to whether individuals or entities may appropriate parts of Antarctica. In my view, Article IV of the Antarctic Treaty, albeit not explicitly, indirectly rules out the possibility of appropriation.

As far as the seabed beyond national jurisdiction is concerned, Article 136 of the UN Convention on the Law of the Sea goes a decisive step further. It states that no such claim or exercise of sovereignty or sovereign rights or such appropriation shall be recognized. Thus, the prohibition of occupation and appropriation has been given a legal status, the effect of which is similar to that of *jus cogens*. Moreover, Article 137 of the UN Convention on the Law of the Sea is phrased as an obligation of all states and not only the States Parties to the convention. One of the objectives of the common heritage principle is to preserve the present legal status of the international commons against all states and, as indicated by the term "appropriation," all private persons. The latter has far-reaching consequences. It means that an illegal appropriation will not result in a title of ownership for the entity in question. States Parties are therefore obliged to modify their law on private ownership accordingly. This constitutes a viable mechanism to preserve the common interests in the resources of the deep seabed.

DUTY TO COOPERATE

The regime of utilization, furthermore, establishes the obligation of all states to cooperate internationally in the exploration and exploitation of the deep seabed. The institution through which such cooperation is to be achieved is the International Seabed Authority (ISA). A corresponding duty of states to cooperate in the peaceful exploration and use of outer space, including celestial bodies, has been formulated as a principle immanent in space law. Such an obligation to cooperate on deep-seabed and outer space matters surpasses the requirements of international law in general.

Although the obligation to cooperate constitutes a strong element in the Antarctic legal regime, it has not been institutionalized in a way similar to the one for the deep seabed. There is no question, however, of the interstate cooperation between states and between states and nongovernmental organizations at the Antarctic Treaty Consultative Meetings. Cooperation is a dominant feature of the Antarctic legal regime and even more evident in the day-to-day activities in Antarctica.

INTERNATIONAL MANAGEMENT

Apart from its negative side just described (i.e. nonoccupation and nonappropriation), the common heritage principle introduces a revolutionary new positive element into the law of the sea by indicating that the control and management of the deep seabed is vested in mankind as a whole. Mankind, in turn, is represented as far as the deep seabed is concerned by the ISA, which is the organization through which States Parties organize and control deep-seabed activities (Article 157, paragraph 1, of the UN Convention on the Law of the Sea). Thus, States Parties are meant to act as a kind of trustee on behalf of mankind as a whole. It is in this respect that the common heritage principle introduces a fundamental change in the legal regime governing the deep seabed. However, no other international agreement implementing the common heritage principle, not even the Agreement Governing the Activities of States on the Moon and Other Celestial Bodies (Moon Agreement) follows this approach.

A particular legal regime governs the use of the geostationary orbit. The legal regime governing the geostationary orbit involves the International Telecommunication Union (ITU) in the administration of that part of outer space, although to a comparatively lesser extent. Many scholars hold that the establishment of an international management system like the ISA is a necessary feature of the common heritage principle. I beg to differ. In my view, it is perfectly possible to serve the interests of the international community even without establishing an international organization.

REGULATED UTILIZATION

The key provision on the system of exploration and exploitation of the resources of the deep seabed (Article 153 of the UN Convention on the Law of the Sea) avoids referring to the freedom of such uses. Instead, it states that activities in the international seabed area shall be carried out by the Enterprise (an organ of the ISA) and, in association with the ISA, by States Parties or their nationals when sponsored by such states. In that respect, the deep-seabed mining regime differs from the one governing the high seas as well as the one governing outer space. On the high seas as well as in outer space all states enjoy freedoms, although such freedoms are to be exercised under the conditions laid down by international law. The main difference between the two regimes rests in the fact that the freedoms of the high seas are to be exercised with due regard to the interests of other states, so as to coordinate the exercise of such freedoms and to protect against negative effects from such exercise, whereas the restrictions imposed upon the utilization of the deep seabed are also meant to protect the interests of humankind. In particular, when the legal regime concerning the utilization of the deep seabed was discussed, it was emphasized that the common heritage principle was meant to replace the freedom-based approach that traditionally governs the use of the high seas.

The approach pursued by the Antarctic legal regime is somewhat different. The Protocol on Environmental Protection to the Antarctic Treaty (Environmental Protocol) and its annexes are much more concrete than Part XI of the UN Convention on the Law of the Sea, which makes supplementary rules for deep-seabed activities necessary. In this respect, the so-called mining code of ISA is borrowed from the draft Convention on the Regulation of Mineral Resource Activities in Antarctica (CRAMRA) and the Environmental Protocol to the Antarctic Treaty. That was particularly true for the liability regime.

DISTRIBUTIVE EFFECT

Controversy over the utilization system concerning the deep seabed centered upon the question of how to make sure that deep-seabed mining would benefit all mankind. The term "benefit" mentioned in the UN Convention on the Law of the Sea should be understood broadly. What matters, on the one hand, is the immaterial benefit, i.e., the extension and deepening of mankind's knowledge concerning the international commons. On the other hand, the benefit thought of is the one that can be derived from the use of the resources of the seabed and ocean floor as well as of outer space and its celestial bodies. According to Article 140 of the UN Convention on the Law of the Sea, activities in the deep-seabed area should be carried out for the benefit of mankind as a whole, taking into particular consideration the interests and needs of developing states. This article merely describes a legal framework from which no specific legal rights and obligations can yet be drawn. However, the UN Convention on the Law of the Sea formulates further, more specific obligations: equal participation of all states despite their technological or economic development, sharing of revenues, transfer of technology (so as to provide for equal participation), preferential treatment of developing countries, protection against adverse effects of deep-seabed mining on land-based mining, and cooperation. The UN Convention on the Law of the Sea attempts to achieve the objective of equal participation by the following means: (1) restrictions imposed upon potential deep-seabed miners, (2) affirmative action benefiting nonmining states, and (3) conferring of jurisdiction over deep-seabed mining activities on the ISA so that all States Parties can equally, though indirectly, participate therein. This utilization system represents an attempt to provide for distributive justice. It is in this respect that the Implementation Agreement has introduced modifications, in particular concerning a production policy and the obligation for a transfer of technology.

The introduction of the term "mankind" combined with the word "heritage" indicates that the interests of future generations have to be respected in making use of the international commons. More specifically, it requires that deep-seabed or outer space activities should avoid undue waste of resources and provides for the protection of the environment. An important part of the intertemporal dimension of the common heritage principle is the concept of sustainable development. Articles 145 and 209 of the UN Convention on the Law of the Sea provide for the protection of the marine environment against harmful effects of deep-seabed mining.

This concept of sustainable development is well enshrined in the Antarctic legal system. The Environmental Protocol, including its annexes, and the Convention on Antarctic Marine Living Resources are based thereon.

HIGH SEAS AND MARITIME AREAS UNDER NATIONAL JURISDICTION

Although the common interests in the oceans are most explicitly expressed as far as the utilization of the deep seabed is concerned, they influence the legal regime for the high seas as well as for maritime areas under national jurisdiction. This point will be highlighted regarding fisheries and the protection of the marine environment.

According to Article 61, paragraph 2, of the UN Convention on the Law of the Sea, coastal states shall ensure that the maintenance of the living resources in their exclusive economic zones is not endangered by overexploitation. Paragraph 3 continues to state that populations should be maintained and restored at levels whereby they can produce the maximum sustainable yield. In short, coastal states are entrusted with the management of the living resources in their exclusive economic zone, but they are not totally free in that respect. They are under an obligation to manage fisheries in a way that the resources in question will contribute to the nourishment of their populations or the populations of other states. The fact that coastal states are not totally free in their own policies is highlighted in Article 73, paragraph 1, of the UN Convention on the Law of the Sea, which indicates that they may only enforce such national laws and regulations on fisheries adopted in conformity with the convention. At last instance the implementation of this obligation is monitored by the International Tribunal for the Law of the Sea.

As far as the high seas are concerned, the flag states are originally mandated to ensure the sustainable management of the living resources (Article 119 of the convention). The UN Agreement Relating to the Conservation and Management of Straddling Fish Stocks and Migratory Fish Stocks has significantly clarified this approach, reflecting the common interest in a management regime dedicated to sustainability as the precautionary principle.

Part XII of the UN Convention on the Law of the Sea, which deals with the protection and preservation of the marine environment, again clearly mirrors the common interests in the oceans. According to Article 192 of the convention, all states have the obligation to protect and preserve the marine environment. This obligation is all-encompassing; it is further detailed in Part XII, which describes the distribution of the functions between coastal states, port states, and flag states.

The same approach applies to Antarctica. There the main responsibility rests upon the state whose nationality the expedition or the station concerned represents.

CONCLUSION

Let me conclude by stating the particularities and strengths of the Antarctic legal regime in pursuing common interest. These are (1) the flexibility of the governance system, (2) concentration on science and the protection of the environment, and (3) reliance on the interchange of science, politics, and law.

It has been indicated that the Antarctic Treaty Consultative Meeting (ATCM) and its secretariat were inadequate to deal with the complexities of Antarctica. I venture to disagree. The ATCM has proved to be remarkably flexible and effective if one compares the situation today with the one 20 years back. Such a metamorphosis would have been impossible had the original signatories decided to establish an international organization. To underline my point, I recommend considering the G8 Summit, which follows exactly the same pattern, although I doubt that its founders were aware of the Antarctic legal system. Modern international law is moving away from the establishing new international organizations. Instead, more informal fora are established, such as meetings of States Parties, some of them enjoying more substantial functions than traditional international organizations. The ATCM, in my view, is a forerunner of this development, although it is rarely considered as such.

I see the second strength of the ATCM in the concentration of the Antarctic legal system on science and protection of the environment. This has not been duplicated elsewhere. Both objectives serve common interest, which makes it easier to solve conflicts that may and have developed.

Finally, I see the particularity and strength of the Antarctic legal system in its reliance on the interchange of science, politics, and law. Attempts to follow this pattern have been made in the context of the law of the sea with the Continental Shelf Commission. But there the integration was not well thought through. This interplay between science, politics, and law is the most valuable asset of the Antarctic legal regime—its primary export article—and it should be nourished and protected.

Governing International Spaces: Antarctica and Beyond

Oran R. Young

INTRODUCTION

The Antarctic Treaty System (ATS) is one of the most successful arrangements created during the twentieth century to address the need for governance at the international level and, therefore, to supply governance in a society that lacks a government in the sense of a supranational body endowed with the authority to make decisions binding on its individual members. This makes the ATS a subject of intense interest not only to those concerned with the fate of Antarctica itself but also to those interested in addressing a wide range of other issues generating a need for governance at the international level.

In this chapter, I take the case of the ATS as a point of departure for a broader assessment of issues relating to the governance of international spaces or, in other words, regions and resources that lie beyond the jurisdictional reach of individual states in international society. My argument proceeds as follows. The first substantive section deals with the nature of international spaces and provides some summary information concerning their location and extent. The next section discusses the legal and political status of international spaces and introduces emerging concepts in this realm, such as the "common heritage of humankind." The sources of the need for governance regarding human activities taking place in international spaces or affecting international spaces are the focus of the following section. A discussion of the options for supplying governance for international spaces with particular reference to innovative approaches emerging as human uses of these spaces rise is the theme of the penultimate section. The concluding section provides a brief commentary on future directions in the governance of international spaces.

WHAT ARE INTERNATIONAL SPACES, AND HOW EXTENSIVE ARE THEY?

International spaces are regions and resources that lie beyond the reach of the legal and political jurisdiction of the individual members of international society. Outer space and sizable segments of the world's oceans belong to this category, at

Oran R. Young, Bren School of Environmental Science and Management, University of California (Santa Barbara),4518 Bren Hall, Santa Barbara, CA 93106-5131, USA. Correspondence: Oran.Young@gmail.com.

least in part, by virtue of their remoteness and the limited capacity of states to exercise jurisdiction in these relatively remote regions. (Nevertheless, states can and do assert jurisdiction over their nationals operating in international spaces aboard ships, aircraft, spacecraft, and so forth.) But as these examples themselves suggest, international spaces are in large measure socially constructed. Technological advances can and often do increase the capacity of states to exercise authority in remote regions. States may assert jurisdictional claims in far away places (e.g., Antarctica), even in cases where their capacity to exercise authority is severely limited. The expansion of jurisdictional claims sometimes reflects the realities of economic and political influence more than any compelling rationale rooted in the requirements of sound management or sustainability. The emergence of coastal state jurisdiction over exclusive economic zones extending seaward 200 nautical miles from the coast, for example, owes much to such economic and political pressures. Shifts in prevailing attitudes and discourses constitute yet another force capable of generating changes in the scope of jurisdictional claims. The development during the latter decades of the twentieth century of the concept of the "common heritage of humankind," for instance, has played a role in curbing some efforts to expand the jurisdictional claims of states at the expense of international spaces.

For the most part, we have construed the category of international spaces to encompass spatially delimited material entities like the oceans, outer space, and (with some reservations) Antarctica. Because these entities are essentially fixed, the category of what I will call traditional international spaces is finite. More recently, technological advances have opened up a range of resources that raise similar concerns about governance, though they are not material entities like Antarctica or the oceans. The category of what I will call "new" international spaces includes such entities as the electromagnetic spectrum, the stratospheric ozone layer, the Earth's climate system, and, arguably, the Internet. As these examples suggest, new international spaces are more difficult to locate in spatial terms. It is likely that additional members of this category will emerge with the growth of knowledge and the development of new technologies over time. Yet these resources are sufficiently similar to traditional international spaces with regard to the issues of governance they raise to make it appropriate to include them in the discussion to follow.

The oceans cover about 70% of the Earth's surface. Subtracting the exclusive economic zones, which collectively account for 10%–12% of the oceans and are now subject to the jurisdiction of coastal states, leaves about 60% of the Earth's surface as international space. Antarctica is a special case because most of the continent is subject to (sometimes overlapping) territorial claims articulated by seven states during the first half of the twentieth century. But the 1959 Antarctic Treaty established a regime under which the parties have managed the south polar region for all practical purposes as an international space over the last 50 years. The prospect of any change in the basic character of this arrangement occurring during the foreseeable future is remote. Since the Antarctic continent covers a little over 6% of the Earth's surface, we can conclude that something like two-thirds of the surface of the Earth currently belongs to the category of international spaces. The areal extent of outer space is harder to determine because of ambiguities regarding both its inner and outer boundaries. States now exercise jurisdiction over the air space above their territories. But there is a lack of precision regarding where air space ends and (outer) space begins. Similarly, space has no clear outer boundary. Functionally, the outer boundary of space is determined by the capacity of humans to use space or to act in ways that affect space in such forms as altering the Earth's climate system. Defined in this way, the outer boundary of space is subject to change over relatively short periods of time.

Thus, the extent of traditional international spaces is great. The issue of extent is more complex with regard to new international spaces. How can we characterize the Earth's climate system, much less the Internet, in areal terms? Even the electromagnetic spectrum and the stratospheric ozone layer are dynamic, so that it is impossible to calculate their extent in a manner comparable to calculations of the extent of the oceans or Antarctica. Equally if not more important is the fact that the significance of the new international spaces is functional rather than spatial. So long as the stratospheric ozone layer inhibits the penetration of UVB radiation, its spatial characteristics are unimportant. Much the same is true of the Earth's climate system whose significance lies in the regulation of radiative forcing rather than in any measure of its size or extent. As we move toward a growing concern with the governance of new international spaces, therefore, questions regarding the extent of international spaces are likely to become less prominent. This may have implications for efforts to draw lessons from experiences in governing traditional international spaces that are relevant to addressing issues of growing importance regarding the governance of new international spaces.

WHAT IS THE LEGAL AND POLITICAL STATUS OF INTERNATIONAL SPACES?

International spaces are widely construed as belonging to the class of things known to international law and international politics as *res communis*, or common property. This ensures that they are not subject to the assertion of property rights or exclusive jurisdiction on the part of individual members of international society. But the doctrine of *res communis* has two major variants that differ sharply in their implications for governance. One variant asserts that the region or resource in question is open to entry (and exploitation) on the part of any member of international society acting on its own authority with no obligation to obtain the consent of the other members of this society. The other variant asserts that the members of international society have the authority as a group to promulgate and implement rules governing the use of international spaces on the part of individual members and perhaps even the authority to approve or reject specific plans on the part of members to use a region or resource. This variant may also allow members of international society, as the idea of the common heritage of humankind suggests, to lay claim to a share of any proceeds arising from uses of international spaces on the part of individual members.

It is easy to see that the two variants can and often will generate different outcomes when applied to specific situations. So long as the resources are plentiful and not subject to depletion or degradation as a result of the actions of individual users, the two variants may produce similar results. But the first variant of the doctrine of *res communis* can lead directly to situations exhibiting the characteristics of the tragedy of the commons as the demands of individual users of the resources grow. It is this realization that has led communities at other levels of social organization to adopt, formally or informally, a variety of rules applying to uses of common property and to develop the social and intellectual capital associated with the idea of governing the commons (Ostrom et al., 2002). Familiar as this perspective is at the local level, however, it is a development that some powerful actors have resisted at the international level. The views of many American policymakers and industrialists regarding access to the mineral resources of the deep seabed constitute a prominent example. Nevertheless, it is probably correct to say that we are witnessing today a marked shift in the form of the evolution of customary law toward acceptance of the second variant of the doctrine of *res communis* with regard to issues involving the governance of international spaces.

Once we accept the proposition that there is a need for governance in guiding human uses of international spaces and observe that governance systems are, in fact, emerging for a variety of these spaces, the distinction between constitutive rules and operating rules comes into focus (Ostrom, 1990). Constitutive rules provide broad frameworks within which human activities occurring in or affecting a particular region or resource are permitted to go forward. Constitutions are familiar arrangements that perform this role at the national level. The most extensive constitutive arrangement now in place for an international space is the set of rules and procedures articulated in the 1982 UN Convention on the Law of the Sea (UNCLOS). As it has evolved from the initial Antarctic Treaty of 1959, the Antarctic Treaty System has come to assume increasingly the role of a constitutive arrangement covering human activities in the high southern latitudes. Despite the existence of specific agreements relating to space (e.g., the 1967 Treaty on Principles Governing the Activities of States in the Exploration and Use of Outer Space, including the Moon and Other Celestial Bodies, or Outer Space Treaty), the constitutive system for space remains underdeveloped. Not surprisingly, a critical topic for debate today concerns the extent to which we should attach high priority to developing or strengthening constitutive arrangements for a variety of international spaces and, in particular, what I have called new international spaces.

The existence of a constitutive arrangement is important, but it is not sufficient to meet the needs for governance relating to any specific international space. Constitutive arrangements are frameworks. They provide a necessary foundation for the supply of governance, but by themselves they do not and cannot meet needs for governance with regard to specific issues. Ocean governance again provides a clear illustration (Oude Elferink, 2005). Important as it is in constitutive terms, UNCLOS does not deal in a substantive way with a range of concrete issues regarding matters like marine shipping, ocean dumping, pollution from land-based sources, the exploitation of highly migratory stocks of fish, and so forth. These matters require the development of operating rules through the actions of authorized bodies like the International Maritime Organization or the development of issue-specific agreements, such as the 1972 Convention on the Prevention of Marine Pollution by Dumping of Wastes and Other Matter (London Convention) and the 1995 UN Straddling Fish Stocks Agreement dealing with fish stocks that are highly migratory or cut across boundaries between adjacent exclusive economic zones or between exclusive economic zones and the high seas. Whereas constitutive arrangements are meant to be relatively long-lasting and stable (though not beyond interpretation to meet changing circumstances), operating rules are intended to be more adjustable, shifting over time as existing activities change and new activities become prominent. In a well-functioning governance system, constitutive arrangements and operating rules operate in tandem, providing both stability and flexibility in addressing shifting complexes of human activities. Such systems are comparatively rudimentary with regard to the governance of international spaces. Even the governance system for the oceans is primitive compared with parallel systems that have evolved to deal with needs for governance arising in national spaces. The governance systems for most other international spaces are less developed. But as human activities occurring in or affecting international spaces expand, questions pertaining to the governance of international spaces are destined to emerge as increasingly important items on the international agenda.

WHAT ARE THE SOURCES OF NEEDS FOR GOVERNANCE REGARDING INTERNATIONAL SPACES?

Governance emerges as an issue of public concern when the actions of humans give rise to unsustainable practices (e.g., depletion of stocks of living resources), interfere with one another's goal-directed activities (e.g., degradation of neighboring properties arising from the actions of nearby property owners), or lead to more general problems of public order that are harmful to members of the community (e.g., breaches of the peace or acts of aggression). Typically, the need for governance is low when the number of users is small relative to the availability of resources or the density of users is low in a given space. There is little need to develop regulatory arrangements to avoid the tragedy of the commons, for example, when individual users are few in number and harvesters have a limited capacity to capture or consume living resources. But the need for governance grows, often exponentially, as human numbers and human capacities grow.

Needs for governance regarding international spaces arise from several distinct sources (Young, 1999). We are apt to take for granted the existence of public order as a precondition for success in most human endeavors. But because international spaces lie beyond the reach of the jurisdiction of states in a realm that lacks a government in the ordinary sense, we cannot adopt a similar attitude regarding these spaces. It is therefore easy to understand the concern for the development of alternative means for ensuring the maintenance of public order in many efforts to devise governance systems for international spaces. Both the 1959 Antarctic Treaty and the 1967 Outer Space Treaty, for instance, contain specific provisions regarding peaceful uses of these areas. The Antarctic Treaty specifies that human actors are to use Antarctica for peaceful purposes only. Both this treaty and the Outer Space Treaty contain provisions prohibiting the deployment of nuclear weapons or weapons of mass destruction. Given the importance of naval forces in the arsenals of powerful states, no such treatment of the world's oceans is politically feasible. Even so, UNCLOS does contain a provision (Article 88) stating that "the high seas shall be reserved for peaceful purposes," and the convention does include a number of provisions (e.g., those pertaining to transit passage) spelling out rules designed to govern the activities of naval vessels and the use of marine systems for military purposes.

The new international spaces may seem less susceptible to problems of public order. Yet it would be naïve to suppose these spaces are immune from the impacts of hostile actions intended to harm or weaken unfriendly human actors. The concerns that led to the negotiation of the 1977 Convention on the Prohibition of Military or Any Other Hostile Use of Environmental Modification Techniques offer testimony to this fact. Advances in technology over the intervening decades have enhanced the capacity of states and a variety of nonstate actors to engage in hostile acts regarding new international spaces. Rising concerns regarding hostile or aggressive uses of the Internet offer a prominent example.

Assuming we are able to meet the need for public order regarding international spaces in a manner that allows normal human activities to proceed, a variety of other needs for governance come into focus. Some of these have to do with familiar problems of depletion arising from unregulated harvesting of living resources or of congestion arising from intensive uses of flow resources like favorable shipping routes or the electromagnetic spectrum (Brown et al., 1977). Technological advances can alleviate, if not eliminate, some of these problems. Increases in the technological sophistication of broadcasting systems, for example, have made it possible for large numbers of users to exploit the electromagnetic spectrum for purposes of broadcasting without interfering with one another's activities. But many cases present classic problems of governance requiring the introduction of mechanisms like catch shares and rules of the road to allow users to make use of the resources of international spaces in a manner that is sustainable and efficient. Parallel challenges arise in cases where security of tenure is an important factor in motivating prospective users to make the investments required to use the resources of international spaces. Licenses to use broadcast frequencies in the electromagnetic spectrum, for instance, would be of little value if they were not secure against encroachment on the part of outsiders. Similar considerations underlie the concerns of those who have advocated the creation of a system of secure licenses, if not full-scale property rights, in segments of the deep seabed as a precondition for success in the development of deep-seabed mining (Eckert, 1979). In all these cases, the challenge is to find ways to address demands for governance in international spaces in the absence of anything resembling a world government.

A somewhat different class of problems encompasses situations in which there are existing or anticipated conflicts among alternative uses of international spaces. Two types of conflicts, both of which loom large in efforts to govern international spaces today, are worth distinguishing in this connection. In the most direct case, a decision to designate an area for a particular use can have the effect, implicitly if not explicitly, of prohibiting other uses of the area. Classic cases involve trade-offs between consumptive uses and nonconsumptive uses. The decision to set aside the 1988 Convention on the Regulation of Antarctic Mineral Resource Activities and to move forward with the adoption of the 1991 Protocol on Environmental Protection to the Antarctic Treaty (Environmental Protocol), for instance, is a development of far-reaching importance precisely because designating Antarctica as a "natural reserve" means banning the extraction of both nonfuel minerals and hydrocarbons as a matter of policy. Debates about the merits of establishing large marine protected areas in various parts of the world's oceans prohibiting or severely limiting traditional activities like fishing raise many of the same concerns. Even with regard to major consumptive uses, trade-offs involving conflicts of use can and often do give rise to needs for governance. Interference between the operations of fishers and shippers in marine systems is a case in point.

Short of direct conflicts between alternative uses, the occurrence of a wide range of externalities or unintended side effects has become an important source of the need for governance regarding international spaces. These are situations in which the activities of those engaged in normal and lawful activities generate side effects that are harmful to resources that are valuable to others. Common examples involve the harmful effects of trawl fisheries on benthic communities and of commercial shipping on marine mammals. A major development in this regard, which poses particularly challenging problems of governance regarding international spaces, centers on what we have come to think of as the destruction or degradation of ecosystem services resulting from a variety of human activities. The removal of key species can cause large ecosystems to undergo dramatic changes or even to collapse. Intentional or accidental discharges of oil at sea can produce far-reaching environmental impacts. The rise of the concept of ecosystem-based management with its associated intellectual capital has drawn increasing attention to this class of problems and the need to create governance systems to address them (McLeod and Leslie, 2009).

As these examples suggest, some externalities arise from activities occurring within international spaces whose impacts are felt within the same spaces. But there is another class of externalities in which activities occurring wholly or largely outside international spaces have impacts that are felt within these spaces. Prominent cases include the growth of dead zones at sea, the thinning of the stratospheric ozone layer, and rising concentrations of greenhouse gases in the Earth's atmosphere. Dead zones are largely products of agricultural practices taking place in national spaces and often far from the coast. The production and consumption of ozone-depleting substances arose in response to the demand for a range of products on the part of consumers located within national spaces. Emissions of greenhouse gases are, for the most part, by-products of human activities taking place within national spaces. The protection of international spaces from the impacts of these externalities poses a particularly serious challenge for governance. Decisions about the regulation of agricultural practices, the production and consumption of ozone-depleting substances, and the emission of greenhouse gases are all made within national governance systems in which international spaces are essentially unrepresented. No one represents the stratospheric ozone layer or the Earth's climate system in the policymaking of states. The citizens of individual states have an interest in what happens to international spaces like the stratospheric ozone layer or the climate system, and it is perfectly possible for states to band together to devise international governance systems designed to regulate externalities of this sort. Nevertheless, the demand for governance is different in such cases than it is in situations where users of fish stocks, shipping lanes, or the electromagnetic spectrum must join forces to devise governance systems that allow them all to benefit from sustainable uses of the relevant resources.

WHAT ARE THE OPTIONS FOR SUPPLYING GOVERNANCE FOR INTERNATIONAL SPACES?

The specific mechanisms needed to govern human uses of international spaces differ from case to case. Yet some useful generalizations are possible in this realm. In every case, it is desirable to establish a combination of constitutive provisions, in the sense of broad framework arrangements intended to provide an enduring matrix within which to address a range of more-specific issues, and operating rules, in the sense of more-detailed regulatory arrangements dealing with substantive and often functionally specific issues. The relationship between UNCLOS as a constitutive arrangement and the specific provisions of the 1972 London Convention dealing with the discharge of wastes at sea illustrates this proposition. It is always desirable, moreover, to strike a balance between stability in the sense of providing governance systems with some measure of staying power and flexibility or agility in the sense of endowing these systems with the capacity to adapt to changing circumstances. All governance systems require some administrative capacity in the sense of organizational arrangements that can make decisions, apply these decisions to the complexities of concrete situations, address matters of compliance, provide authoritative interpretations in cases where parties disagree regarding the meaning of specific provisions, and mobilize the funding needed to operate the system.

The Antarctic Treaty of 1959, the Outer Space Treaty of 1967, and the 1982 UN Convention on the Law of the Sea are all constitutive in the sense that they seek to establish broad frameworks covering human activities relevant to the international spaces in question. But they are not equally effective in terms of providing foundations for the development of full-fledged governance systems. The Antarctic Treaty System is particularly evolved in these terms. The Antarctic Treaty itself has proven successful both in creating a mechanism for making collective decisions about the south polar region and in laying the basis for the maintenance of public order in the area. With the addition of the 1991 Environmental Protocol, the parties to the ATS simplified the governance problem by designating Antarctica a "natural reserve, devoted to peace and science," and explicitly banning mining or the extraction of nonrenewable resources in the area. The effect of these actions has been to avoid potential conflicts among competing uses and to minimize governance issues arising from competition among users of material resources. The protocol has created a basis for developing a variety of operating rules pertaining to matters like waste disposal, the conduct of environmental impact assessments, the establishment of protected natural areas, and the promulgation of liability rules. It established a Committee on Environmental Protection to administer the resultant governance system. The functional integration of the Scientific Committee on Antarctic Research (SCAR), officially a body belonging to the International Council of Science (ICSU), into this governance system has helped substantially in addressing the need to provide advance notice of changing conditions calling for the development of new operating rules or the adaptation of existing ones. This does not mean that this governance system is immune to the impact of stress or able to operate without challenges (Young, 2010: chap. 3). Many complex issues remain regarding efforts to practice ecosystem-based management under the terms of the Convention on the Conservation of Antarctic Marine Living Resources dealing with consumptive uses of fish and other living resources. Some of the most severe threats facing Antarctica during the foreseeable future will arise from large-scale occurrences, such as the thinning of stratospheric ozone, climate change, and ocean acidification, that are largely beyond the control of the ATS.

By comparison, the governance systems we have put in place for the world's oceans and for space are less adequate to meet emerging needs for governance in these international spaces. The UNCLOS does provide a constitutive system for the oceans, and more or less elaborate operating rules have emerged to address a range of functionally specific activities like shipping, fishing, deep-seabed mining, tourism, and environmental protection (Oude Elferink, 2005). But the capacity of these arrangements to meet the rising demand for governance is limited. Despite the provisions of Article 88 of UNCLOS, it is an illusion to suppose that the high seas are reserved for peaceful purposes. The track records of most regional fisheries management organizations leave a lot to be desired. The governance system for the deep seabed, rooted in Part XI of UNCLOS, has never become operational and remains a bone of contention among powerful actors in the system. Major issues relating to the management of marine shipping are looming on the horizon. It is hard to make progress toward implementing the ideal of ecosystem-based management in the oceans because of the effects of externalities arising both from the exploitation of marine resources (e.g., commercially valuable fish stocks) and from land-based activities affecting marine systems (e.g., contaminants associated with agricultural production). What is more, the existing governance system for the oceans has little or no capacity to stem the impacts of a variety of large-scale processes, like ocean acidification, arising from human activities having nothing to do with the use of ocean resources. There is a need for a major upgrade in the governance system for the oceans treated as an international space.

The case of space poses yet another set of problems. The 1967 Outer Space Treaty does create a constitutive arrangement for outer space in the sense of providing for public order; banning the establishment of military bases, installations, or fortifications on the Moon and other celestial bodies; and prohibiting the extension of jurisdictional claims on the part of states to these bodies. But there is a disconnect between these constitutive arrangements for space and the development of operating rules dealing with a variety of functional concerns. Some of these concerns (e.g., the protection of the stratospheric ozone layer, the control of climate change, and the use of the electromagnetic spectrum) may lie outside the scope of the 1967 treaty. Others (e.g., the management of space debris and the development of space-based forms of geoengineering intended to address the problem of climate change) involve issues unforeseen during the 1960s. There have been some successes in meeting specific needs for governance relating to atmospheric issues. The ozone regime is rightly regarded as a success story, and efforts to address a range of issues relating to broadcasting have met with substantial success. Still, we are left in the case of space with a fragmented or incoherent governance system in which the constitutive arrangements do not encompass efforts to address specific matters, such as broadcasting and climate change, and the functionally specific regimes, such as the arrangement for the stratospheric ozone layer, do not serve to strengthen the constitutive framework. A fundamental question in this realm is whether to make an effort to link these arrangements together, thereby creating a governance system in which the whole is greater than the sum of the parts.

Turning to the class of new international spaces, the first question regarding the supply of governance concerns the relative merits of assimilating these spaces into existing governance systems versus treating them as separate cases with regard to issues of governance. As the preceding paragraph suggests, we could treat matters relating to the stratospheric ozone layer, the Earth's climate system, and the electromagnetic spectrum as issues of concern to space and seek to subsume them within an expanded constitutive system for space when it comes to matters of governance (Soroos, 1997). For the most part, however, this is not the approach that the international community has adopted in efforts to supply governance for these new international spaces. The constitutive provisions of the Outer Space Treaty have little bearing on the operation of the ozone regime and the climate regime. The efforts of bodies like the International Telecommunication Union (ITU), the World Administrative Radio Conferences (WARCs), and the International Telecommunications Satellite Consortium (INTELSAT) to regulate broadcasting and to manage uses of the electromagnetic spectrum more generally have little to do with the overarching provisions of the Outer Space Treaty. What lies ahead in this realm? As things stand now, it is hard to foresee any serious move to integrate efforts to address a variety of specific issues like climate change or the use of the electromagnetic spectrum into some overarching constitutive arrangement for space. Yet this could change as we find ourselves thinking more about matters like the management of space debris or geoengineering that pose important questions relating to the provision of public order (Royal Society, 2009).

WHERE DO WE GO FROM HERE?

The challenges of governing international spaces highlight the importance of finding ways to address needs for governance in the absence of government (Rosenau and Czempiel, 1992). As human activities occurring in or affecting areas that lie beyond the jurisdiction of states intensify and as new international spaces become objects of attention, needs for governance in this realm are destined to grow. For this reason, it is desirable to identify and draw attention to success stories in governing international spaces. The Antarctic Treaty System has not only maintained public order in the south polar region over the last 50 years, it also has demonstrated a capacity to come to terms with major issues regarding competing uses of Antarctica's natural resources and ecosystems. The ozone regime has proven successful in bringing about drastic reductions in the production and consumption of a large number of ozone-depleting substances; it also has brought about greater reductions in emissions of greenhouse gases than the climate regime itself (Velders et al., 2007).

Yet pointing to these successes provides no basis for adopting an attitude of complacency regarding the governance of international spaces. The existing arrangements leave much to be desired in meeting current needs for governance. They are even more inadequate when it comes to tackling growing challenges like the disruption of marine ecosystems caused by industrial-scale fishing and the dramatic consequences of climate change and associated phenomena, such as ocean acidification. What is needed in this connection is an approach grounded in the idea of stewardship, based on a tighter integration of constitutive arrangements and operating rules, and alert to the need for adaptive capacity to cope with changes that are often nonlinear, frequently abrupt, and commonly irreversible (Chapin et al., 2009). We have made progress in addressing such issues, but the challenges before us are great when it comes to achieving governance without governance of the sort required to meet the need for stewardship in the use of international spaces.

LITERATURE CITED

Brown, S., N. W. Cornell, L. L. Fabian, and E. Brown-Weiss. 1977. *Regimes for the Ocean, Outer Space, and Weather.* Washington, D.C.: The Brookings Institution.

Chapin, F. S., G. P. Kofinas, and C. Folke, eds. 2009. *Principles of Ecosystem Stewardship: Resilience-Based Natural Resource Management in a Changing World.* New York: Springer.

Eckert, R. 1979. *The Enclosure of Ocean Resources.* Stanford: Hoover Institution Press.

McLeod, K., and H. Leslie, eds. 2009. *Ecosystem-Based Management for the Oceans.* Washington, D.C.: Island Press.

Ostrom, E. 1990. *Governing the Commons: The Evolution of Institutions for Collective Action.* Cambridge: Cambridge University Press.

Ostrom, E., T. Dietz, N. Dolsak, P. C. Stern, S. Stonich, and U. W. Elke, eds. 2002. *The Drama of the Commons.* Washington, D.C.: National Academies Press.

Oude Elferink, A. G., ed. 2005. *Stability and Change in the Law of the Sea: The Role of the LOS Convention.* Amsterdam: Brill.

Rosenau, J. N., and E.-O. Czempiel. 1992. *Governance without Government: Order and Change in World Politics.* Cambridge: Cambridge University Press.

Royal Society. 2009. Geoengineering the Climate: Science, Governance and Uncertainty. RS Policy Document 10/09–RS 1639. September. London: Royal Society.

Soroos, M. S. 1997. *The Endangered Atmosphere: Preserving a Global Commons.* Columbia, S.C.: University of South Carolina Press.

Velders, J. M., S. O. Andersen, J. S. Daniel, D. W. Fahey, and M. McFarland. 2007. The Importance of the Montreal Protocol in Protecting Climate. *Proceedings of the National Academy of Sciences of the United States of America,* 104: 4814–4819.

Young, O. R. 1999. *Governance in World Affairs.* Ithaca, N.Y.: Cornell University Press.

———. 2010. *Institutional Dynamics: Emergent Patterns in International Environmental Governance.* Cambridge, Mass.: MIT Press.

Workshop on Arctic Governance: Drawing Lessons from the Antarctic Experience

Francesca Cava, David Monsma, and Oran R. Young

This daylong workshop, convened 3 December 2009, provided an opportunity for informal discussion among approximately 40 participants in the Antarctic Treaty Summit focusing on insights from experience with Antarctic governance over the last 50 years that have current and legacy value for all humanity and particularly for those concerned with the transformative change now occurring in the Arctic.

The objectives of the workshop were to examine parallel or differing experiences regarding the development and implementation of the Antarctic Treaty System and Arctic governance systems, lessons learned from Antarctic governance that may be applicable to current efforts to deal with governance needs in the Arctic, and any other inferences to be drawn from the political, legal, or ecological management of the Antarctic that are relevant to Arctic governance.

The workshop included four separate sessions, each starting with several speakers invited to initiate the discussion by offering reflections derived from the presentations and discussion at the summit:

1. general insights from the Antarctic Treaty Summit: Robert Corell, Vladimir Golitsyn, and Marie Jacobsson;
2. the relevance of the Antarctic experience with regulatory measures in addressing emerging Arctic issues: Peiqing Guo and John Hocevar;
3. the role of monitoring, reporting, and verification systems in the Antarctic as they pertain to the Arctic: Anders Karlquist and Yeadong Kim; and
4. lessons from the Antarctic experience that may help to strengthen the science/policy interface in the Arctic: Fred Roots and Paul Berkman.

Session 1 began with a synthesis of the summit presentations made earlier that week. History played a crucial role in the development of policy in the Antarctic. The 1959 Antarctic Treaty, for example, was influenced by the cold war, leading signatories to find common ground in the importance of science. History also played a role in the Arctic, but it did not culminate in the signing of an Arctic Treaty. More recent developments, including climate change and globalization, are now affecting Arctic policy.

Francesca Cava and David Monsma, Aspen Institute, One Dupont Circle, NW, Suite 700, Washington, D.C. 20036-1133, USA. Oran Young, Donald Bren School of Environmental Science and Management, University of California, Santa Barbara, California 93106-5131, USA. Correspondence: francesca.cava@aspeninst.org.

History is not the only factor that differentiates the two polar regions with regard to governance. There are significant geographical, political, and social differences. The Arctic is an ocean surrounded by land; the Antarctic is a continent surrounded by an ocean. Governance in the High Arctic is an extension of the sovereign jurisdictions of five coastal states; governance in the Antarctic features a multilateral treaty that does not support specific sovereign claims. The Antarctic has no permanent residents; the Arctic has significant numbers of culturally distinct indigenous peoples as well as long-term settlers. Another major difference between the poles involves matters of security. By treaty, the Antarctic is demilitarized and denuclearized. In contrast, Arctic nations have significant security interests that extend into the Arctic. These differences, summarized in Table 1, make it essential to exercise extreme care in seeking to transfer experience regarding governance from one polar region to the other.

Session 2 extended these general findings through a more focused discussion of regulatory issues in the polar regions. The Antarctic Treaty System has grown into a comprehensive governance system in the Antarctic. It promotes the use of Antarctica exclusively for peaceful purposes and emphasizes the role of scientific investigation. This has resulted in a dramatic expansion of regional research and in insights leading to historic advances in environmental protection, such as the response to the discovery of the ozone hole through the development of the 1987 Montreal Protocol on Substances that Deplete the Ozone Layer. Antarctic science also has fostered efforts to achieve the common good rather than promoting the interests of individual nations. The conduct of science has promoted international cooperation and the development of shared infrastructure; it has provided a venue for states to work together outside the constraints of national policies. Participants in the workshop recommended that science play a similar role in the Arctic in the future, providing a mechanism to focus on global priorities in addition to national interests. In the next 50 years, the Arctic will experience massive physical and social changes, which will make it critical to ensure that scientific knowledge is incorporated into decision-making processes and that the interaction among science, law, and policy is strengthened.

TABLE 1. Polar contrasts relevant to governance.

The Antarctic	The Arctic
A continent surrounded by ocean	An ocean surrounded by land
No permanent residents	Many permanent residents
Jurisdictional status frozen	Multinational jurisdiction
No large-scale industry	World-class industry
Demilitarized	Highly militarized
Denuclearized	Nuclearized

Session 3 explored the role of monitoring, reporting, and verification systems in the Antarctic and the relevance of this experience to the Arctic. Discussion focused on the success of the Antarctic's practice of sharing data and information. In the face of anticipated changes due to climate change, the Arctic nations should adopt similar practices as data integration and comparability become increasingly critical to understanding the health of the Earth's socioecological systems.

In Antarctica, science has given rise to practices in areas such as environmental assessment and data management that allow a common approach to regional monitoring, reporting, and verification. Development of similar standardized data collection, management, and analysis procedures among the Arctic nations will be needed to integrate, interpret, and feed this information into policymaking processes in the future. Similar procedures will prove beneficial to assessments carried out by the Arctic Council's Working Groups.

Session 4 of the workshop focused on whether the Antarctic experience can suggest ways to strengthen the science-policy interface in the Arctic. The growth of a common scientific "culture" in the Antarctic has contributed to the development of informal consultative practices and a less-hierarchical approach than is typical in national or multilateral governmental forums. In addition, this approach has contributed to progress by encouraging open discussions in which parties emphasize "consent" rather than consensus. Environmental nongovernmental organizations have also played an important role in the Antarctic, increasing decision-making capacity and advancing goals outside the formal structures of governance.

There may be a lesson here regarding the role of informal governmental structures as Arctic stakeholders strive to find common ground, define the common good, and achieve compromises. Future challenges in the Arctic will be transnational and often region-wide in scope. In some cases, the effects of decisions regarding Arctic issues will be felt at the global level and vice versa. The global dimensions of Arctic governance will challenge the capacity and the authority of Arctic states to exclude others from participating in decision-making regarding Arctic issues. The Arctic will require adaptive management strategies to meet future challenges, especially in the case of climate change.

Economic development, increasing in both polar regions, is a major concern in the Arctic. It is important to consider adopting substantive arrangements in the Arctic, similar to those developed in the Antarctic for activities like tourism and bioprospecting. Similarly, Arctic nations and the Arctic Council will need to work closely with international organizations like the International Maritime Organization to develop regionally appropriate regulations for matters like shipping, search and rescue, and emergency response.

The International Polar Year (IPY) was successful in bringing significant investments in science involving both polar regions. Participants in the workshop recommended that ways be found to continue IPY efforts, perhaps through the extension of the IPY to an International Polar Decade.

The designation of marine and terrestrial protected areas is emerging in the Antarctic as an important mechanism to promote both environmental protection and scientific research. The Arctic can benefit from this experience through an effort to achieve international agreement to identify and designate sensitive areas for protection and further research.

Antarctica has captured the interest and the imagination of the public through the exploits of famous explorers, the plight of charismatic species (e.g., whales and penguins), and the impact on popular thinking of dramatic events like the discovery of the ozone hole. This high profile has produced tremendous public support for international cooperation in the Antarctic and should become a model for those concerned with the Arctic.

Workshop participants concluded that over the course of the next 50 years there will be a need to adapt Arctic governance systems to address impacts arising from the interaction of climate change and globalization and to promote the achievement of sustainable development and social justice for Arctic residents. The region will experience environmental change resulting from melting ice, a seasonally ice-free ocean, and thawing permafrost along with increasing pressure to develop natural resources.

In the Antarctic, by contrast, the impacts of these forces will not be as profound. As the Arctic changes, we should continue to look for lessons in both polar regions. The Arctic will remain vulnerable to environmental degradation attributable to activities occurring in other parts of the world. There is a need for increased public understanding about how changes in the polar regions will exacerbate climate change and greatly impact global systems. This workshop provided a venue to consider the importance of the polar regions, to look to them for lessons of broader significance, and to stress the need to continue to learn about and protect these regions for their own value as well as for the roles they play in maintaining planetary systems.

Acknowledgments

The Aspen Commission on Arctic Climate Change and the Arctic Governance Project cosponsored this workshop. David Monsma of the Aspen Institute and Oran Young of the Arctic Governance Project served as cochairs. Francesca Cava of the Aspen Institute was the rapporteur.

Conclusions

Paul Arthur Berkman, David W. H. Walton, and Oran R. Young

GOVERNING ANTARCTICA

Throughout human history, nations and empires have colonized territories across the Earth and claimed jurisdiction over these areas, resulting too often in conflicts. To end the battles and wars, protagonists have signed treaties, such as the Treaty of Westphalia in 1648, which solidified the concept of the nation-state, blending cultural and political authority within geographic boundaries. Curiously, just a few years before, in 1609, the Dutch jurist Hugo Grotius published *Mare Liberum*, a treatise articulating freedoms of the sea existing beyond the jurisdiction of nations (Bull et al., 1990). Together, these legal paradigms developed in the seventeenth century reveal a global governance dichotomy that is with us still and that features national spaces governed by states acting on the basis of national interests juxtaposed to international spaces in which all nations have common interests.

Three centuries later, Antarctica was no different than other areas on Earth where nation-states assert their sovereign jurisdiction (Lüdecke, this volume). Like a pie, the division of Antarctica started with the letters patent from the United Kingdom in 1907 and continued with additional claims by New Zealand, France, Australia, Norway, Argentina, and Chile by 1943. With the aide-memoire and draft agreement that the United States transmitted in secret to the seven claimant nations in 1948, Antarctica was positioned to become just another domino in the history of territorial expansion.

This nation-state trajectory in Antarctica shifted course dramatically with the emergence of the vision underlying a Third International Polar Year (renamed the International Geophysical Year) and the statesmanship of President Eisenhower of the United States in the early 1950s (Berkman, this volume). The International Geophysical Year (IGY) of 1957–1958 provided a coordinated international avenue for synoptic studies of the Earth as an interconnected geophysical system combining land, air, and water with forcing from the Sun. This was followed by the International Biological Program (1964–1974), an attempt to apply the big science approach to ecosystem functioning and productivity at a global scale (Worthington, 1975). Biological dynamics of the Earth as an interconnected system, as illustrated by the Gaia hypothesis (Lovelock and Margulis,

Paul Arthur Berkman, Scott Polar Research Institute, University of Cambridge, Lensfield Road, Cambridge CB2 1ER, UK, and Donald Bren School of Environmental Science and Management, University of California, Santa Barbara, California 93106-5131, USA. David W. H. Walton, British Antarctic Survey, Natural Environment Research Council, High Cross, Madingley Road, Cambridge CB3 0ET, UK. Oran R. Young, Bren School of Environmental Science and Management, University of California (Santa Barbara),4518 Bren Hall, Santa Barbara, CA 93106-5131, USA. Correspondence: pb426@cam.ac.uk.

1974), would be investigated subsequently on a planetary scale with the inception during the 1980s of the International Geosphere-Biosphere Programme and the growth of Earth system science. It was satellites with their unmistakable rocket relationship to ballistic missiles, however, that became the national security item that most engaged the superpowers during the IGY in the 1950s.

Ultimately, the IGY paved a diplomatic path, underlain by science, to establish the region south of 60°S, encompassing nearly 10% of the Earth's surface, as an international space where all claims to territorial sovereignty would be held in abeyance (Jacobsson, this volume).[1] Adopted on 1 December 1959 in Washington, D.C., the Antarctic Treaty articulates the premise that

> establishment of a firm foundation for the continuation and development of such cooperation on the basis of freedom of scientific investigation in Antarctica as applied during the International Geophysical Year accords with the interests of science and the progress of all mankind.

The two world wars of the twentieth century underscored animosity on a global scale. In contrast, reflecting unparalleled international cooperation, institutions have evolved since 1945 to prevent or resolve disputes transcending national boundaries. Most of these institutions relate to issues that cross national boundaries. However, there is a suite of institutions that has emerged to manage regions beyond the reach of national jurisdiction in the high seas (1958), Antarctica (1959), outer space (1967), and the deep sea (1971). On Earth, these international spaces extend across nearly 70% of our planet's surface (Young, this volume). The Antarctic Treaty reflects a new vision of an interconnected global society starting with Antarctica "forever to be used exclusively for peaceful purposes."

The Antarctic Treaty was crafted by the seven claimant nations along with five nonclaimant nations (Belgium, Japan, the Republic of South Africa, the Union of Soviet Socialist Republics, and the United States of America). As of August 2010, there are 47 signatories to the Antarctic Treaty (Retamales and Rogan-Finnemore, this volume), including Monaco as the most recent Acceding Party (Albert II, this volume). The origin, development, and implications of the Antarctic Treaty are intimately associated with science, revealing lessons that offer hope and inspiration.

For the benefit of present and future generations—the global challenge is to balance national interests and common interests. Science diplomacy is the international, interdisciplinary and inclusive process to achieve this global balance for the benefit of all life on Earth.

SCIENCE DIPLOMACY LESSONS FROM ANTARCTICA

The origin, administration, and development of the Antarctic Treaty are intimately associated with the conduct of science. The lessons we draw from the Antarctic experience regarding science diplomacy will be of lasting and global significance. The opportunity here is to understand these science diplomacy lessons and to identify their implications for meeting governance needs at the international level. In this section, we identify a number of major lessons emerging from the Antarctic experience. The following subsections explore these lessons with relevance beyond the confines of Antarctica.

Science as an Instrument for Earth System Monitoring and Assessment

Recognizing that science extends across a continuum from basic to applied research (Berkman, 2002), science diplomacy is strongly influenced by discoveries and insights that have practical benefits for society. Such applied research is commonly seen in terms of monitoring and assessing human impacts on natural systems.

In the Antarctic Treaty System (ATS), environmental impact assessment is integrated into the 1991 Protocol on Environmental Protection to the Antarctic Treaty (Madrid Protocol), which introduces the concept of a "minor or transitory impact" (Orheim et al., this volume). On one hand, "minor" involves subjective elements associated with values that have been articulated in diverse ATS measures,[2] including the "value for global baseline monitoring," "unique ecological and scientific value," "value of increasing public knowledge," "value of cooperation," and the "outstanding geological, glaciological, geomorphological, aesthetic, scenic, or wilderness value."

On the other hand, transitory involves objective elements associated with rate-related processes defined in the ATS, such as "changes in the marine ecosystem which are not potentially reversible over two or three decades" (Miller, this volume), as articulated in Article II of the 1980 Convention on the Conservation of Antarctic Marine Living Resources (CCAMLR). As a whole, the concept of a "minor or transitory impact" is a microcosm of the science-policy coupling that has been evolving in the ATS throughout its first 50 years, bringing together both subjective and objective elements that are necessary for good decision making.

Science as the Essential Gauge of Changes over Time and Space

Science is a process of discovery based on a method of hypothesis testing to assess the dynamics of systems: natural and social, small and large, young and old. At the heart of this process is investigation of changes over time and space (Thiede, this volume). Science provides a framework to look backward and forward in time to characterize rates and durations of phenomena as well as their feedbacks. Science places events in context, such as regional weather patterns operating within our global climate system. Importantly, for the benefit of our global society, science reveals interactions between natural and anthropogenic processes at multiple scales.

Time and space are blurred over cosmological dimensions back to the origin of the universe. "The farthest we can see is 13.7 billion light years distant, to a time that was only 350,000 years after the big bang" (Stark, this volume).

Climate, which is a planetary process that has oscillated regularly between glacial cold and interglacial warm periods for the last few million years with principal forcing from the Sun, illustrates temporal and spatial variability in the Earth system (Petit, this volume). The "sawtooth" pattern of climate changes, seen from high-resolution ice cores in the East Antarctic Ice Sheet and Greenland Ice Sheet, reveals that the current warm period is anomalously long compared to previous interglacial periods during the past 800,000 years. The ice core records also demonstrate that carbon dioxide concentrations and temperatures in the atmosphere have been increasing since the beginning of the industrial era (circa 1850) to current levels that are well above any seen in the Earth system over the past eight climate cycles. The inferred atmospheric variability also mimics sea level changes that have been deduced from marine sediments. Such proxy records demonstrate variations in the Earth system over years and decades embedded within centuries and millennia.

These long-term proxies are complemented by real-time measurements that have been made by various types of instruments, producing records of modern events and phenomena as they are happening. In Antarctica, there is a continuous daily weather record at Orcadas Station going back to the Scottish National Antarctic Expedition in 1903 (Zazulie et al., 2010). Starting in 1958 during the IGY, continuous atmospheric carbon dioxide measurements have been made at the South Pole (as well as at Mauna Loa in Hawaii), showing seasonality and increasing global concentrations of this greenhouse gas (Scripps CO_2 Program, 2010). Such real-time measurements reveal changes in the Earth system over days and seasons embedded within years and decades.

Together, the proxy and real-time records provide the context to understand events (e.g., a once in a century flood or warmest decade in the last millennium) that impact humankind. Science contributes to fundamental understanding about the magnitudes, rates, and dynamics of Earth system phenomena that must underpin any adaptation and mitigation policies. The challenge is to design and implement the appropriate strategies over time spans that far exceed the electoral cycles of the decision makers.

Science as a Source of Invention and Commercial Enterprise

Although scientific activities may be initiated with national funding for basic research purposes, discoveries also can reveal opportunities for potential or actual commercial gain. A living resource example from the Antarctic, as from other regions beyond national jurisdictions, is the potential exploitation of genetic resources from unique species that can be amplified, patented and marketed (Berkman, 2010a). This biological cousin to the exploitation of geological deposits constitutes an emerging challenge known as bioprospecting (Joyner, this volume).

The more well-known challenge focuses on mineral resources, as illustrated by scientific results of the *Glomar Challenger* expedition from the Deep Sea Drilling Program in the early 1970s (Walton, this volume), which were suddenly and wildly interpreted in the *Wall Street Journal* as offering the prospect of hundreds of millions of barrels of oil and trillions of cubic feet of natural gas on the Antarctic continental shelf. The mineral resource potential of Antarctica awakened intense international interest, opened the door for questions to be addressed in the United Nations, and led to the development of the Convention on the Regulation of Antarctic Mineral Resource Activities, a legal instrument that has never entered into force (Scully, this volume). Subsequently, the Madrid Protocol prohibited any activity relating to mineral resources, other than scientific research (Golitsyn, this volume).

In addition to identifying potential resources, science plays a role in developing the technologies needed to exploit these resources. However, there is a key difference between commercial and scientific activities, which is demonstrated by the issue of access to information.

Commercial activities restrict information access. To avoid this trajectory, with leadership of the Scientific Committee on Antarctic Research (SCAR), for marine geological resources, at least, the Antarctic Offshore Stratigraphy project (ANTOSTRAT) has been working since the late 1980s to share seismic data that companies otherwise would hold as proprietary (Cooper et al., this volume). Thus, scientific activities facilitate information access and transparency in such a way as to extend cooperation and prevent conflict.

Science as an Early Warning System

Scientific research often yields insights about impending abrupt and irreversible changes in the dynamics of natural systems (Erb, this volume). The pace of global changes seems often to be more rapid in the polar regions than elsewhere in the Earth system (Holland and Bitz, 2003).

Measurements of the changes in the mass balance of the Antarctic ice sheets will provide an early warning of the impacts of sea level rise (Kennicutt, this volume), a global change that will affect the stability of nation-states and the lives of billions of people. Such early warning will also be important to understand the changing flows of Antarctic Bottom Water and North Atlantic Deep Water, which are important drivers of the circulation and biogeochemical cycling of the ocean as well as the global inventory of carbon dioxide (Rintoul, this volume), which impact marine and terrestrial ecosystems across the Earth.

Data on atmospheric ozone depletion, which allows higher concentrations of ultraviolet radiation from the Sun to reach the Earth's surface, have served as a particularly urgent early warning (Solomon and Chanin, this volume). Because of genetic damage, most notably in the form of skin cancers that would ensue worldwide, the 1985 Convention for Protection of the Ozone Layer (Vienna Convention) and its 1987 Protocol on Substances that Deplete the Ozone Layer (Montreal Protocol) were quickly adopted in response to this global threat (Sarma and Anderson, this volume). The ozone story at once reveals unequivocal anthropogenic impacts to the Earth system on a global scale, while highlighting the central roles and responsibilities of the international scientific community in providing early warnings about impending threats that can be translated into adaptation or mitigation policies.

Uncontrolled fishing in the Southern Ocean in the early 1970s alerted the SCAR marine community to a potential ecological disaster of the type that had occurred elsewhere in the world (Walton, this volume). Rapid action to investigate these Antarctic fishery impacts provided the basis for international agreement and regulation through CCAMLR.

Science as a Determinant of Public Policy Agendas

Antarctica and its surrounding seas drive much of the Southern Hemisphere weather systems, form bottom waters that propel the global ocean conveyor (Broecker, 1991), absorb a major component of atmospheric carbon, reflect much of the solar radiation that enters the Earth system, and contribute significantly to global sea level. All of these natural phenomena are of major importance, not just for the Antarctic Treaty nations, but for life on Earth.

Antarctic science has become topical, essential, and strategic. It may be expensive, but evidence from the last 50 years is that we need more not less research there if we are to predict the future state of the world accurately enough to plan for our survival. Fortunately, the ATS has become increasingly aware of its responsibilities for Antarctic diplomacy and science, providing an important foundation for international and interdisciplinary research that reveals the dynamics of the Earth system with direct relevance to humankind.

Scientific advances often give rise to policy issues where they did not exist before, especially in relation to natural phenomena and technological innovations. In some cases, the policy process itself exposes solutions or challenges that can be generalized. Two science-policy examples from Antarctica involve ecosystems and climate.

In 1976, a SCAR Group of Specialists was formed on Biological Investigations of Marine Antarctic Systems and Stocks (BIOMASS) to assess keystone relationships of krill (*Euphausia superba*) to other species in the Southern Ocean south of the Antarctic Convergence (El-Sayed, 1994). This assessment led to a recognition that a species-by-species approach was insufficient to manage harvesting impacts effectively in the Antarctic marine ecosystem. In contrast to the 1972 Convention on the Conservation of Antarctic Seals, it was necessary to consider the interactions of species with their habitats across trophic levels from the phytoplankton to the krill and bird, fish, seal, squid, and whale predators. Embodied in Article II of CCAMLR, this ecosystem approach called for maintaining the "ecological relationships between harvested, dependent and related populations" (Miller, this volume). The underlying concept of interdependence was further elaborated in the 1991 Madrid Protocol to "enhance the protection of the Antarctic environment and dependent and associated ecosystems."

Policy measures emphasizing the term "ecosystem" were adopted for Antarctic protected areas in 1964, well before other regions around the world, as reflected by the Digital Library of International Environmental and Ecosystem

Policy Documents that spans the period from 1818 to 1999 (Marine Mammal Commission, 2007). Today, ecosystem-based management is a widely accepted approach applied to address human impacts in marine systems around the world (Levin and Lubchenco, 2008) as well as to issues involving freshwater and terrestrial systems.

Since World War II, international environmental and ecosystem agreements have grown at an exponential rate (Berkman, this volume), with connections to scientific discoveries that are unmistakable. These discrete solutions dealing with all manner of Earth system phenomena have expanded into an integrated fabric of policies on a planetary scale, as represented by climate. This policy trajectory also is mirrored in the Antarctic, where the value of the environment for global baseline monitoring was recognized in the 1960s, two decades before climate research was incorporated into the policy measures. These global science-policy developments are coupled with technological advances, most profoundly involving data collected by satellites that yield perspectives of the Earth system and its dynamics.

Climate, like science diplomacy, is merely a term for a process that has long been understood. In 1882–1883, for example, 12 European nations convened the first International Polar Year (IPY) with a national security focus on glacial weather conditions that had impacted their agriculture and economies for the preceding four centuries during the Little Ice Age (Berkman, 2003). During the nineteenth century, science already was tasked with contributing to international policies that relate to climate as we define it today and for the same reasons.

Science as an Element of International Institutions

Science contributes fundamentally to the implementation of sustainable development strategies that seek to balance environmental protection, economic prosperity, and social justice into the future. When regions or resources, natural phenomena, or technologies are the policy focus, science is built into the institution. At the international level, the Antarctic Treaty is a seminal illustration of scientific contributions to institutional design and implementation (Jacobsson, this volume).

Starting with the Preamble, which articulates the vision that "Antarctica shall continue forever to be used exclusively for peaceful purposes and shall not become the scene or object of international discord," the contributions of science are incorporated into the major elements of the Antarctic Treaty. To construct this firm foundation, science is elaborated in Articles I, II and III with regard to peaceful purposes, scientific investigation, and international cooperation, respectively. Together, these three articles emphasize the freedom of scientific investigation along with the open exchange of scientific observations, results, personnel, and program plans. To further facilitate information exchange and provide for essential continuity between meetings, an important recent addition to the ATS has been its secretariat (Huber, this volume).

In addition, to ensure competent advice, cooperation is established with "international organizations having a scientific or technical interest in Antarctica" (Cohen, this volume). As recommended at the First Antarctic Treaty Consultative Meeting (ATCM) in 1961, the first scientific organization to be recognized was SCAR (Walton, this volume), whose "most valuable contribution" preceded the Antarctic Treaty.

This marriage between science and policy in the Antarctic Treaty generated the 1972 Convention on the Conservation of Antarctic Seals with its policy-making arm and key contributions from SCAR to "achieve the objectives of protection, scientific study and rational use of Antarctic seals, and to maintain a satisfactory balance within the ecological system." The science-policy architecture of the Antarctic Treaty also was transferred into CCAMLR, which has a commission with a Scientific Committee and a secretariat to achieve its objectives (Scully, this volume).

In all, the Antarctic Treaty uses the terms science, scientific, or research in the Antarctic Treaty 18 times. The central importance of science is integrated into Article IX, which refers to consultation on matters of common interest. Facilitation of scientific research and international scientific cooperation are two of the six common interests. Importantly, as opposed to any political, economic, or cultural criterion, Article IX establishes "substantial research activity" as the standard a state must meet to become an Antarctic Treaty Consultative Party (ATCP), giving rise to a two-tiered system that also includes signatories that have acceded to the Antarctic Treaty without becoming Consultative Parties (Triggs, this volume).

In practice, the complex and expensive logistics needed to conduct scientific research in Antarctica require ongoing support from national programs. Since 1988, with the involvement of the 28 ATCPs, the Council of Managers of National Antarctic Programs (COMNAP) has provided a regular forum to coordinate the ships, helicopters, planes, and research facilities for delivery of the science that is fundamental to the success of the ATS (Retamales and Rogan-Finnemore, this volume).

At once, the Antarctic Treaty demonstrated how science can imbue an international institution with the resilience needed to establish a policy-making system that can evolve and respond effectively to ever-changing circumstances (Scully, this volume; Wolfrum, this volume). This is not to say that the ATS is without a need for improvement, as noted in several contributions to this volume (Huber, this volume; Barnes, this volume). Moreover, there are growing concerns, as with the case of tourism (Landau, this volume), about the need for the ATS to improve its oversight to ensure human safety and environmental protection in the region south of 60°S latitude. Nonetheless, the demonstration is clear and compelling that the ATS has become a model of international cooperation to resolve varied and complicated issues over the past half century, largely because science has a been a key element of its design and implementation.

Science as a Tool of Diplomacy

The Antarctic Treaty emerged during the height of the cold war, creating a firm foundation that promotes cooperation and prevents conflict among adversaries and allies alike "on the basis of freedom of scientific investigation." Although the scientific roots of this international collaboration in Antarctica are deep, extending back to the nineteenth century (Roots, this volume), the imperative came from the terrible losses encountered by all humankind when our world was urgently seeking strategies to build trust, identify common interests, and promote lasting peace among nations. This global imperative is no less critical today, and there is no room for complacency in learning and applying the lessons from our past.

Following the devastation of World War II, which President Eisenhower understood firsthand as a supreme Allied commander, it was vital to promote cooperation and prevent such conflict from ever happening again on a global scale, especially with the development of ballistic missiles capable of carrying nuclear weapons over intercontinental distances (Berkman, this volume). Yet the United States and Soviet Union, the two superpowers with nuclear capacities, were locked in cold war brinksmanship without the ability to negotiate on issues involving ballistic missiles, as demonstrated by the unequivocal rejection of the Open Skies proposal in 1955.

It was providential that the IGY was being planned for 1 July 1957 through 31 December 1958, with the anticipated initial launch of Earth-orbiting scientific satellites suggesting a need for rules involving freedom of space much like the freedom of the sea. Even though they were launched for peaceful purposes, scientific satellites were unmistakably related to the rockets that would become ballistic missiles. Satellites also were the national security concern that had attracted the Soviet Union to participate in the IGY, opening an avenue of cooperation for the two superpowers to collaborate with other nations in shared international investigation of the Earth system. The timing of the first satellite launch, accomplished with Sputnik during the IGY on 4 October 1957, was the historic consequence of science diplomacy with contributions from influential scientists like Lloyd Berkner (Needell, 2000).

With science as a tool of diplomacy, the IGY inspired international cooperation that enabled the United States and Soviet Union to take the lead in establishing the Antarctic Treaty as the first nuclear arms agreement, despite their inability to negotiate on this issue elsewhere. The Antarctic Treaty similarly stimulated peaceful collaboration between the United States and Japan on an equal footing when such interactions were barely imaginable so soon after World War II (Yoshida, this volume).

With the precedent of the 1959 Antarctic Treaty, the 1967 Treaty on Principles Governing the Activities of States in the Exploration and Use of Outer Space, Including the Moon and Other Celestial Bodies (Outer Space Treaty) became the next legal regime to prohibit the emplacement of nuclear weapons in an international space that had never been armed (Kerrest, this volume). The third demilitarization regime was the 1971 Treaty on the Prohibition of the Emplacement of Nuclear Weapons and Other Weapons of Mass Destruction on the Sea-bed and the Ocean Floor and in the Subsoil Thereof (Deep Sea Treaty). Together, these three regimes along with the 1958 Convention on the High Seas (since incorporated into the 1982 United Nations Convention on the Law of the Sea) established four international spaces that humankind has elected to manage beyond the reach of national jurisdiction.

The nuclear issue arose also in connection with the "Question of Antarctica" that India placed on the United Nation agenda in 1956 "to affirm that the area will be utilised entirely for peaceful purposes and for the general welfare" (Jacobsson, this volume). The scientific focus of the Antarctica Treaty subsequently encouraged India to conduct "substantial research activity" and to become an ATCP itself in 1983. That same year, Malaysia along with Antigua and Barbuda raised the Question of Antarctica again in the United Nations, this time due to an interest in mineral resources (Scully, this volume). The engaging contribution of science as a trust-building tool of diplomacy will be further highlighted when Malaysia accedes to the Antarctic Treaty.

Science also creates functional links among disparate institutions, even when their only formal connections are the policy issues they have in common. For example, the issue of iron fertilization in the sea, as a strategy intended to mitigate greenhouse warming by stimulating phytoplankton production that would sequester atmospheric carbon dioxide, illustrates the institutional interplay between the 1991 Madrid Protocol and other international agreements that relate to marine pollution (VanderZwaag, this volume).

Comparisons between the provisions of the Antarctic Treaty and the Outer Space Treaty illustrate conceptual interplay among institutions relating to international spaces (Race, this volume). Regimes created to govern international spaces that can be neither occupied nor appropriated by nations, where science has fundamental roles and responsibilities to promote cooperation as well as provide advice for policy making and implementation, further reveal an emerging alphabet of common interests for the benefit of our civilization (Wolfrum, this volume)

Over time, additional international agreements have arisen to deal with issues beyond the jurisdiction of nation–states, with transboundary issues that also transcend sovereign jurisdictions. The 1992 United Nations Framework Convention on Climate Change, for example, acknowledges that "change in the Earth's climate and its adverse effects are a common concern of humankind." Similarly, the 1992 Convention on Biological Diversity, affirms that "conservation of biological diversity is a common concern of humankind." In view of functional relationships across the boundaries of nations, the 2003 World Summit on the Information Society has determined that "knowledge is the common wealth of humanity" (Electronic Geophysical Year, 2007)

In general, the unique international value of science is reflected by its principles (Elzinga, this volume). The scientific process is open, producing results that are shared and transparent, promoting cooperation, and preventing conflict. It is telling that the 2007 Nobel Prize to the Intergovernmental Panel for Climate Change was awarded not for chemistry or physics, but for peace. As a lingua franca free of political, cultural, and economic agendas, science fosters international, interdisciplinary, and inclusive dialogues that are crucial to protect our common welfare and the world we live in.

GLOBAL SIGNIFICANCE OF THE ANTARCTIC EXPERIENCE

It is a natural step, then, to ask whether the experience in science diplomacy in Antarctica also holds lessons for those concerned with governance in international society in general terms and more specifically with the governance of global commons. Any lessons we are able to glean from the Antarctic experience will be relevant not only to those interested in traditional international spaces but also to those in search of effective approaches to governing an expanding range of issues (e.g., climate change) that have become matters of intense concern at the global level in recent years and that are destined to become even more important in the future.

In this section, we draw attention to several facets of the Antarctic experience that highlight strategies and precedents for the governance of other international spaces. We also explore similarities and differences between the Antarctic and the Arctic with regard to the needs for governance arising in the polar regions and the role of science in fulfilling these needs.

Governing International Spaces

International spaces are commons in the sense that they are not subject to the rights and rules that we associate with systems of public property, much less systems of private property (Ostrom et al., 2002). At least since the publication of Garrett Hardin's well-known article on the "tragedy of the commons," many have come to regard situations of the sort prevailing in Antarctica and other commons as a recipe for disaster with regard to the management of human-environment relations and to the achievement of effective governance more generally (Hardin, 1968). But no such tragedy has occurred in the case of Antarctica. Although there is no shortage of issues that generate needs for governance in the south polar region, Antarctica is well governed by a system that has demonstrated a considerable capacity to grow and adapt to changing circumstances over a long period of time. How is this possible? What are the implications of this success for efforts to govern other international spaces?

Success in situations of this kind requires both the establishment of structures of rights and rules that serve the interests of the major players in the relevant systems and the development of decision-making procedures capable of adjusting and adapting these arrangements to address changing circumstances. In the case of the ATS, this has meant, first and foremost, accommodating the interests of major claimant and nonclaimant states and setting up the ATCMs as a venue for collective decision making about matters of common interest. But there is more to this story that will be of interest to those concerned with the governance of other international spaces.

The negotiations that culminated in the signing of the Antarctic Treaty on 1 December 1959 profited from both the knowledge and the relationships of trust emerging from the 1957–1958 IGY experience. The criterion for consultative party status in the resultant regime is framed in terms of the level of scientific effort. The governance system that has evolved from this point of departure recognizes the role of the science community operating through SCAR and accords considerable prominence to the work of scientists in prioritizing and framing issues for consideration at the ATCMs and in providing the information needed on a regular basis to assess the results of decisions taken by the ATCMs.

The science community has emerged also as an essential player in the implementation and administration of the ATS. The occupants of the research stations in Antarctica constitute the only human residents of this international space. The provisions of the Antarctic Treaty relating to freedom of movement for scientists and to the conduct of inspections of the activities taking place at individual research stations ensure a high level of transparency with regard to human activities in the region. There is little chance that any substantial violation of the rules governing human activities in the region could escape the attention of members of the science community. Because this community is well known for its international character and for its tendency to avoid becoming enmeshed in the pursuit of national interests, these arrangements have operated to produce both a high level of assurance among the members of the regime regarding compliance with the major provisions of the ATS and considerable confidence regarding the absence of unregulated interventions on the part of nonmembers.

Although no two international spaces are alike, much of the Antarctic experience seems relevant to other international spaces. The high seas, the deep seabed, and outer space are all affected by a variety of human actions. But, like Antarctica, they do not have long-term resident populations that form the basis for powerful interest groups.

Particularly striking in this context is the role that science can play with regard to the implementation and administration of governance systems for international spaces or, in other words, what we now think of as science for diplomacy. Because scientists tend to see themselves as operating in a domain that has little to do with policy making or governance, this role may seem alien to many members of the science community. Yet whether we are thinking of the deep seabed or outer space, scientists are key players in the human activities taking place in or associated with these systems. As in the case of Antarctica, decisions about human uses of these spaces will apply in many instances to the activities of scientists, and scientists will often find themselves in a good position to monitor the extent to which parties comply with the rights and rules of the relevant governance systems. Some may worry that this policy-relevant role of science will have the effect of distracting scientists from their main role as producers of knowledge. But as the concept of Pasteur's Quadrant makes clear, the idea that science has a role to play in addressing matters of public policy is hardly a new one (Stokes, 1997). It is destined to grow in importance during the foreseeable future.

Governing the Arctic

The assumption that there are important similarities between Antarctica and the Arctic with regard to issues of governance is a persistent one (Cava et al., this volume). Yet, as Table 1 makes clear, the dissimilarities between the two polar regions are profound. Aside from the presence of a cold climate and the importance of ice, the antipodes differ from one another in most respects. In terms of our discussion of lessons to be derived from the experience of the ATS, it is critical to note that most of the Arctic (all except an area in the central portion of the Arctic Ocean) does not constitute an international space. The coastal states have jurisdiction not only over all the lands located north of 60°N but also over the waters of their exclusive economic zones (EEZ) stretching seaward from their coasts. The Commission on the Limits of the Continental Shelf is currently addressing issues relating to coastal state jurisdiction over the seabed extending beyond the EEZs in the Arctic Ocean.

Yet the thought that there are lessons to be learned from experiences in each polar region that are relevant to the other will not go away. Despite the dramatic differences between the two regions, there are still insights to be gained from comparing and contrasting Antarctica and the Arctic, with particular reference to science diplomacy. The key to this puzzle lies in the character of the science-policy interface in the two polar regions.

Scientific cooperation in the Arctic and Antarctica has a long history that includes the first IPY in 1882–1883 and runs through the IGY in 1957–1958, the fourth IPY in 2007–2008, and the current effort to extend this collaborative effort by launching an International Polar Decade. Just as SCAR predates the signing of the Antarctic Treaty in 1959, the International Arctic Science Committee (IASC) preceded the creation of the Arctic Environmental Protection Strategy in 1991 and the Arctic Council in 1996. The IASC, much like SCAR, has become an

TABLE 1. Comparison of Arctic and Antarctic characteristics. Adapted from Berkman (2010b).

Characteristic	Arctic	Antarctic
Location	The high-latitude region surrounding the North Pole (90°N latitude)	The high-latitude region surrounding the South Pole (90°S latitude)
Geography	Ocean surrounded by continents	Continent surrounded by ocean
Ecosystems	Strongly influenced by solar cycle poleward of Arctic Circle (66.5°N)	Strongly influenced by solar cycle poleward of Antarctic Circle (66.5°S)
Sea ice	Year-round, mostly multiyear	Seasonal, mostly annual
Continental shelf	Broadest, shallowest on Earth	Narrowest, deepest on Earth[a]
Humans	Indigenous people over millennia	No indigenous people
Science	International Arctic Science Committee	Scientific Committee on Antarctic Research
Territories	Recognized sovereign jurisdictions	Claims to sovereignty[a]
Access	Restricted	Unrestricted
Living resources	Ongoing exploitation	Ongoing exploitation
Mineral resources	Ongoing exploitation	Exploitation prohibited
Ecotourism	Extensive	Extensive
Military presence	Extensive since World War II	Nonmilitarized region
Nuclear weapons	Extensive since World War II	Nuclear-free zone
Common interests	Sustainable development and environmental protection[b]	(1) peaceful purposes only; (2) facilitation of scientific research; (3) facilitation of international scientific cooperation; (4) facilitation of the exercise of the rights of inspection; (5) questions relating to the exercise of jurisdiction; (6) preservation and conservation of living resources[c]
Legal framework	Law of the Sea[d]	1959 Antarctic Treaty[e]

[a]Described and mapped in Berkman (2002).
[b]Defined as "common arctic issues" in the 1996 Ottawa Declaration on the Establishment of the Arctic Council (http://www.international.gc.ca/polar-polaire/ottdec-decott.aspx?lang=en).
[c]Defined as "matters of common interest" in the 1959 Antarctic Treaty, Article IX, paragraph 1 (http://www.ats.aq/documents/ats/treaty_original.pdf).
[d]As expressed in the 2008 Ilulissat Declaration, the five Arctic coastal states "remain committed" to the law of the sea (http://www.oceanlaw.org/downloads/arctic/Ilulissat_Declaration.pdf). The Arctic states all have adopted the 1982 United Nations Convention on the Law of the Sea (UNCLOS Searchable Database, http://lawofthesea.tierit.com), with the exception of the United States.
[e]Antarctic Treaty Searchable Database (http://aspire.tierit.com).

influential source of scientific knowledge underpinning the work of the Arctic Council. Both SCAR and IASC are affiliated with the International Council of Science (ICSU).[3] A sizable proportion of those engaged in polar research are active in both Antarctic research and Arctic research, and SCAR and IASC have begun to collaborate in organizing jointly sponsored scientific meetings and in developing research agendas that make it possible to compare and contrast findings from the antipodes in a rigorous manner.

In the process, activities centered on the polar regions have come to play a prominent role in the development of new perspectives on the science-policy interface. Sometimes discussed in terms of the idea of the coproduction of knowledge, these new perspectives highlight a much more collaborative effort encompassing active cooperation in framing research questions and in setting research priorities as well as in delivering the results of scientific research to policy makers who have played a significant role in guiding scientific research from the outset (Jasanoff, 2004). In both regions, an important result of this collaborative process has been the conduct of what we now know as scientific assessments and the infusion of the results of these assessments into the policy process (Mitchell et al., 2006).

The practices that have evolved in the two regions differ in some significant ways. In the Antarctic case, what are known as SCAR groups of specialists have emerged as central mechanisms in carrying out scientific assessments. In the Arctic, in contrast, the Arctic Council's working groups, operating often in collaboration with IASC, have taken the lead in the preparation of policy-relevant scientific assessments. But as the delivery of the Arctic Climate Impact Assessment (ACIA) to the Arctic Council ministerial meeting in 2004 and the submission of its Antarctic counterpart, the report on Antarctic Climate Change and the Environment (ACCE), to the ATCM in 2009 make clear, this emerging relationship between the science community and the policy community is a progressive step in the creation of effective governance systems in the antipodes. This relationship is not always trouble free. The friction associated with the process of drafting the ACIA policy statement in the months leading up to the Arctic Council ministerial meeting in November 2004 provides a sharp reminder of the fact that the concerns of the two communities are never identical and can diverge substantially in specific cases (Nilsson, 2007: chap. 5). But this case also demonstrates that the polar regions have emerged as key venues for the development of new practices regarding the science-policy interface that are now producing major shifts in our thinking about the interactions between the science community and the policy community with regard to efforts to govern complex systems on a large scale.

THE FUTURE OF SCIENCE DIPLOMACY

In its 2010 report on science diplomacy, the Royal Society observes that "interest in science diplomacy is growing at a time when international relations are changing" (Royal Society, 2010). No one expects the state to wither away during the foreseeable future as the basic element of international society. Yet the role of civil society is growing as a force to be reckoned with in determining the trajectory of world affairs. We know that this is the case with regard to the influence of corporations and environmental nongovernmental organizations (Pattberg, 2007). But the science community has emerged also as an important force in a wide range of issue areas. Sometimes, this is a matter of enhancing human capabilities in ways that lead to the emergence of new issues on the policy agenda, as in the cases of the development of nuclear weapons and the creation of genetically modified organisms. In other cases, scientific advances help to solve problems, as the successful effort to stamp out smallpox and the development of alternatives to ozone-depleting substances attest.

Although it is true that the cultures of science and policy making differ sharply in some respects (Royal Society, 2010), the experiences of recent decades in both the Antarctic and the Arctic suggest that science can thrive in settings involving extensive interactions between the science community and the policy community. Taking advantage of the resultant opportunities and steering clear of the potential pitfalls requires sophistication and vigilance on the part of leading members of both communities. But success in this realm is perfectly possible. Perhaps the broadest legacy of the first 50 years of the ATS is the development of a suite of practices that are useful in any effort to ensure that interactions between science and policy produce positive results for both communities in addressing a wide range of large-scale issues for the benefit of humankind and the world we inhabit.

NOTES

1. Antarctica is a transitional case in these terms. Although the territorial claims of the seven claimant states still exist on paper and are protected under the terms of Article IV of the 1959 Antarctic Treaty, Antarctica has emerged in practice as an international space for the purposes of governance.

2. Terms in measures that have been adopted by the Antarctic Treaty Consultative Parties can be comprehensively discovered and integrated from 1959 to 2007 with the Antarctic Treaty Searchable Database, 8th ed., http://aspire.tierit.com. Adopted measures in the Antarctic Treaty System also can be searched through the Antarctic Treaty Database, http://www.ats.aq/devAS/info_measures_list.aspx, from the Antarctic Treaty Secretariat.

3. Formally, SCAR is an ICSU committee, and IASC is an international associate of ICSU.

LITERATURE CITED

Albert II. 2011 (this volume). "Foreword." In *Science Diplomacy: Antarctica, Science, and the Governance of International Spaces*, ed. P. A. Berkman, M. A. Lang, D. W. H. Walton, and O. R. Young, pp. vii–viii. Washington, D.C.: Smithsonian Institution Scholarly Press.

Barnes, J. N. 2011 (this volume). "The Antarctic Treaty System: Perspectives of Environmental Nongovernmental Organizations on Addressing Key Issues." In *Science Diplomacy: Antarctica, Science, and the Governance of International Spaces*, ed. P. A. Berkman, M. A. Lang, D. W. H. Walton, and O. R. Young, pp. 277–280. Washington, D.C.: Smithsonian Institution Scholarly Press.

Berkman, P. A. 2002. *Science into Policy: Global Lessons from Antarctica*. New York, Academic Press.

———. 2003. International Polar Year 2007–2008. *Science*, 301:1669.

———. 2010a. Biodiversity Stewardship of International Spaces. *Systematics and Biodiversity*, 8(3):311–320.

———. 2010b. *Environmental Security in the Arctic Ocean: Promoting Co-operation and Preventing Conflict*. London: Royal United Services Institute for Defense and Security Studies.

———. 2011 (this volume). "President Eisenhower, the Antarctic Treaty, and the Origin of International Spaces." In *Science Diplomacy: Antarctica, Science, and the Governance of International Spaces*, ed. P. A. Berkman, M. A. Lang, D. W. H. Walton, and O. R. Young, pp. 17–27. Washington, D.C.: Smithsonian Institution Scholarly Press.

Broecker, W. S. 1991. The Great Ocean Conveyor. *Oceanography,* 4(2):79–89.

Bull, H., B. Kingsbury, and A. Roberts, eds. 1990. *Hugo Grotius and International Relations.* Oxford: Oxford University Press.

Cava, F., D. Monsma, and O. Young. 2011 (this volume). "Workshop on Arctic Governance: Drawing Lessons from the Antarctic Experience." In *Science Diplomacy: Antarctica, Science, and the Governance of International Spaces*, ed. P. A. Berkman, M. A. Lang, D. W. H. Walton, and O. R. Young, pp. 295–297. Washington, D.C.: Smithsonian Institution Scholarly Press.

Cohen, H. 2011 (this volume). "Public Participation in Antarctica: The Role of Nongovernmental and Intergovernmental Organizations." In *Science Diplomacy: Antarctica, Science, and the Governance of International Spaces*, ed. P. A. Berkman, M. A. Lang, D. W. H. Walton, and O. R. Young, pp. 271–276. Washington, D.C.: Smithsonian Institution Scholarly Press.

Cooper, A., P. Barker, P. Barrett, J. Behrendt, G. Brancolini, J. Childs, C. Escutia, W. Jokat, Y. Kristoffersen, G. Leitchenkov, H. Stagg, M. Tanahashi, N. Wardell, and P. Webb. 2011 (this volume). "The Antarctic Offshore Stratigraphy Project Legacy: Science Collaboration and International Transparency in Potential Marine Mineral Resource Exploitation of Antarctica." In *Science Diplomacy: Antarctica, Science, and the Governance of International Spaces*, ed. P. A. Berkman, M. A. Lang, D. W. H. Walton, and O. R. Young, pp. 223–229. Washington, D.C.: Smithsonian Institution Scholarly Press.

Electronic Geophysical Year. 2007. About eGY. http://egy.org/about.php (accessed 8 December 2010).

El-Sayed, S. Z., ed. 1994. *Southern Ocean Ecology: The BIOMASS Perspective.* Cambridge: Cambridge University Press.

Elzinga, A. 2011 (this volume). "Origin and Limitations of the Antarctic Treaty." In *Science Diplomacy: Antarctica, Science, and the Governance of International Spaces*, ed. P. A. Berkman, M. A. Lang, D. W. H. Walton, and O. R. Young, pp. 59–67. Washington, D.C.: Smithsonian Institution Scholarly Press.

Erb, K. A. 2011 (this volume). "International Collaboration in the Antarctic for Global Science." In *Science Diplomacy: Antarctica, Science, and the Governance of International Spaces*, ed. P. A. Berkman, M. A. Lang, D. W. H. Walton, and O. R. Young, pp. 265–270. Washington, D.C.: Smithsonian Institution Scholarly Press.

Golitsyn, V. 2011 (this volume). "Balancing Sovereign Interests beyond National Jurisdictions." In *Science Diplomacy: Antarctica, Science, and the Governance of International Spaces*, ed. P. A. Berkman, M. A. Lang, D. W. H. Walton, and O. R. Young, pp. 51–58. Washington, D.C.: Smithsonian Institution Scholarly Press.

Hardin, G. 1968. The Tragedy of the Commons. *Science,* 162:1243–1248.

Holland, M. M., and C. M. Bitz. 2003. Polar Amplification of Climate Change in Coupled Models. *Climate Dynamics,* 21:221–232.

Huber, J. 2011 (this volume). "The Antarctic Treaty: Toward a New Partnership." In *Science Diplomacy: Antarctica, Science, and the Governance of International Spaces*, ed. P. A. Berkman, M. A. Lang, D. W. H. Walton, and O. R. Young, pp. 89–95. Washington, D.C.: Smithsonian Institution Scholarly Press.

Jacobsson, M. 2011 (this volume). "Building the International Legal Framework for Antarctica." In *Science Diplomacy: Antarctica, Science, and the Governance of International Spaces*, ed. P. A. Berkman, M. A. Lang, D. W. H. Walton, and O. R. Young, pp. 1–15. Washington, D.C.: Smithsonian Institution Scholarly Press.

Jasanoff, S., ed. 2004. *States of Knowledge: The Co-production of Science and Social Order.* London: Routledge

Joyner, C. C. 2011 (this volume). "Potential Challenges to the Antarctic Treaty." In *Science Diplomacy: Antarctica, Science, and the Governance of International Spaces*, ed. P. A. Berkman, M. A. Lang, D. W. H. Walton, and O. R. Young, pp. 97–102. Washington, D.C.: Smithsonian Institution Scholarly Press.

Kennicutt, M., II. 2011 (this volume). "New Frontiers and Future Directions in Antarctic Science." In *Science Diplomacy: Antarctica, Science, and the Governance of International Spaces*, ed. P. A. Berkman, M. A. Lang, D. W. H. Walton, and O. R. Young, pp. 153–160. Washington, D.C.: Smithsonian Institution Scholarly Press.

Kerrest, A. 2011 (this volume). "Outer Space as International Space: Lessons from Antarctica." In *Science Diplomacy: Antarctica, Science, and the Governance of International Spaces*, ed. P. A. Berkman, M. A. Lang, D. W. H. Walton, and O. R. Young, pp. 133–142. Washington, D.C.: Smithsonian Institution Scholarly Press.

Landau, D. 2011 (this volume). "International Cooperation and Management of Tourism: A World within a World." In *Science Diplomacy: Antarctica, Science, and the Governance of International Spaces*, ed. P. A. Berkman, M. A. Lang, D. W. H. Walton, and O. R. Young, pp. 241–244. Washington, D.C.: Smithsonian Institution Scholarly Press.

Levin, S. A., and J. Lubchenco. 2008. Resilience, Robustness, and Marine Ecosystem-Based Management. *BioScience,* 58:1–6.

Lovelock, J. E., and L. Margulis. 1974. Atmospheric Homeostasis by and for the Biosphere: The Gaia Hypothesis. *Tellus,* 26:2–10.

Lüdecke, C. 2011 (this volume). "Parallel Precedents for the Antarctic Treaty." In *Science Diplomacy: Antarctica, Science, and the Governance of International Spaces*, ed. P. A. Berkman, M. A. Lang, D. W. H. Walton, and O. R. Young, pp. 254–263. Washington, D.C.: Smithsonian Institution Scholarly Press.

Marine Mammal Commission. 2007. Digital Library of International Environmental and Ecosystem Policy Documents. http://nsdl.tierit.com (accessed 8 December 2010).

Miller, D. 2011 (this volume). "Sustainable Management in the Southern Ocean: CCAMLR Science." In *Science Diplomacy: Antarctica, Science, and the Governance of International Spaces*, ed. P. A. Berkman, M. A. Lang, D. W. H. Walton, and O. R. Young, pp. 103–121. Washington, D.C.: Smithsonian Institution Scholarly Press.

Mitchell, R. B., W.C. Clark, D. Cash, and N. M. Dickson, eds. 2006 *Global Environmental Assessments: Information and Influence.* Cambridge, Mass.: MIT Press

Needell, A. 2000. *Science, Cold War and the American State: Lloyd V. Berkner and the Balance of Professional Ideals.* Amsterdam: Harwood Academic Publishers.

Nilsson, A. E. 2007. *A Changing Arctic Climate: Science and Policy in the Arctic Climate Impact Assessment.* Linköping, Sweden: Linköping University.

Orheim, O., A. Press, and N. Gilbert, 2011 (this volume). "Managing the Antarctic Environment: The Evolving Role of the Committee for Environmental Protection." In *Science Diplomacy: Antarctica, Science, and the Governance of International Spaces*, ed. P. A. Berkman, M. A. Lang, D. W. H. Walton, and O. R. Young, pp. 209–221. Washington, D.C.: Smithsonian Institution Scholarly Press.

Ostrom, E., T. Dietz, N. Dolsak, P. C. Stern, S. Stonich, and E. Weber, eds. 2002. *The Drama of the Commons.* Washington, D.C.: National Academies Press

Pattberg, P. 2007. *Private Institutions and Global Governance: The New Politics of Environmental Sustainability.* Cheltenham, UK: Edward Elgar.

Petit, J. R. 2011 (this volume). "The Vostok Venture: An Outcome of the Antarctic Treaty." In *Science Diplomacy: Antarctica, Science, and the Governance of International Spaces*, ed. P. A. Berkman, M. A. Lang, D. W. H. Walton, and O. R. Young, pp. 165–173. Washington, D.C.: Smithsonian Institution Scholarly Press.

Race, M. S. 2011 (this volume). "Policies for Scientific Exploration and Environmental Protection: Comparison of the Antarctic and Outer Space Treaties." In *Science Diplomacy: Antarctica, Science, and the Governance of International Spaces*, ed. P. A. Berkman, M. A. Lang, D. W. H. Walton, and O. R. Young, pp. 143–152. Washington, D.C.: Smithsonian Institution Scholarly Press.

Retamales, J., and M. Rogan-Finnemore. 2011 (this volume). "The Role of the Council of Managers of National Antarctic Programs." In *Science Diplomacy: Antarctica, Science, and the Governance of International Spaces*, ed. P. A. Berkman, M. A. Lang, D. W. H. Walton, and O. R. Young, pp. 231–240. Washington, D.C.: Smithsonian Institution Scholarly Press.

Rintoul, S. R. 2011 (this volume). "The Southern Ocean in the Earth System." In *Science Diplomacy: Antarctica, Science, and the Governance of International Spaces*, ed. P. A. Berkman, M. A. Lang, D. W. H. Walton, and O. R. Young, pp. 175–188. Washington, D.C.: Smithsonian Institution Scholarly Press.

Roots, E. F. 2011 (this volume). "Background and Evolution of Some Ideas and Values That Have Led to the Antarctic Treaty." In *Science Diplomacy: Antarctica, Science, and the Governance of International Spaces*, ed. P. A. Berkman, M. A. Lang, D. W. H. Walton, and O. R. Young, pp. 69–72. Washington, D.C.: Smithsonian Institution Scholarly Press.

Royal Society. 2010. New Frontiers in Science Diplomacy: Navigating the Changing Balance of Power. RS Policy Document 01.10. London: Royal Society.

Sarma, K. M., and S. O. Andersen. 2011 (this volume). "Science and Diplomacy: Montreal Protocol on Substances that Deplete the Ozone Layer." In *Science Diplomacy: Antarctica, Science, and the Governance of International Spaces*, ed. P. A. Berkman, M. A. Lang, D. W. H. Walton, and O. R. Young, pp. 123–132. Washington, D.C.: Smithsonian Institution Scholarly Press.

Scripps CO_2 Program. 2010. Welcome to Scripps CO_2. http://scrippsco2.ucsd.edu/ (accessed 8 December 2010).

Scully, T. 2011 (this volume). "The Development of the Antarctic Treaty System." In *Science Diplomacy: Antarctica, Science, and the Governance of International Spaces*, ed. P. A. Berkman, M. A. Lang, D. W. H. Walton, and O. R. Young, pp. 29–38. Washington, D.C.: Smithsonian Institution Scholarly Press.

Solomon, S., and M.-L. Chanin. 2011 (this volume). "The Antarctic Ozone Hole: A Unique Example of the Science and Policy Interface." In *Science Diplomacy: Antarctica, Science, and the Governance of International Spaces*, ed. P. A. Berkman, M. A. Lang, D. W. H. Walton, and O. R. Young, pp. 189–196. Washington, D.C.: Smithsonian Institution Scholarly Press.

Stark, A. A. 2011 (this volume). "Cosmology from Antarctica." In *Science Diplomacy: Antarctica, Science, and the Governance of International Spaces*, ed. P. A. Berkman, M. A. Lang, D. W. H. Walton, and O. R. Young, pp. 197–208. Washington, D.C.: Smithsonian Institution Scholarly Press.

Stokes, D. E. 1997. *Pasteur's Quadrant: Basic Science and Technological Innovation*. Washington, D.C.: Brookings Institution Press.

Thiede, J. 2011 (this volume). "Modern Research in Polar Regions." In *Science Diplomacy: Antarctica, Science, and the Governance of International Spaces*, ed. P. A. Berkman, M. A. Lang, D. W. H. Walton, and O. R. Young, pp. 161–164. Washington, D.C.: Smithsonian Institution Scholarly Press.

Triggs, G. 2011 (this volume). "The Antarctic Treaty System: A Model of Legal Creativity and Cooperation." In *Science Diplomacy: Antarctica, Science, and the Governance of International Spaces*, ed. P. A. Berkman, M. A. Lang, D. W. H. Walton, and O. R. Young, pp. 39–50. Washington, D.C.: Smithsonian Institution Scholarly Press.

VanderZwaag, D. L. 2011 (this volume). "Ocean Dumping and Fertilization in the Antarctic: Tangled Legal Currents, Sea of Challenges." In *Science Diplomacy: Antarctica, Science, and the Governance of International Spaces*, ed. P. A. Berkman, M. A. Lang, D. W. H. Walton, and O. R. Young, pp. 245–152. Washington, D.C.: Smithsonian Institution Scholarly Press.

Walton, D. W. H. 2011 (this volume). "The Scientific Committee on Antarctic Research and the Antarctic Treaty." In *Science Diplomacy: Antarctica, Science, and the Governance of International Spaces*, ed. P. A. Berkman, M. A. Lang, D. W. H. Walton, and O. R. Young, pp. 75–88. Washington, D.C.: Smithsonian Institution Scholarly Press.

Wolfrum, R. 2011 (this volume). "Common Interests in the Ocean." In *Science Diplomacy: Antarctica, Science, and the Governance of International Spaces*, ed. P. A. Berkman, M. A. Lang, D. W. H. Walton, and O. R. Young, pp. 281–286. Washington, D.C.: Smithsonian Institution Scholarly Press.

Worthington, E. 1975. *The Evolution of IBP*. International Biological Programme Synthesis Series. Cambridge: Cambridge University Press.

Yoshida, Y. 2011 (this volume). "Japan and the Antarctic Treaty after World War II." In *Science Diplomacy: Antarctica, Science, and the Governance of International Spaces*, ed. P. A. Berkman, M. A. Lang, D. W. H. Walton, and O. R. Young, pp. 73–74. Washington, D.C.: Smithsonian Institution Scholarly Press.

Young, O. R., 2011 (this volume). "Governing International Spaces: Antarctica and Beyond." In *Science Diplomacy: Antarctica, Science, and the Governance of International Spaces*, ed. P. A. Berkman, M. A. Lang, D. W. H. Walton, and O. R. Young, pp. 287–294. Washington, D.C.: Smithsonian Institution Scholarly Press.

Zazulie, N., M. Rusticucci, and S. Solomon. 2010. Changes in Climate at High Southern Latitudes: A Unique Daily Record at Orcadas Spanning 1903–2008. *Journal of Climate,* 23:189–196.

Appendix

The Appendix contains documents that celebrate the fiftieth anniversary of the Antarctic Treaty. The documents reaffirm the tenets of the Antarctic Treaty and its contribution to science and scientific cooperation. Included are:

- Signed affirmation by UN Secretary-General Ban Ki-moon
- U.S. House of Representatives Concurrent Resolution, no. 51
- U.S. Senate Resolution, no 365
- Signed Forever Declaration of the Antarctic Treaty presented to the United Nations.

Also included are photos from the Antarctic Treaty Summit, which was convened at the Smithsonian Institution between 30 November and 3 December 2009.

NATIONS UNIES

THE SECRETARY-GENERAL

--

VIDEO MESSAGE ON THE FIFTIETH ANNIVERSARY OF THE SIGNING OF THE ANTARCTIC TREATY

Washington, D.C., 1 December 2009

Excellencies,
Distinguished guests,
Ladies and gentlemen,

The Antarctic Treaty is a unique example of international cooperation. Its main focus is to ensure that Antarctica is used for peaceful purposes only.

As new issues have emerged, the Treaty has evolved.

Antarctica has been designated as a natural reserve – the world's largest conservation area. It has been the scene of successful international scientific research on challenges such as climate change and the depletion of the ozone layer.

International cooperation in and for Antarctica provides an example for all.

After half a century, new challenges are emerging. Commercial activities could jeopardize the integrity of the fragile Antarctic ecosystem, in particular unsustainable fishing, adverse impacts of tourism and biological prospecting.

But the greatest threat is climate change.

I urge you to do your part to ensure that this month's conference in Copenhagen lays the foundation for a legally binding climate treaty. This is crucial if we are to protect Antarctica's fragile environment and prevent devastating sea level rise.

All these challenges will require strengthened cooperation -- not just among Parties to the Antarctic Treaty and the Antarctic Treaty system, but across the entire international community.

I urge all concerned to work in harmony – for Antarctica, for science, for the progress of all humankind.

In that spirit, I wish you a most successful celebration of this important Treaty.

Ki Moon Ban

BAN Ki-moon

111TH CONGRESS
1ST SESSION

H. CON. RES. 51

CONCURRENT RESOLUTION

Whereas the Antarctic Treaty was signed by 12 nations in Washington, DC, on December 1, 1959, "with the interests of science and the progress of all mankind";

Whereas the Antarctic Treaty was established to continue and develop international "cooperation on the basis of freedom of scientific investigation in Antarctica as applied during the International Geophysical Year";

Whereas the Antarctic Treaty came into force on June 23, 1961, after its unanimous ratification by the seven countries (Argentina, Australia, Chile, France, New Zealand, Norway, and the United Kingdom) with territorial claims in the region and five other countries (Belgium, Japan, South Africa, the Soviet Union, and the United States), which had collaborated in Antarctic research activities during the International Geophysical Year from July 1, 1957, through December 31, 1958;

Whereas the Antarctic Treaty now has 47 nations as signatories that together represent nearly 90 percent of humanity;

Whereas Article IV of the Antarctic Treaty states that "no acts or activities taking place while the present Treaty is in force shall constitute a basis for asserting, supporting or denying a claim to territorial sovereignty in Antarctica";

Whereas the 14 articles of the Antarctic Treaty have provided a lasting foundation for maintaining the region south of 60 degrees south latitude, nearly 10 percent of the Earth's surface, "for peaceful purposes only";

Whereas the Antarctic Treaty prohibits "any measure of a military nature";

Whereas the Antarctic Treaty has promoted international nuclear cooperation by prohibiting "any nuclear explosions in Antarctica and the disposal there of radioactive waste material";

Whereas the Antarctic Treaty provides a framework for the signatories to continue to meet "for the purpose of exchanging information, consulting together on matters of common interest pertaining to Antarctica, and formulating and considering, and recommending to their Governments, measures in furtherance of the principles and objectives of the Treaty'';

Whereas common interests among the Antarctic Treaty nations facilitated the development and ratification of the Convention on the Conservation of Antarctic Marine Living Resources;

Whereas the international cooperation represented by the Antarctic Treaty offers humankind a precedent for the peaceful governance of international spaces;

Whereas in celebration of the 50th anniversary of the International Geophysical Year, the Antarctic Treaty Parties in their Edinburgh Declaration recognized the current International Polar Year for its contributions to science worldwide and to international cooperation; and

Whereas the International Polar Year program has endorsed the Antarctic Treaty Summit that will convene in Washington, DC, at the Smithsonian Institution on the 50th anniversary of the Antarctic Treaty: Now, therefore, be it

Resolved by the House of Representatives (the Senate concurring), That the Congress—

(1) recognizes that the Antarctic Treaty has greatly contributed to science and science cooperation worldwide and successfully ensured the ''use of Antarctica for peaceful purposes only and the continuance of international harmony'' for the past half century; and

4

(2) encourages international and interdisciplinary collaboration in the Antarctic Treaty Summit to identify lessons from 50 years of international cooperation under the Antarctic Treaty that have legacy value for humankind.

Passed the House of Representatives September 30, 2009.

Attest:

Clerk.

The Library of Congress > THOMAS Home > Bills, Resolutions > Search Results

NEW SEARCH | HOME | HELP

Print Subscribe Share/Save

H.CON.RES.51
Title: Recognizing the 50th anniversary of the signing of the Antarctic Treaty.
Sponsor: Rep Tiberi, Patrick J. [OH-12] (introduced 2/12/2009) Cosponsors (33)
Related Bills: S.RES.365
Latest Major Action: 10/1/2009 Referred to Senate committee. Status: Received in the Senate and referred to the Committee on Foreign Relations.

Jump to: Summary, Major Actions, All Actions, Titles, Cosponsors, Committees, Related Bill Details, Amendments

SUMMARY AS OF:
9/30/2009--Passed House amended. (There is 1 other summary)

Recognizes that the Antarctic Treaty has ensured Antarctica's peaceful use and the continuance of international harmony for the past half century.

Encourages international and interdisciplinary collaboration in the Antarctic Treaty Summit.

MAJOR ACTIONS:

2/12/2009	Introduced in House
9/30/2009	Passed/agreed to in House: On motion to suspend the rules and agree to the resolution, as amended Agreed to by voice vote.
10/1/2009	Referred to Senate committee: Received in the Senate and referred to the Committee on Foreign Relations.

[+] FEEDBACK

ALL ACTIONS:

2/12/2009:
Referred to the House Committee on Foreign Affairs.
9/30/2009 1:52pm:
Mr. Berman moved to suspend the rules and agree to the resolution, as amended.
9/30/2009 1:52pm:
Considered under suspension of the rules. (consideration: CR H10106-10108)
9/30/2009 1:52pm:
DEBATE - The House proceeded with forty minutes of debate on H. Con. Res. 51.
9/30/2009 1:57pm:
On motion to suspend the rules and agree to the resolution, as amended Agreed to by voice vote. (text: CR H10106-10107)
9/30/2009 1:57pm:
Motion to reconsider laid on the table Agreed to without objection.
10/1/2009:
Received in the Senate and referred to the Committee on Foreign Relations.

TITLE(S): (*italics indicate a title for a portion of a bill*)

- OFFICIAL TITLE AS INTRODUCED:
  Recognizing the 50th anniversary of the signing of the Antarctic Treaty.

COSPONSORS(33), ALPHABETICAL [followed by Cosponsors withdrawn]: (Sort: by date)

Rep Austria, Steve [OH-7] - 6/4/2009
Rep Baird, Brian [WA-3] - 7/14/2009
Rep Bartlett, Roscoe G. [MD-6] - 6/24/2009
Rep Berman, Howard L. [CA-28] - 9/29/2009
Rep Bordallo, Madeleine Z. [GU] - 2/12/2009
Rep Calvert, Ken [CA-44] - 2/12/2009
Rep Carson, Andre [IN-7] - 9/24/2009
Rep Connolly, Gerald E. "Gerry" [VA-11] - 2/12/2009
Rep Crowley, Joseph [NY-7] - 7/23/2009
Rep Dahlkemper, Kathleen A. [PA-3] - 2/12/2009
Rep Ehlers, Vernon J. [MI-3] - 2/12/2009
Rep Faleomavaega, Eni F.H. [AS] - 6/11/2009
Rep Farr, Sam [CA-17] - 2/12/2009
Rep Fudge, Marcia L. [OH-11] - 7/16/2009
Rep Gordon, Bart [TN-6] - 2/12/2009
Rep Hinchey, Maurice D. [NY-22] - 2/12/2009
Rep Inglis, Bob [SC-4] - 2/12/2009
Rep Jackson-Lee, Sheila [TX-18] - 7/23/2009

Rep LaTourette, Steven C. [OH-14] - 7/16/2009
Rep Lipinski, Daniel [IL-3] - 7/17/2009
Rep McCotter, Thaddeus G. [MI-11] - 2/12/2009
Rep Michaud, Michael H. [ME-2] - 6/4/2009
Rep Pascrell, Bill, Jr. [NJ-8] - 7/16/2009
Rep Pence, Mike [IN-6] - 7/23/2009
Rep Peters, Gary C. [MI-9] - 7/16/2009
Rep Petri, Thomas E. [WI-6] - 2/12/2009
Rep Poe, Ted [TX-2] - 2/12/2009
Rep Schmidt, Jean [OH-2] - 7/17/2009
Rep Sires, Albio [NJ-13] - 7/23/2009
Rep Turner, Michael R. [OH-3] - 2/12/2009
Rep Watson, Diane E. [CA-33] - 7/23/2009
Rep Wilson, Joe [SC-2] - 7/23/2009
Rep Wu, David [OR-1] - 7/17/2009

COMMITTEE(S):

Committee/Subcommittee:	Activity:
House Foreign Affairs	Referral
Senate Foreign Relations	Referral, In Committee

RELATED BILL DETAILS: (additional related bills may be indentified in Status)

Bill:	Relationship:
S.RES.365	Related bill identified by CRS

AMENDMENT(S):

NONE

THOMAS Home | Contact | Accessibility | Legal | FirstGov

III

111TH CONGRESS
1ST SESSION

S. RES. 365

Recognizing the 50th anniversary of the signing of the Antarctic Treaty.

IN THE SENATE OF THE UNITED STATES

DECEMBER 1, 2009

Mrs. BOXER submitted the following resolution; which was considered and agreed to

RESOLUTION

Recognizing the 50th anniversary of the signing of the Antarctic Treaty.

Whereas the Antarctic Treaty was signed by 12 nations in Washington, DC, on December 1, 1959, "with the interests of science and the progress of all mankind";

Whereas the Antarctic Treaty was established to continue and develop international "cooperation on the basis of freedom of scientific investigation in Antarctica as applied during the International Geophysical Year";

Whereas the Antarctic Treaty came into force on June 23, 1961, after its unanimous ratification by the seven countries (Argentina, Australia, Chile, France, New Zealand, Norway, and the United Kingdom) with territorial claims in the region and five other countries (Belgium, Japan, South Africa, the Soviet Union, and the United States), which had collaborated in Antarctic research activities during the International Geophysical Year from July 1, 1957, through December 31, 1958;

Whereas the Antarctic Treaty now has 47 nations as signatories that together represent nearly 90 percent of humanity;

Whereas Article IV of the Antarctic Treaty states that "no acts or activities taking place while the present Treaty is in force shall constitute a basis for asserting, supporting or denying a claim to territorial sovereignty in Antarctica";

Whereas the 14 articles of the Antarctic Treaty have provided a lasting foundation for maintaining the region south of 60 degrees south latitude, nearly 10 percent of the Earth's surface, "for peaceful purposes only";

Whereas the Antarctic Treaty prohibits "any measure of a military nature";

Whereas the Antarctic Treaty has promoted international nuclear cooperation by prohibiting "any nuclear explosions in Antarctica and the disposal there of radioactive waste material";

Whereas the Antarctic Treaty provides a framework for the signatories to continue to meet "for the purpose of exchanging information, consulting together on matters of common interest pertaining to Antarctica, and formulating and considering, and recommending to their Governments, measures in furtherance of the principles and objectives of the Treaty";

Whereas common interests among the Antarctic Treaty nations facilitated the development and ratification of the

Convention on the Conservation of Antarctic Marine Living Resources;

Whereas the international cooperation represented by the Antarctic Treaty offers humankind a precedent for the peaceful governance of international spaces;

Whereas in celebration of the 50th anniversary of the International Geophysical Year, the Antarctic Treaty Parties in their Edinburgh Declaration recognized the current International Polar Year for its contributions to science worldwide and to international cooperation; and

Whereas the International Polar Year program has endorsed the Antarctic Treaty Summit that will convene in Washington, DC, at the Smithsonian Institution on the 50th anniversary of the Antarctic Treaty: Now, therefore, be it

Resolved, That the Senate—

(1) recognizes that the Antarctic Treaty has greatly contributed to science and science cooperation worldwide and successfully ensured the "use of Antarctica for peaceful purposes only and the continuance of international harmony" for the past half century; and

(2) encourages international and interdisciplinary collaboration in the Antarctic Treaty Summit to identify lessons from 50 years of international cooperation under the Antarctic Treaty that have legacy value for humankind.

○

NEW SEARCH | HOME | HELP

Print Subscribe Share/Save

S.RES.365
Title: A resolution recognizing the 50th anniversary of the signing of the Antarctic Treaty.
Sponsor: Sen Boxer, Barbara [CA] (introduced 12/1/2009) Cosponsors (None)
Related Bills: H.CON.RES.51
Latest Major Action: 12/1/2009 Passed/agreed to in Senate. Status: Submitted in the Senate, considered, and agreed to without amendment and with a preamble by Unanimous Consent.

Jump to: Summary, Major Actions, All Actions, Titles, Cosponsors, Committees, Related Bill Details, Amendments

SUMMARY:

NONE

MAJOR ACTIONS:

12/1/2009	Introduced in Senate
12/1/2009	Passed/agreed to in Senate: Submitted in the Senate, considered, and agreed to without amendment and with a preamble by Unanimous Consent.

ALL ACTIONS:

12/1/2009:
Submitted in the Senate, considered, and agreed to without amendment and with a preamble by Unanimous Consent. (consideration: CR S12089; text as passed Senate: CR S12089; text of measure as introduced: CR S12072)

[+] FEEDBACK

TITLE(S): (*italics indicate a title for a portion of a bill*)

- OFFICIAL TITLE AS INTRODUCED:
  A resolution recognizing the 50th anniversary of the signing of the Antarctic Treaty.

COSPONSOR(S):

NONE

COMMITTEE(S):

NONE

RELATED BILL DETAILS: (additional related bills may be indentified in Status)

Bill:	**Relationship:**
H.CON.RES.51	Related bill identified by CRS

AMENDMENT(S):

NONE

FOREVER DECLARATION

Declaration on the Occasion of the

50th Anniversary of the Signing of the Antarctic Treaty

Presented for Signature on 1 December 2009

At the Antarctic Treaty Summit Held in Washington, DC

<u>Presented to the United Nations to be Preserved for Posterity</u>

28 January 2010

FOREVER DECLARATION

Declaration on the Occasion of the

50th Anniversary of the Signing of the Antarctic Treaty

Presented for Signature on 1 December 2009

At the Antarctic Treaty Summit Held in Washington, DC

The Antarctic Treaty Summit, consisting of a group of people – as part of civil society – have adopted the following Declaration in the city where the Antarctic Treaty was signed on this day 50 years ago by the original 12 Signatory States;

Recognising that the establishment of lasting peace on Earth represents the primary condition for the survival of humankind and considering that the Antarctic Treaty has provided the means and the inspiration to ensure peace, security, environmental protection and international co-operation in the Antarctic region.

Acknowledging that increased commitment to the objectives and principles of the Treaty has been demonstrated by its increased membership to 47 States Parties that together represent approximately two-thirds of the world's population;

Aware that the template and visionary nature of the Antarctic Treaty have been employed to good effect in other treaties seeking to promote international co-operation;

Noting the indefinite nature of the Antarctic Treaty and that Antarctica should remain a natural reserve forever devoted to peace and science;

Bearing in mind the fundamental principles of international law set forth in the Charter of the United Nations, and that the Antarctic Treaty Parties have pledged that:

(a) Antarctica shall be used for peaceful purposes only;

(b) There shall be prohibited, inter alia, any measure of a military nature, such as the establishment of military bases and fortifications, the carrying out of military manoeuvres, as well as the testing of any type of weapons;

(c) Any nuclear explosions in Antarctica and the disposal there of radioactive waste material shall be prohibited;

Noting that the environmental principles and mechanisms developed for the protection of Antarctica and its dependent and associated ecosystems have inspired the development of international environmental law at large and that such a role of the Antarctic legal regime should continue to be developed progressively;

Convinced that continued scientific research in Antarctica and the effective dissemination of its results are vital to our understanding of the Earth's systems, especially in relation to climate change, and thus is crucial to the interest of all humankind;

THE ANTARCTIC TREATY SUMMIT:

Reiterates the view that Antarctica should remain a continent devoted to international co-operation, the pursuit of scientific endeavour, and that it should be used exclusively for peaceful purposes;

Believes that the pristine nature of Antarctica as well as its aesthetic value will provide inspiration to present and future generations;

Affirms that the Antarctic Treaty, strengthened by the constituents of the Antarctic Treaty System, remains the effective legal means to provide for the international governance of the continent and its surrounding waters;

Encourages all States with an interest in the future of Antarctica to accede to the Antarctic Treaty and its associated instruments, thereby strengthening international commitment to it;

Calls on all States to align themselves with the fundamental principles of peace and international co-operation, including importantly co-operation through science and to recognise that such principles are the cornerstones that guide activities in Antarctica;

Further calls on all States to continue to improve and broaden co-operation in Antarctica taking into consideration that the interests of the international community are best served through such means;

Supports the efforts of the Scientific Committee on Antarctic Research: to encourage scientific research in Antarctica which at the same time meets the requirements of excellence and relevance; to continue to foster co-operation amongst the international scientific community; and to facilitate assistance for those with limited resources and experience;

Urges all States, organizations and individuals to eliminate impacts such as climate change, pollution or over-fishing that stem from outside the Antarctic Treaty area but which are harmful to the Antarctic environment;

Encourages all States to draw on the lessons learned from the Antarctic experience in creating effective governance systems for spaces beyond national jurisdictions:

Calls on all States in co-operation with the relevant non-governmental and inter-governmental organizations, to continue to improve and broaden co-operation in Antarctica recognizing that the interest of the international community are best served through such means, and urges that far-sighted, innovative and imaginative policies be developed to ensure that activities in Antarctica continue to be undertaken with the view to benefit humankind.

Encourages other like-minded people to support this Declaration.

This Declaration shall be distributed widely and shall be communicated by the coordinator of the Antarctic Treaty Summit to the General Assembly of the United Nations, the Secretary-General of the United Nations and the governments of all States Parties to the Antarctic Treaty.

FOREVER DECLARATION

Original Signatories on Behalf of Global Civil Society

On behalf of civil society - the *Forever Declaration* was signed originally by collaborators at the Antarctic Treaty Summit on 1 December 2009 and remains open for digital signature by anyone anywhere in the world (see www.atsummit50.aq). The *Forever Declaration* includes 113 original signatories (please see below and high-resolution image on the website), which include the following individuals who were involved in the ceremonial signing at the Antarctic Treaty Summit:

- **His Serene Highness Prince Albert II of Monaco**

Members of the *Forever Declaration* Drafting Committee

- **Ambassador Jorge Berguño** (Former Ambassador to the United Nations; Council for Antarctic Policy, Ministry of Foreign Affairs: Chile)
- **Dr. Michael Richardson** (Former Head of Polar Regions Section, Foreign & Commonwealth Office: United Kingdom)
- **Judge Rüdiger Wolfrum** (Director, Max Planck Institute for Comparative Public Law and International Law; Former President and Current Judge, International Tribunal for the Law of the Sea – Germany)

Members of the International Board for the Antarctic Treaty Summit

- **Professor Paul Arthur Berkman** (Chair, International Board for the Antarctic Treaty Summit; Head of Arctic Ocean Geopolitics Programme, Scott Polar Research Institute, University of Cambridge: United Kingdom; Research Professor, Bren School of Environmental Science and Management, University of California Santa Barbara: United States)
- **Dr. Marie Jacobsson** (Principal Legal Advisor on International Law, Ministry for Foreign Affairs; Member, International Law Commission of the United Nations: Sweden)
- **Dr. Yeadong Kim** (Former Director of the Korean Polar Research Institute: Republic of Korea)
- **Mr. Michael Lang** (Director, Smithsonian Marine Science Network and Director, Smithsonian Scientific Diving program, Office of the Under Secretary for Science, Smithsonian Institution: United States)
- **Dr. José Retamales**, (Director, Chilean Antarctic Institute; Chair, Council of Managers of National Antarctic Programs: Chile)
- **Professor David W.H. Walton** (Vice-Chair, International Board for the Antarctic Treaty Summit; Professor Emeritus, British Antarctic Survey, Cambridge; United Kingdom)
- **Judge Rüdiger Wolfrum** (see *Forever Declaration* Drafting Committee)
- **Professor Oran R. Young** (Professor, Bren School of Environmental Science & Management, University of California Santa Barbara; Chair, International Human Dimensions Programme on Global Environmental Change: United States)
- **Professor Abdul Hamid Zakri** (Director, Centre on Global Sustainability Studies, Universiti Sains; Vice President, Third World Academy of Sciences; Former Director, United Nations University – Institute of Advanced Studies: Malaysia)

'FOREVER' DECLARATION

Declaration on the Occasion of the
50th Anniversary of the Signing of the Antarctic Treaty
Presented for Signature on 1 December 2009
At the Antarctic Treaty Summit Held in Washington, DC

The Antarctic Treaty Summit, consisting of a group of people – as part of civil society – have adopted the following Declaration in the city where the Antarctic Treaty was signed on this day 50 years ago by the original 12 Signatory States;

Recognising that the establishment of lasting peace on Earth represents the primary condition for the survival of humankind and considering that the Antarctic Treaty has provided the means and the inspiration to ensure peace, security, environmental protection and international co-operation in the Antarctic region;

Acknowledging that increased commitment to the objectives and principles of the Treaty has been demonstrated by its increased membership to 47 States Parties that together represent approximately two-thirds of the world's population;

Aware that the template and visionary nature of the Antarctic Treaty have been employed to good effect in other treaties seeking to promote international co-operation;

Noting the indefinite nature of the Antarctic Treaty and that Antarctica should remain a natural reserve forever devoted to peace and science;

Bearing in mind the fundamental principles of international law set forth in the Charter of the United Nations, and that the Antarctic Treaty Parties have pledged that:

(a) Antarctica shall be used for peaceful purposes only;
(b) There shall be prohibited, inter alia, any measure of a military nature, such as the establishment of military bases and fortifications, the carrying out of military manoeuvres, as well as the testing of any type of weapons;
(c) Any nuclear explosions in Antarctica and the disposal there of radioactive waste material shall be prohibited;

Noting that the environmental principles and mechanisms developed for the protection of Antarctica and its dependent and associated ecosystems have inspired the development of international environmental law at large and that such a role of the Antarctic legal regime should continue to be developed progressively;

Convinced that continued scientific research in Antarctica and the effective dissemination of its results are vital to our understanding of the Earth's systems, especially in relation to climate change, and thus is crucial to the interest of all humankind;

THE ANTARCTIC TREATY SUMMIT:

Reiterates the view that Antarctica should remain a continent devoted to international co-operation, the pursuit of scientific endeavour, and that it should be used exclusively for peaceful purposes;

Believes that the pristine nature of Antarctica as well as its aesthetic value will provide inspiration to present and future generations;

Affirms that the Antarctic Treaty, strengthened by the constituents of the Antarctic Treaty System, remains the effective legal means to provide for the international governance of the continent and its surrounding waters;

Encourages all States with an interest in the future of Antarctica to accede to the Antarctic Treaty and its associated instruments, thereby strengthening international commitment to it;

Calls on all States to align themselves with the fundamental principles of peace and international co-operation, including importantly co-operation through science and to recognise that such principles are the cornerstones that guide activities in Antarctica;

Further calls on all States to continue to improve and broaden co-operation in Antarctica taking into consideration that the interests of the international community are best served through such means;

Supports the efforts of the Scientific Committee on Antarctic Research: to encourage scientific research in Antarctica which at the same time meets the requirements of excellence and relevance; to continue to foster co-operation amongst the international scientific community; and to facilitate assistance for those with limited resources and experience;

Urges all States, organizations and individuals to eliminate impacts such as climate change, pollution or over-fishing that stem from outside the Antarctic Treaty area but which are harmful to the Antarctic environment;

Encourages all States to draw on the lessons learned from the Antarctic experience in creating effective governance systems for spaces beyond national jurisdictions;

Calls on all States in co-operation with the relevant non-governmental and inter-governmental organizations, to continue to improve and broaden co-operation in Antarctica recognizing that the interest of the international community are best served through such means, and urges that far-sighted, innovative and imaginative policies be developed to ensure that activities in Antarctica continue to be undertaken with the view to benefit humankind;

Encourages other like-minded people to support this Declaration;

This Declaration shall be distributed widely and shall be communicated by the coordinator of the Antarctic Treaty Summit to the General Assembly of the United Nations, the Secretary-General of the United Nations and the governments of all States Parties to the Antarctic Treaty.

Signed this 1st day of December 2009:

Antarctic Treaty Summit Participants, from left to right: Jim Barnes, Gillian Triggs, Scott Miller, Cornelia Lüdecke, Michael A. Lang, Paul Arthur Berkman, Olav Orheim, Nina Federoff, H.S.H. Prince Albert II of Monaco, G. Wayne Clough, Aant Elzinga, Marie Jacobsson, Michael Richardson, R. Tucker Scully, David Walton, Stephen Rintoul, and Jorge Berguño.

Index

Figures in **bold**; Tables in *italics*